LUGARD

The Years of Authority

1898-1945

Frederick Lugard about 1895

LUGARD

The Years of Authority

1898-1945

THE SECOND PART OF THE LIFE OF
FREDERICK DEALTRY LUGARD
LATER LORD LUGARD OF ABINGER
P.C., G.C.M.G., C.B., D.S.O.

By
MARGERY PERHAM, C.B.E.
Fellow of Nuffield College, Oxford

COLLINS
ST JAMES'S PLACE, LONDON
1960

To My Sister

On the stage their act hath framed
For thy sports, O Liberty!
Doubted are they, and defamed
By the tongues their act set free,
While they quicken, tend and raise
Power that must their power displace.

From 'The Pro-Consuls' by
RUDYARD KIPLING

INTRODUCTION

THIS SECOND part of Lord Lugard's life is being published four years after the appearance of the first. Much of the original Introduction will serve for this volume and I must hope that it will be read or re-read by those who take up this second half of the story.

In the first introduction I gave the reason why the first Volume was being published before the writing of the second was finished. I rashly promised that the interval would be no more than eighteen months and I therefore owe both an apology and an explanation for the longer delay. I can do no more than plead the pressures upon my time which has to be given to many tasks other than research and writing, above all to observing and visiting a continent which in Nigeria as elsewhere seems to be reaching the climax of changes which Lugard was one of the first to set in motion.

In January 1957 Major Edward Lugard died. I missed his efficient help which, with the amazing devotion and vitality of his family, he gave me up to the last week of his ninety-third year. It is worth remarking in order to get the record of these volumes, not to speak of current events, into perspective, that as I write this introduction, Lugard's *elder* sister, Mrs. Roper, who was born nearly half a century before East Africa and most of Nigeria were first occupied by Britain, is still alive.

ACKNOWLEDGMENTS

MANY OF those former Nigerian officials who supplied me with information and documents about Lugard's work, and with whom I had already been in contact in the 'thirties over my book on Nigerian Native Administration, have now died. Chief among them were Lugard's Residents, Sir Charles Orr, Sir William Gowers, Sir Richmond Palmer, Mr. R. P. Nicholson, and his first Chief Justice, Sir Henry Gollan. Sir George Tomlinson who was also one of Lugard's Residents has helped me. The late Dr. J. H. Paterson wrote to me of the earliest days and supplied the photograph of Lugard in the Emir's palace in Kano. Lady Vischer most kindly helped me to fill in the story of her husband's long association with Lugard.

In reconstructing some picture of the Colonial Office in the first eighteen years of this century I had help from many who had served there. They include Sir Frederick Butler, Lord Davidson, Sir Harry Batterbee, Sir Ralph Furse, and Sir Cosmo Parkinson.

Sir Winston Churchill was good enough to look at those chapters in which he appears as Under-Secretary of State for the Colonies.

I owe much to those who kindly read my Hong Kong chapters or supplied pieces of information: Sir Alexander Grantham, Professor Lancelot Forster, the late Mr. J. R. Wood, Mr. G. B. Endacott.

My academic colleagues in the African field have been generous with help and advice. Mr. J. E. Flint allowed me to see his then unpublished work on Sir George Goldie and Miss Sonia Graham (now Mrs. Parkinson), her thesis upon Sir Hanns Vischer. Mr. Peter Lloyd, historian of the Nigerian Yoruba, shared with me his knowledge of their intricate constitutions. Mr. Colin Newbury gave help in this same field. Mr. Edward Hawkins read my one economic chapter. Miss Cherry Gertzel, working on the Holt papers, made me a present of some interesting quotations. Mr. George Bennett kindly read the pages dealing with Closer Union in East Africa.

Dr. J. H. Oldham was good enough to read through the last three chapters and allowed me to use his own papers on the period. Lord Harcourt and Lord Altrincham gave me access to their fathers' papers which were relevant to the later sections. The late Professor William Rappard sent me his impressions of Lugard on the Permanent Mandates Commission, and Miss Margaret Bates, an American student engaged upon a study of Tanganyika, con-

Acknowledgments

tributed some valuable facts and ideas upon the same subject. Miss Townshend, who lived in Lord Lugard's house as his secretary during the last fourteen years of his life, deserves recognition for her information and also for her wonderfully orderly documentation. Miss Florence Robinson, first Lady Lugard's personal maid, and later Lugard's housekeeper, told me much about the more intimate life of the house on Leith Hill.

Sir John Macpherson, as Governor-General of Nigeria, and Sir Clement Pleass, Sir John Rankine and Sir Bryan Sharwood-Smith as Governors of the Regions, all helped me upon a final visit to the scene of Lugard's Nigerian service.

I am grateful to Mr. Cheeseman, the Colonial Office Librarian, for much help and understanding, and to the always helpful services of the Librarians of Rhodes House and the Royal Commonwealth Society.

Thanks are due to those who entrusted me with photographs for the illustrations—Major Cyril Lugard for that of his father and of Lugard in Hong Kong; Dame Flora Macleod of Macleod for that of Sir Charles Temple; Mr. Maurice Antrobus for that of his father, Sir Reginald Antrobus; Mrs. Oldham for that of her husband and Lady Vischer for that of Sir Hanns.

I am also grateful to the following for permission to reproduce illustrations: The Central Press Photos Ltd. for the photograph of a view of Kano; The Radio Times Hulton Picture Library for the photographs of a Nigerian chieftain and of Lord Harcourt; The Keystone Press Agency Ltd. for the two photographs of Nigerian Emirs; The Hong Kong Government Information Services for the photograph of Hong Kong University and *East Africa & Rhodesia* for the cartoon of 'the Joint Committee on Closer Union'.

I must thank Mrs. George Bambridge and Messrs. Methuen & Co. Ltd., for permission to quote one verse from Rudyard Kipling's *The Pro-Consuls* as an epigraph to this volume.

Finally I must thank the research assistants so generously allowed me by my College. Miss Isabel Ferguson (now Mrs. Glyn Roberts) worked with me for nearly four years. Mrs. Hedley Bull, though in London, continued to assist with this volume, in such time as she could spare between acting as assistant editor for the Lugard Diaries, and then working as Research Secretary at the Institute of Commonwealth Studies. The pleasure of working with these young assistants and the patient goodwill shown towards me by the Warden and Fellows of my College during this long task, have greatly lightened its weight.

Nuffield College   MARGERY PERHAM
January, 1960

CONTENTS

xi

Contents

PART THREE

NIGERIA 1912-1918

PART FOUR

THE LAST YEARS 1918-1945

PART ONE

Northern Nigeria 1898-1906

CHAPTER I

FROM SOLDIER TO ADMINISTRATOR

IN THE last pages of Volume I Lugard was pictured in March 1898 returning to England from that strange little campaign in which he had warded the French off the Middle Niger and created the West African Frontier Force. We saw that, although he could not know it, this return voyage on the Elder Dempster steamer was taking him away from one half of his life towards the other. It was as though Fate had said to him: "You wanted Britain to annex large areas of tropical Africa—you trekked for this end, fought for it, wrote for it, very nearly died for it. Now justify your actions! Here is a great slice of virgin Africa. Govern it and show what you can do with it!"

But as his ship steamed down the Niger and along the West Coast this imperative had hardly reached his mind. It was set more upon the past and present than the future. He was still the commandant of the Frontier Force and he was thinking of his loyal friend and second-in-command, Colonel Willcocks,[1] and the officers and men he had left behind him and to whom he expected to return. There was still much he had to do for them in England if they were to be kept healthy and effective in their remote station.

He came home a sick man, worn out by the anxieties of his politically hazardous task and by the ceaseless administrative effort of organizing a new force and maintaining it so far from its sources of supply. He had also been paying the price of his reluctance to delegate. What had been almost a virtue when he had been the spear-head of action as a caravan-leader became, as he moved nearer to the base of operations, a fault and might become a vice. He had also felt the strain of adjusting himself to the heavy yoke of that imperial authority which, though he had desired to take it upon himself, chafed his independent

[1] See Vol. I, p. 46.

spirit. The policy he had just carried out had not been his own: it had been imposed upon him against his better judgment by Chamberlain who had duly thanked him for successfully playing his allotted part. He may, during his voyage home, have pondered over the capriciousness of public reputation since he knew that his earlier expeditions, for which he had received little or no official approval and even a measure of censure, had been much more original and far more dangerous than the latest achievement. But by the end of the voyage, or very soon after he landed, he had shown again the powers of recuperation possessed by his wiry body and industrious mind and had already thrown aside both sickness and depression.

He went to his old rooms at 63 Jermyn Street and plunged at once into urgent work for his West African Frontier Force. There were new officers to select, terms of employment to settle, stores to obtain and dispatch, and, of course, battles to fight upon all these matters with the War Office, the Colonial Office and the Crown Agents. He was, for example, infuriated to find that there was no Treasury sanction for appointing a new officer to replace one invalided out until the latter had completed his sick leave and been crossed off the strength of the Force. This, with the heavy sickness rate on the Niger and the length of the journey to military headquarters! There were doctors and many other categories of staff to be interviewed. Lugard would not even accept clerks without his personal inspection although "this class of animal, viz. a sucking accountant, seems hard to catch . . . . The only thing they want to impress on me is how well they are connected." His economical mind fretted against the extravagance of government departments; he damned the Crown Agents in the belief that they favoured extravagances because they drew a percentage on their transactions; he longed to place contracts with men and firms of his own choosing and so save the government 45 per cent "or, in other words, I would have 45 per cent more to spend for I have no intention of saving Government anything." (L. to Willcocks, 3 November 1898).

For all his preoccupation with his current patch of Africa, he kept wider views in mind and upon each return from the bush to London, like the good surveyor he was, he re-checked his own position against the changing political landmarks of his world. The scene upon which he looked in the autumn of 1898 had a sombre background and an almost lurid foreground. A few weeks after his return he had the privilege of hearing it explained by no less an exponent than Chamberlain himself. He could have had no better informant since, according to the expert evidence of Sir Edward Grey, the Colonial Secretary was at this period, "the most sensitive barometer by which to record tendencies in foreign policy."[1] During the last week-end of October—in those days of crowded diplomacy each day had its significance—he stayed at Highbury, walking round the cherished garden upon which the murk of Chamberlain's Birmingham was advancing, or strolling up and down the long corridor full of orchids and promising his host some tropical additions to this costly collection.

The sombre background was England's continuing isolation in a troubled world. Only to the west was the prospect clear. True, America was in process of becoming a colonial power by conquering Spain's empire, but imperial Britain had succeeded, thanks in large part to Chamberlain, in remaining on reasonably good terms with her during this war of acquisition. In Europe, however, there was not one amongst the great powers upon whose friendship, to use that most misleading diplomatic term, Britain could rely.

At a time when there was already a development towards "one world", Britain had to watch the almost weekly oscillation of the balance of power as its sensitive needle quivered day by day in response to events which were then happening as far away as Samoa and the China Seas. Russia, so long the cartoonists' bear, had become the devil himself in Chamberlain's famous "long-spoon" speech earlier that year. Germany, with whom the minister had favoured some kind of *entente*, had remained pilotless after the dismissal of Bismarck and was following an erratic and threatening course under her new imperial captain. Milner was at that moment steaming home from South Africa with a very disturbing report. But the foreground at the moment for Lugard, and, indeed, for Chamberlain too, was filled by France, whose imperialism was clashing with that of Britain in almost every quarter of the globe but, most gravely and instantly, in tropical Africa.

The storm-clouds which had piled up over the Niger during midsummer had been dispersed largely by the policy of Chamberlain and its execution by Lugard, but they had only rolled away to the east, following Captain Marchand, as, for some eighteen months, he pushed

[1] Viscount Grey of Fallodon, *Twenty-five Years, 1892–1916* (1925), vol. i, p. 49.

with slow inflexibility towards the Nile. They now hung over Fashoda.[1] This was a spot on the flaccid White Nile which impressed the writer, visiting it nearly half a century later under its tactful re-nomination of Kodok, as presenting the same look of dreary insignificance which in 1898 had contrasted with its dramatic importance along the European telegraph wires. Here Marchand ran up the tricolour on July 10th, 1898. Lugard, looking northwards from Lake Victoria, had long before warned his countrymen to mark this name as he judged that it would represent the point of conflict.[2] The British government had ordered Lugard's former enemy and successor in Uganda, Colonel Macdonald, to march north towards this focal point on the Nile but he had been delayed by the tragic mutiny of Lugard's old Sudanese troops. The summer had seen an ambitious plan by France to bring Ethiopian forces down on to the Nile to link up with Marchand, a junction they only just failed to make. This was part of a typically Gallic continent-wide plan which would have driven a west-to-east axis from Senegal to Somaliland to break the proposed north-south Cape-to-Cairo axis. This was a vision of Cecil Rhodes, one derided by Goldie and Lugard, and not a sustained British policy. The French also hoped by this action to threaten the hated British position in Egypt by controlling the waters of the Nile. On September 2nd Kitchener, driving down the northern section of this axis with the help of a specially built stretch of railway, defeated the dervish army at Omdurman. Chamberlain heard the news in America and his first comment to the reporter was the prophecy that this young man would live to see the railway reach to the Cape,[3] a prophecy which is still unfulfilled.

But it was not the French who were to provide the obstacle to its construction. On September 10th, a few days after the British people had thrilled to the news of Kitchener's victory, they learned of the French intrusion. We saw how anti-French the British press and public had become during the Niger crisis. Now the anger was doubled and both political parties voiced it. France, running a high temperature as

[1] There is a very large literature, much of it contemporary, upon the Fashoda crisis. For a valuable chapter, with bibliography, see W. E. Langer, *The Diplomacy of Imperialism* (2nd edition, New York, 1951), pp. 537-80; also G. P. Gooch and H. Temperley, ed., *British Documents on the Origin of the War*, vol. i (1927); J. L. Garvin, *The Life of Joseph Chamberlain*, vol. iii (1934), pp. 224-37, gives the Chamberlain side of the episode, and A. L. Kennedy, *Salisbury* (1953), pp. 278-95, that of Salisbury.
[2] F. D. Lugard, 'The New African Crisis with France and Germany', *Blackwoods Magazine*, vol. CLVI, July 1894.
[3] Garvin, *op. cit.* p. 227.

the Dreyfus case reached a climax, seemed vehemently resolute. Both nations were urgently arming. The Kaiser expected war and seemed to hope for it. In Lugard's view "the crisis with France is the most serious since the Battle of Waterloo. It is at present even betting whether there will be war or not." (L. to Willcocks, 3 November 1898). In Britain there was certainly a readiness, in some quarters even an eagerness, to take to arms, an attitude which points the contrast between the world of 1898 and our own, a contrast upon which Lugard's account of his talks with Chamberlain throws an intimate light. War on the Nile meant war on all fronts, including the Niger. It was thus in very actual terms that the two discussed the prospects.

"Chamberlain", Lugard told Willcocks, " was full of the question of war with France and could talk of nothing else." The two men worked out the military measures that would be needed in West Africa. Lugard, who had already discussed the matter fully with Goldie, had his plans prepared. He proposed the temporary abandonment of Borgu—poor King of Kiama![1]—and the retention of his headquarters at Jebba with the help of gunboats only. Willcocks should cut Dahomey in half by seizing Carnotville and then march south to take Porto Novo, with the navy attacking it by sea and cutting off all reinforcements. The whole of the interior would then drop helplessly into their hands.

This was exciting enough. But Chamberlain, who was quite determined to buy out Goldie's Company once the French issue was settled, was not so obsessed by military urgencies that he could not make plans for the future administration of the northern region. They worked out how the frontier should run between this and the two southern administrations. "The whole of Nigeria proper, which will include the Hausa states, Bornu, Borgu, Ilorin and the Benue districts, will be under a Governor or High Commissioner. This appointment Chamberlain offered me and I accepted." In this almost casual way Lugard reported an item of news which affected not only his own future but that of his second-in-command. "He assumed that you would remain commandant of the W.A.F.F. and I most sincerely trust that he assumed rightly."

On the military question it need hardly be said that Lugard argued for separate forces for the north of Nigeria rather than a general force

---

[1] See Vol. I, pp. 507-10 and 708-9.

upon which all three territories could draw. Rabeh, the bold military adventurer from the Eastern Sudan, whom the Company and the Foreign Office had once thought of using as an ally,[1] was still dominating the Lake Chad region and Lugard explained his plans to deal with him in the following autumn. This led to a revealing little exchange between the politician and the soldier, both convinced of the rectitude of expelling the Sudanese invader. There must, said Chamberlain, be a very sound ostensible reason for precipitating war, such as an appeal from the rightful king of Bornu, or an outrage or some such thing to avenge " so as to have a case which will be unanswerable before Parliament, and will satisfy the faddists in this country." Lugard laughed as he replied, " I can give you forty valid reasons when the time comes if you want them." In his absolute confidence in his own and his country's purposes, he would not have understood, at least at that time, an accusation of cynicism in this matter. It is relevant, if his approach is to be understood, to record that he went on at once to extract from Chamberlain a promise that Goldie's prohibition of the liquor traffic in the north should be retained, and that there should be " industrial schools for teaching carpentering, brick-laying etc. and also a scientific department for geologists, botanists and commercial experts. You know," he added, " I am awfully keen about this." (L. to Willcocks, 3 November 1898). Keenest of all, of course, was his interest in the suppression of slavery.

Before Lugard left Highbury there was a reference to the last crisis in Borgu. Lugard, we know, had criticized Chamberlain; he had resisted and condemned his instructions and had certainly not enjoyed carrying them out. But all these memories had melted away in the warmth of success and the prospect of future co-operation. So, when Lugard praised Willcocks' spirited conduct at Betikuta and pressed his claims to succeed as commandant of the Frontier Force, they could even discuss in amity those vexed " chess-board " instructions.

" I hope", Chamberlain said, talking now without discretion—and here Lugard quoted him within inverted commas—" my instructions were as they ought to have been—quite pacific, but I can tell you now that I should have been most thankful if you had brought about a fight."[2]

[1] John E. Flint, *Sir George Goldie and the Making of Nigeria* (1960), p. 296 draws attention to the evidence for this strange scheme in " Messages to Rabeh Zobeir", F.O. 2/118.

[2] This remark of Chamberlain's is written in ink in the margin of the typewritten copy of

With the Fashoda crisis still unresolved, however, all plans for the future administration of Nigeria had to be held in suspense. Lugard went straight from Highbury to the Intelligence Department of the War Office to work out his plans for war in West Africa. He then went on to discuss these plans further with Goldie. On November 4th, the day after Lugard wrote his long letter to Willcocks, Salisbury told the country that France had decided to withdraw Marchand from Fashoda. This did not cure the war-fever as it was still uncertain whether this meant retirement from the whole Bahr-el-Ghazal region. Salisbury and Chamberlain were firm about this and had the support of the Opposition and of a public opinion increasingly stirred by what Chamberlain called the French policy of "pin pricks". Kitchener's advance up the Nile strengthened the British hand though the future was shadowed by the growing danger of the position in South Africa. It was not until March 21st in the new year 1899 that France finally withdrew her claims, and not until June 13th that she reluctantly ratified the Niger Convention, in the achievement of which, during the four years of the diplomatic and military game of poker, Lugard had played his part.

Lugard could not enter into his new kingdom until the Charter of the Royal Niger Company was officially terminated. This was a long-drawn-out process but we need only remark those aspects which concerned Lugard.[1] We have already seen how wholeheartedly he espoused Goldie's cause against that of a government resolved to terminate his Charter and how he had supported him in an attempt to retain for the company its administrative powers while shedding its commercial activities. This plan had been put forward on the precedent of the East India Company by Sir John Kirk in his report on the Brass raid.[2] But though Mary Kingsley and some of the Liverpool merchants still played with some such idea in the hope of retaining Goldie's great abilities and of setting up a kind of council of West African traders in London, Chamberlain's concept of the Colonial Secretary's imperial

---

[1] The thirteenth chapter of Flint's *Sir George Goldie* describes fully the termination of the Royal Niger Company's charter. This has made it possible to abbreviate the present chapter and refer the reader to this valuable study which throws much light upon the character of Goldie and the uses and abuses of his Company.

[2] These proposals are to be found in F. O. 83/1382, 25 August 1895. They were not printed in the published *Report by Sir John Kirk on Disturbances at Brass*, Africa No. 3 (1896), C. 7977.

Lugard's letter to Willcocks though it is not in Lugard's writing. The assumption is that the typist copied Lugard's written corrections and additions from the top copy.

estate was incompatible with any such schemes and Goldie knew this too well to lend himself to the plans.[1]

Soon after the hostilities on the Niger, the government had appointed a departmental committee to discuss the future administration of the Company's territory. With the Under-Secretary of State for the Colonies, Lord Selborne, in the chair, it was composed of Goldie, the governors of Lagos and of the Niger Coast Protectorate,[2] Sir Clement Hill of the Foreign Office and Antrobus[3] of the Colonial Office. It reported on August 4th in a document that carries the unmistakable mark of Goldie's decisive mind. In view of the later history of the relationship between the several parts of Nigeria, a problem which may still not have found its final solution, it is interesting to see how this early, expert committee approached the question.[4] They recommended amalgamation as an ultimate aim but advised in favour of two governments, " a Maritime Province and a Soudan Province ", the first to the south based on Lagos, and the second north of the ninth parallel with a capital at Lokoja. The first reason they gave for not appointing a Governor-General over the whole region is the interesting one, always much emphasized by Goldie, that under the bad conditions for health only a young man could do efficient work in West Africa and even he would have to be away from his post for one third of the time. They advised an amalgamation of military forces in Nigeria, and preferably in all West Africa, under one commandant normally resident in England. Sir George Goldie was especially named as the source of two recommendations, one that there should be no direct taxation of natives and the other that there should be no attempt to seize the Muslim states in the north by " a general *coup-de-main*". The British, he advised, should go forward gradually and refrain from sending unsupported Residents ahead of the military advance. A railway should be built from Kano to the navigable Niger. Finally, they proposed January 1st, 1899, as the date for the transfer of administration.

This date proved over-optimistic. The government, Lugard told Willcocks, was unwilling to act until after the ratification of the Niger

[1] Flint, *op. cit.* pp. 303-6.
[2] Sir H. McCallum and Sir R. Moor.
[3] Antrobus (later Sir), Reginald, K.C.M.G., C.B., 1853-1942; 1880-9 private secretary to successive Colonial Secretaries; 1889-90 acted as Governor of St. Helena; 1898-1909 Assistant Under-Secretary of State for the Colonies; 1909-1918 Senior Crown Agent for the Colonies.
[4] 'Report of the Niger Committee', 4 August 1898, C. O. 446/3.

Convention by France, and the Fashoda crisis had, of course, thrown this into suspense. By the end of September the Foreign Office wrote to the Niger Company that the date of transfer would be January 1st, 1900. Lugard, for his part, had to postpone, and finally give up, his intention of returning to his military command in Nigeria before this date as he was incessantly taken up with discussions about the transfer and with plans for future administration. During the first three months of 1899, he was busy working out with Goldie what land, buildings, equipment, military stores, ships and other plant the government should take over from the Company in the north and at what price. His estimates of revenue and expenditure, customs, liquor control, mineral rights and many other matters had to be made.

In April it was decided that the British Niger regions should be under three governments, not two. To the south were the Lagos Colony and Protectorate and Southern Nigeria, the new name of the Niger Coast Protectorate upon its transfer from Salisbury's Foreign Office empire to that of Chamberlain's Colonial Office. What should the new Protectorate be called? It was Flora Shaw who first pressed for " Nigeria " in an article in *The Times*.[1] Lugard had wanted "Niger Sudan," but she rejected " Sudan " as confusing the area with French territory and with the Nile basin. The origins of the word Niger went back to the early Greek geographers, in whose works are references to a great river, an extension of the Nile, and it was taken up by other writers in the early Christian era, including Pliny and Ptolemy.[2] Lord Scarbrough chaffed Flora about her choice of a name, arguing that the Latin form should have been Negretia, which the Royal Niger Company kept as their code word. It appears that at one time " Goldesia " had been proposed: Goldie claimed that he had rejected this kind of memorial which had been given to Rhodes.[3] The name Nigeria appears to have been first used officially in Lugard's Letter of Appointment, dated the first day of the new century.

On June 15th, 1899, two days after the French ratified the Niger Convention, Lord Salisbury wrote to the Treasury a formal letter

[1] *The Times*, 8 January, 1897.
[2] This paragraph is largely based upon information supplied to the writer by Dr. C. K. Meek, who shared with me the results of his learned researches into the origin of the name and also showed me a letter to him from Lugard, written in 1940, upon the subject. See also C. K. Meek, *Land Tenure and Land Administration in Nigeria* (1957), page 7, and Mr. Kirk-Greene's article in *The Times Colonial Supplement*, second quarter, 1959.
[3] Dorothy Wellesley, *Sir George Goldie, Founder of Nigeria* (1934), pp. 98-9.

giving the reasons of public policy for the transfer of the Company's administration.[1] The last stage in the process of creating the Protectorate of Northern Nigeria was the formal revocation of the Company's Charter and the acceptance by parliament of the new acquisition and of the obligation to compensate the Company.

All these long-drawn-out transactions were of the deepest interest to Lugard. Always sensitive to public opinion, he was eager to learn the attitude of parliament and public opinion to the new territory he was to govern. But as one who had served the Company, though often critical of it, he was almost equally interested in the nation's judgment upon its record and its treatment of his close friend and fellow-worker, Goldie.

The Chancellor of the Exchequer—most unwillingly we are told, for he had no enthusiasm for this act of purchase[2]—introduced a resolution on July 3rd, 1899, to pay the Niger Company out of the Consolidated Fund a sum not exceeding £865,000. This was built up by the following items:

£300,000 for the Company's public debt on account of administration.

£300,000 compensation for the expense of developing the territory.

£150,000 for land and mineral rights.

£115,000 for plant (buildings, ships, etc.)[3]

In a sensible but uninspired speech Sir Michael Hicks-Beach gave a brief history of the three Niger administrations, one under the Foreign Office, one under the Colonial Office, one under a Company but with an imperial force operating within it. They had not worked in harmony. The Company had diverted much of its commercial profit to administrative expenditure but had yet succeeded in paying a dividend of 6 per cent each year to shareholders. But he admitted that the Company, in despite of the Charter, had succeeded in maintaining a virtual monopoly. The most immediate need for the transfer had arisen from the French threat which the Company had neither the duty nor the power to meet. The government had therefore been obliged to build up a West African Frontier Force with the inevitable waste and friction where two authorities were operating in the same region. The Company would now be entirely commercial. In defending the terms

[1] *Papers relating to the Revocation of the Royal Niger Company's Charter and to the Government of the Niger Districts* (1899), C. 9372, p. 3; this letter is discussed in Flint, *op. cit.* p. 308-9.
[2] Flint, *op. cit.* p. 308.   [3] *Parliamentary Debates*, 3 July 1899, IV. 73. 1293.

of purchase he referred more than once in the debate to the help he had had from Colonel Lugard in selecting and valuing the plant to be taken over from the Company. Since, he concluded, the new territories covered a million square miles and held 30 million people, " it may fairly be said that the Company has founded an Empire."

This measured statement struck the highest, indeed the only high note in the debate. For the Opposition, Sir Henry Campbell-Bannerman gave a tepid acceptance of the resolution, remarking both " the conveniences and the dangers and difficulties attending government by chartered companies through which a country may be insidiously led on to a somewhat rapid extension of its responsibilities." He agreed that the Company's measures for the suppression of drink and slavery might be held to outweigh any of its " trifling sins ". Much of the debate followed this grudging and negative line, some members scrutinizing each item of the bill and others saying that the Company was transferring its liabilities and keeping its assets. There was a gloomy feeling that the country was being let in for a bad bargain. Dillon asserted that the newspapers' reception of the first day's debate showed the greatest possible doubt in the country and O'Connor that the Chancellor, with his hints about minerals, was just like a company promoter taking in the confiding public with hopes of gold. Why should a Company which had broken its charter, established a monopoly, made large profits, and brought us to the verge of war with France, be so generously treated at the cost of the taxpayer?

Chamberlain, the main mover in the whole transaction, professed himself to be reduced to silence by reason of his holding of some £3,000 worth of Company shares. But when, on July 19th, the bill was read a third time, it was felt that he alone could tell the House whether or not the nation's new investment would be efficiently run or would turn out a dead loss. At last he rose. He took the opportunity of announcing that Lugard would govern the new region which was to be called Northern Nigeria. There was to be a customs union but absolute prohibition of spirits in the north. He said that Lugard had suggested, as a further precaution, a neutral zone in which spirits could be sold but not stored. On this subject and on slavery it was clear he had been fully coached by Lugard. He spoke with cautious hope of the financial future: trade from the north should now come down to the coast; Northern Nigeria would begin with a deficit but he hoped it would not be large and that in time it would disappear. He spoke with dryness and brevity; no one who heard him could have guessed from his speech how much of his thought and hope had gone into the new venture. He made no attempt to commend the achievement and the opportunity with the virile confidence that marked so many of his speeches. He concluded, not perhaps without irony, " I do not think that even as a pecuniary bargain this country will have any reason to regret the change they are asked to assent to."[1] On July 27th, the bill passed its third reading by 181 votes to 81.

These debates show Britain in the act of adding a great new province to her empire at a cost, not counting the plant, of less than three-quarters of a million pounds, and yet many of the country's representatives passed the measure grumbling and grudging every penny, accepting the change mainly for the negative reason that it would cease to endanger relations with France. Although this is generally characterized as a time when the imperialist spirit was at its height, we find throughout the debates hardly one word of satisfaction and not one of enthusiasm for this large act of imperial expansion. Not that there was much eloquence on the negative side. The deeply-founded suspicion of imperial adventures and annexations which had inspired the Liberal party in opposition and perplexed them in office had almost died away with the generation of Gladstone and Harcourt. It was only the Irish Dillon, speaking as one who saw British power from the underside, who appealed to fundamental issues and brought some heart and imagination to the human side of the question.

" . . . I refuse to recognize as a great gift to this country an addition of 35 millions of unknown people. It is out of the power of this country and still more out of the power of this House to discharge to these helpless, silent, inarticulate races those moral duties which are entailed in the government of a great empire. In the years to come crimes may be committed in our name and slaughter may be perpetrated which it may be impossible for the already overburdened Ministers of the Empire to investigate and nobody can forecast the extent of the evil that may result from this great accession to the territory of the British Empire."[2]

Dillon's appeal must have sounded meaningless to Lugard in the gallery. He had been so active in pushing out Britain's frontiers and

---

[1] *Parliamentary Debates*, 19 July 1899, IV. 74. 1293.
[2] *Parliamentary Debates*, 26 July 1899, IV. 75. 378.

was to carry on his shoulders the future responsibility at which Dillon shuddered. For Lugard acted on his conviction that humanity in Africa demanded the assumption not the renunciation of responsibility. He must have smiled, too, to see Labouchere, flanked by the Irishmen, once more vainly trying to stand across the way he was to go as in the old days of the Uganda controversy.

Yet he cannot have found the debates wholly satisfactory. True, he was fortified by the steady support from all quarters of the House for the measures against slavery and liquor which meant so much to him. But there was not much public appreciation for what had been achieved on the Niger, and he could not feel that his countrymen were looking forward with any great interest to what he meant to do there. Rather would they be asked to scrutinize every item of his miserly budget, for the Liberals' tradition of economy had not yet declined to the same extent as their anti-imperialism. His main satisfaction was to know that the Colonial Secretary had chosen him, and he hoped that this strong minister could now be relied upon for whole-hearted under-standing and support.

If for Lugard, at forty-one, the revocation of the Charter meant the ending of one half of his life and the beginning of another of perhaps even further importance and renown, for Goldie, at fifty-one, it was an end and nothing more. Nothing, for him, could ever take the place of the Company. For twenty years it had been his life. He had created it and had fought off every enemy who had appeared, using the weapons of commerce, diplomacy or war, as occasion demanded. For him, economic success was always subordinate to the imperial purpose. As his hope of retaining the Company as an administrative agency faded, so did his own interest in it. He claimed to have given the Company service " which no pecuniary reward, however great, could have induced me to give " and he was determined that his name should not be remembered " as chairman of a Nigerian financial company which . . . . will necessarily exist for purposes of profit alone."[1]

Yet, for all this, as trustee for his shareholders, he fought the Treasury hard in their interests. The historian of the Company asserts that Goldie made a very good bargain and that some of the disapproval and sus-picions of the critics in the Commons, especially with regard to watered capital, were well-founded.[2] The item with which Lugard

---

[1] Wellesley, *Sir George Goldie*, p. 73.   [2] Flint, *op. cit.* pp. 309-11.

was most concerned, the £115,000 representing the total value of the stores and equipment, part of which he selected to take over for his new northern administration, raises the most obvious question. As Dillon pointed out, this was stated to cover only part of the Company's assets in Nigeria. Yet the Company's balance sheet showed *all* of these as being worth no more than £113,282![1] No comment from Lugard upon this strange discrepancy has survived.

An interesting question remains. Did the government offer Goldie the governorship of Northern Nigeria before approaching Lugard? Or even, perhaps, the governor-generalship of West Africa? Mr. Flint brings some evidence to show that this was done.[2] Yet it seems strange that after their prolonged and difficult relations with the head of the Company, who from first to last was so often openly and bitterly critical of the government, the ministers should have wished to carry him over into the new regime. Goldie himself absolutely denied that any offer had been made. In an interview with Reuter on July 5th, 1899, asked whether he was to be given some responsible appointment, he vehemently denied the suggestion, adding that he could not have mixed up financial negotiations with any discussion about his own future. And early in the New Year, writing from a liner steaming to the Far East, he confessed to his most intimate colleague, Lord Scarbrough, his chagrin that no offer had been made. " I have given up all idea of government ever utilizing my services for the Empire. My eyes were opened by Flint's[3] name not appearing among the C.M.G.'s on the 1st January; when half a million square miles and 30 millions of people were transferred to the Empire. I asked for nothing for myself; as I prefer to feel that the country owes *me* something; but it is clear that Lord Salisbury has forgotten the services of the United African, National African and Royal Niger Companies.

Chamberlain, I know, believes in me; for to a friend who had spoken highly to him of my 'talent' he said 'it is not talent; it is positive genius.' But then he is not Prime Minister . . . . No matter. I can serve the country (and humanity in general) as a free lance— perhaps better than if I was trammelled by official ties."[4]

When Goldie presided for the last time over the general meeting,

[1] *Parliamentary Debates*, 26 July 1899, IV. 75. 371.   [2] Flint, *op. cit.* p. 307.
[3] Joseph Flint was one of the two Agent Generals of the Company in Nigeria.
[4] Wellesley, *op. cit.* p. 79.

the nineteenth, of the Niger Company he outlined the history of the Company's great achievements in West Africa. This was in moderate tone, but there was issued to the shareholders at the same time with the balance sheet, a printed statement from " an authoritative source." The anonymity was torn away by the mordant style of the author. The document is an angry vindication of the terms of transfer; it asserts that " the government gave nothing to the Company except the doubtful privilege of taking all responsibilities and all risks in acquiring at its own cost, rights which are now to be conveyed to the Empire . . . The Company never received the slightest Imperial assistance in dealing with the dense native population of its territories . . . " The government had allowed interest on one item at 2 to 2½ per cent: " For the risks run prior to the Bida-Ilorin campaign the rate should have been 1000 per cent. The last misapprehension to deal with is that the Governor of the Company would not have negotiated these terms unless they were satisfactory. This is not true. In dealings with the masters of many battalions, no doubt it is prudent for the Company to come to terms, however unsatisfactory: but it is annoying to have these terms treated in certain quarters as if they were generous or even just."[1]

There seems no doubt that Goldie, for all his efficient pugnacity, had grown tired of being an Ishmaelite. Certainly an authority at once more powerful and less ringed with detractors was now needed in Nigeria. In a typically economical phrase he once wrote, " An Imperial Administration may steal a horse while a Chartered Company may not look over a hedge."[2] On the copy of a document, left in the Lugard papers, Goldie has scrawled, "It is *odious* having to boast of the work done by the Company but circumstances leave me no choice." And in that same Reuter interview of some eighteen months later, he compares the government to a highwayman who not only robs his victim but strips him of his very clothes.[3]

It was left to Lord Salisbury to respond to an appeal from Goldie to vindicate his reputation. In a short speech in the Lords he said: " I think no one doubts for an instant the main object of the Company was philanthropic and political and that it was not a mere monetary

---

[1] Appendix to the *Report of the Council of the Royal Niger Company*, 15 August 1899, presented on 23 August 1899.
[2] In a memorandum on Bornu in the Lugard Papers dated 8 December 1897.
[3] Wellesley, *op. cit.* pp. 71-2.

17

speculation." He proceeded to give the Company, in words that also covered Lugard as its agent, that unqualified recognition of the past and that hope for the future that had been so lacking in the Commons debates:

> " They succeeded in reserving for England influence over the vast territory which represents the Niger Company . . . an enormous territory which we believe is full of wealth and full of inhabitants which is being gradually brought under the civilizing influence of English government and which I have no doubt there is every prospect in the future will yield a rich harvest to the British Empire . . . We cannot sanction this great step without expressing our deep gratitude and high esteem for the advent-urers and patriots to whose efforts the preparation of this territory is due." [1]

This was high commendation. But the measure of Goldie's right to the title " The Founder of Nigeria", inscribed upon his grave in Brompton Cemetery, has been a matter of controversy in which the writer was once most unhappily involved.[2] The poetess, Lady Gerald Wellesley, wrote her vivid and moving memoir of the friend and partner of her step-father, Lord Scarbrough, in a spirit of hero-worship and of indignant vindication. She was right to claim that his work and his name had been too much forgotten, though happily, in Mr. Flint, he has now found his biographer. But there should be no controversy, and certainly no rivalry, between his claims and those of Lugard. Their major tasks were different both in time and character. True, there was some clash between them, which has yet to be des-cribed. But on the record no one can withhold recognition of Goldie's achievement in upholding his country's claims to this great hinterland even though others had won the coastlands and had still to occupy most of the north. That modern Nigeria stretches from the sea to the fringe of the Sahara, that it has the area and the population to become the greatest African negro nation, is due to the vision and the almost single-handed struggle of Goldie over twenty-three years. If in the last years he over-reached his resources; if Company rule was in parts anaemic and disjunctive; if it was harsh to the native traders and monopolist to

[1] *Parliamentary Debates* (Lords), 1 August 1899, IV. 75. 1003. The note of enthusiasm was sounded again in *The Times* when the transfer was at last recorded. In an article, doubtless written or inspired by Flora Shaw, at this time Goldie's unqualified admirer, his Company's record was described as " unstained by crime, undimmed by failure " and paralleled only by that of the East India Company.

[2] See *The Spectator*, 21 December 1934, 4 January 1935, and 18 January 1935.

the European, the responsibility lay squarely upon the government which authorized a private agency to carry out a public enterprise and to fill the gap left by a nation which was "letting 'I dare not' wait upon 'I would'". Almost the same words were used in an earlier chapter in a post-mortem upon the Imperial British East Africa Company. Yet one Company succeeded where the other all but failed. The difference between their achievements lay partly in the greater population, accessibility and commercial sophistication of the Niger peoples, but in no small measure in the contrast between the soft metal in the character of the Scot, Mackinnon, and the steely composition of the Manxman, Goldie. For both Companies Lugard extended his whole energy of will and of body to make up the large discrepancy between their pretensions and their power.

The partnership between Goldie and Lugard had ended; would the friendship survive? How different the situation had been less than two years before! " Not you administrator nor I, but both—" Goldie had written, and Lugard had pledged himself to work under Goldie, his " ideal man,"—Goldie in Britain and Lugard in Africa.[1] The changed situation would have been embarrassing for the most selfless of men, and both of these were confident individualists. But Goldie was, at times, amazingly realistic; he could accept some hard facts while he fought others. The decisions had, after all, been taken at a level above his reach. And it was useful as well as congenial for Goldie to carry out some of the difficult negotiations of the final winding-up with a man who was his intimate friend, and to hand over a responsibility that had been so large a part of his life to a successor who could be trusted to carry it strongly and well.

So, for the present, the friendship stood the strain. One of the last intimate pictures we have of Lugard before, as High Commissioner, he began the second part of his career, has been left for us by Nell, his brother's wife. Edward was abroad soldiering. Nell had taken a small house near Haslemere and Lugard, in between crowded engagements in London, stayed with her. He was trying to fulfil his old dream of the African bush and was planning to build himself a house on land he had bought in this area. Nell's letters to her husband give us a picture of Lugard and Goldie, doubtless in their caps, knickerbockers and Norfolk jackets, cycling together, Goldie meaning to buy or to

[1] Vol. I, pp. 653-6.

build a big house so that he could settle near Lugard when he came back from his long voyage.

Of Lugard himself the picture given by his sister-in-law is of mixed light and shadow. His health is again superlative; he walks immense distances, but is so indifferent about time and food that she asks "Would he not drive a wife wild?" Though she is already not a little jealous of Edward's selfless allegiance to his brother—does he put him even before his wife?—she herself still feels the power of Fred's integrity and strength. But, herself a devoted Christian, she is able to measure the void left in his nature by the loss of a faith round which his early life had been built. Asked by his sister what difference there was between Paradise and Heaven " after his jaunty answer that she would know when she got there, he said in a kind of aside, ' I don't suppose I shall ever get to either.' " He feared that his family must now regard him as a hopeless atheist and "They are not far wrong." If Nell Lugard could diagnose as a Christian she could also do so as a woman and she was not long in discovering that other irrecoverable wound of the heart that lay close to the spiritual injury. " Poor old Fred . . . He seems to have found all false in life where falsehood should not have been. He has no faith at all in *anything* . . . it's too sad. Ned darling, *you* must try to bring Faith and love and happiness and peace to dear old Fred. *You can.* I know he would be greatly biassed by what he sees *you* believe. I can only pray for him." (Mrs. Lugard to E. J. L., Good Friday 1899). Yet, to the outside observer, Lugard, as he approached what was to be his greatest and most arduous task, must have given the rare impression of a man as near to perfection of strength in body and mind and therefore in self confidence as is humanly possible. It is only now through the evidence of private diaries and letters that we can learn of the deep inner disorder which he carried over into the second half of his life.

CHAPTER II

BIRTH OF A PROTECTORATE, 1900

THE ROYAL NIGER COMPANY had been legislated out of its chartered existence; Goldie was seeking oblivion in a voyage to China. Only a few preliminaries stood between Lugard and his new task. First he had to have one more round with a War Office under which he was still a commissioned officer and with which he had still to work out his rank, status, and the exiguous pension to which he would be entitled after all other deductions had been made for his frequent excursions away from his military duties. He was given what he called " the silly title of Brigadier-General . . . though I said I did not want these spurious, local and temporary ranks." Goldie thought it a scandal that he was not given his knighthood, if only to equate Northern Nigeria with its two southern neighbours. For that he had to wait only until the 1901 New Year honours, when he was created a K.C.M.G.

He had also to be appointed formally to his new post. The Company's sphere in the north, now placed under him, was proclaimed a Protectorate. Its small southern portion along the Niger was attached to the Protectorate of Southern Nigeria. The Office had not come easily to its demarcations. The three governors were said to be jealous of each other and Sir William MacGregor was so keen on opening up new country that he had wanted Northern Nigeria to be added to his Lagos territory.[1]

British governors hold their offices directly from the Sovereign. On December 1st, therefore, Chamberlain officially submitted Lugard's name to the Queen as the High Commissioner for Northern Nigeria. " Colonel Lugard," he wrote, " is an officer of great distinction and experience in African affairs."[2] Lugard's official instructions emanated

---

[1] Minutes by Antrobus on Sir R. Moor to Chamberlain, 18 August 1898, C. O. 446/3 and on Hicks-Beach to Chamberlain, 26 September 1899, C. O. 446/6.

[2] *The Letters of Queen Victoria*, Third Series, 1886-1901, ed. G. E. Buckle (1930-2), vol. iii, p. 427.

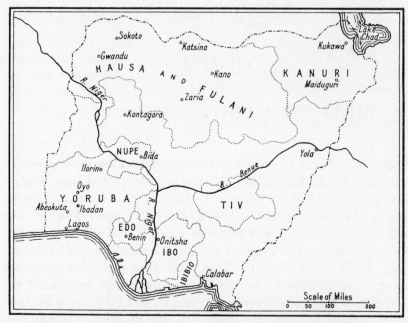

Nigeria showing approximate areas of main tribal groups.
Based on Map 5 of the *Report of the Commission appointed to
enquire into the fears of Minorities and the means of allaying them*
(1958), Cmnd. 505

from the Queen as an Order in her Privy Council, dated December
27th, 1899, Instructions under the Royal Sign Manual and Signet
of December 29th, and a Commission of Appointment of the same
day.

The waxing democracy within Britain still had need of autocracy
across the seas. It was therefore useful to be able to claim that " by
treaty, grant, usage, sufferance and other lawful means, Her Majesty
has power and jurisdiction in the said territories."[1] By the use of
these and other ornate and antique words " given at the Court at
Saint James's " the British government seemed able to dignify and
even to justify the powers they were conferring. The parliamentary
authority for the action was to be found in that morally questionable
but practically essential Foreign Jurisdiction Act of 1890. The intrusion

[1] *Northern Nigeria Order in Council*, 1899.

22

of Britain's armed power and alien law into tropical Africa was really beyond legal endorsement and its justification could be found only in the use that was now to be made of it. This depended mainly upon Lugard himself since, according to these documents, his authority under the Queen and her Secretary of State to make and execute laws was complete, untrammelled by even so much as the minimum control of an executive council of officials. The Colonial Office realized that this would have been difficult to collect over the vast distances.[1]

Lugard was not, as we have seen, indifferent to fame, and he might reasonably have continued to hope that this new acquisition would arrest some public attention in England and, above all, hold the interest of Chamberlain to whom it represented the climax of five years of diplomatic and other effort. But he was unlucky. South African affairs had increasingly distracted public attention from Nigeria and from many other minor matters as the year 1899 went on. In October the South African war had broken out; while Lugard was on his ship the country had been through the shock and humiliation of Black Week and as the young officers of the Frontier Force paraded for the inaugural ceremonies at Lokoja, they were not thinking about the future of Nigeria but wondering eagerly how soon they could get away from it and find their way to the battlefields in the south of the continent where many of them were to be killed. Lugard's friend Willcocks who, as commandant of the Frontier Force, played second to Lugard's lead at the opening ceremony, recognized " the joy of strife written on their faces " and mused that " It is strange but true how soon British officers imbibe the bloodthirsty spirit which gives promise of strife."[2]

Lugard sailed from England on December 4th, and arrived at Lokoja with exact timing on December 31st, 1899. He brought with him a young lawyer, Henry Gollan,[3] as his private secretary. From Gollan's account given to the writer in 1945, and from another supplied by the Reverend J. V. F. Willcocks, Chaplain to the Frontier Force, it is possible to picture the event of the following day.

The nineteen-fifties has seen the impressive inauguration of a

---

[1] Minute by Antrobus, 13 November 1898, C.O. 446/3.
[2] Sir James Willcocks, *From Kabul to Kumassi* (1904), pp. 235-6.
[3] Gollan, (later Sir) Henry Cowper, K.C., 1868-1949; 1891 called to the Bar; 1899 private secretary to Lugard; 1901 Chief Justice, Northern Nigeria; 1904 Chief Justice, Bermuda; 1911 Chief Justice, Trinidad; 1918 Attorney-General, Ceylon; 1924-30 Chief Justice, Hong Kong.

number of new nations emerging from their state of dependency. Their entry into that state was seldom quite so ceremonious. The birthday of the Protectorate of Northern Nigeria, however, was marked by military formality and by speeches which were soberly appreciative of the event. The affair seems to have been well-staged as far as the handful of Europeans in a very make-shift cantonment could contrive. The main event took place on the parade ground at Lokoja, a space cleared out of the bush not far from where the waters of the Benue pour into the wide Niger. The Royal Niger Constabulary and the 2nd battalion of the W.A.F.F., with a battery from each contingent, were drawn up to form a hollow square. At one corner from a tall flagstaff the flag of the Royal Niger Company flapped in the early morning sunlight. At 7 a.m. Lugard and his exiguous civilian staff walked on to the ground and he read the Queen's proclamation " in a distinct and impressive manner". The Company flag was hauled down; the Union Jack was run up; the guns fired their salute; the African military band played the national anthem and the black troops gave three hearty cheers for their new and, to them, quite unimaginable sovereign. The British officers and non-commissioned officers, led by their three colonels, Willcocks, Morland[1] and Lowry Cole,[2] all names of some importance in this first phase of Nigeria's history, stepped forward and Lugard read the Royal Warrant of his appointment. Willcocks then administered to him the oath of allegiance. After the march past, Lugard congratulated the troops upon their excellent appearance and formally took over the Company's Constabulary into the Frontier Force. He administered the oath to William Wallace, the Company's Agent-General, who after 22 years' work for the Company was entering his own service as a first class Resident and his deputy.[3] The Queen's Proclamation was then read to the troops in their two main languages, Hausa and Nupe. Both then and during the two days of sports which followed, the troops and the watching

---

[1] Morland, Gen. (later Sir) Thomas Lethbridge Napier, K.C.B., K.C.M.G., D.S.O., 1865-1925; 1897-8 and 1901-3 served in Nigeria; 1905 Inspector-General, West African Frontier Force; 1910-13 Brigadier-General commanding 2nd Infantry Brigade, Aldershot; 1914-18 served in European War; 1922-3 General Officer Commanding-in-Chief, Aldershot command.

[2] Cole, Brig.-Gen. Arthur Willoughby George Lowry, C.B., D.S.O., 1860-1915; 1885-7 served in Burma; 1898 in West Africa; 1900 in N. Nigeria; 1901-2 in South Africa; 1906 in Sokoto Expedition.

[3] Wallace, (later Sir) William, K.C.M.G., F.R.G.S., 1856-1916; 1878 joined Royal Niger Company; became one of the Agent-Generals; 1900 Resident-General; 1900-10 Deputy High Commissioner, Northern Nigeria.

crowds showed an intense enthusiasm though it must have been of a somewhat uninstructed kind.

The entire British population, some fifty persons, more than half of them military, met that night at a dinner given in the W.A.F.F. mess-house which had been hastily run up in the preceding month. Inevitably, it was a night for compliments. After the toast of " The Queen " Lugard, who loathed public speaking and turned readily to Shakespeare and his Bible for their help, gave that of the Niger Company and took the occasion to sketch its achievement up to this conclusion. " Thus far, gentlemen, The Royal Niger Company has laboured and we have entered into their labours." He went on to praise his friend Goldie—his genius, his marvellous foresight, his courage in the field, his public spirit. "Though a man of wealth upon whom lay no necessity for work, he has for many years worked longer hours than city men do for gain." There followed testimonies to Flint, now to succeed Goldie as head of the Niger Company in its new, wholly commercial existence, and for Wallace, upon whose long experience, Lugard said, he would greatly rely. After-dinner compliments tend to be inflated but upon this night Lugard could be wholly sincere in these tributes and enthusiastic when he turned to Willcocks, " the close friend of many years", whom he had summoned from India to work with him in creating the Frontier Force and in its first operations. Willcocks could reply with an equally sincere and affectionate testimony to his chief.

But the speeches were not all a chorus of mutual British admiration. " Gentlemen," said Lugard,

" though we lightly pledge this toast on an occasion devoted rather to camaraderie than to serious meditation, it is not one that I at least can treat lightly. We drink to the success of Northern Nigeria—that success is not a thing which will grow of itself, or which fate will give or withhold like a Merry Christmas, or a Happy New Year. It is in the hands of each one of us; it is we who are selected to mould the young beginnings, to set the precedents and set the tone and, in short, to make or mar this work. Perhaps the thought is in your minds that the chief influence in either direction will be that of the High Commissioner. Gentlemen I do assure you that I enter on this task with a deep sense of responsibility, and of doubt of my worthiness for it, and though (as our greatest Poet has said) it is not in us to command success, I shall at least endeavour to deserve it. In the words of the oath I swore this morning—words which recall those of the Preacher of old ' I will endeavour to do right to all manner of people, without fear or favour, affection or ill-will ' and I trust that when the time comes for me to ' hand in my cheques ' and look back on my tenure of this office, it may be said of me that to the extent of my ability I did my duty—not sparing myself. But, Gentlemen, if instead of a very indifferent and mediocre man, it had pleased the Secretary of State of his kindness to select the Archangel Gabriel to run this Protectorate, he would make but a poor job of it unless he had your loyal help in all things great and small . . . "

He referred to the war which was in all their minds.

" Gentlemen, personal matters are too paltry to claim our attention in the face of the work before us. The Empire we love is strained to meet the greatest crisis any man here can remember. We are charged to hold in peace and good order this vast Territory, no mean part of that Empire. Whatever may betide elsewhere, we have a charge to fulfil."

The speeches were over, the flag was up and the next morning Lugard sat down in his makeshift office and faced the cold realities of his assignment.

On the writer's table lies the same pile of rather smudged typewritten and handwritten papers at which Lugard was now looking. They comprise a bundle of proclamations dealing with justice, lands, the powers of officials, customs, spirituous liquors and other matters which he had drawn up in his last months in London and on the voyage. Besides these lie three and a half pages of pencilled foolscap in his small neat writing headed " General Policy to be pursued in Northern Nigeria". Of this seminal composition there will be more to say later. Perhaps the most revealing document is a much worn, folded map upon which, with coloured chalk and pencil, he has marked the first provinces he hoped to occupy and administer and also alternative lines by which a railway might one day run from Lagos to Kano. On the map he has written " Northern Nigeria as we took it over 1.1.1900. The greater part quite unexplored. The rough idea of the future provinces is indicated."

These documents illustrate his position. He had been given full powers: he could devise policy and draw up proclamations. But how, and above all, where, could he carry them out? The hard-won international boundaries, heavily coloured on his map, had been agreed at last, but only on paper. They had still to be traced on the ground.

Within them lay an area of nearly 300,000 square miles, and a population of unknown size.[1] Only a fraction of the area, lying in the south and west, had been occupied; the rest was not only unoccupied but unexplored. Half a dozen dotted lines would have shown the track of the few Europeans who had traversed it in half a dozen precarious expeditions before Joseph Thomson reached Sokoto in 1885 on behalf of the Niger Company. Leaving out the deadly cost in lives of the early voyages of exploration up the Niger, the expeditions to the northern part of the territory after the complete loss of Mungo Park's party in 1805 and up to Barth's expedition in 1850-5, had employed some fifteen men and of these only five had survived. The complete lack of communications in a country which had never attained to the wheel and where even camel and pack-ox served only the northern belt, had restricted the Company to the wide but navigationally seasonal waters of the Niger and the Benue and there were few places where its agents had penetrated as much as fifty miles from its banks; in many places they had not penetrated one. There was thus some point in the jibe of the still unconquered and hostile Emir of Kontagora who encouraged his followers to believe that the white intruders were a species of fish which would die if they went far from water. Some of the Company stations were hulks moored in the river which the new government was only too glad to inherit.

A colonial governor can seldom have been appointed to a territory so much of which had never even been viewed by himself or any other European. The vast majority of the inhabitants were not only completely unaware that they had been allocated to Britain but were ignorant of the very existence of such a country. Nor were the bulk of these peoples primitive and unorganized tribesmen whose subjection, when Britain was ready to claim it, could be taken for granted; the region contained some of the most highly developed and civilized Muslim states of tropical Africa, centred upon walled cities and defended by armies of horsemen.

In the first volume Lugard's story took us twice to the Niger country but, for all its international importance, his work was mainly

---

[1] The figure generally given at this time was 30 to 35 millions. It could be only the wildest guess. By the end of his High Commissionership Lugard gave it as 8¾ millions. The first attempt at a proper census was in 1931 which gave 11,434,924 for the Northern Provinces. The latest figure (mid-1959) is 19,158,000 for the N. Region, (35,284,000 for the whole of Nigeria including the Cameroons), which must, of course, represent a large increase over that of 1900.

in the rather backward frontier region of Borgu and though we saw him going up and down the Niger the rest of the territory lay largely outside his concern and was therefore only briefly outlined. A somewhat fuller sketch of Northern Nigeria is needed now if his work in this new Protectorate is to be followed.

In Nigeria, as in the West African coast-lands generally, the interweaving of the physical and the human factors makes a fairly simple pattern. Climate, in latitudinal bands, makes the woof through which the peoples' movements, mainly from north to south, make the warp. Rainfall is the governing condition. From east to west four main zones can be distinguished—the southernmost strip of deep rainforest; a strip of more open rain forest; then, forming much the widest sector, comes one covered by that park-like savannah or orchard bush which makes the pervading scene through most of tropical Africa. Finally, this thins out to the north into the fourth and narrow strip of dry open plain with thorn-scrub, verging into the semi-desert of the southern Sahara.

It is dangerous enough to try to summarize geography but to apply this treatment to anthropology, which is still, year by year, exploring further the races and cultures of Africa, is to ensure criticism. Yet the attempt must be made. We are told that Africa's western coast is the home of the true negro. But through the centuries and, indeed, the millennia, other races, Hamitic speaking members of the European group, have been moving, generally, it seems, in a south-westerly direction, pressing upon the black prognathous Sudanic negro, producing various degrees of mixture and relaying feebly, across vast distances, cultural forms from the earliest homes of civilization where Asia and Africa meet. We shall have to consider later, when Lugard undertook their government, the peoples who had, at least, in part, been sheltered from these penetrations and influences within the protecting forests of the south, and especially of the Niger delta and the south-east, in which the newcomers' cattle and horses could not live. Lugard had seen a little on his Borgu expeditions of the Yoruba, who were more open than the people of the deep forest to external influence, and were grouped into states centred upon large towns. The north of the future Nigeria, with which we are now concerned, lay still more open to the peoples moving across the vast plains from the regions of the Mediterranean and the Red Sea.

In the northern part of Lugard's territory Hamitic migrations and influences, playing upon an amalgam of negro tribes for an unknown number of centuries, had bred one of the largest and most famous cultural and linguistic groups in West Africa, and indeed, of all negro Africa, that of the eight million Hausa. Claiming descent from a mythical migrant from Baghdad, the Hausa had developed their seven original states, which included Kano, Zaria, Daura, Gobir and Katsina, at much the same time that Normans and Angevins were hammering England into shape. These pagan kingdoms, growing up round what were for Africa considerable walled cities, with a constellation of lesser towns around them, were probably not very unlike those of the Yoruba. But in what has come to be called the middle belt, the region lying across the south of Northern Nigeria, the tribes had largely escaped consolidating influences and, though there were some small and very interesting kingdoms, the majority were still dispersed in their small lineage groups amongst scattered villages and without any political unity.

The medieval Hausa states were no isolated centres of civilization. They tended to be in a borderland between large empires. These flourished to their east, north and west from at least the eleventh century, when Muslim records throw the first clear light upon the hidden centre of western Africa, until the seventeenth. An uneven line can be traced across Africa between latitudes 12 and 15, approximately between the Gambia and Senegal rivers in the west and running eastwards until it loops south to include the highlands of Ethiopia. This line represents the borderland between the mainly pastoral and the mainly agricultural spheres. Along this line, through all the ages into which we can peer, the mobile people of the plains with their horses and cattle and, later, their camels, and with their contacts, however distant, with the active springs of civilization, have pressed down upon the more sedentary peoples. These contacts can be seen by historians as fertile marriages between the masterful people from the north and the settled agriculturists, between " the Desert and the Sown ", and a series of kingdoms and loose empires have risen and flourished for at least as long as the thousand years into which history or tradition can reach. Often the northern migrants must have provided little more than ruling castes, accepted for their superior ideas of religion and chieftainship. Some anthropologists have discerned in the widespread belief in the sacred attributes of African chiefs a reflection of the ancient Egyptian concept of the divine king, whose life represents the vitality of his people and of their crops and herds, and who must, therefore, never be allowed to grow old. In parts the non-negro dynasties of the ruling caste retained an associated cult based upon their pastoral tradition.[1] The writer has had the privilege of being entertained by some of the " divine kings " along this line, from the Aku of the Jukuns near the Benue, to the Mek of the Shilluk on the Nile, some fifteen hundred miles to the east. It was the convention that these beings needed neither to eat nor to drink, or that they left no footsteps, somewhat embarrassing pretences when in the company of a merely mortal and unbelieving European. Similarly a visit was made to a Hima chief on the western shore of Lake Victoria who kept his royal cattle and hung his ritual milking vessels in his own hut. In the eighteen fifties, Barth records how, on the other side of Africa, the emir of Kano in his day, though a Muslim, still retained a somewhat odoriferous cattle byre in the heart of his palace.[2]

The long-lived kingdom of Kanem, in close touch with the Mediterranean foci of Islam and flourishing east of Lake Chad, dominated a large region eastward of that mysterious piece of water. It mastered most of the Hausa states and ate its way southwards into the pagan tribes, even writing its name upon the hazy maps of contemporary Europe. Moving its centre in the usual south-western direction and building up the Kanuri " nation ", the kingdom of Kanem became in the sixteenth century the kingdom of Bornu, with its capital west of Chad. It was a great point of departure for the caravans of slaves sent due north to Fezzan, and so to Tripoli or Egypt.

Islam extended gradually and superficially through Bornu and Hausaland, overlaying the old pagan kingdoms but leaving, especially away from the towns, much of their animist culture. The new faith brought with it a unifying and settled culture.

This leads us on to the event which was all-important for the new British administration. This was the Fulani *Jihad*, or Holy War, which occurred in the first decade of the nineteenth century. The Fulani need

[1] There is a large literature dealing with this wide subject from Sir James Frazer, *The Golden Bough* (1890), to many later studies. See especially, for Nigeria, C. K. Meek, *A Sudanese Kingdom* (1931). Professor C. G. Seligman has discussed the subject brilliantly in brief in *Egypt and Negro Africa: a Study in Divine Kingship* (1934). See also E. W. Bovill, *Caravans of the Old Sahara* (1933).

[2] H. Barth, *Travels and Discoveries in North and Central Africa* (1857), vol. ii, pp. 103-4.

some introduction.[1] They are a people widely dispersed, roughly along
that latitude of contact which has been mentioned, from Senegal on
the Atlantic coast to the border of the former Anglo-Egyptian Sudan.
In what may be called their natural state they are a cattle people moving
over wide beats in the search for pasture. Their way of life presents an
attractive picture to the European eye. The writer has a very striking
memory of camping in Katsina Emirate beside a group of these people
(called Cow-Fulani, or Bororoje, in distinction from those who have
become sedentary, the Fulanin Gidda). They were wholly non-
negroid, with slim figures, skin of a lovely bronze colour, fine-drawn
European type of face, and straight, dark hair. The women, gay with
beads, braided plaits and golden ear-rings, looked especially graceful:
Barth called them "slender as antelopes". Equipped with boldly
decorated vessels they went about their milking and other duties.
Their only houses were little shelters of branches and mats carried
about on their pack-animals, and simpler even than the movable housing of those other Hamites, the Somali, at the eastern extremity of the
pastoral line. Smoky fires were lit to keep away the flies and round
these crowded the biddable cattle, as handsome, of their kind, as their
owners, being almost pure white with black noses, hoofs, ears and eye-
lashes. These people, highly skilled pastoralists, penetrating right across
Africa in their dispersed family groups, were tolerated almost everywhere among the sedentary tribes, as they seemed to offer no danger
while the products of their herds were highly valued.

But while the Cow-Fulani remained shy, innocuous and mostly
pagan, those of their kind who settled in the towns and were converted
to Islam became very different people and were often fanatical in
religion and racially arrogant. It was in 1804 in the kingdom of Gobir
that, as has so often happened in the history of Islam, a puritan revival
led to political struggle and to war. It was inspired by a Fulani holy
man, the Shehu Usuman Dan Fodio. In his sermons he denounced the
surviving paganism of the Hausa. After quarrelling with his Hausa
ruler in Gobir, Dan Fodio called for a return to the pure discipline of
Islam and for the faithful to expel all lax or heretical rulers. The Fulani
clans, scattered widely about the states which they knew so well, were

[1] The Fulani, who are given different names in their several regions, still present some
mysteries as to their origins and there is a growing literature about them. A recent book which
summarizes some of the present knowledge and contains a bibliography is D. S. Stenning's
Savannah Nomads, 1959.

ideal material for spies, rebels and cavalry though it appears that many of them remained outside the struggle. The leaders of revolt obtained flags from the Shehu and within a few years, sometimes easily, sometimes after bitter fighting, the old Hausa rulers had almost everywhere been replaced by Fulani. The impetus of the movement carried its leaders beyond the limit of the former Hausa kingdoms and new lordships were imposed over the pagan tribes which lay in the middle belt, though in many of these, above all in Adamawa far to the south-west, a mere handful of these alien conquerors remained isolated in a sea of unconverted and mostly primitive negro tribes. Even the advanced Yoruba group lost their large northernmost city, Ilorin, to a flag-bearing conqueror and to his Muslim faith.

It does not seem, however, that even in the Hausa states there was anything like a general civil war. In some parts the population, as was to be Lugard's own later experience, remained aloof from the struggle for power over them; in others the Hausa might even help the intruders. To the north-east Bornu remained independent of the Fulani rulers and hostile towards their suzerainty over this new loose empire. This suzerainty was divided between Usuman's son, Bello, who took the lion's share east and south of his chosen headquarters at Sokoto, and his brother, the Emir of Gwandu, who presided over the smaller part, west of this. By the time of the death of Usuman in 1817 the first wave of conquest had swept over most of what was to be Northern Nigeria and, indeed, beyond it. But the country was troubled for many years by rebellions led by deposed Hausa rulers, especially in the region nearest to Sokoto, and sometimes by struggles between Fulani dynastic rivals. The control exercised by Usuman's successors was one of lordship rather than government. They confirmed new rulers, and exacted an annual tribute, mainly in slaves. But, as so often in the history of Islam, the puritanical zeal of the revivalists waned with military success and the worldly luxury which followed it. Moreover, rulers with a pastoral tradition always tended to push their boundaries too far, a failing encouraged in this region by the lack of natural frontiers, and also to ignore tribal or cultural forces amongst their subjects.[1] Since the decline of the Muslim culture along the Mediterranean coast, the caravan traffic which still extended across the Sahara brought less stimulus than in the great days of the past. The region was tending to

[1] Bovill, *op. cit.* pp. 264-8.

isolation between the partially obstructive desert and the pagan wall in the south. As the nineteenth century wore on, the ocean was bringing to these despised pagans a deepening contact with the western world in which the northerners had no share.

It is not easy for Europeans, coming in suddenly as masters, to understand their new subjects and a Muslim people present a special kind of obscurity. The fairest way to enter into the realities of Fulani and Hausa culture is to re-read the absorbing records of the first travellers who went in as equals, or even as suppliants, and stayed long in intimate and dependent association with the people, perforce studying their language and customs. Clapperton, Denham, Lander and Barth can give us pictures which no later comers could paint. They show us at once the limitations and the high achievements of these societies, with their organized trade and wide contacts, their custom of supplying housing, food and escort to travellers, and their capacity to breed individuals of high character and intelligence. We see Sultan Bello, the son of the leader of the *Jihad*, discussing with Clapperton, the first European he had seen, the signs of the Zodiac and asking him whether he was a Nestorian or a Socinian Christian.[1] We have to think ourselves back into a medieval setting in which luxury could alternate with primitive poverty, hospitality with fanatical xenophobia, nobility with sadistic cruelty, while the islands of civilization were always threatened and often overrun by storms of destructive warfare. The whole society was based not only upon slavery but upon slave-raiding and trading and the friends of Denham could laughingly and contemptuously kick the skeletons of the slaves whose bones he saw tracing the caravan routes across the desert and heaped around the camping sites.[2]

There had, it seems certain, been some decline from the best days of the Habe—as the pre-Fulani Hausa were often called—and also from the height of the Fulani past. Yet at the date of Lugard's coming, as he was to see more clearly upon closer contact, there was still nothing in untouched negro Africa to compare with the political and cultural sophistication of these ancient Hausa states, with their walled red cities, crowded mosques, literate mullahs, large markets, numerous crafts in metal and leather, far-ranging traders, and skilled production

[1] D. Denham, H. Clapperton and W. Oudney, *Travels and Discoveries in North and Central Africa in 1822, 1823 and 1824* (1831), vol. iv, pp. 85 ff.
[2] *Ibid.* vol. i, pp. 140-6.

of a wide variety of crops. Served by cattle, camels, horses and donkeys, and by slaves whom early travellers to Kano reckoned as half the population, not only the ruling class but the more prosperous of the Hausa had some of the luxury of leisure coupled with a standard of living very rare in tropical Africa.

Many qualifications could be made of the broad picture which has been given of Northern Nigeria, but only one is essential to our understanding of Lugard's problem. The uniformity of the pattern of east-west cultural stripes was broken wherever nature had provided the primitive pagans with conditions which served, like the southern forests, to protect them. Thus there were in hilly or forested regions pockets of pagan tribes even in the far northern zone while the great bare hump of the Bauchi plateau and the spine of hills along the eastern frontier were the refuge of considerable numbers.

Hitherto Lugard's story has been one of movement and adventure. These were not to be wholly lacking in his new command but most of his adventures now took place in his mind or on paper as he sat at his desk in some makeshift office; the action, the trekking, the danger and the fights were for the men whom he moved from place to place, but always, gradually, forward, as if the map were some giant chess board and he were playing a game against the Fulani power. Indeed, at almost this same date, Sir Charles Eliot, the first governor of British East Africa, engaged in a rather different version of the same task, remarked that " White checks black in a very few moves ".[1] But the rules of the West African game were not quite the same as in the East: indeed, the whole analogy cannot be pushed very far. For as Lugard extended his power step by step into new provinces, no settlers followed him, no man lost his land, the black pawns were not swept off the board and even such kings and knights as were taken were replaced, if not in their proper persons, then by almost indistinguish-
• able pieces of their own kind and colour. Rather, returning to the metaphor of weaving, should we see the British bringing new strands of influence working up against the old north to south movement and introducing a new colour, the imperial red, which tended year by year to enrich and diversify the old pattern rather than to obliterate it.

[1] *East Africa Syndicate—Correspondence re Eliot's Resignation and Concession* (1904), Cd. 2099, p. 26-7.

CHAPTER III

THE FIRST TWO YEARS, 1900-1902

LUGARD'S FIRST fifteen months were filled with desperate work. Before he could penetrate the intermediate zone or even think of occupying the great northern emirates, he had to establish or re-establish European authority along the southern part of his protectorate. His resources seemed absurd in face of the immensity of his task. He had the Northern Nigerian Regiment, which was that part of the W.A.F.F. allocated to his Protectorate. It consisted of two to three thousand Africans with some 200 British officers and N.C.O.s, about a third of whom were always on leave or sick. He began with five political officers. By March he had nine.[1] By 1901 his total civil staff, as a result of continuous badgering of the Colonial Office, numbered 104.[2] And it must be remembered that this number covered every kind of post, including doctors, police, engineers, marine department officers, accountants, telegraphists, storekeepers, public works staff, clerks and a number of other minor and major indispensable white men. Of these, moreover, a substantial fraction would at any time be on leave, invalided, or sick. With unseasoned men and the lack of buildings and of doctors the sickness rate was very high. His political staff at the beginning, and actually in Africa, consisted of two Residents and three Assistant Residents. Small wonder that a stream of dispatches and telegrams went to the Colonial Office appealing for more staff. But Northern Nigeria was wholly dependent upon a grant-in-aid. It had as yet, of course, no revenue of its own except an allowance on customs from Southern Nigeria, some £45,000 in 1900-1, and the Office had to submit every request to a very stern Treasury.

During the spring and early summer of 1899 Lugard played a game

---

[1] *Northern Nigerian Gazette*, Vol. I, 1900, pp. 6 and 65.
[2] *Annual Reports, Northern Nigeria*, 1905-6, p. 107.

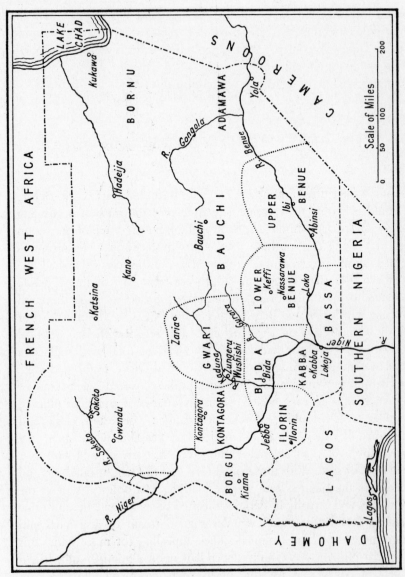

Northern Nigeria 1901. Based on Lugard's map of this period

against the Colonial Office in which the counters were figures of such diminutive size that they must astonish the student of later colonial finance. The game merits recording. Lugard horrified the Colonial Office by asking for a grant of £134,000.[1] Antrobus cut it to £75,000, including a limit of £10,000 for administrative staff. Chamberlain, upon whom Lugard had relied so much for support, remarked that Colonel Lugard's estimates " are impossible and £75,000 seems very large indeed ".[2] By the end of April Lugard had managed to cut his demand to £91,809. But this diminution merely incensed Antrobus, who felt sure that if MacGregor, governor of Lagos, who had run New Guinea on £15,000 a year, " had been told to do what he could in Northern Nigeria with £50,000 or even £30,000 a year, he would set to work to do the best he could " and he remarked it was a pity he could not now change places with Lugard.[3] Chamberlain still declared that even £70,000 was too much and laid down £60,000 as a maximum. Lugard was ordered to cut to £50,000, or £60,000 at most. He submitted a revised demand for £88,000. Antrobus admitted defeat: even he could not now see what could be cut and Chamberlain was forced to agree that the Treasury should be approached. So, against the strongest opposition, Lugard won the first round with the Office—the all-important round of finance. Yet, his fighting spirit having triumphed, his sense of economy came into play and, incredible though it may seem, in his first year, on a revenue from the grant-in-aid and customs of £135,000, he spent only £96,407. The saving of £35,593 was largely made up of the salaries of posts which were filled late or not at all.[4]

To his brother Edward, about whom he was desperately anxious since he had gone to the war in South Africa—"you are playing the man's part and I am fooling here"—he wrote, "Only 8 weeks (barely) are past since I landed and this Administration is a going concern." There follows a list of all that had been done—incorporating the Company Constabulary, housing and posting them; declaring Lokoja and Jebba cantonments and drawing up their regulations and appointing magistrates; starting a postal service; enlisting a police force; en-

---

[1] Lugard to Chamberlain, 2 February 1899, C.O. 446/7.
[2] Minute by Chamberlain, on Lugard to Chamberlain, 2 February 1899, C.O. 446/7.
[3] Minutes by Antrobus, on Lugard to Chamberlain, 2 February 1899, and 10 May 1899, C.O. 446/7.
[4] *Reports*, 1900–1, p. 18.

gaging and allocating 100 native clerks; organizing medical, telegraph, transport services and public works and marine departments; establishing a preventive service against liquor imports; arranging for an Anglo-French boundary commission; above all, initiating and instructing a political department. And, lest at this distance of time we should think of the High Commissioner as a detached administrative mind we might read the last sentence

> " In addition I have had a double-barrelled attack of fever and have been laid up for some time with *most painful* boils (on my stern so that it was painful sitting) but neither stopped me working."
>
> (L. to E.J.L., 25 February 1900).

In creating his administration almost from zero, in the same way that he had only just finished creating the Frontier Force, he had to struggle with every imaginable obstacle. He had no proper office or office staff. He had no printing press, so all laws had to be typed. He had no government house, only an old two-roomed mission-building at Lokoja which he and Gollan used. There were some wooden huts but most of the civil officers had to live in tents. It was not even certain where the protectorate's headquarters were to be. Lugard, with something of a soldier's desire to be near the scene of coming action, was impatient to go further north and he moved up-river from Lokoja to Jebba a few weeks after his arrival. But the difficulty was first to extract building equipment out of the Crown Agents and then to get it shipped and finally to push it upstream to the right places, wherever these might prove to be, while the rivers were navigable.

He began by proclaiming three provinces: firstly the Middle Niger, to include the country west and north of the Niger with Ilorin and Bida; secondly the Benue to cover the country north and south of that river, including Muri, Bauchi and Adamawa, all three of which had still to be occupied; thirdly, Kano, to consist, quite simply, of " the remainder of the Protectorate", in other words, all the main states of the far north which, with Bornu, had lain clear outside even the influence of the Company. The grim fact was that only Ilorin, itself restless, the mainly pagan lands immediately along the two rivers near their junction, and Borgu, which as a result of the operations against the French was under some military control, could be regarded as open to the new administration. To the east, at Yola, the Emir of Adamawa was defiant; the Company agents were almost prisoners on their hulk. Bida, lying just north of the Niger, between the two key British points of Lokoja and Jebba, and an all-important trading centre, had thrown off its allegiance, and Goldie's campaign, only a few months after its conclusion, had been undone by the return of the slave-raiding Emir he had expelled and his forces were still raiding almost up to Lokoja. The turbulent Munshi pagans were massed close to Ibi. Lugard posted one of his four Residents at Ilorin, and the other three on the river at Lokoja, Loko and Ibi. His administration therefore, ran only along a narrow belt, some three hundred miles long, close to his southern frontier.

We are thus brought to the conclusion, which a senior Colonial Office man, who was by no means partial to Lugard, supported, that, at its foundation, only one-tenth of the new Protectorate showed any trace of organized British control.[1] The main reasons for this lay in the utter inadequacy of the Company's resources for its immense task and the enforced concentration of its agents upon the trading aspect of its responsibilities. Added to this was the very natural tendency during the last two years, when the end of the Charter was under discussion, to allow the machine of administration, such as it was, to run down. Thus Mr. Flint quotes Goldie as remarking to Lord Scarbrough that " what happens in Northern Nupe is not vital to us so long as we hold the waterway."[2] The Company admitted that they did not care to " go to any special trouble in administering their territories " at this stage.[3] Goldie had said much about the Empire getting a new territory from him at bargain price, but in the early weeks of 1900 Lugard must have been wondering how much of what had been bought had actually been delivered.

With all these difficulties and uncertainties and with a political staff of less than a dozen, with a Colonial Office quite incompetent to guide him in the immense and novel task the department had just taken over, Lugard did not have to grope his way towards a system of government. He had already worked out his principles and, to some extent, his methods. His system is such an important part of his life, and had such deep and lasting effects not only in Nigeria but in the rest of

[1] Sir George Fiddes, *The Dominions and Colonial Offices* (1926), p. 141.
[2] Goldie to Scarbrough, 30 August 1897 (in the possession of the Earl of Scarbrough), quoted in Flint, *Sir George Goldie*, p. 298.
[3] Minute by Butler on Salisbury to Chamberlain, 9 March 1899, C.O. 446/5.

Africa, and indeed beyond, that we shall have to devote chapters at a later stage to its discussion. Yet the narrative would be quite incomplete if we made no reference year by year to his main administrative measures as he took them.

He had decided, drawing upon his observations in India, his experience in Uganda and upon the ideas and initial measures of Goldie, that he must rule "indirectly" to the utmost possible extent through native institutions, instead of destroying or ignoring these and trying to administer the people directly. The part played in this decision by sheer necessity and that derived from principle must bulk largely in the later discussion. From the first he decided that his chief administrative officers should be called Residents to indicate that they were advisers rather than executives, and that he would try to use, under British sovereignty and guidance, the emirate system and the ability of the Fulani ruling caste to the highest measure of which they were capable. As part of this policy the Supreme Court was limited in its jurisdiction to cases concerning non-natives and government cantonments. A Native Courts Proclamation[1] (no. 5 of 1900), provided for the setting up of Native Courts to try natives by native law and custom. There was the usual formula that cruel punishments and those repugnant to natural justice and English law should be prohibited. These measures were imposed partly by shortage of judicial staff but they left the Supreme Court with very little to do, though the control of the Native Courts imposed a heavy burden upon the Residents and upon the High Commissioner.

Another basic law, and perhaps the one nearest of all to Lugard's own heart, was the Slavery Proclamation. As this large problem required a clear and immediate decision we must consider it here. Slavery may seem to the layman an extremely simple question of right and wrong, of bondage or freedom. It is, however, highly complex. The position of the farm slave may vary through all the gradations from the complete chattel status similar to that which marked the slave on a white man's plantation in the new world, through many grades of serfdom until it merges into a burdened and strictly controlled tenancy of land. Again, especially in a Muslim

[1] As Africans advanced in political self-consciousness and knowledge of English they generally rejected the term "native" as a word of inferiority. It is usual today to use the term "African". It would, however, be unhistorical in this book to ante-date the change, and for the most part, the usage of the time, especially, of course, where it is official terminology, will be employed.

country, the distinction between concubinage and slavery is hard to draw, much more to enforce. Then there is the difficulty of the act of liberation. What is " freedom " to some ignorant pagan, perhaps a mere child, taken from some distant region that cannot be identified, much less reached? Lugard had already, as we have seen, come to grips with slavery on the east African coast. He had written at length about it in his book upon that region.[1] Since then he had much more experience of the subject in West Africa and many opportunities to discuss it with his friend, Sir John Kirk, the leading expert, and with Goldie. They were all agreed that under West African conditions a law simply abolishing slavery would be either a dead letter or would provoke economic chaos, and, perhaps, rebellion. Where a population lives by subsistence farming with practically unlimited land and no incentive to work more than their low standards of well-being de-mand, there could be no natural supply of wage-labourers. There was only a rudimentary monetary and exchange system and the ruling class, or men of exceptional enterprise, could hardly obtain the labourers their activities required except by compulsion. Thus slavery was built into the Hausa economic system which would have been completely disrupted by wholesale manumission, and hordes of un-employed people who had lost their lands and their tribes would have been thrown out to starve or to thieve.

The method favoured by Lugard and his friends was the abolition of the *legal status* of slavery. This meant that after a given date, in this case April 1st, 1901, no *new* slaves could be made. It also meant that no owner could restrain or re-capture a slave who appealed to the courts. Thus, by degrees, slaves who desired their freedom and especi-ally those who were ill-treated, could claim their emancipation, while all their children would be free. Before judging this compromise too harshly, as did many zealous reformers in England, it should be remembered that domestic slaves once attached to a household were not usually ill-treated, and when they belonged to the rich and power-ful they might even prosper. Slaves, indeed, because of their lack of competing ties, could become the most trusted servants of a ruler and even rise to high office. They were frequently used in Africa, as else-where, as the personal janissaries of kings and princes. As late as 1910,

[1] F. D. Lugard, *The Rise of Our East African Empire* (1893), vol. i, chapters III, VII and VIII vol. ii, chapter XLII.

so a Resident of this period told the writer, an official, when asked by the chairman of a committee enquiring into land matters in London how the taxes were collected, replied " By the head slaves." " But we abolished slavery in 1900!" exclaimed the astonished chairman and ordered the reply to be expunged from the record. It followed that a number of slaves preferred, where the choice was offered to them, to remain attached to the households of the great than to take up the hard life of the peasant farmer. Not many years ago the writer saw large numbers of people, generally fat and well-liking, in the compounds of great Nigerian chiefs: these were in fact, though they could no longer be in law, slaves in a light and self-chosen servitude. Goldie, after his successful Bida campaign, had abolished the legal status of slavery though, for obvious reasons, the decree must have been a dead letter. It remained in force, however, and it was not until April 1901 that Lugard issued his own Proclamation (No. 2 of 1901) which covered also slave-raiding and slave-trading.

It was in these that the chief vice of African slavery lay and here the anti-slavery reformers who, during their campaigns, had exhausted all superlatives in the vocabulary of horror, had not over-stated their case. From the beginning of history there appears to have been a demand for negro slaves in the lands bordering the eastern Mediterranean and further east, and especially for eunuchs, who fetched a high price since barely one in ten victims are said to have survived the rough surgery of their captors. Slaves were therefore the main merchandise sent up from the western Sudan in exchange for the luxuries of the Mediterranean and indeed, of Europe; and slaves were themselves also a currency. As we have said before, the Christian nations, who were so lately profiting from African slavery, are in no strong position to pronounce moral condemnation. Even the horrors of the Saharan slave-routes could be well matched by those of the " middle passage " on the ships. It is not, however, only the cruelty but the economic stupidity of the dominant groups which was so striking in West Africa. Economic self-interest can explain the system by which European traders collected slaves at the coast to produce sugar in depopulated West Indian Islands. They had no interest in the well-being of West Africa. The Arab slave-raiders in eastern Africa, also, need feel little concern about the ultimate effects of their activities upon regions which were merely distant slaving grounds. But the chiefs of Northern

Nigeria who, year after year, century after century, went out on regular expeditions to raid the closely neighbouring pagans, destroying, it might be, a dozen for every human prize of proper age and condition which they obtained, were setting rigid bounds to their own prosperity and even to their own dominions. There are poems of the eleventh century exulting in the murder and misery inflicted by the ruler of Bornu in his raids and eight centuries later Barth found his successor still ravaging and burning. After accompanying the Sultan's commander on one of these forays he asked the obvious question, "Why not let these people cultivate in tranquillity and levy tribute from them," and received a stupid and savage answer that showed the limit of the semi-civilization of the Muslims of the western Sudan.[1] The whole region, but above all the intermediate zone north of the forest barrier, was kept static and impoverished by this perpetual man-hunting. In his first annual report Lugard wrote:

"There is, probably, no part of the 'Dark Continent' in which the worst forms of slave raiding still exist to so terrible an extent, and the slave-raiders are not even provident of their hunting grounds, for those who are useless as slaves are killed in large numbers, villages burnt, and the fugitives left to starve in the bush." In Kabba "hundreds of ruins attest the former existence of a population and a prosperity which have gone. Deprived of their hunting grounds, and anticipating the advent of European control, with its prohibition of slave-raiding, the Fulani and Nupes began early in the year to ravage the districts nearer home and with Kontagora, the 'Gwamachi' (destroyer) . . . laid waste the country from the Niger banks, on the west and south to the eastern highlands, and to the north as far as the borders of Sokoto and Zaria" and the two armies "raided for slaves almost to the banks of the Niger and close to Jebba . . ."[2]

Thus the Fulani slave-raids were pushing into the centre of Nigeria as British power moved north to meet them, just as Livingstone and his successors arrived to find the Arab slavers penetrating into the heart of central Africa from the east, and as Gordon had found them pressing down alongside him in the southern Sudan. The effects of this raiding were a grave and increasing threat to the population and the economy of the continent when seen in general terms, and unspeakably horrible

[1] Margery Perham, *Native Administration in Nigeria* (1937), p. 45.
[2] *Reports*, 1900–1, p. 13.

43

when seen in detail. The new firearms which gave the eastern slavers such easy mastery had, fortunately, not yet come in any numbers to the Fulani or their devastations would have been even more complete. The critics of imperialism are impatient today of all opposing arguments but they should weigh the historical fact that European control, though it may in some parts have produced local and temporary decimations of its own, stopped a movement which was already well on the way towards the demoralization and extermination of Africans over immense regions of the continent. Moreover, once man had become an article of commerce, the ruling class did not seek their goods only from pagan " enemies ". The nineteenth century travellers record large regions ravaged of their at least nominally Muslim populations in the north. A book which gives a fascinating and intimate picture of life near Kano shows that even respectable Muslim citizens were sometimes kidnapped into slavery.[1]

Lugard's shortage of civil officers and lack of police obliged him to make every use of his troops as instruments of occupation and order. He sent two companies to patrol the southern border as a preventive service against the import of liquor. Others he sent on what were really pioneer explorations, to probe and survey northwards from the Niger up its Kaduna, Gurara and Okwa tributaries. Their orders were to avoid all hostilities and to make every effort to win the confidence of the people, to report upon the economics and geography and, as Lugard was determined to advance from Lokoja, to look for a new site for his capital. With his friend Willcocks in command of the regiment, the co-operation of the military was assured. It was therefore a severe shock to Lugard when, only three months after he had taken over, the warlike Ashanti caused a sudden crisis in the neighbouring British dependency, and he was asked to send immediately all the troops and guns he could spare. Willcocks, who was put in command of the expedition, took 1,200 men and fifty officers and N.C.O.s. Lugard was obliged to withdraw both his northern expedition and his southern patrols. Not only was there no immediate hope of bringing the Emirs of Kontagora and Bida to order but his position at Jebba, after he had moved his headquarters there, could have been wiped out if these two men had had the intelligence and resolution to do something more than raid right up to it for slaves. This was only one more

[1] M. Smith, *Baba of Karo* (1954). See also Perham, *op. cit.* pp. 44-6, and 49-50.

example of the slightness of the forces which Britain, out of economy and half-heartedness, and in contrast with other colonial powers, sent out to occupy vast areas and control large populations. That so few disasters resulted from Britain's economy of force was not due to any lack of forward policy. The reasons were partly military in that, although great risks were taken, the fire-power of the invaders, as we saw in Uganda, to some extent made up for the absurd disparity of numbers. As Hilaire Belloc said in *The Modern Traveller* with brutal brevity,

> "Whatever happens we have got
> The maxim gun and they have not."

The important political result was that the modest size of the military forces reinforced the natural British moderation which studied the other side and sought for bases of co-operation and understanding.

Chamberlain sent a special cable of congratulation to Lugard for the speed and generosity with which he had sent his force to Ashanti. The troops took this as a compliment to the Regiment but Antrobus minuted that the telegram had referred personally to Lugard and Chamberlain endorsed this.[1] Willcocks could not say enough to the credit of his Nigerian troops in the stiff Ashanti campaign. " I *never* served with finer fellows. How I love them! Always cheerful, plucky, brave and uncomplaining. Rippers! ! ! "[2] Later, in December, the minister was able to congratulate Lugard again " upon the tact and discretion which you have shown in avoiding hostilities " in Nigeria, while it was denuded of troops and also upon the fine record in Ashanti of a force which he had so lately created and trained.[3]

When, thus covered with honour, the troops returned at the end of December 1900, Lugard was able to resume his plans to push British power upon the next stage towards the north. While waiting for the return of the main body he had sent out small patrols which had been attacked by the Kontagora horsemen.[4] In January, 1901, he sent a strong force against Kontagora under the Acting-Commandant, Colonel Kemball R.A., a soldier for whom he had himself asked from

[1] Minutes on Lugard to Chamberlain, 24 June 1900, C.O. 446/10.
[2] Willcocks to Lugard, 7 September 1900, L.P.
[3] Chamberlain to Lugard, 17 December 1900, *Correspondence (1899–1901) Relating to the Administration of Lagos and Nigeria* (1902), African West No. 580.
[4] *Reports*, 1900–1, pp. 14 ff.

India.[1] The force marched along the banks of the Niger then swung round from the north in order to cut off the retreat of the Emir. The town of Kontagora fell easily; the Fulani horsemen were helpless against disciplined gunfire. The old Emir, the "Destroyer", hard pressed by pursuers, escaped with only a handful of followers. When, much later, he was captured and reproved for his slave-raiding, he retorted with the defiant question, "Can a cat be stopped from mousing?" and declared that he would die with a slave in his mouth. The troops managed to save his town from incendiarism or disorder and as they marched out again through the surrounding country the villagers demonstrated their joy at the fall of the oppressor. But in some parts there was silence where large stretches of the country had been depopulated and nothing remained amongst the re-conquering bush but hundreds of clay circles, large and small, to show where the huts and granaries of the murdered tribes had been burned.

Lugard himself joined in the next move, the reoccupation of Bida. Here, as we saw, the Emir Abu Bakri, expelled by Goldie, had returned, and had, perforce, been accepted by the Company as it could not afford to mount another major campaign against him. Lugard offered this man honourable treatment if he would meet him in peace, but he fled. Lugard went with the troops to the town of Bida, assuring the lesser chiefs that not a shot would be fired unless his party were attacked. They marched into the town and formed a large hollow square. Here Lugard, before the assembled crowds, installed as emir the Markum, the chief Goldie had put in place of Abu Bakri, and a man, it appeared, who had good claims to the position. Lugard did not feel much confidence in the Markum's character, and he was quite frank with Chamberlain about his motive.

"It was not without some reluctance that I reinstated the Fulani rulers but, as in the case of Mwanga of Uganda, I did so 'faute de mieux'. He is of the Royal House which exerts great influence."[2]

Lugard described his first achievements thus:

"Two of the most powerful of the Fulani Emirs have been deposed,

[1] Kemball, Maj.-Gen. (later Sir) George Verro, K.C.M.G., C.B., D.S.O., 1859-1941; 1878 joined Royal Artillery; 1879-80 served in Afghanistan; 1895 Chitral Relief Force; 1897-8 North-West Frontier, India; 1901-5 Inspector-General, West African Frontier Force; 1909-13 Assistant Director and Director at War Office; 1914 Maj.-Gen. and Brigade Command, India; 1915-16 served in European War: 1917-19 Divisional Commander, India.

[2] African (West) No. 580, pp. 97-101.

because after repeated warnings, they would not desist from laying waste the whole country and carrying off the people as slaves. Both the fine cities, which were the Fulani capitals, have been preserved from destruction. The loss of life has been confined almost entirely to the Fulani horsemen, viz: to the slave-raiders themselves, and they have suffered heavily, while the peasantry and slaves have suffered little. The Emirs themselves have been pursued with such energy that they abandoned everything, and reached Zaria, or elsewhere, in so miserable a plight that the effect will be very far-reaching indeed, and will not admit of the usual misrepresentation. The Fulani rule has been maintained as an experiment, for I am anxious to prove to these people that we have no hostility to them, and only insist on good government and justice, and I am anxious to utilize, if possible, their wonderful intelligence, for they are born rulers, and incomparably above the negroid tribes in ability."[2]

The departed Emir of Kontagora collected an army of free-booters and set up as an independent slave-raider, preying upon the pagan areas of his neighbours of Zaria and Katsina. In spite of this defiance and disorder Lugard decided to establish his new capital much further north in what was, in effect, an advanced frontier position near the Kaduna river. His idea was partly that once all the Protectorate was occupied, this would be a fairly central position, partly that it would be a healthier place, being in the dry belt and well away from the Niger. Desiring to be near a river that was navigable to steamers for at least part of the year and yet away from any river-valley, he chose a spot about 12 miles from the Kaduna river. On his working map, upon which he first marked the approximate spot, the word Goldilla is written, presumably to commemorate Goldie, but later the native word Zungeru was restored.

For the moment Lugard could do no more in Nigeria. He had passed fifteen strenuous months and in April 1901 he went back to England for seven months, leaving the experienced Wallace to act for him. His first annual report, covering the whole fifteen months, was written on the boat and during his first days of leave. The files of the Colonial Office make it very clear that after this, instead of leaving Nigeria in the temporary oblivion in which governors generally put their territories for at least part of their leave, Lugard was busily engaged in trying to run it from London. The Colonial Office officials

[2] *Reports*, 1900–1, p. 15.

and even Chamberlain himself, though most of his attention was now upon the south of the African continent, seem to have lent themselves to this arrangement. Perhaps, still largely ignorant of Northern Nigeria and regarding it as full of military and financial dangers, they did not at this time altogether deprecate Lugard's authoritative and resolute presence passing in and out of their gloomy offices in Downing Street. Later they were to regret their indulgence.

There were three major affairs which, by this arrangement, he was able to guide. One was a south-eastward projection of British power. This stretched, as we have seen, only as far as Ibi on the Benue. Further up this river the easternmost Fulani Emir ruled his province of Adamawa, part of which lay on the German side of the frontier. The Fulani ruling group at the capital, Yola, being almost surrounded by very backward pagans, had preserved much of their purity of blood along with their language, and this was still true of them even when the writer visited the place over thirty years later. They had also preserved their uncompromising Fulani attitude, and they had no intention of accommodating the white intruders. The Emir, living in his mud palace beside the river, had forbidden the Company agents to land on the river banks and even made them haul down their flag. He was well placed to form a great centre for the slave-trade, and immense numbers of captured pagans were sent from here to the northern states. In August, 1901, a small expedition of 365 men under Colonel Morland went up the river and, conciliatory offers having been refused, attacked the town. The Emir, strengthened by sixty deserters from Rabeh's forces with modern rifles and by two cannon given him by a French officer in 1892, was able to inflict some casualties before the palace was stormed. The Emir escaped and " The acknowledged heir was installed in his place on the usual conditions of appointment."[1] This action was sanctioned by the Colonial Office with the minute that, though Lugard would not like the idea of the work being undertaken by anyone except himself, he would have had to find good reasons for delay.[2]

The second matter Lugard directed from afar was more complex. It will be remembered that as long ago as 1894 he had half-expected to have been diverted from his Borgu expedition to the far north-east

[1] *Reports*, 1901, pp. 7-8.
[2] Minute on Wallace to Chamberlain, 4 August 1901, C.O. 446/16.

to deal with the extraordinary thrust from the eastern Sudan of the bold adventurer, Rabeh. The French, who had arrived in the Lake Chad area shortly afterwards, had defeated and killed Rabeh who, in dying, had charged his son, Fad-el-Allah, to put himself under the jurisdiction of the British. Unfortunately British jurisdiction was still a long way from the kingdom of Bornu where Rabeh had established his power. It was difficult for Lugard to decide whether to treat Fad-el-Allah, who was reported to be a most courageous and able man, as a usurper or, in view of his inability from sheer lack of power to expel him, to recognize him as the ruler of Bornu. Lugard's account of the matter shows the difficulty of making quick decisions. He at first favoured recognition[1] but afterwards changed his mind. "Apart," he wrote,

" from the natural hesitation in receiving as a friend the man who had been fighting the French, was the important consideration that so large and well-armed a body of seasoned veterans would constitute a serious difficulty in that part of the Protectorate. Their methods and mode of life for years had been those of uncivilized victors among a ruined and conquered people, and I know too well, by my own experience,"—he was, of course, thinking of Uganda—" the barbarities of which the Nilotic Sudanese are capable when unrestrained, to suppose that their rule and their methods would be tolerable to us." [2]

The French saved the British from their embarrassment by chasing Fad-el-Allah a hundred and fifty miles into British territory and defeating and killing him there. Chamberlain, always sensitive where the French were concerned, registered his anger about this "unwarrantable intrusion of French officers into the British sphere"[3] but in reality their action cleared the way for the British, when they were at last able to reach Bornu, to restore the native dynasty of this ancient kingdom to the throne. Rabeh's adventure has left nothing behind it but a most impressive fortress at Dikwa. When staying once within its stark crenellated walls of red earth, the writer was informed that they were cemented by the grim raider with the blood of a builder who complained of his difficulty in achieving a firm mixture.

Lugard's third major concern was to make all possible preparations for the transfer of his capital to the site he had so carefully chosen. He

[1] Lugard to Chamberlain, 12 April 1901, C.O. 446/15.
[2] *Reports*, 1900–1, pp. 10–11 and 1901, pp. 8–9.
[3] Minute by Butler on Lugard to Chamberlain, 28 December 1901, C.O. 446/17.

had induced a very reluctant Colonial Office to sanction the position and also the light railway that was to link it with the Kaduna river, twelve miles away. In the teeth of every difficulty, just before he left for England in April 1901, Lugard had somehow forced all the available building material up the Niger and its tributary to this furthest navigable point, had it all carried by porters from Wushishi on the river to the new site at Zungeru, and got his Director of Public Works, Mr. Eaglesome,[1] and a man after his own heart, to begin the earthworks. While at home he had directed his impetus to the English side of the proceedings, the provision of all equipment needed, and he was able to write, with his usual intense pride in speed of action,

" In May the final sanction for the line was given, and the rails were rolled in Leeds, and the first steps for the location were made in Africa, and before Christmas the first train steamed into Zungeru."[2]

" My little railway is in working order," he told his brother,

" and two trains run per diem. I have been to the new site and finally planned the situation of every house and building."

(L. to E. J. L., February 1902).

The story of Lugard's little railway has a parallel version in the Colonial Office records, but it is one shorn of enthusiasm. After getting their grudging agreement in November 1900, we find Lugard asking for more money for it in April 1901,[3] with Antrobus minuting that it was too late to ask Parliament for more and that Lugard had never explained that his transfer of headquarters was dependent on a railway. Antrobus could not help thinking that if he knew he was not going to get the money he would find some way out of the difficulty. Chamberlain was emphatic that the request to the Treasury for more money should not be made. In August 1902, the question comes up again: the Niger, Lugard said, had fallen very low, so he must have a longer railway. Antrobus remarks in exasperation that Lugard seems very unfortunate in his choice of his headquarters.[4]

Upon Lugard's return to Nigeria in November 1901 his first impor-

[1] Eaglesome, (later Sir) John, K.C.M.G., M.I.C.E., 1868–1950; 1890–1900 served in Public Works Department, India; 1900 Director of Public Works, Northern Nigeria; 1907 in charge of Baro-Kano railway; 1912–19 Director of Railways and Works, Nigeria; 1916 services lent to Ministry of Munitions.
[2] *Reports*, 1901, p. 5.   [3] Lugard to Chamberlain, 9 April 1901, C.O. 446/15.
[4] Minute by Antrobus on Lugard to Chamberlain, 17 August 1902, C.O. 446/24.

tant action was to send Colonel Morland to carry the British flag north-east to the ancient kingdom of Bornu. The expedition, consisting of 515 troops, and thirteen officers with two 75mm guns and four Maxim guns, set off early in February. Wallace accompanied it with orders to stop at Bauchi, the capital of an important emirate on the way. The Emir here had a large slave-market from which the slaves from Yola and the pagan areas surrounding Bauchi were distributed to the Hausa states further north, and in 1900 he seized the large " town " of Guaram and massacred or enslaved the whole population. The Emir, whose attitude to the British was known to be hostile, fled without fighting. The new Resident, Mr. Charles Temple,[1] hurried into the town before a panic could set in and at great personal risk calmed the people so that not a shot was fired and there was no disorder or destruction. Wallace called the headmen and chose the Emir's heir to succeed him. Lugard records that bonfires were lit by the people to show their joy at his deposition. The former Emir was later found and sent to live in Ilorin on a small pension. Lugard instructed Temple to do all he could to make peaceful contact with the wild, shy pagans on the hills near Bauchi. But these had had too little cause ever to trust strangers from the plains and some initial conflicts could not be avoided.

Colonel Morland marched on. He had to throw off a determined attack by a militant old man, the Mallam Jibrella, who was trying to imitate the Mahdi of the eastern Sudan, and whose courage showed what a difficult conquest Lugard would have had if religious fervour had been more widespread. Lugard makes a characteristic comment on his capture.

" Jibrella was a white-haired old man of a fine type. The dash and pluck shown by him had won the admiration of our officers, and he was well looked after till his arrival in Lokoja, where I placed him in charge of the local chief with a small subsidy for his maintenance. He is very feeble and no longer a danger."[2]

Pressing on Colonel Morland found himself on the black cotton-soil plains of Bornu, flat dry land patched with thorn-scrub. Here he

[1] Temple, Charles Lindsay, C.M.G., 1871–1929; 1898, 1900 and 1901 Acting Consul, Paraguay; 1899 Vice-Consul Manaos, Brazil; 1901 Resident, Northern Nigeria; 1910–13 Chief Secretary, N. Nigeria; 1914–17 Lieutenant-Governor, N. Nigeria.
[2] *Reports*, 1902, p. 8.

entered a country left ravaged and masterless after the invasion of Rabeh and his son. He found, too, that the French had deported the rightful emir, the Sheikh Shefu Garbai, and were imposing a heavy war indemnity upon the people through their own nominee. Colonel Morland thus arrived in the guise of saviour rather than conqueror. He stopped the indemnity, invited Garbai to come back to his headquarters and left a company of the Regiment there to help to restore a sense of security.

Thus, wrote Lugard, commenting on all these operations, " An enormous area, some 60,000 square miles was brought under administrative control with little bloodshed."[1] He warmly commended Morland for, as Willcocks, who should have known, declared, "Lugard is not the man to allow anything to obscure good work done by his subordinates."[2]

These were major measures of occupation. A great deal by way of clearing trade routes of robbers and of trying to get into touch with the many small pagan groups had to be done in the southern region where occupation was still limited to the rivers and a few main routes and posts. Some of the small Muslim emirs, who represented the southernmost fringe of the Fulani wave of conquest, were the most troublesome.

Lugard's records of the occupation seem to pulse with the urgency and enthusiasm of those crowded months of his life. A rather critical contemporary called his style " dithyrambic ".[3] The moral theme runs strongly through the reports—Lugard and his envoys seem to dash about the country like knight errants, punishing wicked people and liberating the oppressed, overthrowing cruel kings and elevating good ones. This was what Lugard willed to do and what he believed himself to be doing and no doubt he imposed his will and his idea upon his subordinates until they believed with him or, at least, reflected back his own policy in their reports. The events recounted are all true, and since slave-raiding rulers, some decadent, some oppressive, were being brought under a relatively humane and progressive government, the interpretation may, as a whole, be accepted. But it is permissible to doubt whether *all* those deposed or punished were so wicked and all those who replaced them were so much better,

---

[1] *Reports*, 1902, p. 8-10.   [2] Willcocks, *From Kabul to Kumassi*, p. 235.
[3] Sir W. N. Geary, *Nigeria under British Rule* (1927). Sir Nevill was for much of his life an independent barrister on the West Coast and took a usefully detached view of British rule.

and whether the welcome given by the people to their new masters was everywhere quite so warm as it seemed.[1]

A glance at the map will show that by the middle of 1902 Lugard had extended his occupation, in so far as the marching of his scanty troops and the posting of some dozen political officers can be given that name, up to the eleventh parallel with an extension up to Lake Chad where the Sultan of Bornu had given his allegiance. But the most formidable Hausa states to the north-west, Kano, Katsina and Sokoto, had not been entered. The story of that advance demands its own chapters. So does the administrative system which in principle and in practice Lugard had been improvising from the moment of his appointment. Our attention hitherto has been upon the large movements by which Northern Nigeria was, province by province, brought under control. But these were not the only matters which kept Lugard at his desk ten hours a day or which gave him the greatest anxiety, and we must presently try to see his administrative system as a whole. But in the middle of 1902 there occurred that great event which, for him, more than with most public men, changed the colour of his life. We must, therefore, like Lugard himself, make a sudden interruption in the story of his break-neck advance in Nigeria and turn aside into the sphere of his personal life.

[1] It may be of interest to readers that when two of the most widely experienced Residents of the period read this chapter in draft, one of them, Sir William Gowers, wrote in the margin of this paragraph " A fair comment. Of course they applauded the victors." The other, Sir Richmond Palmer, dissented generally, writing " I don't think there was much welcome." This difference of opinion illustrates the difficulties of writing even recent history. Perhaps, before the stories of the old men are all forgotten, some Hausa historian will write his account of these events.

CHAPTER IV

MARRIAGE

In 1902, during his second tour in Nigeria, Lugard took two weeks' special leave, went to Madeira and there, on June 11th, married Flora Shaw.

There may have been eminent men whose personalities were completely engrossed in their work and others who succeeded so well in keeping apart the two sides of their lives that the one hardly affected the other. It might, at first thought, be assumed that Lugard was one of those men whose work was his life. It had been spent, for the most part, in remote and dangerous places beyond the reach of white women. And there was a proportion of iron in his character which might have seemed enough to harden him against the entry of what are generally—perhaps mistakenly—called the softer emotions. We have, however, already seen how untrue this was, and how he was driven right out of the ordained course of his life and thrown into Africa as a despairing, penniless adventurer by the force of his devotion for Celia and the violence of the check it received. Since then, in spite of the loss of his faith in her, he had not been able, though it seems that he had a justification which would have sufficed most men, to evict her and all thought of her from his life. Upon her side it appears that as he rose in the world and she declined, she tried to revive her old claims. She had, after all, been a woman of high spirit and some culture and was still able to follow his exploits intelligently. There is a story that at the height of his fame, at the time of the Uganda retention campaign, as he came out from his lecture to the Royal Geographical Society and his distinguished audience crowded round him, Celia tried to force her way towards him. Some brother officers from his old regiment who knew the story lined up to bar her way. Yet on and off during the years the two were in contact. Lugard did not

54

easily give affection and trust and, having given Celia the utmost he had of both, he could never, while she lived, forget or abandon her, still less it seems—for we are here in a realm partly of conjecture—since she had become poor and *déclassée*. There was an inner conflict between his revulsion from the misery she had caused him, and the bond with one who had given him the only deep sexual experience of his life. Tied, as it were, to the ghost of the past, with the loss of faith which it represented, he felt himself cut off from the hope of marriage and family life. This may not have been the sole cause of the dark moods which sometimes overwhelmed him, but it certainly made them heavier. Here even his brother could not help, for, very naturally, Edward bitterly resented the damage which he believed this woman had done to his brother's life. There seems to have been only one occasion when, with some well-meant family contrivance, Lugard made a half-hearted proposal to a most eligible young lady, but the refusal, which she had the sense to make, was soon regarded by him with relief and gratitude.

We have seen that he had been able to enjoy the friendship and co-operation of two of the most interesting women of his time, Mary Kingsley and Flora Shaw.[1] The second friendship was closer and more prolonged.

Flora Shaw has a place of her own in the colonial history of the nineteenth century: indeed the change into Lady Lugard was in a sense the end of a remarkable public career. Her life has now been written and all those who wish to see the full-length portrait of the most unusual woman whom Lugard married should turn to the biography by Miss Moberly Bell, the daughter of Flora's friend and colleague on *The Times*. This is the official life, for which both Lugard and his brother helped to prepare the material.[2]

She was born five years before Lugard. On her father's side she belonged to a distinguished Irish Protestant family. Her grandfather, Sir Frederick Shaw, Bt., was a well-known public figure who became Secretary for Ireland in 1846 though he had to resign almost at once for reasons of health. He had the house and estate of Kimmage near Dublin. Her father, General Shaw, C.B., was a gunner who served in the Crimea but was mostly at Woolwich during Flora's girlhood. He

---

[1] The most important references in Vol. I are on pp. 571-2 and 646-7.
[2] E. Moberly Bell, *Flora Shaw*, (*Lady Lugard, D.B.E.*) (1947).

married a beautiful and aristocratic Frenchwoman, Marie de Fontaine, daughter of the last French governor of Mauritius, whom he met when serving in that island and who was alleged to be descended from Louis XV. Marie Shaw was delicate but, like Lugard's mother, and nearly all women until our own century, she had to bear children irrespective of her state of health. After presenting her husband with fourteen children, of whom Flora was the fourth, in closest succession, she became a complete invalid and required constant nursing until her death in 1871.

It will be seen that there was much in Flora's birth and upbringing which resembled Lugard's. Both were of gentle birth but both held, with the best of their class, the principle which may have helped to save Britain from social revolution, that privilege is inseparable from duty. Both came from families which on each side were in active service to the state and empire. Flora's grandfather would teach her his own creed of obligation to society, " It's the privilege of a gentleman," he would tell her, " to get the worse of any bargain throughout life."[1] Both were brought up strictly in the Protestant faith—though Flora's mother was a Roman Catholic—and both lost prematurely a much-loved mother. Both, again, were spurred to energy not only by ambition but also by poverty. Colonel Shaw's pay could barely sustain and educate his large family and when her mother died, her elder sister Mimi being married, Flora, at the age of eighteen, had to take charge of ten younger children, assist with their tutoring and run the financially precarious household. Her health was already affected by the strain of nursing her mother and by all her subsequent responsibilities. Yet, in spite of all this, she had a happier youth than Lugard. She was gay and intelligent; she had good looks and great beauty of colouring with her auburn hair, brilliant blue eyes and slight and graceful figure. She had from the first immense powers of affection and sympathy and in the large family parties at Kimmage, where the summers were spent, and in visits to the almost feudal chateau of her mother's people in France, she was able to exercise her high spirits, her intelligence and her genius for friendship. She rejected the respectable offers of marriage in any one of which her special powers would probably have been buried in a contented and maternal obscurity. She might be regarded as self-educated. Like the young Mary Kingsley,

[1] Bell, *op. cit.* p. 12.

she had the run of a good library, the soldiers' library at Woolwich, to which the house of the Commandant, occupied by her father, had access. Even today—a fact which should cause misgivings amongst our educationists—the exceptional and independent mind can often be traced to some divergence from the usual course of schooling which has given both stimulus to thought and freedom to read at will. To this freedom a fine stimulus was added for Flora. Ruskin came to lecture at Woolwich and noticed the beautiful girl who joined the military audience. A deep friendship grew between them: through him she met Carlyle and other writers and new worlds of the mind were opened up to her.

From this time she not only gave free rein to her intellect but followed its movements by action. After studying the poverty of the labouring class surrounding her home at Woolwich she opened a co-operative shop at which goods bought in bulk could be sold at wholesale price to the workers' wives. She penetrated into the east end of London to work there in its terrible 1880 conditions of labour and prostitution. Her determination to pay for further education for her younger sisters turned her mind to money-making and in 1877 she published a novel, " Castle Blair", based on the happy experiences of Kimmage, a book which ran through eight editions, the latest being printed by the Oxford University Press in 1929. This success led to further writing for journals. While staying with friends in Gibraltar in 1886, she had long talks with the notorious adventurer, Zebehr Pasha, then in exile, but reputed as a great slave-trader in the Southern Sudan, whose affairs had been tragically mixed up with those of Gordon, and whose foster son, Rabeh, has appeared in this story. By writing up his story for the *Pall Mall Gazette* she established her reputation as a first-class journalist and also helped to obtain the Pasha's release.[1]

From this point she made her pioneering way step by step upwards in her new profession. Working for the *Pall Mall Gazette* and the *Manchester Guardian*, she visited Morocco and even, with the help of Sir Evelyn Baring and other notables, disentangled the complex financial and political situation in Egypt. She was still spurred on by the need to make money for though her father's second marriage had allowed her to resign her most arduous duties, her elder sister Mimi

---

[1] *Pall Mall Gazette*, 28 June 1887; see also 'The Story of Zebehr Pasha', *The Contemporary Review*, Vol. LII, September–November, 1887.

and her large family were in financial difficulties. Having happened by accident, when walking on the slopes of Leith Hill, upon two of those enchanting old cottages of sandstone and red tiles which are so often to be found hidden away in the beech and pine woods of Surrey, she established herself in one of these called Parkhurst. From here she went to and from London and entertained her friends with her gaily brilliant talk and her French cooking. Ruskin was among the visitors who frequented her cottage. She had also some distinguished country neighbours, including George Meredith, who lived nine miles away at Box Hill, a distance which would daunt most moderns but which she frequently traversed both ways on foot. Meredith brought her into touch with Robert Louis Stevenson, W. T. Stead and other notables. " Come and see Flora Shaw to know whom is to look through an eyelet into the promised land " Meredith wrote to Admiral Maxse. " In matters of abstract thought as well as in warm feelings for the poor muddy fry of this world, you will find her unmatched. She is Irish and French—that's why. Quite as delightful to talk to as to look at."[1] There is plenty of other evidence that Meredith's feelings had not carried him beyond the truth. Flora would seem to be a very close model for Diana in Meredith's most famous novel and the story was told to the writer that she pleaded successfully for Diana's life when the author had a mind to kill her off.

By 1889 Flora, who ceaselessly read up the background for her current observations, had become an acknowledged expert upon Mediterranean affairs. She was mixing more and more in the official and literary society of her day, interviewing public men and writing articles and reviews. There is no evidence at all that the novelty of her sex was of any assistance to her in the world of journalism as it would have been later; it was, rather, the reverse. She made her way by sheer intellectual and literary power, and especially by her capacity for surveying all sides of a question as far as possible by personal observation, and summing it up in terms at once vivid and judicial and in the widest range of its historical context. If the Victorian age had been as rigidly conventional as some members of later generations have pictured it, this young woman's career would have been not merely remarkable but impossible. She had, of course, to carry her sex with

---

[1] Bell, *op. cit.*, pp. 44-5. The whole chapter 'Abinger 1883-1886' gives a delightful picture of Flora and her literary and other friends.

discretion. She always wore black and she never played the woman as a short cut to her professional objectives. Even so, her beauty, and especially the warm temperament that found its outlet in her expressive eyes and shone through the reserve and dignity of her manner, seemed to add a glow even to her purely intellectual activities. Public men, however cautious, found it surprisingly easy to give away official information to such an interviewer.

To work through the records of her life and that of Lugard is to gain an impression of their moving, as if according to some predestined plan, step by step, but all too slowly, towards each other. For Flora was drawn more and more into colonial affairs. A Mediterranean expert in the late 'eighties could no longer regard the north of Africa as nothing more than the southern border of Europe, for beyond the deserts of its hinterland lines of exploration and of occupation were being hastily scribbled upon the great tropical spaces which had always hitherto been blank. Moreover, in South Africa, at least, there were British colonies and a masterful dreamer in that continent was trying to draw lines between the two known extremities across the unknown. Flora naturally met Rhodes—it was in the winter of 1889—and, as we have already seen, was instantly captured, too completely perhaps, by the imaginative scope of his plans and the force which he put into their execution. But her own mind had long been ready for this extension of view. As a girl in east London, she had watched the ships in the docks and wondered whether the answer to the poverty around her was to be found in the trade and emigration offered by the almost virgin lands of the empire. When, therefore, C. P. Scott of the *Manchester Guardian* asked her to attend the International Conference at Brussels on the slave-trade and other African questions in the autumn of 1889, she was very ready to accept. She studied the anti-slavery literature and the Blue Books on tropical Africa and rubbed shoulders in the lobbies of the Hotel de l'Europe with all the leading European experts upon Africa. These included Sir John Kirk, with whom she inevitably made friends. She may for the first time have heard from him or another the name of the still obscure but promising pioneer who was just then encountering slavers in east Africa as he explored the Sabaki route into the interior. The rough notes she left behind show a thorough grasp of the slavery issue and an acute characterization of the European representatives.

Her way was now clearly marked and her further progress along it can be briefly told. The next year, 1890, thanks in part to a friendship formed in Egypt with Mr. Moberly Bell of *The Times*, who had a deep appreciation of her powers, she began to write, mainly upon colonial questions, for that paper. A passage in her first interview with the editor, George Buckle, deserves recording. She asked him to do something to make colonial news more important, assuring him that it would cost him no extra space. He replied that if she could devise such a thing he would do it. " Your Foreign and Colonial column," she said, " will you in future call it Colonial and Foreign?" " You win !" replied Buckle and ever since it has been so, with the later substitution of the word " Imperial " for " Colonial ".[1]

The work was now very hard; there were long days and late nights; there was much to earn for the many family dependents, mainly the children of her sisters. As with all professional women, she had to add to her man's work those extra obligations, large and small, belonging to her sex which could not be set aside without impoverishing her nature. Partly to relieve her endangered health her friends at Printing House Square suggested in 1892 a professional visit to South Africa. Her reports from South Africa were so successful that she was instructed to go on to Australia, New Zealand, and from there to Canada via California. Everywhere she worked with intense energy, meeting people of all walks of life in the cities and pushing on by every means of transport to the frontier regions in order to understand the life and economy of forests, sheep-stations, mines and ranches. Her reports to *The Times* gave its readers not only knowledge of the colonies but communicated to them some of her own strong faith in their future. She achieved a balanced appreciation on the one hand of colonial nationalism and on the other of the mutual interests binding together colony and mother country. Upon her return in the autumn of 1893, at the age of 41, she became the colonial editor of *The Times*.

She now had to draw information from every part of the empire and after her absorption in the settled colonies she turned her attention to the dramatic spectacle of the scramble for Africa. Already the friend and confidant of Rhodes, she met another man of vision and action who was making the new Africa. This was Goldie, whom she found not only, as we have seen, a great public figure, but a man of personal

[1] Bell, *op. cit.* p. 92.

fascination who seems to have become, among the other sex, her closest and most admired friend. It was just after her return from South Africa that she first met Lugard and the story of their meeting over her review of his East African book has been told. This was the first of many meetings when, between their travels, they happened both to be in England. He gave her his news from the frontiers and his views on policy and she, being in general agreement with these, was able to work them into her articles and editorials. We have seen how closely she, Goldie, Kirk, and Lugard worked together over the West African crisis. Through her close friendship with Chamberlain and other public men, her ideas about the possibilities for the empire, including its latest acquisitions in Africa, were built up and widely communicated.

Flora assisted Lugard in his early relations with Chamberlain though the minister was not slow to grasp his value. We have seen how Lugard found Chamberlain serving up to him the very same views which Lugard had been pouring into Flora's ears a day or two before, and how closely Lugard consulted her about his Kalahari expedition. In 1895 she proposed to *The Times* that she should extend her travels to central Africa and travel from the Niger to the Sudan, then in the grip of the Khalifa, a suggestion that Moberly Bell met, though in polite terms, with the answer it deserved.

While on questions of the strategy and tactics of imperialism the two friends were generally agreed, there was one question upon which they decisively parted company. This was about the character and methods of Rhodes.

Feeling as he did about Rhodes and deprecating Flora's allegiance to him, Lugard must have watched with painful interest the crisis that the Jameson Raid caused in her professional life when her public reputation was suddenly imperilled and with it that of the great newspaper which employed her and of the Colonial Secretary himself. Allusion has already been made to her arraignment before the Parliamentary Committee set up to enquire into the Jameson Raid. She stood the ordeal splendidly but it drew heavily upon her inadequate reserves of strength. It certainly would seem that under the spell of Cecil Rhodes she had improperly mixed up her professional and her private action. But those who would judge, as Goldie seems to have done, that here for once she was betrayed by her sex, should remember how many men were swept into allegiance by the force of Rhodes' personality. In 1898, partly to refresh her health, which was again failing, Flora went off after this incident for her most desperate adventure, crossing the wilderness of forests, waters and ravines to camp alone among the rough men of the Klondyke gold rush, taking her long black skirts into log-shanties and Indian canoes just as Mary Kingsley had trailed them amongst the crocodile-infested creeks of West Africa.

The cold Klondyke and Canada seemed to take Flora away from interest in Africa. But when she returned to take up her work on *The Times* in the autumn of 1898 there was much to draw her back into the continent of Lugard's choice. The clouds were threatening over South Africa, and week after week Flora analysed in *The Times* the situation there and put the case of the Uitlanders. There was also the final stage in the crisis of the Niger bend to be explained, with Lugard's help, in her paper. Their letters were still written in the formal manner of their time and were filled with colonial interests. But their tone became more intimate. " You are going out," she told him, as he left England for West Africa in the spring of 1898, writing with full knowledge of his grievances,

" to do important work the development of which it is at present impossible to foresee . . . if you are, with perhaps good reason, dissatisfied as to some of the conditions under which it has to be done you have to console and encourage yourself by looking back on the long list of heroes whose best work has been achieved in spite of not dissimilar imperfections. We have all of us to be content if we can do a part of what we dream . . . If I may give a friend's last word it would be—Don't waste your work in friction one scrap more than can be helped. Don't break your heart in striving for the impossible but accept the legitimate joy of service rendered.

Yours always truly,
Flora Shaw (4 March 1898)."

To this Lugard replied from the Niger,

" I admit your unwritten reflection that I am a very pig-headed and obstinate person—with however the qualification that (in my own view at least) I am mainly so only on *points that matter* and, after all, they are very few!" (25 April 1898).

Marriage

When Lugard returned during 1899 he found himself meeting her more and more often and discussing all his hopes and plans for West Africa. Under such stimulus she raised again the possibility of her making a journey across Africa and, probably under Rhodes' inspiration, it was to be from Cairo to the Cape. Putting the proposal before Moberly Bell she admitted:

" The difficulty would be to persuade Lord Kitchener " (who had just conquered the Sudan) " to let me through from Fashoda to Uganda. Knowing as I do the ease with which I adapt myself to all conditions of travel, I have little doubt inwardly that I could get through . . . I really have a practical gift for travelling without hurting myself . . . When I slept soundly on shingle in the Klondyke, the men told me that I ought to try sand which, they say, is the hardest thing there is. Obviously the desert is required to complete my experience."[1]

When she went to Goldie and Lugard with this plan they were both dead against it. Lugard's opposition arose from his strong appreciation of her value.

> 63 Jermyn Street, 23 February, 1899.
>
> "Dear Miss Shaw,
>
> Your letter only reached me yesterday, and I was out all day and so dead-tired on my return that I could not manage to reply in time to catch the early country post. I am *extremely* sorry to hear of your projected journey from North to South of Africa.
>
> Sir George of course was *quite* right—I am *quite* sure you will succeed, and achieve more information and *see more* than anyone else has done; but any brainless and energetic person can *travel*—whereas *you* are very urgently required for far more difficult and important work. I shall be delighted to call at the first leisure moment I can secure, and more than pleased to be of any use I can to you."

Flora's disappointment was keen. It came at an unhappy time for her. Mr. Buckle was not wholly in sympathy with her views about South Africa and especially about Rhodes, and with this subject filling the horizon as war drew nearer, such a rift was serious. Against the clash of war and in the spate of war views her rational voice had less chance of being heard. Her always delicate health was again in danger and towards the end of the year 1900 she felt she could no longer continue to hold a regular appointment for *The Times*. She had served

[1] Bell, *op. cit.* p. 225.

the paper for ten years and had been Colonial Editor for seven. She resigned in September of this year, to the regret of her colleagues and with promises to write for it whenever she could in the future. It is not easy to assess her contribution. In writing as a member of the staff, in guiding editorial policy, and selecting information her work had been fused into the daily issue of authoritative print that all the people of education and influence in the country, and many outside it, —certainly the " top people " of the day—had been reading. She had raised the importance of colonial—meaning, in the main, what were later called Dominion—affairs in the national newspaper and helped people to see what Chamberlain was urging with the greater force and the authority of office, the relation of the colonies to the economic needs of Britain. She was also able to feel the throb of young nationalism beating in these new communities and to warn her countrymen against an excessively maternal approach to them. Through her close relations with the new men of Africa and especially with Goldie, Rhodes, Kirk and Lugard, she was able to reveal, stage by stage, the penetration of its tropical interior. She told Lugard in 1899,

" I look upon it as a part of my personal work to endeavour to bring all the influences which I believe to be working for good in Africa into harmony with each other."

When Lugard went to Nigeria for his first tour as High Commissioner their friendship had deepened but it was no more than friendship. He wrote to her each mail and during his six months' leave from April to October in 1901 he was a frequent visitor at her cottage. But by October something happened which changed Flora's life. It was an event strangely similar to that which had broken Lugard's into two parts. These events have left no written evidence, and only the barest facts can be given. Flora, for how long is uncertain, had been in love with Goldie. Lady Goldie died in 1898 and Flora not only seemed to expect that, in proper course, she and Goldie would marry but wanted this to happen with the great strength of that side of her nature which, largely by reason of her career and family cares, had always been denied. But—the expected event did not happen. That there was some final crisis in the affair at this time can be guessed only by its effects on Flora. Strong though she was, she seemed all of a sudden to be completely broken down, with health impaired and happiness destroyed.

Marriage

It is difficult to understand how, with her character and experience, she could have loved the Goldie portrayed in Dorothy Wellesley's memoir. Yet Goldie was a man who, as this writer vividly reveals, had a strong fascination for women. Dorothy Wellesley reports a strange remark of Goldie's. " He once told me that, immediately after Lady Goldie's death, an intimate woman friend had written to him proposing marriage. 'What did you do?' I said. 'I sent her a copy of Rosmersholm!'"[1] Since this remark has appeared in print it seems necessary to emphasize here that the allusion to a most grim play, which describes the tragic supplanting of a wife, could not possibly apply to the eminent and dignified woman described by Miss Moberly Bell and further revealed in the Lugard papers. The recipient of this disgraceful communication from Goldie, if, indeed, it was not just a piece of male *bravura*, must have been another and, fortunately, anonymous friend. "He was very fond of women," the author of his memoir writes, "and no man admitted it more frankly. Reports of his personal relationships certainly reached the ears of Queen Victoria and I have been told (I can scarcely believe it) that she refused for this reason to recognize his enormous services to the country!"[2] It is probable that those familiar with Ibsen's play need not take the allusion, to whomever it may apply, too literally.

The effect upon Lugard of this crisis in the affairs of his two closest friends may be imagined. And the result could be predicted. He saw the successful, self-reliant Flora struck down just as he had been many years before. His one desire was to help her in any way possible. Sharing so much, everything, indeed, short of that kind of love which both of them believed that after its betrayal they could never experience again, there was one step which they could take. On October 12th, 1901, Lugard wrote to Nell Lugard:

" I have asked Miss Shaw to be my wife. She has refused—but not *I think* in terms which preclude hope. She has had a blow which has broken her down mentally and physically, and I think from what I hear that she has barely escaped brain fever. Hence she could answer in no other way. I go to see her tomorrow. I feel sure you will like me to tell you this— and perhaps it will account a little for my silences and abstraction. Matters in this connection have been ceaselessly in my thoughts of late."
(F. L. to Mrs. E. Lugard, 12 October 1901).

[1] Wellesley, *Sir George Goldie*, p. 120.   [2] *Ibid.* p. 113.

He was right. He asked again, and Flora agreed. How could she refuse? The union gave her the help she so much needed; it seemed to grow naturally out of their close friendship as that had grown in turn out of their long partnership in public work. But the decision to marry Flora Shaw throws new light upon Lugard's character. He was marrying a woman with an independent and notable career, something still at that time widely regarded as unnatural, and one whose eminence was exactly in his own field. While in some sections of that field his position was undisputed, there were others where she had the advantage of him. Her wit and social charm, added to her professional position, had given her a settled status in the more serious and politically influential circles of London Society where he was known mainly by name and by his occasional incursions from another continent. She commanded an influence which led even such a giant as Rhodes to court her interest. As a writer she was Lugard's superior. She could not write from such deep experience as his but her range was wider: she saw the empire as a whole in relation to Britain and the world, and in years of study, of interviewing and of discussions at Printing House Square, she had built up a great body of knowledge and a confident sense of political and economic realities. Her reading of history had given perspective and richness to her writing. Whereas Lugard was a very silent man and fluent only on paper, Flora was an accomplished talker and became the natural centre in any group. Even as a traveller she competed in some measure with Lugard by her arduous and courageous journeys. All these achievements and qualities Lugard did not merely accept. He admired them with a humility not easy to credit in a man, and a man of his generation, and one so virile and ambitious.

The decision taken, plans had to be quickly made. As Lugard was to leave in a matter of days it was agreed that she should come out to Madeira in the following June. He would meet her, and they would be married there, after which she would come on to Nigeria with him for the rest of his tour. Her two cottages at Abinger were to be enlarged and, as Lugard's plans for a house at Haslemere had come to nothing, that would be their English home.

Yet, when he had gone, Flora felt restless. The news from South Africa of the prolonged war, the loss of life upon both sides, and finally the accusations against Britain of harshness, especially in the " concentration camps" into which Boer women and children had been collected, were all painful to one who had so sensitive a public conscience and who had exercised an important influence in South African affairs. She therefore filled in the interval by going to South Africa on behalf of *The Times*, and there, as before, she travelled as widely as the spread of war allowed, talking with everyone of importance from Lord Milner downwards and especially visiting the camps. The purpose of this visit was, indeed, more to influence than to report events. Flora was an imperialist, but she set a high standard of humanity for her empire. Her expedition was one of reconciliation as well as of humanity. She threw all her energy into the attempt to persuade the Dutch leaders in the Cape and the Orange Free State to come out upon the side of an honourable peace and the beginning of a new partnership while all her influence with her own people was used against policies of revenge or severity. And she was, of course, writing in this sense to *The Times*. British dealings with the Dutch after their defeat were by the standards of history generous. It may be that Flora Shaw in her last activity under that name had some share in this result.

During this strenuous tour she wrote frequent letters to Lugard in Nigeria but as communications were such as to prevent his replies reaching her she felt as if " she were continually writing into space." She reached home in March very tired and somewhat anxious. She therefore went off to Madeira early in May to rest before the wedding.

It was very natural that upon both sides there should be some fears and doubts. Both were in the 'forties; both had given elsewhere if not the best that was in them at least that full energy of love that with serious natures generally comes once in life. For both, these past events threw shadows upon the coming alliance. Celia died at about the time of the marriage but just before her death ended the long unrest she had brought into Lugard's life, she did what she could to wreck the marriage by writing letters of bitter reproach and self-justification. She inflicted some injury but her weapons were blunted by the absolute frankness between the two: each not only knew of the other's experience but could enter imaginatively into it, and there was no pretence that they now came together as anything but as great friends.

" I do, indeed," Flora told Edward Lugard, " recognize in your brother a nature apart from all others in its devoted unselfishness and sweet distinction. I only feel, and feel very deeply, that he should have had a fresh young life to make all his own—not one which the strain and sorrow of life has worn."

To Lugard himself she wrote from Cape Town at the end of December 1901.

" I hope you look upon our marriage as I look on it—and I think you do— that is, as a loyal friendship made absolute for life by the public tie with which we bind it. Such a friendship is among the great good things of life . . . Do you remember Sir Philip Sydney's lines about the ' quiet joy ' of happy marriage—

> *Friend without change, playfellow without strife,*
> *Food without fulness, counsel without pride,*
> *Is this sweet doubling of our single life."*
>
> (29 December 1901).

Again: " You once said you would win my *love*. I, too, hope to win yours . . . We cannot force it. Let us not try on either side: but let us be content to marry as friends." And a few days later: " We shall both of us wish to work on. The greater part of our energy must always be given to the public thing."

There was little room here for misunderstanding. The gravest threat to the happiness of their marriage arose from the unusual kind of life both had lived. Flora had been independent as were few women of her generation, and in struggling for years to carry all her family and professional responsibilities she had been obliged to strengthen the tissue of her character and harden her will. There were times now when she wondered whether she could bring herself to that dissolution of her own life and career into that of her husband which she had decided was her right course in the future.

If she doubted whether her profession had disqualified her for marriage he had as much reason to fear the same for himself. Those dark moods of his increased with the growing strain of the work in Nigeria. It seemed as though they were the payment he made for the periods of excessive activity when he drove himself and everyone else upon his small staff to attempt the impossible. He had long realized this himself and had more than once apologized to his brother for his

" three-cornered moods ". When Flora came back from South Africa to find his accumulated letters she was dismayed by the growing tendency to gloom which they revealed. She continued to receive such letters even after her arrival in Madeira. From here on May 28th she wrote to Hilda Brackenbury, the daughter of her dead sister Mimi, and the niece who was closest to her in intimacy,

> " I don't recognize him in his letters of the last eight months. I feel sometimes as if I were in a strange nightmare of being married to a stranger, but what fortunately remains always solid and unshaken is my trust in his goodness. He is a man whose life is worth sharing and who is worth helping even if it were so to happen that one got no personal happiness at all. And I don't believe that will be the case. When we meet, I think all will be well. I am expecting him any day after tomorrow . . . I am planning to give him a really restful pleasant little holiday, and shall try to do his health good and to make him happy first of all."
>
> (31 May 1902).

Lugard fully shared her fears, wondering whether he could conquer this sombre tendency.

There was still another danger hanging over this unusual marriage but this was one which lay much further outside their control. Flora was by now a very delicate woman. She had from girlhood drawn much too heavily upon her physical strength and had tried to fill the gap by the misuse of her nervous energy. This was because in almost every action she had had to make the additional effort, half conscious though it might ultimately become, to disarm active prejudice or, at least, to transform the instinctive attitude of her male colleagues towards her sex into an equal relationship purely professional in character. The strain of her prolonged journeys, with their ceaseless interviewing, absorbing, observing, and writing were probably, for all the momentary stimulus they gave, too great a demand. Lugard, by contrast, was at the height of his powers and was strenuously dedicated to the service of his country in an unhealthy continent.

May found Flora resting in the warmth and highly coloured beauty of the island. She was enjoying a relaxation such as she had hardly ever known, with time to read the many books she had brought, to walk, to day-dream, to write to Hilda and her other friends, and even, as a woman who had regarded black as her professional wear, to think about her clothes. "I have become quite accustomed to wearing white.

It seems natural in this bright sun. But I still don't like myself in colours." Passing boats sometimes brought momentary visitors, among them Dr. Jameson, who was " . . . like Sir Frederick in being *real* and good. It is now one of the saddest faces I know." She made friends with all she met and especially, in a way characteristic with her, with the servants at the hotel and with the poor. She prepared a large sitting-room at her hotel overlooking the sea and filled it with comfortable cushions, books and flowers in order that it might greet Lugard with a home-like look. For the honeymoon she borrowed Camacha, the house of a doctor in a very secluded position high up in the hills above Funchal.

Early in June Lugard arrived from Nigeria. He had asked the Colonial Office for special leave to Madeira on full pay. Antrobus put the conclusive official case against such an irregularity but ended with the remark that as the leave was for marriage it might be granted. Chamberlain minuted his agreement with the case against the grant, noted the inconsistent decision and then benignly permitted the union of his two friends with the question " who will say after this that Downing Street is bound by red tape?"[1]

We have a picture, drawn with some journalist's licence, of the appearance of the two on the eve of their marriage. Flora is described as

"brown-haired, of neat, *svelte* figure, the slender almost angular proportions of which give an impression not of constitutional delicacy but of compact, wiry strength and nerves of steel . . . She looks what she is, a woman to go anywhere and do anything: the woman to write three columns of good copy for a newspaper on the back of a portmanteau in a desert."

As for Lugard:

" Africa has marked him as her own. Tall [*sic*] gaunt, angular, dark as a Spaniard, the High Commissioner of Northern Nigeria has the yellow skin, the hollowed cheeks, the sunken eyes, the indented temples which mark the man who has struggled for life with the fever-fiend. Square-jawed, with forehead like a cliff, ferocious moustache and keen black eyes, Sir Frederick is a relentless disciplinarian, and stern when he must be. This is in ' business hours ' for he can unbend and be as gentle as a woman."

[1] Minute by Chamberlain on Lugard to Chamberlain, 24 July 1902, C.O. 446/24.

Marriage

Of the marriage itself we have some of their own evidence. On the eve of the event Lugard was, as he confessed to his brother, full of diffidence. Flora from the first fully entered into the unusual intimacy and affection which bound the two brothers. Already she could write freely to Edward, then in India with his regiment, of the event which must mean so much to him.

" 10 June, 1902. Reid's Hotel,
Madeira.

My dear Ned,

We are to be married tomorrow and I must write you one line today to thank you for the kind and reassuring letter which has just reached me.

You ' know ' that I shall make him happy you say. I trust with all my heart it may be so, for I have not the slightest doubt that he will add to my happiness in a way which only one who knows as you do the chivalrous generosity of his nature can understand. I believe there is nobody else in the world who knows him as you do, and for you to think that I shall be able to make him happy gives me confidence and encouragement. You may be sure that I shall do my very best, for he is well worth making happy. He has been tenderness and kindness itself to me since he arrived here just a week ago. We have one more week here before we start together for Nigeria. In the life that lies before us there is no-one, after Fred, to whose help in doing what I want to do for him I look forward more confidently and more affectionately than to yours.

Yours,
Flora L. Shaw."

The marriage took place on June 11th and there are letters from both of them that give some picture of the event.

"June 16, 1902. Camacha,
Madeira.

Dear old boy,

Well here I am in a most absolutely ideal place in the mountains surrounded by roses and camelias, and vast trees of rhododendrons, and masses of colour (geraniums etc.) with the expanse of blue sea stretching to the far horizon spread out 2,000 ft. below us. Funchal, the town and capital, where we lived till the day we were married is simply an idyll of flowers. What we know as plants are here trees. The Jacaranda with its mass of mauve blossom, the masses of roses, geraniums, lilies—of plumbago, and bougainvillia and ten thousand other clusters and festoons of colour make of it a place like nothing else I have seen in my life. Flora, of

71

course, had created round herself a circle of friends—every man, woman and child in the island, whether of the Residents and gentry or of the bare-footed peasants, seemed to love her and to vie with each other in rendering homage. The ' caro ' men fought for the honour of driving her caro—the residents made of our room a perfect bower of flowers with their daily tributes of exquisite baskets of beautifully arranged flowers. All respected our wish that the marriage should be absolutely quiet, and denied themselves the pleasure of coming to the Church. So we were married at the Consulate, and then went quietly to the Church, and Archdeacon Lindon and the Chaplain read a dignified and impressive service. When we returned to the Hotel (at Funchal) we found that the good feeling of the people had vented itself in a deluge of flowers and a perfect little lunch arranged in our sitting room. Then in the evening we came up here. The emotions of the day, and her delicate state of health, had completely overcome her, and for the first two days I nursed her as an invalid. In the evening each day I take an hour's violent walk to the top of some hill . . . "

For her part, Flora wrote to Hilda:

Camacha.
" I can hardly tell you how entirely at rest I felt—and feel . . . Nothing could exceed his kindness and tenderness to me nor the gentle care with which he is surrounding me . . . It seems all dreamlike still, and I find myself from time to time looking at my wedding ring with a kind of surprised remembrance that it is there for life and that this new companionship is not to fade away, but to grow I hope clearer and more real as life goes on . . . I never thought before what a comfort the taking of hands is in the marriage-service . . . From the moment that we took each other's hands to plight our troth I had no feeling but of perfect peace in the service." (13 June 1901).

Up at Camacha Flora had time to show her husband some of the congratulatory letters that had rained upon her from her many friends. As a rule such letters, not always written quite spontaneously or with strict objectivity, are as ephemeral as the atmosphere of the moment which evokes them. But this was a marriage of public interest and one with an almost story-book suitability of the parties. A few quotations will illustrate the general opinion. None were better able to assess the public significance of the marriage of their admired colleague than Flora's friends at Printing House Square. Her old chief, George Buckle, wrote

Marriage

"I only know him rather at a distance, but what I do know has always filled me with respect and admiration. It is a worthy match for you; and I very fervently trust that you, who have done so much, for so long, for the happiness of your many relations, may now find your own (about which you never worried) assured for the future.

Metaphorically I do, what I presume your dusky subjects in West Africa will do literally—kiss your feet." (24 February 1902).

Edward Wilson from the same address wrote that he knew all about Lugard "and I feel that you and he have done as much as any two people living for the cause of the Empire and the credit of the British name." Another leader writer, Mr. Capper, sent, on behalf of many others, at the office

"our *congratulations* (though that is not the customary thing to say to a lady)—for Sir Frederick Lugard is one of the few Englishmen prominent in public life whom I have always unreservedly respected and admired. You know under what a bright and special light we view our public men from P.H.S.; so this is no small thing to say. Indeed, to onlookers so warmly interested in you as this household, the 'arrangement', if I may say so, seems positively ideal."

But among the many distinguished felicitations none were more generous or unexpected than the one Labouchere, so long the political opponent and critic of both of them, printed in his paper *Truth*, in words in which an opponent described Flora at one of the most critical moments of her life.

"I congratulate Sir Frederick Lugard on his marriage with Miss Flora Shaw. My acquaintance with the lady is only a professional one, for it is limited to having had the honour to examine her for an hour or two before the Raid Committee of the House of Commons. A more difficult lady to induce to say what she did not want to it would be difficult to find. Her manner was most charming. When asked a question, she went off at a tangent, and made a clever speech on things in general. If I mildly suggested to her that, however interesting the speech, I had not got a very clear answer to my question, she smilingly expressed her regret, and did it in such a pleasant way, that everyone thought that it was due to my abnormal density of apprehension. Then she made a second speech of the same character. And so well did she do it, that had I persisted in an attempt to get the answer I should have been regarded as a ruffian lost to all sense of courtesy towards a lady anxious to tell me everything. I remember that one of my brother Committee-men near, who was an old stager in the wiles of charming women in the witness-box, handed me down a slip of paper on which was written, ' Take care not to push her too far, for if she bursts into tears we are lost.' I got nothing out of her that she wished to conceal, but I conceived an unbounded admiration of her charm and of her cleverness. Sir Frederick Lugard seems to have been more fortunate than I was in getting a plain answer to a plain question."

There was great pleasure, too, in the good wishes of Lord Scarbrough who knew them both so well and must have been almost the only other person who could have known the truth about the blow which had recently fallen upon Flora.

" I do hope," he wrote to her, " you have found happiness, I am sure you have found one in ten thousand—knowing him as I do I cannot imagine a more loyal or unselfish nature and I am more glad than I can say that he has got his reward." (10 March 1902).

Lord Curzon wrote to Lugard from India, where he was Viceroy, " If it be *the* Miss Flora Shaw I congratulate you. If it be another may she be equally brilliant and not less charming." And there were congratulations to Flora from Lady Kirk who spoke of the joy of her husband at the marriage " of his greatest friend."

The brief interlude on the island was happier than either had dared to hope. The only cloud arose from Flora's health; the excitement of the re-union and the ceremony affected her so much that Lugard had to play the nurse rather than the husband. He confessed to his brother that he was selfish enough to find some satisfaction in this as it gave him at this first all-important moment an opportunity to wait upon her and taught her, for all her independence, to accept his ministrations. Nine years afterwards he reminded her of an occasion when, coming down a steep path at Camacha, she had clung to him for support and he had quoted a line of Euripides, " ὁποῖα κισσὸς δρυός, ὅπως τῆσδ' ἕξομαι".[1] "You asked me what it meant and I said 'As the Ivy clings to the Oak so will I cling to him.' You had taken my arm in a clinging way, and you said you liked the line." It does not matter that Lugard slightly misinterpreted a line in which Hecuba referred to her daughter. Nor, perhaps, that the metaphor was one it would have

[1] The quotation comes from line 398 of Euripides' *Hecuba*.

been unwise to pursue to its exact arboreal meaning. Happily, except perhaps in matters financial, its more ominous significance was never to apply to this union.

On June 20th they embarked, with Flora's 46 trunks and cases, and her English lady's maid, upon the s.s. *Jebba* and steamed along the West African coast and then up the Niger on the river steamer *Empire*. It was now, ironically enough, she who was well and Lugard who was down with fever, and needing her care. In spite of this, the voyage as recorded by Flora to her niece, was peaceful and happy. These letters to Hilda allow us to see the first months of this marriage of friendship through her eyes.

26 June 1902.   s.s. *Jebba*.
  " I can hardly tell you how easily and naturally I have taken to this *vie à deux*. I am astonished myself to feel how little I am disturbed by it. It sounds a rather feeble way of putting it, but I think you will understand. I had rather expected beforehand that, though I should greatly value the kind and affectionate companionship of a friend for life, I should also perhaps at first find the detail sometimes a little difficult to manage. But I don't. It is partly no doubt due to an exceptional kindness as well as tact on his part, but it comes partly as an inevitable part of the new intimacy and trust. He never is in my way . . .

From what Fred tells me (I hope you observe that I always write his Christian name quite properly now though I may confess that I have not yet learned to use it fluently) it will be far more civilized than his letters led me to believe . . . Instead of not seeming to know me by sight as of old, Fred notices everything I put on, and I think he is pleased that I should have pretty white things which, as far as I understand, are just what I shall want. I should like you to see how smart he is growing himself too. I am sure you would like it, for I think it means that he too is feeling just a little naturally happy."

Hilda received confirmation of this from Lugard himself, who was as eager to enter into Flora's affectionate family relationships as she was with regard to his.

" She continually says that she feels younger every day—and she looks it—and she adds that she cannot recognize herself in this gay and youthful frame of mind . . . How pleased you will be at my report, and the contrast it is to this time last year when I came to Abinger. I earnestly hope (with many misgivings) that I may be able to continue to make her happy, but

I do not think she should remain long in West Africa and away from all of you whom she loves so devotedly."

Yet, watching her husband keenly, Flora saw that even now, especially when malaria came, the old melancholy was still ready to seize upon him from time to time. She saw, too, and marvelled at the completeness with which he could submerge himself in his work. Flora's letters give us our first intimate picture of Lugard at work in what had become his natural setting of tropical Africa. They are also the comments of one of the most effective imperialists of the day upon the beginnings of British administration in this immense new Protectorate.

8 July 1902.   s.s. *Empire*.
" Here we are steaming steadily into the heart of Africa . . . I wrote to Lulu from the Niger mouth when we still seemed to form part of the life of the outside world. Here we have left that behind and now realize as we pass between banks deeply fringed with palms and occasional flowering shrubs and trees that we are on one of the better known highways of the tropics. The river since we left the many creeks and outlets of its mouth behind us has become a noble stream and in places the banks recede so far as to seem like the shores of a lake where we take out our glasses to be able to look at the hippopotami and crocodiles that disport themselves on the sandbanks. In other places the banks narrow sufficiently for us to be able to study with the naked eye the foliage and flowers of the woods that border the water . . .
. . . Time passes on board rather like a dream. We get often what I remember to have felt very specially once in the Suez Canal, an illusion that we are ourselves standing still and that the scenes on the banks are defiling before us, and it seems to me in my present passive mood to be somewhat typical of life. It is all very gentle and kind and restful and unreal. I have only the dreamiest perception of what the next turn in the channel may bring. In the meantime there is much that is pleasant and I have no wish for tomorrow . . . Fred is of course at work again and plods in these hours through the piles of papers which form the machinery of office work. Some of them are interesting and then he hands them over to me to read too and they serve to initiate me gradually into the lines of his work . . .
. . . I do see however that the climate is likely to prove depressing and I can understand that years of it go a long way to account for the habit of melancholy which I hope to see gradually lessen in our daily life . . .

On days when he shakes off the depression he can shew himself in a new witty aspect which he scarcely gave a hint of at Abinger. I shall consider his 'cure' to be well advanced when that brighter mood becomes habitual and the other the occasional interval. But the sorrow of life is not to be cured in a day. All I can hope for the present is that we may form round us a little charmed circle of light against that dark background and I shall be content if by degrees the light spreads."

For all his absorption in his work Lugard must have been holding his breath as he watched tropical Africa introducing itself to his delicate wife. They stopped at Lokoja where they camped in an empty Government House while waiting for the Niger to rise sufficiently to carry them on to Zungeru. Here Flora, taking her first settled view of the country that she meant to be at least half her home, was agreeably disappointed. From the raised site of the house she could look out at a circle of hills and within them the two great rivers met and she could watch the tropical sunset and sunrise over their double flood. But as Flora passed into the status of the official's wife in a tropical country, with Lugard away for many hours of the day, her high spirit and intelligence found too little upon which to exercise themselves and they began to turn inwards. She wrote from the verandah " where so far my life is practically passed,"

28 July 1902   Government House
                                                      Lokoja.
" The days as they pass at present are absolutely without incident. I wake between four and five. Early tea is brought at six. I send round to Fred's room to let him know that it has come. He comes in very sleepy to have a cup and then goes away to his office where piles of papers await him . . .
. . . At six Fred stops work. The sun then is just on the edge of setting and we go for a tearing walk in the dark which gives us exercise and brings us in streaming with perspiration to an extent which makes all my clothes seem exactly as if they had been dropped in the washtub . . . After dinner there is an hour on the verandah and between ten and eleven we usually separate for the night.

I have not yet managed to get myself really interested in local affairs and Fred's time and thought are necessarily almost wholly absorbed in them, so that for the moment I feel somewhat dull and depressed and have lots of time to miss you all very badly. But I have no doubt that will pass. I shall gradually be able to feel that all these strange things are my concern and to settle down to some sort of enjoyment of the life itself. I have

D   77

begun today to organize some little improvements in Government House garden, which is at present merely a cleared enclosure.

The black labourers are absurd, just like a crowd of children, but I think I can get on with them and both in the house and garden they seem to be working quite willingly. . . In the house too they are learning our ways wonderfully fast and I am glad to say that Fred found the little dinners we have given since we arrived here better than anything he has ever had in Nigeria. The table is easy to make pretty with good linen and a new lampshade and fresh flowers, and the waiting being organized makes everything go smoothly.

Some of the civilian staff are hardly perhaps what we should call gentlemen, but even then they are intelligent and well-mannered and keen about their work. Some are everything that one could wish in the way of cultivation and charm and among the officers there seem to be some particularly nice fellows. Everyone is kindness itself to me . . .

Books will I expect give me my principal companionship and this will be in one sense a permanent advantage; for life of late years has been so pressing that the habit of reading has fallen into abeyance and it will be a real good opportunity here to get back to it. I have started on Grote and hope to get through all the beginnings of European history again . . . "

By August they had been able to move on to Zungeru, the little capital which through her husband's energy had sprung up almost in weeks. Her letters to Hilda Brackenbury bring back the atmosphere of earlier days in Africa and of their effects upon the exiled Englishwoman.

30 August 1902   Government House
                                                                Zungeru.

" . . . The isolation of tête-à-tête life in Africa is very great and Fred is so constantly occupied with Government business that I am thrown almost wholly on letters from home for human intercourse. You can think of us as having quite a pretty house. . . Everything is much farther in the way of civilization than I expected. Zungeru is a little town looking rather like a pretty English suburb with white houses nestling among trees and in the distance hills rising to an occasional mountain against the sky.

The pace at which Fred works is really wonderful and under his stimulus the place is rushing up like a crop of mushrooms. Every day new houses begin to appear and new roads are cut. The electric light plant is getting into order... It seems a curious contrast with hyaenas prowling round and puff adders in the garden! We were counting up how many people we ought to ask if we gave a big inaugural dinner and we found that there are over thirty civil and military officers of sorts. There are also the non-commissioned officers and subordinates in the civil departments . . . Everyone now is asking me about bringing their wives out and there is a general set towards civilization.

It is sweet of you, dear, to write as you do about last summer. It was the end of a long sad period of life to me, but on looking back the sorrow is all illumined by the love and loyal sympathy by which I was surrounded. The memory of that will live I hope long after the sorrow has been put away . . . We have probably to get over a little difficult time first until we have learned how to manage our lives. Fred is so entirely good, so sincerely kind, and is by nature such a simple, sweet, heroic soul, that it would hardly be fair if he cannot find some definite increase of happiness in a marriage which he certainly seemed at one time to want . . . One must I suppose be uprooted before one can be replanted and in my case circumstances have contributed to make the uprooting very complete."

There were some ominous phrases in this letter. But Flora was not the woman to imprison her mind in her own difficulties or to allow her view of Nigeria to be bounded by the walls and garden of Government House and the rough jumble of rocky, wooded hills around it. She tried to fill her mind by setting it to work upon the problems of Nigerian government and development and analysed the part her husband was playing in these tasks. At the same time, the writer throws further light upon her own difficulties. She writes to her colleague and great friend Moberly Bell:

16 August 1902.   Moreji on the Niger.
" I . . . am beginning to realize the really big work which is involved in the administration and especially the administration with inadequate means of a Protectorate of this size. Every office is under-manned and the extra work has to be got through somehow by expedients which all have their source in the High Commissioner's office. Sir Frederick is fortunately immensely interested in it all, and is content to work hard every day from six in the morning till night falls. Sundays are the same as week-days and except at meals I rarely see him.

I have not yet myself been able to pick up the threads of the life and as the Doctor has persuaded Sir Frederick that I must on no account be permitted to go out in the sun, I spend the greater part of my time in solitary confinement . . . I confess that the first effect of the climate is very trying. It is not so much excessively hot as it is excessively enervating . . . To judge by the amount which everybody does they can't be seriously enervated . . . I was astonished at Lokoja, which from being a mere trading settlement under the Niger Company has become a considerable town . . . We were there for Coronation Day and I managed with the help of a little borrowed crockery from the Mess to give a dinner party of 20 people. I was a little nervous beforehand as a hyaena had paid one or two surreptitious visits to our cookhouse and I feared lest he should walk off with the turkeys—or with the cook which would have been still worse! But fortunately no contretemps of the sort took place. We had the table patriotically decorated with roses (which alas came out of my band-boxes, as they do not grow here) and we drank the King's health with the band playing ' God save the King ', and a black crowd of servants and others clustered round the open windows ejaculating ' Good King! Good King!' . . .

I myself was struck with the thought as I looked down the table and noted the fine type of English gentleman's face which presented itself in rows on either side, that it really is a phenomenon of our Empire that we should be able in the heart of Africa to bring together for dinner twenty wellbred English officers of as fine a type as you would hope to meet in the most civilized centres of London.

. . . One of the young Residents who dined with us on Coronation Day is on his way out to a post just a thousand miles distant. There is of course no railway and as yet no telegraph, but he goes out there practically alone to deal as he can with the problems which arise and to maintain his authority practically by the prestige of the British flag.

The pace at which the country is being civilized is not realized at home; but a great deal more money is needed to do what might be done. Sir Frederick practises the most rigid economy and nearly all that he has goes of necessity to maintain the military force. He has 13 provinces to hold and thousands of miles of frontier to defend with only two battalions at his disposal and Sokoto and Kano are now writing that there can be nothing between us but war. These are the two most distant provinces which are still not annexed. Near us the people are realizing all the value of peace. Cultivation is extending rapidly, trade is opening, and the Niger Co. which has at present the European monopoly is reaping a golden harvest . . .

At present I enjoy the distinction of being the only idle person in the Protectorate. . . "

A little later she wrote to the same friend from her new home.

" We are at Zungeru . . . Little more than a year ago this spot was undiscovered jungle, where hartebeest fed on the luxuriant wild grass and lions fed on the hartebeest . . . our army of black servants are getting drilled into capital shape and really if you chose to spend a week-end with us you would not be too uncomfortable. By the same mail I am giving the same invitation to Mr. Chamberlain, so if he comes will you be of the party!

Empire-making goes on here on a scale to suit you. Sir Frederick has been ill lately and has been ordered by the doctors on pain of their resignation to take an overland trip into the higher air of one of the interior provinces. It will be a 12 days' ride and to reconcile him to spending the time the Resident of the Province has just represented to him that there are two Kings to put on their thrones and one to depose, which he might do *en passant!*"

There followed an account of the administrative structure and the beginnings of economic development.

" The economies which have been practised would be almost laughable but that the strain of living in severe discomfort and working without proper appliances costs good lives in a climate like this.

Sir Frederick has nearly killed himself—and I think a fair proportion of his staff too—with overwork. Yet they like it. After all they are working for an idea, and that is more than all men can say. It is a great idea too and fills one more and more as one thinks of it—this conception of an Empire which is to secure the ruling of the world by its finest race—the best plane for the exercise of justice and liberty and individual effort which the world has seen." (29 September 1902).

Flora did not hesitate to write, and write at immense length, to Mr. Chamberlain both as Flora Shaw to her old friend and also as Lady Lugard to the Colonial Secretary. She was confident she could use her own position in her husband's service, a claim that even Lugard cannot at first have found altogether easy to accept. In the autumn of 1902 she sent Chamberlain a letter that was almost a dispatch with its full account of the work that had been achieved in Northern Nigeria. She did not scruple to impress upon the man of power how greatly this work was handicapped by lack of means and, knowing just what his political difficulties were, she gave him the arguments which might help him to extract funds from a grudging House of Commons. Here are some extracts from a letter which, when copied, covers nearly a dozen foolscap pages of typescript.

"You have seemed at different times to take so lively a personal interest in this new acquisition of the interior of West Africa that I fancy you may like, now that I am in a sense prevented from writing publicly on the subject, to have a private letter telling you how the place impressed me as a new and—naturally—much interested observer."

There followed a picture of the physical character of the country as seen upon her journey from south to north.

" The progress which has been made in the annexation and organization of the inland territories lying back from the highway of the river and untouched except in theory by the Niger Co., seems to me almost incredible when I think of it as having been done in so short a period as two years with the means which, as you well know, are so very limited. It does, I confess, raise in my mind a spirit of extraordinary satisfaction with the British race. One understands looking at this sort of thing why we are the first people of the world.

Two years ago there was nothing in the whole of this vast country but a military cantonment and trading store at Lokoja, something of the same sort at Jebba and an advanced line which held a frontier against the French in Borgu. The officers of the force were living huddled together in the smallest huts which could protect them from the weather. British administration in the interior provinces did not exist.

Now if you could see it you would, I am sure, be keenly interested, for it owes its creation to your initiative. If you had not grasped—at a time when no-one else who had the power to act was thinking about it— the immense possibilities of this field of enterprise and insisted upon the formation out here of the Frontier Force and the stiffening at home of Lord Salisbury's back, it would have been a mere matter of time when the whole of this fertile country should have passed into French hands."

She turned then to sketch the achievements in administration, especially from the humanitarian standpoint, with the spread of peace and justice and the cessation of slave-raiding and trading.

" It strikes me looking on as almost a phenomenal bit of work that a territory of this size . . . should have been brought out of a condition of barbarism and slave-raiding and perpetual local war to such a state of relatively civilized organization within a period of two years and with an income which for civil purposes does not amount to more than from £50 to £80,000 a year.

I can't but think that all this will be a satisfaction to you to know, for whether the great public will understand and will be disposed to grant the means for development within a period reasonable enough to permit of your openly adding the fresh laurels of an achieved success here to your crown or not, it will still remain your work that the estate was kept within the Empire. The principal, perhaps, the only serious obstacle to the successful development of the country appears to me to be the effect of the climate upon Europeans . . . there remains the fact that almost everyone is enervated, that the slightest carelessness in regard either to chills or sun results in fever and that gradually everyone who stays here appears to become permeated through and through with malarial poison more or less virulent in its effects. The result . . . is a distinct lowering of vital force showing itself in loss of energy, irritability of nerves, depression of spirits, premature ageing etc. . . . There can be no trustworthy continuity of administration until men can safely bring their wives and families to the country . . . "

She passed on to what Chamberlain must have recognized as the kernel of the letter.

" Under the circumstances it is not for me to say what I think of the way in which Sir Frederick has done the work which was entrusted to him. Your knowledge of the details of administration will have told you that the creation of an entirely new government with all its departments under the condition of the Protectorate and with a necessarily rigid regard for economy in men, money and materials cannot have been carried to a successful issue without ceaseless labour. It was necessary for him to have not only the brain to organize but the industry to carry out. He considers himself to have been most loyally—even, in some instances, devotedly—supported by his staff, but in the nearly always short-handed and sometimes non-existent condition of certain departments he has been forced personally to do the work as well as to plan how it should be done. The Residents are in many cases young and inexperienced men and require his close supervision. The details of the insufficiently manned Secretariat alone threaten to swamp him daily with office work. He used himself to work for the greater part of the night as well as the day, but, though he prides himself on an iron constitution, no frame can stand so continuous a strain in the climate of the tropics and it has, I grieve to say, told somewhat severely on his health . . . The doctors are urging upon me that he should seek employment at home or in some more healthy portion of the Empire before his strength is permanently sapped . . . I am most anxious if possible to support him in carrying the development of the Protectorate some stages nearer to substantial success, but I fear there can be little doubt that at any rate under present conditions there is a necessary limit to the term of working activity in West Africa.

He has also added considerably to his labour . . . by a system of confidential memoranda by means of which it has been his practice to obtain the opinion of all the more important officials and Residents on any new steps which he proposed to take. In this way, though the government is nominally autocratic it becomes really a system of government by consensus of the best opinion and gains in strength and efficiency by the wholehearted support which it commands. I imagine however, that if his staff spoke all their mind they would say that he works them harder than human nature can long endure . . . "

Finally, she invited him to come and visit him, and playing upon his favourite hobby, she assured him he would find

" not lions but orchids in the woods. You could be back in England in little over two months having had such a complete rest and change of the conditions of your life as I suppose you are not fated to have in this world. Imagine the astonishment of Europe if you were to give us such a pleasure! The least that France would think it meant would be the extension of Northern Nigeria to the Nile! . . .

Forgive me for once more taking up time which has been so often generously at my disposal. I have learned to trust perhaps too implicitly to your power as well as your readiness to find time for all the working interests which present themselves."

There would be much of very real interest to Chamberlain in this letter, and a little perhaps to make him smile. He may also have frowned at the thought that marriage might mean the loss to Africa of the chosen and most effective agent of his policy. But there could be no question at such a moment of visiting Nigeria: he had other and greater matters in hand.

"20 November 1902.   The Colonial Office.
Dear Lady Lugard,

Before this reaches you you will have seen the announcement of my intended voyage to South Africa. We start on Tuesday, and I am overwhelmed with work in consequence, and cannot reply fully to your most interesting letter.

You are right in thinking that I take the greatest interest in the development of our new West African possessions, and you may be assured that I recognize the great service which your husband has accomplished in so short a time. I am very sorry that his health is suffering and that he will not be able much longer to continue in that climate. Here indeed is our greatest difficulty. Men who are fitted to accomplish pioneer work on a great scale are very rare, and unfortunately they cannot give more than a limited portion of their life to the work for which they are so exceptionally qualified. I hope that in the course of time conditions will improve and the period of service may be extended. Unless we can secure this the tropical possessions of the Crown must always be the most difficult to administer.

We have been moving in Nigeria more rapidly than I expected, and indeed more rapidly than I would have desired to do if it had been possible to avoid it. To have brought all this territory under control, and indeed some sort of orderly Government, while we were still carrying on a big war, and expenses of every kind were increasing upon us, is truly a gigantic feat which no other nation could accomplish. . . .

Now I must break off. Give my kind remembrances to your husband and with the same to yourself,

Believe me, Yours very truly,

J. Chamberlain."

The third paragraph of the letter contained a hint of reproof or at least of warning which Lugard heard but, as we shall see, was resolved not to heed.

To watch and to comment upon her husband's work in Nigeria, to write letters to her many friends and relations, to order the house, the kitchen and the garden, were no more than distractions to Flora Shaw. Her problem remained. She had asked too much of herself and, Lugard, without knowing it, had asked too much, or perhaps too little, of her. Yet Flora, who had at least no doubt where her duty lay, would have continued her struggle to achieve it if her health had not again failed her. No doubt her active mind affected her body. She found uncivilized Africa at close quarters poor soil for intellectual cultivation by a mind which had so long busied itself upon the recorded histories and the heritage of art in the civilized world, or at least upon the adventures of her own people in building up new nations in the more temperate wilderness. She knew, and was soon to show, that the western Sudan had a long history but at the moment it seemed to her stagnant but for the stirring her own husband and his staff had brought to it. In any case, it could not be studied at Zungeru. In the heat and unfriendliness of the African scene, the cool wooded hills of Abinger seemed more than ever desirable. Soon, with this state of mind and with malaria, most depressing of infections, she was living the life of an invalid. To his brother on November 3rd, 1902, Lugard wrote hurriedly:

" The doctors peremptorily ordered her home and I insisted too and she has with the utmost reluctance consented—agreeing that it is beyond doubt best. She is devoted to *you*, says she could tell you alone of anyone in the world all that she feels, for she knows that you are my *alter ego* and says you understand me."

The attempt to live and work together in Africa had broken down. If in either of their characters there had been selfish flaws this initial failure might have turned a marriage of friendship into coldness and misunderstanding. As it was, both were highly unselfish and affectionate; they had been brought up in the ceremonious courtesy of their caste and did not discard it at the doors of their private lives. There was, moreover, complete frankness between them and both were intelligent enough to understand the difficulties which faced them. When they parted, therefore, five months after their marriage, it was in some sadness and doubt as to the future, but also in the hope that they would achieve in time some measure of that quiet mutual satisfaction which was all that they had promised to give to each other.

CHAPTER V

EXPEDITION TO KANO, 1902-3[1]

BY THE autumn of 1902 Lugard had occupied some two-thirds of the
territory allotted to the new Protectorate. The number of provinces
had now increased. Ilorin, Borgu, Kabba, Muri, Bassa and Nassarawa
he had inherited, at least as far as their headquarters on the Niger or
Benue banks were concerned, from the Company. Bida, Kontagora,
Yola and Bauchi had been conquered or re-conquered by force. The
vast kingdom of Bornu, thanks to Rabeh and the French, had submitted peacefully and gratefully. Zaria city had been entered without
open conflict. But this occupation did not represent administration:
the greater part of these so-called provinces, and especially the numerous pagan groups they contained, had not been so much as visited by
the handful of newly appointed Residents. This was true even in the
extreme south, in much-oppressed Bassa and Kabba.

A glance at the map on page 36 will show that the still unoccupied
area lay in the north and north-west and that it contained the most
ancient and dominant of the true Hausa Muslim states: those of the
two suzerains of Sokoto and Gwandu, the famous city-state of Kano,
Katsina, and a number of lesser but still ancient and proud emirates
clustered around them.

It had been recognized from the earliest days of the Company's
Charter that the occupation of these states would be no facile business.
This theme is reiterated in the files of the Company and of the Colonial
Office. It had been emphasized during an episode at the very end of
the Company's régime when, with Lugard still in England, there had
been a violent quarrel between the Company agents on one side and
Willcocks and some of his staff on the other, about the insulting treat-

[1] Lugard's account of the Kano-Sokoto expedition was put together immediately after the
events. When historians are able to sift such evidence as can still be found from Hausa-Fulani
sources new light may be thrown upon the story.

87

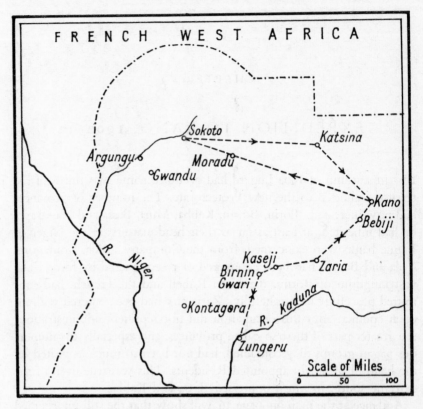

North-western Nigeria, showing the approximate route of
Lugard's march on the Kano-Sokoto campaign of 1903

ment of imperial officers and their troops by local rulers.[1] Our main
interest in the affair is in the views expressed about the treatment of
Nigerian rulers. " If," wrote Goldie,

" a reign of the sword is to suspend statesmanship, if England can spare the
force and the money to smash the Central Sudan into an amorphous
condition and then reorganize it on a new basis, I raise no objection. It
may be the best policy. But it must be deliberately planned and systematically carried out and not by spasmodic efforts."[2]

These were words to make blood in the Colonial Office run cold.
For they were authoritative words. Had not Goldie himself tried

[1] Some account of this is given in Flint, *Sir George Goldie*, pp. 298-301.
[2] Goldie to Chamberlain, 17 October 1898, C.O. 446/1.

" spasmodic efforts " on a large scale against Bida and Ilorin with very incomplete results? On the same day upon which Goldie wrote these words to the Office, and following a discussion in which he, Lugard and Lord Selborne took part, a telegram was sent to Nigeria which stated that " Her Majesty's Government strenuously desire to avoid collision with Sokoto at present,"[1] and soon afterwards the Colonial Office was hoping that " Colonel Lugard will be able to obtain a personal ascendancy which will prevent the necessity for strong measures."[2]

If Lugard was already inclined to dissent from this view it was evidently in silence. His knowledge of the country was still insufficient and he would not have wished a strong policy to be begun before he had taken over control. But as the date of his departure drew near, and as his demands for revenue mounted, some doubts began to arise. Goldie thought that the military would put pressure upon him to start unnecessary expeditions.[3] Chamberlain feared that " he wants to go too quickly."[4] The view—the hope—was expressed in the Office that " civilian work must for many years to come be confined to maintaining amicable relations with the chiefs and encouraging trade . . . "[5] Chamberlain heavily underlined this policy by his congratulations to Lugard for avoiding any hostilities during the Ashanti trouble in 1900,[6] and a few days later Chamberlain added " We must not have another native war."[7]

Was humanity the reason for this restraint? Partly. But there were other more practical reasons. Native wars cost money. Hostilities abroad were reflected in major engagements in Whitehall between the Colonial Office and the Treasury, and also perhaps, with the War Office, faced by the dissipation of its scanty military resources. There would be questions in Parliament inspired by economy, humanity, or sheer party politics. And always there hung over each minor operation the dread of a disaster which would shock public opinion and might cause serious political embarrassment to a government. The names of some recent disasters re-echoed ominously in the Offices on both sides

[1] Chamberlain to Willcocks, 17 October 1898, C.O. 446/1.
[2] Minute by Butler on Willcocks to Chamberlain, 8 November 1898, C.O. 446/1.
[3] Minute by Antrobus on Salisbury to Chamberlain, 18 October 1899, C.O. 446/5.
[4] Minute by Chamberlain on Salisbury to Chamberlain, 18 October 1899, C.O. 446/5.
[5] Minute by Mercer on Lugard to Chamberlain, 2 February 1899, C.O. 446/7.
[6] Minute by Antrobus on Lugard to Chamberlain, 23 August 1900, C.O. 446/10.
[7] Minute by Chamberlain on Lugard to Chamberlain, 23 August 1900, C.O. 446/10.

of Downing Street and it was well known that they were most likely to occur in " new " countries and in places far from the waves which at that time Britain still ruled. Not very long before, in 1890, there had been the somewhat similar prologue to the Zululand disaster of Isandhlawana; and, more famous and more prolonged, the indecisions and cross-purposes that had led to the Gordon tragedy.

Lugard knew this. Had he not played a major part in the campaign for the retention of Uganda with all it had taught him of the ambiguous position of politicians where imperial expansion was concerned? He now acted with unusual care. In his annual report of 1900 he merely directed attention to the unsolved problem of the north. He reported that he had not succeeded in opening up friendly relations with the distant Fulani emirates. Acting, however, with great propriety, he formally recognized the pre-eminence of the Sultan of Sokoto and even, on March 18th, 1901, sent a message to him, after the deposition of the Emir of Kontagora, to ask him if he would like to exercise his traditional right and nominate a successor.[1] He reported that no answer was returned to this request and that he was still unable to make any contact with the rulers of the north-western emirates.[2] About May, 1902 he did receive a message from Sokoto. It was brief, uncompromising, but hardly surprising.

" From us to you. I do not consent that any one from you should ever dwell with us. I will never agree with you. I will have nothing ever to do with you. Between us and you there are no dealings except as between Mussulmans and Unbelievers, War, as God Almighty has enjoined on us. There is no power or strength save in God on high."[3]

This letter was taken by Lugard as a denunciation of the treaties made with the Company in 1885, 1890 and 1894. In the 1902 report (which he carried over into 1903 in order not to spoil a good story, that of the Kano-Sokoto expedition) he summed up the causes which had lead to his taking military action.[4]

In stating this case he did not show himself to be blind to the moral issues involved; he settled them in his own mind, not only by the fact that we had undertaken international treaty obligations which he always accepted as overriding all other rights, but that these obligations

[1] *Reports*, 1900–01, p. 15, and 1902, pp. 99-100.
[2] *Ibid.* 1901, pp. 6-7 and 9, and 1902, p. 101.
[3] *Ibid.* 1902, p. 101. [4] *Reports*, 1902, p. 16 ff.

were to enforce law and order and above all to check any traffic in slaves or in spirits. The position of Sokoto was bound up with slavery: slaves were its annual tribute from the emirates. While this continued there could be no end to raiding and trading. On the political side, Britain had agreed to join the French in a boundary commission along their treaty-made frontiers and so long as Kano and Sokoto were un-occupied, he could not guarantee the commissioners' safety on the British side of the line. There were, therefore, in his view, compelling international as well as moral reasons why he should hasten to assert effective control of the whole region.

There were also pressing internal reasons why action should be taken and taken immediately. Though one emir after another had been forced to bend or break before the advent of British power, there was still, he reported, a widespread belief amongst the people that Sokoto and Kano would not so easily fall. The Sultan of Sokoto, though no autocrat like Menelik of Ethiopia, bore the same dignity of a " King of Kings" and strengthened his temporal position with his religious emin-ence. Although Lugard had actually recognized his primacy in his letter he was determined that it should be exercised only under the new supreme British suzerain. So long, argued Lugard, as the revered Sultan was still recalcitrant, so long would all the Fulani emirs be troubled by a double allegiance; spies and agents would pass from palace to palace; some of the newly appointed emirs would, like the now apparently " loyal " rulers of Ilorin and Bida, be distressed and uneasy, while others would openly or secretly ally with the head of their religion. The supreme religious authority of Sokoto was but-tressed to the east by the far-famed political and commercial power of the emirate of Kano. The great market-town of this state, to which merchants came from a wide area, had a population which fluctuated seasonally between thirty and fifty thousand. With its army of mailed horsemen and its great wall it was regarded throughout the northern states as impregnable. Aliu, the Emir, was reported to be bitterly hostile to the British and in the middle of 1902 he did something for which, in Lugard's view, there could be no exoneration.

Nassarawa province, lying northwards of the Benue and just west of its junction with the Niger, had given Lugard trouble from the first. An administrative officer, the Hon. David Carnegie, had been murdered there in June, 1902; a native Christian missionary had met the same fate. In this province lay the small Fulani chieftainship of Keffi which was directly under Zaria, the important emirate lying in the very middle of Northern Nigeria. The old chief of Keffi was dominated by one of his palace officers called the Magaji who refused to accept British authority and continued to raid for slaves. The Resident, Captain Moloney, even though he had a premonition that the Magaji would one day kill him, was determined to try peaceful influence before resorting to force and to urge him to change his conduct. Crippled from a previous wound inflicted at the time of the Brass raid, he was carried into the palace, unarmed and in a hammock. The Magaji killed him with his sword and then fled to the north. He was received with honour by the Emir of Kano and appeared in state riding at his right hand.[1] " If," the Emir of Kano was reported as saying, " a little town like Keffi could do so much, what could not Kano do?"[2] Lugard commented:

" If the life of a European can be taken with impunity the prestige of the Government would be gone, and prestige is another word for self-preservation in a country where millions are ruled by a few score. In my opinion Government owes it to every British officer called upon to serve in distant districts among turbulent people to take prompt and effective measures in such a case, or the lives of its servants would not be safe. This has ever been a cardinal principle with the Indian Government, and a frontier tribe shielding the murderer of a British officer has been held to have declared war against the State. I felt that I had no option but to attempt the arrest of the Magaji to the uttermost limits of the Protectorate, and if ever the day shall come when any other policy may prevail it will not be long before it is followed by disaster."[3]

These political problems had, of course, their strategic side. Lugard's forces were small; his communications gravely difficult; his new headquarters was within the hazardous Zaria emirate and on the very borders of the hostile states. He was obliged to disperse his troops and send expeditions hither and thither to parade or to use their strength. Sokoto and Kano were reported to be busily collecting arms and men, especially deserters from French and British forces with their rifles, and strengthening the walls of all their hundreds of towns. The possibility could not be ruled out that the combined forces of the northern emirs with their immense numbers of horsemen might attack and over-

[1] *Reports*, 1902, pp. 12-13, and 1904, p. 60.   [2] *Ibid.*, 1902, p. 17.   [3] *Ibid.* pp. 17-18.

whelm Zungeru at a moment when most of the Northern Nigeria Regiment was dispersed. And by the middle of 1902 the ambiguous situation in Zaria seemed to open the way to an attack.

The Emir of this large and centrally placed state had only accepted British authority when he was forced to appeal to Lugard for help against the deposed and fiery old Emir Ibrahim of Kontagora who, turned out of his own city, was ravaging Zaria for slaves and sustenance. The Sultan of Sokoto, who was Ibrahim's near relative, encouraged him to attack an emir whose loyalty was doubtful. Fulani rulers at this time were not notable for humanity but, according to Lugard, Zaria was an expert in cruelty. He had a way of burying people up to their necks and leaving them to die. Another of his customs was to invite anyone to whom he objected to stay in his house from which they never emerged, dead or alive, as they were interred in their guest room. The Emir, who seems to have been a man of humour, would grimly explain that they had gone upon a long journey. He was able, also, to go about his country perpetrating even worse cruelties than before the coming of the British because he could now claim their authority and put the responsibility upon them.

It was hard for Lugard to convey to the Colonial Office the difficulties of trying to occupy, still more to administer, a country in this state of uncertainty. He had to consider not only the safety but also the morale of his Residents. The tension felt amongst the handful of British administrators charged to hold this huge country, whose rulers were stirring restlessly under their prentice hands, is revealed in the letters which were later given to the writer by one of the Assistant Residents, R. P. Nicholson.[1] He was sent up to Zaria in April 1902 under Captain Abadie, formerly Lugard's A.D.C. and a man for whom Lugard had almost a father's affection. There, with one company, they had to keep the Emir, distracted as he was by constant appeals for action from Kano and Sokoto, at least on the fence, if not on the right side of it. They could not stop hundreds of slaves being hawked about in the streets in irons or a tribute of a 100 being sent off to Sokoto. They knew from their spies that the Emir was always on the verge of

[1] Nicholson, Reginald Popham, C.M.G., 1874-1956; 1900 private secretary to Lugard and subsequently a political officer until 1906; 1903 served Sokoto-Kano Campaign; 1906 attached to Colonial Office, East African Department; 1908 Colonial Secretary and Registrar-General, Bermuda; 1915 Administrator of St. Vincent; 1922 Colonial Secretary, British Guiana; 1926-9 Colonial Secretary, Cyprus.

wiping out their little encampment with his bodyguard of gunmen and his thousands of cavalry. Often Abadie was away on patrol. This left the young Nicholson in charge. The telegraph had not reached Zaria. "It is difficult," he told his mother, "for you home-folk to realize what communication is in this country; Kontagora, 9 days off, Bauchi 10 days and Keffi 10 or 11 days, all by runner." Abadie, coming back to Zaria from Kontagora, had to swim across dozens of rivers. It was not until September, with the arrival of another W.A.F.F. Company, that they had risked arresting the Emir. The next month came news of Moloney's murder which naturally had its impact on all the exposed political officers. "It just shows," Nicholson wrote, "what a policy of bluff it is out here. The Fulani could have done the same in every station wherever they liked." The deposed Emir was invited to live, in suitable style, at Wushishi. "It had been a source of regret to me," Lugard commented,

> "that the inclusion of each new Province under administrative control had been accompanied by the deposition of the ruling Emir, and Zaria was the solitary exception. I had, therefore, been unwilling to depose him, and I now hoped that a period of enforced banishment would be a sufficient lesson to him that he must amend his conduct."[1]

During 1902 it was common knowledge among the Residents, and it certainly seemed commonsense to them, that Lugard meant to march against the north. Even before he went to Madeira for his marriage in June it was being discussed. The country was full of native rumours which Lugard, with his elementary intelligence service, was unable to check. Anything seemed possible. At the end of October he heard that the Emir of Kano was marching to attack nearby Zaria and turned back only because he heard of the death of the Sultan of Sokoto. After his return, Lugard felt obliged to strengthen the small garrison at Zaria and to send up supplies of food and ammunition for them. This was, of course, at once widely known and it was assumed that the long expected attack on the northern emirs was now to begin. Zaria was, indeed, to be the base of operations. Lugard therefore found the two additional arguments against further delay: it would have the psychological danger of appearing to be timidity and the practical dangers of consuming the hardly collected supplies and damping the possibly

[1] *Reports*, 1902, p. 14.

evanescent ardour of his native soldiers. Upon a small as upon a great scale, war, once envisaged, creates its own forward compulsions.

Lugard felt that he was unlucky in two things at this crisis. Chamberlain had gone to South Africa. He could not therefore get into immediate contact with the chief who, he might hope, though the records now show that the hope was vain, would trust him and believe in forward action. His other problem was more serious. We have seen that Lugard had arranged for a Colonel Kemball to come from India to be second in command to Willcocks. When Willcocks, to Lugard's great sorrow, left West Africa in 1901, Kemball succeeded to the command. He and Lugard were not in sympathy and the relationship between a very masterful High Commissioner, who was also a soldier with great experience of Africa, and the officer commanding the Force—the very Force that the High Commissioner had himself recently created—was likely to turn a little sour unless it was sweetened by friendship or at least by respect.

Kemball, after he had been promoted to the post of Inspector-General of the West African Frontier Force, went on to threaten Lugard upon a very vulnerable side. Lugard not only liked whole-hearted colleagues: he also liked to be in sole command of them. The very idea of subordination fretted him. We have seen how he evaded de Winton's control in Uganda; how Macdonald's clumsy assertion of power was to him a mountainous outrage and how, again, in 1897 he struggled against the suggestion that the Governor of Lagos should be, even in form, his superior. Now, just when he had planned his special kind of campaign and arranged for it to be under the command of Colonel Morland, who was very much his own man and completely initiated by Lugard in the delicate political side of the coming campaign, the whole position was endangered by Kemball in England. He was advising the Colonial Office that Lugard's forces were insufficient and that reserves should be called up from Lagos and the Niger Coast Protectorate. This would have four results, all equally objectionable to Lugard. One was that, with an inter-colonial force, Kemball would be substituted for Morland in the command; secondly, an officer of higher rank would be more likely to contest his own control of the campaign; thirdly, he would have to accept help from the neighbouring, and to some extent, rival, governors; fourthly, there would be delay and difficulty in collecting these dispersed forces. Our earlier knowledge of the lengths to which Lugard would go in order to avoid losing his autonomy gives the key to his conduct now. With an absolute conviction of the rightness of both his political and military judgment he decided that action was urgent, that it could be successfully achieved with the modest force he commanded, and that he would take the risk of being checked or even disavowed by his masters at the Colonial Office.

Between December 10th, 1902, and January 28th, 1903, there took place an exchange of telegrams and dispatches between Whitehall and Zungeru which throws further light upon Chamberlain's fears of 1898-9 and vividly illustrates the process by which in a democracy a party government controls, or tries to control, the frontiers of its empire. Willing success but shrinking from failure, and still more, from responsibility for failure, temperamentally unsympathetic towards the men of decision to whom they were obliged to commit the frontiers, the officials and ministers of the Crown sometimes seem to cut poor figures at these moments of action. The sympathy of posterity is generally with the soldier but it must be remembered that the minister from whom he draws his authority and his funds is himself drawing that authority from an ill-informed and fickle master, an electorate which in England usually prefers peace and economy to military glory.

On December 5th, 1902, *The Times* printed a statement from Reuter that operations were to be undertaken against Kano. There was consternation at the Colonial Office. There was also indignation when it was learned that the intention to start a campaign was known among West African merchants and even in France. To a question in the House of Commons on December 9th, Austen Chamberlain, the Postmaster-General, answered for his father who was in South Africa. He was obliged to say lamely that the report in the papers appeared to refer to preparations which Lugard was making to ensure the safety of the British and French Boundary Commissioners.[1]

On December 10th, Lord Onslow, Chamberlain's Under-Secretary, telegraphed his fears to Lugard,

" Reuter states that it has been decided to· undertake hostile operations against Kano, but I presume that you are only taking necessary pre-

[1] *Parliamentary Debates*, 9 December 1902, IV. 116. 449-50.

cautions for safety of Boundary Commissioners. Telegraph outline of proposed arrangements and strength of force to be employed."

Lugard's wire in reply was packed with all, or almost all his reasons.

" 12 December. No. 124. Referring to your telegram received this day, see my dispatches of 24th November, 28th August, 7 October. Information received that Kano preparations completed for provoking war, demonstration in favour of murderer of Moloney. Safety of garrison of Zaria, prestige of British Government, possibility of delimitation of frontier, depend on energetic action. Paramount chiefs in this country await result and if action deferred they would attribute to fear of them (with) possibility of deplorable result. Probable number of troops, 1000. Dispatch sent."[1]

Onslow's reply to this cannot have been unexpected by Lugard.

" 19th December. Telegram received No. 124. As you are aware, His Majesty's Government are anxious to avoid military operations in West Africa. We have full confidence that you will not engage in them unless they are absolutely necessary for defensive purposes, but if in your judgment they are necessary we leave you full discretionary powers as to manner in which they should be carried out. We understand that you have resources in men sufficient to meet all contingencies ".[2]

Lord Onslow went on to demand detailed information as to Lugard's plan of action, his forces and his reserves. This telegram made it clear to Lugard that his move was unpopular and, in the customary game within the public services of passing responsibility, it put upon him the onus of proving that he was acting purely on the defensive, and also that he had a sufficiency of force.

Three days later Onslow telegraphed again. He had now looked up the dispatches to which Lugard had referred him and had found nothing in them to indicate the coming campaign. On the same day, advised presumably by Kemball, and without waiting for Lugard's agreement, he telegraphed to Moor in Southern Nigeria to hold in readiness 300 men and two 75 mm. guns. " Although the High Commissioner for Northern Nigeria has not asked for troops, His Majesty's Government fears that forces at his disposal may be found not to provide sufficient reserve of men in certain eventualities."[3] Two days

[1] *Northern Nigeria: Correspondence Relating to Kano* (1903), Cd. 1433.
[2] *Ibid.* p. 2. [3] *Ibid.* p. 2.

later, while still awaiting Lugard's answer, Onslow's anxiety increased, and he telegraphed:

" His Majesty's Government must have information asked for before any expedition starts for Kano."

The next day, the 25th, Onslow at last got Lugard's statement as to his plan of action, sent on the 23rd. In this he repeated all his arguments in favour of the campaign, concluding:

" Situation has been forced by circumstances referred to; for safety and for defensive measures I am compelled to take energetic action. Total strength: 1,000 native troops, 7 Maxim guns, 5 75 m.m. guns, 50 Europeans which are considered quite sufficient. In reserve 270, 1 75 m.m. guns, 2 Maxim guns, defensible position Argungu; Kontagora, 100, 1 7 pr. R.M.L. guns, 1 Maxim gun; Zungeru, 310, 4 7 pr. R.M.L. guns, 3 Maxim guns. Impossible to estimate enemy's forces: Wallace anticipates large number of rabble, fixing maximum at mounted troops 4,000. I do not personally anticipate so many; Emir unpopular; Hausa population and traders on our side; majority in the field will not fight. I shall impress on them that I consider action proposed absolutely unavoidable . . . "[1]

The Colonial Office minutes on the correspondence show that while they had great confidence in Lugard's ability to direct a campaign, and were even ready to be convinced by him that it had to be fought, they were inclined to censure him for springing the plan upon them in this way.[2] His earlier incidental references could not possibly have been taken to mean that he was planning a campaign. The Colonial Office was actually less well informed than the outside world. And yet Ommaney[3] was bound to minute on December 27th, " I do not suppose that H.M.G. will desire to forbid the responsible man on the spot to undertake an expedition that he holds to be absolutely necessary."[4]

The expedition might have to be sanctioned but Onslow and his advisers could not quite shut out their fear of a disaster. So telegrams were sent to Southern Nigeria and the Gold Coast as well as to Lagos ordering the governors to prepare forces while, on January 1st, Lugard

[1] Cd. 1433, p. 3.
[2] Minute by Strachey on Lugard to Chamberlain, 12 December 1902, C.O. 446/26.
[3] Ommaney, Sir Montague Frederick, G.C.M.G., K.C.B., I.S.O., 1842-1925; 1864 entered Royal Engineers; 1877-1900 Crown Agent for the Colonies; 1900-07 Permanent Under-Secretary for the Colonies.
[4] Minute on Lugard to Chamberlain, 23 December 1902, C.O. 446/26.

was again asked if his forces were sufficient. Three days later, as Lugard had feared, in view of the addition of troops from other colonies, General Kemball was sent out to command.

By now parliament and public opinion were becoming aware of what was in the wind. As one of Onslow's officials minuted later, Lugard might succeed, in his usual way, in carrying out operations against Bida and Kontagora quietly without attracting attention until the coup had been made, but it was a very different matter when such well-known places as Kano and Sokoto were concerned.[1]

There was another aspect. It is seldom, indeed, in English public life that there is no one to speak for the enemy. Sir Charles Dilke began on December 9th asking questions in the House which suggested that the northern emirs might have a case and that it was the British who had broken their word by not paying the subsidies promised in the original treaties made by the Company. He returned to the question again with Emmott on December 16th, pressing for further information upon this point. Austen Chamberlain, still unsure as to the facts, answered in guarded defence of Lugard. On January 2nd Lord Onslow wrote off to him for information which would enable him to answer these questions fully.[2] On the 8th he telegraphed that the government

" desire to impress on you that there is strong feeling in this country amongst those most deeply interested in West Africa, even though approving generally of the policy pursued in Northern Nigeria, that military operations should be avoided, if possible. The information in possession of His Majesty's Government is not so complete as they could have wished."[3]

Lugard had already telegraphed, on January 17th, before getting this, that he had given orders for an immediate advance, but the next day, upon receiving it, he threw the responsibility back at them by saying, " please inform me definitively whether you desire that I should stop advance of expedition started already . . . I deprecate responsibility incurred by delaying under existing circumstances."[4]

He knew very well that it was one thing for Whitehall to prevent the launching of an expedition and quite another to stop it in the field and make it turn back. On January 19th, Onslow sent the only

[1] Minutes on Lugard to Chamberlain, 17 April 1903, C.O. 446/31.
[2] Cd. 1433, pp. 4-5, and *Parliamentary Debates*, 9 and 16 December 1902, IV. 116. 449-50 and 1336-8.
[3] Cd. 1433, pp. 5-6.   [4] *Ibid.* p. 6.

possible reply which Lugard received with grim satisfaction.[1] As generally happened, he had got his way.

He was, however, very angry. The appointment of Kemball was the chief cause. In a dispatch of January 16th he did not conceal his hurt.

" In your telegram of yesterday you order me to consult with General Kemball as to the sufficiency of the Forces at my disposal etc. I very humbly and respectfully desire to remind you that in 1898 you saw fit to entrust me with the entire command of the troops (including part of the West India Regiment) in the Field in the French crisis, with the plan of operations, and the organization and raising of the West African Frontier Force. I believe I achieved the results you desired. I am senior in service to General Kemball with somewhat more extended experience especially in African service. An opinion as to sufficiency of our troops can only be formed in relation to the probable forces of the enemy, and the political conditions and state of feeling of the people throughout the Protectorate. These conditions it is impossible for General Kemball to know better than myself."[2]

If, he continued, Colonel Morland were superseded in the field while no other troops than the Northern Nigeria Regiment were operating, he would resign and Lugard would lose " the very best of Commandants ". He spoke of the strong feeling about this among the officers, and of the confidence of the troops in their own Commandant. General Kemball should wait with reserve forces and come in with them only if their use should prove necessary.

He was angry too, with less justification, at the movement of opinion in England against war and in favour of conciliatory measures. His conviction was that no one could be more moderate and more averse from war than himself and he resented the implication that he needed any restraining by humanitarians. He repeated his point about the murder of Moloney and the safety of men, " who are to the best of their ability doing the Empire's work here and honestly working for the good of these people." He then went on to the wider issue.

" The advocates of conciliation at any price who protest against Military

---

[1] " Jan. 19 . . . I do not desire that you should stop progress of expeditionary force, but I think reserves should be brought up into Northern Nigeria without delay." Cd. 1433, p. 9.

[2] Lugard to Chamberlain, 16 January 1903, C.O. 446/30.

Operations in Northern Nigeria appear to forget that their nation has assumed before God and the civilized world the responsibility of maintaining peace and good order in the area declared as a British Protectorate and that the towns of Kano and Sokoto are ruled by an alien race who buy and sell the people of the country in large public slave markets daily, these being now—thanks to British rule—the last remaining centres of this traffic . . . Underground dungeons in which men are placed and left to starve, public mutilation in the market places, bribery in the so-called Courts, oppression and extortion in the whole scheme of rule. The Military Operations so much deprecated have, in the great cities of Bida, of Kontagora, of Yola, of Bauchi, of Ilorin, of Zaria and elsewhere led to the suppression of these things, while the Fulani caste, though aliens, have been re-instated and treated with honour and consideration. The bulk of the population is on our side, those who oppose us are their oppressors. The task upon which I am employed is one of prevention of the daily bloodshed which has already denuded this country of probably half its population and even the suppression of the forces of tyranny and unrest has been achieved with almost no bloodshed at all. After reading the misconstruction of motives and the designs which some persons appear to delight in ascribing to those in responsible positions in Africa, you will, I trust, forgive my wish that my words could reach Sir Charles Dilke and others in their places in the Parliament of the Nation."

The year 1903 does not, perhaps, mark one of the highest moral tides in the ebb and flow of humanitarian impulse in Britain. It does seem, however, that following the military hysteria shown in the early part of the Boer War the British public had already swung back with revulsion from jingoism to their usual love of peace. As long ago as the summer of 1900 Goldie, an acute observer, had sent Lugard an interesting analysis of the popular mood, with the advice which he derived from it.

"I lay stress on maintaining peace because the Boer War has brought about a great change in public opinion at home. I believe that ' the 40 millions, mostly fools ' as Carlyle says, who have the last word in our policy are heartily sick of the idea of war anywhere and for any object. The timidity shown in the treatment of the Chinese question by journals which formerly beat the drum on every trivial opportunity is one of many proofs of this remarkable change. The Ashanti affair has fallen quite flat and publicists talk of it and other little wars as nuisances. No one can say how long this reaction will last; but I think it must be for some years. I throw this idea out for your guidance as the result of wide and careful enquiry since I arrived home."

(Goldie to L., 31 August 1900).

Perhaps Lugard's awareness of this pacific mood was another reason why he went so softly about the preparations for his little war.

It was not, however, a mere relapse into a blind pacificism that he had to consider. Dilke's was not the only intelligent voice that was being raised in favour of conciliatory methods and just conduct even upon a dangerous and little known African frontier. It was very proper that Lugard should be asked whether, on the question of the immediate necessity of the campaign, his arguments were valid. To his sense of innocence Lugard should not have added one of injury. Yet the reply just quoted, which he made to this question, and which resembles his defence of his conduct in Uganda, is one that the critics of empire must answer in their turn.[1]

Before we go back to the Nigerian scene we must see how Lord Onslow tried to tie up the ragged ends left by Lugard's precipitancy into a decent conclusion which the Colonial Office could present and Parliament could accept. On January 28th he signed a dispatch to Lugard, which he published a few days later as the final document in the papers presented to Parliament.[2] In this he repeated Lugard's case for immediate action, and in the main accepted it, while at the same time he tried to clear the reputation of the government by saying that they had always wanted to avoid a rupture with Sokoto and would have preferred a policy of delay which might have allowed of friendly negotiation with the Sultan. It was part of the total situation that the position of the Conservative government was not at that moment strong enough to stand much criticism. Indeed Onslow was shortly afterwards confessing to Chamberlain that bye-elections had gone badly and that thirty per cent of their members were in a state of mutiny.[3]

Onslow took the occasion of this dispatch to approve Lugard's policy with regard to slave-raiding and his administrative policy as set out in his first annual report. But he complained that there was no hint of any plan to attack until Lugard's telegram of December 23rd, received on the 25th. That was some three weeks after the newspapers,

[1] See Vol. I, pp. 358-86.   [2] Cd. 1433, pp. 10-14.
[3] Onslow to Chamberlain, 13 March 1903, Chamberlain Papers. Mr. Julian Amery kindly gave me access to these.

through Reuter's Agency, were reporting that operations had been decided upon. The sting of the dispatch was in the last paragraph.

" His Majesty's Government regret the necessity which has arisen for taking action against Kano. They think that you should have kept them more fully informed of what was passing, and that you should have given them an earlier opportunity of considering, with the knowledge which they alone possess of the general situation in other parts of the Empire, whether it was necessary to send an expedition to Kano and whether it was expedient to do so at this time and with the force which is available. But they agree with you that in the circumstances the action which you are taking was inevitable. They have your assurance that you consider the forces at your disposal sufficient to accomplish the object which you have in view, and they trust that the operations will be successful."[1]

Was this a censure upon Lugard? Opinions differed. " I hope," wrote Onslow privately in his weekly letter to his chief in South Africa, " that you will not think that I went too far in saying what I did." Yet he told Chamberlain that:

" Dilke and some newspapers characterized the dispatch as a censure on Lugard though *The Times* and others termed it a ' dignified rebuke '. My feeling is that it is impossible for a pro-consul in a distant part of the Empire to know what are the conditions everywhere and what liabilities His Majesty's Government may at any time be under. For instance he would not know the extent of our liability in Somaliland[2] nor of the ' mess ', as it has been called, in Venezuela and though he has accomplished the first step ' off his own bat ' if anything went wrong he would need to be supplied by troops from some other part of the Empire and they might but ill be spared.

The public, too, is anxiously looking for an early closing of the doors of the Temple of Janus."[3]

The last sentence endorses Goldie's opinion. Actually Dilke, in discussing Onslow's dispatch which, with the whole correspondence, had been laid before parliament, had said:

" The Kano expedition has led to a most painful censure upon a very

[1] Cd. 1433, p. 12.
[2] This was the third expedition against the Mad Mullah which necessitated extra troops being sent from Aden and India to strengthen the local force. See D. Jardine, *The Mad Mullah of Somaliland* (1923).
[3] Onslow to Chamberlain, 26 February 1903, Chamberlain Papers.

distinguished officer, namely the Commissioner of Nigeria, in words which are very strong. What the House ought to be quite clear about is that censure is deserved by the Commissioner and not by the Government."[1]

This stirred Austen Chamberlain to declare the government's confidence in their Commissioner.

" The right honourable Baronet would make a great mistake if he supposed that the Government had in any way lost confidence in Sir F. Lugard . . . We retain full confidence in that most experienced administrator and we are quite certain that he will act with all forbearance and with great discretion in dealing with the circumstances which arise in the great area under his control."[2]

The Times, weighing up the arguments in the finely balanced scales of one of its leading articles, called Lord Onslow's words " a temperate remonstrance " and added its own restrained criticism of Lugard's failure to secure the approval of the authorities before he " practically committed them to war ". But

" We all admire and respect Administrators who in time of need do not flinch from responsibility—even when it is responsibility of so grave a kind as that which Sir Frederick Lugard did not hesitate to assume."[3]

It may be concluded that, on the home front at least, Lugard's daring had certainly won him a victory though not without some days when the issue hung in the balance.

Following the British side of the story has led us to anticipate. The parliamentary discussion on the papers presented was held when the first phase of the campaign had already been reported. But we must return to Zungeru where Lugard, after receiving Lord Onslow's reluctant consent of January 19th, was working twelve hours a day in his hot, makeshift headquarters. He took all this perturbation at Whitehall and Westminster with astonishing unconcern. His eyes were fixed on the map to the north. "The government," he wrote, in a later letter to his brother, " were in an insane funk re Kano. Cabled to me not to hesitate to ask for troops—would have sent a British Army Corps—censured me for going at it ' without asking Mamma' as the *Pall Mall*

---

[1] *Parliamentary Debates*, 17 February 1903, IV. 118. 120-1.
[2] *Ibid.* 129.   [3] *The Times*, 18 February 1903.

puts it, and if we'd messed it, I should have been broke." (L. to E. J. L., 11 May 1903).

On January 29th Lugard had sent Morland ahead from Zaria to march to Kano with 722 men, 24 officers, 12 British N.C.O.s, 4 guns and 4 Maxims. On February 2nd he himself turned as far as he could— for he still had to send telegrams and dispatches back to London as he rode—from these preparations to the action itself. Against the doubts of Goldie and his masters, he had staked everything upon his military and political judgment that the famed power of the northern emirs and their vast armies would melt away or be easily defeated by his little force. True, he was not able to shake off General Kemball who now arrived. He did, however, refuse to call up the reserves from the other colonies and these were left waiting at Lokoja. (At the Colonial Office, when these dispositions were reviewed later, the opinion was expressed that Lugard had been ungenerous to Kemball in that when he knew that he was coming he sent Morland ahead to Kano before Kemball could take any part.[1]) Lugard was, of course, unable to command the operations himself, but he meant to follow on the very heels of the soldiers to carry out the political settlements. Although he was travelling into unknown country with very serious business on hand, he showed his usual almost boyish pride in breaking some imagined record for his unique journey.

He left Zungeru in the evening of February 2nd, and marched eight miles to his first camp; the next day he marched twenty-five miles. He had with him his young private secretary, Hopkins, who, dragged from his office table to the saddle, rode in on the first night in an almost fainting condition. There was also an officer for survey work, a young doctor and Eaglesome, who came along with his chief upon the first stage to see the possibilities of railway construction. Lugard brought his favourite African servant, John, and other natives of his household who had simply insisted upon coming with him.

On the surface no story could seem more simple and straightforward than the record of this war-like journey. Yet Lugard was living upon three different planes as he rode north. There was the major action that lay on the surface—the march—the fights—the political settlement—all that found its way into his published reports and became a first chapter in the history of the new Nigerian state. Then there was

[1] Minute on Lugard to Chamberlain, 2 May 1903, C.O. 446/31.

the more secret history of that ego, the very energy and assertiveness of which, while it drove towards rapid and successful action, chafed against the limits within which it had to act, wounding itself and others. For he was in conflict not only with the northern emirs but with the Colonial Office and with Kemball, with all that would limit his independence of action or question his judgment. But he was living also upon a third and deeper plane, that of his great affection for his wife. She was still more friend than wife but for Lugard's nature, after all these years of distress and embitterment where women were concerned, the relationship of mutual tenderness and loyalty was something new and precious. Although, therefore, on this amazing round journey from Zungeru and back, with the long hours on horseback and all the reporting, correspondence, interviewing and political negotiation he had to do in the hours when he was out of the saddle, he found time to write long letters to Flora. When night came and the others were asleep he could indulge in his private thoughts, and he could now pour them out in letters to a mind at least equal to his own in intelligence and in appreciation of the significance of what he was doing. He knew that his daily actions would be read with pride and affection; with how much more, after their rather unhappy parting, he could not be sure. He had promised her that he would be at Lagos to catch the April boat back to England and he dramatized the long and eventful journey on this secret plane, as a journey back to her, even when he was marching away from his base.

By February 7th Lugard could report to Flora that they had covered 100 of the 165 miles to Zaria. Each morning he rose at 4.30, had breakfast and started while it was still dark. He would walk 8 or 10 miles and ride the rest, averaging 18 to 20 miles a day. He would have gone faster but the 200 carriers had to catch up on their feet with the tents, food and other camp gear. As he rode Lugard scanned the caravan track ahead anxiously for runners coming back from Colonel Morland who had left Zaria five days before Lugard left Zungeru. The lives of the little force, white and black, and perhaps his own, depended upon his judgment of the sufficiency of Morland's troops. He was convinced that he was right: he *must* be right. And, yet, in a letter to his brother he confessed to an " if ". " If I don't come to grief over the Kano-Sokoto business with my inadequate forces for a country a third the size of India . . . " He knew that after Morland had crossed the frontier into Kano emirate he would meet a series of walled towns leading on to the capital and that many of the Hausa soldiers in the force carried surnames showing that these towns were their homes. Significantly, before setting out, he made his will.

He was just approaching Birnin Gwari, some 60 miles west of Zaria as the crow flies, when runners brought him the first news. The force had come upon the first important " enemy " town, Bebiji, eight miles over the Kano frontier.[1] Captain Abadie, sent on as political officer with the force, rode up to the red earth walls of the town and parleyed with the defenders who were lining them, trying to persuade them not to fight. But the Emir of Kano had threatened with death anyone who opened the gates to the white men. Abadie asked for the chief of the town but the people answered that he was not there and without his orders they could not open. A shell was therefore fired into the gate and blew it open, killing the chief, who was actually standing behind it, and his headmen. The storming party then went in with little resistance. Lugard could report with satisfaction that there was no looting or destruction in the town and that non-combatants were unharmed.

Then, one after another, the towns on the way to Kano opened their gates to Colonel Morland and his men. The Fulani head of each town, with his immediate following, fled to Kano. The people, who now knew, wrote Lugard, that

" contrary to all their own experience and custom in warfare, the British troops would not harm them remained quietly in their towns and brought ample supplies of food and water for the troops. These were duly paid for as though no war was being waged, for, indeed, we had no war against the people of Hausaland, but only their Fulani rulers."[2]

Lugard went on to emphasize this " striking testimony " to the discipline of the troops and the government's reputation for humanity: the usual procedure in the country was for everyone to run into the bush at the slightest alarm.

So far, so good! But the great walled city of Kano still lay ahead. Here all the Fulani irreconcilables had fled and here would be met a large army of horse and foot, presumably led by the Emir. Many times as Lugard followed up the force he must have wondered if he

[1] *Reports*, 1902, pp. 27-8. [2] *Ibid.* p. 28.

had been right, in his correspondence with the Colonial Office, to "play down" so emphatically the strength of Kano. He had not succeeded in one of his reasons for so doing, since General Kemball was now pursuing hot foot the expedition which he was to command. But Morland was ahead and Lugard longed to hear that he had reached Kano and had won his battle before being superseded.

The news reached Lugard as he camped at Kaseji, not much more than a march from Zaria. Morland had approached Kano unopposed. Since Clapperton's discovery in 1824 very few Europeans had looked upon the city. Morland found it even more formidable than he had expected. Now, as then, the traveller sees in the distance the long line of its walls drawn like a dark red band on the open plain. From the air or from high ground within the walls the crowded flat roofs in their thousands of rectangles make one continuous mass of the same red colour. The two strange abrupt hills of rock are the highest objects within the walls but the minarets of the mosques and the larger buildings of the Emir rear their incised and crenellated walls above the one-storey level of the houses. The wall, now crumbling away, runs for eleven miles and was pierced by thirteen gates. When Morland and his men looked at this wall and its gates they could see that these had been fully repaired against them. The wall varied from 30 to 50 feet in height: it was 40 feet thick at the base and had a double ditch in front divided by a triangular wall. The main wall behind was crenellated and loopholed at the top with a banquette running round on the inside to serve the loopholes. The cow-hide gates were fixed in towers "fifty feet long and tortuous" while some of them were elaborately designed to allow of attackers being enfiladed from the walls. But, putting all this work in jeopardy, some of the gates were inferior in strength to the others.

Morland began by shelling Zaria gate, at which he first arrived, for an hour. As he failed to breach it, he turned to the next, made a breach in this and flung a small storming party against it. These, to the sound of a call from the massed buglers, dashed at the breach with axes and ladders. The defenders on the walls could easily have annihilated this small party as it struggled through the gate: as it was, they kept up an ill-directed fire which succeeded only in wounding fourteen of the attackers and, as soon as the first of the party got into the gate, the defenders streamed from the walls and fled. The attackers must have

Lugard working at his desk in the Emir's Palace
immediately after the capture of Kano, 1903

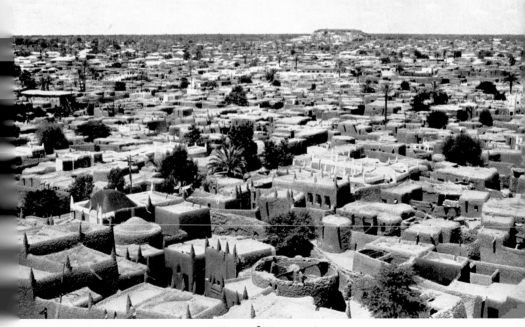

View of Kano

A Northern Nigerian ruler

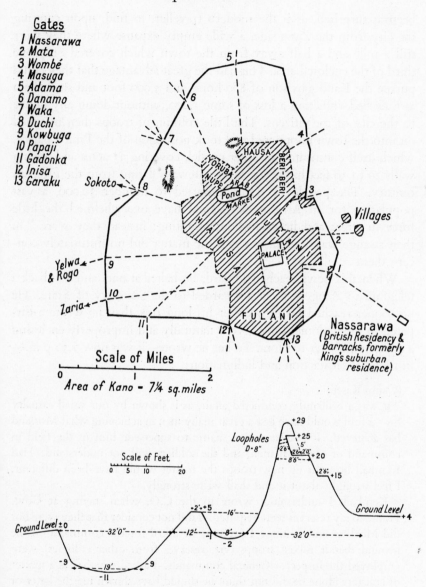

Gates
1 Nassarawa
2 Mata
3 Wombé
4 Masuga
5 Adama
6 Danamo
7 Waka
8 Duchi
9 Kowbuga
10 Papaji
11 Gadonka
12 Inisa
13 Garaku

HAUSA

YORUBA · ARAB
NUPE
Pond
MARKET

BERI-BERI

Villages

H
A
U
S
A

PALACE

FULANI

Nassarawa
(British Residency &
Barracks, formerly
King's suburban
residence)

Sokoto

Yelwa
& Rogo

Zaria

Scale of Miles

0 ——— 1 ——— 2

Area of Kano = 7¼ sq. miles

Loopholes
D · 8"

+29
+25
5'
2'6" 26·20" +20
8'6"
2'6" +15

Scale of Feet
0   5   10   20

Ground Level
+4

+2'·+5
16'

Ground Level ±0

-32'0"   -12'   -8'   -32'0"
-2

-9   -19'   -9
-11

Plan of Kano city and section of city wall, 1903. Taken from
the diagram in *Annual Reports*, Northern Nigeria, 1902, p. 165

been as surprised, as is the modern traveller, to find, upon entering the city from the Zaria side, a wide empty expanse where they were still a mile and a half away from the town which covered only one third of the enclosed area. This had the great advantage that they could pursue the Kano garrison of 800 horse and 5,000 foot and shell them as they fled, inflicting a loss of some 1,200, without doing any injury to the city or the citizens. The little column of troops then marched on into the town unopposed and took possession of the Emir's palace, which itself constituted an inner citadel, covering 33 acres and having walls 20 to 30 feet high, one of its gateways dating from the fifteenth century. The people of Kano, reported to number 30,000, a vast population for an African city, could have overwhelmed the little force in street and house-to-house fighting: instead they were " in their strange way looking on as if the matter did not intimately concern them . . . "[1]

When this news reached Lugard, he halted at once and sent back a telegram to Zungeru to be forwarded to the Secretary of State. He no sooner reached his camp after his long trek than he wrote a dispatch to the Colonial Office, very naturally and improperly enclosing a copy in his letter to Flora. To her he wrote—it was now 7.30 p.m.— in mingled satisfaction and indignation:

(Camp Kaseji)
" It was a brilliantly conducted affair, as is shown by our small casualty list—a fool would have lost a great many men in achieving what Morland has achieved. It is a *monstrous* shame to supersede him in the field in command of our own men, and the soldiers will not understand. Had Kemball brought up new troops the matter would have been different. I feel strongly about it and shall write strongly.

Kemball, I understand, wrote to the C.O. when staying at Govt. House to say reserves were required. *I* did not consider that they were nor did Morland and Festing. I presume he asked for the command on the ground that if mixed troops (viz. reserves from other colonies) were employed the Inspector General commands. I asked whether as a matter of courtesy alone he did not think he should have shown me the letter or informed me of it. He made some lame remark that I had not mentioned the Kano affair to him (why should I? It was not his affair and he is junior to me) and that I had evaded the subject. It is by such acts as this that the C.O. wound the feelings of the best men they have—men who

[1] *Reports*, 1902, p. 29.

are working double tides and often spending private money for the State. I cannot write much tonight, dear, for as I said I only got in at 5 p.m. and had a long dispatch to write, and have now just bathed and shaved, and it is dinner time and I have asked everyone to dine with me to celebrate Morland's success in a bottle of champagne. I think the whole Protectorate feel the unjust way in which he has been treated, civilians and soldiers alike, and I don't conceal my own view.

I don't know whether Kemball will manage to stop him and take command and supersede him. I have officially told Kemball what *I* think. He is due in Zaria today or tomorrow, and I shall be there on 11th, 3 days later." (L. to F. L., 8 February 1903).

Then, remembering his ultimate destination, he scribbled in conclusion, " This will be almost or quite the last letter to which you will be able to reply. Even if I go round by Sokoto I hope to catch the boat of April."

He reached Zaria on February 11th. He found this somewhat rickety emirate, with its many pagans, tending to fall to pieces in the absence of the peculiarly brutal Emir, who, it will be recalled, had been suspended. His deputy was loyally helping the Resident but tribes and towns were defying both and refusing to pay taxes. This and other matters kept Lugard busy at Zaria for five days. Writing to Flora, he seems to have been struck by the contrast between the rough business he had in hand and the character of his correspondent, though he knew she shared his belief that there was moral justification for his action.

Camp at Zaria
" . . . I told you in my last that our little corps of Mounted Infantry had ' got into ' the Fulani and killed 200. This will be invaluable for the moral effect it will cause, but it is all very hateful, is it not? What idiots we little mortals are, as though life were not short enough but we must hack each other to death as well. We have still the Emir and his force to deal with, and after all I don't believe a country of the size of N.N. has ever been annexed with less bloodshed . . . "

Then he went on to announce a theory about his own powers of which much more was to be heard.

" . . . It will not be long now and I shall be glad when I can lay down this ' white man's burden ' (in part at least) for a time—but of course I am equally responsible for N.N. whether at home or here, and whatever goes wrong is due to my fault and policy, and it is I and no substitute who must account for it. And now, goodnight dear, I hope before you receive this you will have seen the telegrams in the papers that all is well and finished." (L. to F. L., 12 February 1903).

He left Zaria at dawn on February 17th to follow the troops on the 82 mile stage north-east to Kano. To ride, almost without escort, into what was a hostile state, with the Emir and his army at large and un-defeated, seems, at first sight, a wholly unjustifiable risk for the civil head of the government to take. But he continued to back his judg-ment though even he was astonished when, on his way to Kano, thousands of the local population, walking with their laden donkeys, met him on the track and smilingly greeted him as they passed. There were even women journeying alone who did not turn aside from the track as they met the party. Lugard claimed this as another testimony to the good reputation of the British which had so far outrun their presence.[1] So it was, but it was also a tribute to the defeated rulers under whom, whatever their crimes against pagan tribes, this wide-spread trade had flourished in the Muslim regions by reason of the good security which, between their dynastic wars, they had enforced along its routes. Here, perhaps, lies one explanation of the easy accep-tance by the people of their new conquerors, especially in the great city of Kano. They were a people of traders and they were quick to grasp that the invaders were striking only at their rulers while offering peace and order to themselves.

Lugard covered the 82 flat, featureless miles to Kano in three and a half days. He would have moved faster but for the carriers who are—or were for they are becoming a feature of the past—always an un-avoidable drag upon African trekking. They were suffering severely from the pace and from the contrasts between the fierce heat of the day with its hot wind, the *harmattan*, blowing down from the Sahara charged with sand like a fine mist, and the bitter coldness of the night. As he drew nearer to the city he was able to see the dense population, the excellent agriculture, the manuring and the occasional essays in irrigation. The party reached the city on February 21st.

Kano.

" I got safely here without any trouble on the road, though I was not

[1] F. D. Lugard, ' Northern Nigeria ', *Geographical Journal*, vol. XXIII, January 1904. There are also photographs of Kano.

without anxiety yesterday morning and I am anxiously awaiting the result of the action which the Force has gone out to fight . . . Yesterday afternoon the mail of Jan. 10th bringing me yours of Jan. 7th . . . and a photo of you with New Year wishes. You little thought it would reach me sitting in the wonderful Hall of Audience of the Emir of Kano on Feb. 21st. I *like* the photo. It is *vastly*, incomparably better than those you had before. Thank you much for everything, dear."

" . . . I am in a room which I am told was a private Audience Chamber— others say the room of a favourite wife. It is a marvellous place. 18 ft. square—walls of mud very thick. At each corner about 8 ft. from the ground . . . runs a curved arch of mud but excellently finished to the opposite corner . . . tapering to the centre of the domed roof . . . walls about 18 ft. and centre of dome, say, 24 ft. Round the room runs a black dado 4 ft. high, above it at 6 and 10 ft. are bands. While the whole wall is coloured in all kinds of quaint designs and shapes in white, black, pale blue and yellow, the latter being of ground up mica which glitters. The door is carved. Great quantities of Arabic writings have been found and interesting correspondence with Sokoto. The arsenal contained enormous quantities of every conceivable kind of ammunition and even, I am told, some of home manufacture. I have been writing all day and I have not had time to go out and look round. The fortifications are marvellous. All is quiet."   (L. to F. L., 21 February 1903).

When he did have time to go out and look at the city he was deeply impressed, especially by its size and its fortifications. It was the first time he had seen the Kano type of mud building with flat roofs which here had its southern limit. He exclaimed that he had never seen nor even imagined anything like it in Africa. He was equally struck by the evidences of the cruelty of the government. It had been the centre of a great trade in slaves. Lugard, true to his dominant idea, had ordered Morland to close the slave-market immediately upon arrival. " So well, however, is our policy known that the slave-market had closed itself . . . " He had also given orders for an immediate visit to the gaol.

" I visited the dungeon myself. A small doorway 2 feet 6 inches by 1 foot 6 inches gives access into it. The interior is divided (by a thick wall with a similar hole through it) into two compartments, each 17 feet by 7 feet and 11 feet high. This wall was pierced with holes at its base through which the legs of those sentenced to death were thrust up to the thigh, and they were left to be trodden on by the mass of other prisoners till they died of thirst and starvation. The place is entirely air-tight and un-ventilated except for the one small doorway, or rather hole, in the wall through which you creep. The total space inside is 2,618 cubic feet, and at the time we took Kano 135 human beings were confined here each night, being let out during the day to cook their food, etc., in a small adjoining area. Recently as many as 200 have been interned at one time. As the superficial ground area was only 238 square feet there was not, of course, even standing room. Victims were crushed to death every night and their corpses hauled out each morning. The stench, I am told, inside the place when Colonel Morland visited it was intolerable, though it was empty, and when I myself went inside three weeks later the effluvium was unbearable for more than a few seconds. A putrid corpse even then lay near the doorway . . . One of the great pools in the city is marked as the place where men's heads were cut off; another near the great market is the site where limbs were amputated almost daily."[1]

Absolute order and quiet reigned throughout the city. Captain Abadie had at once taken charge and put himself at the head of the city's government. The headmen of the fourteen quarters reported to him: a rate of exchange was fixed between the local currency of cowrie shells and British silver while an old man who had been head of the market for 40 years played his part so well that, three days after the capture of the city, it was " Business as usual ", and three large trading caravans had set out for Zaria. So deeply had Lugard impressed upon the officers his determination to maintain the discipline of the troops in their dealings with the people that only one outrage was recorded. A soldier killed a civilian. He was condemned to death by court martial and " I directed," wrote Lugard, " that some of the chiefs of Kano should witness this vindication of British justice."[2]

The fighting was not over. Indeed, as Lugard expected, the worst was still to come. Aliu, the Emir of Kano, all the Fulani leaders and the bulk of his army had fallen back to link up with Sokoto.[3] Having heard of Lugard's practice of appointing the nearest heir in place of an irreconcilable emir, Aliu had taken the precaution of collecting and taking away with him every possible claimant and of giving orders that any one of them trying to get back to Lugard was to be killed. Three thus lost their lives. The situation was confused and difficult.

[1] *Reports*, 1902, pp. 30-31.   [2] *Ibid*. p. 31.
[3] For contemporary native evidence of the Emir's cowardice, see the Nigerian paper *Gaskiya* No. 156.

Lugard wished through negotiation to avoid more fighting but it was difficult to get into touch with the responsible leaders and it seemed certain that the Emir's great host would attack the small force of 600 men which, after leaving a small garrison in Kano, was marching on towards Sokoto. An even more serious possibility, since Morland was going through quite unknown country, was that the enemy might slip back past the little force and attempt to recapture the lightly-held city.

Lugard had ordered Morland to send forward a reassuring letter to the Sultan of Sokoto impressing upon him that, though the white men had come to stay, they had no desire to fight with him but would confirm his position and respect the Muslim religion. The Magaji of Keffi, must, however, be given up. With this letter went off a gift of five pieces of brocade. A highly evasive answer was received.[1] Another friendly letter was sent to the Emir of Katsina who replied courteously and sent a present of two fine horses.

General Kemball had arrived in Kano on February 13th, and had taken over the command. The expedition left Kano on February 16th, and marched a hundred miles westwards towards Sokoto. At this point they ran into a belt of thick waterless scrub. The Emir's army was said to be encamped on the further side. The force therefore made a detour to the south, and Kemball sent Captain Wright with a small scouting party of 45 men of the Mounted Infantry, an arm in which Lugard had taken a special interest, to reconnoitre to the south of the obstacle while the main force followed on more slowly. It was later learned that the Kano army, as it halted at Kaura, was divided in its councils. The Emir was there with his two chief brothers—he had sixty-four in all—who held the titles of Waziri and Wombai. It appears that Aliu, who, according to Lugard, was a tyrant, was as much afraid of his own men as of the enemy, and he therefore decided to desert the army in the night, and disappeared, disguised as a salt merchant, towards the frontier with a few followers. The Emir's younger brother, the Wombai, decided to make peace and broke away with his own men. The Kano army under his brother, the Waziri, fell in with Captain Wright's little scouting group of mounted men. This officer, though he had warning in time to allow him to retreat, decided to advance against them. Otherwise, he must have feared they might, in this wide

[1] *Reports*, 1902, p. 101.

and unknown bush country, have slipped past the main force to attack Kano where they would have found Lugard with a garrison of only 80 men.

It seems, from a letter written by Lugard on March 6th to Flora, that the Waziri also had offered to make terms and Lugard had sent orders to his forces that he was not to be attacked. These did not arrive in time and unfortunately " the Waziri mistook our people and they, of course, opened fire." This was " just what I wanted to avoid." In February 1960, when this book was already in proof, the writer discussed the question of this fight with the present Emir of Kano in his palace, and he suggested that the Kano force might have been seeking a " holy death ".

However the battle began, it proved to be one more example of what a combination of courage, discipline and modern weapons could do against a superiority in numbers that must be almost unique, even in this kind of warfare. The Waziri had 2,000 footmen, some of them armed with guns, and 1,000 horsemen against the 45 native soldiers and their two white officers. The Kano cavalry were an impressive sight as they advanced in their high turbans and flowing robes, armed mostly with shields and spears and mounted on horses covered, in a fashion that had come across north Africa from the model left by the crusaders, in an armour of quilted cloth. Wright had only recently come to the country, but he had trained his men himself and he had already established such an authority over them that they remained perfectly steady in the face of such appalling numbers of their own countrymen. Wright formed a square, put the horses in the middle, and set some men to cut branches of mimosa thorn to act as a screen. The Waziri and his chiefs did not spare themselves but led the horsemen and charged the square ten times. Wright's men withheld their fire each time until the horsemen were within fifty yards range and then fired only at the word of command. The dead piled up, many of them only fifteen feet from the square. Even so the mass of attackers must have trampled down the little square if their horses had not flinched away at the last moment from the vollies of rifle fire. Their own fire was wild and ill-directed. The attack went on for two hours and it was only when the Waziri, seven of his principal chiefs and many others lay dead, that the army drew off. Wright, who appears to have had no fatal casualties, followed them but could not attack again as his men were down to fifty rounds. At this moment he was startled to hear a sudden outbreak of firing: it was the retreating Kano horsemen revenging themselves upon their footmen for not having supported them better.[1] For his action Wright was afterwards awarded the Victoria Cross.

Another small detachment of the Mounted Infantry stung the Kano army as it retreated. Then, in this extraordinary war, as if to fulfil all that Lugard had prophesied, the people of the towns and villages shut their gates against the Kano forces, and thrust them off the walls while one village actually made a sortie to rescue a British officer who had been cut off, took him in and shut out their own army. After these defeats, which must have made the main force very jealous of the Mounted Infantry, the Waziri's army simply dissolved. Many of the men, in the usual way of feudal levies, dispersed to their homes but the bulk joined up with the Wombai and agreed to follow him in peace to Kano. So, from their enormous mob of soldiers and refugees, the Wombai sent a message to Lugard asking if he could bring them back to the city and make his submission.

Lugard was ready for them. He had been waiting impatiently for news, though making good use of his time dealing with the papers that followed him, studying Kano and interviewing the big merchants who included white Arabs from Tunis and Morocco. He could now confess to Flora that the message was a great relief as the Kano army

" has been a source of some anxiety to me. I did not think they would offer any serious resistance to our force which had gone out to meet them but I thought they might give that force the slip and come back here and make some trouble . . . "

In reply to the Wombai, he said that he would cordially welcome the return of all fugitives; that the fighting was done; there were no old scores to wipe out and he had no grudge whatever against those who had fought him fairly.[2]

To his wife he described the sequel.

Kano.
" I sent out a reliable native Agent to bring them to within 6 miles and then to bring in the Wombai. It was difficult work as they were so scared and suspected treachery. He came in today and I reassured him

[1] *Reports*, 1902, pp. 32-3.   [2] *Reports*, 1902, pp. 33-4.

and sent him back to bring all his people. These were made to file through one of the gates and as they passed they had to give up their fire-arms. I allowed them to keep their swords, and shirts of mail and spears . . . The numbers were estimated variously at anything between 800 and 4,000 horsemen and at least 10,000 all told. They were fewer than they would have been because they have dispersed to the towns around or come in quietly by night during the last few days. Then the Wombai and a few Chiefs came back and I spent several hours settling things . . . Altogether it was a most satisfactory interview. Their suspicions are allayed and there will be no worry during the night. They were greatly delighted at all I said, and apparently frankly and fully accepted the situation. I need not say that Abadie has been invaluable, and indeed it is largely due to him that these results have been achieved. Doubtless they are most glad that I am going to Sokoto. Once I settle Sokoto they will all settle down all right." (L. to F. L., 6 March 1903).

By now, because he must go on to Sokoto, his hopes of catching the April boat were sadly fading. But Flora, ill and anxious, must understand his reasons.

Kano.
" I am told, that my coming here has had a great effect. That the people all say that this is no mere foray of troops and that as the Governor himself has come and sat down in the Emir's house at Kano it means that we have come to stay. The effect will be much greater if I go to Sokoto. Moreover you are aware that a prestige attaches to the Sultan of Sokoto. It is the crowning act of a policy I have very steadily pursued for three years, and I feel I should *always* regret it if now at the last moment I were to hurry home and leave this thing only half done. Do not *you* think so too? I *hate* not coming on the date I had fixed, but I am sure you will agree with me, and that you would be the first to wish that the fact of my being married should not interfere with my public work. . . . Marching thus I shall have about 740 miles to cover to get back to Zungeru, say 50 days actual marching . . . The programme I have sketched is a severe one, but if my carriers and camels can do it I shall accomplish it."
(L. to F. L., 25 February 1903).

Three days later he had the satisfaction of receiving a telegram of congratulation from Flora. It was not the only one.

Kano.
" With it came the following (I quote from memory). ' I am commanded by H.M. the King to convey to you and to the Kano Expeditionary

Force his sincere congratulations on the successful occupation of Kano.'
This will delight the officers exceedingly. Those here who have seen it
are *greatly* delighted. It seems to me that they have been creating a great
scare in England. Hopkins tells me his wife said she had seen some papers
which announced that there was an absolutely certain disaster about to
take place here, and that they were glad to see I was on my way home and
so was out of it! Meaning I suppose that I had bolted! I reached Kano a
week after it was taken, and had there been any check here, I would have
brought those powers of resource with which you always so liberally
credited me into play. There were more ways than one of capturing this
city." (L. to F. L., 28 February 1903).

A few days later another telegram reached Kano. It was from
Chamberlain in South Africa; he sent, Lugard told Flora,

" congratulations on successful occupation of Kano ' by which a large
number of people had been released from tyrannical oppression '. These
words indicate not merely congratulations on military success, but on my
policy, and approval of what has been done which is a very different
matter, and I am accordingly very pleased." (L. to F. L., 6 March 1903).

Knowing that Flora could give him very substantial help in explaining his actions and ideas to her friends at the Colonial Office, at Printing House Square, and other places where policy was made or modified, he wrote to her on February 28th to expound the pacific and
political intentions which kept him close upon the heels of the soldiers.

Kano.
" I have written to Kemball that if a friendly letter is received from
Sokoto (of which I do not think there is any doubt) in reply to mine, I do
not want the Force to march on that place but to return here, and the
' Kano Expeditionary Force ' can then cease to exist. I shall not see the
Abinger woods in spring. But there is no doubt that I *cannot* leave this
task in the middle. The place will not settle down until the H. C. himself
and no other has seen the Sultan of Sokoto and then the people will say
that ' the palaver is finished ' . . . The Boundary Commission can then go
round the arc and past Katsina without fear. I shall leave a garrison at
Sokoto and another at Katsina and another at Kano, and install the
Residents at each place. I can then feel that another stage has been reached
in my work and that I administer *all* Northern Nigeria. Very much of
course remains to do, and with our slender staff we cannot adequately
put everything right, but there will no longer be a defiant state to harbour

the murderer of a Resident . . . I thought you would like to know all this and to be able to tell those whom you think it advisable to tell. My full account and vindication of my acts will be reserved till it is all done. . ."

(L. to F. L., 28 February 1903).

Lugard was deeply anxious that there should be no more fighting, above all at Sokoto, but it irked him that the issue should be in the hands of Kemball, who was now reaching the end of his 300 mile march from Kano to Sokoto.

Kano.
" I go pretty fast as you know and having got through this business in one day, I start for Sokoto tomorrow. The force has apparently gone on there greatly to my regret, for they will scare Sokoto, who I am certain does not want to fight. Kemball has accepted a grave responsibility in doing so, for all my letters have been in the contrary sense, though I could not issue positive orders while events were so uncertain. He was to write every third day *at least*, but I have had no letter since one dated Feb. 23, and today is March 6th. . . . I have about 500 miles to cover before I get back to Kano . . . and every mile I cover will be one off the long total of 750 which intervene between me and my *Home*. It sounds so strange to write the word, for I have never had a *home* since I was a boy and even then it was not entirely a joy to return to it, and in later years, as I grew up, it was the reverse of a pleasure. Henceforth I have a *Home*, and I am trying to realize it and that wherever *you* are there is my Home . . . "

As he wrote the word "home" he looked up. In the room in which he wrote his officers were still talking to the Kano chiefs and the contrast of his words and thoughts struck him as he looked at this

" strange Moorish-African room I occupy. The gilded arches and lofty dome—the mud floors. On the latter is spread a handsome Turkish rug (loot of the 'Palace') and on it sits the Wombai (Emir-elect) in a snow-white pugari—a cloak of white satin with yellow silk inside, and voluminous gowns and embroidery. Around him sit others in embroidered gowns and highly worked riding boots. In my old deck chair, in a suit which has lately been much torn and mended, I sat (near your photo) with Abadie, Cargill (Resident) and Phillips (Junior Resident) beside me while I laid down the lines of future rule in Kano."

(L. to F. L., 6 March 1903).

March 6th had indeed been an important day both in Lugard's life as an administrator and in the history of Nigeria. In his talk to the chiefs he had laid down more than the future rule of Kano, and it was very proper that this full explanation of his policy should have been made to the representatives of that Hausa State which, even though it was not the highest in status, was the most rich and renowned of all. Lugard at this moment was at the height of his powers and every physical and mental capacity had been exercised to its utmost in this expedition. The very essence of the man was shown in this talk with the chiefs—the strength which came from his absolute certainty of the rightness of his action and of his ideas; the range of his plans from high principles to those details which he knew were all-important; the courtesy and consideration of his attitude towards men who a few days ago had been in arms against him; the pith and economy of this working speech. Here was shown the art of the good administrator who, neither subordinating himself wholly to circumstances nor trying to violate them, fits his own design to their structure.

The full meaning of this speech must be discussed later when general consideration is given to his system of Indirect Rule. But these words to the silent men, sitting cross-kneed under the red arches of the Emir's hall in their flowing white and blue robes and the high indigo-dyed turbans which swathed their heads and necks, and Hausa-fashion, covered their mouths, must be given here in its proper place. It represented Lugard's first recorded exposition of his policy. As such it must be quoted in full. For ease of reference some headings have been inserted and the speech has been broken into paragraphs.

British sovereignty

" The British Government would in future, I said, be the Suzerain of the country, but would retain the existing rulers, exercising the right to appoint not only the Emirs but the chief officers of state. The rights of succession, nomination, or election customary in the country would not as a rule be interfered with, but the High Commissioner would retain his right of veto, and the king or chief would lose his place by misconduct.

Law and justice

Similarly in the matter of law and justice; Mohamedan law, so long as it was not contrary to the law of the Protectorate would not be interfered with, and the Emir's and Alkali's courts would be upheld and strengthened under the supervision of the Resident. Mutilation and imprisonment under inhuman conditions would not be allowed, and no death sentence would be carried into execution without the prior concurrence of the Resident. Bribery and extortion would be checked, and certain classes of offences would be tried in the Provincial Court, in which alone all cases affecting non-natives and Government servants would be heard.

Taxation, trade and land

Government would impose such taxes as the High Commissioner might see fit, to pay for the cost of administration, but these would not be of an oppressive character. Traders and caravans would be encouraged, and were not to be taxed by the Emir, whose levies would be subject to the approval of the High Commissioner. The Fulani, I observed, had lost their domination, and in future the ultimate title to land and minerals would be vested in the British Government, but the owners would not be deprived of their land unless it was needed for necessary public works or Government requirements.

Slavery

I emphatically forbade all slave raiding and all transactions in slaves, while saying that it was not my intention to interfere with the existing domestic slaves; but these would, like anyone else in the land, at any time, have a right of appeal to the Resident, and, if they proved cruelty on the part of their masters, would be liberated. We recognized, I said, no less than they did, that labouring classes must exist, and I had no desire to convert the existing farm and other labourers into vagrants, idlers, and thieves, but I hoped they would by and by see the advantage of paid free labour, which we considered more profitable and better than slave labour.

Armed forces

In future, I said, neither the Emir nor any chief would be allowed to have recourse to armed force, and the 'Dogari' (gunmen) would be abolished. If the Emir were unable to enforce his legitimate orders he would refer to the Resident, for in the British Government alone was to be vested the task of policing the country. Consequently firearms would not be required and must be rendered up, and, unless in special cases authorized by permits from the Resident, their possession would involve punishment. All supplies would be fairly paid for and they need have no fear in taking to the Resident all complaints against soldiers or other Government servants who might commit any violence or deal unfairly. The garrison would be located outside the town and soldiers would not be allowed to enter it with their arms.

Expedition to Kano

Religion and custom

When I added that liquor was prohibited, there was a motion of appreciative assent, and to the announcement that they were absolutely free in the exercise of their religion there was a quite remarkable expression of joy and relief. Sokoto, I said, would remain the religious head, but no tribute of slaves might be sent to him in future. I added at the close of my remarks that it was not the desire of Government to upset and to change such native laws and customs as were good, and that it would be our desire to study them so as to understand the people . . . .

Interpretation of the speech

It is important to note that on each occasion I had the best interpreters in the country and the words were paraphrased into simple English. The interpretation was checked at Sokoto by Major Burdon and at Katsina and Kano by Dr. Cargill (the two most fluent Hausa scholars), and at Zaria by Captain Abadie. All of them frequently corrected the interpreter when he had not thoroughly grasped the sense. The intelligent comments and questions of the chiefs showed that they thoroughly understood.

Succession to the emirate

Turning to the circumstances of Kano itself, I declined to appoint the Wombai as Emir until I had returned from Sokoto, whither I proposed to go at once, judging that this period of probation would not be without good effect, while for my own part I was unwilling to act with precipitation even though the circumstances, as I saw them at the time, seemed to leave no alternative and though we appeared singularly fortunate in the candidate proposed. Meanwhile he was left in charge of the town but was not to occupy the King's quarters until finally installed . . . With these conditions the chiefs appeared well satisfied. They had entered my room in a state of extreme nervousness and we parted with much cordiality."[1]

The last sentence, as the conclusion of a report upon the capture of a large city, *vi et armis*, could be claimed as characteristic of the writer and, surely, not without some satisfaction, of the country for which he was acting.

---

[1] *Reports*, 1902, pp. 34 6.

CHAPTER VI

FROM KANO TO SOKOTO, 1903

LUGARD'S SPEECH to the chiefs of Kano was made upon March 6th. The next day, in the evening, he left the city to follow up the troops on their way to Sokoto. It was two miles from the Emir's palace to the gate in the walls by which he left the city and the Wombai and his squadrons of horsemen rode with him. At the gate the proud Fulani saluted his new master in front of all his people. This Lugard took to be a good sign.

> " In return I shook hands with him and said I hoped to be back in 30 days and if he had done well in the meantime to install him as Emir. I like this Wombai—he is a gentleman . . . a fullbred Fulani with a very pleasing smile. I think he has 'cottoned' to me too, and he smiled with what I thought quite a genuine air of pleasure as he saluted."
>
> (L. to F. L., 8 March 1903).

That evening the little party marched only five miles; the next day Lugard rode five and walked fifteen, which was all the mileage he could get out of " these troublesome camels ". (It is impossible not to sympathize with any men and animals who had to trek with Lugard and the unhappy donkeys of the race to Nikki come to mind). He hoped, however, that the men would "soon get fully into marching conditions", and the camels " get into our ways ". He was himself tormented that night in camp by an eye trouble which made it difficult for him to write very much to his wife by lamp-light. He did, however, record with some natural complacency, that his cook and cook's boy, having looted a gown and a sword from a passing native, had been duly tried and sentenced to flogging and imprisonment under the Protection of Natives Proclamation; the sentence being confirmed by the High Commissioner and the flogging publicly carried out with " good effect "—presumably both upon the victims and upon public opinion, though not, presumably, upon Lugard's commissariat. In the next 72 hours Lugard covered 80 miles. But the camels and carriers were beginning to drop off along the route. The water contained soda and potash and upset him internally; yet it was impossible, in the heat and thirst of the march, to refrain from drinking. He was still sending letters back to Flora but could not hope to get anything from her as he was now outpacing the mail runners. He noticed the wide, sweeping sandy dunes, with their thinning bush, which lead on to Sokoto, land so arid in the dry season that it seems amazing that it can carry an agricultural people. Lugard, even more than hitherto, was now marching into considerable danger. He had with him only a small escort composed of some 70 Yoruba soldiers under a young subaltern who had recently arrived in the country. It was difficult for him to know exactly what was happening to the force ahead of him. But he knew that between Kemball, who stated that he only " accompanied " it and yet, according to Lugard, continued to issue commands, and Morland who was nominally in charge, there was almost bound to be division of responsibility, and his own improperly outspoken comments cannot have done much to bridge this dualism. On March 13th, when he was four to five days' march from Sokoto, a letter came back from Kemball to say he had turned south towards Argungu to meet and pick up Merrick, who was the British member of the Anglo-French Boundary Commissioners. These gentlemen had come up from the state of Gwandu, the Emir of which had, fortunately, decided not to fight, and were now halted on the western frontier waiting to venture nearer to Sokoto. Kemball wrote that he assumed that Lugard was not following as it would be " a proceeding which would be full of grave risks ". Lugard fulminated in his letter to Flora that his advice to Kemball had been to march steadily all the way by the southern route, picking up Merrick on the way. He was especially disturbed by the sudden southward divergence when already in face of Sokoto, as the Sultan had called in all his councillors and was trying to decide whether to fight. Morland, knowing Lugard so well, was sure he would be hastening forward and would realize the danger to his chief of Kemball's action. (L. to F. L., 13 March 1903). He was, therefore, as Kemball himself admitted, opposed to what Lugard called " this retrograde move ".[1] If the Sultan decided on war and

[1] Lugard to Chamberlain, 22 March 1903, C.O. 446/30.

moved quickly, Lugard's little party would be swamped under an avalanche of horsemen.

His great hope, as he pressed forward, was still that fighting could be avoided and a peaceful meeting with this suzerain ruler attained; he was harassed by his fear that Kemball would not carry out the pacific spirit of this policy. Yet he could see the comic side of the danger as he, the greatest prize the enemy could kill or capture, went on with his little company, " dodging round this beehive of populous towns, all under Sokoto, on whose capital the Force is marching ", and whose army was still undefeated in the field. Each day, in this heavily populated country, they passed four or five " enemy " towns with walls and moats, some of these groups of settlements numbering 30,000 to 40,000 people. Lugard's resolution to go forward was proof against even an insubordinate stomach, for, with the bad water and the long marches in blazing sun, he was violently upset and had to starve for three of these strenuous days. At one of these towns the Jekada, or headman, who had come out to greet Lugard, suddenly recognized in a veiled man, posing as a trader from the far north, one of the chief men of Kano. He tore aside his veil and the man fell to the ground expecting immediate execution at Lugard's hands. He was at once reassured, told to go and put on his proper dress, supplied with a letter to the Resident in Kano and was soon keeping the British party in roars of laughter over his humorous, inside account of the taking of his city, while Lugard, too ill to sit up and join in the conversation, lay under a nearby bush listening. (L. to F. L., 15 March 1903).

On the 17th, after pushing on another 25 miles to Moradu, he guessed he was within about 30 miles of Sokoto. There were rumours that a fight had taken place and they actually ran into two men from the town riding with drawn swords in pursuit of the messenger Lugard had sent ahead with a letter for Kemball. They were just able to save him and captured the two men: again there was general astonishment at Moradu that Lugard did not kill them. On they went again, the rocks on the track so hot that it hurt the horses' feet.

Meanwhile, ahead of Lugard's advancing party, the expeditionary force had not made contact with the army of Sokoto. The pacific letters which, on Lugard's orders, had been sent to the Sultan had been met by the one vague answer and then by silence. When on

March 14th the troops came in sight of Sokoto from the south they saw the plateau and open slopes in front of the walls covered with an army of some 15,000 horsemen and 3,000 footmen. It was clear that this army, unlike that of Kano, meant to fight in the open to defend their city. The British combatant force now contained 650 rank and file, 25 officers, four guns and two Maxims. They advanced steadily towards the city. It soon appeared that only a handful of the enemy were ready to die for their cause. These flung themselves in ones and twos upon the attackers to certain death while the vast majority, in face of the small oncoming ranks of trained native soldiers, with their mobile patrols of mounted infantry on each flank, broke up and dispersed in all directions. Colonel Morland directed his force towards a point where a few men stood round their standard and died in its defence. The square then formed column and marched into the walled city. They found it almost deserted. In this light battle the loss to Sokoto was about 100 killed: on the British side one carrier was wounded by a stray shot and later died.[1] The Sultan and the doomed Magaji of Keffi fled. We may anticipate their fate. They found their way, gathering other irreconcilables, to the borders of Bornu. Here at Burmi in a fierce engagement on July 27th, 1903, both the ex-Sultan and the Magaji of Keffi were killed.[2]

On the morning of March 19th Lugard, gaunt and dusty, and looking anything but a High Commissioner, reached the city. He put on a clean white coat, mounted his medal ribbons and rode up to the walls. Kemball, Morland and the other officers rode out to meet him. With them came the Waziri, a blind old man, and the other senior chiefs, to make their surrender. Lugard reassured and reinstated them. He was grieved that any fighting had occurred and he told them he wished to find and restore the fugitive Sultan or, failing that, to appoint a successor of their choice. He told them to keep their horses and swords but to give up their fire-arms. No one would suffer except the ex-Magaji of Keffi. The chiefs quickly chose a new Sultan, Atahiru. A strong claimant to the throne, he had retired quietly to his farm at the recent death of the last Sultan in order to avoid a civil war with his rival, and had also refused to join in fighting the British.

[1] *Reports*, 1902, pp. 37-8.
[2] *Reports*, 1902, pp. 39-40n., and 1903, pp. 8-9. Mr. D. Muffett is making a study based largely upon the evidence of survivors of this event which should round out the story of this brave but hopeless campaign from the Fulani side.

Lugard took one look at him, made one of his instant decisions—" a man whose face and manner greatly prepossessed me in his favour "— and agreed to install him the next day. Atahiru was to rule Sokoto well for many years to come.[1]

Lugard allotted only three and a half days to the settlement of Sokoto so they had to be typical Lugardian working days. His first and most congenial action was to disband the expeditionary force and to say good-bye to Kemball who then left immediately. Lugard ordered the unwanted and unused reserves from Southern Nigeria, which had now crossed the border, to be sent back. He had to deal with the French and British boundary commissioners and direct them on a way now made safe for them. Most happy of all tasks, he had to congratulate Morland and his officers and give a dinner in their honour. A mass of official papers had now at last caught up with him and these had to be dealt with. There were telegrams and dispatches to send to his anxious masters in Whitehall.

The main event, however, was the installation of the Sultan, the suzerain of most of the Muslim rulers of Northern Nigeria and, until European invaders drew their unhistorical boundaries, of lands beyond. On March 21st Lugard had a long talk with the chiefs; he explained to them about the treaty with the Royal Niger Company. He showed them the letter in which the ex-Sultan had declared war[2] and explained to them with very careful interpretation—a point upon which he was always insistent—the conditions upon which the new government would rule and the reasons for the British action. While he covered much the same ground as at Kano, there were special points for addition or emphasis at Sokoto, above all the assertion of sovereignty by conquest.

" The old treaties," he declared, " are dead, you have killed them. Now these are the words which I, the High Commissioner, have to say for the future. The Fulani in old times under Dan Fodio conquered this country. They took the right to rule over it, to levy taxes, to depose kings and to create kings. They in turn have by defeat lost their rule which has come into the hands of the British. All these things which I have said the Fulani by conquest took the right to do now pass to the British. Every Sultan and Emir and the principal officers of State will be appointed by the High

[1] See note at the end of this chapter for an African's account of the conquest.
[2] *Reports*, 1902, p. 106.

Commissioner throughout all this country. The High Commissioner will be guided by the usual laws of succession and the wishes of the people and chiefs, but will set them aside if he desires for good cause to do so. The Emirs and Chiefs who are appointed will rule over the people as of old time and take such taxes as are approved by the High Commissioner, but they will obey the laws of the Governor and will act in accordance with the advice of the Resident. Buying and selling slaves and enslaving people are forbidden . . . All men are free to worship God as they please. Mosques and prayer places will be treated with respect by us . . . It is the earnest desire of the King of England that this country shall prosper and grow rich in peace and in contentment, that the population shall increase and the ruined towns which abound everywhere shall be built up, and that war and trouble shall cease. Henceforth no Emir or Chief shall levy war or fight, but his case will be settled by law, and if force is necessary Government will employ it. . . . You need have no fear regarding British rule, it is our wish to learn your customs and fashion, just as you must learn ours. I have little fear that we shall agree, for you have always heard that British rule is just and fair, and people under our King are satisfied. You must not fear to tell the Resident everything and he will help and advise you."

The next day the public installation was held. Lugard rode into the town: the troops were drawn up in a hollow square. Round them stood the assembled masses. Lugard made his announcement.

" It was marked by the really extraordinary murmur of deep satisfaction from the assembled masses when I announced the complete freedom of their religion, and by a prayer recited aloud by the Mallams so soon as I had installed the Sultan."[1]

The next day, March 23rd, having appointed Major Burdon,[2] an expert in Hausa and a former Company man, as Resident, Lugard left Sokoto. He struck north-east with an escort of 60 mounted infantry for the northernmost emirate, Katsina. He left with a high heart and a justified sense of achievement. The new Sultan and throngs of chiefs and horsemen insisted on riding with him even in the burning heat of the day

[1] *Reports*, 1902, p. 40.
[2] Burdon, Major (later Sir) John Alder, K.B.E., 1866-1933; 1897 Niger-Sudan campaign; 1898-9 Commandant, Royal Niger Constabulary; 1900 Resident, Northern Nigeria; 1903-6, 1909-10, Resident, Sokoto; 1910-15 Colonial Secretary, Barbados; 1915-25 Administrator St. Kitts; 1925-31 Governor, British Honduras.

" which the Fulani feels as much or more than a European, and our parting in its cordiality almost resembled that of old friends. They thanked me profusely for all that had been done . . . astonished to find that the British are not the ogres which they expected. . . . We told them that they had made a more plucky stand than Kano had, for they faced us in the open, while the Kano warriors had only fought behind their stupendous walls, and had bolted at the first assault. This seemed to please them greatly, and to be all they cared for."[1]

If there were an element of induced illusion in this last belief it was at least one likely to have beneficial effects upon the psychology of both conquerors and conquered. Nor was his optimism only for official use. " Had you been present dear," he wrote to his wife, as he camped that night, seven miles from Sokoto,

" you would have thought I was saying goodbye to old and cordial friends instead of to men who surrendered three days ago, and who this day week were opposed to us and defeated in battle. The Sultan in especial—a most prepossessing man—grasped my hand with evidently sincere goodwill. One and all, even to the blind old Vizier, I believe they are heartily glad to have the crisis over which has been impending over their heads for a couple of years past . . . and they have been treated not only with honour and dignity, but as gentlemen with cordiality and friendship. Really I think the auguries are good, and I am most delighted with the success of the settlement."   (L. to F. L., 22 March 1903).

It did, indeed, sound almost too good to be true. But there was one incident which confirmed its truth. The Sultan of Sokoto, as chief suzerain, had never received any present upon his installation: rather it lay with him to bestow a present upon the emirs he confirmed. But now, as the chiefs themselves pointed out to Lugard, the ceremony would be incomplete unless the High Commissioner made him a present, thus signalizing that the supreme power had passed from Sokoto to Britain.

An unhappy scene marred Lugard's departure from Sokoto. Hundreds of slaves, who had broken away from their masters during the disturbances, stole out of the city and crowded into his camp and hundreds more clambered over the city walls and followed him. They were seeking the freedom which, for the first time in their lives, seemed to have been brought within their reach. Lugard, however,

---

[1] Reports, 1902, p. 41.

could at that moment do nothing to help them. He had promised, for reasons that have been given, not to perform any immediate and wholesale act of emancipation. In any case, he was setting off upon a forced march through unknown country, where he would have no food and little water for extra mouths, while the economy of Sokoto would suddenly be ruined by this exodus. There was nothing to do but to send them back with orders to the Resident to enquire into all deserving cases. Then it was discovered that the neighbouring Emir of Gobir with 400 wild desert horsemen was hunting down the masterless wretches and collecting them for himself. This at least could be stopped.

It was on the afternoon of March 22nd that Lugard left Sokoto. He sat outside his tent that night, under the stars, but with no moon to throw its silver over one of those night marches which are a relief and joy to the traveller in such country. He had told the Wombai of Kano that he would be back there on April 5th and he was determined to keep his word if he could, although harsh and waterless country lay between him and Katsina. His thoughts wandered from the dim quiet camp.

"Your description of the bird sounds at Abinger," he wrote to Flora, " of your walks in the brisk, keen, spring morning, are like a mental draught as one plods along the scorching track . . . the garden and early bulbs must now be growing interesting. I wish I were there to see them, but I have, and I know *you* will have, a satisfaction in knowing that my task is being *well* done, and fully done before I leave it."

His thoughts, in a mind always alert for anniversaries, ranged further. He remembered that the next day was his brother's birthday. The day was the anniversary for that brother of the Manipur disaster and, for himself, of McNeill's Zariba in Suakin. Only a few days before, when tormented by thirst, to satisfy which there was only tepid, brackish water, he had thought of all the places of thirst to which his work had taken him—the Khyber—the blazing plains of sand and stones in the Jellalabad valley—the cholera camp in the Punjab—the dust storms on the plains of the Indus—Suakin, where water was issued by the pint— the Kalahari desert. All bad places, but never had he suffered so much as on these Nigerian marches, when the water was of a kind that only added to his thirst.

In the march to Katsina, which turned out to be 167½ miles from Sokoto, he broke all his own records. In spite of the lack of the moon and the shortage of water, he did the stretch in 6 days, 28 miles a day without pause. People had smiled when he said he would try for the May 19th boat: he now set himself the "almost impossible goal" of catching the May 5th boat. He and his party were still not out of danger. With a gesture of superb confidence in his policy and in the word of his late enemies he had disbanded the Expeditionary Force and had ridden on alone with a small escort into the still unknown north. It was true that the Emir of Katsina had sent him a letter disassociating himself from the hostile policy of Kano but this might have been due to chicanery or fear, and with the ex-Sultan of Sokoto still at large with his cavalry, Lugard's manner of approach offered a splendid opportunity, almost an invitation, to attack. Indeed, secret news came to Lugard as he made his way towards the city that there *was* a war-party in the town urging the offensive. Some thirty years later the writer heard the Emir of Katsina, who in 1903 had been a senior chief, describe to Lugard, when a guest at his house in Abinger, how the Emir and chiefs had debated all night as to whether they would not ambush and wipe out the little party at a favourable part of the track. Nothing, he vividly demonstrated to us, could have been easier. This chief, who was soon to become one of the most progressive and loyal emirs, was among those who had argued against the attack. It was this Emir Muhammadu Diko, C.B.E., who in 1939, at the Muslim festival of Id el Fitr, set a bronze tablet at the Yandaka gate to commemorate Lugard's entry there on March 28th, 1903. In his speech the Emir said

"The gentleman in whose memory we are gathered here is still living. I see him whenever I visit England . . . My earnest prayers are that God gives him and us long life and health, as it was that gentleman who made it possible for us to be in the British Empire, which has given us peace and prosperity. We pray that the Empire of His Majesty the King will long endure. Amen."

So Lugard entered Katsina in peace; proclaimed British sovereignty; confirmed and instructed the Emir; complimented him on Katsina's reputation for learning; lectured him on the value of a stable currency; fixed a rate of exchange between silver and cowries; chose a site for a Residency; declaimed upon the advantage of peace and good order, and in two days was on the march south.

Far from being exhausted by this breathless enterprise Lugard grew fitter the faster he went each day. " I am extraordinarily well," he told Flora on March 30th, " I have a monstrous appetite . . . I am so renovated by this hard physical life that I feel I could begin another tour of service." The routine of the march was now firmly settled. Reveille was at 4; then came some thirteen miles before the first halt: then another 6 or 7 miles; another halt and then the rest of the day's 24 to 28 miles, getting in to camp between 4 and 6 p.m. for a drink of tea, a bath and shave. Then Lugard would get out his block, write to Flora and draw up his reports. Dinner would follow with his favourite officer, Abadie, who had joined him at Kano and was writing his own report on his chief to Flora. Dr. Cargill, the Resident of Kano, who had come up to Katsina to meet him, was there and two or three other Englishmen. Lugard would sit for a while and smoke a cigar before turning in at 10 p.m. for six hours' sleep. There was no time to read. The little book of Spenser's love poems Flora had sent had not arrived. But at least the English newspapers had caught him up just before he reached Sokoto and he worked through these in his conscientious way. They told him that Flora was still doing for him as wife what she had so long done as friend and admirer,

Camp Douke.
" Your article in *The Times* re Kano was excellent and most accurate.[1] My annual report for 1902 (which will include these three months of 1903) will give my full defence and reasons for this Kano affair, and I think they will pretty well carry public opinion. The mail also brought me a cablegram from you saying that the Kano business had been mentioned in the King's Speech, and there had been a debate on the subject in which I scored." (L. to F. L., 18 March 1903).

He got back to Kano, having dealt with some minor rulers on the way, on April 2nd. Some of his party, including most of his servants, were exhausted, but he felt " fit to go for my life ". The Emir-elect, a thousand horsemen and an enormous mass of people came out to meet him and to escort him to the site of the new Residency. The next day, with due state, he installed the Wombai, Abass Muhammadu, the fugitive Emir's brother. He was to reign as Emir until 1919 when he

[1] *The Times*, 20 January 1903.

was succeeded by his brother. Lugard followed the special tradition of Kano and fastened upon him a sword and a dagger and opened a state umbrella. There was also a mountain of papers to meet him with " various worrying matters from Zungeru, friction between the civil and military as usual, and sheets of recriminations and various other matters which have not been conducted in my absence as I would wish."

On April 7th he reached Zaria, was met by the chiefs and marched into the city in procession amidst clouds of dust. Having washed this out of his throat with " a delightful glass of claret and water " he set to work to settle the affairs of this emirate. The old cruel and irre-concilable Emir was deposed and another man, proposed by the new Sultan of Sokoto and accepted by the local chiefs, was installed, with a new set of office bearers, upon the usual terms and with the usual public ceremony.

" There followed a discordant hubbub of eight-foot trumpets, of drums, and various other instruments which can be sounded only for a duly appointed and accepted emir and which no *locum tenens* may use. This is the signal to the populace of the final appointment of the Emir. I then shook hands with him before his people, and according to custom led him into the interior of the royal enclosures which thenceforth became his residence."[1]

From Zaria came the last lap to Zungeru. The pace quickened: the ultimate goal was exercising all its magnetic power. His letters to Flora, still dashed off in his few spare moments, preserve little pictures of his mind and his journey.

Kaseju.
" If you follow my course on the map, you will see at what a phenomenal rate I am striding over it. Each hour of the day and night brings me a mile nearer Abinger . . . The sun is furiously hot, for the early rains and tornadoes are long overdue. I nearly brained myself the other day by bashing my head against a limb of a tree when I was asleep on horseback. One can't keep awake after only 4½ hours sleep at night. So, dear, I am losing no time, and probably I shall be with you a week after you get this."   (L. to F. L., 10 April 1903).

Upon April 17th he was back in Zungeru, almost as pleased with the physical, as with the military and the political achievements, and it

[1] *Reports*, 1902, p. 16.

was on this note that he concluded his account of these transactions in his report to the Colonial Secretary.

" It was just 38 days since I had started from Kano, and in this period close on 800 miles had been traversed (in 32 marching days giving an average of 25 miles per day) and matters settled at Sokoto, Katsina, Kano, and Zaria, a really wonderful record when one considers that loaded carriers covered this distance in a waterless country at this time of the year."[1]

It is perhaps needless to record that he caught the boat on May 5th and three weeks later was at Abinger walking with Flora in the garden, where the azaleas were just at their height, and in the beech woods outside, where the bluebells, which flow like a lake round three sides of the little estate, were in the brief prime of their colour.

In this thirty-eight days of fighting, marching, and political settlement Lugard had, as upon other occasions, exactly carried out his own plan in his own time. He had imposed his will not only upon the Hausa states but upon the Colonial Office. His masters there had desired the end but feared the means; Lugard knowing this, had backed his own judgment and powers and had deliberately begun without their full knowledge and consent, to strike a blow which could not be arrested half-way. Before the speed and steely resolution of the little force— the fighting men never numbering more than some 700 Africans and up to 35 British—and of the High Commissioner who impelled it forward, the remaining grandiose but fragile superstructure of the Sokoto empire had collapsed, hardly affecting in its fall the life and organization of the peoples over whom it had been erected. The loss of life had been very small and, in Lugard's view had been suffered only by the most irreconcilable members of the ruling caste and their followers.[2] We are left to judge as best we can whether Lugard was right, the policy of annexation being accepted, to sweep them away with one violent gesture or whether he should have attempted the gradual methods favoured by the authorities in Britain—if, indeed, in their remoteness, they had any plan—of achieving control with their attendant risk of prolonged sporadic resistance and so, perhaps, of more

[1] *Reports*, 1902, p. 44.
[2] Lugard may have been too optimistic in always insisting upon the small loss of life on the Fulani side. General F. P. Crozier gives a somewhat different account in his book, *Five Years Hard* (1932), pp. 131-55. But his recollections are written in a style which seems meant to shock the reader and cannot be regarded as very serious evidence.

bloodshed.[1] The officials at the Office, in the privacy of their internal communications, gave him best. " Yes," wrote Antrobus, after getting the Kano dispatch, " the event has shown that Lugard was right with regard to the opposition to be met with at Kano and it is not unnatural that he should feel rather aggrieved at the decision to place Kemball in command of the troops." But he went on to say that it was Lugard's fault not to keep them informed.[2] When his Sokoto dispatch arrived with its criticism of Kemball the Office made him re-write it. But they admitted that Lugard had worked wonders in the few weeks he had had in which to settle the northern emirates.[3]

Conquest was to Lugard no end in itself: his impatience sprang not from bellicosity—though he had this quality to release at need—but from his determination to realize those principles of government which he had long before prepared and for which Northern Nigeria, from frontier to frontier, was now open and waiting.[4]

---

[1] It may be of interest to quote the only comment made by an actor in these events, the late Mr. R. Nicholson, after he had read this chapter. It was upon this sentence which, he said, " is one which could not have been written by anyone who knew the character and mentality of those gentry. Everyone there, especially 99 per cent of the people, and they were the ones who mattered, not politicians or the ignorant public elsewhere, knew not only that no other course was possible, but that no other course *could* be right."

[2] Minutes on Kano Dispatch, 15 January 1903, C.O. 446/30.

[3] Minutes on Lugard to Chamberlain, 21 April and 2 May 1903, C.O. 446/31.

[4] When in Sokoto in 1955, the writer was able to study the scenes of these events and to have talks with the Shehu and with a number of old men who remembered the days of the fight and of the occupation. Some extracts will therefore be printed from the account given by a magnificent-looking old man, with hawk-like face and tall spare figure who had just been on a flight to Jos for a meeting of the Nigerian History Society! His name was Mallam Nagwammatse Sokoto. His account was translated by Mr. Hanson Smith, an administrative officer then in Sokoto. These rather discontinuous extracts must, in the main, speak for themselves. Interpolations are in square brackets. He first described earlier rumours of " strangers with white skins but whose hair was dark. They were called by some, Touaregs but . . . they wore no long clothes. Some of us kept saying that they could only be devils as their eyes were green like cats' eyes . . . [Later he went on to the arrival of Lugard's first letter.] Atahiru Ahmadu was then the next Sultan and during that year (1900) the Europeans sent a message for the third time. So the Sultan assembled all the elders of Sokoto. He said ' There, you have heard what the infidels have asked of me! Am I to fight or to give in? What do you all think?' The elders became as silent and stiff as if they had been drowned. Then Mallam Akali said ' Oh Sultan! put your trust in Allah and remember what has gone before. All those of us who may be killed will die for the glory of Allah: should we drive them out then shall we be victorious and blessed with the spoils of a Holy War. But, should you flee, then only the wood-ants will be fit to crawl upon your neck.' All the elders echoed the words of Mallam Akali and vehemently agreed with what he said. The Sultan thanked them and they took their leave. He ordered that a reply be sent to the Christians saying that he would fight them."
[News came of the subjection of Keffi and Bida.]
"In 1903, after the hot season and on the 10th day of the month Zulhajji, we prayed on the prayer ground in the morning. The news then came that the British had come upon us from the east. It was now the time to combine and resist them. The Sultan, having left the Friday mosque, went outside the town to one of his houses and then dismounted near the Gaugu dye-pits, where all his nearby chiefs and their followers had assembled and here, on the open ground outside Atikule gate, was gathered a countless host of horsemen and infantry. From the evening

and all through the night the drums beat while everyone stood to their arms. The British spent the night at Bodinga.

On Saturday, the 11th day of Zulhajji, the Muslims advanced to the banks of the stream and there halted and made ready for battle " . . . [The Waziri and a few others were killed that night in a preliminary engagement.] "By the morning of the 12th, a Sunday, by about 9 o'clock there had arisen such a cloud of dust that everyone sought water to drink. The Sultan had taken up position under a palm-tree. The bullets were falling like rain and soon his horse was shot from under him. Another was brought for him to mount. On that day they killed " [about ten prominent men.]

"As soon as the Sultan realized that the day was lost he spurred his horse forward and led a wild retreat, his horsemen pouring after him like water from a cracked pitcher. When the horses heard the noise of the machine-guns, they reared and fought. We never saw the Christians who were hidden, lying down, in a small depression, but they kept firing at us.

All the people of Sokoto were in a panic. They cried out and thought only of escape, and they poured out of the gates, not knowing whither they were going." [The British Cavalry pursued the Muslims.] "The British then returned to the Lakyes Hill near the river where they pitched camp. They posted sentries at all the gates but there were few people left there, only the inveterate sight-seers and hangers-on. On hearing that the city was not going to be burnt and that the British were exhorting us to return, Mallam Akali brought a lamp and we returned in stealth to our home by night. When dawn broke we were glad we had done so as the soldiers were everywhere, entering the houses and taking what they wished with nobody to stop them." [Evidently Lugard's orders against looting could not always be enforced. Later, a message was sent to Mallam Akali asking him to go and interpret for the British Commander. He said:] " ' Well, you elders, what do you think?' and they answered and said. ' As this will be for the general benefit of the Muslims, let us saddle our horses and go. Should we be killed then Allah shall know the truth and that is all that matters.' . . . On the 16th the Waziri and other chiefs sent their greetings which Mallam Akali again translated . . . and immediately after he was made to write answers saying that there was no more war and everyone should therefore return peaceably to their homes . . . The people returned to their homes and peace came to the land and food was very cheap and plentiful."

CHAPTER VII

INDIRECT RULE: THE IDEA

No PART of history is more difficult to record intelligibly than administration. This is especially true of good administration, for while the
bad is generally advertized by the protests of the administered and
sometimes defined by the resulting investigation, the good is likely to
produce the happiness that has no history. Again, at a later stage, a
good system of administration is liable to a peculiar penalty. Created
by men, or more likely, by a man, of high ability, it may become
sanctified by its own success and be reverently or lethargically prolonged by lesser men until it ceases to meet the changing needs of the
time. It can then be displaced only by vigorous action in which condemnation is employed less as a rational process than as an instrument
with which to sweep away the obsolete structure. This is to some
extent true of Lugard's system which later evoked much criticism.
The earliest attack came from the first generation of western-educated
Africans, to whom " Indirect Rule " stood for an alliance made between
imperial and tribal authority to restrain their own advance. By the
mid 'thirties criticism was being voiced far beyond this group.

But the period with which we are dealing now was one of creation.
By the time Lugard left Northern Nigeria, he had constructed both
upon paper and in the practice of the men, British and African, who
worked under him, what can claim to be the most comprehensive,
coherent and renowned system of administration in our colonial
history. This was his greatest and most famous work, the achievement
of his prime. Not to attempt some analysis of it would be to leave out
the main reason why his life deserves to be recorded in full. But there
must be a difference in the treatment of such a subject in a biography
and that proper to a study of government or of Nigerian history.[1]

[1] A more general and historical account by the writer will be found in Perham, *Native
Administration*.

The full account of Lugard's administrative work, based upon the mass of his official documents, demands a volume to itself. In this chapter and the next, half-way through the narrative of his tenure of office as High Commissioner, we shall do no more than picture him at work at his desk and upon his administrative tours, and consider the nature of his administrative achievement, not omitting to scrutinize it for faults.

His work was shackled by the poverty of his revenue. Today, in Britain and even in Africa, administration is conducted upon comparatively lavish standards, with a parliament which seems willing to vote millions with less reluctance than in Lugard's day it voted thousands. He had to open up a vast region and create a new administration upon a civil revenue made up largely by a small and reluctant grant-in-aid. If he were to administer according to his own standards, which, as we shall see, were wholly different from those of the department he served, he had to make up for its inadequacy by the extra energy he forced out of himself and his staff. Shortage of staff, moreover, with shortage of military force, brought closer the possibility that he might at any moment land the imperial government in an expensive and embarrassing disaster.

For the task set him, Lugard was so exactly fitted that his life up to this moment might have been a training especially designed by Providence. He was experienced in every activity that the newly annexed country demanded: in transport and supply; in survey work; in prospecting for minerals; in dealing with Africans, whether potentates, raw tribesmen, or wage labourers. He knew Africa and Africans as did few men of his time. He was a soldier, and a jungle soldier, in a job that was still half military and he had himself created the Regiment he employed. He knew his region, having worked around the middle Niger for six years, helping to win its western frontiers. He had been in contact with Islam and he was an expert upon slavery in a region where it was a major problem. His physique allowed him to do two men's work in a climate and in conditions which halved the capacities of most men. But no list of qualities, however long, would have met the needs of the work if they had not been fused within an ardent temperament and directed by a will of exceptional strength. He entered upon his work with complete confidence. The contrast is arresting between the indeterminate soldier he had been in 1898, when

obliged to carry out Chamberlain's directions, and the new administrator with, at least in the earlier years, almost entire freedom of
action. Reference has been made to an undated and pencilled paper
in his writing which must have been written while he was in England
soon after he was appointed or upon the voyage out. In this he laid
down the main principles upon which he meant to administer the
country.

" In the earlier stages of British rule," he jotted down, "it is desirable to
retain the native authority " (an expression which was to achieve a widespread technical meaning as a result of his system) " and to work through
and by the native emirs. At the same time it is feasible by degrees to
bring them gradually into approximation with our ideas of justice and
humanity . . . In pursuance of the above general principles the chief civil
officers of the Provinces are to be called Residents which implies one who
carries on diplomatic relations rather than Commissioners or Administrators."

In the less organized areas, however, their functions would be more
administrative and less diplomatic. Legislation would at first be mainly
permissive and would be fully enforced only in the most accessible
and docile areas and it would allow of great variety in its application.
He went on to sketch the legal system through Native Courts and to
plan how far he could use his expensive military force as an auxiliary
to his inadequate civil service without undermining its discipline and
essential character. These and other ideas in his early notes he exactly
carried out. The word instinct must not be misused, but at least he had
such an aptitude for administration that he hardly seemed to need the
processes of reasoning or discussion, either with himself or with others,
or even of experiment.

The administrative principles which Lugard developed during the
High Commissionership are generally summed up in the words
" Indirect Rule ". Was there, then, an antithesis that could be called
direct rule and were there other contrasting methods? To answer this
a glance over the earlier phases of British colonial government is
needed.

The first stage of British expansion had, in the main, seen British
colonists carrying their representative institutions, laws and judicial
system with them to the new lands in their ships. When territories
inhabited by native populations that lay near to commercial stations or

to white settlements were annexed, as along the Guinea Coast or the Straits Settlements, the tendency was still to extend, as far as possible, British institutions without, at first, their representative element. This was introduced gradually and in closely restricted fashion in the form of legislative councils in which officials preponderated over nominated unofficials. Generally speaking, the British authorities, even if they made use of native agents and to some extent recognized native laws and customs, tried to introduce their own institutions and worked in an assimilative spirit. This policy, though the expression somewhat overstates the British form of it, has been called the policy of identity.

This policy seemed desirable when confidence in British civilization was at its maximum—a period which just lasted into Lugard's day—while at the same time both understanding of native society and respect for it were at their minimum. It seemed also a practicable policy, in regions where British rule was developed piecemeal over relatively restricted areas. This was true of the first annexations of tribal South Africa or the first exiguous footholds on the West African coast. But as the nineteenth century wore on, the British, like the Romans before them, found that it was impossible to draw an imperial frontier and the pace of annexation quickened. Sometimes at a stroke, whether by the use or threat of force or by consent, large tribal or monarchical states were added. No British government of the last century would face the cost or the effort of attempting direct administration of the old kind over such large acquisitions. Lugard's policy of ruling " indirectly " through the Nigerian emirs cannot therefore, *as a general principle*, be claimed as either inventive or original. Clearly the choice demanded little invention from a governor confronted on the one side with large, semi-civilized but not unco-operative principalities, and on the other by his own absurdly inadequate staff and revenue. Nor, since many other conquerors from the earliest days of history had been faced with much the same position, was the choice very original. Any intelligent conqueror, however self-interested, who had come from a country with a reasonably high standard of order, would hesitate to destroy the structure of a subjected society unless he has some overriding reason for such action and the means to carry it through. Rome, as Tacitus said, making even kings the instrument of her rule, was of course the most famous empire to adopt this expedient and the story of the three trials and sentence of Jesus Christ is a familiar example of its working. Britain herself, in India, in the Pacific, in South Africa, and even in territories much closer to Lugard's domain, found herself increasingly obliged to recognize princes and tribal chiefs by treaty or by usage and the very term " protectorate ", though it was soon to lose what constitutional meaning it originally had, represented at first a self-imposed restraint by the ruling power.

Lugard as a soldier in India had at least shot tigers in the Indian States. In Nyasaland he had known only backward and broken tribes. But in Uganda, in 1890-1892, he had encountered the most advanced kingdom in the whole of East Africa and had been upon intimate terms with its elaborate hierarchical structure. This had led him to publish in 1893, the principle upon which he believed British administration should be based in that country.

" With regard to internal control in Uganda, in my opinion the object to be aimed at in the administration of this country is to rule through its own executive government. The people are singularly intelligent and have a wonderful appreciation of justice and of legal procedure and our aim should be to educate and develop the sense of justice . . .

An arbitrary and despotic rule, which takes no account of native customs, traditions, and prejudices, is not suited to the successful development of an infant civilization, nor, in my view, is it in accordance with the spirit of British colonial rule. The King has been proved incompetent and useless, but the Resident should rule through and by the chiefs."[1]

We can now see that the application of the indirect principle in Northern Nigeria was original, but not the idea. That great administrator in India, Sir Thomas Munro, had urged it nearly a century before. We have already met in these pages Lord Stanmore who practised this principle in Fiji. Mary Kingsley aired it in her very individual way.[2] Lugard's neighbouring Governor in the Niger Coast Protectorate stated that the paucity of European staff necessitated rule through the chiefs.[3] Coming still nearer to Lugard, Goldie held ideas which appeared to run closely upon these lines and which he defined with characteristic force and clarity.[4] For both the welfare and pacification of the natives, he wrote, " the general policy of ruling on

[1] Lugard, *East African Empire*, vol. ii, pp. 649 and 651.
[2] Mary Kingsley, *West African Studies* (1899), pp. 382-3.
[3] Sir R. Moor to Chamberlain, 18 August 1898, C.O. 446/3.
[4] See Goldie's statement given in S. Vandeleur, *Campaigning on the Upper Nile and Niger* (1898), p. 239.

African principles through native rulers must be followed for the present." But he added the interesting idea that European methods might be employed in specially suitable districts to serve as models and also as "cities of refuge" for more advanced individuals. Goldie must often have discussed his ideas with Lugard in the period of their co-operation. But, as we have seen, Lugard inherited very little by way of a working administration from Goldie's Company. In spite of his defeat of Bida and Ilorin in the field Goldie was unable to retain sufficient control over these emirates to establish much more than diplomatic and commercial relations with them. It would not seem, therefore, that Lugard owed much more to Goldie than the confirmation in terms of Nigeria of a principle which he had already defined before he knew either the man or the country. He took over, of course, the same conditions of limited resources in face of strong native states which seemed to impose a tentative "indirectness" of method.

To emphasize these two conditions in order to disparage Lugard's reputation is to mistake the nature of his achievement. His claim rests not upon his adoption, still less his invention, of the indirect principle, but upon the special methods through which he applied it. It is possible for imperial rulers to use it as a temporary device until they are strong enough to dispense with it as was sometimes the French method, or to express it in terms of mere ultimate sovereignty with the very minimum of intervention in internal affairs, as with Indian states. Or, to take the example of the South African High Commission territories, it was possible, in a spirit of limited liability dictated by economy and the evasion of responsibility, to take over a few superior functions of government and leave the subordinate society to continue to carry out the rest, with little attempt at integration or even at supervision. This last, in varying degrees, was the course already being followed in more than one part of tropical Africa when Lugard took over Northern Nigeria.[1] The distinction of Lugard's system was that he not only preserved native initiative but tried to direct it and, indeed, to incorporate it into his own system. To use his own words, in the first *Political Memoranda* he issued—and of which more presently—he did not ordain

[1] The policy now being developed in the Union of South Africa is the most extreme form, indeed a perversion, of the indirect principle. Under it Africans who are in large measure economically part of a dominant European-run State are being thrust back politically under artificially revived tribal rule in the attempt to retard and divide them.

" two sets of Rulers—the British and the Native—working either separately or in co-operation, but a single Government in which the Native Chiefs have clearly defined duties and an acknowledged *status*, equally with the British officials."[1]

They were to be an integral part of the machinery of the administration. Such a purpose had nowhere been so consciously attempted: it could not be attained by decree but only by laborious and unceasing efforts in nearly every department of government.

It has been admitted that, principles apart, shortage of political staff was a sufficient reason for a large delegation at first to native authorities. We have seen that in the first two or three years, owing to limitations of finance, Lugard could seldom post more than two political officers to each of the immense provinces he was creating, and often one of these would be sick or on leave. The actual number of men under Lugard was as follows.[2]

	1900–1901	1901–1902	1902–1903	1903–1904	1904–1905	1905–1906	Probable 1906–07
Civil	104	155	163	231*	248	266	288
Military	200	163	157	186†	207	208	187
Total on Estimates	304	318	320	417	455	474	475
Should be in Africa	202	212	214	278	310	323	326
Actually‡ Present	—	—	—	—	270	277	—

* Increase due to inclusion of Hausa States (Kano, Sokoto etc.)
† Increase due to new Mounted Infantry Battalion.
‡ No explanation is given for the omissions under this heading.

It should be noted that the civil staff gradually overtook and passed the military in number. We have already observed that " civil " staff given here covered all ranks down to foremen of works and masters of the

[1] *Instructions to Political and other officers on subjects chiefly Political and Administrative* (1906), p. 191. This will be referred to as the *Memoranda*, 1906.
[2] *Reports*, 1905–6, p. 107.

many vessels on the rivers. According to a Colonial Office report upon Lugard's grumblings the number of political officers in the total rose from 9 in 1900 to 40 in 1903, and to 75 in 1905-6.[1]

Lugard did not find it easy to recruit men of the calibre he demanded since he began his administration just as the outbreak of the Boer War called many of the most adventurous spirits to another part of Africa. He was therefore obliged, in face of the paucity of senior civil staff, to make all the use he legitimately could of military officers and he defended this course in words that reveal what he desired from his officers. They were " an admirable class of men for this work. They are gentlemen: their training teaches them prompt decision"; their knowledge of military law and of survey were assets, they had shown a sympathy and understanding with the people. " It is, indeed, a characteristic of the British officer that when in civil employ his rule is often marked by less ' militarism ' than that of the civilian and he is more opposed to punitive operations."[2] Oxford and Cambridge were, however, now coming forward with offers to train graduates for colonial service and Lugard's men from this source formed a creative nucleus for the new Colonial Service. It is difficult to understand how, with the small number of political officers he had at any one time in the field, especially in the first three years, he and they were able to accomplish so much. The leave system, necessary but costly in time and money, meant that only two-thirds of his establishment could be at their posts, while there was a large expense of time in laborious travel, in accompanying military expeditions, and in sickness.

What were the tasks Lugard asked of his Residents and Assistant Residents? To say they were to rule through the chiefs does not take us very far. An immediate question to be answered was "What chiefs?" Was it to be the Fulani who had ousted earlier rulers and imposed themselves over the Hausa population? The British, coming in, judged them cruel and oppressive; the test of war showed that their own subjects had little active loyalty towards them, and at first sight they cannot have seemed very promising partners for government.

An attempt has been made to picture Hausa society in the nineteenth century. We must now look more closely at the Fulani ruling class themselves as Lugard studied them as candidates for authority under

---

[1] Minute by Strachey on Lugard to Lyttelton, 26 March 1905, C.O. 446/44.
[2] *Reports*, 1902, p. 50.

his control. It is easy to reconstruct the picture these men presented to him, so little in many outward things had the country changed when the writer first travelled there, sometimes trekking on horseback, in the early thirties. They and their large families and many courtiers, comfortably settled into the seats of their predecessors, played their parts as the great men of their world with that dramatic ostentation which, in industrial civilization, wealth and rank has largely discarded. In their high turbans, with the characteristic swathe round the chin to keep the blown dust out of their mouths, their flowing cloaks and brilliantly coloured equestrian trappings, they would ride out among the earth-stained Hausa peasantry who would fall prostrate in the fields at their passing. The rulers had palaces of red mud, with crenellated walls which extended over acres of ground in the capital cities: these had high arched halls patterned with arabesques; courtyards; warrens of rooms for retainers; quarters for slaves and horses and, shut away in the care of eunuchs, large collections of women of many tribes. These last, invisible to Lugard or any other European man, at least until recent days, were shown to the writer by more than one Fulani emir, who, passing down the long row of chambers, called each occupant to the doorway and explained how and from where she had been obtained, as a horse-breeder shows off his stud. It was through this luxury and indulgence that many of the emirs, following some greater oriental rulers, had sunk from the physical and religious energy of their conquering forefathers and had drawn negro blood from wives and slave concubines into their Hamitic race, darkening, in many of them, their light colour and thickening their fine drawn Fulani features and slender limbs. Yet the decline can be over-stated: they still had the habits and the capacities of command and Lugard, obliged to make use of his quick judgment of men, declared them fit to rule.

Had he, indeed, we must ask again, as we approach his situation more closely, any choice? In his *Memoranda* he stated the alternative policy of discovering and reinstating the former Hausa dynasties, and Sir Richmond Palmer[1] informed the writer that a number of Hausa claimants at this time were collected in Gobir hoping to be reinstated. But it is difficult to believe that this restoration could have been possible

[1] Palmer, (later Sir) Herbert Richmond, K.C.M.G., 1877-1958; 1904 Assistant Resident, N. Nigeria; 1917 Resident, Bornu Province; 1925-30 Lieut.-Governor, N. Provinces, Nigeria; 1930-3 Governor, the Gambia; 1933-9 Governor, Cyprus.

with his scanty staff and his need for a rapid and tranquillizing settlement. Such a substitution would have ruled out the break-neck speed of his king-making expedition in the spring of 1903. And once a partnership had been made with the interlocked Fulani dynasties, it would have been difficult in honour and in policy to break it.

The indifference, if no worse, of many of the Hausa towards their Fulani ruling caste served, of course, to make these, once the spell of their power was broken, very dependent upon their new masters.[1] The Fulani may have been in some ways able rulers but the evidence of the early European travellers shows how destructive their *Jihad* had been, especially where, as in Katsina, fighting had been prolonged.[2] There is evidence that after nearly a century of assimilation with their subjects they were still regarded as a dominant group, a distinction that was often close to hostility. The Hausa woman, Baba, though she ran into her hut when she saw the first white face, could remark "We Habe [Hausa] wanted them to come. It was the Fulani who did not like it. When the Europeans came the Habe saw that if you worked for them they paid you for it, they didn't say like the Fulani, 'Commoner, give me this! Commoner, bring me that!' Yes, the Habe wanted them; they saw no harm in them."[3]

The situation might demand the recognition of the Fulani rulers but there was still a wide margin of choice as to their exact status and their powers, and it is at this point that we must begin to distinguish what was peculiar to Lugard's application of the indirect principle. He confessed to the writer, many years afterwards that, though he later quoted the example of the Indian States in his *Memoranda*, when suddenly confronted with the northern emirs after their rapid collapse, he could only scrape together the vaguest recollections about the position of these States, and was, indeed, amazed at his own ignorance. He had to devise what seemed to fit the immediate situation. It was true that he had thought out the main lines of his settlement long before and had enforced them in Bida but it was now necessary to be more detailed and definite. Lugard's speech in Kano has already been quoted; it shows the main indirect principle; he still had to go a long

---

[1] *Memoranda*, 1906, No. 18, pp. 263-4.
[2] See for example Barth, *Travels and Discoveries*, vol. ii, pp. 39 ff., and 70, 80 ff. for the original Fulani attitude justifying the *Jihad*. See also Sultan Mohammed Bello's own account of the Hausa ' evil doers' in *The Rise of the Sokoto Fulani*, ed. E. J. Arnett (Lagos 1922).
[3] Smith, *Baba of Karo*, pp. 66-7.

way in developing it into a system of administration suited to the country.

First, because constitutionally basic, was his determination that there should be no uncertainty whatever upon the question of sovereignty. This, half-consciously perhaps, must have been a main reason for his launching his 1902-3 expedition. The alternative would have been to attempt to secure a treaty, at least with the suzerain state of Sokoto. Or he might have made one of those agreements which elsewhere have tended to confuse both sides by their ambiguous legal status and their tendency to crystallize societies at the very time when annexation was going to bring rapid changes. Lugard's first demand, whether he was looking at authorities above or below him, was always for a free hand. He had not forgotten the hazardous uncertainties of his relationship with Mwanga. So he laid down that the Fulani had lost by defeat the powers—he had then little idea, as he told the writer, what those powers were—that they had won by conquest and recent conquest at that. Now, by grace and not by right, some of these powers would be returned to them by delegation, to be kept according to good behaviour. This settlement, by implication and usage, was made to cover those states which, like Bornu, had acceded by consent and not as a result of conquest. It was upon this constitutional foundation that the Residents were to stand, willing to advise and help, but able, with full statutory power, to control and to command. He was quite definite about the contents of this new power. " This suzerainty involves the ultimate title to all land, the right to appoint Emirs and all officers of state, the right of legislation and of taxation."[1] He goes on, in this second of his annual reports, to give the underlying reason for his policy.

" But in my view the tradition of British rule has ever been to arrest disintegration, to retain and build up again what is best in the social and political organization of the conquered dynasties, and to develop on the lines of its own individuality each separate race of which our Great Empire consists. That has been our policy in India; and Northern Nigeria, though but a third in size, and many centuries behind the great Eastern dependency, still presents to my imagination many strangely parallel conditions. I believe myself that the future of the virile races of this Protectorate lies largely in the regeneration of the Fulani. Their cere-

[1] *Reports*, 1902, p. 25.

monial, their coloured skins, their mode of life and habits of thought, appeal more to the native populations than the prosaic business-like habits of the Anglo-Saxon can ever do. Nor have we the means at present to administer so vast a country. This, then, is the policy to which, in my view, the administration of Northern Nigeria should give effect, viz., to regenerate this capable race and mould them to ideas of justice and mercy, so that in a future generation, if not in this, they may become worthy instruments of rule."[1]

These passages are important for, in spite of the comparison with India, meaning of course, the Indian States, it is quite clear from the powers he claimed that his system was to be fundamentally different from the almost diplomatic supervision of the British Residents at the courts of Rajahs. The oath of allegiance which each Emir had to take was uncompromising.

" I swear in the name of Allah, and of Mahomet his Prophet to well and truly serve his Majesty King Edward VII and his Representative the High Commissioner of Northern Nigeria. To obey the laws of the Protectorate, and the lawful commands of the High Commissioner and of the Resident, provided that they are not contrary to my religion. And if they are so contrary, I will at once inform the Resident, for the information of the High Commissioner. I will cherish in my heart no treachery or disloyalty, and I will rule my people with justice and without partiality. And as I carry out this oath, so may Allah judge me."[2]

(Even in an official declaration the Emirs are made to follow Lugard's habit of splitting his infinitives!)

Undisputed sovereignty was one of Lugard's principles. The integration of British and native power was another; the two were not to lie together in impermeable strata.

" The effect is to still further recognize the Native Administration as an integral part of the machinery of the Government of the country, and to amplify and regularize the position already accorded to it in Proclamations Nos. 1 and 2 of 1906 (Native Revenue and Native Courts). These three important statutes practically contain the whole policy of Government regarding the position, authority, and emoluments of the Native part of the Administration of the Protectorate.

The prestige and influence of the Chiefs can be best upheld by letting the peasantry see that Government itself treats them as an integral part of

[1] *Ibid.* p. 26.   [2] *Memoranda,* 1906, No. 9, pp. 191-2.

the machinery of the Administration. . . . They should be complementary to each other, and the Chief himself must understand that he has no right to his place and power, unless he renders his proper services to the State."[1]

The words are clear and firm but their implementation was not easy. Indeed, as we shall see when discussing the judicial system, there were contexts in which Lugard wished to emphasize dualism rather than integration. He made no attempt to deceive himself or his staff about their difficulties. He discussed them frankly and summarized these discussions in his *Political Memoranda*, especially in the one entitled " Fulani Rule ".[2] In this, it must be admitted, he tended to run together three related but separate issues—firstly, whether the Fulani should rule or be replaced by the old Habe dynasties; secondly, how far Muslim rule should be restored or extended over pagans; thirdly, the question in what measure the power of the emirs should be retained or increased. Immediate decisions answered the first two questions but the last remained, and continued to remain until the eve of independence, open to varying political practice. Not surprisingly, there were differences of opinion among Lugard's first Residents. There was at first a feeling against the emirs who had been in the field as " the enemy" and in favour of the underdog, the peasantry. This was followed by an early realization that it was impossible, as Lugard pointed out, to take over, or even, indeed, to supervise very closely, the large administrative work of the Fulani rulers. And as many of these quickly showed their intelligence by a co-operative acceptance of their new status most Residents entered into some degree of partnership with them.

The Residents fell into two schools of thought, though these were perhaps not very clearly defined. One, led by Major Burdon, first Resident in Sokoto, and a student of the local culture, wished to go a long way in supporting Fulani rule, even so far as to rebuild the pre-eminence of the Sultan of Sokoto. Temple, a little more moderately, supported him. Hewby stood at the opposite side and would even have restored the Habe dynasties. Lugard listened to both sides and held his own course. Upon the extent of the emirs' power he came, as we shall see more clearly later, into opposition with some of his most active Residents through his own belief that the sphere of British

---

[1] *Memoranda*, 1906, No. 9, p. 192.   [2] *Ibid*. No. 18, pp. 263-268.

action, especially as operated from the centre, should be larger than they wished.

" On the general question of the advantage of Fulani rule," Lugard wrote, " it is premature to dogmatize " . . . However, as some directives had to be given until fuller knowledge could be gained, he went on that, since the staff was inadequate for such a vast Protectorate, " it is obvious that we cannot in any sense *administer* it, nor is it intended that Residents should be *administrators* in the true sense of the word." (See Memo. 1. para. 2). And, again, " Hence we must utilize the existing machinery and endeavour only to improve it."[1]

This seems clear enough yet the more searchingly Lugard's system is analysed the more difficult does it become to rationalize it. There are recognizable extremes of indirect and direct methods in the all-but-independent native state on the one hand and in the employment, on the other, of a hierarchy of agents, alien and native, acting directly upon the native population according to the orders of the European official. Both extremes could have a fairly static character. But, in Northern Nigeria, British sovereignty, having been first uncompromisingly declared, was then fitted gradually and selectively over native institutions, here weakening or destroying, there retaining and reforming. Allowance has also to be made for differences both in the circumstance and in the personalities, black and white, in each province, and also for a continuous process of change, planned and involuntary.

The two sides soon found that there was a considerable area of agreement. Both the Hausa peasantry and the Fulani emirs understood the meaning of conquest and the working of a hierarchical system. To the people the addition of one more tier of authority over the many-tiered structure above them seemed, especially in the early years, no revolutionary change, though it soon appeared that it was one for the better. The emirs, after the first shock of European conquest, were relieved to find how many of their powers were left to them almost undiminished. They were quite ready to strike a bargain on these terms with their incomprehensible conquerors. With a will to co-operate on both sides the emirs and the British officials came some way towards understanding each other and the more intelligent of the emirs learned to appreciate the advantages, if only to themselves, of better order, larger trade and some of the comforts and ingenuities of western civilization. But

[1] *Ibid.* pp. 264-5.

the great benefit they received, one for which they knew they could hardly pay too high a price, was security for their status as princes, an even greater security, whether against their suzerain of Sokoto, their fellow princes, their own subjects, or the other white invaders operating along the frontiers, than they had possessed in 1900. For this advantage they desired to pay the minimum in the reduction, visible or invisible, of their powers, and in interference with their pleasures, perquisites, the advancement of their families, their religion and customs.

Here we come upon the area of disagreement. For the British authorities, while anxious to upset the power, especially the visible power, of the emirs as little as possible, wished to introduce the maximum of change in the direction of good administration, freedom from slavery and oppression, and economic development. The source of disagreement lay, of course, in the difference of ideology from which the two sides came to seek their area of co-operation. For the British administrators drew their political philosophy, with the rest of their mental and moral equipment, from a society that, however imperfectly it expressed its ideals, was both Christian and democratic. Islam had, of course, its own lofty ideas. But most of the Fulani rulers of 1900 appear to have done little to express these in humane and honest government. Thus the British officials found themselves confronting and indeed, collaborating with a society that was authoritarian and Muslim and they had been obliged solemnly to recognize a religion which almost entirely insulated rulers and people from the sources of those western ideas which governed their own action. The gap between the two standards was narrowed partly by forcing the emirs to act according to British standards. But it was sometimes closed by the administrators themselves meeting the emirs half-way, by partially suspending their own ideals, by supporting at times a corrupt and selfish aristocracy and teaching themselves to regard as irremediable a measure of abuse. Some of the early Residents, while admitting the danger, urged upon the writer that direct rule being quite impracticable, some acceptance of abuse was inescapable if the whole structure of the indigenous society were not to break down. And they could claim that the margin of oppression was far less than that tolerated in many Indian States.

The Residents' dilemma was accentuated by the order which Lugard felt bound to issue that the authority of the emirs had to be supported. In spite of the arrival of a foreign ruler, the people must continue to regard their own princes as their masters. This demanded a deliberate self-effacement of British officials in their work. They were to restrain themselves from frequent and, above all, open interference with the emir and his entourage in his conduct of affairs, unless gross disobedience or abuse should demand deposition. Influence should be brought to bear upon the emir himself rather than that his prestige and sense of responsibility should be undermined by British officials taking open and direct action at lower levels to right some wrong. Subordinate appointments should be made in the emir's name: his public dignity should be maintained with all traditional ceremony and the Resident himself should show a proper respect for his office according to a ritual elaborated in full detail by Lugard.[1] He gave the reason, " for, if a Native Chief has lost prestige and influence to such a degree that he has to appeal to Government to enforce his orders, he becomes not merely useless but a source of weakness to the administration." On the same page, observing that the people were less ready to obey their Chiefs, now that they had seen them conquered by the British, he asserted, "I am anxious in every possible way to counteract this tendency and to support the authority of the Native Chiefs . . . "

It is now easy to see in many parts of Africa that where the vital current of a chief's responsibility running downwards to his people was diverted into responsibility towards an alien power suddenly imposed above him, the whole character of his office was changed. The change was intensified because, at the same time, the chief was often expected to use his new and increased power to enforce novel measures. It was as if the institution of chieftainship was a hollow statue, out of which the real traditional content of native power was almost imperceptibly draining away while the white ruler was, equally unostentatiously, pouring in his own power in substitution, the outward shell of the institution looking the same while its inner substance was gradually changing. Certainly, the colonial government in attempting to make use for its own purposes of a power developed in other times for other ends, was likely to run the risk some day of deceiving its subjects and, perhaps, itself. The emirates, because of their strength, size and advanced development, probably suffered less

[1] See especially *Memoranda*, 1906, No. 9, pp. 191 ff.

than any other institution of rule in Africa. But they could not be quite immune.

To look so far ahead into the future of his system is, perhaps, unfair to Lugard's initial years of work, though it is intended to protect it from inapplicable criticism. There were large and immediate gains from this policy in its first stage. One was to be found in the achievement of an immediate contrast with what had been. Another was the avoidance of the shock and dislocation which generally accompany conquest. A period of peace and goodwill was secured which could allow of a reasonably smooth adjustment to change. Economic activity, already advanced, was increased. The beginnings of social services were at least planned, and oppressive and extravagant methods of government checked. With the Muslims restrained from the wastefulness of their own war-like activities, and the pagans freed from the terror and loss of slave-raiding, the energies of both could be absorbed in peaceful exertions which in a hundred unseen ways brought a new contentment and well-being to both peoples. These were immense gains and their achievement was due largely to Lugard's system of Indirect Rule and to the immense energy with which both he and his Residents put it into operation.

CHAPTER VIII

INDIRECT RULE: THE STRUCTURE

THE LAST CHAPTER dealt with the principles of Indirect Rule. The responsibility given to the Residents was so wide and their application of Indirect Rule to the varying conditions in Northern Nigeria so protean that principles are easier to record than practice. But the system had to be expressed in measures covering the several spheres of what came to be called " native administration ", the judicature, and public finance, such simple economic development as was possible, and lastly the question of slavery. Between 1900 and 1906 a series of proclamations dealing with these matters were issued by Lugard under his sole legislative power, most of them being amended more than once.

The administrative and political side of Lugard's settlement can be studied in his annual reports, and in his *Political Memoranda* of 1906,[1] and in the measures collected in the *Enforcement of Native Authority Proclamations in 1907*. Chiefs obtained their new legal authority only through their appointment by the High Commissioner. There were to be five grades of independent chief, each holding a special staff of office, and ranging from the great emirs to small pagan elders. Emirs appointed, under the supervision of the Resident, their own subordinate chiefs, headmen and office holders. Lugard urged reduction of these last since they tended, partly owing to the immense families of the chiefs, to be very numerous. But this was certainly one of those interests so dear to the emirs that his attempt was not very successful. One of his most difficult reforms was the concentration of the scattered fiefs held by the district headmen. The emirs, following a common custom of autocrats, kept these important men in attendance at their palaces. Lugard insisted that they should go out and administer their

---

[1] The *Memoranda*, 1906, dealing most closely with native administration are: 1. Duties of Residents. 3. The Law and the Courts of Justice of the Protectorate. 5. The System of Tribute and Taxes. 6. Slavery. 8. Native Courts. 9. The Position of Native Chiefs. 18. Fulani Rule.

fiefs and so dispense with the rapacious crowd of agents and messengers, passing to and fro between the capital city and the district head-quarters. The highest emirs had their judicial councils, which were administrative courts somewhat reminiscent of the Star Chamber in their functions; they retained their personal police and could enforce their orders in the Native Courts.

In the emirates, as we have seen, the Resident was to be as far as possible an adviser rather than an administrator but in pagan areas, with their small scale and rudimentary organization, he would have to undertake many of the functions of government himself. Upon the very delicate question of Muslim claims to rule pagan tribes Lugard laid down that although pagans might voluntarily come under a Muslim rule, yet, " No independent or revolted pagan tribe will, however, be included in his jurisdiction, without the express sanction of the High Commissioner."[1] But peaceful penetration under the new *pax Britannica* was to do what centuries of wars and raiding had failed to achieve. Some at least of the smaller groups more accessible to Muslim influence were to be assimilated to the superior culture of their old enemies who could now come freely amongst their naked-ness and poverty wearing the long Muslim gown and carrying the Koran. But this was hardly clear at this early stage. Indeed, there still remained many pagan areas where administration in any full sense did not yet reach. Most of the pagan tribes, especially where they had the refuge of hill or forest, remained wild and shy. Nor were they always innocent parties. Humane administrators in Northern Nigeria then, and for many years after Lugard's day often risked, and sometimes lost, their lives in the attempt to make friendly contact without act or show of force.

There have been many references to Lugard's *Political Memoranda.* There is, as far as the writer knows, nothing quite like them in the varied documentation of the empire. The idea of them had come to him before he sailed for Nigeria or, at least, upon the ship. As early as 1902 he wrote to his brother,

" In the organization I am codifying and memo-writing and reducing all subjects to a set of general principles and rules of policy. I will send you these—they are of real interest and well epitomize my work here."

(L. to E. J. L., September 1902).

[1] *Memoranda*, 1906, No. 18, p. 264.

His letters to his wife often show him detaching himself with difficulty from the pressures of the day in order to give time to writing and re-writing these *Memoranda*. Issued as a bound collection in 1906, they were twenty-three in number and covered 319 closely printed pages. They dealt with every aspect of administration from discussions of high policy, from which quotations have been made, through the major branches of government down to canoe registration.

The main impression given by the *Memoranda* is of comprehensiveness. In the range of topics, and in their depth, from guiding principles to details about form filling, or characteristic advice upon economizing in stationery, everything is covered. His pages breathe a sense of order and confidence. But he went too far. It is almost impossible, as the reader pauses for a moment, crushed by the perfectionism of the instructions, to visualize the state of the country, still only partly occupied as the orders were written, and the few, scattered, inexperienced officers who were to carry them out. In the chapter, " Books, Returns and Office Records," he lists some thirty sets of records to be kept or sent in, dealing with courts of justice, finance and taxation, slavery, police and prisons, post, and registers of oaths, letters, caravans, canoes and many other matters. When it is remembered that in the early years there were either no clerks, or, at best, native apprentices of insignificant competence and responsibility, and very inadequate office equipment—both Sir William Gowers[1] and Sir Charles Orr[2] told the writer that in desperation they had to buy their own typewriters— we must conclude that Lugard's instructions were far from being always honoured in the observance. In addition to the Memoranda, there was the usual colonial issue of Government Standing Orders,[3] less original but all carefully revised by Lugard himself: these were also collected in book form in 1906 and contained 80 separate orders and covered 248 pages. And we must remember that to laws, memoranda, and general orders, were added an unceasing flow from Lugard's office to the Residents of general and particular letters,

[1] Gowers, (later Sir) William Frederick, K.C.M.G., 1875-1954; 1899-1902 British South Africa Company (Southern Rhodesia); 1902 entered Colonial Service, Northern Nigeria; 1921 Lieut-Governor, Nigeria; 1925-32 Governor, Uganda Protectorate; 1932-38 Senior Crown Agent for the Colonies.

[2] Orr, (later Sir) Charles W. J., K.C.M.G., 1870-1945; 1895-9 served in Royal Artillery, India; 1902 South African War; 1903-9 Resident, Northern Nigeria; 1911-17 Chief Secretary, Cyprus; 1918 Intelligence Department, War Office; 1919 Colonial Secretary, Gibraltar; 1926-31 Governor, the Bahamas.

[3] *Government Standing Orders of Northern Nigeria*, revised to September 1906.

and of verbal advice and instructions given upon their visits to Zungeru or during the High Commissioner's tours of inspection.

We must turn now from the administrative system to the judicial settlement. The Supreme Court, under the Chief Justice, had a very narrow jurisdiction. Under it were the magistrates' courts in the cantonments, the name given to the few purely European-made military and administrative centres. The Supreme Court dealt with cases in which non-natives and government officials were concerned: the Court also had concurrent jurisdiction in the most southerly, and therefore accessible provinces, with the Provincial Courts. These last were the really important British courts. Each Resident had jurisdiction in his own province and under him all administrative officers could hold commissioner's courts. These courts were under the control not of the Chief Justice but of the High Commissioner and it rested with him to transfer a case from the Provincial to the Supreme Court, while the monthly cause lists of the Provincial Courts went not to the Chief Justice but to himself and served automatically as appeals. No lawyers could plead in these courts. All sentences of over six months' imprisonment, 12 strokes or a £50 fine had to be formally confirmed by the High Commissioner.

The great bulk of the litigation in the Protectorate was, however, carried out in the Native Courts. In the emirates there was a recognition of the existing judicial system in which the native judge, the Alkali, had behind him the Maliki code of Muslim law, and the authority and dignity of some centuries of tradition. These were under the supervision of Residents who could freely transfer cases from them to the Provincial Courts. Lugard refused to follow the example of the French and of the governments in Southern Nigeria by putting European officers into the Native Courts. " I prefer," he wrote, " to keep the British and Native Courts distinct so that the latter may not feel that they have lost all power and initiative and become merely advisory to the British Administrator."[1] Following this policy of trust in 1904 he recognized some of the Courts in the leading emirates as 'A' courts with powers in criminal cases, under the Resident's supervision, of life and death. They had practically unlimited jurisdiction in civil matters. At the other end of the scale were the small pagan courts, though in these early years the insufficient staff could

[1] *Memoranda*, 1906, No. 8, p. 169.

make only a beginning with them. From the Native, as from the Provincial Courts, lawyers were excluded.

Recognition of the separate existence and traditional authority of all these courts did not mean, as in some less considered applications elsewhere of the " indirect " principle, that they were left to act as a completely separate system with the minimum of supervision. Lugard arranged for the closest supervision that was possible by his small staff. In judicial as in executive matters, however, he had to draw a very fine distinction between too much and too little intervention. Thus, he laid down that " Care should be taken not to intervene unnecessarily so as to lower the prestige of the court in the eyes of its members or of the people . . . "[1] Yet every effort was to be made for the gradual and reasonable reform of the Courts in their procedure and sentences. To preserve the clear distinction and responsibility of the courts, the native authorities were to carry out their own sentences—the major emirates inflicted capital sentences by beheading—and run their own prisons, for he did not wish British officers to carry responsibility for sentences that might not accord perfectly with British standards of justice.[2]

He had to face in its earliest and acutest form the problem of punishment which has continued to confront European administrators in Africa. The horrified condemnation of mutilation and of imprisonments which were not far removed from burying alive, had left the native authorities so uncertain of the principles of their new rulers that they swung to the opposite extreme of a lenience in which, Lugard said, " flogging is a mere farce and prisons often do not exist." It was not easy to assure humane and sanitary imprisonment in the administrative conditions of those early years while to pagans imprisonment seemed like a European continuation of slavery. Such considerations as these have often induced British administrators to favour flogging as a punishment that was not only quick and obvious but also relatively humane. In Northern Nigeria it was the rule that the flogger had to keep some cowrie shells in his armpit to prevent him striking too hard. But Lugard believed that with the abolition of all the old severe and cruel punishments, floggings should be severe enough to be deterrent. He also considered keeping the native punishment of the stocks so that public disapproval and derision could be

---

[1] *Ibid.* p. 176.   [2] *Reports*, 1902, p. 76.

called in to support the law. But on such matters there is often a breach between a realistic governor and officials in London responsible to British public opinion, and the Colonial Office, even though it was half-convinced by Lugard's arguments, flinched from the task of facing parliamentary questions on the use of the stocks in a British colony.[1] It was also somewhat sensitive on the question of flogging and Lugard, confident of his own humanity, was indignant at being questioned closely upon his use of this penalty, and furious when General Kemball commented adversely in the Office upon the severity of the whip which was in use.

This system of courts relieved the British officials from the crushing burden of carrying on the whole judicial administration in what were often highly litigious communities, for they left as much as possible to the Native Courts. Even so they still had duties of supervision over Native Courts and as judges of the Provincial Courts. Lugard's principle has sometimes been called, generally in criticism, one of "administrative justice" and it is true that his so-called "political officers", most of whom had had no legal training, combined judicial with administrative control. In the condition of Northern Nigeria there were decisive practical reasons of finance and communications for this fusion of powers in the same officer. But Lugard from first to last defended it as positively desirable in preference to an extended jurisdiction of the Supreme Court.[2] The unsophisticated north appears to have accepted the combination of powers and the virtual exclusion of British courts with passivity but the subject, as we shall see, was to become controversial with educated African leaders, and especially African lawyers in the south.

A system by which the same man might deal administratively with an offence and with every stage of the prosecution and trial could not indefinitely be harmonized with British conceptions of justice, the more so as before the flood of circumstantial or corrupt evidence he was often, as judge, obliged to fall back upon his "insight" into the workings of the native mind or a "sort of instinct".[3] But only time and progress could reveal these flaws and it is for the critic to show how higher standards of justice could have been achieved at that stage or,

---

[1] Minute by Antrobus on Lugard to Lyttelton, 30 December 1904, C.O. 446/38.
[2] *Reports*, 1900–01, p. 16, and F. D. Lugard, *The Dual Mandate in British Tropical Africa* (4th edition, 1929), pp. 536-69.
[3] C. W. Orr, *The Making of Northern Nigeria* (1911), pp. 232-5.

Indirect Rule: The Structure

perhaps, at any time before Sir Donald Cameron set about his judicial reforms in the early thirties.[1] But this is to approach the controversy that lay in store for Lugard upon his return to Nigeria in 1912.

Lugard looked upon the judicial side of his system as among its most important and successful parts. Although the original delegation of judicial power was largely dictated by sheer practical necessity, he did not, as his administrative hold on the country increased, begin to reduce the powers of Native Courts. On the contrary, as we have just seen, he increased them, and his later reports abound in commendation of the striking success of the courts in the emirates. His policy here expressed exactly his three principles; generous recognition of native capabilities and institutions; the integration of the latter into the new system of government; and the wide discretionary powers of the Residents in the interests of reform.

Throughout tropical Africa the judicial side of tribal life is generally the most advanced aspect and has been that most successfully retained and developed under British guidance. This was especially true of the law and the courts of the Nigerian emirates. But the initial success was due largely to the immense interest and energy which Lugard put into this side of his work. This is frequently shown in his letters to his wife. Here is an extract which shows the system in action and his part as the head of it towards the end of his period.

"Tuesday is my judicial day on which I act as an Appeal Court, and review all the Cause Lists of the Provincial Courts brought to me by the Attorney General—sign death warrants, and exercise the Royal prerogative of pardon etc. I cannot but think that it would interest you greatly to listen to a morning of this work. I think the system I started here is a very sound one and has worked well. The Residents, men without legal training as a rule, administer Justice in the Provincial Courts. They submit Cause Lists with a précis of the case, and full minutes of every sentence over 6 months, for this needs my Confirmation. The full instructions in my Memos have resulted after these years in very tolerably good results as regards the actual judicial work and the forms of trial etc. The Attorney General reviews these carefully and writes his notes (or remarks that he has 'no comment') on every case from the legal point of view. In going thro' the minutes he marks in red ink all hearsay and inadmissable evidence, comments on any irregularity and suggests which is omitted. Then I review every single case—add further notes on points in the Memos

[1] Perham, *Native Administration*, pp. 337-43.

161

which have been disregarded, and reduce any sentence, and confirm (with or without reduction) the cases over 6 months. My review is on wholly different lines. I am not hampered by legal technicalities, but I bring to bear a long African experience and a knowledge of native custom. I endeavour to promote uniformity throughout the whole Protectorate, and I above all endeavour to bring to bear a strong 'common sense' point of view. Frequently I set aside the Attorney General's recommendations and I think I *never* fail to get him to concur in my judgment when I have thrown on the case my own particular point of view and experience. I think that for substantial justice it would be hard to beat this system. It involves the greater part of one day in every week . . . "

(L. to F. L., 23 January 1906).

It should be explained in conclusion what law these Courts enforced. Under an early Proclamation (No. 4 of 1900), the "Fundamental Law" of the Protectorate was declared to be the Common Law and Statutes of England as in force on January 1st, 1900. Upon this basis, subject to any British Orders-in-Council which had overriding authority, law was built up by the Proclamations of the High Commissioner, issued upon his sole authority subject, of course, to Colonial Office assent. In cases concerning natives, however, the Proclamation 6 of 1902, recognized native law and custom when not repugnant to natural justice or any law of the Protectorate. The law-making power was one of the heaviest burdens upon Lugard as in the first years of his rule he was obliged to frame, with very little expert help, large numbers of laws, covering every aspect of administration. He issued seventeen of these in his first year, including laws on such questions as the Courts, the Cantonments, Finances, Liquor, Slavery, and Land, and year by year there was a steady output of legislation.[1]

It was over this issue that Lugard had a conflict with Gollan who, from being his private secretary had, in 1901, become the Chief Justice. The relations between a colonial governor and a chief justice have in them the possibility of rivalry as the chief judicial officer, since he draws his commission directly from the Crown, is, alone in the colony, in a position of some independence towards the otherwise all-embracing power of the governor. It is very probable that Gollan, himself a most able and spirited man with a high sense of his office,

---

[1] These were issued in collected form in *Order-in-Council and Proclamations and rules, regulations, Government notices and orders thereunder in force in the Protectorate of Northern Nigeria on the 1st Day of October 1904* (1905).

resented the small sphere in which he was allowed to act. He had been so much used as a legal maid-of-all-work by Lugard that he seemed to find it necessary, upon his promotion to the august position of chief justice, to assert the dignity of his office, partly by refusing to continue the exacting work of helping to frame legislation and partly by an attempt to extend the sphere of his Supreme Court. The Colonial Office appeared to have had some sympathy with his first cause for resentment but upon the second they had already accepted Lugard's policy of granting more extensive judicial powers to executive officers than was customary in other colonies.[1] This controversy greatly distressed Lugard. He was obliged to take the opposition of a chief justice seriously and it was probably difficult for him to adjust himself to this situation with a man whom he had taken out as his private secretary. Early in 1904 they were writing each other long and formal memoranda, and in the end Gollan insisted that the whole correspondence should be sent to the Secretary of State.[2] " The question," Lugard told his wife, " is the whole judicial system here and the position and duties of the chief justice and the jurisdiction of the Supreme Court." Although Lugard had a very high regard for Gollan's capacity and character he was relieved at his departure later the same year and the substitution of a chief justice who, it seems, gave no further trouble upon the points at issue.

Lugard's administrative structure was, of course, governed largely by his financial resources. It is here that we find the cloud that hung perpetually over his head these six years, rousing rather than chilling his administrative a-dour. Northern Nigeria was a poor country. True, its more advanced peoples lived far above the general African standard and there was some long established trade, both internal and across the new international boundaries drawn upon this land-locked region. But, by European standards, the condition of the country made it largely self-sufficient; its people grew and consumed their own food and made their own cotton cloth and their implements for fighting and agriculture. There was no seaboard at which trade could be tapped for a customs' revenue. Distances were vast and communications, which were dependent upon camels, pack-oxen, donkeys and the flow of the inconstant rivers, left large areas untouched.

---

[1] Minutes on Lugard to Lyttelton, 23 July 1904, C.O. 446/38.
[2] Lugard to Lyttelton, above dispatch.

The two southern dependencies, close to the sea, with their ready and accessible export crop of palm oil and their crowded negro population eager to import clothes, hardware and gin, were fully solvent while Lugard, with his domain on a grant-in-aid and always asking for more, was very soon unpopular with the Treasury. We saw how he managed by sheer importunity backed by irreducible estimates to push his grant-in-aid up to nearly £90,000 and then, from shortage of staff, to make a large saving. In addition to his grant for civil expenditure parliament voted more than twice as much, £200,000, for the West African Frontier Force.

To Lugard these figures represented an almost intolerable anxiety. He studied from the first moment how he could augment them from the terrtiory. Before he went out it had been agreed that nothing could be expected at first from direct taxation and he soon found that this caution had been only too fully justified. First he had to occupy or conquer the whole country and this was not accomplished until 1903. Then he had to complete his political settlement. Next, following his usual principle, he had to set his overworked Residents to study the existing methods of raising revenue and they found a multiple system of taxation to be unravelled in the emirates. Finally, he had to be sure that he could impose taxation with the co-operation of the emirs and without provoking widespread resistance which he would not have the strength to overcome.

By 1904, however, he began to see that taxation could be so shaped as actually to give added solidity to his political settlement. He found that he had to support the emirs' rights to taxation which had been shaken in the peoples' eyes by the conquest. The emirs had a number of dues: the old Koranic right to the tithe, tolls upon the movement of merchandise, taxes upon arable land, upon irrigated crops, upon stock, and upon accession to office. There was also a levy upon all forms of handicraft and trade; this covered dyers, butchers, leather-workers and even dancing girls and prostitutes. These many and elaborate taxes were not all unjustifiable in principle but they were too often oppressive in collection, especially as some of them had been granted out by the emirs to the numerous fief-holders who lived at the capital and employed agents to collect them. Other taxes were farmed out. There might be a chain of people drawing their proportion of a tax, or probably much more, before the residue finally reached the emir.

Yet the very structure of the emirs' government would collapse if the flow of revenue were checked by hasty reforms. Lugard's first action, therefore, had to be an instruction to his Residents to support the emirs in the collection of their dues. It was not until 1904 that he felt himself able to issue a Proclamation dealing with the revenue system. He defined its purpose in these words:

" The object in view is to retain, as far as possible, the ancient forms of taxation known to the people, and sanctioned by tradition; to utilize the existing machinery, while simplifying the mode of collection, which in the past lent itself to great abuses, and was extremely wasteful; to introduce as far as possible, some uniformity and equality of taxation in the different Provinces; and, finally, to preserve the old Jurisdictions as far as possible, and to maintain the individuality of the institutions of the country."[1]

The plan showed clearly the financial aspect of his partnership with the Muslim rulers. He recognized their system and assured them their revenues, taking one half for the central government—only a quarter from Sokoto—and leaving the residue for all public and personal expenses. This allowed Kano, for example, in 1905–6 some £20,000 with £8,000 for the emir's personal salary while other emirs drew sums proportionate to their positions.[2] At the same time he canalised the spreading and turgid movement of taxation into a single stream of revenue, justly assessed and regularly collected. The assessment of revenue, as Indian experience had shown, is the most realistic and penetrating aspect of administration and Lugard, building his reforms into the native system, set his officers to study the resources and structure of each village, or convenient taxable unit, to report upon its total income and liability and to give its own natural authorities the task of distributing the incidence and collecting the dues. All this, though at first a very rough and ready assessment, represented a heavy task for an overworked service but it taught the British officers to know their people as nothing else could have done; it imposed an important and stimulating duty upon the village authorities, and it gave Northern Nigeria a more justly graduated system of taxation than that of any other colony in British Africa.

Lugard had a philosophy as well as a system of taxation, and he claimed for what most men regard as an unfortunate necessity a sur-

[1] Land Revenue Proclamation, No. 4. 1904; see also *Reports*, 1904, pp. 8-21.
[2] Sir F. Lugard, *Memorandum on the Taxation of Natives in Northern Nigeria* (1907), Cd. 3309. See especially table on p. 64.

prising number of advantages, even to the payers. In a country of slavery and serfdom direct taxation was " the State recognition of the rights and responsibilities of the individual ... the moral charter of the independence of a people." More than this, " in a country so fertile as this, taxation is a moral benefit to the people, by stimulating industry and production." In Kabba, for example, after the British conquest " the male population, deprived of the necessity for producing a surplus to pay their taxes, and of the pastime of war, have become indolent and addicted to quarrelling and drinking."[1] Taxation would thus be synonymous with economic and moral reform. Lugard believed also that the payment of tax was an act of acceptance by the subject of his sovereign and, as such, an essential part of good government and the recognition of British rule.

The pecuniary results of this policy, especially in view of the government's modest share, were not impressive by modern colonial standards. The local revenue, apart from the customs contribution from Southern Nigeria, did, however, rise from just over £4,420 in 1901–2, to £54,000 in 1903–4, and to £110,500 in 1905–6, Lugard's last year. Expenditure was, of course, rising each year, far outrunning the laboriously won increase in Lugard's direct taxation. The figures given by Lugard for his period set out in simplified form, ran as shown on the next page:[2]

There was little Lugard could do in the three years of his full occupation of the country to increase its productivity. White settlement, which he had once advocated for the empty regions of the East African highlands, or even white plantations, which would have been somewhat more practicable, would have been alien to his whole policy. It was as an African country that he saw Northern Nigeria, both politically and economically. Communications were the key. He bought all the ships and built all the telegraph lines for which he could get approval. His mind was set from the first upon the possibility of a railway. But all he could do in the time was to draw up alternative plans for extending to the north the few miles of line from Lagos and build his miniature railway to Zungeru. As for commerce, he looked enviously at the palm-oil trade in the south and set to work to study the possibilities of cotton with the help of the British Cotton-Growing

---

[1] *Memoranda*, 1906, No. 5, pp. 85-7. This long memorandum *Taxation*, pp. 85-134, gives a full account of the ancient taxes and the new reforms.

[2] Based on table in *Reports*, 1906-7, Appendix IV, pp. 93-4.

	1901-2	1902-3	1903-4	1904-5	1905-6	1906-7
Revenue						
Local Revenue	4,424- 0- 2	16,315-11-11	53,726-17-10	94,026- 6- 0	110,544-11- 5	142,067- 6- 6
Imperial Grant in Aid (Civil and military)	280,000- 0- 0	290,000- 0- 0	405,000- 0- 0	405,000- 0- 0	320,000- 0- 0	315,000- 0- 0
Contribution for customs from S. Nigeria	34,000- 0- 0	34,000- 0- 0	50,000- 0- 0	50,000- 0- 0	60,000- 0- 0	75,000- 0- 0
Do. do. Lagos				10,000- 0- 0	15,000- 0- 0	0- 0- 0
Deferred Pay and Reward Fund W.A.F.F.		16,693-13- 6				
Total Revenue	318,424- 0- 2	357,009- 5- 5	508,726-17-10	559,526- 6- 0	505,544-11- 5	532,087- 6- 6
Expenditure. Military	132,583- 1- 8	142,416- 1- 7	191,445- 9- 2	190,259- 5- 0	188,712-12- 4	169,586- 1- 4
Civil	165,936- 4- 4	246,975- 0- 1	307,540-15- 8	330,286- 6- 5	309,547- 4- 1	329,262- 5- 3
Total	298,519- 6- 0	389,391- 1- 8	498,986- 4-10	520,545-11- 5	498,259-16- 5	498,848- 6- 7

Association. The exports in 1905-6 amounted to no more than £148,000, and among these much the largest item (£101,207) was what was to prove the ephemeral one of forest rubber. He was very critical of the lethargy of the merchants and he included his old employer, the Niger Company, in the condemnation although the Colonial Office had continued to hold their conviction that Lugard was so much under Goldie's influence that he favoured it unduly.[1] For reasons to be explained the personal relations of the two men cooled and he was able to judge the Company wholly from the standpoint of a governor. In a letter to his wife, in which allowance must be made for the strong language with which he often relieved his feelings in writing to her, he said:

> " As to development—It is folly to talk of real development, when we have no sea-board and no Customs of our own, and when we are hampered as I have shewn you by C.O. officials, and while the Niger Company block all enterprise. They are now the curse of Nigeria. Wallace said the other day that their greed and grasping were worse now than even ' in the old Goldie days '. Scarbrough attacks me in his Annual Statement for imposing ' crippling taxation ' because I re-introduced an old Company's tax on salt. It was a book entry merely *then*— it hits them *now*. They are ' *coining money* '. Wallace tells me that they have passed huge sums to their reserve—they have spent thousands (£50,000, I believe they say, £100,000 Eaglesome estimated) at Burutu [their southern port]—and are paying good dividends etc., but will do nothing here, except undersell every competitor, and close the river by engaging all crews and pilots. . . . It is simply stupendous folly paying £450,000 a year for N.N. for the Niger Company alone to reap any commercial profits, and then to prate of ' crippling taxation '."
>
> (L. to F. L., 1 September 1904).

He was critical also of the Company's failure to encourage local traders. He did not want to see southerners coming north to block the way for the northerners, especially as they tended to be as commercially static as white traders and were much given to litigation. He thought the Company might have extended trade by making advances to small northern merchants and using them as agents. But his most serious disapproval was directed against the Company's right to a half share in the royalties from minerals extracted from a large area of the country. Indeed, Lugard, prompted by his own strong will

[1] Minute by Antrobus on Lugard to Chamberlain, 3 January 1903, C.O. 446/30.

and self-confidence as well as by the special conditions in Africa, was very much of a socialist while the creed was still that of a daring minority in England. But this was less the outcome of any social theory than of his belief that his government could perform such tasks as railway construction better and more cheaply than any private company.

Flora, for her part, did her best whether from Nigeria or in England to persuade the Colonial Office into a bolder conception of Northern Nigeria as a good investment. She had, perhaps, a wider view of economics than her husband and, writing to Mr. Chamberlain from Nigeria in October 1902, she played upon his conception of the imperial estate waiting for development. Everything, she said, "was necessarily held in embryo for want of means." The ideas of her husband can be read in her more flowing style. She told Chamberlain of the good cotton grown over vast areas, of the emirs' eager acceptance of better seed, and went on:

"It is not only of cotton that samples have been collected. Packets arrive here at the High Commissioner's office by every mail from the interior containing specimens of commercial products, various grains, nuts, dyes, barks, rubbers, etc. . . . The country is simply teeming with promise. But for want of an economic department it is literally and physically impossible to make its resources known at the present moment to the public . . . Everything is politically speaking ready for the downward movement of a heavy volume of trade from the northern provinces . . . The opportunity is ripe for us to capture the whole of the trade of Kano with the Mediterranean, but again we lack the machinery—good roads, wheeled transport, to substitute for the cumbrous and expensive system of caravans, and perhaps a light railway from the Niger to Kano. The Niger is itself a splendid highway if it could be reached with greater ease from the rich district of the interior. Such a movement of trade, if it took the proportion which we have a right to hope would of course necessitate a far larger staff of British officials than we have at present at our command . . . The common public would perhaps hardly be able to understand in this stage what has been achieved, but you who are accustomed to the grasp of positions intellectually would, I am sure, fully appreciate the fact that nothing is now needed to make a great public success here but the flow of means."

But Chamberlain, in the year 1902, could not afford to act upon his earlier golden hopes, and he answered:

" You will see by my official letters that I am endeavouring to get the Treasury to consent to an increase in the W.A.F.F. which has become absolutely necessary to the development of the country. If I were a despot I would make a large investment in railways, but we must not go much in advance of public opinion for fear of a reaction. I am afraid the slow progress and the enormous cost of the Uganda Railway has rather influenced public opinion against too rapid progress, and until the promise of trade is more evident than can be expected at present, it would be difficult to obtain a grant for any very large undertaking which would appear to people in this country to be speculative."

(Chamberlain to F. L., 20 November 1902).

The initiative was thus left to private capital and commerce was the least speculative enterprise. The Niger Company may have been making good profits at this time, but Lugard's views were not free from prejudice. He seems to have had little or no desire to please the merchants and he was certainly not popular with them.

" They are a class I much distrust," he told his wife, " Their aim is purely dollars but they talk with an excess of unctuous righteousness . . . I could never have the patience to sit at the same Council table with them. They would loathe me and I them, and I should forget and become sarcastic, which irritates a commercial magnate more than cayenne pepper does a dog." (L. to F. L., 11 March 1906).

And harking back to his old differences with Mary Kingsley, and a little unfair to his old friendship with her, he wrote of the Liverpool merchants:

" Miss Kingsley flattered them by calling them ' Lords of Trade ', and telling them that West Africa existed for them alone, and they alone ought to rule it, that our officials and our system were vastly inferior to the German and the French, and were merely their servants. They adore her memory. I do not worship at her shrine myself, and I think her undoubted ' cleverness ' did a good deal of harm. You are a very, very different person from Mary Kingsley, and what you say will do them good so far as they are capable of receiving it . . ."

(L. to F. L., 2 October 1904).

The Marxist critic will continue to assert that Lugard and his colleagues were impelled, even if it were unconsciously, by the deep economic needs of the capitalist state in its attempt to find new fields of investment and so stave off its own destined collapse. On the economic side it may well be asked whether conditions in Britain or, considered as a field of investment, in Nigeria, can be made to fit the demands of their theories. The self-interested elements in Chamberlain's concept of colonial economic policy were perfectly clear, but he never seems to have pressed them upon Lugard. Like many other colonial governors of his class and education, Lugard seemed mainly concerned, in the interests of the native people as he conceived them, to control, or even in some spheres to prohibit, the business enterprise of his nation. Such governors could not be reckoned very effective agents of the forces they are supposed to represent. African leaders now assuming power and suddenly aware of the facts of economic life, and their own retarded development might justifiably criticize their colonialist predecessors for allowing not too much but too little " capitalist exploitation ".

Normal economic development could hardly go forward while slavery still existed. No part of Lugard's work interested him more than the suppression of this institution. We have seen the problem as it presented itself at the outset of his rule and his initial action in dealing with it. It is surprising that this policy did not cause greater overt resentment upon the part of the emirs or more difficulty in execution. Here, as in so much of his administration, Lugard had to guide his Residents upon a narrow and sometimes almost tortuous line between the strong and historic principles of the nation he represented and the local need to prevent disaffection and economic disturbance. Chamberlain had been nervous about this question: he had asked that Lugard should not proceed with measures against slavery until after the return of the troops from the Gold Coast. Fortunately, the policy of gradualism which lay behind the abolition of legal status, justified Lugard's hopes. One valuable witness, Baba of Karo, records how the male members of her family went out with apparent resignation into the fields to do the work formerly done by their slaves.[1] The reports of the Residents showed that there was no sudden break-away of slaves; that a gradual shift over to wage-labour, in which the government set an example, was beginning, and that the ruling classes were being reassured. This was only possible because the Residents were instructed to use all their influence to discourage wholesale or unjustified emancipations, a restraining role which some of them probably found

[1] Smith, *Baba of Karo*, pp. 67-8.

painful at times. We saw that the intention of Lugard's policy was that no discontented or ill-treated slave could any longer be held by his master and it seems that the threat of losing their property and being unable to draw upon a new supply was inducing masters to treat their slaves with much greater consideration than in the past. As time went on Lugard was able to stiffen up his legislation and its execution, and also to suppress almost entirely slave-raiding and slave-dealing—two evils which admitted of no compromise.[1]

Lugard lavished much personal attention upon his Slaves' Home and the education and the nourishment of the children. He often visited the Home and inspected the gardening, smithing, the dress-making, drill, and other activities which went on there. It was, however, a sad task. A high, though with the years, decreasing, mortality resulted from the emaciated condition in which the children were generally found.[2] He established another home at Bornu where the neighbour-hood of the Germans, who seemed indifferent to the traffic in slaves, made suppression especially difficult.

In harmony with the spirit of his rule Lugard did his best to get the emirs to understand this policy and even to co-operate with him in the suppression of slavery. Instead of trying to override or to ignore them, he studied their own restraints upon slavery and their methods of emancipation and encouraged them to handle slavery cases in their own courts. At the end of his period he was able to report that the enfranchisement of over 3,000 slaves had passed through the records of his officers but this was only a small proportion of the numbers of those who had simply returned to their homes or been freed by the Native Courts without registration.

While suppressing indigenous slavery, Lugard was careful that his own labour policy should be above reproach. He was, indeed, well in advance of his period here since forced labour was used in wholesale fashion by his German and French neighbours and, to a lesser extent, for public works, in some British colonies. In the earliest stage of the introduction of European rule, with its need for roads, government buildings, and other minimum equipment of the new state system, some way has to be found to induce a self-subsistent and suspicious peasantry, with no knowledge of money and no need of what it can

[1] *Reports*, 1902, pp. 73 ff. The laws dealing with slavery are No. 11 of 1900, No. 2 of 1901 and No. 27 of 1904. See also *Memoranda*, 1906, No. 6, p. 135.
[2] *Memoranda*, 1906, No. 6, pp. 135-59.

buy, to leave their farms and undertake the wage labour without which no development is possible. European governments in a hurry, and especially their local agents, have not always been scrupulous in choosing methods of persuasion, hence the grim and even blood-stained record of the earlier dealings with African labour. Lugard, however, laid down, even at this early, difficult and penurious moment, that the employment of any kind of unpaid labour was prohibited, and that even customary labour used for the repair of local roads was to be employed under strict rules and was always to be paid.[1] It was by this early experience in humane regulation that Lugard qualified himself in later years to handle questions of labour with authority in international councils.

In surveying the branches of a system of administration in the colonies today one of the first points of interest would be the social services, especially health and education, and the proportion of revenue spent upon them. There is little that can be said under this heading during the first years of British administration in Northern Nigeria: the tentative beginnings in education will best be reviewed at a date when a real effort could be made in this field. But the record of Lugard's first governorship, with the country only half occupied at its beginning, and his lack of men and money, explain why in this brief period he felt himself unable even to begin those services which the people would one day regard as most important of all and, indeed, the main justification for conquest.

---

[1] *Memoranda*, 1906, No. 11, pp. 213-4.

CHAPTER IX

THE HIGH COMMISSIONER

THE MAIN branches of government upon which Lugard built his system of Indirect Rule have been surveyed. We still have to consider his way of working, his relations with others, and the impress of his qualities upon the system he was creating. This is not difficult as he poured himself out day by day upon paper, in a spirit of release from official reserve.

First, as to his manner of work. The design of a large oriental carpet does not reveal on the surface the minute, patient years of stitching which went into its making. So with Lugard. He certainly had a clear design in his head from the first but it was by no grand, proconsular " turn of eye, wave of hand " that he brought it into being. Even during his adventurous past pen and paper had been at least as important a part of his equipment as compass, tent and gun. As a governor, once the phase of conquest was over, he was a man of the desk. He admitted that he could hardly think without the help of paper, a limitation more usual in the scholar than in the administrator. His friends declared that during the six years of his High Commissionership he worked sixteen hours a day while in Nigeria, and eleven hours while on leave, and the records show that the exaggeration was slight. At his desk he interviewed white men and black; there he wrote letters, reports, instructions, telegrams and dispatches, drafted laws, drew up financial estimates and reviewed judicial decisions. All these individual administrative acts must have totalled tens of thousands and all but papers of the merest routine bore the stamp of his mind.

" The work got through under this regime is really enormous. I suppose some 20 more or less difficult legislative proclamations have been dealt with, and are now in process of being printed or on their way home etc. The dispatches to the Secretary of State average I think about 25 a week (about 250 since Jan. 1st) . . . some are long dispatches drafted by myself on difficult subjects. Sokoto Rising, such as I have sent you—Tolls, taxations, etc. I write no more than I can possibly help, usually and chiefly replies to dispatches from home . . . This of course is in addition to correspondence with our West African Governors . . . on various matters which arise, and the whole internal correspondence with 17 Residents and all departments!" (L. to F. L., 15 March 1906).

Yet, in spite of constant reference to his overwork, he did not ask for sympathy.

"I love to have more work than I can do and it exhilarates me sometimes to find really useful work and interesting work accumulating—but I do assure you, dear, that to properly and efficiently do the work of the Protectorate, now that it includes the *whole* area, is more than any living man can do with the staff I have. Why, there is not a man in the section or my office who can draft an ordinary dispatch, or be relied on to correct a proof except Ned, and no one can write a précis of my notes on a report etc." (L. to F. L., 6 May 1904).

In spite of great physical strength he was frequently ill with fever, or from boils, or upset by bad food and water. Here is a record, not untypical, of three of his days at Zungeru, just before he set out upon a tour.

"*Sept.* 13. I had a touch of fever. I am in consequence very headachey and cheap today, with but little voice left, but I shall be quite right to-morrow. Ned looks drawn and ill too, I think. He is harassed by the amount of work, which is more than two men could do. The trip will do him a great deal of good. But the time at Lokoja will be one of high pressure, and of a very worrying class of work to which I do not look forward with any pleasure at all . . .

Sept. 14. I am quite all right today and full of energy and work so you see my fever wasn't very bad, nothing like so bad as the last go. The time for my leaving Zungeru draws very near now . . . of course there are endless matters on which my ' decision is required before I leave '.

Sept. 15. A tremendous storm last night with crashes of thunder so monstrous that Wallace and Ned thought the house struck, deprived me of my evening mouthful of fresh air, and brought us over an inch of rain. Again tonight a violent tornado at sunset with deluges of rain stopped me from going except just to inspect an office . . . and tonight the sandflies and mosquitoes are quite intolerable and I cannot even sit on the verandah . . . "

When he went on tour the discomforts were even worse, and he did little or nothing to make things easier for himself or his companions. Here are a few quotations from letters to his wife dashed off while he was on trek.

Seygina.

" It was a bit of singularly bad luck that all of a sudden yesterday forenoon I felt that I had a touch of fever on me, and felt very cheap indeed. Nevertheless I had to interview the Commissioner of Police etc., but after lunch I went and lay down under blankets. I was most unwilling to upset all arrangements. The baggage and escort had already gone on. So I made a considerable effort and dragged myself off the bed and started with Ned to walk. On the other side of the Kaduna two miles off my horse awaited me, but I had perspired very heavily indeed and thought it better not to sit on a horse in wet things in the night air. So I made up my mind to ' stick it out ', and I walked the whole way to Garam Baggas (about 9 miles in all) where we arrived at 8.15 p.m. I was pretty well ' played out '. This morning we started with the first break of dawn, and I walked 7 miles when we stopped for breakfast. I rode the next 7 into this place. I am not *quite* all right yet, but am taking quinine and shall throw off the malarial effects entirely tomorrow I expect."

(L. to F. L., 2 February 1904).

And again,

" I felt so seedy I had to lie down, and Dr. Tichborne looked in—but in the morning the two French boundary commissioners had arrived, and I had a dinner of 14 in the evening, and had to be there. I pulled through all right, though it was heavy work, and today I remained in bed till late to make up (they stayed till near midnight) and I have done but little work . . . with my inability to *speak* French it has been difficult work, requiring undivided attention and brain work!"

(L. to F. L., 2 May 1904).

And a few months later, while canoeing up the Gongola,

" *Oct. 11th.* We got off about 6.40 a.m. after a tremendous racket of yelling negroes, and blowing off of steam, and bumpings and things, which woke me up before daylight, though I had only turned in at midnight up to which time I was writing my last letter to you . . . The little steam launch has a canoe on each side of her—one of which is occupied by Ned and me, and the other by my office clerks and other such persons . . . We had a violent storm of rain in the afternoon, but were well protected and only a few of Ned's papers and little of his bed got slightly wet. I am a very old stager at this game, and a storm usually finds me fully prepared . . . I have done a very steady day's work at this most confounded Memo. . . . but it is *not* good for the liver to have positively no exercise at all. It is impossible to get out and walk for half an hour, for there is no path, and the banks are swamps up to your waist for the most part—but perhaps higher up there will be an opportunity."

" *Oct. 12th* . . . ' What am I doing in this lovely Easter weather?' Well it registered 96° of a damp heat at breakfast and 100 later, and the smuts of the engine are in my food and my papers and my bed."

" *Oct. 16th.* On my canoe there are Ned and I—8 polers, and one clerk and at least 9 servants including Da Silva's and the Orderly and Interpreter etc. That means over a ton of human flesh . . . "

" *Oct. 28th.* Zungara. We did 21½ miles today . . . crossing the Gongola, here very broad and shallow, but it was up to our horses' girths in places . . . We are now 25 miles from Bauchi, and the feeling I know is strong against doing it in one march. Today's march of 21½ miles tired the men considerably. So I only go to Yuli tomorrow (16½ miles) and march into Bauchi early next day . . . "

Lugard always claimed that no hard work or hard climate could knock him over for more than a few days at a time. This was not, however, medical opinion. On the writer's table lies a document with evidence upon this subject.

" From the Principal Medical Officer to General Sir F. D. Lugard, K.C.M.G., C.B., D.S.O.

" We have the honour to inform you that we have had a consultation re your present state of health and have formed the following opinion:
That you are suffering from Malarial Cachepia.
That you have a dilated stomach.
That you should abstain *absolutely* from any brainwork for the present . . .
That we are strongly of opinion that you should not remain in West Africa over your tour of service, no matter whether you are feeling fit or not.
That you should not return to West Africa after your present tour of service.

(Signed) D. K. McDowell, P.M.O.
Zungeru, 29.9.02   S. M. Langley, S.M.O."

Grave and uncompromising medical advice! Lugard ignored it, stayed on in the country, worked harder than ever—and survived until 1945!

As High Commissioner Lugard had not only to create from the ground upwards a system of administration but also a service to carry it out. The Colonial Service was in time to develop traditions of its own and to accumulate its essential corpus of experience. But in 1900 the Service, above all in Africa, was in its earliest beginnings. It has been said that Lugard's past experiences fitted him well to deal with almost every aspect of administration in Northern Nigeria. But for the all-important task of building up a staff he was not so well prepared. His long records of success in carrying out his work as a " one man show " had, as we have seen many times, made it difficult for him to work with superiors. But neither, of course, had his experience helped him to deal with subordinates, especially men of senior status. He had either worked with almost equal partners such as Williams in Uganda, his brother in Bechuanaland, and Willcocks in Borgu or, for the rest, with wholly inexperienced juniors.

But now he had a service, absurdly small at first for its immense task, but steadily growing in numbers and experience during the six years. How did he use them? The writer for the purposes of this book and for earlier researches, was for many years in touch with some of Lugard's first generation of Residents, most of whom have since died, so that their evidence can be added to his.

Lugard was fortunate in his first senior officers. He inherited the highly experienced William Wallace from the Company to act as his second. No one called him a great administrator but that was not what his Chief wanted or, indeed, could have borne. As it was, with 22 years' service in the country by 1900, he was docile, popular— Lugard generally referred to him as " a dear "—and a living encyclo-paedia of local knowledge, especially of the southernmost provinces. This was a capacity especially useful in a country which had no records. Lugard also took over from the Company Major J. A. Burdon, who had commanded the Royal Niger Constabulary, and Mr. Hewby. Burdon was made the first Resident in Sokoto and Hewby the first in Bornu, two highly important posts. Colonel Morland, though com-mander of the W.A.F.F., should be mentioned because he was full of political knowledge and sense, and was a tower of strength. To these

Lugard added Orr, Gowers, Temple and Palmer. Four of his original group became governors;[1] three wrote important books on Northern Nigeria.[2]

In his relations with these and others of his political staff there were three aspects, though not very easy to disentangle from each other, the personal, the administrative and the political.

On the personal side we have seen that Lugard asked from his officers unreserved devotion to the service. But he was still happier when his officers added to this an allegiance to himself based upon a whole-hearted acceptance of his policy, and he was happiest of all when this allegiance was warmed by a personal affection. What administrator, indeed, does not offer up heartfelt thanks when fortune blesses him with such a relationship with his subordinates? But the greatest administrators are those who have learned to distinguish personal from professional loyalty and to turn to good use instruction and even criticism from below. These capacities, even harder to exercise in a colony, and especially a new colony, than in Britain, were ones which Lugard found it difficult to acquire. It was therefore fortunate that he was able to draw from many, though not quite all, of his senior officers a whole-hearted allegiance. This was true also of many in the lower ranks of the service, some of whose touching letters of admiration and of gratitude for his unobtrusive personal kindness Lugard treasured to the end amongst his papers.

The happy relations Lugard could have with some of his colleagues will be best illustrated by an extract from a letter sent to the writer by one of his earliest Residents, Sir Charles Orr.

" I went home on leave in May 1904, and stayed two or three nights with Lugard at Government House in Zungeru on my way down to the coast, so meeting him for the first time in person. Instead of the hard, stern man I had led myself to expect, I found to my surprise a small man with a charming smile, a rather shy manner, and a friendliness which took me captive at once. Obviously he was absolutely engrossed in his work, and never spared himself. Except at meals I never saw him until after dinner, when we would sit out on the verandah, and he would then ask me search-

---

[1] These were Orr, of the Bahamas, Gowers of Uganda, Palmer of the Gambia and Cyprus and Burdon of British Honduras.

[2] Orr, *The Making of Northern Nigeria*; C. L. Temple, *Native Races and Their Rulers* (Cape Town, 1918); H. R. Palmer, *The Bornu Sahara and Sudan* (1936). Palmer also published some translations of Arab chronicles dealing with the Western Sudan.

ing questions about my work and every detail of it. But what struck me most was that he asked me constantly for my opinion about various matters of administration, evidently genuinely seeking for knowledge, although I felt positive that he knew infinitely more about such matters than I had even begun to learn. But it gave me the impression that he regarded me as one of a team with which he was working, and that he just happened to be the captain. My whole previous life had been, as I have said, spent in the Army, where in those days no one was supposed to think for himself . . . Lugard was in fact a revelation to me. Here was a man that I could serve with my whole heart and soul. And he somehow encouraged one to reveal oneself frankly . . . for he could read one like a book and could not be hood-winked or deceived. And during those few evenings I began to feel that he trusted me, and believed that I was just as genuinely keen on the job we had in hand as he was himself; and in the very act of believing this of me and showing me that be believed it, he bound me to the job as firmly as he was bound himself. I became then and there ' one of Lugard's men ', and to the day of my death I shall be prouder of that title than of any other that could be bestowed upon me. Lugard founded a kind of school of men, and from this school his influence spread like the ripples in a pond . . . With him, one's job was indeed everything and took precedence over all one's private and personal interests."

Another officer, who was for a time Lugard's private secretary, felt a similar devotion to his master, which he described to the writer.

" His view was that difficulties were made to be overcome. Political Officers who stood up to them received encouragement, as did all constructive suggestions and a recital of things *done*. In all his comments on progress reports one felt a master mind at work whose grip of broad principles was firm and sure and he assuredly knew how to get the best out of his instruments."

So far so good! But when the enquiry is pushed more widely amongst his staff we find a conflict of evidence and even some hints of criticism or discontent. Time, of course, affected the relationship. During the first years Lugard towered above his staff in authority and experience. But as a small group of first-class Residents emerged who had an increasing knowledge of their provinces, and also an increasing self-confidence in their own ideas of administering them, his domination had either to be adjusted in response or to be brought at least a little into question. In the last half of his Commissionership there were signs, here and there, of some strain within the service.

A senior officer in Nigeria whose work obliged him, some years later, to go through the papers of this period, informed the writer that he was surprised and even shocked to read Lugard's distrustful and discouraging comments to some of his Residents. He noted especially a letter from Burdon, Resident at Sokoto, to Lugard complaining that it was impossible for him to say how discouraged he was by the carping and criticism that came from the High Commissioner.

How could Lugard show two such different selves to different men? The answer lies in the peculiarities of his temperament. Either the long-drawn-out conflict of his love-affair, or the years of lonely travel, had left him the victim of alternate moods of black reserve and of a longing for affection. It was, therefore, a hard blow of fate that when, having late in life achieved a happy marriage, the Nigerian climate decreed a separation. Not surprisingly, he found the perfect assistant, because the perfect friend, in his brother Edward. They shared the bond of family, the same military training and, except that the brother never lost his faith in Christianity, the same general outlook upon life. Edward's affection was joined with a whole-hearted admiration, a homage rooted in his own humility. As he remained unprovoked by his brother's cold, dark moods the older man could indulge them without fear of offence or misunderstanding. In 1903 Lugard persuaded the Colonial Office to appoint Edward as Chief Clerk, Office of High Commissioner, with the rank of Second Class Resident. The Office later became critical of this unusual appointment but at the time they accepted it in their conviction that Lugard was not the man to recommend his brother unless this were the best thing for Nigeria.[1]

Lugard recognized what he owed to his brother, and confessed it freely to his wife.

" In a certain clerical ability on my office stool I ' pass ' Ned (as the local phrase goes)—and in some other ways I am the ' predominant partner ', but in human worth—in self control—in unselfishness, in ability to make others happy—as well as in a certain application of *nous* to the ordinary affairs of life, he beats me, dear—quite beats me."

(L. to F. L., 1 August 1904).

[1] Minutes on Lugard to Chamberlain, 1 March 1903, C.O. 446/30.

Edward was working neither for pay nor ambition: he was ready to go on to all hours and had to be ordered away from his desk.

> " I have sent Ned off for a shoot in the jungle. He was most reluctant to go, dear boy—wanted to ' clear his table ' etc., I told him he would continue to want that till he left N. Nigeria, and bundled him off—I miss Ned so much when he is away like this . . . and I do hope, dear, that I shall grow more conversational and less three-cornered thanks to his influence . . . I marvel how he can stand me sometimes—but he makes allowances and though I hurt him and often rile him dreadfully, he forgives instantly and his wonderful affection for me dwarfs all my shortcomings. It is a wonderful thing." (L. to F. L., 26 March 1904).

Unfortunately, the very comfort of having this other self as his chief assistant may have relieved Lugard from the effort of making friends with those of his colleagues whom he found less congenial. His wife tried to use her influence in the right direction and he was frequently obliged to defend himself against her gentle criticism. His replies showed that while understanding and affection could unlock all the hidden kindness of his nature, it might be wintry weather for those officers who came with opposition or challenge or merely, perhaps, with the natural self-assertion of an independent spirit. For Lugard was a severe man. The Nigerian correspondence of these early years, and the minutes upon his papers, show at once the persevering thoroughness with which he pushed every query—and these were numerous and detailed—right through to the firmest possible conclusion and also his unhesitating infliction of punishment, including dismissal, upon any member of his service who transgressed his strict laws of personal and professional behaviour. One political officer was dismissed for shooting three giraffes without a licence and there are other instances of dismissal for offences of no great depravity. It is possible that in his lonely eminence in a new country and with an inexperienced service this was the only way in which he could have achieved the rapid execution of his policy. Those whom he most valued did not escape his discipline but they also experienced his trust. Among those of the inner circle were Morland, Abadie, Nicholson, Eaglesome and Orr: in the outer circle were Kemball, Temple, Burdon and Gowers, with Palmer perhaps in a half-way position.

On the administrative side the main charges of Lugard's critics were that he over-centralized and that he overworked his staff.

Lugard's besetting sin was undoubtedly his unwillingness to delegate. The trouble began at the centre. Lugard complained of the utter inadequacy of his headquarters' staff, relieved only by the entry of his brother, and the crushing load of routine work this put upon his shoulders. But the Colonial Office was informed otherwise, and believed what it was told. We can now see one of the reasons for Lugard's attitude towards General Kemball. As early as September, 1900, Lugard wrote to his brother that Kemball, who had just taken over the Frontier Force from Willcocks, had disheartened him by accusing him of " doing everything oneself and not trusting others or of writing too much " and the soldier took his criticisms to Downing Street. Here it was noted that one of Lugard's chief assistants at headquarters resigned because he was not given any responsible work to do,[1] and two years later Antrobus remarked that Lugard did not know how to make use of a trained Secretariat.[2] One of his difficulties arose from his very love of work: because he *could* do everything, he *would* do it. " I do not," he told his wife, " merely look on it as ' something usefully done '—there is to me the pleasure in the doing of it . . . I hope I may not bother about the results achieved till I am on the wrong side of eighty." (L. to F. L., 24 December 1903). It was this which made it difficult for him to distinguish between work proper to him and the less important duties.

" I am rushed," he wrote, in what was in fact a confession, " from early till late with endless details of no importance which strangle the work one wants to do. But I simply *can't bear* to see the details mismanaged or badly done and so I do them or supervise them and my time goes and the things that matter get squeezed out! . . . It is in a sense a curse of Nature. I must and am trying to alter it." (L. to F. L., 27 December 1903).

The effect of this upon the administration as a whole can be imagined. "A born centralizer," was the opinion of one of his more detached colleagues, given to the writer, while another spoke of " his passion for centralization. He seemed to be constitutionally incapable of delegating responsibility." On this question, too, his wife added her tactful pressure. He had represented himself to her once as the plodding bricklayer who did not arrogate himself to be architect or builder, and she had turned this against him as a reproof.

[1] Minute by Antrobus on Lugard to Chamberlain, 6 October 1900, C.O. 446/11.
[2] Minute on Lugard to Chamberlain, 17 November 1902, C.O. 446/25.

" In theory," he replied, " I am fully of your view as regards delegation of work (*à propos* of my being bricklayer instead of only Architect and Builder) but I will talk to you of this presently, when I come home—and you shall refer to Ned too, and he can explain how impossible it is to delegate, when delegation means that I have eventually to do it all over again in a longer form. I do, however, delegate a *very great deal* neces-sarily—especially to Ned."   (L. to F. L., 10 December 1904).

The last three words are all too-revealing. For the period of the High Commissionership Lugard's fault was kept in bounds by the conditions of the country which at this time made any really damaging over-centralization impossible. Until the telegraph reached the main centres of administration, as one officer of this period explained to the writer, " political officers had to act rather on their own judgment and initiative almost every day in their dealings with novel situations un-known in settled dependencies." Lugard tried to enclose this initiative within the bounds of his policy through his very full *Memoranda* but in these he himself recognized—and it is important to remember this— that in political matters there must be some freedom of action and variety of method. We have seen from the evidence of one Resident that Lugard did listen to his senior staff and the writer owes to Sir Richmond Palmer the valuable point that his chief tried to impose an administrative rather than a political centralization.

But in so far as Lugard did achieve centralization, a case can be made out for it during these six years or at least during the first four of them. He not only was, but had to be, the sole originator of policy. The Colonial Office had little or no experience of the immensely difficult problems he was attacking. Even in the succeeding years leading on to colonial independence the Office never developed anything compar-able to a general staff, and gave little, if any, positive guidance in the handling of those political problems which are generally individual to each territory. In what direction, indeed, in his isolation and with the need for quick decisions, could Lugard either delegate or look for guidance? His handful of political officers were, it must be repeated, utterly inexperienced and untrained. "There may have been more ", his then private secretary told the writer, " but in my five years I only came across one who had had previous administrative experience. For that reason the whole pattern of provincial administration had to be set out in detail; hence the number of memoranda and directives.

Exactly how far the success and durability of the Northern Nigerian administration was due to their execution by the Political Officers is impossible to say, but I can say that in a totally unknown country with an untrained administrative staff, instructions that lacked the clarity, precision and detail of Lugard's, would most certainly not have resulted in the enduring success and administrative stability which ensued . . . "

The second administrative fault with which Lugard was charged was that of seriously overworking his staff. In the early years of the Protectorate deaths were so frequent that it was decided, because of the depressing effect, not to mark the occasions by flying the flag at half-mast. "I can testify," the late Mr. R. Nicholson told the writer, " that of the nine Europeans in Muri in 1905 all were dead by 1908 except myself and all were men in the late twenties or early thirties except one who was just over forty." But apart even from death or formal sick-leave, there were the days or weeks when men in lonely stations struggled to work while half their strength was drained away from them by malaria, by the effects of bad food or water, or of extremes of heat or damp. These had to be endured in makeshift quarters while time and energy had to be given to long tours on foot or in the saddle. Here the fundamental query which hung over Indirect Rule and which has been discussed theoretically obtruded itself into practical administration. Already, it seems, some of Lugard's officers wanted to push its principle of delegation to Africans further than he wished. Orr, because of his personal devotion to Lugard, was able to speak frankly to him and he complained not only, as we have seen, of overwork, but of the reason for overwork in that political officers were being asked to do what, in his view, should have been left to the emirs. We need not repeat all his arguments, but this is what he wrote on the margin of his correspondence. " 'Jekadas [tax collectors] are corrupt,' says Sir F. L. ' Sweep 'em away; natives can't be trusted. Residents must personally assess,' etc., etc., and so we are being broken down with overwork and the natives are sullen and discontented."[1]

Though devoted to his chief, and quite willing to work himself to death if necessary, he was moved to question this necessity. In his report for Zaria province for 1905, an unpublished report sent to the writer, he complained that

[1] From papers given to the writer by Sir Charles Orr. This is undated but appears to be 1905.

" . . . the congestion of work is appalling, and I do not think the strain can be continued indefinitely. I find it necessary to continue work throughout Saturdays, Sundays, and holidays just as on other days, and even so arrears accumulate and work has to be skimped. I think it right to lay these facts frankly before Your Excellency and submit that if the European staff cannot be increased or casualties filled, some change in the system is unavoidable: the change I would indicate is to leave more work in the hands of the Native Administration, and to watch and guide it rather than to take the details out of its hands."

Lugard replied sympathetically, asking for Orr's views about delegation, and it was typical of Lugard's thoroughness that later, when he was spending his leave revising the *Political Memoranda*, he sent Orr a copy of his reply remarking " This is very old date but I do not recollect having received any reply." Orr therefore wrote at length urging that the emirates should have been run as " Native States, with the British Government keeping well in the background."

" It is an invidious task to complain of overwork, and very thankless. But when I think of the death roll and invalidings and shattered constitutions and put it down as I do far more to the effects of constant overwork than to climatic conditions, I naturally ask myself if it is not possible by some radical change to lessen the strain without at the same time permitting culpable misrule and oppression under the aegis of the British Government. If it *is* impossible, then I accept the death-roll."

(Orr to L., 26 September 1908).

Lugard's reply is interesting " I have not any accurate knowledge of what the regime in an Indian protected State is, but I think that on the whole in general principles the system established in N. Nigeria is not very dissimilar, except in matters where more direct control is in the nature of things unavoidable." He went on to show that in the conditions of Northern Nigeria neither tax collection, police nor the army could, as in India, be handed over to the emirs. " If you consider these things I think you will concur that the India ' Protected States ' system cannot be adopted in its entirety, but I think we have got a fairly good compromise between pukka Administration and it." He ended with a most characteristic remark, " I think myself that work does not kill, it is the bad food and bad housing, the latter especially, which is I think accountable for the death-roll." " No," wrote Orr, in the margin,

" it is ceaseless overwork *combined* with the bad houses and the bad food." (L. to Orr, 29 October 1906).

Lugard's contacts were not only downwards with his officers but upwards with the Colonial Office. In Northern Nigeria he seems at first sight to be behaving as if he were an autocrat. As the friend and personal choice of Chamberlain, dealing with a novel and dangerous kind of dependency, he might have expected to be run on a very loose rein from Downing Street. His private letters and the Colonial Office archives tell a very different story and show that in so far as he ran free it was only by pulling hard on the bit and sometimes by bolting. It is with a sense of shock that the discovery is made that this now famous piece of work was carried on under an almost constant fire of disapproval from the Colonial Office which was bitterly repelled by Lugard. The three officials most concerned with his administration at this time were Antrobus, Ommaney and Strachey.[1]

The evidence must, however, be used with caution. The average official who writes brief confidential minutes on a governor's correspondence is largely concerned to point out flaws, inconsistencies and dangers, while on Lugard's side we learn his reactions mainly from his very uninhibited correspondence with his wife. Thus the evidence tends to be the extremes of negative criticism upon one side and the maximum of angry retort on the other.

Seventy years before his appointment the civil servant in the Colonial Office had been satirized as " Mr. Mother Country ", the very ordinary bureaucrat who " has a modest home in the outskirts of London " upon whom the ever changing Secretaries and Under-Secretaries of State have become helplessly dependent; who has established secret and irresponsible but steady rule over the colonies and thinks that he and his associates in " the Office " are the only people in the world who understand anything about the colonies.[2] There was still, or so Lugard would have said in his most resentful moments, some truth in Buller's description of the Colonial Office official of his day, and the resentment of the man of deeds for the man of words was always ready to flare up in Lugard's mind at every sign of bureaucratic insensitiveness to

[1] Strachey, (later Sir) Charles, K.C.M.G., 1862-1942; 1885-99 Foreign Office; 1900 Colonial Office; 1919 represented Colonial Office at Peace Conference; 1924-7 Assistant Under-Secretary for the Colonies.

[2] Charles Buller, *Mr. Mother-Country of the Colonial Office* (1840), reprinted in E. G. Wakefield, *A View of the Art of Colonization* (1849), pp. 279-296.

the harsh realities of his task. One day, for example, going up the Benue near Yola, he ran into an area of famine.

" The wretched people have eaten their seed corn, and have none to plant, and so there are no crops coming on. They are eating grass and dying by hundreds, and the corpses are floating down the river . . . It is pitiful. I telegraphed long ago to the Secretary of State, ' What are you prepared to sanction for famine relief?' and the reply was, ' the estimates must not be exceeded '. . . . The pagans are selling their children for 1s/- to 2s/- and we lately caught a caravan of over 100 bought on these terms for a few handfuls of grain. These I must somehow accommodate in my Slave Home. Dear, doesn't it strike you as wonderful how these things can go on, and the Mandarins sit in their office chairs—the Stracheys and the Antrobi—and find fault and talk indifferently of the whole matter, wagging their legs, seated on a table edge . . . I am face to face only with what I have so often been before—viz. the appalling waste of life and misery of Africa before we came. This, I say to myself, is what has gone on through the ages—it is foolish to fret because the misery of ages cannot be cured in a year or two. We have done much—yes, dear, I your husband, can feel that I have done very much to alter all this—and we must just be patient and bow our heads to the rule of the office clerk, and do our best with the means allowed us. I have strained my tether as you know, I have gone for Sokoto and Kano without official sanction. I have over-spent my estimates. But from the Administrator's point of view, this is the psychological moment to get in touch with all these tribes, to bring them under our rule without firing a shot—at the expense of a few tons of corn, instead of costly expeditions and money spent in ammunition."

(L. to F. L., 7 October 1904).

Lugard's uneasy relations with the Colonial Office arose, however, from something more definite than their contrasting views of his task as seen from the Niger and the Thames. Before questions of policy were reached there was criticism of much smaller points, the technique, for example, of his correspondence. It is surprising to anyone who knew the military orderliness which in later years reigned on Lugard's desk and in his library, to read the harsh minutes penned in Whitehall condemning his " vicious habit of mixing subjects ", or of ignoring later correspondence " with his usual facility "; drawing up " slovenly " proclamations, sending a pensions list that was " a careless performance ", and perpetrating inaccurate arithmetic and unsound estimates.

To Lugard the picture of an official sitting comfortably at his desk and censuring him for some technical error while he, overwhelmed with work, sweating with heat, sick with fever, perhaps, struggling single-handed with endless sheets of figures was, almost in the literal sense, maddening. Worst of all, he had to start with no administrative precedents.

" . . . I must get all my next year's Estimates done first, and as there is no previous Estimate, including the W.A.F.F. to go upon, and the whole concern has to be reorganized in every department, and no departmental officer knows how to prepare his estimate, I have to do every single figure myself and it is a colossal task. First a rough estimate down to a button—then each reassessed and pared down to get the whole within the mark, and this must be done a dozen times before I shall succeed, and I never get a clear spell of time to get at it."   (L. to E. J. L., 13 December, 1900).

The two larger questions which caused the greatest flow of angry ink were those concerning Lugard's finances and his staff.

When he was defeated upon the main financial issue he did all he could in small ways, and especially by what most Colonial Service officials would regard as legitimate sleight of hand over the estimates, to get money for his favourite schemes. Early in 1903, for example, he wanted to get some more money for his Zungeru railway but this provoked a caustic minute that the original demand, by the process of automatic growth common in Lugard's estimates, was now quietly replaced by a greater sum.[1] The minute declared firmly that neither the Colonial Office nor the Treasury would acquiesce in his methods. When Lugard pleaded for more money for his telegraphs the officials refused, remarking that every piece of work in Northern Nigeria, since it was on a grant-in-aid, involved an extraordinary appeal to the Treasury. Four months later Lugard was accused by Antrobus of trying to force their hand again over his beloved little railway. At the end of the same month Strachey identified another of Lugard's stratagems, that of calling expenditure on Public Works "Extra Capital Expenditure", and assuming that for this he need not keep within the estimate but could take what he wanted from his balances. (Lugard found this exposure especially hard. For what, in his thrifty way, had he been saving for at all except for some cherished project?) In August, 1902, however, he managed to push his estimates up by

[1] Minutes on Lugard to Chamberlain, 30 January 1903, C.O. 446/30.

£35,000 to £390,000 and to get them approved. In his minute of acceptance, Chamberlain stated with a defensive glance at the Treasury, " The situation has altogether changed, not by our fault or initiative, since we first took over the country."¹ This financial truce was temporarily shattered by Abadie, infected with his Chief's enthusiasm for the railway, buying an engine and truck for it out of his own pocket while on leave. This greatly affronted the Office as it was felt to be a dodge to force their hand as they would now be practically obliged to purchase it.²

Another quarrel arose from the restless fertility of Lugard's mind. He wanted to hasten the process of Nigerian civilization by borrowing from somewhat more advanced countries. Over his demand for a consignment of mules a little storm blew up. Antrobus, perhaps the least severe of his Whitehall critics, delivered himself of a general indictment of the High Commissioner's methods which, it is fortunate to remember, Lugard never saw.

" Sir F. Lugard has many good qualities. He has plenty of ' go ', he is full of ideas, and he is not afraid of taking responsibility. But he is not a prudent or far-seeing administrator, his schemes are not well thought out, and he has more than once involved us in heavier expenditure than was contemplated. We have not hesitated to let him try experiments when it seemed worthwhile to do so."³

The Office set itself to work to a total expenditure of not more than half a million and though the opinion was privately given to the Secretary of State in 1904, that " it is remarkable that such an administration as we have now in Northern Nigeria should have been established with such a small capital account," while even " the ordinary expenditure was not excessive,"⁴ it does not appear that Lugard was ever allowed to overhear this admission or be released from the anguish of grinding economy.

Lugard had two major quarrels with the Office over staff. He was angry because, when he was doing all he could to train and encourage his overworked staff, composed largely of men he had selected himself, the Colonial Office would suddenly impose upon him some " old chestnut " or " old coaster from Sierra Leone " and demand that he

¹ Minute on Lugard to Chamberlain, 28 August 1902, C.O. 446/32.
² Minutes on Lugard to Lyttelton, 13 January 1904, C.O. 446/38.
³ Minute on Lugard to Lyttelton, 16 September 1904, C.O. 446/40.
⁴ Minute by Antrobus on Lugard to Lyttelton, 26 September 1904, C.O. 446/40.

should be put over some able and aspiring officer, whose devoted work Lugard had been meaning to endorse and encourage with promotion. It was not, he told his wife, their " clucking " at him that worried him but their sending out incompetent men and so endangering the whole edifice which had a very narrow margin of safety.

But he was also continually demanding more officers and complaining bitterly when refused. The Office would justify themselves by indignantly minuting that they had not in fact refused his demands. Moreover, although Chamberlain had wanted a unified military force in West Africa, he had given way before Lugard's passion for independence and allowed him his separate Northern Nigerian regiment which gave him greater freedom to use his military officers in support of civilian administration.

What fused the two issues of finance and administration was Lugard's proposal, in 1905, to introduce a full system of direct taxation with all the extra work this would involve. The officials declared—and here we come upon the fundamental disagreement—that if his political staff were grossly over-worked, it was because Lugard had embarked upon a system of government of an ambitious kind that had never been intended when the country had been taken over from the Company. This condemnation of Lugard's policy will serve, if history finally approves the High Commissioner's administration, to deny the Colonial Office much share in the credit for the achievement. In 1905 Antrobus minuted upon Lugard's plans for raising more local taxation:

> " The policy to which Sir F. Lugard is anxious to commit the Government in Northern Nigeria is not the policy which was laid down by Mr. Chamberlain when he took over the Niger territory. Sir F. Lugard wants to incur a much heavier expenditure, and to interfere much more in the administration of the country than was intended . . .
>
> Sir F. Lugard was bitterly disappointed, for as Sir G. Goldie told me, he had expected to have the spending of millions and he found himself limited to a few hundreds of thousands . . . "[1]

The effect of this view upon Lugard could easily be imagined. We have, indeed, his own words, written a little earlier, when the official attitude was first revealed.

" What has vexed me as you know is their lack of appreciation of great

[1] Minute on Lugard to Lyttelton, 26 April 1905, C.O. 446/45.

interests. I sent you an extract from the one which was the worst (together with my reply) when they said that they did not desire N.N. to be
' administered ', all they required was to carry on as cheaply as possible in
the circumstances and N.N. had not reached the higher level of administration necessary in other W. African possessions. Dear, it is profoundly
irritating to reach such a declaration after one had worked very hard for
seven years. I myself (perhaps vainly) think that the stage we have
reached here is beyond that of S.N. and some other places. But it shows
such profound lack of interest, such ignorance of facts, such ignoring of
things that they must know. It is therefore more disheartening than any
lack of personal courtesy, and it was contained in the dispatch reviewing
the annual estimates, which Lyttelton[1] must have seen (or should have
done) for it is one of the most important dispatches of the year, and it is
printed and circulated to every other Colony. My reply was I think
strong in its simple and brief exposé, but that will not be printed or
circulated I expect! . . . They do not worry me, but they cause me to feel
that the C.O. and myself are working for opposite ends, and that is a bad
thing for a Governor to recognize and admit to himself. Bad for the
Empire, and bad for the C.O. They will not make the slightest difference
in my work or my policy by letters of this sort—they only create a
divergence and a lack of confidence. I am ready to resign at a shadow of
hint if they wish it, and prefer to put in a man who will carry out their
own retrograde policy. But while I am here I will only work for my
conceptions and my ideas of what is best, so they had better if they disapprove get someone else and not write letters which merely tend to make
me desire to keep them uninformed and ' run my own show ' without
their aid, and free of their opposition."

(L. to F. L., 2 March 1905).

These were strong words for a servant of Whitehall, and they were
addressed to a wife who could, and did, go back to her old haunts at
the Colonial Office and confront the officials with the effects of their
conduct upon her husband.

The Colonial Office developed their ideas further later in the year
when Lugard was still pressing his taxation proposals. They pointed
out that Lugard had always acted on the wholly erroneous sequence of
ideas that if he could raise more local revenue he could follow a more
ambitious policy; that for this he created more staff to collect the
revenue, and he therefore made his Residents believe that their promo-

[1] Lyttelton, the Rt. Hon. Alfred, P.C., 1857-1913; 1895-1906 M.P., Leamington; 1903-5
Secretary of State for the Colonies.

tion depended upon their zeal in collecting taxation. The Office protested that they had never pressed him to collect more taxation, still less to impose such heavy duties upon his staff.

" He also seems to have persuaded himself and has conveyed the idea to others that we are always urging him to produce more local revenue which is not the case. I don't believe we care a straw whether the local revenue is £50,000 or £100,000," [There was a marginal note here that the Treasury might care!] " and though we naturally prefer that something should be contributed by the country towards meeting its own expenses, we do not want this put forward as a reason for putting on the screw either by imposing taxation or by trying to get more than can fairly be expected out of the staff."[1]

All that the Office wanted was administration upon a " care and maintenance " basis with the utmost economy combined with a high degree of delegation to the native rulers. "Emphasize the fact," wrote the Secretary of State, Mr. Lyttelton, " that we have not pressed the increase of revenue upon Sir F. Lugard however glad we may be to have it when it is obtained without undue sacrifice."[2]

Lugard made a final attempt to get his way in 1905 when he went to the Colonial Office while on leave. But he failed.

Emphasis may have been given here to the negative side of Lugard's relations with the Colonial Office; the great bulk of day-to-day contacts were positive or at least neutral. Yet all the official correspondence is bleak reading, so little warmed is it by a sense of common purpose, still less by any shared enthusiasm for a large and adventurous task. Once, when his wife reported to him a talk with Antrobus in which the civil servant revealed his very decided preference for the neighbouring—or rival?—Governor, Sir Ralph Moor, Lugard replied in words which showed how much he felt this under-valuation.

" For myself, dear, I do not think it is a matter of great moment how Antrobus regards me, but I deplore and do not feel inclined to laugh at the result upon the interests I have at heart. I have long felt that there is a steady wall of dislike and opposition to me and my methods at the Colonial Office. Were you to be in my office you would find ample proof of what I say, I think. It is a pity for the work's sake and I fear it is

[1] Minute by Strachey on Lugard to Lyttelton, 26 March 1905, C.O. 446/44.
[2] Minute on Lugard to Lyttelton, 26 April 1905, C.O. 446/45.

the fault of my own impatience and contempt for some of their methods, and the little pains I have been at to disperse it . . ."

(L. to F. L., 19 August 1904).

If there were times when Lugard raged against the " maddening indifference " of the Colonial Office, yet there were others when he almost enjoyed the conflict. " I really do believe," he exclaimed once, " I should like my work less if I had not this C.O. obstruction to contend against!—It is essentially a part of the difficulty to be overcome, and anything that lessened the difficulty would lessen the interest in the work." (L. to F. L., 13 April, 1905).

There is support for this view in the surprising fact that his personal relations with his two chief official bugbears, Antrobus and Ommaney, when he met them on leave, were not unfriendly. After working with them in London, he would throw back to Flora from the boat amiable comments upon the pair. While agreeing with his wife's view that there was at the Office " a determination not to admire or praise anything done in Northern Nigeria," he good-humouredly, if somewhat ironically, excused Antrobus on the grounds that he, Lugard, was, after all, " a complete outsider ", " a mere officer of Foot " imported from the Kalahari desert to the dignity of High Commissioner and that he ought to have shown more gratitude and consideration to the officials. After all, " I think I might have fared very much worse than by having Antrobus at the head of the Department . . . " He might indeed! It is an illuminating comment on the situation, and a very necessary one since we have seen the Colonial Office from the Niger through Lugard's somewhat distorting spectacles, to quote a passage from a letter from the son of Antrobus to the writer. This shows how utterly unaware this official was, as he went conscientiously about his work, of the degree of frustration Lugard was feeling. " My father always talked so enthusiastically about Lord Lugard and all the work in West Africa which he, Lord Lugard, and Mr. Chamberlain did together."[1]

If the most important and original part of Lugard's work was carried out in despite of the Colonial Office rather than with its support or understanding, there was always one exception to this rule. Once military action had begun, though not before—for we shall see again how greatly the Office distrusted Lugard's *approach* to such action—

[1] Mr. M. E. Antrobus to M.P., 28 October 1959.

all questions ceased. There was an absolute confidence in his ability as a fighting man. To Lugard this was a poor consolation: it was as an administrator that he wanted freedom and appreciation.

A further explanation of the difficulties of his position lies in the ignorance and indifference of the British public which, unavoidably, perhaps, in face of the number of the colonies and the unfamiliarity of their problems, was reflected in Parliament and left the Colonial Secretary and, still more, the departmental authorities with very little guidance or check. Hence the colonial governor, himself with insufficient knowledge of the many metropolitan considerations which dictate decisions in Downing Street, was left to face a group of officials with equally insufficient knowledge of the realities in a given colony. The colonial peoples themselves, unable in the first period of annexation to understand what was happening to them or what their new masters were attempting to do with them, failed, except by irrational outbreaks of violence, to express *their* opinion. The two sides, Colonial Office and colonial governor, were thus left to hammer out policy, largely by means of dispatch and telegram, without the controlling direction which, in handling domestic matters, ministers draw from public opinion through parliament. Only a strong and knowledgeable Secretary of State, big enough to choose and to trust big men for posts overseas and with time enough in office in which to create and carry out a policy—and how many of these have there been?—could master this conflict. Only a thoroughly informed and interested public could close it. Lugard, deprived, first by Chamberlain's South African distractions and then by his resignation, of the strong and sympathetic support upon which he had counted, tried to continue, in spite of the limitations of his position, the appeal to public opinion he had begun as a freelance. There was a clear purpose in the immense amount of reporting which he achieved and it was not one which was likely to endear him to the officials whom he was endeavouring to outflank. At the end of 1905 he explained his policy to his wife.

" The reviews of my Annual Report are very encouraging and kind. If one can command public interest and attention, one can afford to treat the Treasury strictures with indifference. For after all the Public are our Masters, and it is the Nation that pays the grant-in-aid. I have this evening been reading a long Treasury censure upon me for exceeding certain

Votes, some of it was rather strong . . . I regard the Annual Report, therefore, as a great opportunity and one which with the expenditure of some time and labour may do more to further the interests of the country and to strengthen my own position than can be achieved by much patient labour out here, and still less by writing long expositions and apologies to the Treasury . . . while acknowledging the S. of S. as my Chief, and the authority of the Treasury as fully as possible, I do not consider myself to be their servant but the servant of the King and the Nation. In the ultimate resort it is to these I wish to justify my action, it is these I wish to convert to the view that present expenditure is needful and is being usefully spent as capital outlay on a great estate, and it is to these that I wish (through my Chief) to give an account of my Stewardship. That is a conception of my duties which raises me above the level of a subordinate, and makes me able to accept the criticism of the Antrobi, and the more hostile microbes of the Treasury, with comparative indifference."

(L. to F. L., 29 December 1905).

His wife replied with a not wholly imaginary account of how each official, first for one timid reason and then for another, had cut a piece out of one of his reports and she reflected that, had the Colonial Office been more fully staffed, nothing would have been left of the document.

Yet, in the six years of his High Commissionership, Lugard did learn some degree of docility, at least outwardly. This was due in part to advancing years and wisdom, in part to the mellowing influence of his marriage, but mainly to his success in keeping a very large sphere for free action especially in the political and closely connected military affairs which meant most to him. As a result he was the victor at least for the moment. He succeeded, at great cost both to his officers and to himself, in forcing through a policy which the imperial government had not been prepared to sanction because it was unwilling to provide the necessary money and staff.

Though our analysis has led on to the listing of his administrative merits and defects there must be something unrealistic about such a distinction. His quality was indivisible. He took the whole burden on himself, made decisions and saw them carried through to the last penny, the last man, and the last syllable of a regulation. He combined this hard will and a swift decisiveness in action with the character of an immensely laborious administrator. There was truth in his own view as expressed to his wife:

" . . . I have accepted this job on my shoulders and I run it right through whether on leave or in Nigeria . . . Most men have a second . . . I really have none. Hence the pressure—and hence (as *I* think) whatever of success I have achieved, for tasks of this kind can't be shared. The time will come later on when I can decentralize more, but *creation* is the task of an individual, not of many." (L. to F. L., 1 December 1903).

The claim seems just and the qualities we have discussed in Lugard, if they would count as faults in other situations, were for these pioneering years the virtues that made possible his success. And they were such as can leave no doubt that, whatever measure of advice he did accept from below, whatever changes took place later, he was the creator of the system of Indirect Rule. All his papers on the subject, from the one he wrote before he landed in Nigeria, to his last Annual Report and his revised *Memoranda*, lead to this conclusion.

We must now turn to quite another aspect of the work of these six years. In our generation, which has seen a development towards colonial, and certainly Nigerian, self-government of a kind never imagined by Lugard and his colleagues in the first decade of this century, interest has shifted to the native side and indeed the native view of the imperial association. Already, among the millions of Africans, the first few hundreds, if not more, are studying the beginnings through foreign conquest of a modern state in their country. Their first question must be " What of us, and what of our fathers? How were *they* treated and how regarded?" And the standard that many of them will apply—are already applying—is not their own old standard, or even that of the Europe of half a century ago. It is the highest reached or professed today in those many pronouncements which the party conflict and the colonial and world situation has evoked from British politicians. By these standards Lugard will be judged to have fallen short unless a sincere effort is made to see him as he was, working within the beliefs, purposes and conditions of his day.

When the avowedly Christian nations of Europe decided to occupy tropical Africa with its anonymous and uncivilized millions, they sent their agents into a moral as well as a physical wilderness and these very often lost sight of their domestic standards of conduct. Lugard claimed for himself that he represented the humanity and justice of the best type of English gentleman. He was also responsible to a Parliament and public opinion which, in the main, took its lead from that type, still self-consciously existing. He was further subject to the criticism of organized humanitarian groups, some of them Christian. It would be difficult to estimate whether, in the invisible scales of his consciousness, his personal standards or his official accountability to his nation weighed the most. There were occasions when he believed himself obliged, in order to fulfil his commission, to take action from which the Colonial Office and others in England tried to dissociate themselves. This attitude he condemned as unrealistic and hypocritical. He believed that his standards were higher than those followed by other occupiers and rulers of Africa in his day, and, in the main, in the face of great difficulties and temptations, he adhered to them, though there are two important incidents that may later invite question.

In the use of force we have already seen that he did all he could to avoid bloodshed or at least to restrict it to the few who were the core of resistance or of rebellion. His reports abound in examples of this scrupulous economy, and of his satisfaction when positions were taken with a minimum of loss to the peoples both of life and property. Upon punitive expeditions he held strong views. " Yesterday," he told his brother (a fellow-soldier and the last person to whom he would have struck an attitude even if that had been one of his habits), " I got the backs of the troops up by some straight talking on the subject of punitive expeditions and the laws of humanity, and I was told that I had a bias against soldiers and neither trusted them nor believed them to be anything but fools." (L. to E. J. L., 29 July 1900). It especially distressed him when measures had to be taken against the fierce, shy pagans. But when it is remembered that these often wiped out whole caravans of traders and also that, for lack of famine relief, which British administration alone could bring them, they sold their children and even themselves wholesale into slavery as an alternative to starvation, the single sharp lesson which might be necessary to bring them within the *Pax Britannica* might seem a small price to pay for its benefits.

> " So called 'punitive expeditions', which leave behind them only the memories of a raid and bloodshed, are detestable from the point of view of the Administrator, but the protection of peaceful tribes from wanton aggression, and the introduction of the benefits of civilization by perma-

nent occupation are objects which justify recourse to force when other methods have failed . . . "[1]

But he was never content with laying down rules or even giving proper orders. One of the valuable results of his passion for detail was his ability to think out the exact administrative measures without which the most beneficent principles would have stayed upon paper. This is obvious in his exhaustive provisions with regard to slavery, but it can also be seen in his Memorandum upon " Political Offences and Punitive Expeditions ". Among the many rules and restrictions by which such actions were to be governed was the prohibition of operations by night, because of the danger to women and children; or of the destruction of granaries, except to a limited extent in very serious cases, and the absolute ban upon the destruction or seizure of property except as an ordered fine. Yet, in a clear-sighted way, in the paramount interest of order, he could be severe.

" When," he laid down, " the use of force is necessary, I prefer destruction of life to destruction of food; for the former falls upon those who are directly responsible for the original cause, and has an immediate effect, whereas the latter causes suffering later on to the non-combatant portion who are the less responsible—for women and children, the aged and the weak, are the first sufferers from famine. Experience has shown that, where the resistance is determined, the only way of avoiding recurrent expeditions is to inflict severe punishment, for uncivilized man, regrettably, only recognizes force, and measures its potency by his own losses. The punishment must, therefore, be such as will thoroughly deter the people from a repetition of crime."[2]

A humane democracy, which puts its representatives into positions which demand such severity, is always in a morally undignified position when it is obliged to face the results of its action. So Lugard in one of his recurrent brushes with the Colonial Office over flogging, unburdened himself to his usual correspondent.

" Tonight I got a telegram from the Colonial Office telling me to report by telegram the number of floggings in the W.A.F.F. in 1905. What are they at now! Is this some fresh interference? Imprisonment is most unpopular with the men, and there is no other punishment. I suggested the Pillory and Stocks but they want to deal with a primitive people on the lines of 20th century England, instead of on the lines of 15th century

[1] *Reports*, 1905-6, p. 39.   [2] *Memoranda*, 1906, No. 7, p. 163.

England. Flogging and mutilation are their own traditional punishments. We rightly prohibit the latter but we cannot yet dispense with the former. Nor is it possible on the line of march to give imprisonment, and every prisoner means that others have to do his guards and duties. Well, if they brush aside all means of enforcing discipline, on sickly ' Chinese slavery ' and ' Methods of Barbarity ' grounds, this Government will find itself with one or two Mutinies on its hands presently, and men like myself will not be inclined to shield them from the responsibility for their acts. I look on this kind of thing as signs of decadence and absence of virility. Decadence I take it either shows itself in horrible cruelty and despotism as in later Rome, or else in the opposite extreme of kid-glove sentimentality. Do the Colonial Office arrogate to themselves a greater humanity and sense of abhorrence of drastic punishments than men selected to govern dependencies possess? Am I less an English gentleman because I am here?— I still hope that I have preserved the instincts of Mercy and Sympathy and do not need to be taught them by Churchill and Antrobus."

(L. to F. L., 7 April 1906).

The only completely logical people in this controversy were those who wanted to abandon imperial expansion altogether because of these very moral risks which it entailed. But these forces had been in retreat since the days of Gladstone and Harcourt and were not to advance again until they did so for a time under the banner of the young Labour Party. To Lugard in the earliest years of the century his critics seemed to use the term humanity too often in the merely negative sense as the restraint of cruelty or its renunciation. He would claim to use it in the full positive sense in which he felt himself to be bringing humanity, as expressed in order, law, and good administration, to a people whose life, in its isolation, seemed to be cruel and stagnant.

Lugard, at least, treated his new subjects fully as men. He regarded them neither with a sweeping contempt as uncivilized nor—an attitude which is almost as offensive—with an undiscriminating philanthropy. He knew the full meaning of savagery—using the word in its technical sense as the opposite of civilization—and also that there were men in Africa who could rise above it and peoples who had advanced no small distance into civilization. To such men and groups of men he gave a proper respect and he liked to win the same respect from them for himself and his colleagues. His attitude is well shown in his account to his wife of a visit to the Emir of Kano early in 1905;

" . . . This evening . . . I went with Cargill and Ned to call on the Emir at his own residence. He received us in the very room I used to occupy . . . We drank tea with him, but it was almost liquid sugar and nearly made me feel sick! I have really quite a friendship for Abbas of Kano. He is a most charming man, so frank and dignified, and so wonderfully well-mannered, courteous and courtly. In conversation he is extremely shrewd, and one had ' to keep one's wits about one ' when arguing a matter with him . . . You would have been quite delighted and interested to hear his replies and the general conversation in fact between us. I am convinced that these dignified yet cordial personal relations go a great way towards the real effective Administration of a country like this. Two years ago— rather less—Kano was armed to fight us, and all the tyranny of barbarism was practised within its walls. Today I drank tea alone and unarmed with the Emir as his honoured friend, and I know he is really glad to see me, and you can walk anywhere you like in the city or the country alone and unarmed and as safe as in London. The people all smile and salute. Nor is this a result of suave methods, and a negrophile kow-towing policy . . . Not only all slave raiding, but any form of slave-dealing is now rigor-ously repressed . . . "   (L. to F. L., 4 January 1905).

Two days later he continued the story of his relations with the Emir.

" I have just paused to scribble a line of acknowledgment and farewell to Abbas. It may interest you.

' I am very pleased with my visit to Kano and I am glad to have seen you again, for I regard you as my personal friend, in whom I place entire confidence and trust. And I much desire that you shall regard me as your personal friend to whom you can speak all that is in your heart without any reserve. And if it become thus between us, then the country will prosper and though we are men of different races and different creeds we shall understand each other, and know that each has only the word of absolute truth and sincerity in his lips, and no second thought in his heart. Your friend. The Governor.'

It may be egoism or self-conceit dear, but do you know I quite squirm at the thought lest some successor to me in the near future should treat these chiefs in a different manner from my own. Either with less cordiality and friendship, and courtesy—summoning them at unreasonable hours with thoughtless lack of tact, or on the lines of Macgregor of Lagos (which would be *worse*)—treating them as superiors—as Royalties—and incurring their astonished contempt that the King's representative—the conquering dynasty—should so behave. Alike in India and Africa I have made friendships, and I think won respect and esteem on these lines."

(L. to F. L., 6 January 1905).

Lugard also recognized the need for long and serious study of the people under his rule. Fortunately there have been a number of British governors who approached colonial peoples in this humble and scholarly attitude, notably Sir Stamford Raffles and Sir George Grey. Even so, such men are probably in a minority in their class and it might have been thought that Lugard's natural self-confidence and his long periods of isolation from studious and enlightened circles in his own country, might have bred that confidence in an " instinct " for dealing with " natives " to which men in positions of colonial authority have sometimes laid claim. But Lugard had the attitude of mind of the anthropologist even if he had neither the competence nor the time to be one himself. Though, regrettably, he never mastered Hausa, he valued and encouraged its study among his staff. His attitude was markedly respectful towards the alkali class, the Muslim judges in the emirates. He saw in them " men of much learning, with a keen appreciation of the impartiality and supremacy of the law ".[1] He wished to gather them together in a conference to discuss and settle points of law and, when events prevented this, he set all his Residents to elicit and report their opinions. Even the customs of the backward and obscure pagan groups were to be studied with respect and this as early as 1902, when the greater part of the country had still to be occupied. " For in this, as in all other matters affecting subordinate races, I hold strongly that the hasty introduction of revolutionary ' improvements ' is to be deprecated and I have impressed upon Residents that systems eminently suitable for Europeans and Asiatics are often opposed to the prejudices and root ideas of Africans."[2] Already the future promoter of research into African customs and languages was taking shape.

He had only to look around to see a fulfilment of his best hopes far more swift and dramatic than comes to most men. Doubtless in his reports he made the most of all that was good. No man liked appreciation better than Lugard when he felt he had earned it but there was one quarter from which he most valued it.

[1] *Reports*, 1902, p. 75.   [2] *Ibid.*

The High Commissioner

"It would interest you dear if I could tell you of the general results of the work here. The extraordinary reports I get of the change that has come over the country from the cessation of the chronic warfare and raiding. Today I read a report (among several in the same sense) saying that a Resident had found that a man had turned his gun barrel into a hoe saying that people no longer wanted weapons!—I have just been conducting operations against some intractable savages who from time immemorial have murdered all caravans etc. Instead of fining them for offences in coin which they can't pay I have ordered that their bows and arrows should be taken. I think the total is 5,000 bows and 200,000 arrows given up or seized!—And already caravans are coming through the heart of the country which they dare not enter before. Is this not good?"

(L. to F. L., 8 May 1904).

His question could be put more widely, and the reader might answer it on the record up to this point. But it would be better to wait, for we have still to return to the narrative of Lugard's last years in Northern Nigeria and to see what additional light, and, perhaps, what shadow, they throw upon this picture of the High Commissioner.

CHAPTER X

LEAVE AND WORK, 1903-1905

IN ORDER to consider Lugard's system of administration we turned aside from the narrative of Lugard's actions with the end of his rapid campaign against the northern emirs. It will be remembered that on his march, in his determination to sail for England and his wife on the appointed day, he was attempting to break all records. Unfortunately for the record, neither before nor afterwards was there such a king-breaking and king-making expedition over such a course with which any comparison would be possible.

He *did* catch his boat early in May. It was the first time he had met Flora as his wife in England and in normal conditions. Much as both had longed for the reunion, they approached it with certain fears. For it was not only for reasons of health that Flora's brief attempt to share his African life had failed. Lugard, upon his side, was wondering whether he could learn to put aside his tendency to gloomy silence and to fierce concentration upon his work. As he marched through the heat and the blistering wind of the *harmattan*, he thought much of these things and of how little she still knew of his real self. " Will you, I wonder," he asked " like or love *me* when you know me !" But he also had a healthy longing for England, not only for the flowers and bird-songs of Abinger but for such material things as " a pat of rich yellow buttercup butter and English bread and a tankard of English ale."

The leave, which lasted from May to November, was a success. They spent it partly in London where Flora had taken a furnished house in Cadogan Place and partly at Abinger. He had always longed for a real home and she had taught him to love the richly wooded hills, so accessible to London, and to plan and to watch the reconstruction of the house was a delight they could share to the full. And in London she could draw him gradually into the several circles of her friends, journalistic and political, and help him to take pleasure in the round of calls, dinners, receptions, and week-ends which filled the London season.

Yet for Lugard leave could never be all holiday: he had to force himself to relax as other men force themselves to work. He finished writing his long report for 1902 running over into the first quarter of 1903. He carried on a busy correspondence with Nigeria, visiting the Colonial Office and intervening in the settlement of any important questions.

Among other activities, upon November 4th, Lugard gave a lecture upon Northern Nigeria to the Royal Geographical Society. It was now, after his marriage, that he must meet Goldie again. Their friendship had weathered the potentially difficult passage of the transfer of administrative power over Northern Nigeria from the one to the other and Goldie continued, during 1900 and 1901, to help and advise Lugard. He had come back from a trip to China feeling, he said, twenty years younger and " bursting with capacity for work which *will* find an outlet. While physically and intellectually I feel young— I feel a 1000 in sensation. I believe I have reached a plane of stoicism (not hard heartedness) from which nothing can dislodge me." He had now to look round for some task large enough to use the great powers he had already shown and which he now felt to be renewed. But he would not be easy to please.

" Nothing would have induced me even to consider the Parliamentary Under-Secretaryship at home; so long as C. remains Secretary. You know I like him and could work under him but I know he would not support me in sweeping change and I could not work under the old system."

(Goldie to L., 20 July 1900).

Lugard was evidently a little anxious for his friend, especially with regard to his loss of his long and fruitful absorption in Nigeria, but Goldie brushed this sympathy aside.

" . . . do not fear on my account. I did not think of the Nigeria idea until I was 31, nor begin to work hard at it until I was 33. If I was able to fill my life without it for the first 12 years of my manhood, I can do the same for the last. I have no fear of degenerating or running to seed. I know too well my only strong quality, will power: I am, like a hen, sitting at present (since my return from China) as I did between 1877 and 1879. There must be an interval between great efforts, but we will discuss this on your return . . . I am looking forward with great pleasure to seeing you once more . . . I still have friendship left on the emotional side. Take care of yourself." (Goldie to L., 21 January 1901).

Nothing could have been more intimate and wholehearted than these letters of 1900–1901, " I have a few friends," Goldie said," (you among the chief) and I want no more," and he signed his name with the word " affectionately " which was rare in those more formal days. This was the end. From the time of Flora's breakdown and her engagement to Lugard, his friendship for Goldie came to an end. The problem remained as to how they were to conduct their public relations especially as, surprisingly, Goldie did not seem to have expected the reaction of the Lugards.

For some reason very hard to understand—was it that Chamberlain had not forgiven him for his high-handed conduct over the transfer of the Company?—no post worthy of his great abilities had come Goldie's way. When Lugard first came home Goldie was away cruising on his yacht and it was not until the end of October, a few days before Lugard was to give the lecture, that contact was made.

In those days, and, even more, a little earlier, when there were still new lands to explore and describe, meetings of the Royal Geographical Society could be very dramatic occasions and Lugard's first account, as its Governor, of the new Protectorate was an important event for the *cognoscenti* of the colonial and geographical worlds. The sudden possibility arose that, as once long before with Speke and Burton, it might be stirred by a personal encounter. On October 30th, five days before he was due to speak, Lugard received the following letter from Goldie.

" My dear Lugard, 29 October 1903.

I had determined, privately, to go to your R.G.S. address and (while adhering to my fixed rule not to speak on Nigeria) to introduce a well-earned eulogy on yourself; provided always that the President, as seemed probable, called on me to speak.

This morning, I got from Keltie [Secretary of the Royal Geographical Society] a copy of your address, for my report to the Council—a formal matter. Up to Page 8, I found only three or four minor points, which to my mind needed alteration.

My chief disagreement with you was as to the introduction of my name. You know my motto—'*L'oeuvre c'est tout, l'homme c'est rien.*' But I know that your kindly impulse *compelled* you to speak of me in the very handsome way you have done. Then *I came to Page 8*! ! I do not want to *have* to stand up and *flatly* contradict your main points—in a score of words.

Could you breakfast, lunch, dine or sleep here, or all of them? I am at your disposal until Tuesday. Please send me a wire. Your credit does not depend on minimizing the work of the Company.

> Yours very truly
> George Taubman Goldie."

We do not know exactly what were the offending words. But, from what Lugard had discovered about the extent and nature of the Company's control of its territory, it is possible to guess. He answered the letter on the day he received it at Abinger, withdrawing the offending page but maintaining its truth.

" Dear Sir George,   Abinger, 30 October 1903.

I have just received your letter relative to my R.G.S. paper, telling me you are prepared to ' flatly contradict the main points on page 8—in a score of words.' There is nothing there but what I should have thought you would yourself have thoroughly agreed in, had we been conversing on the subject, and I was careful to emphasize the reasons which had made it impossible for the Company to set up an effective Administration in what is now Northern Nigeria prior to 1900—viz., foreign aggression, trouble with Nupe, and lack of funds. I should indeed be sorry to accord to the Company and to yourself anything else than the fullest possible mead of praise which is its and your due. Nor would it be in good taste either to raise a controversial point, or to insist on reading my paper as it stood, or not reading it at all. I will therefore, if you wish it, erase the whole passage referring to the Company on p. 8 from the word ' natives ' in line 18 to the word ' country ' in line 37. There is nothing in this passage which, so far as my information goes, is not absolutely in accordance with fact, and if in any point I am less or more than the fact, I should be *extremely* glad to be informed, and that the emendations should be *proved*. With regard to the inference that I desire to enhance my own reputation by minimizing the work of the Company, I have nothing to reply to anyone who thinks that that is my character. It is a matter of opinion—and everyone is entitled to his own—but I should not myself have thought that it was borne out by the way I have spoken of the Company during these past years."

He then went on to give overwork and his wife's health as reasons for refusing all Goldie's suggestions for a meeting. And he had now become

> "Yours very truly,
> F. D. Lugard."

There was a postscript:

" P.S. I gather from your letter that you do not intend to be at the R.G.S. on the 4th? It is kind of you to have at first intended to eulogize me, but I am sure you will not misunderstand me when I ask you in no event to do so."

Posts were faster, it seems, in the first than in the sixth decade of the century and Goldie received and replied to Lugard's letter on the same day it was written. The strong man was now on the defensive, both as administrator and friend, and he was generous enough to reveal it. But he maintained his claim about the extent of the Company's grasp upon the north and this deserves to be recorded. In the first lines he announced his acceptance of a position, one hardly equal to his capacities.

" My dear Lugard,   30 October 1903.

I am, I expect, as much pressed as yourself. That is saying a great deal; but you will understand it when I tell you that I have accepted a Vice-presidency (jointly with Grey) of the British South Africa Co. and that I am starting on the 20 November to have a look at Rhodesia. This means that I have (in four weeks time) to master the complex conditions that have sprung up during the last 15 years . . .

My letter to you yesterday was written in the midst of urgent work and interruptions . . . I never had the absurd thought that you *intended* to minimize the work of the Company. How could you imagine that I should suddenly and without any ground, alter my opinion—no, my *knowledge*—of your character, and think you capable of trying to enhance your reputation at the expense of anyone, let alone an old friend like myself?

My meaning was that the *effect* of your statements would be to minimize the work of the Company; and lest you might think that I did not fully appreciate your great work of settlement, I added that it needed no such foil.

Leave and Work

I am more sorry than I can say that you have interpreted my phrase in the way you have; because it shows me that you no longer have the faith you once had in my affection and respect for you. What have I done to deserve this?

I *do not* want to enter into any controversy with you. It is so easy to misunderstand letters, and I hope you may find some opportunity of seeing me in London before we leave. Thank you for cutting out the passage you propose. I *could* not have spoken after you without flatly contradicting the statement that ' it was not safe for their agents to travel far from their warehouses'. Hewby—who is, I suppose, still with you— could, I am sure, give you a very different account of the Company's work in the Bakundi and Donga regions, between 1890 and 1900. Nor could I admit that the diplomatic relations of the company with Nassarawa, Muri and Bauchi (which effectually checked the slave-raiding across the Benue which existed up to 1890) were not a form of administration, although of course not comparable with the effective occupation that you have established.

But most of my fear of misconception falls to the ground if you cut out the passage to which you refer.

Of course, I do not like the expression ' *trading* depots at Egga, Jebba and Ibi ' etc. For nearly three years before 1st January 1900, *Egga* and *Jebba* were the centres of political influence over Southern Nupe and Ilorin. *Jebba* had been a military station of the Company. I have not access to the papers now, but I expect that the Company's troops had been withdrawn from Jebba to make way for the W.A.F.F. You will remember whether this is so.

Ibi had been since 1890 a principal military station of the Company. At one time, fully one half of the force was kept there, the strength being diminished to carry out the Bida Ilorin expedition, immediately followed as that was by the incursion of the French into Borgu. I will not enter into controversy but will leave it to you to decide whether the phrase ' trading depots at Egga, Jebba and Ibi etc. etc.' is accurate. I would not, on any account, suggest anything that would lessen the magnitude of your work of settlement. I am only anxious, as I am sure you are, that the work of the Company should not be minimized—unintentionally— I know it would not be otherwise.

I have never varied in my intention to be present at the address to do you honour. How could I do otherwise? And if, as is probable, the President calls on me to speak, why should you object to my expressing my *appreciation* of your work? I apologise for the Greek form—*eulogy*. I hate the word. It has, I don't know why, a sickly sound which is absent from the Latin word. But the substance is the same; and I shall think that I have lost your friendship if you maintain your objection. I have been a Fellow of the Society for more than a quarter of a century, and a member of the Council for a dozen years or more and I have had a very close connection with Nigeria and (I thought) a very close friendship with yourself. For me not to attend or to say nothing about you would be simply shocking—at any rate to me.

Yours ever,
George T. Goldie.

P.S. You are a nice man to ask me not to ' eulogize ' you when you have ' eulogized ' me so freely in your address."

The possibility of an open conflict seemed to be removed by the restraint shown upon both sides. But a public discussion of the relative claims of Goldie's Company and Lugard's administration might have been too severe a test for their restraint. They were not put to the trial. The next day Goldie wrote to say that the sudden death of an aunt prevented him from coming. " As to your paper," he wrote, " I leave everything in your hands—as I shall not be present, I shall not have the heavy responsibility I should have had."

At his lecture Lugard gave a general account of Nigeria, more political than geographical. He left out his remarks upon the slightness of the administration he had inherited from the Company. He gave Goldie " the credit of having secured Nigeria to the British Crown ", but his reference to his old friend upon an occasion, and at a period, when compliments tended to be lush, were brief and restrained. The President read a letter from Goldie, which brought his apologies, ran over Lugard's great services, and concluded with the remark that if they were not properly appreciated it was because Lugard had " a weakness shared by many other truly great men—excessive modesty." The President then reminded the audience that the Society's first gold medal had been given to Richard Lander for his discovery of the mouth of the Niger in 1830 and complimented Lugard with special emphasis upon his survey work. These compliments were tepid beside the quite tropical warmth of a tribute by Sir Harry Johnston who had carried through that settlement of Uganda which Lugard had longed to make. He declared of Lugard that before he went to play the part of Warren Hastings in Nigeria, he had been the Clive of Uganda. " Uganda," he went on, " certainly owes its incorporation in the

British Empire to the really remarkable efforts of Sir Frederick Lugard." This was very handsome, all the more so as, in its main lines, his career ran so closely parallel to Lugard's that " little Johnston ", as Lugard always called him, was the nearest he had to a rival.[1]

The meeting was thus a great success. It does not appear that, in the brief period of his leave remaining to Lugard, he and Goldie met. They did meet from time to time in later years. But the friendship which, certainly on Lugard's side, had been so deep, so effective and almost romantic was over. In the writer's experience, in his later life, Lugard could hardly be brought to speak of Goldie. From about the time of the incident Goldie's star, as far as public office and honours went, continued to wane, leaving his pride at war with his bitterness to make the strange, still vital and arresting yet unhappy figure of Dorothy Wellesley's later portrait.

Lugard returned to Nigeria in November 1903, taking with him, as we saw, his brother who had returned after service in Ngamiland, the South African war and India. He put in a seventeen months' period. Much of his time was given to the day-to-day administration and especially to the reordering of the system of taxation. He did, however, break away from his desk in order to carry out an arduous tour in which, covering 2,000 miles by land and 1,000 by water, he inspected every one of his fourteen provinces except Sokoto. In the course of this journey he visited and, where still necessary, formally installed the emirs, and explained personally to them the aims and methods of British rule; inspected the administration and the official records of each Resident, and settled permanent sites for the provincial headquarters.

Some of the main incidents of the tour are worthy of record. The first expedition in February was to Kontagora, to visit Ibrahim, the famous " Destroyer ", the man who had devastated the whole surrounding country for twenty years, leading out his slave-raiding army every dry season and who only two years before had even threatened Lugard in Jebba. Captured at last and deposed, Lugard had found that such was the dread of this terrible but able man that, so long as he lived, no successor dared take his place. So Lugard, depriving him of his much-raided pagan provinces, had put him back and was now going out to confirm him.

[1] F. D. Lugard, ' Northern Nigeria ', *Geographical Journal*, vol. XXIII, January 1904.

In contrast with the vast mounted hordes which represented an emir's power, Lugard (himself at the time weak with fever) walked out from Zungeru with 25 native soldiers, his brother Edward, Eaglesome, the Director of Public Works, one British military officer and a string of carriers. The day's march would be from fifteen to twenty miles. In front of his little procession, as it wound through the narrow African bush paths which allow room for only one pair of feet and go round every little obstacle, an orderly carried the Union Jack. After six days' marching Kontagora was reached, still half ruined and deserted within its five miles of walls, while a little apart, in a few native-built thatched huts, was the Resident and his assistant.

Ibrahim came out with all his family and retainers to meet Lugard. He was riding a showy black horse, the royal colour, with the Fulani double-pommelled saddle. He wore long fanciful boots with spurs and his head was swathed in the usual high indigo turban. The High Commissioner's party was impressed by his quiet dignity in defeat, his absolute command over his people and the singular intelligence of his face, with its keen eyes and aquiline nose. They might have concluded that, so long as his deeds are not sins in his own eyes, a man may spend a lifetime of bloodshed and yet retain something that seems not ignoble.

The next event of interest was the arrival from Sokoto of an embassy from the Sultan to greet the returning High Commissioner and bring presents of horses, cattle, and bright saddlery. This was a striking testimony of submission and a credit to the Resident, Major Burdon, whose enthusiasm for the Fulani rulers had won a marked response from them. The envoys themselves were impressed by the magic of the furniture, baths, and electric light of Government House which Lugard expounded to them.

The next visitor was the Emir of Kano who came with his Resident, Dr. Cargill, in order to demonstrate his loyalty in the face of disturbing rumours that were being spread by his brother the ex-emir, then in exile at Lokoja. He presented Lugard with the tribute of horses, formerly payable to Sokoto, but without the customary string of slaves which had always accompanied them. Edward Lugard, whose journal here expands his brother's letters, keenly watching his behaviour in the strange setting of Zungeru, characterized him a gentleman, somewhat nervous but thoughtful and observant. It was only on the

British side that a social solecism was committed. His eldest son, the Chiroma, was placed opposite to him on the little train. It was noticed that the Emir turned away: by Fulani custom the king's son must never look upon his father's unveiled face.

A day or two later a very different kind of potentate came to pay his respects, no dignified mounted emir with crowds of horsemen but a simple chief of a pagan tribe with a small following. Yet no African visitor could have been more welcome for this was the " King " of Kiama into whose hands ten years ago, Lugard, in a desperate gamble, had entrusted his life. The High Commissioner turned on all the ceremony, the band and the guard of honour, for this simple Bariba chief as he had for the great Fulani emirs. The visitor had none of their studied dignity and grave Muslim calm. He fell upon the High Commissioner with a happy, cheery, independent, hail-fellow-well-met kind of air, assuring him as a continuing sign of their old trust, that he would eat what he ate and would sleep with him. But though, as Edward Lugard drily remarked, " Fred had other plans ", everything possible was done to honour the chief who went about smiting himself on the chest, when excited or pleased, to inspect the wonders of Zungeru. He pointed out that he was wearing, in compliment to his host, the same embroidered garments that Lugard had given him at their first meeting. He brought lion and leopard skins and guinea fowl as his present. Edward Lugard was immensely pleased with the old man, " a first rate ruler, a fine type of a native Chief, a good horseman and a brave man . . . I was introduced to him personally and he literally stroked me down with delight at finding I was F's own brother!" He went back to what was now " the best behaved province in the Protectorate ", having shown how the response of human nature to honour and courage can spring across barriers of race, religion, colour and culture. The moving story of Kiama's virtue and subsequent troubles had had a very happy sequel.

There followed a succession of provincial tours, with much that was the same in each, but always something that was different. In the middle of April it was the turn of Bida, won, as already related, by Goldie's expedition, lost and won again by Lugard only three years before this visit. The Company's emir, Mahomadu, now restored, was a loyal and able ruler, but his twenty stone of weight made it difficult for him to show his allegiance according to local custom. This demanded that he should dismount from the unhappy little Nigerian horse that carried him, kneel down, touch the earth with his forehead crying "Zaki, Zaki," (Lion, Lion) and then, in order to reach the very acme of submission, turn round and repeat the genuflexion with his back to his suzerain. When all was over and Lugard took his leave, the Emir, with great physical distress, executed the valedictory honour of leading his horsemen in a mock charge which ended—always a distressing moment to the lover of horses—in their being jerked to a dead halt. Lugard, his brother said, "feared this valuable twenty stone political factor might succumb to heat apoplexy" so he forbade him, after this, to ride out upon the customary mileage of leave-taking.

Ilorin was next on the programme. The party had to go up the Niger at its June level in canoes. At Jebba they climbed the high bank to see the remains of Lugard's old house and station, already overgrown with jungle like some ancient city, and looked up the familiar view to the great "juju" rock. From here they went on by land. At Ilorin they were in a great Muslim Yoruba city in the far south of the Protectorate, the northern fringe of that lively turbulent Negroland that, for its larger pagan part, was under the Governor of Lagos. Here, as contrasted with Hausaland, there was more colour, and more animation among the crowd of 10,000 which came out to see the great white man. Indeed, so Lugard told Flora, "the women of Ilorin had struck work saying they must have their hair done for the occasion (a work as you know of hours and days)." Yoruba society was not so autocratic or centralized as that of the Hausa emirs, and as a result 48 crowned "kings" and 400 chiefs—the Resident's reckoning—had come together for this great occasion. Many of these had never met before; many had been enemies and there was much peace-making and many vows of allegiance made to the Emir whose primacy was now confirmed. Lugard made a not very impressive arrival. He had been carried, half dressed, over the Oyo river on the shoulders of carriers, and then, mounting his dripping horse, which had swum the river, he rode through a mile of massed people who, he confessed "were obviously much at a loss to know which of the whitemen was the Governor and would have preferred something more after their own style . . ." The Emir, in receiving Lugard, was surrounded by all the hundreds of lesser chiefs who wore strange traditional headdresses, and even golden crowns, and robes of many coloured plush, "such,"

Lugard said, " as curtains in ducal London houses are made of." Afterwards there was a visit to the great, sprawling city with its reputed 100,000 inhabitants and its warren of rectangular thatched houses that contrast with the round huts or flat-roofed mud buildings of the north.

There followed a short journey to return Kiama's visit, the party poling upstream in canoes and then plunging into the wet bush, full of elephant and buck, which Lugard remembered so well. On the way Lugard observed the French " enclave " on the Niger, about which so much diplomatic ink had flowed, a neglected stockade inhabited by a native caretaker. The French themselves crossed the much disputed border to meet him at Kiama and Lugard had cause to admire, in contrast with his own service, their more simple and spartan life, their living on the produce of the country and their longer tours. " Really," he exclaimed, " these Frenchmen give us points!"

In September 1904 Lugard set off upon a very long tour. First down to Lokoja, then along the fast falling Benue to visit the stations along the river, Loko, Ibi and Numan. He went in his steam yacht, the *Corona*, " a floating palace," Nicholson called it, " that jars his economic mind at every turn of its latest pattern twin screws." They came finally to Yola, that great slaving centre of yesterday, and here he installed an emir in place of the one defeated two years before. Leaving the *Corona* to find her way down the Benue while there was yet time, the party tried to push up the Gongola river in canoes, but the current was so fierce that their impatient leader, finding he was growing " a liver like a Strasbourg goose," broke away and marched through the emirate of Gombe to that of Bauchi. Here they found one of his most interesting and expert Residents, C. L. Temple, in charge.

The usual ceremony of installing the Emir took place. He presented Lugard with a horse of the royal black, with oxen, fowls and hundreds of eggs (Lugard remarked that they must have been collecting them for months). But when the Emir jibbed at taking his oath of allegiance before his people, Lugard was firm. As was his custom, the High Commissioner marked the occasion by releasing political prisoners. In this case they were the so-called " dangerous fanatics " who had fought to the last for the old Sultan of Sokoto the year before at Burmi. " There I had up," wrote Lugard, " a decrepit, miserable lot, most of them grey-headed and I released them and gave them an ox to eat. Their gratitude was touching. Their imprisonment was never sanctioned by me." (L. to F. L., 31 October 1904).

From Bauchi the party marched the dull straight sandy 300 miles to Bornu. Here they were able to exchange the carriers for pack-oxen. They had left the Fulani emirates and the Hausa people and were going into the ancient Kanuri kingdom of Bornu. Lugard reported the enthusiastic reception by the Shehu at the old capital of Kukawa. There were long and detailed discussions about the new conditions of government, after which thousands of his people saw their ruler take the oath of allegiance.

" Thirteen months ago there were 60 residents here, and the vast ruins were full of leopards, hyenas and wild beasts. Today there are at least 20,000 to 30,000 in a growing city, in which houses and walls are being repaired in every direction. The people are extremely loyal, and it seems to me that they are really attached to us; for it is we who have restored the dynasty and brought peace and prosperity to the country. It is wholly different here to what it is in a Fulani city. Different, too, was the taking of the oath.

It was not administered by the Alkali, but the Shehu, who is a magnificent figure of a man—stood up and took the book, and facing me asked if there were anything in the Oath he was asked to swear which would interfere with his religion. (I had already assured him on this point). I said No. ' Can I (he said) observe all the customs of my forefathers?' ' As regards religion: Yes ' I said. Then he said ' for the rest I swear to observe all the conditions you described yesterday and I agree to all you say,' etc., and touched the Koran. It was rather impressive."

(L. to F. L., 30 November 1904).

A week later, he wrote in retrospective mood.

" It was here at this spot that Rabeh defeated Kiarai, the last of the Bornu Sultans who had fled here with the remnants of his army after the sack of his capital. The Sultan was captured, and Hewby tells me that his throat was cut and he was thrown into the river. This happened I believe in '95, when I was in the country—little thinking I should have so much to do with its future—and just before I went to S. Africa, when our heads were all full of ' the Jameson Raid '. As I strolled out for a few minutes at sunset, I came on a human skull and bones, for they lie scattered still among the mealie stalks, and the crops which have grown from the blood of the dead. It is strange to think of—Rabeh with 10,000 men camped on this very spot, in all the barbaric splendour of a conqueror, and now a British Governor in a humble straw shanty and in khaki. Yet the one represented an ephemeral and retrograde power, the other represents a new era, and the ' British Empire '."

(L. to F. L., 7 December 1904).

The party now struck back westwards and slightly north for the small Emirates of Gummel, Katagum and Hadeija. The two first Emirs had never resisted the British and they now welcomed their new suzerain. Lugard wrote,

" I told these chiefs that, as they had from the first received us with friendship, I did not wish to insist on the Oath of Allegiance which I had administered to emirs appointed by the Government. I later, however, received a message from both of them saying that they wished to take the oath, and they came next day to do so. Taking the Koran in his hand, Katagum said, ' I believe it is the will of God that the white man has come to my country, and I will therefore obey him. If I am guilty of any double-dealing, may the Koran punish me.' Gummel's self-suggested oath was even more emphatic. Katagum said that, since our arrival, he had received more revenue than before, in spite of the share he paid to the Government."[1]

The neighbouring Hadeija was a very different matter. The people of this small Emirate had a great reputation as fighting men, they possessed a fine breed of horses and a very strongly walled town. Their Emir had shown in many ways his unwillingness to accept the new order. He was a tall man and it was said he refused to stoop to enter a doorway; if any were not high enough the wall must be broken down. Lugard, with his small party could not take the risk of meeting him in his own town or in open country and so he summoned him to Katagum. He came just as the white men were leaving the town and Lugard noticed that as Hadeija and his company came on, the Emirs of Gummel and Katagum with their 1,000 horsemen, although they had been dismissed, stayed on and formed a great watching crescent, ready, if needed, to act in Lugard's defence. The proud Emir appeared, however, to be all humility and his behaviour after this was correct. But it was reported that there was still an irreconcilable party in his town.[2]

---

[1] *Reports*, 1904, p. 39.   [2] *Ibid.* pp. 39-41.

From here Lugard marched on to Kano in order to confirm there the installation of the Emir of that great city and of the Emir of Katsina. Writing to Flora:

" The Emir elect of Katsina performed the very full ablutions prescribed before he could swear on the Koran. Then he alone advanced in a dirty white gown and filthy turban (signs of humility) and to indicate that he was nobody. Then I presented him with a new gown which was put on and a snow-white turban which was bound round his head, after he had taken the oath of loyalty and friendship to the British Government on the Koran administered by the Alkali of Kano. Then I summoned all the leading Katsina chiefs, a most delightful lot (for Katsina is remarkable for the courtesy and friendliness of its chiefs and people). Then I invested the Emir with the traditional insignia, the seal of Katsina, and the sword in a silver scabbard (whose origin is wrapped in fable) covered with Arabic inscriptions, then the drum. On this a particular chief with immense seriousness and concentration of features beat 12 deliberate strokes. That was the signal of his accession, and the drum will not again be beaten till another king is made. It has not been beaten for 18 years. Then I shook hands with the new Emir, and wished him long life etc., and all were greatly delighted. They retired and the emir of Kano came forward alone and I presented to him the Government installation present (deferred till now) a gorgeous saddle—a sword, and a very small Persian carpet. An illuminated Koran is to follow. He was much pleased, and meanwhile the Katsina people were blowing their trumpets and careering round their new King, who is very popular, for his father, who was a former King, was greatly liked and so is he. Then the Emir of Kano retired . . . and I mounted my beautiful black horse (the Shehu) and rode down the ranks of artillery, infantry, and mounted infantry."

(L. to F. L., 2 January 1905).

Lugard had an eye not only for the political and human side of all he saw from his path but also for the physical setting of his journey. He had probably learned much about the vegetable world from his brother who was an expert botanist. Now, with all these political duties, culminating at Kano, behind him, he could afford if not to stand, at least to stare at this world.

"Camp Ruka.
The colours of the spring leaves in the jungle we pass through are like nothing you can conceive. In England the young leaves are green—here they are every conceivable colour. Not the *buds*, but the full young

foliage. There are trees every yard of the way clothed in leaves of deep blood-red—others of a reddish purple with a sort of 'bloom' on it like a peach—others russet, yellow, brown, dazzling green, every shade of each, and all looking as though dipped in varnish, so brightly do they glisten . . . The deep scarlet bell-flowers of the thorny Bombax, the scarlet of the Butea—and the feathery dusters of greenish grey spirea-like flowers which are now in masses on a tree whose name I don't know. Yellow blossoms in great bunches are on two other varieties—while the Shea and another are also in blossom. Another tree is covered with ripe fruit, and many more with ripe pods, for this strange country mixes up spring, autumn, winter and summer indiscriminately, and at all times of the year you will find trees in fruit, in blossom, or in bud at the same time . . . In the early morning, with the fresh keen air, and the rising sun, the feeling is just like a most glorious morning in English spring or early summer. I think that as I ride along (if I have not indigestion!) I feel something of that exhilaration which you describe as the 'joy of living'. It is good to be in so beautiful a world, and I keep wanting you to see it. Only I differ from you in liking to enjoy it *silently* . . . " (L. to F. L., 20 January 1905).

There was still one more province to visit before Lugard could bring this arduous tour to an end, the wooded, hilly, pagan and much raided Kabba. There was nothing very striking to report but as he went by boat or by land, he drew little pictures for his wife of wayside incidents. Here are two of them:

" A man has been sitting on the bank opposite my ship for 2 days dressed in spotless white. At the prayer hours he kneels in prayer and tells his beads. I asked what he wanted. He said he had come to see me, hearing I was arriving. He had come from Timbuktu, and gone to Mecca, and was now on his way back. A fine, respectable looking dignified old man. So I heard his words. His wife had died. He did not think to have another, certainly not till he reached Timbuktu again, but here in a tiny village he had met a woman, the wife or divorcée of someone else, and wanted to marry her, but thought he ought to ask me first. They are strange folk are they not? . . ." (L. to F. L., 30 March 1905).

The next story too had its strangeness but it struck a grimmer note.

" In each case I have asked whether there was any prisoner whom I could liberate (to mark my coming) and here I found that two had been urgently recommended by the doctor as quite unfit to undergo longer imprisonment. He said both would shortly die unless released. So I had them up, and I tell you the story as a typical African experience. Two decrepit old men appeared, one so emaciated he could hardly stand up. They were heavily ironed. One was already half an idiot, the other little better, and they were in filthy rags. It seemed a monstrous thing that such tottering white-headed old men should be still confined in irons, in the state they were in. I ordered them instant release. While the irons were being taken off I enquired for what crimes they had been imprisoned (their cases had of course been fully gone into by me and confirmed). One was in for burying a man alive, the other for cutting off the head of a soldier's brother in order to see what the white man would do! Really the contrast between their appearance and their crimes was so absurd as to be ludicrous, and the feeling of sympathy and pity to which one had given way was so absurdly misplaced when one recalled their crimes, that I was moved to laughter at the absurdity of the situation."

(L. to F. L., 11 April 1905).

But often, as he travelled, his thoughts took wider and deeper range above the events of the day, and there was now someone with whom he could share them.

"Keffi.

. . . There is something unique in night marching in the dark and the silence . . . the ghostly trees, and the sleeping villages . . . a feeling of lack of individual power which perhaps may be a new idea to you. By daylight one depends on one's own keenness of eyesight and of perception, on one's own ability to meet any contingency . . . It is not till one marches at night that one recognizes it by its absence. Sight is nearly useless, for nothing could guard one against surprise or ambush . . . So one has a sense of being in other people's hands—the guide, the escort, and so on. We had ever in front of us the Great Bear which at this time (and now as I write) is upside down, and as the night wears on gradually inverts itself, so that when I reached Laminga at midnight it was taking a header into the horizon . . . I thought of your favourite quotation from Job 'Canst thou loosen the bands of Orion, or (control?) the sweet influence of the Pleiades?'[1] . . . I almost resent the little span that is given to man, and his unspeakable lack of importance in the Universe and in Time. To me it is a depressing thing to think of the cities of Troy—seven distinct cities were there not, each built on the wholly obliterated and buried ruins of its predecessor, of which its builders had no knowledge. In each there were men who led strenuous lives, and advanced the

[1] Correctly, "Canst thou bind the sweet influences of Pleiades, or loose the bands of Orion?" Job XXXVIII. 31.

sum of human knowledge and perhaps of human happiness in their day. Their very inventions have to be invented again and their knowledge rediscovered. There is *nothing* which eventual oblivion does not cover with a brand new city. All our little efforts are of absolutely no account in the world's history. ' Viscerunt Multi ante Agamenon'."[1]

(L. to F. L., 9 April 1905).

From this long and hard tour Lugard returned home in May, 1905, much exhausted. But, no longer alone, he was now a member of a firm, Lugard, Lugard and Shaw, with two of its partners mostly in Nigeria and the third in England working ceaselessly and with the highest competence in its interests.

It was a source of never-ending wonder to Lugard that Flora should have married him. He was always ready to sit humbly and gratefully at her feet and draw upon her intellect and experience. As he told her:

" You have lived and found your friends among the most polished and the best of London—which is England. You have lived from your early girlhood among the best books and, as you say, with the greatest thoughts of the greatest writers. Mine has been so different a life. I have read *nothing*—I have lived all my life largely among my inferiors—very rarely and for very brief moments associated with my superiors, or with ' cultivated ' people . . . Well, we come back to the old mystery. You find, you say, in me the companionship which you would select before all others for close intimacy of thought in spite of my life in the bush and forest and my lack of opportunity to mix with the living great, or hear the words of the still greater Dead." (L. to F. L., 29 December 1905).

In this summer of 1905 they came to know each other well and the respect and friendship in which they had married began to grow into something very different from friendship.

But marriage had its more material sides. Ever since its event Lugard's attitude towards his career had been changing. Before, so long as his debts and family obligations could be met, he had been able to set himself more exciting objectives than money or security. In reading the stories of notable men, and especially perhaps of men of adventurous action, it is easy to forget that even heroes have to earn their living. Lugard was now forty-seven and he was responsible for a wife. Flora was distressed to think that she had not only brought him

---

[1] Correctly, " *Vixere fortes ante Agamemnona multi* ": "Many brave men lived before Agamemnon ", Horace, *Odes IV*, ix, 25.

no dowry but she had added her own heavy family obligations to his though neither of them ever hesitated to meet such claims. She recognized his perfect generosity but she saw that it:

" takes from you that financial independence which you and I together, I venture to say, could readily maintain with our daily work, were we obliged to try outside the bounds of your official career . . . I am at present bearing it as simply the worst thing which I have ever had to bear for my family's sake. When I think of all those helpless beings to be educated and provided for, I have to take prudential views which otherwise I would leave on one side."   (F. L. to L., undated, 1904).

But this was not the worst. The truth must be faced that Flora was extravagant. The French are reputed to be economical and the Irish to be spendthrift: if this is so then the Irish blood in her, reinforced by an Irish childhood, had mastered the French element. Lugard hit it off very neatly in a letter to his brother in 1903—" I must eat bread and she must eat bread and butter." Since she had left the country-house atmosphere of her childhood, Flora had been forced to earn her own and other people's livings but even this had not had its usual effect, one which had been so strongly marked in Lugard. She loved the bright human circulation of London society, to be guest or hostess where there was interesting talk and the men who directed the affairs of the nation were to be met. And she also loved country life: she wanted her Abinger cottage to become the perfect setting for small but distinguished week-end parties. One of the things most corrosive to any kind of human partnership is to hold opposing conceptions of the value of money and it is most remarkable that Lugard, with his own deep-rooted habit of economy that was never to his very last days relaxed, should have resolved not even to attempt to diminish the happiness Flora found in this way of life. He joined eagerly with her in the building of the new house, rejoiced at the skill of the craftsman who carved the newel posts of the staircase to her liking and planned with her a little pavilion amongst the trees where she could retire to write during the summer. He agreed to the taking, more than once, of a house in town; to her having a lady's maid and the servants she wished; to the succession of visits from her nephews and nieces and, of course, the almost continuous expense of doctors and special treatments demanded by her impaired health.

Early in 1904 he decided that they could not live upon the income he was then receiving without a change in their way of life and perhaps having to let their house at Abinger upon which he was already some £3,000 in debt. What was to be done? This was the constant debate in their letters. It was clear she could not join him in Nigeria and there was the possibility that his own health would break down after so many years of hard living in the tropics. He often spoke as though his days in the tropics must be nearly over. Yet there were other times when he felt that he could not tear himself away from Nigeria until he had brought his work there to what he regarded as a proper conclusion. This, as defined by him, was a rather large order—he was to round off all his memoranda and legislation; to put through his scheme of taxation; to make the country self-supporting; and to build the railway. His ideas went even further. As early as 1900 he had told his brother that the three Nigerias should be amalgamated and that *he* wanted to do it. Flora on her side was in mental conflict. She saw that Nigeria divided them: she admitted that she was jealous of the spell it laid upon him. Was it his duty to kill himself with overwork and fever? Was it selfish to long to give him the happiness of a home with her and to cherish his health? Her mind swung to and fro between desire and duty. There were times when he was sufficiently ill or worried or angry with the Colonial Office to seem to agree with her but always his mind righted itself like a shaken compass and pointed again to his true purpose—his determination to finish his work, just as hers would go back to her dominant hope, somehow, somewhere, to live together.

Lugard had also to reckon with the uncertainty and irregularity of his career. After the prolonged if tenuous link he had preserved with the army he was finally retired in 1905. He knew that in the Colonial Service he was an " outsider ": there would be no strong obligation to find him another job. He recognized, not without some pride, that he had done little enough to make himself beloved by the officials who handled the appointments. At other times he feared he had degenerated since the days when he was " more free-spoken and independent and didn't care a damn for any of them " and " did not hesitate to tell Mr. Chamberlain that I thought his policy wrong." (L. to F. L., 9 March 1905).

In these fears and regrets, however, he reckoned without Flora. Her

223

contact with the Colonial Office was continuous, especially with the Secretary of State and his parliamentary Under-Secretaries. It was typical of her position that when at the end of 1902 the Colonial Office did make Lugard the offer of another post, it was she who sent the telegram in cypher on their behalf. The Colonial Office, she said, was anxious about his health and while they would consider his removal an irreparable loss to Nigeria, yet,

" in the kindest spirit of sympathy they desire me to say that the Government of Western Australia, one of the best of climates in the world, is now vacant and if for reasons of health you care to accept an appointment otherwise little fitted for the exercise of your special ability, they wish to give you the opportunity of doing so."

Lugard's telegraphed reply, after receiving this telegram in the middle of his Kano campaign, was brief and decisive. After a word of appreciation, it ran: " respectfully desire to remain in Nigeria. Health excellent."

It was indeed clear that there was little else that for his own sake he would wish to do except to go to East Africa and perhaps amalgamate *those* territories.

" We are agreed," he told Flora early in 1904, " that a Governorship of Jamaica, Ceylon, or part of Australia would be hateful to both of us. I go further and say that I should be wholly unsuited to it and incapable of doing it well. I am no public speaker to open Assemblies or Legislative Councils with ' Speeches from the Throne '. I *could* not do it, though for your sake I would attempt most things, I feel that if I attempted that it would be to fail besides making life very unpleasant. You have the same feeling and would equally hate doing My Lady Gracious on a red carpet."
(L. to F. L., 23 January 1904).

There was no doubt this was *his* view. But was it really Flora's? She could not be sure. Before deciding, however, she could join with him in a strenuous effort to attain the best of both worlds. There, on the personal side, lay the origin for that extraordinary Scheme—for it will merit and must have a capital letter—which from this time onwards, became a major theme of both their private and their public lives.

CHAPTER XI

THE LUGARD SCHEME FOR
CONTINUOUS ADMINISTRATION

WE HAVE now to consider the evolution of the contentious Scheme which the Lugards evolved during the second half of the High Commissionership. To understand its development we have to put together facts that have already been at least suggested. There was Lugard's dissatisfaction with the staffing and organization of the Colonial Office for the new task of large-scale African administration; his own reluctance to delegate; his disinclination ever to take a holiday. He and Flora, both being interested as much in the public as the personal aspects of this situation, discussed the possibility of a new department of African or of tropical administration at the Colonial Office with an experienced permanent Under-Secretary of its own. When all these pieces were fitted together it was found that they made a pattern. Lugard should become a governor who spent half his year in his territory and the other half administering it from the Colonial Office. It will be seen at once that this plan was a perfect solution of their personal as well as their public interests. The summer together and only the winter apart; his health—and hers—safeguarded; his control maintained unbroken; the Colonial Office opposition neutralized. And perhaps from this scheme there might grow a wholly new system of tropical administration centred upon a new department of the Colonial Office.

An early definition of the idea is found in a long letter which Lugard wrote to Kirk, the man to whom he felt he owed some of the basic principles which he had developed in his administration. Lugard, writing in reply to a suggestion from Kirk that there should be an African Department under his friend, referred to his Scheme.

" I love the work but it is time that I had more help, for it grows beyond the capacity of one man to deal with. I would propose that they should appoint a Lieutenant Governor with a second or deputy Lt. Governor to act in his absence. These two men would carry on the routine government . . . This would leave me free to deal with all legislation . . . and matters of general policy. I would propose to have an office in London and remain there for half the year, visiting Nigeria only in the winter for 5 months at most. By this means I should spend, say, 5 months at home at work and one on leave, 5 months in Africa and one on voyages, p.a. This would be a new departure bringing me into close touch with the C.O. at home—not in an unrecognized and irregular way while on leave, but as an official on duty, and I daresay that being on the spot it might be possible that this scheme would originate something of the nature of your proposal very shortly."   (L. to Kirk, 2 April 1904).

Upon other occasions when he defended his Scheme he pointed out that in London, with the telegraph, he would be little further in *time* of communication from the main centres of Nigeria than he was at Zungeru, and that, being within reach of the Colonial Secretary and his officials and also of the commercial world, he would be able to make decisions that would at once be better founded on his side and better understood upon theirs.

Once the Scheme had been conceived Lugard and Flora pursued it with almost passionate concentration. Since Flora was the chief protagonist the main scene of action was not in Nigeria but in England, in Whitehall, Westminster and Mayfair. He gave general directions and supplied memoranda; she set to work to convert all the people who mattered and indeed, in her enthusiasm, many who might not have been thought to matter very much.

Cabinet ministers were naturally at the top of the list. The first of these was Chamberlain. Here we must go back a little to pick up the story of their relationship. Lugard had counted upon having as his chief a man whose most distinguishing characteristic was, as he wrote later "the trust he placed in his Governors and the latitude he allowed to those in whom he had confidence."[1] Deep was his disappointment when Chamberlain was forced to give all his attention to another part of Africa and abandon any really vigorous policy of tropical development. But worse was to come. Chamberlain adopted tariff reform after his return from South Africa and resigned from the

[1] Lugard, *The Dual Mandate*, p. 163n.

Cabinet in September 1903 in order to gain freedom for its advocacy. A political earthquake for Britain, it communicated its own special shock to Lugard. He wrote to Mrs. Chamberlain, a wife who was as well able as his own to write for her husband, and she admitted in reply that

" . . . after eight years continuous work at the Colonial Office it has been a tremendous wrench to sever his connection with it and all those who have so loyally worked with him there. I know how greatly he has been interested in the development of Northern Nigeria and how much he has appreciated your work there, and how he has relied on you to carry it out, with a feeling of absolute confidence in the great ability you have shown there, and he asks me to tell you how truly he regrets that this new departure has broken up that relation with you which he has always valued."

She went on to explain that he believed that

" . . . he can do more to further it from an independent position than from within the Cabinet—at the same time not abating his loyalty to and friendship for the Government. And if this is the best way to serve the cause of Fiscal Reform as we believe it is, we can only be satisfied."

(Mrs. Chamberlain to L., 21 September 1903).

The personal friendship continued in so far as the business of the two men on their diverging paths allowed. But Lugard did not wholly despair of still getting some political help for his territory from the tariff reformer. Later the same year, writing to congratulate him upon one of his speeches, and noting that in Chamberlain's protectionist balance sheet there was to be a surplus, Lugard boldly suggested a use for it.

" . . . my suggestion is that any such surplus should be as it were placed to a reserve account by employing it for the development of the less advanced colonies and protectorates—especially those in the tropics— for the production of raw material only grown in the tropics, and for which we are at present largely dependent on foreign countries—such as cotton, rubber and other essentials . . . To quote your own phrase the surplus would be employed on ' developing the new estates ' to take the place of the older." (L. to Chamberlain, 7 October 1903).

We can appreciate the necessity of such a fund now when, after many years on somewhat more altruistic terms, it has at last been established. But Chamberlain, whatever he had once meant by his policy of development for the imperial estate, brushed aside the proposal without ceremony. He was then in the midst of his strenuous tour of conversion, and there was perhaps something galling at that desperate moment in this allocation of hypothetical funds to be derived from a hypothetical policy.

" 10 October 1903.   Highbury, Moor Green,
                                                                    Birmingham.

You know my earnest desire to develop the colonies, but I must not increase the burden of my task by adding new complications to it. Every proposal, however good, means additional controversy. Let us secure one thing at a time. When we have got our surplus it will be time enough to consider how it may be utilized."

Lugard kept in touch with Chamberlain, finding for him, with the help of his brother, more rare orchids from Nigeria, and continuing to press for his influence in support of a policy of railway and other development. Chamberlain was not very encouraging.

" 22 March, 1905.   40, Prince's Gardens, S.W.

I am very much obliged to you for the trouble you have taken to send me some of your native orchids. They have arrived in fair order and I think that I shall be able to grow them, as I was with some others you sent me some time ago. The Ansellia is common all over Africa and I already have specimens doing well. The Eulophias are pretty and new, and so is the Cienkowskia.

I wish you had time to tell me a little of what you are doing. It is most interesting to think of you bringing your vast province into some sort of order. I hope trade is showing signs of development, but I fear that without great expenditure on railway communication we cannot hope that the country will pay, and the present is not a good time to ask for large sums of money from the British Parliament. Still the foundations will have been laid by you, and the country will justify your work and sacrifices in the long run . . .

I am full of work as usual, but progress is slow and the burden of a new policy is left very much on my shoulders. However, here also I look forward to time to justify what is undoubtedly a Herculean task."

Two months later, he was even more emphatic in discouraging Lugard's hopes of large capital development.

" If I had my way, I should, as I have often told you, treat it as a great estate which must be developed, in the first instance at considerable expense to the mother country.

Unfortunately taxation has reached so high a level that the cry is all for economy, and we must, I expect, wait for a more favourable opportunity before we can make such progress."

(Chamberlain to L., 30 May 1905).

But this is a digression from the story of the Scheme. It need hardly be said that Chamberlain's interest and support for it was solicited from the first. It appears that, although Chamberlain saw the official obstacles that would arise, he gave the Scheme his general approval.

Chamberlain, alas, was out of office but there were others who were in or who, at this time of party confusion, might very soon be in. Chief among the "ins", of course, was the Secretary of State, Alfred Lyttelton, whose personality was of great importance to the Lugards. Flora circled about him, spinning her web of charm and persuasion. Charm was Lyttelton's own most remarkable quality; in the records and memoirs of his time he stands out as a man who cast a spell upon nearly everyone who met him. Tall, handsome, athletic, a proficient cricketer, related to Gladstone, who married his aunt, he was at once a close friend of Balfour and of Asquith. He was drawn into the Cabinet as an intimate of the Prime Minister to fill the breach made by the simultaneous resignation of Chamberlain and other ministers in 1903. To Asquith he was " the happy warrior ". Balfour spoke of his " irresistible appeal ". His kindness made him almost too accessible. It was remarked at the Colonial Office, when he took up his work there, that everyone who came seemed to call him by his Christian name. But something more than personal attractiveness was needed in a successor to the formidably effective "Joe". He held his ministry for three years in that bewildered Cabinet as, jostled between the opposing currents of the tariff reform controversy, it drifted along to its wreck in the 1906 election. His two most prominent activities were not very fruitful. The first was the importation of Chinese labour into the Rand mines, a question which, quite unforeseeably, touched off an emotional reaction in the British public. His other chief activity was to draw up a cautious constitution for the Transvaal which was shortly afterwards swept aside by the Liberal government in its own great act of trust in the defeated Boers.

With the Cabinet so unsure, and South Africa so exacting, Nigeria must have appeared of somewhat marginal importance to the new Colonial Secretary. He seems to have been weak over the Scheme in allowing a reluctant agreement to be gradually coaxed out of him. The officials of his department were certain to oppose the plan. They would not, as the Lugards saw, easily give up a position in which, behind the disguise of the Secretary of State's signature, the " nameless boys " of the Office directed governors, while the senior men manipulated the Colonial Secretary himself.

In Flora's operations amongst the political personalities of the London of 1904 to 1906 timing was all-important. She had to conquer Lyttelton while at the same time recognizing that he represented a retreating power and that the new forces of the Liberal party were just forming their ranks for a promising attack. She had to neutralize, as far as she could, the continual sniping of the senior departmental officials from their strong, well-screened position. Lugard was at first a little uneasy about the way in which Flora was handling the affair. Remarking that he would not himself try to influence Antrobus, he added:

" . . . and I would rather you—as my wife—did not do so either—whether by conversation with Mr. Lyttelton or with persons influential in the Press. That is my *strong* feeling." (L. to F. L., 29 December 1904).

He might as well have asked her to stop breathing, and soon he was writing that: " At this distance I will take no steps myself, but leave it to you to do as you think best." There were times when he wanted to assure himself that in this plan there was no self-seeking and at such moments he could draw that assurance from her superb confidence.

" Neither you nor I need have any shame in the desire to obtain such conditions as will render possible a continued holding of your position as the directing head of the destinies of Nigeria. In doing so the public advantage is quite as much involved as our own. We want nothing which it is wrong to want. Very well then, that being so let us quietly and firmly endeavour to win our point . . .Your plan is a good plan and my working experience is that in England—in spite of all that people say to the contrary—our public is such that good plans when clearly made known do succeed." (F. L. to L., 9 July 1904).

With Lyttelton she had this success—or thought she had. She met him, wrote to him, invited him and his wife to a week-end at Abinger, and saw all she could of them in town. She knew how to handle the *Morning Post*, then a very authoritative newspaper, as well as *The Times*, and in June 1904 the former paper published a long article, in which her hand is obvious, advocating the Scheme, against the broadest background of imperial responsibilities. It concluded:

> " Not the least of these advantages would be that the Colonial Secretary would have constantly at hand the best expert advice obtainable on all matters relating to Equatorial Africa—an advantage which it would be difficult to over-estimate."

The leader which warmly approved the article was also quite clearly under Flora's inspiration. It gave a pretty strong hint to Mr. Lyttelton.

> " The occasion is one that may well furnish a test of Mr. Lyttelton's right to be regarded as something more than a politician in office . . . To lay the foundations of a large and intelligent policy in Equatorial Africa and to provide machinery for giving effect to that policy, is a task worthy of any man's powers."[1]

Flora gained one public man after another to her view. Rumours that Balfour was about to resign set her studying the most probable distribution of posts in the coming Liberal ministry. Sydney Buxton was tipped for Colonial Secretary, so she had long talks with him and won his warm approval for the Scheme. She, in return, pointing out the Liberals' lack of a supporting press, promised, in the interests of the party, to make enquiries for him in the City for financial people interested in journalism. Ministers, junior and senior, politically active peers, members of the House of Commons, writers, journalists and others, pass in procession through her letters. " You have certainly many friends at home and on both sides of politics who recognize the signal service you have done for the Empire and the value of your disinterested ability " she told her husband, and she was as tireless in confirming these good opinions as she was in trying to win new ones for him. While pressing towards the main purpose she could enjoy diversions along the way. At one dinner she met Rudyard Kipling, Sidney Colvin, John Buchan and Monypenny. She found herself next to Labouchere. She had long refused to meet him but now, to her own surprise, they had quite a pleasant talk.

[1] *Morning Post*, 3 June 1904. See also *The Times*, 13 June 1904.

" . . . I asked him if he was in truth the anti-Imperialist which he posed as being, and he said he was and that he would willingly give up all Colonies tomorrow. He asked what good they were to us, and, though it was perhaps rather useless, I was drawn by the intelligence of his conversation to express to him the faith that was in me with regard to the real value of the empire in raising and enlarging our plane of existence and making of us a finer race than history has seen before. Of course he said I was an Idealist." (F. L. to L., 31 March 1905).

The next day she sat next to Grogan, who had earned fame by tracing the famous line from Cape to Cairo on his feet. This resourceful and expressive Irishman, probably in the same attractive conversational style the writer has since enjoyed in Kenya, told her a story most flattering to her wifely pride. It was about a moment on his journey. He was beside a lake-shore; all the natives had refused to provide food, and had taken to their canoes. Faced with starvation, he swam out after them and clung to one of their canoes.

" . . . There in the water, holding on to a canoe with one hand, he told them through an interpreter that he was your ' brother ', and thereupon there was an instantaneous change of attitude. They remembered you perfectly, called you Kapelli, and immediately hailed him as friend and provided him with all he wanted. An Indian judge, who was sitting beside him at dinner, asked if he had ever followed on Stanley's tracks; he said ' Yes,' and was immediately asked ' What was his reputation with the natives?' He laughed and said something vague about his having had a difficult job, and then added, ' I tried the same game once with his name that I tried with Lugard's, and I was very nearly murdered for my pains. They wouldn't have Stanley's brother at any price.' He said that the difference between you and Stanley was known over the whole of East Africa . . . " (F. L. to L., undated, 1905).

Lugard smiled as he read passages of this kind. He was never deceived by praise, especially of the kind offered over the sweets or savoury.

" I discount very largely the pretty phrases which people use to you about me. It is a man's natural resource when talking to a lady and *differing* from her in argument, to praise her husband and use terms which are ludicrously in excess of their real feeling or even opposed to it." (L. to F. L., 9 March 1906).

Flora had the whole empire as her field and could claim in a letter to him " to have helped to rouse the British public to a sense of Imperial responsibility and an ideal of Imperial greatness." Yet, willing now to concentrate entirely upon the new and still relatively minor African colony governed by her husband, she gave two public lectures upon Nigeria. (The sacrifice was, it seems, at first misconstrued. Lugard, in Nigeria, and still a fraction short of the entire allegiance which was to come, is reported as saying, in the only breath of criticism of his wife that is ever known to have come from him—" Could she not have left me my one territory?") Flora's lectures were given at the Society of Arts and the Royal Colonial Institute. At the first, in March 1904, she had the Duke of Marlborough, the Under-Secretary of State for the Colonies, as her chairman. Her historical and literary gifts endowed her lecture with a universal flavour which must have mitigated the fact that it was for the most part an account of her husband's problems and achievements. In the debate that followed at least three eminent men, Sir John Kirk, Lord Scarbrough and Sydney Buxton, gave speeches in which, in their support of a new departure in tropical administration, her direct influence can be detected.[1]

Two months later she lectured to the Royal Colonial Institute with Earl Grey in the chair. This time she shewed what other peoples and civilizations had done for the upper negro belt and called upon Britain to play her part in the beneficent forces of history in this region. Her chairman said that Lugard could be described as " Nigeria's best asset and that would remain true as long as there was no interference by politicians at home."[2]

Since Flora could write as well as lecture she began to plan a large book on Northern Nigeria that should lead up through its obscure history in the pages of Arab chroniclers to the happy conclusion of its occupation by Britain. Upon this last point she had no doubt and she offered her faith to her husband in confirmation of his own. Speaking of this Negroland she was beginning to study, she wrote:

" But I am struck in trying to arrange my material with the fact that for the very first time good government has come to it from outside. It has always been preyed upon. For the first time it is to be developed. To

[1] Lady Lugard, ' Nigeria ', *Journal of the Royal Society of Arts*, vol. LII, 18 March 1904.
[2] Lady Lugard, ' West African Negroland ', *Journal of the Royal Colonial Institute*, vol. XXV, June 1904.

have been the man to initiate a new and happy era in a nation's history is something to be glad of." (F. L. to L., 24 April 1904).

Flora's activities had got thus far when, in May, 1905, Lugard came home. His leaves, however full for him, are, for his biographer, empty periods. Some imagination has, therefore, to be used in order to recreate these months of always increasing happiness and unity with Flora as they moved together in London Society, a much noted pair. From London they would go down to Abinger, where Flora would point out to their guests—the Chamberlains, the Alfred and Neville Lytteltons, the Scarbroughs, the Kirks—his display of African weapons, the trophies of his animal victims on the walls or the floors, and the dark, carved doors of the Emir's palace at Kano, which he had regarded as a permissible souvenir and had made into screens by the hall door. The two would walk about the garden or into the surrounding woods talking, exchanging accounts of their doings while separated, of their plans and ideas, of people, of politics, religion and philosophy.

The Scheme dominated the whole leave and took on growing clarity. Exactly what happened is still obscure. It seems that before he sailed Lugard extracted, by the strong pressure he had directed upon a Colonial Secretary already weakened by Flora's persuasions, a verbal agreement to try the experiment. The sadness of parting was thus relieved by the certainty that it would never again be for so long since, as Lugard said, as he settled down for the voyage in November 1905, " we have together achieved the impossible and got the Colonial Office to undertake a most radical and disturbing reform." And yet he had the faintest misgiving; he wished that Lyttelton was to remain in power, for *he* at least was friendly and " he has committed himself to the first step." He felt that a Bryce or a Morley might not be so amenable. " A Pharaoh may arise who knew not Joseph."

It was at this time that Flora's book on Nigeria appeared. It had been written with astonishing speed. Dedicated, of course, 'To my Husband,' it was a most handsome volume with its 53 chapters, 500 pages, its excellent maps and its majestic sweep of history from the first Arab conquests in Africa to those of Goldie and Lugard.[1] Its introduction was a call to the public, which she had done so much to educate about the white dominions, to recognize that Britain now had a predominantly colonial and autocratically ruled Empire and should

[1] F. L. Shaw, *A Tropical Dependency* (1906).

frankly face her new and wide responsibilities of tropical administration. Of British government of dependencies she wrote:

" It must be more or less in the nature of an autocracy which leaves with
the rulers full responsibility for the prosperity of the ruled. The administration of India . . . is among the successes of which the British people
are most justly proud. The work done in Egypt is another proof of our
capacity for autocratic rule. We are justified, therefore, in thinking of
ourselves as a people who may face with reasonable hope of success still
vaster questions of tropical administration."[1]

She introduced the last few chapters upon British administration
with a proper confession. " The British High Commissioner is my
husband . . . It is impossible for me altogether to clear my mind of
favourable prejudice."

It is a book in the grand manner, written in a tone of authority and
with considerable literary power—more considerable than that of her
husband—and is somewhat of a pioneer work in its use of Arab
chroniclers and other sources. Its chief demerit, for later students, is
the lack of reference to her authorities and of a bibliography. The
book went in a specially bound copy to the King, and also to
Balfour, Rosebery, Milner, Lyttelton and many other leading men
whose letters of appreciation should certainly have been genuine if
they had found time to read it. Shortly after the publication of her
book Lugard's own immensely long report upon Nigeria for 1904 at
last came out, and was summarized in three columns in *The Times*
with much more notice in the rest of the Press than a colonial report
would get in these days.[2]

As the year ended Balfour's temporizing government was making
its exit from the political stage in a last act which rather dragged, and
there were many speculative glances into the wings to see what per-
formers the Liberals were going to send in. It was an anxious time for
Flora. After Lugard's departure she set to work to get Mr. Lyttelton
to commit himself more definitely with regard to the Scheme by allowing her to write an article in *The Times* while simultaneously he was
to publish a communiqué announcing the new system. She wanted
to see the publication of this communiqué before she sent her own
article. But it did not come. Lyttelton wrote vaguely to tell her it
would be issued on an agreed date. On December 2nd she opened her

[1] *Ibid.* pp. 2-3. [2] *The Times,* 24 November 1905.

Times and, having looked for his statement in vain, sent off her own article. On December 4th Balfour resigned before Lyttelton's communiqué appeared. Had the permanent officials taken advantage of the imminent change of ministers to hold it up? The next day, December 5th, Flora's article appeared, well constructed, in her firm, clear style and marshalling every imaginable argument in favour of the new plan. It covered the health of the governors in tropical colonies and their family ties; the frequent deaths or transfers; the long leaves and resultant discontinuity; the need for fresh blood and local knowledge in the Colonial Office; the desirability of much more contact between governors on one side and the Colonial Office and commercial and scientific circles on the other. With the vast increase of work, ill-informed juniors were taking decisions. Then came the idea of grouping territories under Governors-General, and the assumption that the plan would extend not only to Nigeria but to other colonies. The key to the scheme was " that whether in England or in Africa, the High Commissioner will remain the sole working head of the administration."

Editorial comment endorsed the plan warmly. It was one of the administrative testaments left by departing ministers and " a far-reaching scheme of administrative rule to which Mr. Lyttelton has set his hand during his tenure of the Colonial Office." There was the important assumption, for which Flora must have pressed, that this measure, being non-partisan, need not be upset by the change of ministers.[1] Then Sir Augustus Hemming wrote a letter[2] strongly supporting the plan and saying that if it had been in operation in his day the valuable lives of more than one governor would have been saved. This letter, unsolicited and unexpected, was the more valuable in that Hemming had been for thirty years an official in the Colonial Office and had been head of the West African department before going on to be a colonial governor.

The new plan could not at such a moment have attracted wide attention. The next day the new Prime Minister, Campbell-Bannerman, announced his Cabinet. Eagerly Flora ran through the list. It was strong in ability, with Asquith at the Treasury, Grey at the Foreign Office, Lloyd George at the Board of Trade and Haldane at the War Office. Alas! Her friend, Sydney Buxton, was Postmaster-

[1] *The Times*, 5 December 1905. [2] *Ibid*. 26 December 1905.

General, and Lord Elgin was Colonial Secretary. Elgin! The name gave her a shock from its very lack of significance. Hastily she sought information and opinions. A not very distinguished Indian Viceroy, recently retired, the son of a Viceroy, the father of many children, reputed to be honourable, serious, plain, and, as one of her informants told her, " four foot high, four foot broad, but stuffed four foot full of solid sense." But he was said to be—and this was ominous—very shy and inaccessible. And, as Elgin's Under-Secretary, incredible, almost horrifying, no other than Winston Churchill!

There was no need to make enquiries about *him*, young though he was. All the Empire knew the name, which spoke of romantic adventurousness in the military field and reckless irresponsibility in the political. At thirty-one he had been in four campaigns in widely different parts of the world, written striking books, entered the Commons as a Conservative, raked his own government with the stinging fire of his young eloquence, and then walked over to the Liberals. What was to be expected of him in his new office? Who could tell? But Lugard, in Zungeru, shook his head and called the appointment " bad news ".

He proved to be right as far as concerned his own special hopes. Flora had friends inside the Colonial Office and she soon heard that Antrobus was displeased with her article, that the Office meant to persuade Lord Elgin to reverse his predecessor's decision, and that Churchill had joined forces with the officials. " You may be sure," wrote Flora, superfluously, perhaps, " that I will leave no stone unturned that I can move." She went to the Colonial Office, sent in her card—she had no appointment—and asked to see Mr. Churchill. She was shown straight in.

The young man, with the alert eyes and wilful mouth and chin, sat at a desk piled high with files. She went at once to the point. She told him, feeling herself to be in a position to offer her judgment to this— in her eyes—political stripling, that she had heard many good things of him with regard to his work at the Colonial Office. " But amongst the good things, this bad thing had reached me." She told him with some force that the plan he was trying to upset was a definite engagement, in reliance upon which her husband had returned to Africa, expecting to be back in England in six months. Churchill seized on this, and from her account the conversation can be reconstructed.

" But I want him specially to come home this summer. There is all West Africa to talk over with him. There are many things that this new House of Commons won't stand and they will have to be reformed."

" Yes," Flora replied, " Yes, my husband also thinks there are a few things that might be reformed in West Africa."

" Now," Churchill went on, " There is a part of the scheme that I approve of. The idea of a Governor-General for a group of colonies. That pleased me. I think it is very likely that we might want a Governor-General for West Africa." Here he paused and looked at his visitor significantly. But he could not stave off Flora's well-prepared attack by this feint. Having reminded him that before there could be a Governor-General there had to be an amalgamation of the three Nigerias, she stated her case. It soon appeared that it was the very kernel of the scheme to which he most objected, that Lugard should remain responsible for Nigeria while in England.

" The man on the spot must be responsible," he insisted.

" And so," replied Flora, "this lack of continuity must still hinder the development of West Africa as it has for 300 years." Even in England, she argued, Lugard would be " the man on the spot."

" I see," said Churchill (in what Flora was reluctantly bound to admit was " one of his happy phrases which helped in the discussion"). " It becomes really a question of the definition of ' the spot '."

She took up the idea and showed that with the development of modern communications, the " spot " had changed its character and new measures were needed, " horribly shocking no doubt," she said, " to the traditions of permanent officials but good for the service of the Empire and in accord, I imagine, with the spirit of a progressive party."

" That it is new," Churchill replied in a cordial tone, apparently taking this fly, " is all the better."

" It has never been thought of before," Flora pressed. " You have never thought of it. You have not thought of it properly now. You have allowed yourself to accept the arguments of the permanent officials who are, of course—though I think needlessly—alarmed at a startling innovation."

Churchill protested that, having read Lugard's memorandum and the officials' minutes in it, he had been convinced their case was the stronger. It was not that he under-estimated Lugard—he paid him an ungrudging tribute. Nor did it matter that Lugard had left all the officials " spluttering and protesting ". That was their nature. " But," and here again he surprised Flora who had not expected such intellectual power in "the boy ", " there are men of knowledge and men of power. In this office there are men of knowledge, of extraordinary ability and industry." To make up for his disrespectful comments he went on to speak of their long lives devoted to work, of their public spirit, and brilliant intellectual endowments. Flora agreed. " But," he went on, " they have no power. There is only one individual in this Office who has power and that is the Secretary of State. On the borders of the Empire there are men like your husband who have made the Empire by their energy, their courage and inventive genius. These are men of power. Now what you want to do is to bring a man of power and put him in here amongst these men of knowledge. He has knowledge of his own subject as well as power. He is an expert. He knows more than any of us. He can with his knowledge override the Secretary of State himself. Don't you see that you want to endow him with a double position. He has to have what no-one else has here except the Secretary of State. He is to have power as well as knowledge. Surely this is an anomaly?"

Flora was impressed, but she countered with the argument that Lugard would have power only for Nigeria as he always had. "And now," she went on, " let us quit phrases and try to examine together how this thing will in reality act." She sketched for him all her long considered plans for tropical development in relation to the metropolitan economy, ideas about new colonial products, of communications, labour and the rest. She was at her best in this and Churchill's attention was caught. This was not a policy for a dying government, she urged, but eminently one for the new ministry with its long lease of power before it.

" Where are you going to get the local knowledge which is essential to the intelligent development of such a policy? If you want to develop tin-mines in the Malay States whose advice are you going to ask, that of Mr. Antrobus—or Sir Frank Swettenham?"

Churchill raised the possibility of a West African Council. Flora, putting her finger upon one fear which has always militated against this plan, said its personnel would be retired men out of touch with current affairs. Churchill insisted that he would and could consult governors and seemed surprised and vexed to hear that, if the Scheme fell through, he would have to wait until the next summer before Lugard could be at home.

" But he must come home on leave. I for one would say that a man of that sort, a man who has created, so to speak, the whole of the great work on which he is engaged should have the absolute right to command as much leave as he judges necessary. There should be no question as to the amount."

Flora smiled.

" You don't know my husband. He is passionately attached to his work. He won't come home to injure his work and to subject himself again to the ordeal through which he has just been passing in getting through the accumulations which await his return from leave. He can't come home on leave when leave means what it means now !"

She then made her proposal. Let the Scheme be tried as an experiment this year! This would bring her husband home for consultation and then all the parties concerned could try it out. Churchill was evidently shaken.

" Well, I will think the whole thing over again. I want Sir Frederick home. He is a distinguished expert. He knows more than we all know about these questions. He has been doing, while we have all been talking, and I can't say more than that I will do my very best, and of course as you know no decisions lie with me. It is Lord Elgin and Lord Elgin only who can give any decisions. He has not yet read the papers but when he does, I have no doubt he will talk it over again with me and I will do my very best to discuss it fairly with him from every point of view. I think it is very likely he may stand by the scheme."

Flora seized the moment to bring forward her long list of the names of eminent men who supported the Scheme, many of whom she had herself converted. Sir Edward Grey, Buxton, Haldane, members of his own ministry; Lord Scarbrough, Lord Milner, Lord Cromer, Goldie, Kirk, Lord Robert Cecil, Lord Camperdown, Lord Knutsford and others. Churchill seemed impressed. " I had no idea that the whole thing had been so fully discussed. I will do my best. I will think it over."

They parted cordially. " Of course," Flora commented to her

husband, as she thought over what had passed, " it must seem ridiculous that a boy of his age and experience should have the power and influence that he has." Still he *was* the Under-Secretary and a vital one at that. She felt that his interest had been deeply stirred; he had shown his great admiration for Lugard, and she slept better that night than for many weeks past. (F. L. to L., 6 February 1906).

But she did not for a moment rest upon her new hope of Churchill. The next day came an official letter from Lord Elgin's secretary, Bernard Holland—who happened to be a friend and ally of hers—to say, in answer to a letter from her, that his chief was still studying Lugard's " full and able memorandum ". She redoubled her efforts. The next night at dinner, sitting next to Haldane, of whom she was seeing a good deal, and hearing much of his plans for army re-organization, she discussed the Scheme again and also the man who would decide upon it. Haldane gave a frank but favourable account of his Cabinet colleague Lord Elgin. " Disappointing in appearance and presentment of himself, small, insignificant, unready of speech, but on further acquaintance disclosing qualities of shrewdness, ability, grasp of his own subject and tenacity of will which make him, in my opinion, a far more serious man and likely to be a much better Colonial Secretary than Lyttelton."

" But," interjected Flora, " rumoured to be in the hands of his officials."

" No man less so. He is a man who will have his own opinions, but who will not form them till he has full material, and will then carry them tenaciously into action. Already he is absolutely master of the Colonial Office." (F. L. to L., 7 February 1906).

The next day Flora reported a letter from Chamberlain defending the Scheme, but regretting that since " he, too, was fighting with his back to the wall " he could do nothing practical to help. She had a long talk with Lord Robert Cecil, who thought the principle excellent, and sitting at dinner next to " an intelligent young Walter of *The Times*," she got him to say that there could be " no argument for the other side except the usual official obstruction." She gained heart as she found everyone outside the Office in favour of the plan and decided " we are bound to win".

It was at this time, in the middle of February, that Flora had news from Lugard of the rising at Sokoto, to be described later, but she does not seem to have fully realized the gravity of the event and remained absorbed in her own campaign. All her plans to meet Lord Elgin failed and the best she could do was to collect authoritative opinions of the still obscure character of the Secretary of State. Sydney Buxton, whom she met often, said that the more the Cabinet saw of him, the more favourably they were impressed, but that they were all so over-worked at the moment that Elgin had probably not yet studied the question. She was pleased, also, to hear that one of Lugard's Residents, David Carnegie, was half-brother to Lady Elgin. But she was depressed to hear—an interesting leakage—that Churchill, in his minute support-ing the official opposition to the Scheme, had written in characteristic style, that he " could see no reason why the Colonial Office should become a Pantheon for Pro-Consuls." Then she cheered up when she realized that this was written before her talk with him.

Her spirits rose higher again when, operating upon her usual terrain of the dinner-table, she led a former Secretary of State for the Colonies, Lord Knutsford, to say that there ought to be a Permanent Under-Secretary for tropical Africa and

" if Elgin can be persuaded to do it, there is no man so fitted for the post as Sir Frederick Lugard . . . if we only had a few more Sir Frederick Lugards there would be a prospect of carrying out successfully a really grand policy of development."

The tension grew as February ran out. Flora wrote, " I have allowed myself to hope so much . . . " Yet everyone seemed to surrender to her brilliant advocacy. Even Churchill? She could not be sure. If only she could meet Lord Elgin. But " shy, retiring creature that he is, nobody knows him. But I hear Lady Elgin is coming to town. In this case," we can almost see the set of Flora's mouth, " they will have a house and she can be called upon."

Meanwhile she wrote again to Elgin's secretary; she arranged for Lord Camperdown to give him a private letter from Lugard. She dined with Haldane again at the House but he was much too full of his army estimates to give much attention to *her* preoccupation. How-ever, Major Seely was there, a member for Liverpool, a future Under-Secretary at the Colonial Office, and he was won to the Scheme. " Lugard," he said, " is a splendid fellow. He is the very head and front of all our administrators." He added that " he should come home to England and have a berth worthy of him in the tropical administration at home. Will you tell your husband from me that there are some of us who don't forget the work which he is doing on the outskirts of the Empire?" And there was " that able young man, Mr. Amery" of *The Times*, whom Flora found a most congenial fellow-imperialist, who grasped at once the full significance of the Scheme and told her, as he sat next to her at dinner " The precedent for it is the Viceroy of India with Calcutta and Simla. If they weren't such blockheads, they would see at once that Nigeria is Sir Frederick's Calcutta and London his Simla."

While Flora's letters were mostly bulletins on the campaign they also helped Lugard to live with her in the London of her day. "People are moving now fast into London," she writes at the beginning of March, "and invitations shower down." She records the tragic death of her friend Dorothy, wife of Sir Edward Grey, from a driving accident. She tried to comfort him, marking how splendidly, though inwardly broken by the loss, he carried on his public tasks. " I do not complain," he told her, " I have had twenty years such as few men have had." Then, courage deserting him for a moment, he told a mutual friend, " I have not seen her for three weeks. I have never been so long separated from her since we married, and I am only forty-three. I don't know how I am going to get through the rest of life." (F. L. to L., 28 February 1906). This brought home to Flora the reality of death and so their urgent need of the Scheme.

" And yet while death dwarfs everything else, it has also its reflex effect in making one feel, while this little space of consciousness lasts, let us use it to the best of our ability. With the great separation hanging over us, it seems a pity to waste so much of life alone. With only so little life to live, one would like to live it in the best way." (F. L. to L., 13 February 1906).

Lord Milner dined and talked with her. She was greatly indignant about his treatment over the Chinese labour question and, when he had to make his defence in Parliament and was struck, he told her, by " an invincible cold," she wrote to him

" the sort of letter which would I fear have aggravated you dreadfully to receive, enclosing salicin and begging him to gargle his throat regularly with salt. I don't know whether he did it, but I am told that after the first few sentences his voice cleared and held out well to the end."

(F. L. to L., 27 February 1906).

The salicin must at least have done good to her own position with him. Meeting him again at dinner at the Halifaxes, she was able to urge him to see Lord Elgin and talk sense to him. She met " one of the minor lions of the moment," Mr. Smith—afterwards Lord Birkenhead—who made a speech which took the House of Commons by storm and marked him out as a possible future Prime Minister. She heard that the Princess of Wales had said that she and her husband took the greatest interest in the wonderful work Lugard was doing in Nigeria. Mr. George Wyndham told her that

> " a number of the Government side have read my book, and have been much impressed by it, amongst others . . . the most villainous and unscrupulous Little Englander that you can imagine. He was, Mr. Wyndham said, ' most enthusiastic '. Another Little Englander, of no great consequence truly, who had . . . read it with enthusiasm, was Wilfred Blunt. One likes to hear of people of the wrong way of thinking who can read it with sympathy." (F. L. to L., 20 March 1906).

When Haldane told her how he won his army vote against the dissidents of his own party, she encouraged Lugard with the comment that " the Imperial section in the Government are already daring to oppose the ultra-radicals and are *winning*."

But on March 8th, the blow fell. A note came from her friend Bernard Holland, Lord Elgin's secretary, to say that the Scheme had been definitely rejected. To sugar this bitter pill she was also told that a cable had been sent to Lugard asking him to come home for some months during the summer. Flora took the blow even more hardly than Lugard, for he had been preparing himself for it. But her spirit was not crushed. She did not need young Mr. Amery to say to her " But you will not give it up. Sir Frederick will work it some other way," before she was planning means of getting the substance of the Scheme without its formal sanction. For if Lugard brought his brother back to work with him, " we could slip in the thin end of the wedge and start a little C.O. of our own down at Abinger."

Lugard, it appeared, had been right in his fears. Lyttelton had *not* left a written decision behind him. The tone of Lugard's memorandum on the Scheme and of Flora's article had still further alienated the permanent officials and they had done all they could to induce the new ministers to reject an experiment that was both personally and professionally abhorrent to them.

The Lugard Scheme for Continuous Administration

There is more than a suggestion of special pleading in the arguments put forward by Lugard and his wife. Yet it would be a mistake to assume that in this matter they had deceived themselves. Apart from those who, softened into acquiescence by the flattering urgency of a charming and brilliant companion at the dinner table, gave their easy agreement to the Scheme, there were others with the relevant knowledge whose names represent impressive support. Chief among these were Chamberlain, Buxton, Knutsford, Hemming, Goldie, Kirk and Amery, and to them must be added two serving Governors, Sir Frank Swettenham and Sir Ralph Moor.

The Lugards had been checked. But time was to show that they were not defeated.

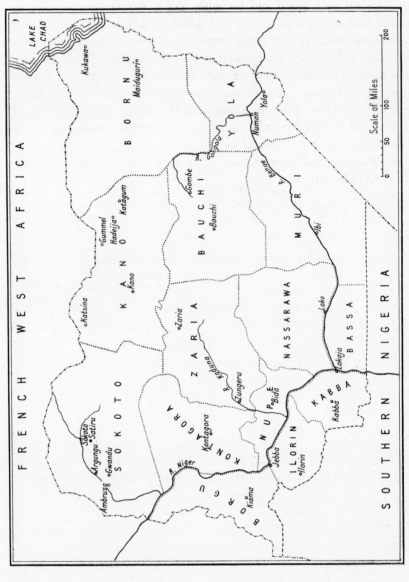

Northern Nigeria 1906. Based on map in *Annual Reports, Northern Nigeria* 1906–7

CHAPTER XII

CRISIS IN SOKOTO, 1906

IN THE first weeks of 1906 a crisis burst upon Northern Nigeria. It came with the suddenness of a tropical thunderstorm, and, like lightning, it throws a momentary flash over the central figure and his Nigerian background and leaves the observer not only startled, but puzzled as to what it was he really saw and what meaning to give to it.

The story began amongst the Munshi people of the open forest lands south of the Benue, one of the regions most inaccessible to the new administration. The Munshi, or Tiv as they are now called, were a numerous and very attractive tribe of pagans, more than half a million strong, who still give—or, since Africa changes so quickly, did give the writer a few years ago—an impression of unsophisticated vigour and cheerfulness. Living in clans in their excellent villages in light rolling woodlands, they had the fearless bearing of those who own no master. But the untamed pagan, for all his air of almost childlike freshness and innocence, does not always make a good neighbour. Early in January, 1906, at the little Niger Company trading post of Abinsi on the Benue, run by an African manager, a dispute broke out between one of the Hausa traders and a woman of the near-by pagan Jukun tribe. They agreed to settle it by the ordeal through the medium of a fowl, but the woman refused to accept the result, and flew at the Jukun man who stabbed her. The Hausas and the Jukuns at the store at once came to blows; the Jukuns called in their fellow-pagans from the nearest Munshi group. These fell upon the Hausas, killed many of them, captured some and drove the rest with their women and children into the river to drown and then, for good measure, sacked and burned the Company's store. The outrage was the more important as the Benue was the main trade-route for north-eastern Nigeria, used by the Germans of the Cameroons as well as by the British, and this disorder closed it to shipping.

The trouble was not, however, upon a scale seriously to disturb Lugard when news of it reached him on January 2nd. He was in one of his most confident moods, as his letter of this date to Flora reveals.

" Telegrams came to say that the Munshis are up, and had burnt the Niger Company's store at Abinsi . . . I have made all necessary precautionary measures, and ordered up a flying column of 100 men for defensive purposes—a bigger expedition must follow . . . —*Everything* is urgent, and one is kept at high pressure from morning till night . . . I love this turgid life of command, when I can feel that the sole responsibility rests on me for everything,whether it be a small crisis like this, with the necessary action to be taken to preserve life, and to re-establish prestige or whether it be, as my day's task has been, to confirm the hanging of criminals or the penal servitude, or the petty punishments of others, watching jealously that the executive officer does not inflict punishments which are unfair, or that the legal adviser does not hamper true justice by technical objections." (L. to F. L., 2 January 1906).

The next day he sent off, almost as a routine matter, a telegram to the Colonial Office.

"January 3. Munshi tribe has destroyed Royal Niger Company's depot, Abinsi. Navigation of Benue closed. Making necessary preparations for strong military expedition.—Lugard."[1]

He had, it seems, forgotten that new ministers were now in power, and that they had old officials to remind them of his precipitancy over the Kano campaign. Precipitancy was a fault of which the Colonial Office was not guilty. After sitting on Lugard's telegram for a fortnight, Elgin and Churchill turned their attention to it. Churchill's reaction was vigorous, and, by implication, very critical of Lugard and of the whole " forward " policy for which he stood, and upon which he had now been acting steadily for more than five years. The minute also reveals the ignorance of the new hand.

" The entire scope and nature of our responsibilities and activities in Nigeria and in the Lagos Hinterland require to be searchingly reviewed and reconsidered by the S. of S. I incline to the opinion that we should withdraw from a very large portion of the territory which we now occupy nominally, but really disturb without governing and that we should concentrate our resources upon the railway and economic develop-

---

[1] *Northern Nigeria: Correspondence relating to Sokoto, Hadeija and the Munshi Country* (1907), Cd. 3620. The account given here is largely based on this document and *Reports*, 1905-6, pp. 8-23.

ment of the more settled . . . regions . . . I see no reason why our occupation should be made immediately effective up the French frontier line; or why these savage tribes should not be allowed to eat each other without restraint, until some more suitable opportunity than the present shall arise for ' pacifying ' them."[1]

Lord Elgin, graver and a little more accurate, followed in the same vein, " We engaged," he wrote, " in the game of grab in the African continent and cannot escape the consequences!" It was sometimes possible to decline responsibility for a hinterland but, he rightly went on, he doubted if the word applied here. Lugard was therefore asked what was the extent of the disturbed area and the size of the expedition he planned.[2]

Having received Lugard's purely factual answer, the two ministers turned to consider the punitive side of the question. In a scathing minute Churchill opined that the expedition had probably started already and the Colonial Office would find itself committed to operations of indefinite character without knowing what it was all about. If the order of the colony depended on it, it would be supported, but H.M.G. seemed to have only a nominal control over these grave matters and yet had to bear the direct responsibility. Elgin agreed that it was most unsatisfactory that he had not been consulted about a military expedition. He did not know what the colonial practice was but in his Indian experience the sanction of the government was required. Nor should it be overlooked that there was a large annual deficit in Northern Nigeria.[3] (This was not quite a fair way of describing a grant-in-aid for a newly annexed territory.) As a result of these discussions, but not until eight days later, this telegram was sent to Lugard.

" Referring to your telegram of January 19, I am not prepared to approve dispatch of large expedition without further information of objects proposed. If these cannot be explained by telegraph, advance should be limited to what is necessary to open Benue navigation and protect any property but should not be carried further without my sanction."[4]

This attitude seems rather surprising in an ex-Viceroy of India. It was still more so in the hero of the Malakand Field Force, the River

---

[1] Minute by Churchill on Lugard to Elgin, 3 January 1906, C.O. 446/52.
[2] Minute by Elgin on Lugard to Elgin, 3 January 1906, C.O. 446/52.
[3] Lugard to Elgin, 19 January 1906, with minutes by Churchill and Elgin, C.O. 446/52.
[4] Elgin to Lugard, 27 January 1906, Cd. 3620, p. 2.

War and other famous military adventures, and the man who was to become probably the most superbly confident imperialist and war-leader in modern British history. Elgin may have been merely register-ing the disapproval of his officials or expressing the tendency of new ministers to try to go into reverse upon their predecessor's policy during the first months of office. But Churchill is harder to interpret. It must be remembered that he was then a Liberal, and a new convert at that, at a time in life when he liked to play with ideas, the more surprising and emphatic the better. But in Churchill's attitude there was another and permanent element, one that, in a man of his com-bative record was probably not understood at the time and which has re-appeared to cause surprise in our own day. This was the sense of generous humanity towards an enemy and the ability to cross no-man's land to see the point of view of the other side. In his book on the Sudan campaign of 1896-99 there will be found passages of sensitive appreciation of the qualities and the sufferings of the Sudanese enemies and, in the earlier editions, outspoken criticism of what he judged inhumane conduct by Kitchener at Omdurman, and afterwards in the desecration of the Mahdi's tomb.[1] In a comment which he made a little later upon Lugard's proposed canoe tax, he exclaimed, " No wonder he wants so many troops and such frequent punitive expedi-tions to impress upon the natives the advantages of British rule."[2]

Churchill had guessed right about Lugard's action—perhaps because it was what he would have done himself. Lugard had never intended to wait; he had already sent an advance force of 100 men from Lokoja and these had found the Company's depot razed and strewn with headless corpses. On January 22nd, five days before the restricting telegram of January 27th was sent, he had dispatched another force of some 600 men and 26 officers which had been collected at Lokoja. Lord Elgin's telegram made him a very angry man. " It is the Kano business over again on a small scale." All the other Munshi and the neighbouring pagan tribes were waiting to see if the aggressors would be punished. If not, they were almost certain to rise themselves.

" With great difficulty I have got together a thoroughly efficient force. It is already practically on the spot and capable of dealing with the whole Munshi tribe. Not a word from the C.O. all this time. Now, when all

[1] W. S. Churchill, *The River War* (eds. 1899, 1902, 1933), pp. 211-14.
[2] Minute by Churchill on Lugard to Elgin, 20 March 1906, C.O. 446/53.

the expense of transport has been incurred and men have worked day and night to do it, they wire they do not approve, and pending full information the expedition is to do nothing. If so the Okpotos will rise and the North bank Munshis and the C.O. will land themselves in a big palaver which might now be crushed in bud. How can one run a country like this on such terms? Such orders are applicable to a young novice, not to a H.C. entrusted with the government of a country and moreover one who has been here as long as I have. The result will no doubt be that the expedition will eventually take place, but the delay will do the greatest harm, make it more difficult—cost more lives—and cost much more money . . .

I am sending a long telegram in reply explaining all I can and ending by asking for immediate orders, and whether I am to cancel the expedition. They have spent 27 days since I telegraphed to say I was sending a strong expedition. Why did they not at once stop it if not approved? Do they suppose I can wait a month for orders in a crisis? It makes one rather sick for it denotes such carelessness and apathy at Home combined with much 'Jack in Office' intention of putting on the bearing-rein and shewing one that one is only a little cypher, whose little plans, after long being laid aside as not worthy of immediate attention, can be squashed whenever the Antrobi and the Secretary of State can find leisure to attend to them." (L. to F. L., 28 January 1906).

But Lugard had had experience of this sort of trouble with the Colonial Office over his Kano expedition and he thought he knew how to deal with it. On January 30th he telegraphed a reply stressing the seriousness and brutality of the attack and the danger of a general rising and ending, " Much regret if I exceeded legitimate action. As I received no further instructions from you, supposed that action proposed in my telegram of 3rd January was approved. Request you to inform me at once whether you order cancellation of expedition. Lugard."[1]

The Kano situation was being exactly reproduced. " Cancel " was a harsh word to a politician mainly concerned to show that he has said the right thing even if other people have done the wrong one. In these exchanges responsibility is quietly pushed around from one to the other as in the old game of hunt the slipper—with Parliament as the hunter. Churchill realized that the expedition could not now be recalled. Elgin was obliged to agree but he replied, on February 2nd,

[1] Cd. 3620, p. 2.

in the sort of terms that infuriate men of action with confidence—over-confidence perhaps—in their own ability and good sense: " I do not order cancellation of expedition but it is most desirable that it should not be carried farther than immediate object renders necessary."[1]

Here again was the classical rift between an imperial government and its frontier agents as to the urgency of extending control. Lugard's argument was that it was bad policy, bad economy, and bad morality to go in for piecemeal advances and that the expedition against one group of Munshis should be used as an opportunity to impress them all, as well as neighbouring tribes. This was coldly received at the Office. Antrobus' minute that they were not obliged to interfere everywhere in Northern Nigeria, or push their administration at once to the frontiers, was most congenial to his chiefs and, indeed, echoed Churchill's own words.[2]

While Lugard was awaiting news of the Munshi expedition, Lord Scarbrough arrived in Zungeru. The relations between the two men were unusual. Lugard was, as we have seen, highly critical of many features of the Royal Niger Company but he was personally devoted to the man who had succeeded Goldie as its head. They had much to discuss, especially mining questions, and Lugard found that although a " delightful man to do business with, he is as obstinate and strong on his own personal views as I am myself." On February 15th, in order to give his guest a full picture of the work of government, Lugard was sitting with him just before dinner in his office and reading out the various telegrams that had come in, and laughingly commenting upon them, when suddenly he found himself reading the following telegram from Ambrusa, near Sokoto.

" . . . whole of C. Company, Mounted Infantry, defeated and annihilated at Satiru . . . Hillary and Scott, Residents, Blackwood, West African Frontier Force, are, I fear, killed. Dr. Ellis severely wounded, Sergeant Slack, R.A. and myself and doctor only men remaining: most urgent. Signed Gosling, Sergeant."[3]

For a moment, Lugard's world seemed to spin round him. It was not the disaster alone, grave though it was, and the first defeat ever sustained by the Force, that made the solid ground upon which he

---

[1] Cd. 3620, p. 2. [2] Minute on Lugard to Elgin, 14 February 1906, C.O. 446/52.
[3] Cd. 3620, p. 7.

thought he stood, seem to shake. It was the utterly unexpected, unexplained stroke falling just as the government was in a moment of great weakness. The bulk of the troops were in the Munshi country in the far south-east, at the furthest possible point, some 500 trackless miles, away from Sokoto in the extreme north-west, and very far from the main centres of administration. The Resident of Sokoto, proceeding on leave, had just left that city and, with his assistant, was on his way down to Zungeru escorted only by the small number of the Sokoto police. His successor had not arrived. There was no force left in the whole region with the exception of 25 native infantry, with four Europeans under Captain Harbord, at the furthest point the telegraph had reached, 80 miles from Sokoto, at Ambrusa. And this place was the capital of Gwandu where the Emir was known to be unfriendly and might well take this chance to rebel.

Later that night, Captain Harbord wired, before leaving his dangerous position at the telegraph and falling back, upon Lugard's orders, on the friendly chieftainship of Argungu. He told Lugard that the rising, so amazingly successful in its first attempt, was headed by a new Mahdi, and that he had captured the W.A.F.F. company's Maxim gun. It was, of course, only later, in this country of difficult communications, that the full story of what had happened came through. But it will be better to record it here.

An outlaw from French territory, Dan Makafo, who was believed to have killed two Frenchmen, had fled across the border and persuaded a certain Mallam Isa to declare himself to be the prophet Jesus. This man's father had declared himself a Mahdi in 1904, had been arrested and had died in prison. The whole population of the small town of Satiru, twelve miles south of Sokoto and well-known as a centre of fanaticism, accepted the claim, and from this arose the excitement and disorder that seem inseparable from such fervour. The Satiru people, indeed, used their exaltation in the first place to pay off old scores against their nearest neighbours.

The acting Resident, Hillary, with his assistant, Scott, Dr. Ellis, and Lieutenant Blackwood, with a white sergeant, some 70 Mounted Infantry and one Maxim gun went out to the place. Confident that he could pacify the people without resort to bloodshed, Hillary, accompanied by Scott, rode well ahead of the troops, not even waiting until the Maxim gun, which was a long way behind, could catch up with the rest. As he approached the town long lines of men suddenly arose from a depression where they had been hiding and rushed at him. There was no chance for him to talk to them, though to the end he was heard calling to the people that he had come to talk and not to fight. But the crowd was in no mood to listen and the force coming on behind must, in any case, have cast doubt on Hillary's words of peace. There was no time to bring up the soldiers. It seems that at the moment of crisis there was confusion and contradictory orders; the lieutenant hesitated between the two courses of forming and keeping square at the point the soldiers had reached or of bringing on the square in face of the enemy in an attempt to save the two political officers. There was confusion, too, as to whether the men were to dismount, and some of the horses bolted. The crowd rushed with savage abandon at each white man they could see. They were armed only with their agricultural implements, hoes and axes, and a few spears and bows and arrows. In a few moments of wild hacking and thrusting they had overrun and killed Hillary, Scott, and Blackwood and speared Dr. Ellis. They then turned upon the soldiers. Many of these were killed and the rest fled in all directions. But some showed great bravery. One rescued Ellis from his attackers and Sergeant Gosling, helped by others, managed to carry the wounded doctor from the field.

When the first news of the disaster reached the Sultan in Sokoto he believed that all the Europeans were killed. The Resident was away. There was only one Englishman, a sergeant, in Sokoto. The spell of the white man's invincibility was broken. If the Sultan, with his religious and political pre-eminence, should join the triumphant rebels, there could be little doubt that, more or less actively, all the emirs would respond to the call of their suzerain. It needed little hatred or discontent to have produced this result; the mere fact of conquest, of the novelty and strangeness of the new masters and their interference with slavery and other customs were motives enough for the ruling class; while the fact that the impulse was mainly religious made the situation more critical. It meant that the danger had now entered that sphere of Muslim passion, of the fierce unifying call of the faith which is the incalculable danger that always haunted the men who carried British power or influence into the world of Islam. The very word Mahdism had a powerful atmosphere peculiar to itself because of its very mysteriousness. It was a force which had shown its power in the Sudan, in Somaliland and elsewhere. It has possessed a strange kind of fascination that has proved readily exploitable in fiction, as Buchan has shown in *Greenmantle*.

Lugard, in his position, and with his temperament, was the last man to feel any romantic thrill in the danger which he had to assess and command from his office desk. He had only one question in his mind. " Would the emirs rise?" They knew very well that the troops were far away in the south-east. There was also a most extraordinary combination of other events to make the moment perfect for rebellion. Not only was the Resident of Sokoto away and exposed to danger, but the Resident of the neighbouring and ill-affected emirate of Gwandu, Captain Ruxton, was also away; the able Resident of the key position of Kano, Dr. Cargill, was very ill with blackwater fever, and his assistant had just been invalided home with the same dangerous complaint. The Resident of Zaria, Orr, was on tour in the bush in the south of his emirate, also out of touch and in danger. Nor was it only amongst the senior grade of the civil government that a general post was in train; both the commandant of the Northern Nigeria Regiment, Colonel Lowry Cole, and his second-in-command were out of the country; even the battalion commander was away, so Lugard had to add to his duties the complete control of the military dispositions.

There were six days of intolerable tension when Lugard did not know whether the whole of the work of the last five and a half years would not be swept out of existence and with it the lives of all the handful of white men scattered about the country. It was the uncertainty that was hardest to bear. When Lugard had ordered the four men away from the telegraph at Ambrusa he could get no further news for a time from Sokoto province. He could not even know if the Sultan was standing firm. Meanwhile other alarming news came in. The situation in Hadeija, further east, was reported as threatening, and this meant that he could not move the desperately needed 250 men he had stationed in that sullen emirate. There was news that other incipient Mahdis were proclaiming themselves in Bauchi, one near the " Holy Hill " of Bima, another in German territory over the border. It was rumoured that the fiery Senussi further north were stirring and there were moments when Lugard, and still more some of the isolated political officers, imagined that the whole western Sudan was secretly smouldering and might burst into a great religious up-rising against the new white infidel rulers.

Lugard, of course, remained outwardly cool. He continued to work in his spare time with Lord Scarbrough. He ordered the recall of the troops from the Munshi country—but they were four days beyond the nearest telegraph station—and ordered them to make a forced march to Zungeru. He cabled to the Governor of Lagos and asked him —an uncongenial request to have to make—to send him some help. The Governor replied that he would send 250 men. These were for a precautionary reserve; they would, of course, arrive too late for im-mediate action. Lugard ordered up the 100 rifles stationed at Lokoja, and managed to collect another 75 from Zungeru and 75 more from Kontagora. Such was the scale of force by which these immense territories were held!

On February 19th, Orr came in to Zungeru. The alarming news had reached him while touring, and Lugard, who had a high opinion of his ability, had called him in for consultation. Marching all night and day he reached headquarters at night and went straight into Lugard's office. Long afterwards he gave to the writer a written account of what happened there. His chief, looking calm but stern, handed him all the telegrams. The situation, Orr thought as he read them, was obviously dangerous in the extreme. The turbulent tribesmen were elated by their success against the white man and his well-armed troops, and their Mahdi had, he read, declared that he would now fall on the depleted garrison at Sokoto, wipe them out and then attack Kano and Zaria. Orr realized only too well how a rapidly moving mob could easily overwhelm in turn each little detachment of troops scattered about the provinces long before reinforcements could be collected.

He and Lugard slept upon it that night and in the morning Lugard showed him a telegram from the O.C. of the Kano troops, a very able soldier. He advised that as the situation was so critical, all out-lying detachments should be called in and concentrated at Kano, from which an attack could be made upon the closely neighbouring and threatening Hadeija. There would thus be concentration of forces, with an impending insurrection at Hadeija forestalled and prestige restored. Lugard asked Orr whether he thought the plan wise. Orr asked in return whether the Resident at Kano, a man of good judgment, had

endorsed this advice. Lugard stated that he had. "Very well Sir,"
Orr said, " in that case I do not see that Your Excellency has any choice
but to concur, and to authorize the O.C. to proceed as he suggests.
After all, these two men are on the spot and must be better able to
judge the situation than we here, 200 miles away."

Lugard was silent for a minute, then he said,

" No, I cannot think that it is sound to show weakness by withdrawing all outlying detachments from Katsina and elsewhere, and it
seems to me sheer folly to utilize all the available troops in knocking
their heads against a formidable walled city. If the attack failed, or even
if it were held up, without reserves we should be helpless and our prestige would receive a blow which might well prove disastrous." His
plan was to send the few hundred troops he could muster directly
to Sokoto, the place of danger.

" But, Sir," ventured Orr, " If the O.C.'s diagnosis should prove
correct and disaster were to occur, Your Excellency's responsibility
would be tremendous if you had deliberately disregarded the advice
of the senior military and civil officers."

" I am perfectly aware of that," rejoined Lugard, " but the whole
responsibility is mine in any case, and I must judge the situation as I
myself see it after careful consideration of all the views expressed and
of the facts before me."

Orr concludes his story,

" He then dictated to his Secretary a reply to the O.C. at Kano, giving the
reasons why he felt unable to accept his advice or authorize the steps he
had proposed to take; and he ordered him, while taking all possible precautions to keep himself informed of events, to stand fast and await further
orders . . . Lugard's courage and level-headedness in the face of this
dangerous situation made a tremendous impression on me, and showed
me something of his calibre."

As five days went by without news of any of the emirs or their
people joining the rebels, the tension, as Lugard told Flora, " relaxed
by mere efflux of time. The first shock has somewhat subsided—one
has got more used to it." There was news of success from the south-
east where the Munshis, properly impressed, gave up their captives
almost without resistance and the commander, Captain Hasler, began
a great march at high speed back to Zungeru. No news from the

northern provinces was most certainly very good news. Everything had turned upon the reaction of the Sultan of Sokoto. " Had he shown the slightest indecision," (this was Burdon's opinion) "I have no doubt that the bulk of the ' talakawa ' (the peasantry) would at once have joined the enemy."[1] But the Sultan did not hesitate for one moment. He at once took the one white man under his protection, succoured the survivors of the defeat when they came in, and began to make defensive preparations at the fort. Then the returning Burdon rode in. The Sultan and his chiefs had taken it for granted that the Resident, upon hearing the alarming news, would continue all the faster on his way to Zungeru. They were therefore astonished to see him—but they also appeared unfeignedly glad and relieved. After a council of war, they sent out the Marafa, the Sokoto commander, with 3,000 horse and foot against Satiru. But, convincing testimony of the dangers of the position, as the assault on the town began, the bulk of the troops refused to attack the people of Satiru and deserted their leaders, who only just escaped with their lives. Meanwhile, from province after province, word came in of the steady loyalty of the emirs. Some even sent telegrams to Lugard expressing their concern and offering every assistance in their power, including contingents of troops. Nupe pressed a body of horsemen upon Lugard and Zaria said he would never break his oath of loyalty sworn on the Koran. And, another major satisfaction to Lugard, the Colonial Office was now entirely co-operative.

Once the seriousness of the crisis was realized there, only one course was possible—absolute support for the man responsible. There was, indeed, a tendency to do even more than Lugard asked and to send Colonel Morland out at once to Nigeria. But Elgin wisely said that all the dispositions must be left to Lugard.[2] Four days later, when Lugard was able to send more reassuring news, there was strong satisfaction at the Office. Though it was complained that Lugard did not send sufficient information, yet there was general agreement that the loyalty of the emirs was a personal triumph for him and that his pride was fully justifiable. Elgin added his praise for the speed with which Lugard had collected and advanced the troops.[3] But the ministers were not ready to go so far as to give Lugard *carte blanche* for his actions

---

[1] Cd. 3620, p. 19.   [2] Minute by Elgin on Lugard to Elgin, 24 February 1906, C.O. 446/52.
[3] Minute by Elgin on Lugard to Elgin, 28 February 1906, C.O. 446/52.

When he urged strongly that he might arrest the Hadeija ringleaders, although Elgin telegraphed agreement on February 26th, he added that the force must be sufficient and also his hope that the Emir would not resist and " that object may be attained without actual fighting."[1] And the next day in the House of Commons, Churchill, answering a question about the disturbances, gave it as his opinion that the circumstances did not call for punitive expeditions but only for reinforcements in the affected district and the arrest and punishment of the promoters.[2]

A very different attitude prevailed in Northern Nigeria, especially after the full news of the disaster came through. Vengeance, it must be admitted, was what most of the white men in Northern Nigeria wanted, and with them in this were those Fulani leaders who had accepted their rule. Burdon was reported anxious only lest the Satiru fanatics should disperse before an example could be made of them. He need not have feared. The exalted and deluded people of Satiru, now busy oppressing their neighbours, were in no mood to disperse, while upon his side, Lugard had concentrated his forces with amazing speed. By March 8th, three weeks after the disaster, by collecting every man available in the north, and sending them on a forced march —the 280 miles from Zungeru to Sokoto were covered in 12 days, guns and all—he got 573 rifles to Sokoto. The commander of the Munshi expedition, Captain Hasler, got back by horse and canoe in seven days to stand by at Zungeru. The Lagos troops moved up country slowly enough for Lugard to draw complacent comparisons with the speed of his own men and he was glad to be able to send them back, with many thanks, unused.

On March 10th, the small government forces, with 30 European officers and some Sokoto chiefs, a 2.95 gun and several Maxims, advanced on Satiru. A rebel force of 2,000, armed as before mostly with hoes and axes, came out to meet them and flung themselves upon the soldiers. The Mounted Infantry in front wheeled aside to draw on the enemy and to allow the infantry fire to take effect. There could be only one result. A Sokoto chief who had been present at the original disaster described what happened with a minimum of words.

" They came on, and the horsemen gave way and went back; no one took any notice. I thought we were all going to be killed as before.

[1] Cd. 3620, p. 4.   [2] *Parliamentary Debates*, 27 February 1906, IV. 152. 1022-3.

Someone gave an order, everyone fired, then a whistle blew; everyone stopped and there was no one left alive in front."[1]

As the troops went on to Satiru and entered the town, however, they met new forces and were repeatedly and bravely charged, and the Satiru people continued to be slaughtered in the town and in the pursuit, while the avenging villagers from nearby joined in the hunt. The bodies of the British who were killed were found and buried with military honours. Then the Sultan called out the whole population of Sokoto and at his orders they razed Satiru to the ground while he pronounced a curse upon anyone who should rebuild its walls or till its fields. Mallam Isa had been killed in the original fight but Dan Makafo, the leading spirit, was captured, tried by the Native Court with other ringleaders, and executed in the market place, where their heads were set up on spears.

It was a terrible vengeance, more terrible than Lugard knew at the time. The executions had been carried out without his confirmation; he at once stopped them. But there can be no doubt that he had intended that the retribution should be complete. Speaking of the expedition, " They should," he told his wife a few days before the news came, with the force and weapons at their command, " *annihilate* them and it is necessary for the recovery of our prestige that the victory should be a signal one." (L. to F. L., 9 March 1906). On March 13th, the news came in and he sent his telegram to the Colonial Office. " I fear," he wrote to her the same day,

" the slaughter of these poor wretches has been terrible—but in the face of the death of three British officers I could hardly order them to treat them with mercy and had to leave it to those on the spot. They fought very bravely indeed. The execution which our weapons can do will have a great moral effect . . . " (L. to F. L., 13 March 1906).

And the next day he told her that Burdon estimated that his figure of 1,500 out of the 2,000 killed had been an underestimate and that the enemy had been exterminated.

The suppression of a *jacquerie*, whether in medieval France, Tudor England, or twentieth century Nigeria nearly always makes terrible reading with its indiscriminate slaughter of humble peasants who, from the moment of their first chance success, are doomed because they have given the powers above them a moment of utterly unanticipated fear.

[1] *Reports*, 1905-6, pp. 17-18.

Yet a merely emotional recoil from the fate of Satiru and its hasty characterization, in the words used by the Prime Minister, Campbell-Bannerman, of another event, as imperialist " methods of barbarity ", must be set against Lugard's reasons for severity. Firstly, the rebels were in arms against the British authorities, but outbreaks against their rulers had occurred before the white man's arrival and the excesses in vengeance taken on the rebels, which were later reported to Lugard, were the work of the native authorities behaving according to their usual custom. Secondly, it must be remembered that the rebels had raided and murdered in the surrounding villages. Thirdly, that they had been the first to attack and had hacked to pieces with hoes and axes men who were trying to talk peaceably to them and had probably died because they had risked their lives in that attempt. Fourthly, these peasants belonged to a dominant Muslim people, themselves raiders and enslavers of weaker tribes and, according to Lugard, one of their chief grievances had been the loss of those slaves which, in suzerain Sokoto, even the peasants possessed. Fifthly, the results of weak and hesitant action must be visualized with the great extension of unrest, fighting and loss of life that must have ensued before order could have been re-established. But behind all the incidentals that explain, if they do not justify, Lugard's severity, lies the broader reason for all such punitive action. The nation which wills the end of imperial power must face the necessity for the means by which it is won and held. This is the theme, with its constant accompanying question, that underlies so much of Lugard's life and work as an agent of his country's advance and the reader who believes, as he did, that it was best for tropical Africa to attain greater unity, peace, prosperity and civilization under European power must accept the responsibility of that power to keep order and impose its will.[1]

Lugard had still two things to do before he was free to obey Lord Elgin's telegram, received in the middle of his crisis on March 9th, which told him that the Scheme was rejected and that he was to return to England for three months of consultation. He had first to deal with Gwandu. Here, fortunately, the Emir surrendered without opposition, and was sent to comfortable exile in Lokoja, while his acknowledged heir took his place.

[1] For a discussion of these issues by a missionary who was then in the country, see W. R. S. Miller, *Reflections of a Pioneer* (1936), pp. 102-5.

The second task was to bring the long recalcitrant Hadeija to order. Lugard's most definite fear during the crisis was that this Emir would take advantage of the moment of weakness and set the example of revolt. Moreover, Hadeija had kept 250 desperately needed soldiers tied to the city. Colonel Lowry Cole, who commanded the Northern forces, had now returned from leave. He collected the troops from Sokoto, took them to Hadeija and on April 23rd, after Lugard had made several efforts to make a peaceful settlement, this force marched on the city. The commandant reported that the request to give up the eight ring-leaders of the opposition was refused and that the government's messenger was struck in the face. Lowry Cole then marched on the Emir's palace. There followed, according to the official account, five hours of street fighting in a temperature of 115 degrees in the shade, with mounted men armed with swords and spears, many covered in chain mail, charging down the narrow streets while slugs and arrows were discharged from windows and doorways. The Emir and his three sons were shot " boldly charging at a few yards range ". It is surprising after this account to read that on the British side only six rank and file were wounded. No figure is given for the number of the enemy killed. So, with what Colonel Lowry Cole terms " senseless bravery ", the famous war-leaders of Hadeija, who had never before met the fire of the magazine rifle, were mown down in all their brilliantly coloured equestrian panoply, the last independent relic of the centuries' old military power of the Hausa and Fulani. The Colonel reported that the troops behaved with restraint: the women and children, who had not suffered, returned, and the following morning the town resumed its usual aspect, the markets were well attended and the next recognized heir succeeded the dead Emir.[1]

After this, it was easy to send the troops on to Bauchi to overawe the tendencies to Mahdism in that region. The rumours of such movements seem to have been exaggerated and the whole Protectorate was soon at peace again.

The Colonial Office pressed Lugard to give reasons for these insur-

---

[1] Cd. 3620, pp. 38-9, 44-5, 52-6; and *Reports*, 1905-6, pp. 27-8.

A correspondence in the Lugard Papers suggests that doubts were raised afterwards as to whether very excessive severity was not used at Hadeija. Enquiries by the writer from the surviving Residents, and by a local British official amongst the oldest townsmen, suggests that this doubt was ill-founded except for the possibility that the Emir, at the last, wished to surrender and was not fighting when killed.

rectionary movements.[1] The Munshi outrage at Abinsi was easily explained as a sudden ignition of the smouldering ferocity of primitive pagans against their old Muslim Hausa enemies and the strange intruding Company with its valuable storehouse of eminently desirable goods. But the Satiru affair was obscure. Movements of protest, whether more or less violent, amongst subjected peoples are worth careful study for obvious practical reasons by the immediate rulers and for more general ones by the imperial authorities and the student. For it is one of the gravest inherent defects in colonial power that it tends to silence the free expression of opinion and even to freeze natural social action among its subjects. Too often the Colonial Service officer lives and works in a cloudy and unreal atmosphere in which complaisant chiefs and delusive interpreters stand between him and the tribal masses who watch silently, unwilling or unable to voice their true needs and grievances. Then, generally abruptly, and quite unexpectedly, the silence is broken by the uninhibited uproar of revolt in which the true strains and grievances, hidden perhaps for many years, are suddenly laid bare in a few hours of action.

Lugard had to ask himself whether Muslim fanaticism was the fire or merely the fuel for the conflagration at Satiru. And why had Burdon, so expert in native ways, so devoted to the Sokoto chiefs that he was called the " white Fulani ", been wholly unaware of what was coming? And why did the Marafa's army desert rather than attack Satiru? " If the idea of treachery is true," wrote Burdon in a significant comment on this event, "it confirms my former opinion as to the sullen disaffection of the 'talakawa', and will have served a very useful purpose."[2] But to what was this disaffection due? Partly, as we have seen, to the loss of their slaves. Not, Lugard argued, to taxation, for Satiru had not even been assessed under the new scheme, still less taxed. Racial feeling might, he admitted, have been a contributing cause, since the rebels were all Hausa and the chiefs, with whom the British had become so closely associated, all Fulani. Why, then, did the rebels attack their neighbours instead of starting a general revolt? There seemed to be a definite " anti-white " feeling to explain the determination with which at the first attack the rebels singled out the British officers for destruction. But, then, why did the surrounding

[1] Cd. 3620, p. 4.
[2] Burdon to Lugard, 21 February 1906, enclosed in Lugard to Elgin, 7 March 1906, Cd. 3620, p. 20.

peasants show such willingness to help not only the white survivors but Burdon and other isolated white men in the region?[1]

We cannot hope on the slightness of the evidence to come to wholly convincing answers to all these questions. But in the astonishing and almost universal loyalty of the emirs, upon which Lugard, rightly in the circumstances of that time, prided himself, was there not that note of warning that has been suggested in the chapters on Indirect Rule? Lugard can be justified for preserving order and the structure of society in the first period of conquest by his policy towards the emirs. But when it is remembered that these men, a few years earlier, had been described as decadent, cruel and oppressive, was it to be expected that a handful of British officers, mostly ignorant of the language and customs of the people, and too often tied to their offices by overwork and routine, could assure themselves that they had been able to bring about that complete change in these Muslim rulers at which they aimed? The very enhanced strength and security the rulers drew from the support of British power made their hold upon the peasantry greater. The whips of their independent days had been taken from them but Indirect Rule may have given some opportunity for the use of scorpions. This, indeed, was the view of the missionary Dr. Miller, watching from his detached but humane standpoint in Zaria the doings of one of the emirs most approved by the British.[2] And it was this dread, as he told the writer, which haunted the mind of one of the ablest of the early Residents, Charles Orr. In a letter of the period which he later gave to the writer, Orr asks whether, perhaps for three or four years, he may not have been the cause of oppressing the peasantry to a far greater extent than they were oppressed before the arrival of the British.

" In this state of civilization the big prey upon the small. Obviously the whole position is utterly hopeless unless one can trust the emir . . . If he is using me to oppress the people, how must they feel towards the government? An alien race, different in colour, ideas, character, habits, religion, backing up the other alien race in oppression—what must they feel? . . . If I am merely an instrument of injustice and oppression, what is the use of me working myself to death in an unhealthy climate amid intense discomfort and in exile from home and friends? . . . Of course there is

[1] *Reports*, 1905-6, pp. 17-22. In these pages Lugard discusses the reasons for the revolt.
[2] W. R. S. Miller, *Have we failed in Nigeria?* (1947), p. 49ff.

only one thing to do, namely to go on probing and probing and trying to get at the truth, knowing that one is doing one's utmost to replace injustice by justice."[1]

So long as officers could ask themselves such a question and give such an answer, there was a good chance that the British occupation would justify its claims. The lesson of Satiru may not have been altogether clear but it at least suggested that, however right and necessary the political settlement had been for its time, there would be need of unceasing vigilance lest, in the future, from the standpoint of the common people, the close partnership of the imperial and the princely power should become harsh, or merely static.

---

[1] Letter written on 10 March 1907. See also his discussion of this and similar issues in *The Making of Northern Nigeria*, pp. 275-86 and in Miller, *Reflections of a Pioneer*, especially chapters VII and XI.

CHAPTER XIII

LUGARDS AND LIBERALS

The immediate responses of the Colonial Office to the happenings in Nigeria have been recounted. But it is necessary to consider their background in Britain. Lugard thought he detected in the Liberal ministers, from the moment of their appointment, an excessive tendency to intervene in his actions. True, at the extreme moment of crisis they gave complete support to the man on the spot. And, to look ahead for a moment, not only then, but publicly and officially when the affair was finally wound up, he was given the fullest credit for his prompt action and for the loyalty of the emirs. Lord Elgin wrote on June 7th, 1906 to congratulate him for

" the promptitude with which you were able to deal with the situation that arose after the engagement at Satiru, and of the rapidity with which the troops were concentrated at Sokoto . . .

I have pleasure also in expressing my recognition of the credit that is so largely due to yourself for the remarkable loyalty shown by the native emirs, which is to be attributed to the policy which you have consistently pursued towards them and to the loyal and intelligent manner in which your officers have interpreted that policy."[1]

But though, on this central issue, there was appreciation, Lugard was quick to feel what he believed was the loss of that measure of faith and sympathy which, in spite of the officials, he had received from the Conservative Government. What had caused him most chagrin in the telegrams from the Office during the crisis was their implication that he was at once too quick and too immoderate in the use of force. Thus, when on March 9th he had been asked whether he could give any reason for the increasing hostility and suspicion of the Munshi people,[2] he exclaimed " The plain insinuation was that I had stirred up

[1] Cd. 3620, p. 37.　　[2] Ibid. p. 4.

the business in order to carry out my policy of repression." (L. to F. L.,
6 April 1906). He had, however, a momentary revenge upon the
Colonial Office for this attitude to his belligerency. When, in their
anxiety at the height of the crisis, they wired to ask him whether he
did not now want to cancel his request that the Frontier Force should
be reduced in favour of more political staff, he replied, as he later
reported to Flora, with great satisfaction:

> " I adhere to my opinion that in the interests of this country it is more
> important to have the increase of Political Staff than the troops I have
> proposed to disband, if it is necessary to choose between the two."
>
> (L. to F. L., 10 March 1906).

Lugard saw in the Liberal ministers' conduct over Hadeija, " a new
line of interference in detail ", which would land Elgin " who seems
to be both weak and interfering " in a disaster. " I think he is likely to
come to grief before he learns the lesson that the local Governors are
responsible, and that Downing Street does not govern directly."
(L. to F. L., 23 March 1906). Why on earth should he, Lugard, wish
to take on this responsibility?

> " Would it not be nicer to leave Hadeija alone and to ensure myself
> elsewhere? and go off to England? . . . But that would not be playing the
> game which with great show of magnanimity they allow me to play.
> Why in the world do these people always seek to take it for granted that
> I am a man who longs for wars and rows . . . So I am *permitted* to carry
> out my plan—permitted to do what I would a thousand times rather have
> undone if it were merely a matter of *personal* wishes."
>
> (L. to F. L., 8 April 1906).

In the game of passing on responsibility, the Government found
themselves caught out on March 31st, when *The Times* published a
Reuter report from Northern Nigeria that it had now been learned
that they had caused the Munshi expedition to be stopped by telegraph
just as it reached Abinsi, where it was kept inactive and then re-called
by the Sokoto crisis, so that the Munshis were unpunished and the
whole work of pacification left to do over again. The Government put
out a very defensive official statement asserting that " there was certainly no intention on the part of the Government to reverse the
decision of Sir Frederick Lugard." But this defence did not save the
Government from a strong rebuke in *The Times* which in a leading

[1] *The Times*, 31 March 1906.

article wove together the Government's current troubles in Natal with those of Nigeria and called them " random excursions in the sphere of Imperial policy." Here were rash interventions followed by embarrassed withdrawals and assurances that there was no intention to interfere with the responsible Governor.

> "There is an ironic flavour about these assurances which would be irresistible if the issues were not so grave. The Government are no respecters of persons. They pay scant attention to the long colonial experience of Sir H. McCallum, and they seem to repose as little confidence in Sir Frederick Lugard, who is probably the ablest administrator of his type at present in the service of the Crown."[1]

A few days later, in answer to a question in the House of Commons, Churchill repeated the Government's defence.

> "Most certainly the Government wish to discourage these and all forms of military operations in West Africa and all other parts of the British Empire under the authority of the Imperial Government."[2]

Lugard was a little worried about this attack on the Government; it looked so much as though he had at least encouraged the provision of that embarrassing information from Nigeria, whereas he was guiltless. Whether Flora had any hand in it, at least in influencing *The Times* leader, is not so clear. She appears to have maintained her close contact with the paper and was writing occasional articles for it. She hoped that Lugard would get " a little satisfaction to see the good incidental smack which *The Times* gives the Government . . . on the stopping of the Munshi Expedition." (F. L. to L., 31 March 1906).

We have seen that Flora had been so concentrated upon her pursuit of the Scheme that she had found it difficult to realize, from the first telegrams about the Satiru disaster, how great a crisis her husband had encountered. When he felt able at last, on March 12th, after news of the retribution at Satiru, to telegraph to her, " Everything alright ", she had been puzzled by this and had assumed that it referred to his state of mind after getting the cable about the rejection of the Scheme or to some plans in connection with it. On March 2nd, indeed, she had published in *The Times* an article in which, as she told him, " you will see that I have taken on the whole an optimistic view of the disturbances." Lugard may have smiled somewhat wryly at this, though

---

[1] *The Times*, 31 March 1906.   [2] *Parliamentary Debates*, 4 April 1906, IV. 155. 497-8.

Northern Nigerian Emirs

Sir Reginald Antrobus, Assistant Under-Secretary
The Colonial Office, 1898-1909

he realized that Flora's easy acceptance of the crisis was due to the strength of her faith in him. She wrote that though she was sorry that the affair had " cost good English lives " she could not help " feeling glad that just at this moment such eloquent testimony to the success of your system should be given by the loyalty of the Emirs." (F. L. to L., 6 March 1906).

In discussing Lugard's relations with the Office and Flora's ideas and actions as his London agent we are always in danger of isolating Nigerian affairs from the total of colonial policy. Flora, as ex-colonial editor of *The Times*, naturally took the wider view and communicated it to her husband. In the first half of 1906 she had to relate his affairs to the three main colonial issues before the country. These were the form of government for the annexed Boer republics; Chinese labour on the Rand, for which Lord Milner had to bear responsibility; and the Natal native rising. These two last especially had some relevance to the handling of Nigerian affairs.

In spite of her very friendly relations with Grey, Haldane and Buxton Flora was very angry about the Cabinet's treatment of Lord Milner over the Chinese labour question, and still more so over the endeavour of the Colonial Office to prevent the execution of the leaders of the native rebellion in Natal. She believed that the only hope of holding the white colonies within the Empire was by the ungrudging gift of self-government. Anxious to believe well of Lord Elgin she tried to put all the blame for mistakes in colonial policy upon Churchill. He was, she told Lugard, justifying the fears which his appointment aroused. Skilled in obtaining inside information, she was able to tell Lugard a story that must have been of the greatest interest to him.

" Did I tell you of how Lord Elgin is keeping that wild Winston in check within the office? He frequently over-rules his opinions. When a question was asked in the House of Commons about the Munshi expedition, Mr. Strachey wrote the answer which you saw, a moderate and sensible one. This went to Winston who said ' This kind of thing will never do for this House of Commons. We must pledge ourselves to no more expeditions,' and wrote an answer to that effect, putting his pen through Mr. Strachey's. The papers went up to Lord Elgin, who calmly put his pen through Winston's and wrote ' stet ' opposite to Mr. Strachey's."   (F. L. to L., 20 March 1906).

(She might have capped this with a rather similar story, told to the

L   269

writer by an official then in the Colonial Office, that when Churchill minuted upon a certain proposal put up to him " I cannot take the responsibility for doing this," Elgin simply wrote " I can.")

A few days later Flora had more to tell him about the debate in which a vote of censure was moved in the Commons upon Lord Milner. As a misunderstood man of action she equated him with her husband.

" . . . Of the Milner debate Chamberlain's speech, as you will see, was fine. Winston Churchill's was a disgrace to the Government and was evidently directed almost entirely to the ultra section of the radicals in the House . . . I had expected better things from what Mr. Haldane told me. But for the moment politics have degenerated into a tactical battle apparently between the two sections of the Liberal party and the interests of the Empire are allowed to take what place they can in the background of the keener strife" (F. L. to L., 23 March 1906).

A few days later she wrote to relate her husband's troubles to the rest of the government's colonial policy.

" . . . For the moment I am so much aghast at the conduct of the government in relation to Natal—that is to the principle of self-government on which the Empire is based—that even my optimistic inclination to have faith in Lord Elgin is shaken . . . I confess myself in despair over a Colonial Secretary who can show so little knowledge of Imperial tradition as to provoke such a crisis. From both points of view of the administration of native races and the self-governing principle of the white portion of the Empire, it is as bad as it can be. The same reckless spirit of ignorant interference which would have paralysed your Munshi campaign applied on a wider scale to the disruption of the Empire . . . But what I feel is that while all the wild *talk* about the Transvaal is Winston's, this is Lord Elgin's doing. The solid good sense, which we have heard so much of, seems to have no existence . . . It seems to me that in this short time they have been in office a government could hardly have done more harm than this to the internal administration of the Empire."

(F. L. to L., 30 March 1906).

Her strong faith in the civilizing mission of the empire and her admiration for the men who were its builders made it difficult for her to understand the humane recoil of Churchill and others from paying the account in life and suffering, native as well as British, in Natal as well as in Nigeria, which this expansion presented. In the problem, which

still persists today, of the rights of white colonial minorities over
coloured populations she was untroubled by doubts. Much later, after
his retirement, when Lugard had to deal with the Kenya controversy,
he himself took a very different line. But upon Nigeria there could be
no possibility of disagreement when she wrote:

" What a mess would have been made of Nigeria if anyone less resolute
and less energetic than you had been at the head of affairs! We should
have had all these small people terrorizing us with their reputation and
the fear of what they might do if we did so and so. Sokoto, Kano, Hadeija,
and Bornu would all be independent sovereigns at this moment flying
when the humour seized them at each other's throats, or uniting to fly at
ours and to close the country to our trade. And then an ignorant boy like
Winston Churchill at the C.O. can at a critical moment dash in and seize
your arm just when a sharp blow is essential. Nevertheless men like you
and Lord Milner do their work and the Empire is gradually well built.
That is the comfort of it. And that you have to do your work under great
difficulty and with perpetual hindrance is a common link between the
heroes of Empire dead and living. Nelson, Marlborough, Wellington!
The roll is long as well as honourable . . . "

(F. L. to L., 20 March 1906).

She would have been even more indignant with Marlborough's
descendant if she could have seen the minutes he was writing in the
Colonial Office and how *he* related the affairs of Nigeria and Natal.
When news came of the annihilation of the 2,000 people of Satiru, he
asked,

" How does this extermination of an almost unarmed rabble . . . compare with the execution of twelve Kaffirs in Natal after trial . . . I confess
I do not at all understand what our position is, or with what face we can
put pressure on the Government of Natal while these sort of things are
done under our direct authority."[1]

At the same time he was showing his persistent humanity in desiring
the severe punishment and dismissal of one of Lugard's senior officers
who had been guilty of cruelty to his servant,[2] and his liberalism in
objecting to a press law by Lugard although there was as yet very little
press. In a true Churchillian flash, he minuted, "Nigeria seems to be a
sort of sultry Russia."[3]

[1] Minute by Churchill on Lugard to Elgin, 14 March 1906, C.O. 446/53.
[2] Minute by Churchill on Lugard to Elgin, 5 February 1906 C.O. 446/52.
[3] Minute by Churchill on Lugard to Elgin, 10 March 1906, C.O. 446/53.

Did the official statements and minutes which have been given really amount, as Flora argued, to a new colonial policy? It must be kept in mind what small proportions the affairs of Northern Nigeria assumed in Downing Street and how seldom the administration of this Protectorate caused questions or debate in Parliament. Colonial policy in these years, both during and after the Boer war meant, above all, policy towards South Africa. It would therefore be misleading to consider the occasional decisions of ministers upon Nigerian affairs in isolation from their main pre-occupations.

It has been shown in these pages how Lugard had committed himself to Africa at a time when Britain had not wholly abandoned the anti-expansionist position of the middle years of the century. The dominant ideas of a nation are not quickly or completely displaced by their opposites. Underneath the changing surface of events, there can be detected a rhythmic alternation between Britain's impulses of advance and retreat. Disraeli's forward impulse, after Gladstone's recoil, had been re-asserted moderately by Salisbury and more strongly by Chamberlain, who had given it a conscious colonial direction. This had led up to, even if it had not caused, the South African war. The recoil had followed and it is probable that the opposition would have come in before 1906 if the conflict between the two impulses had not been expressed, not only between the parties, but within the Liberal party ranks. There the old Gladstonian "Little England" theme, with Morley as chief exponent, still persisted, with little sympathy from the new men, Asquith and Grey.

As far as the empire was concerned, the watershed between the two parties did not run quite where it had thirty or forty years earlier. There were few if any Liberals who did not now value the major colonies, which had refused their chance to drift away, were now respectably self-governing and had rallied to Britain in the most heartening way in the South African war. Even the issue of annexing new lands was closed since there seemed to be no more left to annex and few wanted actually to abandon what had been gained. The question now was not *whether*, but *how*, to maintain the empire. Was it to have the fiscal and economic character Chamberlain demanded? Upon this the Liberals, supported by many Conservatives, were united in negation. Was it to be secured in defiance of the democratic and humanitarian principles which were acknowledged at home? Here the Liberals were emphatic and, as is customary in party politics, their emphasis exaggerated the difference between themselves and their Conservative predecessors. The Liberals were for peace, hence there must be no military adventures in the Crown Colonies. They were for retrenchment, so there must be no ambitious and expensive schemes for administration or development. For all these reasons they must keep a sharp eye upon hard and over-active governors and soldiers. In the field of politics words have their changing contemporary flavour in addition to the meaning given by the dictionary. Thus " punitive expeditions " roused a special reaction in Liberals who had been condemning punitive action at the end of the South African war, while the party which was damning Milner for allowing the flogging of Chinese must make sure that no similar excesses took place anywhere in the empire while it was under their control.

One of the most revealing exchanges in Parliament in this connection took place in a debate not on Nigeria but in the vote of censure moved upon Lord Milner for allowing the flogging of Chinese. Churchill put one side: the ex-Colonial Secretary, Chamberlain, put the other, taking that stand which had so endeared him to all imperial servants and which had won the devoted allegiance of Lugard. Generalizing in the course of his defence of Milner upon the wider aspects of the subject, he said:

" Will the House allow me to try and bring before it the nature of the work which is imposed upon High Commissioners, Viceroys and Governors of Crown Colonies throughout the Empire? These men are in a way autocrats, and that brings upon them all the disadvantages from which autocrats have to suffer . . . They are answerable for order, for legislation, for every detail of administration, for every act, be it great or small, of every member, be he important or otherwise, of the whole administration. For all these things they are responsible to this Department and to the House of Commons. They are not infallible. How can you expect to get infallible administration under such circumstances? I do not believe they are to be found anywhere. But certainly you do not offer much temptation. I have never heard of any man in the Colonial Service who in these trying positions and having to submit, as he has now, to the kind of ignorant criticism on the part of people who have none of his responsibility, has become a gold magnate, who has ever made a fortune, who has even been able to provide for those whom he has left behind him,

273

by devotion to the public service, by his interest in the great work he is conducting from the highest motives."[1]

Churchill, while he did not support the vote of censure, afforded what Balfour called "an insulting protection" to Milner, and declared that his methods and policy were utterly discredited. In the course of his speech he answered Chamberlain's general point about colonial governors.

"Under the Secretary of State for the Colonies there are 30 or 40 officials of high rank administering under different forms and varying conditions as many separate and distinct provinces, comprising a population of something like 30,000,000 of human beings of many races, creeds, and of almost every colour. To the Secretary of State all these important officers are responsible, and it is from the expressions which the Secretary of State as the servant of this House, may use, that these officers all over the world must be guided in the character of their administration and in the manner in which they discharge their responsibilities to all these many races over which our authority is exercised."[2]

He went on to say that although foreign affairs might be outside party politics, "The Colonial Office lies in the heart and centre of the fiercest partisanship and controversy."

If this were true, it is small wonder that Flora joined those who passionately defended Lord Milner, and that she found Sir Edward Grey—who abstained from voting on the Milner issue—her most sympathetic friend in the Cabinet. When Milner dined with her in her London house she commiserated with him, and he with her on Lugard's behalf. He remarked ruefully, "We have all been laid upon our backs and we must be content for the present to suffer in good company."

It is, of course, too great a simplification to see the party division as one between more or less humanity, corresponding somewhat with the general rhythm of retreat and advance. Lugard's record constantly faces us with the question as to whether there are not two kinds of humanity, the one of negation or restraint, and the other of action. Both had their own virtues and their excesses. The refusal to undertake responsibility for backward peoples, or the decision to abandon halfway responsibilities already taken up, could result in much suffering and it is not easy to judge whether this was more or less than that arising from the confident imposition and maintenance of alien power.

[1] *Parliamentary Debates*, 21 March 1906, IV. 154. 484.   [2] *Ibid.* 489-90.

On the other hand an assumption of a kind of imperial divine right could tempt its promoters to excessive interference or harden them in the continued use of force or severity. Forward action, moreover, often drew much of its force from the immediate self-interest of the nation while its opponents, however much party advantage might sully the purity of their motives, were often attempting to bring the element of universal principle into their policy.

Whatever may be true of Lugard's more eminent fellow-sufferer, Lord Milner, it seems that even Lugard, moderate and humane as he was for a man in his position, was the better for the checks and questions of his new Liberal ministers, if only because they reminded him to control his own agents. It was almost impossible for any governor not to be to some extent moulded by his immediate world of action and to forget a little the high standards—the inappropriately high standards as they might sometimes have seemed to him—which were accepted in his own country and by which many of its people, his ultimate masters, demanded to judge his actions. The " bearing-rein " of Downing Street, against which Lugard kicked so hard was not only constitutionally proper but usually justifiable in its occasions. It is interesting that it was not the generous and idealistic woman, Flora Lugard, who was stirred to pity and indignation by the fate of Zulu or Hausa rebels, but the reputedly hard-bitten military adventurer, Winston Churchill, a contrast that will shortly be emphasized again. Pity may cloud perspective, and in Churchill at this time, as his minutes suggest, it probably did, but if this tender growth were crushed out of public life there would spread an arid waste of callousness and indifference.

The intervention of the Liberal ministers seems to have had little positive effect upon the actual course of affairs in Northern Nigeria. Under neither party did Lugard show much respect for the warning against military action. Where he believed this necessary he carried it out with a speed and sharpness which made it difficult for his masters to exert their control, and with a success which relieved them of the subsequent embarrassments they feared. Under both parties, he had to work within severe limits of finance, yet in administrative matters he continued to carry out his own ideas with a very large measure of freedom.

Yet he was anxious to get a closer contact with the new ministers, and especially with Churchill. He was half attracted and half repelled by his concept of the Under-Secretary. In moments of irritation when he thought he saw his rough, prentice hand in some exasperating telegram he would call him " that bumptious young subaltern ". But at other times he would try to think better of him. He told Flora:

> " I have only once met him, and when I came back from Herbert Samuel's dinner I told you that, though he had talked utter piffle, and miserable ultra party shop, I was greatly impressed with his appearance. Do you remember? I rarely misjudge a man at sight, and I said to you that W. Churchill had a head the shape of which meant *brains*. Ever since I saw him, I have judged that he is a man to be reckoned with, and no mere fluent speaker whose vanity and loquacity were all his assets. I think so still. He has brains and power." (L. to F. L., 9 March 1906).

Flora was able to obtain some new and intimate evidence for him. In May 1906 she went to stay with the Duke of Marlborough in his grandiose heritage of Blenheim Palace. From there on May 6th she wrote a long letter. She described how one morning she was talking to the Duke in his study, discussing the question of railways in Nigeria about which he was getting up a case in order to heckle Lord Elgin in the House of Lords, when Lord Elgin's colleague, Churchill, walked in and joined in the conversation in a way which she found most discouraging. He was so " hopelessly ignorant in regard to colonial affairs and at the same time so full of personal activity that the damage he may do appears to be colossal." He talked, in her view, rank " Little Englandism ". Yet underneath it all she seemed to feel " there was a certain disappointed perception that he was making a failure of himself," and he showed " a certain openness to new ideas even when he combats them " that made her feel sorry for the young man even in her anger, all the more as he looked ill and over-worked.

They discussed Nigeria. He spoke of his immense respect for Lugard and then went on to say what she thought were such foolish things that she could not imagine that her husband would have been able to listen to them with a proper show of patience. He re-asserted the Office view that Lugard had gone too fast and added " the extreme radical rubbish about holding innocent people tight in the grip of a military despotism." He then threw out his suggestions which, put back into direct speech, were as follows: " Abolish the West African Frontier Force! Give up the greater part of Nigeria, which is much too big for

us to hold! Put an end to the whole system of punitive expeditions
and be content with the peaceful administration of a small part of the
whole."

He did, however, interrupt himself to say that he had not yet formed
serious opinions and that he would not do so until he had discussed the
whole question with Lugard. But these were the directions in which
his thoughts were tending.

Thus provoked, Flora sailed into the argument with all her guns
firing. The Manchester electorate might think that " 250 white men
can govern some 12 to 20 millions of coloureds and put down slavery
and open the country to trade without any military or police force,
without an administrative organization and without any expenditure
on railways and other public works, but we who have the intelligence
and experience know that they are quite wrong." She went on
fiercely: "How is it possible that we should govern uncivilized Africa?
What you are saying amounts to this: that you allow men for whom
you profess to have the profoundest regard to spend their lives in
out-of-the-way portions of the earth, to make every sacrifice that men
can make of happiness, health, and personal comfort " (some of her
bitterness about his rejection of the Scheme came into these words)
" to devote themselves with the utmost fortitude to the accomplish-
ment of a certain work and when it is done—done as you admit with
almost unparalleled success, you say to them by way of reward, ' We
don't want your beastly work and we propose to throw the whole of
it away.' How can you expect an Empire to prosper if these are to be
your methods?"

Churchill retreated a little before this attack, disclaiming the attitude
she denounced but insisting that he only thought that punitive expeditions were expensive and unnecessary.

" Remember," she retorted, " that in England, which has been settled
for upwards of a thousand years, we still have military and police
forces without which it would be impossible to maintain good government. All civilization rests on force as a background. I assure you
that there is nobody in the world less military than my husband; his
government is essentially a government of peace, but he has made it
so by knowing how to repress disorder." She reminded him of
Lugard's recent refusal in the thick of the Sokoto trouble to increase
the Frontier Force. " Every military step he has taken in the Protec-

torate has been forced upon him and it is by his promptitude in dealing with them as they arose that he has averted chaotic disturbances such as those which in another part of Africa have led to the Somali war."

Churchill intervened to assure her in the most handsome terms that he *did* recognize all that Lugard had done in Nigeria.

" Very well," Flora replied, " who then is to be judge in case of a sudden disturbance or riot, in any part of the Protectorate—this man whom you praise as a distinguished administrator or the Manchester mob which governs your party vote?"

Meanwhile, the Duke had not been a mere listener. He had, after all, as a member of the other party, held the same position as his cousin not long before and he warmly supported Flora. He even managed to get information from Churchill with which to attack Lord Elgin with regard to Nigerian development! This led Flora on to her favourite subject of Nigerian development, of its need for railways and its future amalgamation.

Churchill listened and promised that until he could talk it all over with Lugard he would not make up his mind upon these points. He seemed, she thought, ill, irritable and oppressed by the questions he had to answer in the House. That evening, with characteristic magnanimity, he sought her out among the guests and sat by her. He seemed more gentle and human and listened patiently to her views on South Africa " which were necessarily very different from his own ". He seemed very upset about Natal and Flora pointed out to him that it was a great pity from every point of view that he should let the idea gain ground that, holding his position, he was antagonistic to the colonies, by which, of course, she meant the colonists. She said that if it had been Chamberlain who had taken his line about Natal, the ministry there would not have resigned just because they would have had faith in his sympathy with the colonies.

" I beg you to believe," she urged him, " that sympathy is itself a power and if the Colonies believed you to be in sympathy with them they would be ten times more willing to do what you want."

Churchill looked at her, she thought rather pathetically, and said, " That has gone by the board, I am afraid."

She noticed in these talks that Churchill spoke all the time as if he and not Lord Elgin was the Secretary of State.

" I did not ask him for his opinion of Lord Elgin, but I asked the Duke for his, which was very much the same thing. He said he was a man of very inferior ability, incapable of grasping a subject intellectually, but that he was very much a gentleman and could not do anything that was dishonourable."

" And what a couple," was the dismal conclusion Flora sent to Lugard, " at the head of colonial affairs!" However, she was now a little softened towards Churchill, especially when, on the same day, she opened her *Times* to find that at Liverpool, from which he had just come, he had alluded to Lugard as " that distinguished soldier and administrator " and said that he was coming home to confer with the Colonial Office about many things. She thereupon invited him to come and stay at Abinger, to which he replied that there was nothing he would like better.

The concern of the Lugards over the colonial policy of the Liberal ministers was almost inseparable from that over the refusal of the Scheme. Both anxieties, especially after the strain of the Satiru revolt, urged Lugard to get back to England. He wanted to comfort Flora for the defeat in which her long campaign had ended. Indeed, each felt almost more for the other than for self. Lugard had taken the blow hardly but with philosophy and he had no intention, as she feared, of making an immediate resignation in protest. He brushed aside her suggestion that the Scheme might be brought about by degrees in practice without open definition. He had an experience she had not shared—a soldier's service training—and his words had an element of rebuke. " I think," he told her, " the only way to deal with the situation is to loyally accept the decision given by my chief—as I expect my own subordinates to accept mine . . . So that when I come home Churchill and Antrobus and Elgin " [the order of names is significant!] " can only admit that I have loyally accepted my orders . . . These things are a matter of *instinct* and my instinct is opposed to trying to give partial effect to the scheme by any such methods." (L. to F. L., 10 April 1906).

Churchill kept his promise to bring Lugard back for early consultations. He arrived in England with his brother on June 12th, 1906, and set to work at once in the Office and at home upon Nigerian affairs. His first contacts with the Office put an end to any hopes he still cherished that the Scheme might be reconsidered. The prediction that he would find Elgin shy and unapproachable was more than fulfilled: he felt a complete lack of understanding or of any human warmth in the Secretary of State. With Churchill it was different; soon after Lugard's return he came to stay at Abinger. The visit was a success; relations were personally cordial and the Under-Secretary must have realized that the High Commissioner was not quite as much the Russian czar as he had thought. Meanwhile there was much to do for Northern Nigeria, long discussions in London over the future of the railway system, plans for cotton growing, many reports for Lugard to write, and the classic *Political Memoranda* to revise for printing.

The joy of Lugard's reunion with Flora and the quiet months together at Abinger brought them to the conviction that nothing, not even Africa, must part them again. It was a hard decision for Lugard to make. But he could feel that he had completed the conventional term of a governor: he had largely created Northern Nigeria as a Protectorate and carried it through its last crisis to peace and the promise of orderly development. Above all, he felt that the Colonial Secretary had broken his predecessor's promise about the Scheme. In July, therefore, he sent in his resignation, which was tepidly received by Elgin, though the Press was generous in its comment upon his achievements.

The novelty of unemployment was neither to his taste nor Flora's. Their partnership was not of a kind to find its fulfilment in their private enjoyment of each other. They were both to the core public characters, they needed to join together in public work. When, therefore, rather surprisingly, the governorship of Hong Kong was offered, Lugard accepted the offer and, as he thought, finally closed the book of his African record.

PART TWO

Hong Kong 1907-1912

CHAPTER XIV

THE FIRST TWO YEARS, 1907-9

FROM THE moment that Lugard embarked upon his ship for Hong Kong we have again a personal record upon which to draw. Flora was with him but Edward, his other intimate personal correspondent, was not. To him he wrote:

> " The day after tomorrow we reach Hong Kong and to *you* I will confess that as I look back over my life I do not know that I can easily recall any task upon which I have entered . . . for which I feel less aptitude, and from which I shrink more than the one which begins tomorrow."
>
> (L. to E. J. L., 26 July 1907).

This was the mood in which Lugard faced his new work. He had made his sacrifice for Flora's sake. Since she had not allowed her career or her intelligence to desiccate her Franco-Irish femininity, the fitting of his extremely male life into hers had been for him a fascinating adventure. Yet there was still a male corner of his mind which he could enjoy keeping untouched, if only as a vantage point from which to watch and enjoy the transformation which was happening to the rest of him. It was this corner which he would show to his brother Edward in letters which were probably the only papers that were not automatically open for her inspection.

Thus, as they landed in Japan, on the way to Hong Kong, Lugard could report of Flora upon the voyage that " she is simply and enthusiastically interested in a new place and a new environment and asks as many and as simple and as embarrassing questions as a child of six." One day, on the last lap of their journey, he found himself sitting

> " cross-legged between my wife and my A.D.C.'s fiancée, as Governor of Hong Kong with a British Consul to act as showman, while nautch girls danced and the surroundings brought back scenes of unregenerate

days when I was a subaltern of few years' service and less morals—of Ismailia and of Bombay and of days of ' greater freedom and less responsibility '." (L. to E. J. L., 26 July 1907).

The girl to whom Lugard refers here was Hilda Brackenbury, Flora's niece and almost a daughter to her, who was coming out to marry Lugard's aide-de-camp, Captain Taylor.

The introduction to Hong Kong was all that colonial ceremony and an astonishing natural setting could make it. Flora had dressed herself happily in gold and white; Lugard had struggled unhappily into the full levée dress uniform, which had cost him a hundred guineas; the heavily braided coat—Lugard called it his armour plate—the feathered hat and tight breeches in which governors of British colonies grace the tropics. In the misty morning sunlight their steamer passed through the narrow entrance into the great seemingly land-locked sheet of water, its blue surface broken by islands and scattered with Chinese junks and European ships. The series of crests rising from Hong Kong's rocky mass opened out to their view as they steamed on. At the base of the island was a shelf of level land, much of it reclaimed from the sea, loaded with docks and buildings. Facing Hong Kong, across the harbour, and half a mile away from it, lay the Asian mainland. That point of it, Kowloon, which reached out towards the island was British territory and it, too, was covered with the buildings, the wharves and cranes with which Western energy and wealth had crowded a once barren shore. Beyond lay the New Territories, with their bare eroded hills and beyond them again was China itself.

The salute of 17 guns boomed across the harbour: the men of war dressed overall, joined in with their fire, and Lugard bowed to their companies, ranked on deck, as his ship glided past them. He stepped off the gangway on to Blake pier, with its palms, red carpet, and awning under which all the rank and fashion of the Colony were gathered. A band struck up the national anthem. Then came the introductions. Lugard and the Colonial Secretary, who was Acting-Governor, took a quick, deep glance at each other, knowing how much would depend upon their coming relationship. " A somewhat stolid, slow-thinking sort of fellow," was Lugard's first impression, " quite good—devoid of vaseline—gives you rather the idea that you must play up to him than he to you. Plenty of sense. I liked him." Whether Mr. May, the

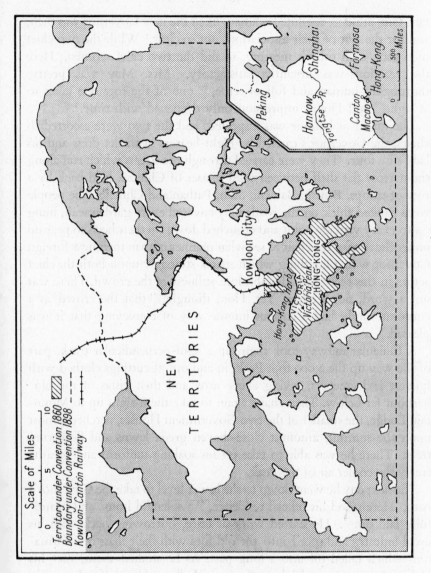

Scale of Miles

0   5   10

Territory under Convention 1860
Boundary under Convention 1898
Kowloon–Canton Railway

NEW TERRITORIES

Kowloon City

Hong Kong Harb.

VICTORIA
Victoria Peak
HONG-KONG

Peking

Hankow

Yangtse R.

Shanghai

Canton

Macao

Formosa

Hong-Kong

0   500 Miles

Hong Kong 1908.   (Based on map in *Annual Reports*, Hong Kong 1908) fair, taut, athletic, resolute Irishman, liked the new Governor was then, and for the rest of their association, not so clear.[1] While the two chief men took each other's measure, so did the two chief women. Here the reaction was instantly satisfactory. Mrs. May was pretty, thoroughly human and full of sense, " one of the sort one takes to at sight," and Flora's impression only deepened with time.

The guard of honour was inspected, and the two were escorted to chairs, the Governor's carried by eight bearers in scarlet dress and his lady's by four. They were carried through the streets which run along the narrow flat shelf between solid masses of Chinese, held back by a row of troops, British, Baluchi, Sikh, Pathan and Chinese. The people were banked thick on the road; they covered every garden wall, hung on to every vantage point and crouched down on their heels to peer up under the roof of the chair to see what manner of man their new foreign Governor was. One thing which struck strangely upon both the chief actors in this scene was the absolute stillness of the crowd. There was not a word, not a cheer. Yet, Flora thought " that the crowd as a corporate body had a curious intense way of conveying that it was pleased."

A funicular railway took them up a semi-perpendicular track, part of the way up the 2,000 foot Peak, in and out of cuttings clothed with flowers and creepers, giving every now and then vistas of the blue harbour far below. Then chairs again to take them right up to Mountain Lodge, the smaller of the two Government Houses, perched almost upon the summit, amongst close-shaven green lawns and flowering trees. There he was able to take off his soaking uniform and breathe freely the cooler air of the Peak.

The next day he went down to the lower level to take the Governor's oath. Here stood his official residence, " a splendid house and beautifully laid out ". He started work at once, burrowing back with his usual industry and speed into the old files with their mass of information which tailed off into a long past. As he studied them, met his Colonial Secretary and other officers, and allowed himself to be gently and firmly settled into the deep and well-oiled groove along which he was expected to proceed, the full depressing contrast between the old and the new work had to be faced. In Nigeria he had been a

[1] May, (later Sir) Francis Henry, G.C.M.G., 1860-1922; 1881 Hong Kong Cadetship; 1891 Assistant Colonial Secretary; 1902-10 Colonial Secretary, Hong Kong; 1910-12 Governor of Fiji and High Commissioner Western Pacific; 1912-19 Governor, Hong Kong.

pioneer and had had to create a government out of nothing: here he was faced by almost three-quarters of a century of precedent and by a large staff of officials, most of whom had spent all their working life in a Colony of which he knew nothing. There he had been king of almost infinite space; here he was confined in an island of 32 square miles. Even with Kowloon across the harbour and the New Territories and a few barren islands, the total was just under 400 square miles. In Africa he had ruled some ten million tribesmen; here, perhaps 400,000 members of one of the oldest and most cultured nations in the world with some 14,000 non-Chinese, including European merchants, lawyers, bankers, and engineers. There he had been an autocrat; here he was shackled by an Executive and a Legislative Council and must work under the running commentary of a free press. There his task had been above all military and political; here, commercial and municipal affairs filled his day and his files. In Northern Nigeria he had been almost out of the world upon its last frontiers with barbarism; here he was in a region where the strongest nations of the world were competing dangerously with each other to exploit the huge bewildered nation at his doors. In Nigeria he had been alone with his handful of assistants, living hard and trekking hard; here, in a luxurious and ordered home, he presided over a great port. Into its waters ships brought distinguished men of all races and types.

Increasingly he felt he had made a grave mistake in coming, and he confessed to his brother that he felt " horribly circumscribed." He liked to work for his pay but here " my role is to perpetually functionalize . . . to endure fools gladly, to sign my name perpetually and agree to the faultless suggestions of the Honourable the Colonial Secretary." He looked back with deep longing to " the man's work I had to do in Nigeria." Not that the new work was altogether easy. Each of the current questions had a long history. One, sanitary legislation, had been the subject of a commission which, to the great bulk of preceding literature, had recently added five or six large volumes. Nor was it merely boredom that threatened him; he had no experience of dealing with a secretariat of the kind he now took over, still less with an Executive and a Legislative Council.

His Colonial Secretary was his chief adviser and the human link between him and the new little world that had been put into his charge. Without an effective contact here no governor can be happy and can hardly be successful. Lugard's fiercely independent temperament and past history as an administrator seemed to guarantee trouble. For May had been in Hong Kong for 26 years (he was to serve it for thirty-eight in all) and there was nothing he did not know about it. He had more than once been Acting-Governor: he was a regular Colonial Service man and he was entirely efficient and very much liked. He had just been running the Colony for months with confidence and success and he now had to hand over to this wild man from Africa.That was what May might have thought. If so, he never showed it. Quiet, impassive like the Chinese amongst whom he had lived so long, unresponsive, brusque in manner, strong in will and opinions, he yet did his full duty by his chief. Lugard told his brother that he was " much in his hands, indeed no more than a puppet ... I can address no-one except through him and he resents my speaking to anyone on official subjects unless he is present." Yet this partnership was a success even from the beginning. " I do not resent it," Lugard said, " for the object is to get the Colony governed as well as we can ... I am not here to assert *myself* and my opinions in order to prove that I am the Governor."

There seems to have been two explanations of this surprising harmony. One was that for all May's personal coolness towards him Lugard liked his Colonial Secretary. There was no soft-soap about him, Lugard told Edward, "He is a desperate keen sportsman and as hard as nails. I like him very much, he is white right through." The other reason must be found in Flora. His happiness with her made him more kindly and less combative and day by day she brought her reasonable and generous mind to bear upon the work. There was a bad period at first. Some of his dark moods, rare since his marriage, came upon him. He was very much depressed and constantly silent in what they had of " home " life. She reported this to Edward " and you know without my telling you how difficult life grows for the rest of us when that is the case." She saw that he was " in his modest way a little bit afraid of some of his new tasks, especially the management of the Legislative Council and social round." Then she remarked his growing confidence. Together they began to understand the new work and to broaden their conception of it.

" It is not only the government and the gentlefolk, but it is the merchants and the poor people, not only the military and naval, but the civilian element, too, which claims his care, not only the European but the Chinese, and all these together make a charge quite important enough to be very interesting when it is faithfully fulfilled."

(F. L. to E. J. L., 21 September 1907).

Lugard was, indeed, beginning to look over the top of his desk and even over the head of his Colonial Secretary. If, he told Edward,

" I contentedly (?) sign my name after the words ' Accordingly please' or ' I concur '—or ' Approved ' yet I usually try to get the hang of it first and I think that if one pursues that line, opportunities for proving of use in the larger issues are sure not to be slow in offering—and indeed they have already offered in many directions."

(L. to E. J. L., 23 September 1907).

Lugard hated the social side but it was impossible to indulge hatred towards something which his wife did so well and with such enjoyment. In Hong Kong there was an important place for a Governor's wife who could play the perfect hostess to the procession of visitors and help her husband to give the right social lead to an isolated British community.

The entertaining was an essential part of governing Hong Kong. Government House was used as a high-class hotel, restaurant and sports club by many of the hundreds of passengers who left their ships to write their names in the Governor's book. There were the globe-trotters who might be as literary as Valentine Chirol or Sven Hedin; or as politically interesting as William H. Taft,[1] Keir Hardie or the Sidney Webbs. Then there were the British official visitors, generals and admirals on tours of inspection, diplomats and experts of many kinds. Socially most exacting were the many distinguished foreigners and Eastern potentates—Chinese and Japanese princes, Indian Rajahs, the Governor of the neighbouring Portuguese Macao, foreign admirals who had to be visited in their warships and later entertained in turn at Government House; ambassadors en route to or from Tokyo or Peking, and many lesser functionaries. The official, commercial, and Chinese residents of Hong Kong were always with them, presenting delicate problems of hospitality in an artificial community, in a day when class division was still almost unchallenged and official hierarchy was exactly reflected in social life.

[1] President of the United States, 1908–12.

Lugard and Flora sustained each other by mutual admiration. After one great occasion he wrote:

> " She has very large ideas—has had a huge stair-case some 12 feet broad with a huge half-way landing constructed outside the Ball room to the garden, domed over with arches and all lit up by electric light. A great conception. Her arrangements for feeding 200 at a time at supper are magnificent."　　　　　　　　　　　(L. to E. J. L., 16 November 1907).

Whatever *his* part in the Colony, " Flora's is clear gain. They have not had a lady at Government House for 15 years."[1] Upon Lugard's form as the head of society, his brother had Flora's account.

> " He really does play up splendidly. We don't ask him to come on show too often but when he does come he does all the right things, talks to the right people, admires the pretty, is nice to the dull ones and kind to all the lame ducks."　　　　　　(F. L. to E. J. L., 21 September 1907).

Lugard even set himself, with his usual dogged thoroughness, to learn the Lancers (" We have done one or two practices but it is a pretty complicated drill ") and he was proud to record that the Admiral said " I did it so well that when he was in doubt he watched me."

But the social duty remained utterly uncongenial. The waste of time irked him most. There was some social occasion each day. He hated " to stand first on one leg then upon another with a glazed grin on my face, or bowing like the Chinese image on the mantelpiece whose head wags for an hour if you touch him under the chin." He urged his brother not to believe a word Flora said about his social or any other kind of success, " She is absolutely unreliable where I am concerned, thank God!"

Lugard's duties were not confined to Government House. Hong Kong's few thousand Europeans were not only divided horizontally into a number of classes, but perpendicularly according to profession. There were battalions of soldiers to be welcomed, inspected or sent off; merchants in their Chambers of Commerce and other societies; associations of engineers and many other professions. There were all the different religious sects with an astonishing number of institutions of every kind run by them which had to be opened, visited, aided through

---

[1] The preceding Governor had been Sir Matthew Nathan. He was a very able man, and the writer can testify from personal experience to his great charm and humanity. Lugard often paid tribute to his work in Hong Kong. In this station he had the demerit of being a bachelor. But his predecessor, Sir Henry Blake, had been married.

concerts or bazaars, or have their prizes given out. There were actually more of such occasions, Lugard claimed, than could be dealt with in 365 days. Then there were all the scores of sporting clubs and events— cricket, yachting, football, tennis, polo, horse-racing and the rest, not to speak of dramatic clubs and chrysanthemum societies. And the same people would sort themselves afresh into still other clubs and national societies in order to meet each other again in new capacities and to fill more nights with dinners and speechifying. For every single or annual event the presence of the Governor or his lady, or preferably both, was regarded as the essential crown, and a speech was always exacted. Day after day he must don his gubernatorial fancy dress, and some-times even ride a borrowed horse in a frock coat and top hat, all the time conning over the speech he had had to learn by heart.

" It gives me a curious feeling of having suddenly been withdrawn from a life of work I understood, to act a part in a stage play which I have not worked up. I don't know my part, and I feel that it is not *I* who am being saluted when I come into a Council or Race course etc., with ' God Save the King ', but some other idiot in whose place I am masquerading, and I feel that it is supremely ridiculous and I ought rather to be riding bare-back or bowling a hoop." (L. to E. J. L., 11 October 1907).

Flora never shared this sense of incongruity. Everywhere she made human and intelligent speeches, duly reported in the local press, and Lugard, for his part, gave sincere little addresses which breathed the confident patriotism of his day.

It may be thought that the Chinese population makes a rather late entry into the story. This only reflects the facts. For Lugard, in his two houses raised high above the densely crowded Chinese areas on the water-line, was at first surrounded by the European community. In the busy life of the crowded commercial centre he had at first little time to look beyond his frontier to China. But as the affairs of the greater and the less became politically entangled he had to set to work to make some study of the history and character of his neighbours.

The continuity of China's civilization and its extension over such a vast area and population through millennia of virtual isolation from the rest of the world, had bred in the people both conservatism and com-placency. This turned naturally into fierce xenophobia when men of distant unknown nations came pricking and prowling in their ships along her hitherto inviolate coasts. The moral problem raised by the contact grows more difficult in retrospect. The right of a numerous people to shut themselves and a great region away from the rest of the world has to be set against the claim of other nations to use force to open it to their trade and influence when consent was refused. Certainly most British people, looking back, are now uneasy about some aspects of their early relationship with China. We may be inclined to accept the humanitarians' plea for the imposition of "legitimate trade," and even annexation, upon Africa, where these could be used to counter slavery and poverty and where the tribes could hardly be credited with a political will, and yet not agree that this principle could be stretched to justify the coercion of an old imperial government like that of China. Though the story is not quite such a simple one as it appears on the surface, few would justify today the attempt to force upon China the trade in opium.

The very existence of Hong Kong as a British possession arose from Britain's determination, and China's refusal, to trade in the early nineteenth century. The Chinese government, which regarded Europeans as contemptible barbarians, red-faced "foreign devils", had insulted and rejected Britain's most dignified envoys and had subjected what trade Britain had been able to force upon the great southern city of Canton to every kind of difficulty and exaction. Finally, in 1839, the Chinese authorities seized great stocks of the merchants' opium stored there. The British, forced out of Canton, found, only a few hours' sailing from that port, a great almost land-locked harbour and an island which was then completely defensible by a sea power. To this island they transferred themselves. It is the British claim that when they took the island it was a barren rock, the haunt of a few fishermen and pirates, and that they have made it one of the greatest ports of the world. China's agreement to the annexation was obtained in 1842, but only after a war in which Britain's naval supremacy allowed her to seize ports at will. Kowloon, the strip of land opposite Hong Kong's city of Victoria, was ceded in 1860 following another war and the seizure of Peking by Britain and her allies. Finally, in the great scramble of 1898, Britain, to balance gains made by other powers, claimed a much larger area lying behind Kowloon and covering 359 square miles. This, a hilly region called the New Territories, was leased to Britain for 99 years. It was at first regarded as a convenient extension for supply and defence, but the enormous growth of population on the island itself has made it wholly dependent upon the mainland for food and water. The Japanese proved in 1941 that with modern weapons the island is no longer the impregnable fortress which Lugard could still believe it to be. But, of course, at that grave moment, the command of the sea had been lost.

But Hong Kong is only one theme in the story of British relations with China and the British were only one among the nations which were penetrating more deeply every year of the later nineteenth century into the land and economy of a country which was as hostile as it was helpless. But the years just before Lugard came to the East had seen a change in the attitude of China. The blind antagonism that had governed her dealings with the commercial powers through most of the nineteenth century had led her to strike out wildly like some large creature trapped in a net which only became more helplessly entangled with each movement. Finally, in 1900, came the ferocious Boxer attack on the foreigners which led to the capture of Peking by the commercial powers and to a penal treaty weighted with heavy indemnities. The event shook further the already weakened loyalty of the Chinese to the Manchu rulers. In spite of all the cunning and vitality of the old Empress-Dowager and her final acrobatics in swinging over to a policy of democratic reform, a revolutionary movement developed.

In 1904-5 occurred an event which made another profound impression, the Russo-Japanese war. The Chinese saw the small Japanese nation, which had borrowed its civilization from them, beat a large Western power at its own game of modern war. The Chinese suddenly realized that their old attitude of angry rejection had been a failure and that they, too, might use Western knowledge to beat the West. Though many Chinese were converted to Christianity and some became friends as well as admirers of Western nations, yet in the people as a whole the deep inner resentment remained. But while it dictated some of their actions, there developed a greater readiness to understand and to accept the new things brought to their doorstep. So they waited while the powers, Britain, France, Germany, Russia and Japan, with America always a little more moderate in her conduct, strengthened their positions in the Concessions and Treaty Ports, competed to provide loans for the railways which would open up the interior; co-operated and quarrelled, and sent their men-of-war, their consuls, financiers, merchants and engineers up and down her coasts and into her rivers.

Britain was only one of the six chief powers which were forcibly opening up China. But in the nineteenth century, her adventurous and commercial impulses had outrun those of her rivals and she had won the largest share of trade in China. The economic penetration of China was only the simultaneous expression in the Far East of the same sudden outburst of expansive energy by which Britain and other Western nations had reached out into Africa and in a few years partitioned that large continent between them. But the conditions were here very different and not only in the character of the country of exploitation. Here there were even more competing nations and they were not all western. If war had been avoided, during the scramble for Africa, though only, as Lugard's activities reminded us, by a narrow margin, it had been partly because there was enough for all the few competing powers. But all the leading nations in the world were jostling in the China seas for trade, and reaching from there into the interior for economic concessions, while Russia, France and Britain were paring away at the soft rim of China's land frontiers. However, since open conflict between them might not only lead to a general war but would weaken them in the face of China's massive resentment, the nations kept the peace until they were joined in one bound by the new Eastern claimant for equality with them. Japan, neighbour and rival of China, had a much greater interest than the other powers in annexation and more ruthless methods of achieving it. It was with Japan that Britain, unable to stretch her fleets to cover all the seas in the face of growing naval construction from more than one quarter, made her alliance in 1902.

We can now see Hong Kong a little more clearly in the Chinese setting. Its function was commercial. As a free port and the best harbour between Indo-China and Shanghai, it was a natural place of call for the growing amount of shipping on the east Asian coast. It was the storehouse for the trade of southern China and especially of the great Kwangtung province, its immediate neighbour, but its trade extended to North China and beyond, and it had become the major banking centre for that part of the world.

Yet the story was not one of unbroken success or of perfect security:

the Chinese still resented the port by which they so greatly profited and Canton, above all, regarded it as a rival. The real feeling of the Chinese towards foreigners had been shown only seven years before, in the Boxer rising, when the Empress had paid a tariff for every dead barbarian, man, woman and child, who could be found and killed within her lands. But Britain had little to fear as yet from China. The insecurity that was of more immediate interest to the great merchant firms which dominated Hong Kong was economic. It was a place which had then little production of its own. A warehouse, a market and, even more, a wharf, it could do no more than reflect every economic condition, good or bad, not only those in the great country beside it, but also on the graph of world trade, its merchants profiting from good times and holding on grimly through years of depression.

A few figures, taken for 1910, the central year of Lugard's governorship, will show the size and character of the commerce of the Colony. In the twenty years before this the tonnage of shipping entering the port had risen from $4\frac{1}{2}$ to 12 million tons, of which over 4 million was British. Over 4,000 ocean ships, 35 per cent of them British, and more than 5,000 smaller steamers entered the port.[1] Out of China's total trade of £114,000,000 the British Empire's share was £59,000,000, or approximately 52 per cent. Out of this Empire trade, Hong Kong accounted for £38,000,000. But Hong Kong was also an entrepôt for trade, the goods being deposited there and imported as required into China by Chinese and foreign merchants.[2] And China was not the only country in the East to receive merchandise from Hong Kong. It was Lugard's first duty to see that this great trade was kept moving. This required, administratively, order and efficiency in the port and, politically, that the government should remain on as good terms as possible with all parties to the trade.

It follows from this that the big men of Hong Kong were the representatives of the great firms engaged in the China and eastern trade, such as Jardine, Matheson & Co. and Butterfield & Swire; the big shipping agents, the owners or managers of the docks, and the bankers. It was around them and their concerns that all the lesser men who were their subordinates, and all the lawyers, doctors, engineers, building contractors and others were ranged.

[1] *Annual Reports, Hong Kong, Report for 1910*, p. 5ff.
[2] *Report for the year 1910 on the Trade of China* (1911), Diplomatic and Consular Reports, No. 4751, Cd. 5465, p. 10.

What then of the Chinese? A few, with some Indians and Anglo-Chinese of mixed blood, were wealthy merchants, while the rest occupied various positions in the long scale of wealth and status which reached down to the coolie level. Here, at the bottom, was found the vast majority of a population which rose from 300,000 in 1906 to 436,000 in 1910. In 1910, 200,000 Chinese lived on Hong Kong island, 80,000 in Kowloon and the New Territories, while 50,000 were classified, not altogether metaphorically, as " floating ".[1] They worked mainly in the docks; others were fishermen and petty traders. No accurate statistics about their movements existed at this time, but the majority were drawn from the mainland, itself overcrowded, into the Colony and pressed out again according to its demand for labour as shown by the fluctuating level of wages. There was, and indeed could be, no control of immigration: the Chinese were almost amphibious and could swarm over by night or day across the narrow water in thousands of craft of all sorts and sizes. In face of the grossly crowded living conditions and the high cost of lodgings ashore, very large numbers lived in their junks. But the Chinese had a cat-like capacity for making any spot where they happened to be into home.

These were the people who constituted Lugard's new charge. Hong Kong presented some of the problems of what has since been termed a " plural " community, one in which people of different races have been drawn together for mainly economic purposes and have developed none of those deeper unities which would bind them into a true society. The position in Hong Kong was simplified by there being, except for some cosmopolitan element, only two races in contact, but the economic basis of their co-operation was more than usually dominant. Yet some of the residents of the Hong Kong of that period have told the writer how much goodwill there was to reach across the barriers of class, caste and race.

Lugard recognized this. He had, we saw, been no enthusiastic friend of business interests in Nigeria. But he had mellowed with time and he knew well enough that he was there to serve a commercial colony. Marriage, too, as we have seen had fostered the kindlier part of his nature.

" We are agreed," he told his brother, " that the people here are very nice. They are all so easily pleased and so anxious to please: there seems

[1] *Report for 1910*, p. 21.

to be so little scandal-mongering and jealousy . . . the men are all frankly
here to make dollars and the women to amuse themselves in a reasonable
and proper way and both seem to do it with success."

(L. to E. J. L., 23 September 1907).

At first it seemed as if the personal gain had made Lugard's sacrifice
worth the professional cost. But soon even that became doubtful. The
first blow, in December 1907, was the sudden death of Flora's niece,
Hilda, soon after her happy marriage with Lugard's aide-de-camp.
Then, in March 1908, Flora's health began once more to cause anxiety.
Even in the cold weather the climate did not suit her. This was partly
due to her ceaseless over-exertion. In addition to the never-ending
social round and public duties, she conducted weekly readings for
groups of the local ladies, practised music and spent two hours a day
learning Chinese " as a relaxation ". In the middle of the month she
suddenly collapsed. Upon examination, she seemed to have almost
everything wrong with her, but, in addition, some serious undiagnosed
disorder. Once more Lugard took the strain. The recent sudden death
of her niece sharpened his fears. He became the perfect nurse and could
hardly bear to leave her room though at the time he was very heavily
engaged. He met the situation by working almost round the clock.
He sent her home in May, confiding her to his brother (" the only
absolutely reliable man on earth ") but warning him against believing
all she would tell him.

" You will find that Flora is in love with me (there's no accounting for
women) and in consequence she will tell you . . . that I am a huge success
here . . . As a matter of fact this is not my *job*, but I toil and spin . . . and I
go through the mill, and am occasionally rapped on the knuckles by my
exceedingly able Colonial Secretary. But don't you go away with any
such crude idea as that I am considered here . . . as anything more than a
willing makeshift for a Governor."   (L. to E. J. L., 22 May 1908).

Lugard felt very solitary after Flora went. The burden of entertaining seemed unusually heavy. He found some relief in reporting it to
Flora. There was, for example, a visit from the Japanese Admiral with
a return visit to his flagship (" not exhilarating . . . his lunch was bad,
so were his cigars.") Next came the brother of the Regent of China, a
stout young man of nineteen, who insisted that Lugard should call on
him first, lost the round, and then arrived unexpectedly for lunch with

twenty-two admirals, generals and other attendants. Then came Lord
Kitchener to stay at Government House and to divide his time between
studying Far Eastern defences, as the barometer of international relations moved steadily downwards, and to collect china with a passion
that was almost indecent: but " collectors have neither morals nor
conscience and are to be judged as partial maniacs . . . He was friendly
and wholly unaffected but naturally thinks a good deal of Kitchener
of Khartoum—as, indeed, all the world does . . . The Press and community here have gone mad about him." Next came a visit from an
American female philanthropist " a dowdy little elderly lady in a sort
of Panama hat with a blue turban or bandage tied around it and a blue
veil." When Lugard greeted her she drew back and looked him up
and down with ill-concealed misgiving. " You, are *you* the Governor?
I had expected to see an elderly man!" She told him her mission was
to get a book called *Black Beauty*—perhaps some readers can
remember how deeply this equine biography moved them in the
nursery—deposited in all the schools. It seemed that it already had a
circulation next to the Bible. It inculcated, said the lady, kindness to
horses. Lugard said that his Chinese had no horses. This did
not deter her and it was a tribute to her determination or his
cowardice that in return for promised supplies of the book free
or for $1\frac{1}{2}$d. a copy he agreed to put it in all the schools. After this he
had the German admiral and all his captains. Next came the American
admiral who gave him a grand dinner, exulting over its chief delicacy,
oysters, which Lugard could not eat but dared not refuse and had to
transfer one by one via his handkerchief into his pocket, no mean feat
for the chief guest at a public banquet. Sir John French came on the
heels of Kitchener to discuss defence and engaged his host for several
days in talk that was deep and fascinating but also highly disturbing.
Then came another Japanese squadron with an admiral and seventeen
captains to entertain, and a return party on board with geisha girls
dancing. Why, the Japanese admiral asked him, with a realism his
nation was one day to express on a dramatic scale, did Britain not
fight *now* instead of waiting for the Germans to grow stronger and
stronger?

Lugard commented not only on the personalities of his guests but
upon their dress and appearance. Some of these comments were startling.

" Mrs. X, whom I took in, was of the well-to-do cook stamp and really she ought not to wear a low dress for the kindest and most unobservant person could not help noticing the colour and texture of her shoulders and arms. They smote one in the face at a distance before she entered the room and were like the skin of an alligator."

He was, indeed, often shocked at the ladies' low dresses since " the Chinese servants stand gazing at them amazed that foreigners should allow their women to expose themselves." None of his visitors aroused so much enthusiasm as a Mrs. Max Muller, the Norwegian wife of a young diplomat from the British Embassy at Peking.[1] He admired her masses of bronze-coloured hair, " her *healthy* look " and " her air of taking life seriously which I so admire in these Scandinavians." She was also highly intelligent.

" She was extremely prettily dressed and I studied it closely for you. It was a salmon coloured silk (or satin) gown (note the word gown) brought over the right shoulder, and circled round the top (where it ceased on her breast) with a sort of leaf pattern of sparkling glitterations (I can't find any word in my vocabulary because of course they weren't jewels.) From the bust of it there were small pendant glitterations, not too pronounced, and the bust part was not of the salmon silk but of a sort of muslin or lace . . . Dresses are quite extraordinarily difficult to describe but I took stock of this so as to give you a full description—but it doesn't seem to read very full and clear?"   (L. to F. L., 12 December 1909).

Flora needed to be cheered by light relief of this kind, since she was ill for almost the whole of the six months she spent in England. By December, however, she took the risk of returning. But she had no sooner delighted him by her arrival than she collapsed again with her mysterious internal complaint and in June he was at once sad and relieved to send her home again.

This meant that it would be nearly a year before, by taking his first leave, he could see her again. More and more he began to think he had sacrificed Africa in vain. He had left because his six months Scheme had been rejected, yet here he had to face separations longer both in time and in distance than when he was in Nigeria. Since their marriage they had been apart for almost the whole of his working life in Nigeria and, what with the lateness of their union and her fragile

[1] Mrs. Max Muller, later Lady Max Muller, wife of Sir William Max Muller, son of the celebrated Professor. The writer, who later enjoyed her friendship, can testify that the admiration both for her appearance and her sense of dress was well merited.

health, Lugard had a desperate sense that he was throwing away the best thing that life, all too tardily, had given him. The anxiety caused by Flora's illnesses was so intense that but for his superb physical strength and powers of self-discipline, it would have subtracted seriously from his efficiency as a governor. And worse was to come. Early in March 1910, while living in a flat in Kensington, Flora was suddenly seized with acute appendicitis. The operation revealed a deep-seated and dangerous abscess. For three days she lay very close to death. It was only later that he learned how nearly she had died.

As this news came to him, the last days of his first term of service in Hong Kong were running out. Public work and private anxiety gave him little leisure to think how the Colony was regarding his departure. It was not that he was indifferent to the public attitude. He had at first been much startled and even angered by what he regarded as the misleading, scurrilous and even libellous attitude often displayed towards his government in the four English daily papers. He did not realize that in a remote tropical colony men's minds craved for strong spice just as their physical appetites asked for hot curry and strong drink. But on the occasion of his departure the press appears to have spoken with one voice in praise of Lugard's character and achievements. What pleased him more, however, was that the Chinese community insisted, in spite of tactful dissuasion, upon an official leave-taking. The whole ceremony was an expression of the Chinese perfection of form and artistic grace. They brought up to Government House a long satin scroll embroidered in Canton and hung it in the reception hall suspended from two silver bats, emblems of good luck. At the top of it was an embroidered phoenix gazing at the sun: this expressed Lugard's high position. Then, in two columns, came the embroidered letters of the address and the list of signatures, all in the beautiful Chinese characters. Below this were two deer, which expressed the Chinese wish—in the circumstances an unselfish one—for Lugard's speedy promotion. A mandarin duck and drake stood for Chinese devotion. A carved red sandalwood box had been made to hold the scroll and it carried Lugard's monogram in silver, with the Chinese addition " Benevolent Governor of Hong Kong." A few extracts from the long address will show its character.

" More than once have the stars and the hoar frosts returned in their course

Lugard as Governor of Hong Kong

Hong Kong University: the original building

since Your Excellency came to Hong Kong: the benevolence and clemency of your virtuous administration is in the mouth of every passer-by in the streets . . . More especially has every movement for the benefit of the Chinese received your heartiest support."

The signatories then went on to congratulate Lugard upon specific reforms and they ended with the hope that:

" you may spend your holiday in happiness in the society of Her Excellency Lady Lugard, our admiration of whose virtues we pray you to convey to her. We trust that you will remember this Colony in your heart and return soon that we may look again upon the dignity of your countenance and hearken to the grace of your commands."

These wishes were fulfilled. At the end of April he set out via Japan and the Trans-Siberian railway upon his four weeks' journey home. Invitations to meet both the Mikado and the Kaiser en route, tributes to his personal fame as well as to his status, were politely evaded in his anxiety to hurry back to England and his wife. Once there, with the interruption of his official papers and of his correspondence with Flora and with his brother, a silence of some five months descends, a silence of happy re-union and of English summer life but by no means of idleness.

CHAPTER XV

THE TEXTURE OF GOVERNMENT

LUGARD, AS we have seen, landed in Hong Kong in the strange position of a colonial governor who had no experience of Crown Colony government. In Northern Nigeria, a raw block of Africa which fitted into no category, staff and government had to be improvised. But in this established Colony the several hierarchies of trained officials were very conscious of being regular Colonial Service men recruited by examination through the system of the Eastern Cadetships (Lugard, in gentle derision, called them the " twice-born "). They mostly spent their whole professional life in this very comfortable colony. Colonial Office opinion at this time was that they wanted new blood. They were certainly efficient; the place was small and administration was conducted according to a system which had been seventy years in the making. There were two things which Lugard had to do, though he could do them well or badly, and a third that he could do if he pleased. The first was to carry out the routine duties of his post. The second, which might give him a little more scope, was to deal effectively with such special problems as might present themselves. The third, and most difficult, was to find for himself some independent activity to employ his creative energy. This chapter mainly concerns his first task.

Even this proved difficult enough. He had to learn how to use the traditional instruments of the Executive and Legislative Council. Fortunately, perhaps, for him, the Colonial Office had not considered Hong Kong a place into which much of the democratic element could be infused. The Executive Council, which was purely advisory, was formed of a few senior officials. The Legislative Council, over which he must preside in person, consisted of seven senior officials and six nominated unofficials, all " big " men in the Colony. Two of them were Chinese and most of them had been members for a long time.

The Texture of Government

Lugard at first found the Legislative Council an embarrassing institution and he was thankful when the ordeal of his first meeting was over.

" I got through moderately well, though grossly ignorant of how to ' put the question ' and all ordinary formalities. When a member rose and asked if he was in order in replying I had to turn to the Colonial Secretary and ask if he was. However, these are things which only fools worry about. I shall learn in course of time, though these kind of Bodies don't like their ' top sawyer ' not to know the ropes."

(L. to E. J. L., 23 September 1907).

There could be no better school in which to learn the lessons of the Colony, since in the course of the year nearly all its public affairs went across the table in the papers and legislation of the Council and any that were at all controversial were hammered out in debate. He very soon realized that, for all his paper autocracy, the Colony was governed very largely by consent. There was, indeed, a double assent to be gained, that of the business men who knew that their interests were the *raison d'être* of the Colony, and, in a somewhat different range of subjects, that of the Chinese. It was easy to know the views of the first: the second were reached by a somewhat mysterious and ramifying system of communication which found its official apex in the office of the Registrar General and depended much upon the help of the two long-established English-educated Chinese members of the Council, Dr. Ho Kai[1] and Mr. Wei Yuk.[2] The system appeared to meet all needs: there was no serious movement for greater self-government. Both the British and the Chinese leaders well knew how impossible it would be to apply the British, or any other, democratic system to this abnormal population, and both were well content with a constitution which was worked by compromise and consent to a degree that could not have been realized from looking at its outward forms.

To an administrator, Hong Kong had some extraordinary features. It was at once a state, with all the constitutional top-hamper of a colonial government, and a municipality. Although the greater part of

[1] Kai Ho Kai, (later Sir), K.C.M.G., 1859-1914; educated Aberdeen University, St. Thomas' Medical College and Lincoln's Inn; married Alice Walkden; practised medicine and law, Hong Kong; founded Alice Memorial Hospital; member of Legislative Council 1890-1914. Knighted 1912.
[2] Bosnan Wei Yuk, (later Sir), K.C.M.G., 1849-1921; educated Stoneygate School and Dollar Institution; 1872-1908 Compradore of Mercantile Bank of India; 1886-1917 member of Legislative Council; prominent in sanitary and railway questions and in Hong Kong—Canton relations. Knighted 1919.

its administration was frankly and often sordidly municipal, it could not have a merely municipal government because it was, in fact, a Chinese city run by the agents of a foreign government operating some 1,300 miles from their own imperial headquarters. Its position raised political and diplomatic questions, especially in relation to the neighbouring provinces of China, which were anything but municipal. Secondly came the formidable problems of a crowded eastern port with an ever-shifting population. And thirdly, there was the peculiar nature of the revenue, at once rigid in character and fluctuating in volume.

In dealing with the first of these questions Lugard had to remember that, whatever his colony was by constitution, by geography and population it was closely related with China's large southern province of Kwangtung. He had to observe also that an increasingly revolutionary situation was developing in China. It was caused largely by foreign influences, many of them brought back by Chinese who had been in Europe or America. The potentate with whom Lugard had to reckon immediately was the Viceroy of Canton and he could not be quite sure how far this functionary was responsive to the behests of Peking or how far, in view of the ancient cleavage between south and north China, he was playing his own game. Lugard was supposed, in all relations with the Chinese, to avoid direct action, and write first to the Colonial Office, sending a copy of the letter to the British Ambassador in Peking, then Sir John Jordan.[1] But for urgent and local matters he could apply direct to the British Consul-General in Canton. As there were a great many points of contact with Kwangtung—piracy and extradition were perennial subjects—Lugard, always independent in his actions, was tempted to deal direct with Canton's Viceroy.

Almost as soon as he arrived, he had to entertain a new Viceroy, Chang Jen Chun, coming by way of Hong Kong in a Chinese warship to take up his new post. This visit was a very formal affair, with exchanges of visits and of nineteen-gun salutes. A large luncheon party was given. The Viceroy had, Flora remarked, the massive face of a man of power, rather unpleasantly half-closed eyes but an agreeable smile. He spoke through an interpreter but seemed perfectly at home with European food and manners. Early in January, 1908, Lugard

[1] Jordan, Sir John, P.C., G.C.M.G., K.C.B., 1852-1925; 1891 Chinese Secretary to the British Legation, Peking; 1898-1906 Consul-General, Korea, Minister Resident at the Court of Korea; 1906-20 Minister Plenipotentiary, Peking.

returned the visit, sailing in the Admiral's man-of-war yacht up the
river to Canton. He and Flora visited the shops and saw the intricate
workmanship of craftsmen whose art had matured over thousands of
years and bought blackwood furniture for their home in Abinger. For
his official call Lugard was carried through miles of streets only six or
eight foot broad and paved with granite slabs. The escort of forty
nondescripts in khaki, slouching along with antedeluvian guns and
sword bayonets, led by a very fat Chinese on a very fat white pony,
was not impressive. The Viceroy provided a magnificent lunch and
pledged Lugard in champagne, sherry, port, liqueur, brandy and
whisky. He proposed the health of the Empress Dowager and the King
of England, after first retiring to discuss the procedure with his assistants, probably to find out, Lugard thought, if England *had* a king or
not.

" He is a jolly, genial old boy—speaks no English at all, and, like all
Chinese, exceedingly courteous and good-mannered. Taotai Wen . . .
was interpreter, but the mixture of wines so got into his head that he
could not remember the six doctrines of Confucius, and I had to help
him out! With one course we had a nice little heap of slices of bread, cut
as thin as possible. I did not know what it was, and asked. Wen said
' Chinese bread but Foreign flour ', and repeated the last words. I observed
that China seemed to have a ridiculous aversion to anything Foreign.
' Our Economic Ideal,' I added, ' is quite the opposite. We think that a
country should make a speciality of what it can produce best and cheapest,
and let the Foreigner supply whatever he can import cheaper than we can
make it. For instance, all our bread in England is of 'Foreign Flour ' . . .
Wen, who had started on liqueur brandy, bucked up, and seemed to
think there was some sense in this, and asked if he might repeat it to the
Viceroy, who received it with a loud grunt."

(L. to E. J. L., 10 January 1908).

This visit, with the Consul-General accompanying him in full uniform, might be accounted a success. In July 1909 the Viceroy, who was
about to take up a new post in Nanking, again visited Hong Kong.
A great party was given for him at Government House and he seemed
genuinely pleased. It was the first time a Chinese Viceroy had ever
accepted such full and friendly hospitality in Hong Kong. Lugard
commented that he had always believed that:

" Hong Kong's prosperity largely depends upon our friendly relations

305

with Canton. It was an object lesson to the swarms of Chinese to see the Viceroy and myself going side by side in the train and laughing and chatting familiarly, and they craned their necks and obviously appreciated the significance of the sight."   (L. to F. L., 30 July 1909).

Yuah Shu, the man who was about to succeed as Viceroy, was reported to be bitterly anti-foreign so Lugard set himself to win his respect and friendly regard. After his visit at the beginning of September 1909 he decided that this reputedly embittered potentate had a nice friendly face. He spoke no English but he told Lugard that both his wife and his son had been educated in England, though, as the Japanese were to prove, this was a circumstance by no means incompatible with hatred for the people whose civilization was being ransacked for its most utilitarian and dangerous items.[1] But Lugard's frank approach appeared to have some effect. Again and again the Viceroy looked hard at his slight, confident but courteous host. Then he told him that he had heard much about him, that he knew he had had excellent relations with his predecessor, that he was said to be conciliatory, just and fair, and that, now that he had seen him, he could believe it. " I smiled at him," Lugard recounted, " and looked as affable as possible and think he really took a sort of liking to me as I did to him." One grave enquiry he made of Lugard was whether his capacity for drinking was good, to which Lugard replied, with regret but with equal gravity, that formerly it had been very good but that it had fallen off of late years. Chinese decorum prevented his guest from pressing his hedonistic enquiries any further.

Upon his next visit to Canton, Lugard was again received with great cordiality and treated, according to a menu which lies on the writer's table in Chinese and English, to a lunch of bird's nest soup, boiled perch, filetted shark's fin, fried pigeons' eggs, crabs with green vegetables, bamboo roots with shrimp roe sauce, roast duck and turnip dumplings, roast sucking pig, and herb puffs.

Relations in general with Canton were surprisingly correct in view of their general background and of the special causes for friction. When, in December 1908, the redoubtable Empress Tz'u-hsi and the puppet Emperor died almost simultaneously, Lugard sent all the correct messages and moved a dignified vote of condolence in the

[1] For an interesting treatment of this theme in fiction see Robert Standish, *The Three Bamboos* (1942).

306

Legislative Council.[1] The event may not have seemed of more than diplomatic interest to Hong Kong, yet the passing of the last able Manchu ruler, after her vain attempt to re-establish the influence of the dynasty by modern reforms, was one more phase in the emergence of a new China, which might prove to be a neighbour very different from the old.

Before he had been in Hong Kong much more than a year Lugard learned how closely the situation in the mainland could affect the Colony. Feeling in China had been intensely hostile to the Japanese since the island people had defeated China in the Sino-Japanese war of 1894-5 and had then defeated Russia, as it were, over China's body. China was the great home of secret societies and there were in Canton some that were militantly nationalist, among them the " Self government Society " and " The National Disgrace Society ". These organized a boycott against Japanese goods which was completely successful in Canton and spread to Hong Kong. Even if Japan had not been an ally, Lugard was not the man to take tamely a challenge in his own territory. When riots broke out the Hong Kong police were caught by surprise and Japanese goods were looted and destroyed, though no lives were lost. Lugard struck with speed and severity. He banished six of the fomenters of trouble who had come in from outside and threatened those Chinese merchants who had taken the lead with the same penalty. Order was quickly restored. But the officials in Downing Street felt that he had been high-handed, not only towards the mischief-makers but, as usual, towards themselves, in acting without giving them sufficient information,[2] and they were further harassed by the legality of the banishments being questioned in parliament.[3] Lugard's writ did not run in Canton, and here the xenophobes effectively boycotted one of the great shipping firms, Butterfield and Swire, following an incident upon one of their ships, the *Fatshan*, and forced them to submit to oppressive demands. Lugard writhed at a humiliation which he could not prevent.

On one occasion the remark of a visiting Englishman, Mr. A. H. Harris, Commissioner of the Chinese Customs, who was discussing this incident, and who appeared to see things too much from the

[1] *Legislative Council Reports*, 1908 Session, 3 December, p. 148.
[2] Minutes on Lugard to Crewe, 12 and 25 November 1908, C.O. 129/349, and 12 June 1909, C.O. 129/356.
[3] *Parliamentary Debates*, 3 December 1908, IV. 197. 1668.

Chinese point of view—an attitude he might well have felt it to be his duty to adopt—stung Lugard into a generalization about the whole situation of a kind he seldom uttered.

> " I came here as an open-minded man whose ideas had not been moulded in a Chinese groove, and my judgment is that China has been treated in an extraordinarily courteous and obliging way by this Colony. Without any reciprocity we extradite her criminals at much cost and labour to ourselves, and we suppress any literature etc., which is seditious. We help her without any recompense or reciprocity to prevent the import of arms, and of prepared opium. We help her to collect her revenue on opium."

He contrasted the liberal and humane action of Britain over the opium trade as compared with that of Portugal and Germany:

> " The trade of China is a part—a great part—of the trade of this port, but China does not send it here to oblige Hong Kong. Nor, on the other hand, has Hong Kong created this great Mart and Port to oblige China. It has grown by the growth of civilization from a barren rock. You say China could kill the trade—let her try! As to your *Fatshan* affair, what was it? Two nations (China and Japan) fell out and the former boycotted the latter. Well and good, it is no concern of mine, but when China tried to enforce her Boycott in the territory of a third and most friendly power I had to put my foot down and say ' No, you shall not do it in Hong Kong.' And hence the *Fatshan* affair! What defence has China of her actions?" (L. to F. L., 21 March 1910).

At this sudden outburst, Mr. Harris, we learn, " coiled up ".

Yet Lugard had a great respect for the Chinese nation. Pondering over the rapid development of the Japanese, he could ask himself:

> " If they can thus excel, what of the Chinese, who by universal testimony are their superiors in physique and in brains and in honesty and capacity. Truly I often wonder whether the dream of the Yellow Peril is not likely to come true some day, and the Chinaman by sheer ability and industry will dominate the commerce of the world."
>
> (L. to F. L., 9 July 1911).

The only consolation was that it would not come in his time. Today the question is whether he was right to confine his prophecy to commerce.

Within an outwardly correct framework of relations with China, Lugard had to handle two very important and most contentious subjects. These were the Kowloon-Canton railway and the opium question: both had been raised before Lugard's time, but reached their climax while he was governor. The opium question demands a chapter to itself but the subject of the railway can best be discussed here.

It was obvious to the British, especially after Kowloon had been developed as a port, that a railway from there to Canton was an economic necessity. But in Chinese eyes railways had come to represent a political intrusion and might be a military danger. They were already the cause of a fierce struggle for concessions among the powers after these had satisfied their claims for vantage points along the coast. It was the intense feeling of the people of a Chinese province over a foreign railway concession that finally touched off the revolution of 1911. The idea of a railway from Hong Kong, a British Colony, was especially obnoxious to Canton, which also feared the effect upon its own shipping and commerce.

Yet Lugard embarked confidently upon the project. In the face of the omniscience of his Colonial Secretary, he felt that colonial railways presented much the same kind of problem everywhere, and fresh from long discussions with Churchill and others about the railway system of Nigeria, he approached the twenty-two miles of his side of the proposed railway with an assurance that turned out to be excessive. The railway proved to be one long struggle; with the Colonial Office over the control of the work; with the engineers over its execution; with his Council over its finance; and with the Chinese over the attempt to get them to make an agreement for the joint working of a line, the longer section of which was to be built and run by them. But the reward for overcoming all these obstacles would be high. No less was at stake, as Lugard told his Council in a long and detailed speech in which, early in 1908, he showed his mastery of the subject, than the commercial predominance of Hong Kong. " It was a question of seeing that the final outlet of the main trunk railway of China should be at Kowloon and at no other place."[1] The line was to be the continuation to the sea of the main interior line running through the centre of Eastern China from Peking through Hankow to Canton. The Chinese Government agreed in 1905 to accept a British loan for building their part of the railway and it was from the repayments of this, paid in instalments, that the British part was to be built.[2]

[1] *Legislative Council Reports*, 1908 Session, 6 February, p. 8.
[2] G. B. Endacott, *A History of Hong Kong* (1958), pp. 272-3.

Lugard did not start on this project with a clean sheet. Surveys and over-optimistic estimates had been made before his arrival. But the greatest disappointment for Lugard was to find that the work was not to be carried out directly by the colony, a method that would have given him the full joy of creation and of practising his favourite virtue of thrift, but by the so-called " Departmental System ". This meant that the work was directly under the Crown Agents with a consulting engineer in London, appointed by them, who in turn appointed a resident engineer to work on the spot. It was not long before trouble started. The structure of the Leased or New Territories beyond Kowloon was difficult and mountainous: there were 49 bridges and 5 tunnels—one at least very long—to be built; land to be reclaimed from the sea; and other land to be acquired right up to the crowded dockland of Kowloon. (It may be worth a remark in passing that the returning Chinese labourers whose presence in the Transvaal mines had caused such a storm in British political life, found a useful opportunity for their new skill in making these tunnels.) The boundary between the responsibility of the resident engineer and the sphere in which he needed the help of the local government was not easy to draw. The Colonial Office was soon complaining that Lugard was interfering too much and Lugard upon his side was throwing doubt upon the capacity of the engineer and the strength of his bridges. Lugard told Downing Street that the co-operation of Government Departments in a work which was taken out of the direct control of Government was difficult to secure in what was called the Departmental System, and the officials were inclined to agree that it certainly *was* difficult to secure—under Lugard.

On the whole, however, Lugard came out best. In the end the Colonial Office changed the resident engineer though they did not appoint the man Lugard had chosen. (" Sir Frederick Lugard will be cross," ran the Minute, " as he always is when he does not get his own way."[1]) They were also dubious about his enthusiastic desire to build rolling stock locally as an economy. If the estimates of cost went jumping up month by month from an original—admittedly very preliminary—estimate of $5,055,500 (about half a million pounds),[2] to ten and then to twelve million dollars, this was not Lugard's fault. But

---

[1] Minute on Lugard to Crewe, 7 August 1909, C.O. 129/357.
[2] In this period the Chinese dollar fluctuated between 2/- and 1/6d.

his Colony had to find the money. He seems to have handled the financial side very well. He also gave much time and energy to devising a form of joint management with the Chinese. He brought the unofficial members fully into the discussion. He worked at the question during his leave in 1910 and took it up at Peking on his way back to Hong Kong. In the end, owing to Chinese suspicion, he failed to get a joint management but fell back upon a Working Agreement, which, after all he had learned of Chinese jealousy and ignorance, was perhaps the better plan. Canton, however, determined not to lose its long-established position for handling merchandise, succeeded in imposing in their city a break between the terminus of the Hankow-Canton line and that of the line from Canton to Kowloon.

The unofficials in the Legislative Council were naturally deeply interested and one or two were highly competent critics. Some of them condemned almost everything about the railway, from the first estimates to the last supplement; the cost per mile was said to be £50,000 and almost the highest in the world. Lugard was in the very difficult position, in which governors so often have to stand, between the imperial government and the unofficials. Sharing much of the disapproval, he had to defend his masters and also take a great deal of responsibility for making the system work. There is perhaps no part of his work in Hong Kong where Lugard's honesty and thoroughness as an administrator, his accessibility, and his impressive mastery of detail, are more evident than in the debates in Council upon the railway.[1] In all their indignation, the unofficial critics excused their Governor. As Mr. E. A. Hewett, one of the sternest of these critics, said in a long and all-inclusive condemnation of the whole enterprise,

" . . . from the first day of your arrival you have devoted every possible spare moment of your time and given all the necessary personal supervision you possibly could to this railway. If there has been any money wasted or any loss of time it is certainly not due to want of any exertion on your Excellency's part."[2]

Before Lugard finally left the Colony all difficulties had been surmounted. He drove the first engine from Kowloon to the Chinese border in April, 1910, and the first through train to Canton ran in July 1911. The railway immediately justified and, indeed, exceeded, expectation by carrying three times the estimated traffic.

[1] See especially *Legislative Council Reports*, 1911 Session, 20 April, pp. 56–63.   [2] *Ibid.* p. 62.

When Lugard withdrew his eye from the wider Chinese scene to his own small Colony, he turned from diplomat into administrator. Hong Kong presented an extraordinary field of administration. The system might appear on paper as tidy and regular as a suburban garden, but this was because the wilderness of the Chinese quarter seemed to defy cultivation and many of its problems were simply left outside the bounds of administration. The whole area of the Colony, even with Kowloon and the New Territory, was small enough, but the bulk of the 300,000 Chinese were concentrated in high, airless tenement houses run up by native landlords along the narrow level rim of the island at the foot of the Peak and a little way up the slopes. Here, according to somewhat later figures, they lived at a density of 1,000 to the acre. Attempts to develop social services met at least four strong obstacles. The first was the lack of revenue. The second was the lack of water: the island was wholly dependent upon rain which fell irregularly and then rushed quickly down the steep slopes of the hills into the sea. Although new works were always being built to catch and store it, the increase of the population, one very wasteful of water, was always outrunning the supply. The third reason was the almost complete lack of any sense of hygiene amongst the Chinese. The fourth, and probably the major reason, one which governed everything in Hong Kong, was the shifting character of the population. It was impossible to develop for any purpose a true community out of this spill-over from the huge population of the mainland, with its daily surge of workers in and out of the Colony.

It would not be true to say that nothing was done for these people: no British Government could leave them in unrestrained disease and disorder in a great international port and their periodic outbreaks of plague gave urgency to the problem. But reforming officials had long ago decided to accept the close limits of the possible. Hong Kong existed for trade: full social services meant heavy taxation and if trade were heavily taxed it would go elsewhere. The Chinese labourers came to get good money in conditions of freedom and safety: to tax or nag these labourers beyond an essential minimum would make the Colony unattractive to them. As one of the British officials said in Council, the choice in Hong Kong was between wealth or health.

In this strange situation in which the Crown Colony system of government meant little or nothing to the Chinese majority, the system had thrown out a great excrescence that almost amounted to a dual system of government. The two Chinese members of the Legislative Council and a few hundred other well-to-do Chinese acted as a link between the colonial government and the Chinese population. To some extent they could also speak for China as a whole and especially for Kwangtung, in which most of them had a second home or at least relatives and property. The dualism was even more formal than that. There was a British officer, at this time, Mr. A. W. Brewin,[1] the Registrar General, who had the function of a secretary for Chinese affairs. He was an expert in the local customs and language and was constantly testing Chinese opinion on all current issues. This officer was the British apex of the Chinese pyramid which spread out at its base into the half million anonymous and shifting coolies. The Chinese had been encouraged to develop a chain of consultative and executive bodies, even down to street committees, which, though they had no constitutional status, to some degree harnessed the opinion and will of their community to the actions of the government.

The best Lugard could do was to associate himself fully with the topmost layers of this pyramid and this he did mainly through the Registrar General. Lugard liked and trusted Brewin: if, he once said, he was very " pro-Chinese " this was really a compliment. He would even allow Brewin to forbid his own delivery of a much-prepared speech to a Chinese gathering. He could not always understand the reason " but I trust implicitly in him." With Brewin's help he entered into the happiest co-operation with the many Chinese committees and boards. He urged Brewin to devise means of getting him into still closer touch with the Chinese—" a weekly levée or something when anyone who likes can bring matters personally before me . . . I am not sufficiently in touch—personal touch—with them " (L. to F. L., 7 August 1909). His mind was sensitive enough to take a deep impress from the dignity, good manners and public spirit of the well-to-do Chinese.

The most important part of the duties of the Chinese organizations concerned sanitation and security, and a body of influential Chinese, which supervised the work of a squad of Chinese police known as the District Watch Force, had become, by usage, the chief Chinese council

---

[1] Brewin, Arthur Winbolt, C.M.G., 1888 cadet, Hong Kong; 1894 J.P.; 1897 Inspector of schools; 1901 Registrar General; 1903 Member of Legislative Council.

to advise and assist the Governor. Membership of this committee was an honour which was eagerly sought.

No institution revealed so impressively both the difficulty of bringing Chinese and Western ideas into partnership and the success by which this difficulty could be met than the Tung-Wah Hospital. There were four government hospitals in the Colony and several run by the Christian missions. But, as large numbers of Chinese were still suspicious of European medicine, a Chinese committee in 1872 started a Chinese hospital, largely supported by subscription but with a grant from the government. Here patients could choose whether to be treated by Chinese or European methods. Lugard and Flora, upon visiting this hospital heard that an increasing proportion of patients were choosing European methods. The Chinese section was clean and beautifully ordered. The majority of the medicines here were herbal but included hedgehog and snake skins, dried lizards, and cockchafers. These items were ground into powder for a broth. Each patient had a small earthenware stewing-pot marked with his own number. In a hall which seemed to fulfil the functions of a chapel there was an altar dedicated to the god of agriculture who is also the Chinese god of healing: this was hung with beautiful embroideries. The distinguished visitors and the hospital committee, greeted with formality, were served with red and green tea, in little silver covered cups. "It was all extremely dainty and elegant," wrote Flora, "and pleased my taste very much."[1] They were impressed by what they learned of the work of the committee which ran an infectious diseases hospital, dispensaries, mortuaries and other services. There was also a refuge home for children and young girls. Most of these institutions were supported by Chinese subscriptions and were carried on through the hard work of the committee in co-operation with those British officials who were experts on Chinese affairs.

Soon after Lugard's arrival he walked into a sharp controversy about the almost unlimited problem of public health of which the Tung-Wah activities could only touch the fringe. His predecessor had appointed a commission upon public health which had sat for about a year and had produced an immense report. It covered such evils as the airless tenements; the slum landlords' device of cutting rooms up into cubicles for whole families of the overcrowded coolies; the Chinese

[1] Lady Lugard's Diary for 7 October 1907, L.P.

habit of depositing dead bodies—over 1,000 a year—in the streets, and the Chinese inability to turn off water-taps. The commission touched the basis of the Hong Kong constitution by proposing something very like municipal government. But the ablest British speaker in the Legislative Council, Mr. Murray Stewart, a local financier, congratulated Lugard when he resisted any encroachment upon Crown Colony government.

> " The leading members of the mercantile community do not want to govern municipally and they certainly do not want to be governed municipally under any so-called popular system . . ."

They desired that authority in municipal affairs should rest with the servants of the Crown.[1] The leading Chinese agreed with him.[2]

Lugard handled the whole controversy well. He realized that there had to be compromise between the standards and the interests of the Europeans upon one side and of the 95 per cent majority of the Chinese upon the other. Grievances cooled off as leaders of both races felt that the Governor had fully studied all their views, and had himself examined the congested waterside areas. In the end he achieved full agreement and won the warm thanks of Dr. Ho Kai on behalf of the Chinese.[3]

Sanitation, however, obtruded itself again, caused by a storm, not in a teacup, but in a spittoon. Lugard, after full discussions, issued an order to control the Chinese habit of spitting in and out of doors. The two Chinese members dissented strongly on the ground that to penalize a universal and almost involuntary habit would antagonize the whole Chinese population. The three long debates on this were most acrimonious. The usually acquiescent Dr. Ho Kai put up a good fight. The Chinese, he said, like other people, prefer to be led rather than driven. The ordinance would either be a dead letter, which was bad for the law, or the whole population would be liable to fines or imprisonment. Lugard announced that he meant to stick to his principles and drove his clause through against repeated amendments.[4] But the Chinese were not defeated. Beaten in the Council, they presented him with a large, beautifully bound volume, two foot by one, and several inches thick. It contained the signatures of 8,000 Chinese of the Colony

[1] *Legislative Council Reports*, 1908 Session, 2 July p. 86.   [2] *Ibid.* 30 April, p. 38.
[3] *Legislative Council Reports*, 1908 Session, 30 April, p. 38.
[4] *Legislative Council Reports*, 1908 Session, 10 December, pp. 154-60, 170-4; 1909 Session, 25 February, pp. 2-3; 1 September, pp. 88-9.

and he was told that 80,000 had tried to sign. It was a petition saying that Chinese feeling was stirred to its depth; the very existence of the Colony as a loyal dependency was threatened.

> " And the reason? Because I took power to make regulations to check spitting on pavements and in public buildings (except in provided spittoons) . . . I believe I am popular with the Chinese. Had I not been so there would have been a Revolution with a big R. So we all make our mistakes . . . I shall deal with the crisis which, I confess, strikes me as somewhat ludicrous." (L. to E. J. L., 1 August 1909).

He dealt with it by giving way and announcing in Council that the Chinese had decided to set up an Anti-spitting Committee of eighty of their leading men " for the total suppression of the habit by educative and persuasive means . . . They proposed to conduct their campaign with energy, earnestness and success." In making his capitulation, Lugard stated, " I have always said in this Council, gentlemen, that methods of co-operation are in every way to be preferred to methods of coercion." So, since " co-operation and coercion cannot exist side by side," he proposed the repeal of the obnoxious legislation.[1] It is by such surrenders and admission of mistakes that a governor can show his strength and win true respect. Meanwhile, however, it is reported that the insanitary habit continues to this day.

When we turn to finance we find that Lugard had not escaped the anxieties of administering a colony upon an inadequate revenue. Perhaps, with his bent towards personal economy, he shouldered it better than many governors. He might have expected, coming to one of the largest and apparently richest ports in the world, that he would be able to draw off a substantial flow of revenue from its river of gold. Unfortunately, being a free port, Hong Kong could provide no customs revenue and the transit trade by which the Colony lived could easily be scared away by heavy taxation. The prosperity of the port rose and fell in response to the smallest movements in the volume of world trade and of the conditions in China, and especially in the rice and wheat harvests of the south. It was Lugard's bad fortune to find the Colony in an economic depression, the fourth year of depression in China's trade as a whole. The end of the Russo-Japanese war had seen a burst of over-trading; then came a wild rubber boom, followed by a failure of native banks and a restriction of foreign capital. China's

[1] *Legislative Council Reports*, 1909 Session, 1 September, p. 89.

currency problem was endemic, but a fall in the price of silver had sharpened its ill effects. All this was reflected in the figures of Hong Kong trade and revenue, just when there were heavy charges for the railway and for defensive works against typhoons. The revenue was between six and seven million dollars during the first three years of his régime, or roughly (with a dollar of between 1/6d. and 2/-) some half million pounds: it was a little higher in 1911.

In colonies where there are unofficial leaders aspiring towards greater constitutional power, the debate on the estimates is the show-piece of the year. But in Hong Kong the four European and the two Chinese unofficials knew too well the limitations, constitutional and financial, which bounded their activities, to press their arraignment of government very far. Each year in the autumn, with growing strength and mastery, Lugard would introduce the estimates to un-officials who, from their commercial positions and long experience of the Council of the Colony, knew a good deal more about his subject than he did. Then each of the Europeans would deliver a somewhat grudging speech, addressed in part to his small audience in the Council chamber and in part, through the press, to his firm, his club, and the Chamber of Commerce. He would complain calmly or with almost ritual indignation about the slow construction of the railway or this or that public building, or about the inefficiency of the Public Works Department as compared with private contractors. After this the Council would go into Finance Committee under the Colonial Secretary, and there hammer out the details in those unrecorded sessions which under Crown Colony government give unofficial opinion an opportunity for which critics of the system have seldom made allowances.

A further element of rigidity provided an annual topic which aroused an almost conventional indignation. This was the so-called military contribution, the 20 per cent of its gross revenue which the Colony had to make to imperial defence. This is a question with a long history at least since the time of the American Revolution. What angered the unofficials of Hong Kong was not so much the amount but the equal incidence in bad times as well as good. Lugard at first, as in duty bound, defended the imperial government and pointed out that though it was the peculiar geographical position of the Colony which made its defence so costly, it was the same position which made it so prosperous a port. He urged that if the contribution were regarded as an insurance, and if the value of the Colony's assets was put at £500,000,000, then the premium was considerably less than 1 per cent. But, as time went on, he began to doubt his own defence. He wrote one of his long memoranda on the subject for the Colonial Office. The officials agreed amongst themselves that it was a very obscure composition and put it aside with a few kind acknowledgments.[1] They deprecated his laying his paper before the Legislative Council.[2] He fell back upon a governor's last, somewhat improper expedient and permitted a strong statement of opinion by the unofficials. But even this debate left the Colonial Office unmoved.[3]

No record of a colonial administrator's life can hope to recall more than the two or three outstanding questions out of the scores which come to his desk. During Lugard's governorship, there were two outstanding tasks, the one forced upon him, the other chosen by him, which deserve to be remembered. It was to them that he gave the largest share of his time and interest during the five years of his work in the Far East. These were the opium trade and the University.

---

[1] Minutes on Lugard to Crewe, 28 October 1909, C.O. 129/358.
[2] Minutes on Lugard to Crewe, 12 May 1909, C.O. 129/377.
[3] *Legislative Council Reports*, 1911 Session, 1 June, pp. 102-10, and 8 June, pp. 120-1. The *Memorandum on Military Contribution* was printed in Hong Kong in 1909 for confidential use.

CHAPTER XVI

OPIUM

THE WORD opium, when linked with China, evokes in most British minds a sense of guilt.[1] It must be admitted, although apologists may advance some measure of extenuating circumstances, that opium had been the main item of the trade in pursuit of which Britain had seized Hong Kong and had extracted other concessions from China. It is claimed that it was the West, represented by the Dutch, which in the seventeenth century had first lured China from indulgence in an excess of alcohol to an excess of opium, by impregnating tobacco with that drug in order to make it more desirable merchandise.[2] One result of Britain's wars with China was to force the import of opium upon a people whose government, however spasmodically and inefficiently, was endeavouring to refuse it both on economic and social grounds. In undeveloped countries the lack of industry and the simplicity of human needs make it difficult for foreign traders to find goods either to offer or to take. But mercantile initiative is not easily baffled and, too impatient to wait for normal economic development, it often plays upon the lower qualities which all men are known to share. Hence the part taken in the earliest exchanges with economically under-developed peoples by such items as slaves, spirits and fire-arms. As the Chinese had small need of any of these, and for long required little from the West except cotton goods, opium was a god-send (or rather, perhaps, a devil-send) to the traders. It was especially valuable to the British because the bulk of it was grown in their own dependency of India.

It was not until after the capture of Canton and Peking (1858-60) that the Chinese were at last obliged to give formal recognition to the

[1] For further reading see particularly J. Rowntree, *The Imperial Drug Trade* (1905), S. H. Bailey, *The Anti-Drug Campaign, An Experiment in International Control* (1936), and W. Willoughby, *Opium as an International Problem, The Geneva Conferences* (Baltimore, 1925).
[2] E. T. Williams, *A Short History of China* (New York, 1928), p. 248.

319

trade in opium. One result was that the cultivation of the poppy now became legal in China and spread with great rapidity though, in view of the superiority of the Indian type and of the growing demand, this did not reduce the import from that country. A nation which had been through the long experience of the anti-slavery movement and which had some knowledge of the effects of the trade in spirits in Africa and elsewhere, seems to have been slow to bestir itself about this highly questionable drug traffic. It was not until 1874 that a British Society for the Suppression of the Opium Trade was formed with Lord Shaftesbury as its first president. The first vote against the abuse in the Commons was obtained in 1891 on the motion that the Indian production of opium was " morally indefensible ". But in 1893 a Royal Commission on the Indian aspect of the problem did not give the reformers the support they needed.

Early in the twentieth century the Americans began to move against the trade in the Far East. As young Chinese with ardent hopes of reform went to the West for education they linked the efforts of their own country with those of the foreign reformers and so strengthened both. They claimed that their government was closing opium dens in the native cities while in the neighbouring treaty ports the foreign municipal governments not only refused to do the same but even tried to suppress the local activity of Chinese anti-opium societies.

In 1906, the year before Lugard came to Hong Kong, the opium question was raised again in parliament after an interval of eleven years. A motion was brought in by Mr. Theodore Taylor, a Lancashire representative, based on the straight moral issue. India, it was said, gained nearly £4,000,000 revenue from the traffic, and " How long were we, the real rulers of India, to go on taking this wage of sin?" The issue should not depend upon China's will to reform. " If China chose to commit national suicide that was no reason why we should help her to do so." " For every soul," declared another member, Dr. Rutherford, " our missionaries send to Heaven from China, the British Government was sending ten to hell by this traffic." John Morley found little room for manoeuvre when faced with an indictment framed in these terms. He was obliged to make various vague promises of amendment. Mr. Taylor's motion was passed unanimously.[1]

[1] *Parliamentary Debates*, 30 May 1906, IV. 158. 494-516.

Opium

The following year, 1907, saw the British Government come a long way to meet China by signing an agreement that the export of Indian opium to China should be decreased by one-tenth a year so that in ten years it could come to an end. The condition was that the cultivation of the poppy in China should be abolished *pari passu* with the reduction of the Indian trade. This threw a great responsibility upon the Chinese Government at a time when it was not in full control of all the provinces and when all those interested in the trade challenged not only China's competence but also her sincerity.

In September, 1907, the old Empress Dowager, bent on saving the dynasty by a large programme of reform, issued an edict which aimed firstly at abolishing the opium habit, *pari passu* with the destruction of the poppy cultivation, in a period of ten years, and secondly, at closing the smoking dens. (The old lady, herself an opium smoker, inserted a clause thoughtfully exempting people over sixty years of age from the prohibition). This strong gesture stimulated the anti-opium societies in Britain to urge their government to action. It was May, then acting-Governor of Hong Kong, the port that was the clearing house of the opium trade for southern China, who had to face the first effects of the new impulse to reform. He replied to the government's new-found morality with such withering realism that Fiddes[1] wrote that he preferred to put this statement upon one side and to ask Sir F. Lugard privately to write " a more tactful dispatch."[2] Lugard had not yet sailed, so he was given an oral initiation into this delicate subject, and he also found it waiting for him on his table when he landed in July, 1907. The British Government was being stung into action by a steady fire of questions in parliament. Lugard was instructed to get into touch with the British minister in Peking, Sir John Jordan; he should take note that the British Government desired to co-operate with China in the gradual elimination of the opium traffic and he should do all he could to prevent smuggling.

Lugard set himself to study the question. He found many teachers at hand led by his Colonial Secretary, and all gave him a very different picture from that presented to him in London. Outside the circle of the missionaries, he found no moral absolutes on the question in Hong

[1] Fiddes, (later Sir) George, G.C.M.G., K.C.B., 1858–1936; 1897–02 Secretary to High Commissioner for South Africa, and subsequently to Transvaal Administration; 1909–16 Assistant Under-Secretary of State for the Colonies; 1916–21 Permanent Under-Secretary.
[2] Minute on May to Elgin, 15 May 1907, C.O. 129/340.

Kong. The position had its analogy with slavery in that a complex economic system had been built up round a trade at a time when, far from being recognized by Britain as an abuse, it was held to be a national asset. In Hong Kong, as in India, Singapore and elsewhere in Eastern Asia, large numbers of people had become participants in some branch of this large, old-established and profitable trade and many were wholly dependent upon it. The sale of opium was a monopoly. The Hong Kong government, finding it embarrassing to handle this itself, had put it up to the highest bidder who became the Opium Farmer for three years. The Farmer, at this time a Chinese merchant from Singapore, carried out the highly unpopular restrictions and the espionage which was necessary to enforce the monopoly with the ultimate backing of the police. He sold his goods to China and in the Colony, where there were over a hundred licensed opium-divans. The public revenues were also involved; nearly a quarter of those of Hong Kong came from the steady source of the Opium Farm, an important item in a free port where taxable assets were so elusive. While, therefore, there was no open defiance of the new policy of abolition, there was great anxiety that it should be carried out justly and, above all, gradually.

But this is not the way in which moral impulses, once aroused, supply their pressures. When they are harnessed to some large abuse the situation resembles that of a powerful motor which, upon being attached to some heavy vehicle embedded in a rut, can only get it moving by a sudden great jerk of power. In May 1908, a zealous back bencher, Mr. Johnson of Nuneaton, being lucky in the ballot (he " won a place for his opium resolution as he might have won a doll in a raffle at a bazaar ", was Murray Stewart's bitter description in Hong Kong Legislative Council)[1], brought in a sweeping resolution which, among other items, committed the Government to bringing the licensing of opium " dens " in Hong Kong to a speedy close.[2] A Liberal Government was in power and its principles bound it to sympathy with the resolution. But the debate followed little more than a fortnight upon the reconstruction of the ministry under Asquith after the resignation of Campbell-Bannerman. This had sent Lord Crewe to the Colonial Office with Colonel Seely as Under-Secretary.

[1] *Legislative Council Reports*, 1908 Session, 24 September, p. 117.
[2] *Parliamentary Debates*, 6 May 1908, IV. 188. 339.

The new ministers were faced with a debate upon a motion which, amongst the three departments which shared responsibility in the matter, concentrated its fire upon the Colonial Office. It ran as follows:

" That this House having regard to its Resolution unanimously adopted on 30th May 1906, that the Indo-Chinese opium trade is morally indefensible, welcomes the action of His Majesty's Government diminishing the sale of opium for export, and thus responding to the action of the Chinese Government in their arrangements for the suppression of the consumption of the drug in that Empire; and this House also urges His Majesty's Government to take steps to bring to a speedy close the system of licensing opium dens now prevailing in some of our Crown Colonies, more particularly Hong Kong, Straits Settlements and Ceylon."[1]

The new ministers were anxious to enter the Commons debate with the claim that they had already freed themselves from the long-accumulated guilt of their country. The Hong Kong Government had been named as a chief offender, therefore, following a hurried debate in the Colonial Office the day before, this telegram was sent to Lugard:

" Matter most urgent. His Majesty's Government has decided that steps must be taken to close opium dens in Hong Kong, as they recognize it is essential in dealing with the Opium question in Hong Kong we must act up to the standard set by the Chinese Government. I propose to make a statement on those lines in Parliament tomorrow night. Dispatch follows by mail. CREWE."[2]

Lugard received this cable the next day. He was aghast at this sudden and unexpected decision which had allowed him no time to give his opinion. He telegraphed immediately asking for " reasonable time " before the matter should be raised in parliament so that he could explain the serious effect of the policy upon the revenues of the Colony.[3] The reply came that it was not possible to postpone the debate but that the necessary steps would not be discussed before Lugard's dispatch arrived. The debate took its expected course, in which the newly aroused consciences of Westminster painted eastern Asia in the most lurid colours. Johnson, who moved the resolution, said that letters and telegrams had been pouring in testifying to the strong public opinion against the British tolerance of the opium vice. China had done all she could to suppress the trade but we had lagged

[1] *Parliamentary Debates*, 6 May 1908, IV. 188. 339-40.
[2] Crewe to Lugard, 5 May 1908, C.O. 489/10.
[3] Lugard to Crewe, 6 May 1908, C.O. 129/347.

behind and, indeed, frustrated her efforts. The India Office and the Foreign Office had done a little, but the Colonial Office "next to nothing" and the Crown Colonies, especially Hong Kong, had done nothing. He drew a moving picture of the effects of the drug, quoting an account which told how " Once this awful vice masters a Chinaman he sells all he has, his land, his wife and children, the roof, doors and windows of his house, in summer nearly all his clothing and dies of cold in winter, stripped and naked in the street." Taylor, in seconding, said that " nothing less than the complete suppression of the consumption of opium in the British Empire would satisfy those who had studied the question." The position in Hong Kong, with a rising revenue from opium, was " appalling ". China was absolutely sincere in her desire to end the vice and to put an end to her own production.[1]

Colonel Seely, making his first speech as Colonial Under-Secretary, found it difficult to defend his department. He could not, as a Liberal, justify the opium trade, yet he had to meet the accusation that the Liberals had done so little over a long period. He showed his embarrassment by excess of zeal. He accepted the motion whole-heartedly. This was a non-party matter; the evil must be eradicated. He was able to defend the Straits Settlements, where a Commission was sitting, and also Ceylon, where reform was in train. As for the chief culprit, Hong Kong, all he could do was to read out triumphantly the telegram which had been sent the day before and which cleared him and his chief and shifted future responsibility on to the local government. " That," he claimed, " is a decisive action." There were certain difficulties " but they will be dealt with." The Government would not recede from the expressions in the telegram; they realized they must act up to the standard set by China. He did, however, in commenting upon the moral issue remind the House that " it is our morals and other people's money." Lyttelton, as the last Conservative Secretary of State, expressed entire agreement. To rub a little salt into the wounds being inflicted by members upon their fellow-countrymen in Hong Kong, a certain Mr. Bennett of Woodstock took the occasion to express his distrust of " that imperialistic fetish called the ' man on the spot ' whose superior intelligence and experience was held to be paramount in deciding great questions of policy and morality."[2] Sir Edward Grey wound up the debate with wisdom and generosity of

---

[1] *Parliamentary Debates*, 6 May 1908, IV. 188. 341-5.   [2] *Ibid.* 372.

mind, congratulating the Americans on their Christian lead. He hoped that China would not be ungrateful. There were some weaknesses in China's position but, " If you are on the side of abuse, of course it is easy to pick out the unsatisfactory points in which no progress has been made and make them an excuse for doing nothing."[1] The motion was agreed. *The Times* emphatically endorsed the policy of the Government.[2]

Lugard and his Colony were both under an implied censure. As soon as he received the disturbing telegram of May 5th, he had set to work to discover the exact effects the policy would have upon his Colony. He ordered one of his officials, the extremely able Chinese-speaking Clementi,[3] to make a thorough investigation of the system of the Opium Farm. He could not bring the matter to his Legislative Council while it was still under urgent discussion with the Secretary of State. But it could not be kept secret, as telegraphed reports of the Commons debate appeared in the Hong Kong press. On May 28th, Murray Stewart, tall, handsome, histrionic and grim, rose to express the " typhoon of protest " that had gathered amongst the mercantile community. He was careful not to aim his oratorical shafts at the centre of the target, the main principle of abolition, but ringed it with darts struck at the inconsiderate and injurious haste of the procedure and the contemptuous over-riding of a Legislative Council in the matter of its revenue and taxation. Here he was raising the basic constitutional issue between Britain and the colonies, never a very robust gesture for legislators who are nominated or who represent privileged minorities. He also tried to rebut what he regarded as the calumnies which had branded them as worse than highwaymen, since they were said to demand from China not " Your money or your life!" but " Your money and your life!" Hong Kong was ready for a gradual abolition of the trade within ten years. Their doubts were not of China's sincerity in carrying out her part of the agreed plan but of her capacity. He moved a strong resolution against the Secretary of State's issuing an order without sufficient notice to the

[1] *Ibid.* 379.

[2] *The Times*, 13 May 1908.

[3] Clementi, (later Sir) Cecil, G.C.M.G., F.R.G.S., 1875-1949; 1899 Cadet, Hong Kong; 1911-12 Acting Colonial Secretary; 1913-22 Colonial Secretary, British Guiana; 1922-25 Colonial Secretary, Ceylon; 1925-30 Governor, Hong Kong; 1930-34 Governor, Straits Settlements and High Commissioner for Malaya.

Colony. Finally, he read some telling passages from a recent parliamentary debate on the British Licensing Bill, when the impracticality of a wholesale and sudden closing of public houses had been emphasized. A Chinese member seconded, in support of " the dignity, rights and privileges of the Council " and its claim to be consulted upon all matters affecting the welfare of " this fair Colony of ours."[1]

Lugard, as he listened to these speeches, felt himself in almost complete sympathy with them and went so far as to admit in his reply " I personally agree with a great deal of what has been said ", but as the matter was still undecided " it was premature to deal in heroics." They could rely, he added, expressing a confidence he did not feel, upon the statesmanship of the British Cabinet and he must reject what was practically a vote of censure upon the imperial government. The unofficials, however, pressed it to a division and all but one voted against the official majority. But on the same day, as an instalment of reform, they passed without a division the second reading of a Bill to prohibit the export to China of opium prepared for smoking.

It was with some satisfaction that Lugard sent a copy of this debate to the Secretary of State with a covering dispatch pointing out the difficulties of hasty action. When, early in June, he received the full text of the debate of May 6th, he realized how complete was the denunciation of his Colony. By then he had started his countermeasures. He had set Flora to work in London and she, fully coached from his immense letters, had been to the Colonial Office to reason with Colonel Seely (whom they both knew well) and also, in view of his part in the debate, with Lyttelton. In the attempt to gain time and to check the drastic policy that had been threatened, Lugard suggested that half the divans should be closed in March 1909 and the remaining half a year later.

This was in June. On July 28th the question was again raised in the House of Commons in a debate on Supply. This time, Lyttelton, now fully primed by Flora, made an effective attack upon the Government for the hasty and high-handed way in which the Secretary of State, departing from the proper methods of consultation with the Colonial authorities, had presented Hong Kong with an ultimatum which reached the Governor only three hours before the statement was made in parliament. Colonel Seely showed his discomfort in face of this

[1] *Legislative Council Reports*, 1908 Session, 28 May, pp. 46-52.

attack by an answer, the ambiguity of which might well be given a harsher name.

> " The right hon. Gentleman had spoken of the opium traffic and said that we took action without consulting the authorities of Hong Kong . . . Although they did their best to ascertain the views of the people, it was quite impossible to get anything like a reasoned opinion from the inhabitants of Hong Kong."[1]

When the press report of this debate reached Hong Kong the watchful Murray Stewart pounced at once upon this loose statement with which Seely had tried to defend himself and tore it to pieces. It was not to be wondered at, he said, if the Hong Kong inhabitants found this a hard saying. Who " did their best?" If His Majesty's Ministers, when and how did they " do their best?" " Did the Hong Kong authorities inform him that reasoned opinion was non-existent in the Colony? I imagine not." He went on to deride the British government's announcement on May 6th. " As a tactical move it was well calculated. The announcement brought down the House: cheers greeted it. The Government scored. From a practical point of view the main object of the opium policy was not advanced a jot." All the " proper steps " had still to be taken. He moved a vote of censure on the Under-Secretary of State, an offensive action even if the position of the un-officials as a nominated minority made the shot, like a blank cartridge, fire and smoke without any lethal charge. Once more it was a Chinese member who seconded him. Then the vote was pressed to one of those divisions by which unofficial minorities in Legislative Councils used to register their impotent indignation.[2]

Lugard defended his masters, as he was bound to do, but with a lack of conviction that seemed to be almost deliberate. He was sure that the impossibility of obtaining a " reasoned opinion " referred only to the time factor; also, that the ministers had not been acting according to party exigencies. He was again walking the familiar tightrope, balanced between the danger of disobeying his chief on the one hand and on the other that of acting in defiance of the strong opinion of the leaders of the local community.

His own judgment was now formed. By September he felt that he understood all sides of the difficult problem and he stated these views

[1] *Parliamentary Debates*, 28 July 1908, IV. 193. 1260.
[2] *Legislative Council Reports*, 1908 Session, 24 September, pp. 116-9.

in a memorandum, the first version of which was printed at this time.[1] He felt himself, he wrote, morally entitled to an opinion because of the work he had achieved in Africa in suppressing two not altogether dissimilar evils, slavery and the liquor traffic. He was in agreement with the main object of the new British policy. But he thought that it was being carried out in feverish haste because an emotional view of its character, and an easy hope of its rapid abolition had been impressed upon the British people and, apparently, upon the Government. He felt, with the community in his Colony, the slur of the uncontradicted statements made about them in parliament. " The Eastern Colonies," he wrote, expressing a claim that was emotional rather than verifiable, " are as much part of the British Empire as the United Kingdom and are animated by the same ideals and have a not less high standard of morality." Hong Kong was the first market for raw opium, mainly from India, and had been handling some £5,000,000 worth a year, with all the indirect benefits to the economy of the port which that amount of trade must bring. The system of the Opium Farmer had been devised mainly in order to canalise the sale of prepared opium for smoking and so make it at once more easy to tax and to control. He protested against the statements made in parliament that Hong Kong had done nothing and he listed a number of measures taken to control or limit the trade.

In his long struggle against slavery, Lugard had been directed by an intelligent and patient study of its character in several regions and by an appreciation of those economic factors of which any reform must take account. So now, standing between the fundamentalist denunciations of the humanitarians in Britain and the reasoned but interested defence of the Hong Kong merchants, he sought to measure the facts for himself and to devise reforms exactly fitted upon them. He came to the conclusion that the smoking of opium was by no means either so prevalent or so vicious as the abolitionists believed. He quoted several authorities to show that only some 1.5 per cent of the total Chinese population and 10 per cent of the adult males were opium-smokers, and a large proportion of these were only casual smokers. As to the viciousness of the habit, Lugard went out to judge the truth for himself. He visited a large number of divans (he deprecated the

---

[1] *Memorandum regarding the Restriction of Opium in Hong Kong and China*, Confidential, Government Printers (Hong Kong, 1908), L.P. (A slightly revised edition was printed in 1909).

term " dens " as deliberately calculated to excite irrational disgust) and
was much surprised at what he found. He spoke of this in his memorandum, but to Flora he gave a fuller account of his investigation.

" Certainly what I saw was very different from what I imagine Colonel
Seely's conception of a ' Den ' is. No-one seemed surprised at or in any
way resented our entrance; the men smiled goodhumouredly and went
on chatting . . . Much more tobacco than opium seemed to be smoked.
The divan was a narrow room, perhaps 20 or 30 feet long, with lounges
(all *very* clean) on either side and a passage down the middle . . . on each
divan two or perhaps three men lounged . . . Then to one of the lowest
class. This was not so clean, and the smell and the atmosphere were
suffocating, as the interior of any Chinese dwelling is, but so far as the
opium was concerned, the experience was precisely the same. Here there
were three tiers one above the other, like shelves, but only on one side of
the room. . . . Here, too, a couple of friends seemed to occupy the divan
and to be chatting together, smoking chiefly cigarettes or tobacco pipes,
with an occasional pull at the opium pipe. All were animated and intelligent, and there were none besotted or stupid. We talked with one, who
said he was a coolie who had been carrying loads to the Peak all day. . . .
He was perfectly sober and intelligent. . . . I must say the net impression
conveyed to one's mind was that the so-called ' vice ' was really a most
extraordinarily temperate and satisfactory substitute for alcohol etc. . . .
You could not find such scenes in English public houses."

(L. to F. L., 30 July 1908).

In his official paper Lugard went on to discuss the effects of hasty
abolition. Prohibition of the external trade with China could make
little difference to that country, since seven-eighths of the opium
consumed there was now produced within her borders. Even if her
government had the will it had not the power to stop this production
in the provinces in any short period. But his strongest argument
against hasty and one-sided action was that, denied his opium, the
smoker would turn to other and more injurious stimulants. He was
able to make a telling counterstroke by showing that, with the first
beginning of restrictions, China was already being flooded with
" anti-opium pills ", containing either opium, and so introducing the
habit of eating which was far more dangerous than smoking, or the
much more destructive morphia, which was being prepared and sold
by a British firm. Large orders were being placed in England for

morphia which was being sent out in unlabelled bottles while hypodermic syringes were being supplied. Thus, the most serious vice of all, that of morphia and cocaine injections, was beginning to spread. He explained that one grain of injected morphia at a cost of 7 cents could produce the same narcotic effect as $233\frac{1}{2}$ grs. of smoked opium costing $1.32! " The profit to the sellers of these pills is also enormous for they are sold at four times the cost price—75 per cent profit. There is little occasion for surprise that vendors and purchasers are alike eager to obtain them!"[1]

He summed up his Memorandum with these final words:

" I have attempted in the foregoing paragraphs to show that those who may claim to be not less interested in the question of the Native Races, and in the welfare of the intelligent, industrious and most interesting population of China, than the Mover and Seconder of the Resolution in the House of Commons, have some doubts as to whether the common object we all have in view can best be achieved by the particular methods proposed.... and I trust I may claim to have vindicated the Colony of Hong Kong from the charge of apathy, and of having made no sacrifices to promote the Policy of the Home Government in this matter."[2]

In his accompanying dispatch Lugard put up his own plans for tightening the controls on the sale of opium by the Farmer, and for a gradual closing of divans by 1910. He also put in a strong claim for compensation from imperial revenues for the progressive loss to revenue. Confident of his case and desiring, as always, to appeal to public opinion, he asked that his Memorandum should both be laid on the table of the Legislative Council in Hong Kong and be published in England.

Neither the dispatch nor the Memorandum were well received in Downing Street. They reflected most unfavourably upon the politicians' surrender to the sudden pressure in parliament for sweeping and hasty action. So the first minute was one of condemnation of " this extraordinary dispatch!" Fiddes, with whom Lugard was to wage a long administrative duel, complained that Sir Frederick had not been very helpful. What was the use of his putting up all kinds of proposals when the Government had already announced its policy? Lugard's job was to find ways of carrying this out, not to put forward new proposals. As for publication, that was preposterous. But the gentler

[1] *Opium Memorandum*, p. 14. [2] *Ibid.* p. 16.

Antrobus, who had known his Lugard longer than Fiddes, counselled " that it would be advisable to accept them " (the proposals) " and, knowing Sir F. Lugard well, I am sure they are put forward seriously and with a full sense of his responsibility, and, as we have reason to know, his opinion carries great weight with the public (irrespective of party) in this country."[1] This advice was sufficiently weighty to induce Lord Crewe to defer the final abolition of the 180 divans until March 1910. But 26 were to be closed at once and the Farmer was limited next year to the sale of 1,000 chests of opium, instead of the usual 1,231. Lord Crewe hoped that Lugard would co-operate.

It may be that when Antrobus wrote the last part of his minute he knew very well that Lugard would find some way of asserting his views even if he were refused the publication of his paper. Antrobus, we have seen, knew Flora as well as he did Lugard, and was probably well aware that she was even then busy interviewing the key people in the controversy before she returned at the end of the year to Hong Kong. But Lugard had gone further. He had already sent the Memorandum, which had been printed in Hong Kong, to Lyttelton. The prohibition against publication therefore made him rather anxious, though at the same time he had the satisfaction of knowing that Lord Crewe had been reluctantly impressed by it.[2] A letter to his brother reveals his state of mind at this time.

> " Did you read my Opium Memo? . . . Have just got a long ' Private and Personal' telegram from Secretary of State practically imploring me to help him out of a hole. My arguments, he says, have greatly impressed him, but the ' Parliamentary difficulties of the situation are great'! ! which means that having made egregious asses of themselves they do not know how the devil to face that Memo. He says ruefully ' your dispatch must eventually be published' and begs me to implore the Farmer to be conciliatory. ' Could you not remind him ' etc.! I roared with laughter when I read it!—but, by Jove! if Lyttelton goes and lets it be seen that he has had access to that Memo (I sent him a copy) I am clean bust up! I pray God you have not let anyone see the copies I sent you? I am fidgety and worried." (L. to E. J. L., 13 December 1908).

Lord Crewe had increasing cause for embarrassment. First there came a long commentary on Lugard's Memorandum from Sir John

[1] Minute on Lugard to Crewe, 27 October 1908, C.O. 129/349.
[2] Crewe to Lugard, 12 December 1908, C.O. 129/349.

Jordan in Peking, the most weighty authority to whom the British Ministers could turn. He wrote that " taking the memorandum as a whole, I am so entirely in accord with what Sir Frederick Lugard says that it is not at all an easy matter for me to offer any observations." His only questions concerned an intrusion by Lugard into his own sphere of Chinese reforms. Here he was inclined to think that quick and vigorous action would be more effective than a policy of gradual repression. In any case " The Chinese nowadays think they know their own business best and are not likely to act on the unsolicited advice of foreign officials." He agreed that Lugard had hit upon the weak point in the Government's policy, the impossibility of knowing how far China was keeping her side of the agreement by reducing her acreage of poppy.[1]

Shortly after this Lugard's views were given even more weighty confirmation. Under American inspiration, an international opium conference met at Shanghai in 1909 and produced a number of resolutions which, although aimed at the suppression of opium-smoking and trading in China, yet used the word " gradual " and were drawn up in such moderate terms, and emphasized so much the great danger of the fraudulent anti-opium nostrums and the new and deadly danger of the morphia habit, that Lord Crewe was forced to admit that the Shanghai Conference had rather strengthened Lugard's position. But his civil servants still grumbled at Lugard's policy of gradualism and complained " These unwilling agents are awkward people to deal with."[2]

On February 25th, 1909, Lugard, as a result of his long and difficult correspondence with the Colonial Office, was able to announce the final decision to his Council. The British government refused to allow him to act as gradually as he wished but they did agree that 1910 should be the date for the final closing of the divans. Moreover, they " will be prepared to ask parliament to give a substantial contribution " towards the Colony's loss.[3] The announcement was greeted with applause which was probably polite rather than warm. But at the Colonial Office Lugard's handling of the matter at last drew some commendation. He had given the Secretary of State " a free expression of his views, but now he comes to business he makes (it seems to me)

[1] Jordan to Grey, 12 October 1909, F.O. 371/616.
[2] Minutes on Lugard to Crewe, 15 March 1909, C.O. 129/355.
[3] *Report of the British Delegates to the International Opium Conference held at the Hague, December 1911—January 1912.* Cd. 6448, pp. 22-26.

a loyal attempt to carry out the policy of H.M.G." Thus Fiddes; while Lord Crewe decided that " The Governor seems to have done his best to meet the necessities of the case and great credit is due to him."[1]

A settlement of the opium question which gave even this degree of satisfaction to the Secretary of State could not please the Hong Kong merchants. When the Opium Amendment Ordinance came before the Legislative Council in June 1909, in spite of Lugard's pleas, the unofficials again pushed their opposition to the second reading to a division in which they voted solidly against it.[2] At the third reading it was only Lugard's personal influence which induced them to change their tactics. They asked Lugard to report that it was only in deference to his personal appeal that they refrained.[3] Lugard emerged from the conflict with credit as an honest and skilful mediator holding to the reasonable middle way against intemperate pressure from both sides. And the British people could feel that they had at last expiated nearly a hundred years of sin by repentance and amendment.

Unfortunately, this last part of the process had to be carried out vicariously by other people in Hong Kong. In a rather gloomy financial situation, revenue had to be found as an alternative for that which had been derived from opium. In the end, sadly sacrificing the complete freedom of the port, a condition of which they were very proud, the business community agreed to the levy of duties upon liquor, and to a small customs service to prevent smuggling, though they insisted that its officers should behave in a very restrained manner.[4]

Lugard now had to use his strongest persuasions in favour of a generous grant from imperial funds to make up some of the imposed deficit. He played up the indignation of the mercantile community for all it was worth. The ministers were, of course, feeling the opposing pressure from the moral enthusiasts who regarded compensation as condonation of vice. In a debate in the summer of 1909 Lugard came under the lash of their reproof. Bennett hoped that Lord Crewe had not made any promise to compensate. If he did, members should resist this attempt to extract money from the British taxpayer for such an improper purpose. He then went on to quote Lugard's warning that the closing of the divans might lead to the substitution of alcohol

---

[1] Minutes on Lugard to Crewe, 19 April 1909, C.O. 129/356.
[2] *Legislative Council Reports*, 1909 Session, 17 June, pp. 43-52. [3] *Ibid.* 24 June, pp. 53-61.
[4] *Legislative Council Reports*, 1909 Session, 13 August, 10, 16, 17 September, pp. 75-8, 94-100, 102-15, 116-26.

for opium. " There is to my mind," said Bennett, flinging back the very epithet that Lugard had applied to his party, and following him even in his grammatical peculiarity,

> " a suspicion of real cant about that kind of statement. I say that these Imperial officials . . . ought not to be permitted to openly thwart the efforts made to better the condition of things in our Colonies. That they should be allowed to do so is really intolerable. It is bad enough to have the work of our Government thwarted by political opponents at home . . . but that paid officials in the Colonies or at home should thwart the action of their own government is an intolerable state of things, and I think that some very sharp reprimand should be administered to officials of this type."[1]

Lugard's reaction to this flagellation in Westminster sums up his attitude to the whole question and also throws some light upon Flora's agency.

> " You will see *inter alia* that I have been much censured in the House of Commons . . . It rather strengthens my hands out here, for they thought I was not ' firm ' enough etc., and now the local papers have to champion me! These pernicious parliamentarians who use this kind of language and have swollen heads because they are M.P.'s for some villa settlement, and criticize what they know absolutely nothing about, do a great deal of harm and make the Colonies hate the Mother country. Nor is it entirely useful for the Chinese to read these censures on their Governor. Your talk with Fiddes was interesting. I am not sorry that I irritated their smug complacency by a few home truths. I am also glad that they recognize that I have done a great deal towards the *real* policy by the very stringent restrictions on opium pills and morphia and cocaine. . . . Col. Seely fore-bore to defend my action when the Faddists attacked me in the H. of C. but I need hardly say that I care not one row of pins for their silly censures. I do, however, care for the fact that the S. of S. told me that my Memo and covering letter must of course be printed and laid before Parliament . . . and that apparently they have suppressed it. I must endeavour to get them to publish it . . . Ill-considered haste finds a proverb in every language I have heard of . . . but these reformers of other people's morals cannot wait a minute—no doubt their own morals can wait, and so, by the blessed injunction of a Christian creed, they sacrifice their own for other people's . . . You say you found Fiddes very sound on the opium question. Fletcher had a talk with him, and found him so ignorant as to be quite amusing.

[1] *Parliamentary Debates*, 27 July 1909, V. 8. 1097-9.

He thought that you smoked opium by chopping it up and putting it in a pipe like tobacco! and Hong Kong was full of men staggering about under its influence!" (L. to F. L., 26 August 1909).

The Colonial Office officials, calculating the financial value of Britain's moral satisfaction, decided that they would recommend as a first instalment £9,000, a sum that was £9,000 too much for Bennett and his friends but which, Lugard pointed out, was only 42 per cent of the loss and a sum which the Hong Kong unofficials condemned as wholly insufficient. Before the second instalment was due Lugard was on leave and able to supply his pressure in person at the Colonial Office. He succeeded in converting the officials. But the Office had to convert an unsympathetic Treasury. The Colony had a good case. A pledge of substantial assistance had been given by Lord Crewe. Lugard could plead not only in the name of justice but also, at that time, of poverty as the Hong Kong revenues were low. In the end the contribution was screwed up from £9,000 to £12,000. The sum at issue seems derisory by modern standards but Lugard could at least go back to his Colony having won on the question of principle.

This transaction was not the end of the opium problem: it has, unfortunately, not yet come to an end. The Opium Agreement of 1907 with China was carried out more effectively than Lugard, Jordan or anyone else had expected. In some of the Chinese provinces opium was reduced by quick and drastic methods. Unhappily, the Chinese revolution, with its administrative disintegration, caused a set-back. Britain, however, adhered to her side of the bargain. But, as Lugard had foreseen, the use of morphia at first greatly increased, and new and strict measures of control had to be devised. The drug was largely supplied from Britain who seemed unable to control this export. China, or rather Canton acting independently, did not keep to the treaty; she imposed heavy extra duties upon the opium that could still be legitimately exported. Japan, severely protecting her own people from demoralization, was wholly unco-operative in controlling trade through Formosa. But the powers, pulling at very varying rates and not always heading in the same direction, were now harnessed to the lumbering vehicle of international regulation, though it had to be dragged over all the successive ruts and hills of diplomatic corres-pondence, delegations, instructions, conferences, signatures, ratifications, legislation and enforcement. The suppression of the drug traffic, in some aspects reminiscent of the campaign against slavery, has proved in the end much the harder to deal with. A more diffused and less visible traffic, it has a legitimate medical nucleus, and the self-interest of the traders is reinforced by the almost irresistible demand of those who are at once their customers and victims.

What has been described is, therefore, only one brief and local incident in a long story. Lugard never struck heroic attitudes; as in his anti-slavery work in Africa he had been Fabian rather than Quixotic. The humanitarians could complain that in his reaction against their zeal, influenced, perhaps, by his Colonial Secretary and his unofficials, he had recoiled too far.

The episode lights up the almost typical figures which appear on the British political stage when any reform with moral significance is in question. At one side are the enthusiasts, moved by absolute and generally religious principles of right and wrong: at the extreme opposite side are people, who, perhaps, unconscious of any pre-meditated wickedness, have become materially interested in what is later branded as an abuse. Then, moving inwards, come the increasingly moderate supporters of each of the two extremes. In a position, generally very near the middle, stand the ministers who have to find the point of political balance between these conflicting ideas and influences and build their policy and their action around it. Then there are the officials, those at home advising the minister on policy and those abroad who have to execute it. When these last, as well as those whose interest it is to defend the abuse, are some thousands of miles away from the fountainhead of ideas and action, and have not passed through the same moral and mental experiences, the construction of policy out of ideas is likely to be an even more clumsy process than usual. Lugard, surprisingly, won the approval of all but the most extreme of the opposing forces. He did this by acting as the most effective mediatory link in the chain of persons between the reformers and the reformed. But it seems that he did not appreciate that but for the zeal of the reformers, so easy to condemn as self-righteous and intemperate, the chain of action might never have been set in motion at all.

CHAPTER XVII

THE UNIVERSITY

IT WILL BE remembered that very soon after his arrival, while allowing himself to be firmly eased into the well-worn routine built up by his predecessors in Hong Kong, Lugard had vowed to himself that he would find some opening for independent action. There appears to be an absolute distinction between the artist and the administrator. The first seems to run as free as a wild horse where his ego drives him while the second seems to resemble an ox bending with his team of yoke-fellows to the heavy weight of the organization to which they are harnessed. Yet it is possible that in every really good administrator there is something of the artist and this element, though it must be under rigid control, urges him to find some task in which he can give it expression. A colonial governor may perhaps find more opportunity for such creative action than a civil servant in Britain, though the brevity of his tenure and the seeming malleability of the material upon which he works, may tempt him to hasten into enterprises that are more striking than sound. Lugard, however, did not as a rule reach out towards attractive projects until he was sure of his stance upon solid experience. But in the task which, more than any other in Hong Kong, he began and carried through as his own, he risked an advance upon ground that was perilously unfamiliar to him.

This chosen personal task was the establishment of a university. After leaving school, his time at Sandhurst had been interrupted after a few weeks by a Russian scare, and since then he had been cut off from almost all influences or contacts that could be called educational in any technical sense. In Hong Kong, however, education was one of the activities of his government. The amount of help it doled out was, by the standards of the modern welfare state, very meagre. At the top were a few government schools. Chief among them was the secondary boys' school, Queen's College, entrance to which was much sought after by the Chinese. There were a number of other English medium schools, many of them run by religious bodies, which received small grants. Some Chinese vernacular schools also had government support. These 70 government or grant-aided schools educated in 1910 just over 6,000 children out of a population of some half million.[1] But unaided schools run by Chinese private enterprise, mostly at a very low level, dealt with many more pupils. The majority of the coolie population was felt to be inaccessible to any regular system of education. There was little scope for advance. Lugard did, however, manage by 1911 to screw the proportion of expenditure up from 1.69 per cent to 2.34 per cent of the revenue.[2] He also set up a Chinese committee to watch over the Chinese vernacular education, and he cut down numbers in the overcrowded upper schools in order to raise the standard of education.

He found it all intensely interesting. " I have never before in my life," he said, " had anything to do with education and as a new subject it interests me immensely. Before I leave this Colony I hope to make very considerable changes—I hope, improvements." (L. to F. L., 13 June 1909). As we have seen, he paid frequent visits to the larger schools, government and mission, and made sincere and sensible speeches. The tolerant Chinese, with no organized church of their own to defend, and with their high respect for the scholar, had no objection to Christian schools so long as there was no active proselytizing in them, and the missionaries, by their selfless service, won the respect and sometimes the souls of those they tried to serve. What the Hong Kong Chinese mainly wanted was the English language and the kind of education that would qualify them for a sedentary, clerical life, either in trade or, preferably, in the profession—so honourable in their own country—of civil servant. Education, therefore, presented no difficult cultural or religious problems, only that of unlimited demand by a China suddenly realizing her need of the knowledge which had enabled the Western nations and their Japanese pupil to impose their will upon her. It was clearly higher education that was the key to power.

Lugard was not, of course, the first man in the Colony to realize

[1] *Report for 1910*, p. 14.
[2] *Legislative Council Reports*, 1911 Session, 19 October, pp. 193-5.

this. Doctor, afterwards Sir, Patrick Manson, the great expert on malaria, started the College of Medicine in 1887. It had neither endowment nor buildings but consisted of a few young Chinese working in the several hospitals of the Colony, especially Ho Kai's Alice Memorial Hospital, under the tuition, in their spare time, of the medical staffs, and earning the title of licentiates. One of these grew into the famous leader, Sun Yat Sen. There was also the "Technical Institute", where local schoolmasters and professional men gave what were called "Evening Continuation Classes" in a variety of subjects, including engineering. The idea of developing a university was thrown out as a vague aspiration in the local press during 1905. But very soon after Lugard arrived, in presenting the prizes at the Anglican School of St. Stephen's, he ventured the large and rather ambiguous hope that Hong Kong might be "the Oxford and Cambridge of the Far East".

This was a daring kite to fly at a time when financially the Colony was in one of its depressed periods. But there was in Hong Kong an Indian, a Parsee, one of those numerous merchants of many races who are to be found in eastern ports and who have been able to prosper under the Pax Britannica. Mr. H. N. Mody, already a fragile and ailing little man, was struck by Lugard's words. He also made friends with Flora, whom he greatly admired, and seems to have talked over his ideas with her. He now wrote to Lugard and offered a total of $150,000 to build a university and $30,000 to start an endowment fund, rather less than £18,000 in all. Lugard was touched by Mody's offer and excited by the prospect of building an institution of such dignity. Flora joined eagerly in the project. As usual with Lugard his plan seemed to spring into his mind, with its reasons, form and prospects, as a complete whole.

First he had to make a thorough study of the prospects. He estimated that some three hundred or more students would be qualified at once for entry into the university from the Hong Kong schools alone. Then there were several hundred Chinese studying in America and Britain, while in Japan there were said at one time to have been 16,000, a number which the Chinese government deliberately reduced to 5,000 as they resented having to learn from this cultural upstart. The abolition in 1905, as part of the last desperate modernizing reforms of the Manchus, of the ancient Chinese system of examination for their Civil Service—a visitor to China at this time saw the ruins of a building with some thousands of examination halls—left an educational vacuum that could be filled only by Western education.[1] Lugard's survey of the routes the Chinese were taking towards the goal of higher education revealed that few found their way to Britain and his country was therefore losing a swiftly passing opportunity. America had been quick to make the generous gesture of using part of her Boxer indemnity—later she used the whole—to endow scholarships for Chinese at her own universities. Germany established a large college at Kiaochow. Even at the obvious economic level, the first Chinese engineers, traders, doctors and the rest, would turn to these countries not only for their ideas but for all the material goods and equipment with which they had become familiar. Lugard saw that in Hong Kong Britain had, lying idle, a cultural asset which she had hitherto lacked the imagination to use. Here was a place that was part of China, yet ruled by Britain, easily accessible, mainly Chinese in population and yet British in its order, efficiency and intellectual liberty, equipped with modern institutions of all kinds and possessing a wealth of engineering and other installations for example and study. Chinese parents in the Colony or on the mainland, he argued, could educate their sons here at a fraction of the cost of sending them to Europe, could keep in touch with them and be sure that, while they would learn all they needed from the West, they would not be denationalized or demoralized by exile.

Like all thoughtful men who have worked on the frontier between West and East, he was forced to recognize the power of the West to destroy the religion and custom of the East without being able to replace them with its own and he saw sheer materialism rushing in to fill the void. As a governor he followed the official policy of granting limited support to Christian missionary institutions. He believed, however, that Britain could offer in secular form those qualities of character which religion had done so much to develop, and he hoped that, if Chinese students could live in a community where these qualities flourished, their own moral standard would be strengthened and materialism kept at bay. And not only materialism, but the revolutionary and even socialistic influences which good Chinese parents must reprobate as sternly as he did himself. He was especially concerned to observe the deep division which higher education made

[1] *The Times*, 13 September 1910.

in the student's nature between his new knowledge and his old culture. This subject had been raised by Valentine Chirol in his book *Indian Unrest* (1910), which Lugard discussed with the writer himself when he visited the Colony. From these ideas sprang his two main safeguards for his university: it must be entirely residential and the British staff must be chosen for their moral as well as their academic distinction. The several Christian missions would be allowed to provide their own hostels but there would also be undenominational hostels and, of course, complete freedom of religion.

Lugard began on March 18th, 1908, by calling a large representative group to discuss the proposal. But its sub-committee was forced to report in the autumn that the potential funds were inadequate. This was a severe blow. But Lugard was not to be defeated. He now suggested that, as a preliminary step, the proposed College of Medicine, for which Chinese benefactors had already subscribed $60,000, should fuse itself and its funds with the university. It would also house the Technical Institute. The Medical College Committee, with great public spirit, accepted this proposal. But this was not enough for Mody, who wanted to see a real university established in his lifetime, and he gave the end of 1909 as the date before which £110,000 must be collected if his first offer was to stand. Lugard's realistic Colonial Secretary threw the very cold water of his financial calculations of the building and running costs over the whole project. Even Lugard faltered. But he decided to go forward, rallied his wavering and half-hearted supporters, and took the offensive against all his opponents.

These were many and powerful. In public enterprises there are often two accounts of the proceedings, a smooth official story of progress, studded with compliments and congratulations to all concerned, and the true unpublished story of the bitter struggles and the personal conflicts through which the success was in fact achieved.

The first obstacle presented itself suddenly in Britain. Lugard was not the only man who realized that Britain was the laggard amongst Western nations in helping the Chinese to draw upon her own civilization. During 1909 two public movements were launched in Britain, the one to assist the work of the missions in the schools and the other, " The United Universities Scheme ", to establish, through an alliance between the British universities and religious bodies, a

university somewhere in the heart of China, probably at Hankow.[1]
This plan threatened to compete most authoritatively with his own in
the limited circles from which Lugard so desperately needed financial
and political support.

There was some very impressive support for the British scheme,
especially in Oxford and Cambridge. A strong list was issued of supporters' names, royal, noble and academic, with those of such leading
English experts on China as Sir Robert Hart and Sir Ernest Satow.
America was expected to co-operate. Poor Lugard must have felt a
very small David when suddenly confronted with this Goliath, but
like David he sallied out at once to battle. He printed a statement
showing in two parallel columns the several points in the new scheme
and the superior proposals of his own. There was a certain woolliness
about his rivals' project which allowed Lugard to slip under their
guard and do considerable damage with his clear-cut and practical
alternative. But upon the difficult moral issue he was thrown upon
the defensive. The supporters of the new scheme were whole-
heartedly Christian. They pointed out the terrible danger that by
education in materialist Japan, or even by living in lonely and demoral-
ising exile in Europe and America, the coming leaders of a vast nation
might obtain the science of the West without its religious and cultural
spirit. Their new university, though its teaching would be non-sec-
tarian, would have religious hostels and the staff would be men of
Christian character. This approach, said Lugard, would alienate the
Chinese from the first; and he argued that there was a kind of morality,
especially, it seems, in Britain, which, though derived from Christianity, could now dispense with it. " Educated British gentlemen may
be trusted to have a high standard of morals . . . If the Ethics and
History either of Christianity of Confucianism are taught as part of an
Arts Course, the teachers will naturally be men in sympathy with
their subject."[2]

He wrote in May, 1909, to Lord William Cecil, the chief agent in
the new movement, enclosing his rather belligerent comparative
memorandum, and suggesting that, as there was neither room nor
money for two schemes, they should be amalgamated. Lord William
pointed out that not only was his university to use Chinese as the

[1] *The Times*, 13 September 1910.
[2] Sir F. D. Lugard, *The Hong Kong University Scheme and the Scheme of the China Emergency Committee*, 7 May 1909, p. 3, Private memorandum, L.P.

language of instruction (the difficulties of which Lugard had most sensibly explained) but it was for that larger section of China which spoke Mandarin and which would never patronize an institution in "a dialect area" such as that covered by Canton. But it was on the religious issue that Lord William, as was to be expected of a Cecil, most decisively rejected Lugard's ideas.

" . . . we do not believe it possible in a country like China to introduce moral apart from religious influences. Exceptional men may do this, but in the long run the enthusiasm and the patience which to most men come only from strong and definite religious conviction are needed . . . "[1]

The new scheme also put the emphasis upon humane rather than upon scientific subjects which Lugard countered with the view that it was these subjects rather than the more utilitarian ones that had created revolutionary unrest in India. Lord William replied that this unrest was caused because

"Young men, yellow or white, are enthusiastic and must have great causes put before them: we Christians put before them the higher moral tone of the individual. A merely Utilitarian University leaves to a great extent the enthusiasm of youth unoccupied and therefore it becomes a hotbed of revolutionary intrigue. The enthusiasm for political reform takes the place of an individual reform."

Lugard condemned revolutionary ideas as whole-heartedly as Lord William but he was confident in his own antidotes. His letter elicited from Lord William the gloomy prophecy that

" . . . two ideas will probably fill your University. Number one, China for the Chinese and death to the foreigner; number two, the equality of man and its two developments, socialism and anarchism. . . . to foster a crowd of bomb-throwing patriots in your midst will be extremely unpleasant."

So Lugard had to pursue his relatively lonely and modest way, with an anxious eye at times on the lordly progress of his rivals. He could not foresee that their large and rather nebulous plans would go through a process of evaporation. He issued his own appeal to the British public. Like most people calling for British support, he skilfully interwove altruism with national, and especially economic, interest, but the stress was on the former, and it was with full sincerity that he

[1] Cecil to Lugard, 8 July 1909, L.P.

included the platitude that " Science is the property of mankind ".[1]

He encountered his second obstacle near at hand. He had confidently hoped that the British business community would follow Mody's lead with a long list of impressive subscriptions. He employed every kind of pressure, personal and indirect. But for long there was no response. In such matters the lesser men tended to look to the great firms, led by Butterfield and Swire and Jardine Matheson and to give to public causes in proportion to their subscriptions. In some quarters there was not so much indifference as reasoned hostility to his plan. It was openly attacked in the press as " the University fad ", but there was also, Lugard told his brother, " a solid opposition in certain quarters, not the less troublesome because voiceless." Then, sweeping and unrestrained in his disappointment, he added, " These money grubbing traders fear that if we educate the Chinaman he may be a serious rival . . . " (L. to E. J. L., 1 April 1911).

Lugard felt isolated and depressed. He told Flora:

" I am by no means liked here. Even the University scheme which you applaud is unpopular . . . never I think in my life have I received such consistently hostile and sneering criticism without even the credit for good intentions . . . " (L. to F. L., 19 August 1909).

Was it, he asked himself, that some of the Europeans did not want to encourage the rise of a western-educated class which might challenge the strong commercial citadel they had built up and which might aim at replacing European staffs? He characterized such fear as "short-sighted even from the point of view of our material interests, while from a larger standpoint it is unworthy of British traditions." As the headquarters of the firms were in England he appealed directly to them and sent his capable agent, Flora, round to interview the big men in their offices. Were they, she asked, prepared to allow the Chinese to subscribe the bulk of the money? The combined Lugard persistence at last produced some result. Butterfield and Swire, a firm which had need to reinstate itself with the Chinese, came forward with £40,000. The China Association, a largely commercial body in London, gave the same sum, and more subscriptions trickled in during the year.

Lugard's third obstacle lay in the Colonial Office. He hardly expected any positive enthusiasm there for his project but he did hope for assent and some financial help, with permission to give a site and

[1] A printed, undated paper, headed " Some Notes for Readers in England " (1909), L.P.

propose a grant from colonial revenue. The proposal got a tepid reception. The university was referred to as Lugard's "pet lamb". "I should be rather inclined to forget to notice the suggestion that Imperial aid would be acceptable "[1] ran one minute which seems to have met with acceptance. The grant of a site, inevitably a small one, was allowed. But what chiefly interested the Colonial Office, in a wholly negative sense, was Lugard's success in raising money from the Chinese Government. Flora had been to see Lord Crewe, and had urged him to obtain an imperial contribution to the university because, as she told him, it might warm up the Chinese government to contribute handsomely. Crewe concurred most warmly and said he would do his utmost. (F. L. to L., 15 July 1909). And Lugard had already approached the British ambassador, Sir John Jordan, who readily supported the appeal and took it to the Chinese government which agreed to contribute a sum of money. Crewe, it seems, had made the mistake of straying away from his office and being acquiescent to a lady. His officials demurred, reminding each other that they had always strenuously resisted the efforts of the Chinese government to get a finger in the Hong Kong pie. Fiddes called Lugard's action " an extraordinarily ill-judged proceeding. I foresee a real danger if Sir F. Lugard is not pulled up."[2] The Governor, moreover, had dared to write direct to the British ambassador. In future he must correspond with him only through the Office. Now he was obliged to telegraph the cancellation to Jordan, and the ambassador wrote to him privately to say that he had been deeply embarrassed. He had repeatedly urged the Chinese government to contribute: now their gift was thrown back at them.

> " You know how sensitive the Chinese are in such a matter. It means great loss of face and they were, Sir John said, in much difficulty about it and did not know how to withdraw and were very much disappointed. This is the way our C.O. helps the man on the spot. It forgets his dispatches for six months, then reverses his policy and brings all kinds of trouble with the local people whom it does not understand."
>
> (L. to F. L., 15 July 1909).

The Colonial Office, however, appear to have had some reason on their side. Flora, in a later interview, admitted that the Chinese govern-

---

[1] Minute on Lugard to Crewe, 12 January 1909, C.O. 129/355.
[2] Minutes on Lugard to Crewe, 12 January, 1909, C.O. 129/355.

ment had asked to be allowed to send an Inspector of Schools to Hong Kong as part of the bargain. This difficulty was finally overcome, and in the end the Chinese Government were told that they were now allowed to subscribe.[1] They gave £25,000, "no great sum," Lugard said, "but very valuable as a public token of goodwill." In the end Crewe cabled his definite permission for the establishment of the university, a concession which Lugard believed he owed largely to Flora's advocacy. All that could be offered from Britain was £300 a year for scholarships and these were to be called King Edward VII Scholarships. Lugard blushed each time he had to play up this paltry gift from Britain with its over-grandiose title.

This was not the last round with the Office. As the year 1909 ran to an end, Lugard at last persuaded the reluctant members of Legislative Council to agree to vote for a grant of $50,000 from the revenue of the Colony and cabled this news to the Colonial Office. The night before the actual vote he sat up late preparing a long and convincing speech. Just before he was to give it the Colonial Office cabled to forbid the grant.[2] Their reason was that a Colony which had obtained £9,000 in compensation for its opium revenue could not now be allowed to afford anything for a university.[3] Lugard was bitterly aggrieved. The opium grant had not been asked for *in forma pauperis* but as just compensation. Could he not be trusted, with all his experienced unofficials, to decide upon a small grant from revenue? How hard it was, in the absence of a strong and imaginative Secretary of State like Chamberlain, for a governor to assert his initiative against the Office in favour of any new and large idea!

In Hong Kong Lugard had to struggle against the indifference and distractions of colonial society as well as its hostility.

" All this is not satisfactory and depressed me for a moment, but on the whole I do not think I mind much. It simply means that I must evoke a new enthusiasm, but I must wait till this cricket week, and the Government House Ball and the St. Andrew's Ball, are past, I fear, for till then no-one can think of anything else."   (L. to F. L., November 1909).

The year, with Mody's deadline hanging over Lugard, ended in a nightmare of engagements, but all the time, with the tenacity of a bull

---

[1] Minutes on Lugard to Crewe, 12 June 1909, C.O. 129/356.
[2] Crewe to Lugard, 15 December 1909, C.O. 129/359.
[3] Minutes on Lugard to Crewe, 9 December 1909, C.O. 129/359.

terrier, he never let go of his university project. He even went ahead with the building plans. When the final estimate for them came to $285,000, far outdistancing Mody's original offer of $150,000, there seemed no chance of collecting the balance by December 31st. The old man himself was rapidly declining in health and he must get the transaction through while he was alive to fulfil his part. Lugard had become devoted to him, and he was distressed to find that his benefaction, far from gaining Mody any local gratitude, had rather brought him strain and even unpopularity. He told Lugard there was " innumerable people who blamed him for having been the source which had brought upon them this ' fad ' and the demand for subscriptions." (L. to F. L., 2 December 1909).

Lugard was obliged to throw himself upon the old man's mercy and plead with him to give more. Thus the end of the year saw a struggle with, or rather within, Mody as to his capacity to give more and also as to his capacity to survive. Flora, in London, was working to get him a knighthood, and the prospect of this reward, which was not without metropolitan precedents, was tactfully hinted at, as a tonic both to his vitality and to his generosity. Mody at the very last agreed to give the whole sum for the building and even laid down that no expense should be spared to make the work as good and as beautiful as possible. Then Butterfield and Swire, also at the last moment, removed a condition which had limited their grant. So, as the last night of 1909 ran out, Lugard could go to his lonely bedroom and write to Flora the news that he had won his university.

There were other compensations besides the main achievement. There had been a surprising amount of support from the local Chinese. From the very first, according to the dualism which ran through all Hong Kong organization, a group of 100 Chinese gentlemen had been formed to work parallel with the main Committee and large numbers of their countrymen had given what they could. The Chinese in the European settlements, on the mainland, and even in Malaya, Saigon and Australia, had sent their contributions. This was very pleasing to Lugard. Here was something he had done for the Chinese and with them, which brought the promise of a deeper relationship than the materialist bargain which was the main link between them and Britain.

The co-operation of the Viceroy of Canton, who sent $200,000, encouraged the Chinese merchants in Hong Kong, many of whom were in no position to get out of step with this potentate. It also encouraged Lugard. He was beginning to feel the joy of creation. To Flora he confessed:

> " My dear, I do really deserve to make this University a success, if long hours of thought and work and the sacrifice of personal recreation and even of almost necessary exercise, can establish a claim. I feel a little pleased with myself—so please be pleased with me too."
>
> (L. to F. L., 6 February 1910).

He could dwell upon a still more valued compensation: the enterprise had been a partnership with her.

> " All my other public schemes have been my own, emanating out of my work. This is yours. I took it up at your strong instigation. Mody . . . knows how keen you are about it, and he has a profound admiration for you . . . if it goes through to success the credit will be yours."
>
> (L. to F. L., 2 December 1909).

Early in 1910 all plans were prepared. The university was to be built on a high shelf levelled out on the hillside. There was to be a central block with accommodation for Medical and Engineering Faculties, the nucleus of an Arts section, libraries, and preliminary hostel room for seventy students. The annual expenditure had been worked out to the pay of the last gardener and stoker and was to run at $117,239 a year.

The foundation stone was laid on March 16th. Lugard was excited and nervous about the event and longing for the leave which was to follow it. It was on March 3rd that the cable about Flora's operation reached him. It was merciful of his brother not to have told him at this moment the full gravity of the position. A handsome illustrated thirty-page foolscap size pamphlet was printed in English and Chinese. The plans, which showed contours rising from 160 to 440 feet in a site little more than 1,500 feet deep, give some idea of the difficulties of building in Hong Kong. The pictures show, in a setting of bunting, flags and pots of palm, a half circle of all the public figures of the Colony: frock-coated officials and merchants, bishops, soldiers, sailors, and the silk-clad delegates from China. Confronting them on the other side of the suspended stone, at two little tables, are the two chief actors, both small spare men and both dressed in black with funereal effect. The Lugard shown sitting nervously holding his silk hat seems an incalculable distance away from the Lugard of Lake Nyasa, Kampala or Borgu. The fragile Parsee, in his big black cap, was so overcome with emotion and physical weakness that he could only just manage to read his speech. It was one which revealed much, not least the setting of the British colony in which this Indian had flourished in wealth and in public spirit. He paid a great tribute both to Flora, who had helped him to form the plan, and to Lugard whose perseverance alone had carried it through.

Lugard, as he sat, looked round at the audience. He was astonished at the enormous numbers present, many of them Chinese who surrounded the inner circle of the important and the official people. He was in a state of tension from his public and private anxieties. This was, perhaps, his most important moment in Hong Kong. He had learned his speech by heart and in his excitement he delivered it with a feeling that he rarely showed in his public speaking. It expressed the faith in which he carried out his work, but it had also a defensive note. After a formal introduction he went on:

" Mr. Chamberlain, whose name is spoken with affection and admiration throughout the oversea Dominions of our Gracious King, called himself a ' Missionary of Empire' and bade us ' think Imperially '. Let us then exercise an Imperial imagination in regard to this University and not confine our view to the horizon of the immediate present. We are endeavouring not only to afford the highest educational facilities to the citizens of Hong Kong, but to hold out the hand of friendship and to assist China to educate her sons without exposing them to long exile and the risk of denationalization by sending them to Europe and America. Shall we by so doing create skilled rivals to compete against ourselves? I refuse to believe that men of British race have come to be afraid of fair and honest competition.

The justification of the British Empire lies in its results. So long as it stands for impartial justice, so long as its aim is to raise and to educate the peoples who are subjects of our King, or who are contiguous to his boundaries, for so long will it prosper, and no longer. It will pass away, as other Empires have passed away before it, but I believe that history will record of it that it was founded on something higher than territorial conquest or national aggrandizement . . .

It has happened to me in past years that I have been the humble instrument by which the confines of the Empire were enlarged in some directions. Those days are past. It is no longer an age of acquisition in which we live, but an age of development . . . And if this Colony becomes . . . the centre of educational progress in South China, you will have achieved a nobler extension of the principles which underlie the British Empire than any which accompany territorial expansion.

. . . the material of the building is to be of the best. It is even more important that the personnel and the organization should be of the very best . . . men like those who have carried through a similar undertaking at Khartoum founded in memory of Gordon, where on the very scene of the cruelties of slave-traders and the oppression and misery of ages, a centre of British education stands like a beacon on the threshold of the desert . . ."

He drew attention to two points: the residential character of the University and the high character of the staff they intended to appoint.

He then sprang a surprise upon the audience by announcing the knighthood of Mody, now to be Sir Hormusjee, and having duly laid the stone, gave way to the Chinese delegate from the Viceroys of Canton and Nanking. His Excellency Wei Han, dressed like Lugard in dark clothes but of very dissimilar cut, was listened to with close, almost suspicious attention. He read his speech in English and in addition to all the proper compliments he was able to present the Chinese attitude to the occasion, and to make some sly hits at the West.

" Geographically, Hong Kong is a portion of China, and what makes for the good of one part must naturally reflect profitably upon the whole country. It is a universal axiom that the man who can make two blades of grass grow where only one thrived before is a worthy citizen, but how much more valuable to the world at large is the country which can ensure the growth of such a tree of learning as is today being planted? China ever has been and always will be a home of study; the nation has not, of course, developed and pursued the line of march taken in the West . . . Foreign countries are prone to blame, if not to censure, China for backwardness in adopting modern sciences. She does not deserve such blame. China is a vast empire, which, centuries before the European nations evolved from the barbaric state, possessed her schools and her regulated system of civilization. That system was eminently suited to her needs up to a certain point, just as the primitive standards of life, and the ' might-is-right ' system of feudal days in Europe suited the people who then existed . . . China is at one with others that feel the impulse at their hearts to acquire what is best of the numerous world-changing advances in scientific, industrial, political, and social life. . . . It is for this reason that a University in Hong Kong is welcomed by the Chinese . . ."[1]

After the ceremony Lugard escaped to his room to share the experience with Flora.

" Well now I have told you ' all about it '. You will like dear old Mody's reference to you—he almost worships you, dear old man—when he read that part in a voice of feeling and an almost reverential tone, there was great applause . . . I am in great spirits tonight. Physically perhaps it is the reaction after the double tension of your illness and this Ordeal, but it is founded on good cause . . . The sunshine of the outer world has got into my heart this evening."   (L. to F. L., 16 March 1910).

So the academic venture was launched. The opening of the University was to come two years later. But this seems the place for some general comment upon its future.

How far has the university fulfilled the hopes of its founder? These were high indeed, how high he did not fully reveal until the opening day but we may quote from this speech here. He said:

" Was ever such an opportunity afforded to any nation as this comparatively small Colony has? Look round the Colonies of Great Britain—aye, of any and every other nation—is there any which has assumed so great a task? When the historian of the next century reviews the progress of the Eastern world it may be that he shall point to this Colony of Hong Kong—a mere speck on the map—as the centre from which emanated an influence which profoundly affected a nation numbering one-fourth of the population of the world."[2]

Lugard did not see all these hopes fulfilled. Forty-seven years is not a long period in the life of a western university and this was an experiment in the Far East. Moreover, the period was broken by two great wars, one accompanied for Hong Kong by destructive foreign conquest. Yet some of the adverse influences which clogged the later advance of the university were already revealing themselves in his time. Chief among them, until very recent years, was the indifference of the British government, of many of the British commercial leaders, and of the local government itself, except under Lugard and later, Clementi.

[1] *Hong Kong University, objects, history, present position, prospects* (Hong Kong, 1910), p. 31.
[2] *Hong Kong Weekly Telegraph*, 11 March 1912.

A university should be an expression, however sublimated, of the ideas and aspirations of the community it serves, but in Hong Kong there was little understanding of what a university should be. The poverty which shadowed the birth of the university, therefore, continued to cripple its youth. Lugard's enthusiasm had forced the institution into existence upon an annual revenue of about £10,000 with little hope of the progressive increase which its advance must require. His policy of making it residential, so desirable ideally, added greatly to the running expenses. Inevitably the university ran at intervals into financial crises; the staff tended to be overworked and this, with their isolation, made it difficult, though many excellent and devoted teachers have served it, to attract enough men of the uniformly high quality Lugard had envisaged. Not until many years later was the interest of the British people and parliament fully evoked and until then the Colonial Office and the Treasury kept the imperial purse closed.

The university was narrowly based not only in finance but in the supply of students. The Colony alone, with its large shifting coolie element, could hardly for many years justify the institution. The flow of the Chinese from the mainland was checked by Chinese nationalism. With that unerring perception of motives which humiliated peoples seem to possess, they detected the element of self-interest in the European gift of higher education. To illustrate this a significant extract from a Peking newspaper early in 1910 may be given.

" Germany has been making plans to establish a University in Tsingtao, and Great Britain in Hong Kong. To all appearances they are very enthusiastic in promoting education; but in reality they are secretly taking away the power of the Empire with regard to education. It is deplorable to contemplate . . . We shall be better served by men who are educated in our own schools and are therefore reliable as patriots and lovers of their country."[1]

This suspicion gained its full growth with the revolution of 1911. Mainland Chinese who were willing to accept educational help directly from the Western nations hesitated to seek it in a European Colony. The time would come when their attitude would be rationalized under Communist inspiration into a defence against " cultural aggression ".

[1] *Peking Daily News*, 19 May 1910.

The University

Lugard's hope that the university might become a great intellectual meeting place for Western and Chinese culture has also remained unfulfilled. The students were mostly too intent upon Western knowledge, especially science, to pursue this deeper, less utilitarian quest. Moreover it was hard for Hong Kong, with Cantonese-speaking students, to rival the best centres of Chinese study where Mandarin was the language of learning, or to attract eminent Chinese scholars. While Britain grudged educational help to China or Hong Kong, the Americans, especially the missionaries, went in to China with both hands open, fostering a dozen colleges for Britain's one.

But the story of Lugard's university is by no means finished. There is no place for an epitaph. With all other Western colleges crushed out of existence under the Communist steam-roller, his university is still vigorously alive and this in spite of all the adverse external factors, culminating in the Japanese conquest and the destruction of much of its buildings. The policy of Britain is now very different from that of Lugard's day and some £15,000,000 has been given to colonial colleges, including about three-quarters of a million to Hong Kong. It is now realized that a conflict of ideas governs the great political divisions of the world. The university has today more students—nearly a thousand in 1959—and they are reported to be in calm pursuit of their studies in spite of the ferment so near to them. Mody's original building has been restored and enlarged; the Lugard and the other five hostels are full of students; local Chinese benefactions have been generous and a residence has recently been built for women. The university offers now a full range of humane and scientific subjects. During its half-century of existence many thousands of young Chinese and of others have spent here happy and profitable years, passing out to be well-trained doctors, with degrees recognized in Britain, engineers and teachers. They have learned to feel some understanding for the other island which lies off the opposite coast of the great Eurasian land mass which divides them.

The University, in its foundation, was the expression of an idea and in the half century of its existence it has continued, at a level deeper than its curricula, to deal with ideas. How difficult it is to estimate their character or their destination may be shown by what Dr. Sun Yat Sen said to the University when he visited it in 1923. He spoke of his education at the Medical College which preceded the University

353

and his reflection when he went from Hong Kong into the outside world. " I began to wonder how it was that foreigners, that Englishmen, could do such things as they have done, for example, with the barren rock of Hong Kong within seventy or eighty years, while in 4,000 years China had no place like Hong Kong . . . That is the answer to the question ' Where did I get my revolutionary ideas from?' It was entirely in Hong Kong. My fellow students, you and I have studied in this English Colony and in an English University and we must learn by English examples. We must carry this example of good government to every part of China."

This public admission, so perfectly meeting the hopes of Lugard and others who served the island, seems to come from another and less prejudiced world. Yet the island has continued to attract more and more Chinese and the good work done in both government and education cannot be without results even if they now win no public commendation from the beneficiaries.

The verdict passed at the time upon Lugard's project at the Colonial Office was that he was too ambitious. There was some truth in this. But it is equally true that then and for very long afterwards the British Government was not ambitious enough.

CHAPTER XVIII

THE LAST TWO YEARS, 1910-12

LUGARD SPENT the five spring and summer months of 1910 in England, during which, among other duties, he studied university administration with the help of some of its leading experts. Flora returned to the Colony with him. They travelled by the Siberian railway. They were in high hopes that after all the illness, anxiety and separation which had marked their marriage, a period of shared work and private happiness lay before them. They came via Peking where Flora hoped that the personalities would interest him even if the monuments left him cold. In that brooding capital the Manchu power, on the eve of its extinction, was vainly trying to limit the demands of the National Assembly it had called. Lugard was better received than might have been expected for a governor of Hong Kong; private motor cars were provided for him and he was even offered some decoration which he was obliged by rule to refuse.

Perhaps the most enjoyable function was a dinner given in his honour by the Chinese who had been educated in Britain. Some forty of them received him at the Students' Club which was banked with glorious chrysanthemums and hung with Dragon flags and Union Jacks. The chief speaker, Dr. Wu Lien Teh, described Lugard as a brilliant soldier; he was now winning battles in the field of education. About the Hong Kong University he made two points, which were remarkable, coming from a Chinese in Peking. He spoke of

" the ideal position of Hong Kong . . . gateway from Europe to the East " as " the right place for the teaching of modern European knowledge to us Chinese."

He welcomed Lugard's decision to use English for instruction

" not only because it is the commercial language, the lingua franca, of the

East, but also because it will enable our students to keep in touch with the latest and best literature connected with science and other branches of modern knowledge . . . such a university, where Young Chinese maintain a proper mode of life and are brought up in a pure Chinese environment . . . will appeal to Chinese parents, especially as the cost to each student will be only one-fourth of what it is in Europe. Gentlemen . . . I would ask you to join me in wishing Sir Frederick Lugard and his co-workers godspeed in their great work, to assist them wherever we can, in making this fine university known to all our people."[1]

Lugard responded with deep feeling. He told them of the progress and moral aims of the University. With an eye upon the anxious Chinese government he added, " Politics and theories of government reform should find no place in a University." He received a personal letter of appreciation on the remarkable reception he had been given in Peking from Lewis Harcourt[2] who had just been appointed Secretary of State for the Colonies following the General Election of December 1910. This reception was:

" a great tribute to your past work . . . The article about you in the *Peking Daily News* (very seldom pro-British) was most satisfactory and you must have been gratified at the banquet of English educated Chinese and their great appreciation of your ' child '—the Hong Kong University." (Harcourt to L., 1 December 1910).

Back in his Government House Lugard took up again all the threads of administration. In January 1911 he learned that his invaluable Colonial Secretary, after 28 years in Hong Kong, was to become Governor of Fiji. Lugard's difficulty in working with him had not decreased with time. He confessed how often May had wounded his vanity by showing openly his disapproval, especially when he thought Lugard—of all men!—was being soft or weak. Yet Lugard admired May unreservedly; his Colonial Secretary was the absolute antithesis of that type he most disliked and which he would sum up as " sketchy fellow ". The two men had worked together in as complete a unison as their duty demanded. Lugard made a farewell speech in Legislative Council that was correct rather than enthusiastic, but the stolid May surprised everyone by breaking down and being almost unable to

---

[1] *Peking Daily News*, 21 October 1910.
[2] Harcourt, (later Viscount) Lewis, 1863-1922; 1881-1904 private secretary to his father, Sir William Harcourt; 1904 M.P. for Rossendale Division, Lancs.; 1905 First Commissioner of Works; 1910 Secretary of State for the Colonies; 1916 resigned with Asquith and raised to peerage.

answer.[1] May was succeeded by W. D. Barnes, who, after a short tenure of office, horrified the Colony by falling dead from his pony as he rode away from a chukka of polo. Fortunately Lugard had the help of the brilliant Clementi, the man who would one day succeed him as Governor of Hong Kong, and whose scholarly mind was of the greatest value to him in the construction of the University.

On the personal side the first six months after his return were among the happiest in his life. The reason was simple—Flora was there and she was well. He was glad to have her with him, for the cool weather visitors were pouring through the port.

The guests in these months were a strange assortment. Among the British were Mrs. George Keppel, the great friend of the King, whom the writer remembers in her later prime as a most lovely and glowing woman, festooned with pearls. There followed, by contrast, the versifier, Ella Wheeler Wilcox; and the usual procession of diplomats, admirals and generals. Also " we have had a plethora of princes. German Crown Prince failed to come but we had all the preparation. Prince Lichtenstein (Austria) stayed here some time, Prince and Princess Fushimi (Japanese) . . . Prince Pistolamtumulok (Siam) due quite soon. Prince Leopold passed through a few days ago." The Queen of Siam arrived with a large entourage soon after Flora had left, so Lugard had the difficult task of describing her attire: " black lace stockings and an intermediate dress between her knees and waist which had the general appearance of somewhat skimpy knickerbockers. The result was enormously grotesque. I don't know if I should have kissed her hand?" The hair " was close cropped like a boy, very black, very coarse, and very straight . . . The scent, a sort of mixture of sandalwood, garlic and a fast restaurant in Piccadilly, was overpowering." A disastrous occasion was the German naval visit in the course of which the Admiral was killed by accident; but the trouble Lugard took to arrange his funeral " as for Royalty " won golden opinions from all the visiting German officers as well as from his own Foreign Office. " So when the shooting begins, I hope they'll aim at something other than Government House!"

With the hot weather coming, it was felt that Flora should go to Japan for four months to escape the heat. So she set off with her elderly maid.

[1] *Legislative Council Reports*, 1911 Session, 12 January, pp. 1-3.

357

Lugard was now beginning to look with anxiety over the hills of Kowloon to the Chinese Empire, where signs of the coming storm were appearing. Disturbances of any kind over there always sent their ripples down the Canton river and into the generally placid waters of Hong Kong. Canton was beginning to seethe with revolutionary ideas, and the pressure of the police, urged on from Peking, was squeezing out the law-breakers, criminal and political, into their nearest refuge. But Lugard was the last man under whom they could expect a secure base for their operations. Disorder was disorder to him, whatever the reasons for it, and he always struck at it almost automatically. He knew that Hong Kong was not the sort of place in which to take risks. He brought in legislation to deal with an outbreak of armed robbery and violence which provided for a five year minimum sentence for serious crime, with whipping for a number of offences. This punishment, with a 50 lash maximum, was to be administered with "an instrument specified by the Court".[1] This was too much for Harcourt who pleaded that he had to allow for the humanitarian tendencies in parliament. Lugard was reminded of the maximum of 24 lashes laid down by Chamberlain in 1902. As the Ordinance was drawn, it might be the bastinado or an iron bar! It was in the Colonial Office that the severity of the measure was curbed, not in the Legislative Council where even the Chinese members agreed to it. Lugard's action may be understood, though it may not be accepted by modern penologists, when his speech in Council is read with its record of brutal attacks by gangs entering houses, boarding defenceless junks, kidnapping girls for prostitution and children for ransom, and often murdering their victims if they proved unprofitable. Lugard wanted the longer imprisonment to encourage the production of evidence, since the criminals terrorized the people, and the proportion of convictions fell steadily as the number of crimes rose. But he also wanted to allow the teaching of a trade to the criminal. As for the flogging, the Colonial Office might hold him to 24 lashes, but *he* chose the instrument and it was the "cat".

On the political side Lugard had to deal with the growth of secret societies and the spread of seditious meetings. At the end of April disturbances broke out in Canton. They spread to the surrounding countryside and the life of the Viceroy, Chang Min Chi, whom

[1] *Legislative Council Reports,* 1911 Session, 20 April, pp. 64-5 and 27 April, pp. 82-4.

Lugard had found so friendly, was for a time in danger. But this was a mere curtain-raiser. During the July and August of 1911 the real rebellion was simmering in the heart of China, in the province Szechwan. The occasion was the struggle between the provincial leaders and Peking over railway construction. The attempt of the Manchus to save their regime by the introduction of a fraction of democracy came, like the similar attempt of the Romanovs, too late. Their advisory councils, following many historical precedents, refused to be advisory and began to turn republican.

From Hong Kong, a vantage point just out of reach of the turmoil, the British could watch the great revolutionary storm sweep over China. All the forces Britain held in Hong Kong were put in readiness for immediate dispatch to Shanghai if republicanism should suddenly be infected with xenophobia. But though Cantonese leaders were playing a prominent part in the north and centre, the great province of Kwangtung was for a time strangely quiet. The leading progressive figure, Dr. Sun Yat Sen, was abroad; it was not until December that he passed through Hong Kong on his way to China where he put himself at the head of the republican provinces. Meanwhile, in Canton, the " Dare to die " and the " Dynamite Bomb ", and other secret societies, were beginning to act. The new Tartar general sent down from Peking was assassinated by a bomb on his way to his house. On November 6th Lugard was asked by the Viceroy to suspend the lately opened railway service from Kowloon. On the same day the arrival of a false rumour that Peking had fallen and that the Manchus had fled, allowed the Hong Kong Chinese to show the feelings which had been held in suspense. To Lugard it was an amazing exhibition. He described it to the Colonial Office.

" The entire Chinese population appeared to become temporarily demented with joy. The din of crackers (the usual method of signifying rejoicing) was deafening and was accompanied by perpetual cheering and flag-waving—a method of madness most unusual to the Chinese."

Lugard appreciated the force of revolution even if he could not sympathize with it, and he made no false move that might have turned wild rejoicing into wild rage.

In Canton the merchants, who had everything to lose from disorder and looting, struggled to make the inevitable revolution a peaceful one, and were largely successful. On November 9th, the Viceroy took refuge with the British Consul who sent him on to Lugard in a naval vessel. He arrived in Hong Kong in a state of collapse. In many parts of China Manchus and their representatives were being murdered, sometimes with terrible cruelty. Lugard appealed to the Chinese community to treat him as a guest in distress seeking the protection of the British flag, and the Chinese leaders responded warmly. Posters were put up in the city to inform the people of Lugard's wishes that no affront was to be offered to the old man, and he left, completely unmolested, on November 17th. Delegates even came over from the new Canton government, which contained some well-known Hong Kong Chinese, seeking money and advice from Lugard and help with the drafting of their new laws. Yet his position was difficult. The abdication of the Manchus did not officially take place until February 12th, 1912. But, recognizing the inevitable, and being assured that the celebrations were mainly for joy, he agreed to an orderly midday demonstration on November 13th, at which £10,000 worth of fire-crackers was exploded. It was clear to all that Lugard meant to stay firmly in control of his island, however much spray from the Chinese storm might reach it.

As the months went on, however, it began to look as if the barriers, moral as much as physical, which Lugard had set up against the revolutionary wave from China might collapse. Hooligans and criminals from the mainland came in increasing numbers over the border. Chinese women had their jewellery torn off them in the street; stones were thrown at the police; there were cries of " Kill the Foreigners " and others that Hong Kong belonged to China and must be taken back. The crowds, in their new excitement, sometimes stopped the police from making arrests. Lugard was in frequent consultation with the Chinese leaders, who responded because they wanted not only security but an early resumption of normal trade. Through them he could still influence Canton since " The leading men here are looked to and consulted by the revolutionary leaders at every step." But he expected some frontier disorder and much crime by riff-raff from Canton and " already there are signs of this pre-liminary of the millennium which all Chinese now expect."

" The situation here demanded active measures. I introduced a special

Ordinance—passed it in one sitting—did not consult the S. of S., but introduced 'the cat' for all offences of violence and intimidation etc. . . . I had daily route marches of troops with fixed bayonets through all the crowded thoroughfares, and adopted a thousand minor performances— personally interviewed the leading Chinese (with *admirable* results) etc. The result is I believe the thing is fizzling out rapidly, and what might have been a serious crisis, will escape almost unnoticed. The Europeans got into a bit of a panic, and I hear many stayed away from the St. Andrew's Ball in the fear that the place would be blown up by dynamite! The Chinese have gone off their heads (the lower classes). Even the Prostitutes have announced in posters and in the press that they are paying half their earnings to 'the Cause' and inviting extra custom from patriotic motives! Where but in China would you find it an act of high patriotism to fornicate?" (L. to E. J. L., 23 December 1911).

Three weeks later the situation was still tense.

" Canton, which is within spitting distance, is a volcano, with a regiment called the 'Assassination' Company, who publicly issue manifestoes to reform in 3 to 7 days or the suspect will be blown up with bombs!
(L. to E. J. L., 14 January 1912).

It was impossible that Lugard could feel any sympathetic response to revolutionary fervour even if it had not presented itself to him mainly as a question of public order. But he did not rely upon force alone. As he said to his Legislative Council:

" Chinese residents in this Colony, I am confident, appreciate the security and safety they enjoy under the British flag, and this has been proved abundantly to me during the course of the last month when I have had most loyal co-operation from leading Chinese residents, of course including the two Chinese members of Council. It is the duty of the Government to show, if people come from Canton to this Colony, that they must behave themselves, and that we shall not allow the city of Victoria to become the scene of turbulence and riots such as, unfortunately, at the present moment exist in some parts of China."[1]

In addition to his other measures Lugard collected all the arms into a strongly guarded central store—did his memory go back to a similar measure in the little fort near Mengo?—and armed the police with revolvers and women with police whistles. When the Chinese revolutionaries in the south wanted to use the harbour to send troops to the

[1] *Legislative Council Reports*, 1911 Session, 30 November, p. 244.

north, Lugard forbade it and ordered out the naval ships. The situation rapidly improved and by December the railway service over the frontier was resumed. By March, 1912, he could look back with some satisfaction upon the steadiness of the Colony and especially praise the loyalty and good sense of the Chinese. Their leaders had been in a very difficult position. Most of them had property and relatives on the mainland: they sympathized with the revolution, and went in fear of assassination if they showed too little fervour in its support. Their moderation was recognized, at Lugard's request, by a knighthood for their leader in the Council, Dr. Ho Kai. This Chinese Christian doctor had won the distinction by many other services, especially to the University, but the time chosen for the award had significance.

This was also a time of intense personal anxiety in which the high hopes of the earlier part of the year that in future he and his wife could live and work together were finally dashed. Flora went to Japan in May; she was deeply interested in all she saw and wrote at first in high spirits. Then early in September, just when he was expecting her to leave Japan, a telegram came "Departure postponed". He guessed rightly that this meant illness, "Just those two words I read this morning have changed all my horizon." The next telegram told him the real truth, that of another operation, and knowing how serious this must be he had to wait for news and to suffer. He wanted to go to her but felt that at such a difficult moment his duty forbade him to leave the Colony. She wired to him daily. One day no wire came. He was suddenly seized with the belief that this meant she had suffered a relapse and was dying or dead. This gave him what he reckoned to be the worst day of his life. The telegram came. It was not only reassuring but with a bathos which was almost stunning, went on to deal with purchases for a coming bazaar in Hong Kong in aid of the University! But the reaction could not diminish what he had suffered. He went up to his room and to the desk where his serial letter to her was lying:

"I have travelled with you how many times through the Valley of the Shadow of Death but I have never penetrated so far into its gloom and terror as I did yesterday." (L. to F. L., 28 September 1911).

It would be a month before Flora could be ready to travel, and in the course of it they had to come to a big decision by correspondence. Just before her illness Lugard had received a letter about his future career. Sir John Anderson[1] (who had recently risen to be head of the Colonial Office) had written to him a private letter:

" We are anxious to amalgamate the Nigerian Administration making one Governor and, say, three Deputies, one for East, West and North. But our difficulty is to get the right man for the job. We are agreed that you are the man if you would take it even if only for sufficient time, say three or four years, to give it a good start. We should not be difficult about salary, but the figure in our minds is £6,000 with a duty allowance of £1,500. Will you kindly let me know what you think?" (17 August 1911).

Even before he had news of Flora's latest illness he recalled a picture, one of those problem pictures of the Edwardian period, which he had seen somewhere called " Twixt Love and Duty ". The first influence won the preliminary round in his mental battle. " First and foremost—indeed nothing matters in comparison with it—is the question of separation and of your happiness." He had come to learn how difficult it was to live without her. And yet—and yet—with the old Scheme for continuous administration—and of course he would not even consider the post without it—would she be so much worse off than she had been in Hong Kong, with half the world between them much of the time? At least there would be certainty in which she would be able to *settle* in London or Abinger. Then he indulged himself by just considering for a moment the appointment apart from personal considerations. It would be an immense task, a burden the weight of which he could well estimate. He had left Nigeria just five years before. He had come to the new task with misgivings as to his fitness for it; he had worked hard at big schemes and small. But it had been, compared with Africa, a mere backwater of life. " The strain of anxiety, and of single-handed personal responsibility are as Nil compared with Africa and I have grown fat and well-fed and lazy and self-indulgent." As for the work, " Must I confess to you, who can read all my thoughts, that the task does appeal to me?" It was at the moment " about the biggest job in the whole British Empire and one of the most difficult . . . it is the turning point in the destinies of that

[1] Anderson, Sir John, G.C.M.G., K.C.B., 1858-1918; 1879 entered Colonial Office; 1904-11 Governor of the Straits Settlements and High Commissioner to the Federated Malay States; 1911-16 Permanent Under-Secretary of State for the Colonies; 1916-18 Governor of Ceylon.

vast country." But he was only putting the pros and cons: he did not want to form any opinion until they could form one together.

Flora returned to Hong Kong on October 9th, still very weak. Before she left Japan, having read through the lines of his letters, if indeed she needed that much evidence, she telegraphed to him about the offer of Nigeria. "Sorrowfully accept." Upon her return they discussed the matter. Flora could watch the demand of Africa becoming stronger every day. Then came a letter from the Secretary of State, Lewis Harcourt, an old friend of hers, containing the very flattering confession that if Lugard did not accept the offer he would probably postpone the amalgamation. Lugard and Flora composed a reply in which, on the grounds of her health, acceptance was made conditional upon their old Scheme by which the Governor of Nigeria should administer the country continuously, spending six months in Nigeria and six in London. This was to be their irreducible condition, but "He may very possibly decline to be dictated to by me," he admitted to his brother. He did. Sir John Anderson replied that while sympathizing deeply with the reason, they felt considerable hesitation about Lugard's proposal.

> "We should look to the Governor-General to be at once the driving and controlling force of the administration, and could not contemplate without anxiety a country so new, and where the unexpected is constantly happening, being left for half the year in the charge of subordinates subject only to control from Downing Street, even though we had the advantage of your presence there.
>
> Your proposal would moreover never permit of your getting a real rest, or holiday, and everyone needs an occasional spell of complete rest." (9 November 1911).

Sir John was, of course, mistaken in his last remark: Lugard, we know, never needed, or at least never took, a rest. But the Under-Secretary, in his obvious anxiety to win Lugard's assent, went on to go a very long way towards meeting him. Instead of six months' leave home after a twelve months tour, he was to have four after eight. And while they hoped he would make the greater part of it a real vacation, there would be no difficulty about allowing him and his secretary to deal with dispatches from Nigeria, and to have a room in the Colonial Office. This was indeed a large advance from the position taken up by the Office in 1906. Anderson also pointed out that his first tour of service could be a short one; he could simply review the general situation and then return and report. On the same day Harcourt wrote to Flora in the most personal and persuasive terms, but he was obliged to add:

" I am anxious to do anything which would be agreeable to you and him, but I am sorry to say I could not possibly assent to the idea of the half England half Nigeria arrangement. I do not trouble you with all the arguments against it, but they are quite conclusive to my mind."

Then, after pointing out the concession he was making, he ended:

" I cannot tell you what great importance I attach to getting your husband to complete his great African work."

(Harcourt to F. L., 9 November 1911).

In face of this, the promises they had made to each other melted away. How could they refuse this? They demanded two weeks in which to think it over. But Flora knew that she had inwardly made her decision. " Fred must accept . . . "; she had felt it from the moment she received the news in Japan. " ' African Lugard '! The words have been like a refrain to my thoughts," she told Edward.

" He is asked now to complete his work, to do the biggest thing that remains to be done in tropical Africa . . . our personal happiness must not stand in the way . . . I am not hurrying to communicate my views to Fred. His own will form parallel to mine."

(F. L. to E. J. L., 5 December 1911).

And soon there followed instructions to Edward to look for a house, and a fairly roomy one, where Fred could come back to dispense hospitality, do his work and find that Flora had kept " his relations with the London world in proper trim." Yet Lugard had told his brother that Flora was in tears when Harcourt's letter came. But then she was ill again and the old anxiety was upon them. So they got out the Bible and read the story of Jehoshaphat's victory over the Moabites and agreed that they would " be not afraid nor dismayed ".[1]

As the year drew to an end, Flora became more ill; her operation had been bungled. The letter to Harcourt accepting Nigeria had been posted. Lugard, impressed by what he regarded as the generous and appreciative attitude at the Colonial Office upon this occasion, decided

[1] II Chronicles, XX.

not to bargain over terms. Shortly afterwards, Flora's condition worsened. In Hong Kong she had been well for only two short periods: for the rest she had either been ill in the East or in England. Yet the short time they had spent together had been almost ideally happy; their relationship had grown into something they could not even have imagined when, disillusioned elsewhere, they turned to each other in friendship.

Their correspondence in this period revealed their growing unity of mind. Perhaps because of Lugard's deep early knowledge of the Bible they studied it together. They were especially devoted to the psalms. Together or apart they read the psalms for the evening every night at the same time. But for God's name in the psalms, they would read " the Ideal " or " Spiritual Law in the Natural World ", substitutes which cannot always have made either for good theology or good literature. He liked the psalm beginning " Take heed unto the thing that is right . . . " " Not on the whole," he commented, " a bad definition of a *Gentleman*. One who strives to do right because it is right and who is ' merciful and liberal '." He felt a sense of relief in this vague religion of nature, understandable after the intense moral pressure brought to bear upon him almost in babyhood. And yet there were things that puzzled him. Emma, the half-sister who had helped to bring him up, died in 1911. " She was as near being perfection of human self-sacrificing love as it is possible to conceive . . . a saint-like life, with no unkind thought for any human soul." And yet, he marvelled, poor Emma was a narrow Christian. Even the psalms were not always to be moulded to the new philosophy. Psalm 22, for instance, how explain that away? " . . . indeed it reads like a forecast of Gethsemane."

On the plane of social and professional life there can be little doubt that Flora was an improving influence. She told Edward that in Hong Kong he had gained a very useful experience of dealing with men, though perhaps she was a little over-optimistic about the future.

" You would be interested to see how he has learned to handle his Council . . . and I anticipate that this experience will enable him to get on with the officials of the C.O. better than he has ever done before. He appreciates as a part of worldly wisdom and administrative skill the importance of not antagonizing men with whom the exigencies of the public service make it necessary to work. He can smile philosophically now where he used to be indignant, and with him, as with all sound hearts, increase of experience has brought a mellowing increase of sympathy."

(F.L. to E. J. L., 14 January 1912).

It cannot be said that he was sorry to leave the Colony. In accepting Hong Kong, he had staked his professional career to win personal happiness and it seemed that he had been completely the loser. But life's gambles are seldom quite absolute in their results. He had gained some personal happiness and he had achieved some professional satisfaction. But as the shadow of war in Europe took on clearer shape and men like Kitchener and Sir John French came out to take stock of Britain's imperial defences, he became restless. When he went on leave in 1910 it was with the wish that he should not return.

It is possible, though by no means certain, that he would have been happier in his work if he had not carried it on in an almost continuous state of friction with the Colonial Office. (On this question Flora had been over-optimistic). The points at issue could not, for obvious reasons, be so fundamental in Hong Kong as they had been in Nigeria. His main charge against the Office now was of inefficiency and his main difficulty arose from his position suspended between an informed and able community and a distant department. He hated the secrecy and even subterfuge to which Colonial Office instructions sometimes drove him.

" I am personally at all times strongly prejudiced in favour of frank and open speaking and facing and owning mistakes and it goes strongly against the grain to gloss over things and make them appear other than they are." (L. to F. L., 12 May 1908).

When Flora, after a visit to the Colonial Office to discuss opium and the University, came away disconcerted " to find how little they knew in the C.O. of the work that is being done in the Colonies," Lugard replied that he understood that Hong Kong was run by a young man called Stubbs,[1] whose dispatches the others signed, and that there was also another, named Harding, " who shares with him the responsibility of approving or censuring the Governor's actions.[2]

[1] Stubbs, (later Sir) Reginald Edward, G.C.M.G., 1876-1947; 1900 Colonial Office; 1913 Colonial Secretary, Ceylon; 1919 Governor, Hong Kong; 1926 Governor, Jamaica; 1932 Governor, Cyprus; 1933-7 Governor, Ceylon; 1938 Vice-Chairman, Royal Commission on the West Indies.

[2] Harding, (later Sir) Alfred John, K.C.M.G., 1878-1953; 1901 Colonial Office; 1909 assistant private secretary to Crewe, and subsequently to Harcourt; 1920 Assistant Secretary; 1928 Director of Colonial Audit.

In reviewing the treatment of Lugard's communications to the Colonial Office in this period it is impossible not to feel some sympathy with him. The proportion of strong criticism seems high and there is something approaching hostility and derision in the tone of some of the minutes. There is "a good deal of nonsense" in one paper; others of Lugard's proposals are "monstrous", "preposterous", "absurd" or "fatuous"; his methods are "bull-headed". He has "despotic tendencies" and is—this was Stubbs—"an Imperialist with a very big I." It is hoped that "the F.O. will inflict the snub which is deserved." Rarely, indeed, does the Secretary of State or his second find time for the minute that might have raised the whole level of comment by some more imaginative and dignified appreciation. Lugard hit back but only to earn further censure: his style is "terse and offensive"; a message is "rather insolent". There was bureaucratic merriment over one of Lugard's vices of style; when he reported that "they would all be prepared to formally consider . . ." the exclamation was "surely they didn't *all* split their infinitives!"

Lugard sometimes got a little of his own back. The young Stubbs was sent out to collect comparative information upon staff salaries. Lugard invited him to Government House but as "a mere guest". When he proposed, before starting his special work, to investigate all the departments, Lugard found his enemy delivered into his hand. With great suavity he asked him if he had the authority of the Secretary of State for this; if he required any information, Lugard himself would be glad to give it him. The young official therefore took a country walk to think it over. Flora was even more blunt, asking him "frankly and sweetly" whether "he felt justified in forming and stating opinions on subjects about which he knew practically nothing." The guest was probably glad that Lugard had never seen his minutes and that Hong Kong officials were not aware of the opinion he had expressed of their service, that "even the cadets were prepared to advance claims to act for the Almighty." In later years, when the young man had become Sir Reginald Stubbs and a very able governor of Hong Kong among other places, he must have smiled grimly as he realized that another generation of young men at the Office were probably polishing their powers of sarcasm at his expense.

The Colonial Office was, however, justified in one censure. Lugard, so eager and self-confident and so little trained in the routine of the

Civil Service, tended to resent " interference " with *his* colony: he was now tempted to control its external relations. The temptation was strong. As we have seen, great men of all kinds were guests at his house and it was natural to him to talk freely and fully with them. He established excellent relations with the Portuguese in their neighbouring settlement at Macao. But the place that really mattered to Hong Kong was Kwangtung and its capital Canton. A few hours away by boat and even less by train when the railway was opened, physically and politically, it was an immense distance from Peking. But that was where the British Ambassador, Sir John Jordan, was posted and all relations with China were in his hands. The Colonial Office complained that Lugard would not see that all these matters bore upon foreign policy and that " Sir Edward Grey knows a good deal more of what is going on than he does."[1] The next year Lugard took the offensive and complained that the Consul-General of Canton had not reported to him serious riots there which might have had repercussions in Hong Kong. Early in 1911, when the new Viceroy on his way to Canton was entertained by Lugard, the two discussed methods of checking the alarming growth of crime on both sides of their border, and later the Viceroy privately asked Lugard to help and advise him over this difficult problem, an almost unprecedented approach. The two concocted successful joint measures for security and extradition.

Through the much aggrieved Consul-General at Canton rumour of this collaboration reached Sir John Jordan and he wrote a very stiff dispatch. He admitted that this was an old difficulty, dating from as far back as 1868, but the procedure had been carefully worked out and there had never before been such a flagrant breach of it. Lugard had been congratulating himself upon the speed and success of his negotiations with Canton and the Ambassador's letter came as a severe shock. He instantly recognized that it was just. He had done wrong and he must face the consequences. He could even wonder whether he would be recalled as a punishment. His frank confession seems to have disarmed the Office. The difficult situation was saved by the " high esteem " in which Jordan said he held Lugard and by the friendly personal letter he wrote upon receiving Lugard's dispatch. " He is a good, earnest, real man with whom it is a pleasure to deal," Lugard told Flora. Finally, when Lugard left Hong Kong, no letter was warmer,

[1] Minute by Cox on Lugard to Crewe, 12 June 1909, C.O. 446/356.

or gave Lugard more pleasure, than a generous tribute from the minister at Peking.

As Lugard's period came to an end it became clear that Sir John Jordan's appreciation of Lugard was shared very widely in the Colony. The unofficial leaders, Chinese and British, made more than one attempt to persuade the Colonial Office to prolong his tenure. Upon his last day in Council he made his dry and modest farewell. Dr. Ho Kai in his speech as senior member drew attention to the financial success which had marked Lugard's regime but above all to his achievements in winning the respect and confidence of the Chinese. The European tribute compared the good feeling between the two sides of the Council under Lugard contrasted with the acrimonious debates of former years. " That good feeling, Sir, is entirely due to the accessibility of your Excellency to all classes of the community." Nor was it light praise when a member of more than twenty years' standing could say of a man of Lugard's unpromising qualifications in this sphere, " You have during your tenure of office done everything you could to foster trade and industry. It is due in great measure to your interest in commercial affairs that the position of the Colony is better than when you came."[1]

But Lugard's real farewell to the Colony came five days later when the University was opened. The University Court was already in being with himself as Chancellor in the chair. An eminent public figure and oriental scholar, Sir Charles Eliot,[2] had been appointed, not without controversy, as the first Vice-Chancellor. The opening was Lugard's great day. Sir Hormusjee Mody had died some months before, having insisted upon naming all the seven scholarships he founded after Lugard. As at the laying of the foundation stone, all Hong Kong society, the leaders of which, like a stage army, appeared at every public function, were there, representatives of many nations. They climbed to the E-shaped building, red brick with facing and colonnades of white stone, crowned with its high clock tower. Such was the narrow financial margin on which the start was being made that a great bazaar was being held to raise money. The ceremony took place in the great hall, with its domed roof, its dais, gallery, teak pillars,

---

[1] *Legislative Council Reports*, 1912 Session, 7 March, p. 18

[2] Eliot, the Rt. Hon. Sir Charles, G.C.M.G., P.C., C.B., 1862-1931; 1900-4 H.M. Commissioner, British East Africa Protectorate; 1905 Vice-Chancellor, Sheffield University; 1912 Vice-Chancellor, Hong Kong University; 1919-26 British Ambassador, Japan.

stained glass windows, and empty niches waiting for the statues of benefactors. For the University song the Colonial Secretary, Clementi, had composed a Latin ode to a Catullan metre with an echo from the Book of Job, and a local musician had composed the music. The University motto was "Light of the Orient", but these ambitious words were later changed to the somewhat more modest claim to "*Sapientia et Virtus*".

Mr. Mody, the son of the benefactor, presented Lugard, as the first Chancellor, with a silver model of the main building. It stood in an honoured place in the drawing room of Lugard's English home until his death.

The University was opened upon March 11th; Lugard left Hong Kong on March 16th, the Colony having been reassured to hear that Lugard would be succeeded by his ex-Colonial Secretary, Sir Henry May. At the final ceremony in the City Hall, Flora made the effort to appear and she was carried on to the platform in a chair, "fashionably dressed" the newspapers record, in a cream satin costume with black revers, a black picture hat with a large upstanding ostrich feather "and carrying a bouquet of red roses". Lugard was presented with an address, read by a leading local merchant. Nothing in it pleased him more than the tribute to Flora, "It is no secret—you have made it none—that you and she are one in all things."[1] From the Hall the two went straight down to the pier, through a guard of honour which, as upon their arrival, was made up of British, Chinese and Indian troops, and the Governor's launch took them off to the mail steamer, bound for England.

Lugard had governed Hong Kong for very nearly five years. There can be no claim that it had been a great governorship. Greatness would, indeed, be difficult to achieve within the cramping physical and political conditions of a Colony which calls for tact and ingenuity rather than for bold innovation and energetic leadership. The newspapers in their final appraisal of his work picked out his sympathetic handling of the Chinese; the ability and economy of his management of the Colony's depressed finances; of his interest in public works and the sensible and courageous way he had guided the Colony through the dangerous months of the Chinese revolution. Finally, of course, his creation of the University was praised, especially by the Chinese,

[1] *China Overland Trade Report*, 25 March 1912.

though even to the end there came from some quarters the reproach that in it he had sown dragon's teeth.

All the appreciation, on the evidence of these pages, seems to be just. His first contribution was his own character. It is difficult for those who have not lived in a colonial society, especially one of mixed races, with all their suspicions of each other and of a semi-autocratic government, to realize the immense importance of integrity in the man at the top. Brilliance, even expert knowledge of the country, are secondary to this in importance. Everyone who met Lugard had only to look him in the eyes and exchange a few words with him to know that he was in contact with an absolute sincerity and simplicity, upon a rock-like basis of physical and moral courage. The British community, official and unofficial, living an uprooted and temporary existence in the tropics, and the watchful leaders of the subject race, could see in Government House an example of perfect married life, of industry, confident patriotism, and generous desire to serve.

In Hong Kong Lugard was not simply marking time between his African appointments. He was constitutionally unable to work upon a " ca' canny " basis and he gave his services without stint to Hong Kong. He studied and admired the character of the people with whom he was dealing. He was even willing to discuss with Flora when, writing from Japan, she raised the question, whether the yellow race was not superior to their own. He agreed that the worst Europeans were below their worst but maintained that the European best were superior to the yellow best. And yet, " I pause when I think of the extraordinary generosity of the merchant class to all charities and education and not merely in money but in personal service and interest." And again, after a Chinese social meeting, " They are really wonderful in the adroitness of their civility and manners." In spite of his necessary pre-occupation with their insanitary habits he could also appreciate the good qualities of the masses. On a visit to Canton, carried through the crowded and filthy streets in a chair:

" The thing that strikes one in the jostling crowd is the *intelligence* of their faces, their diversity within a common type, and the absence of wrangling and quarrelling. Generally speaking, you see a vast number of industrious folk, each in his own cell or pigeon hole, working hard, sallow and intelligent." (L. to E. J. L., 10 January 1908).

Lugard was not quite indifferent to the great moral question-mark which hung over the dealings of the West with China. His papers contain a correspondence he carried on in 1910 with Sir Edward Grey which reveal his state of mind. Pondering over the great need of China for help from the West and her bitter resentment at the terms upon which she was forced to receive it, he groped his way towards a plan which would meet China's attitude and which was in line with his growing realization, remarkable in such an assured patriot, of the part international agency could play alongside the imperial action. The scheme, in a few words, was for a seven-power association for financial and technical development in a selected part of China, carried out in partnership with the Chinese authorities who should draw 50 per cent of the profits and devote them to social reforms in the region. Sir Edward Grey, though recognizing the dilemma the plan was meant to meet, replied that he saw no chance of an adequate response from either the European or the Chinese side. But in the course of the correspondence Lugard put to the Foreign Secretary the unanswerable problems that were troubling him, and which, forty years later, are revealing their full magnitude.

"I confess I cannot myself find an altogether satisfactory and logical answer to the question ' Why assist China to become a World Power and so become a menace, industrially if not by armaments, to Western civilization?' It is true that ' militarism ' is singularly absent from the temperament of the people *at present*. But will it remain so when such a radical change has transformed her? Her action in Tibet is in evidence. But granting her the most pacific of intentions, there remains the industrial yellow peril. The usual answer is I suppose that it is immoral to endeavour to arrest the development of a people and even not to assist in every way."

He asked the question " How is the West to assist China to obtain real progress without danger to itself?" and gave first the realist's answer, that there was no way of avoiding the danger except by partition and separate control by the several nations. There was even the hope that Western civilization would tempt an oriental race into luxury and decadence, " a somewhat cynical view ". The development scheme he had put forward might, with really fine leadership on the British side, be the best reply.

"I have felt that an effort of this sort made by a really disinterested and thoroughly honest Englishman, even if it fails, cannot but show the

Chinese (as I hope my University scheme will also do) that the British have their welfare at heart, and are willing to promote a scheme in which we have no preponderant advantage over other foreigners, with that object in view."[1]

Here we have at least the partial answer Lugard gave to the moral doubt that has been the recurrent antistrophe in the paean of British imperialism from at least the eighteenth century. He dreamed of shifting the basis of the relationship with China from a bilateral basis to one that was more international, and from one of force and self-interest towards one of agreement and common interest. Such a conclusion could hardly have been expected of a soldier and an ex-African Governor, temporarily posted in the Far East, and in the year 1912.

[1] Lugard to Grey, 11 August 1910, L.P.

PART THREE

Nigeria 1912-1918

CHAPTER XIX

THE TWO NIGERIAS, 1912-1914

LUGARD ARRIVED back in England from Hong Kong on April 19th, 1912. He spent six months in London preparing for the large new task which awaited him in West Africa. They were necessary months. Colonial officials serving long periods in the tropics grew into their prime in climates which, in more than a physical sense, were different from that of Britain. Today communications are fuller and swifter. But in Lugard's time, if a governor were to express in his administration the political art and ethics of his own country he needed, during his leave, to breathe deeply its changing and generally invigorating atmosphere.

It is possible that the Britain of 1912 was a little too invigorating for the Lugards. The nine-year period of peacetime Liberal rule which succeeded the ten years of the Conservatives was now well advanced. The crisis over the reform of the House of Lords was over, but Lloyd George was outraging the propertied classes by his first advances towards the goal that was later to be called the welfare state. The Agadir crisis also was over but, for all the shock it had caused Britain and France, they had not read this German omen in its full gravity. The darkest shadow the Lugards could discern over the British scene was thrown from Ireland, Flora's own country. Just as they returned, the Home Rule Bill was introduced in parliament and there were demonstrations in Ulster. In his earlier life Lugard had been fairly open in his political affiliations, being guided by an expediency based frankly upon his plans for Africa. But Flora had more definitely conservative principles so that, though she had friends in both parties, she would write in her letters of " our side ".

" The other side ", however, was for the moment showing itself much more accommodating to the Lugard plans than might have been expected. Mr. Lewis Harcourt, who was Colonial Secretary

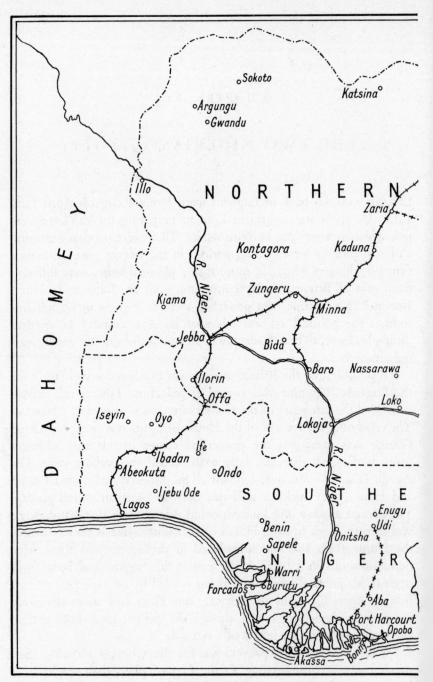

Nigeria 1912

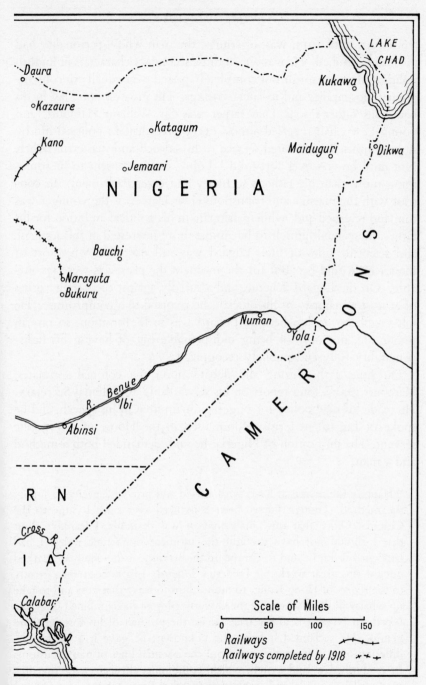

Nigeria 1912

from 1910 until 1915, was, of course, the man whose personality had most to be studied. He was one of those secondary characters in English political life who are almost completely passed over equally in contemporary biographies and in later writings. His greatest fame lay in his being his father's son. That father was Sir William Harcourt, and young Lewis had reversed almost every precedent in political life by sinking himself in devoted service to his adored and masterful father. Not until he was over forty did " Lulu " at last consent to be something more than his father's secretary and enter parliament. In contrast with the massive and robustious elder Harcourt, the younger was thin and reserved and, while passionate in his political ambition for his father, he seemed himself to be almost more interested in the aesthetic and scientific sides of life. Lugard was still uncertain what sort of master he would be. But for the moment the prospects were favourable. On the Lugard Scheme, and assuredly against the strong wishes of at least a majority of his officials, he resorted to a compromise. He felt unable to do less because Lugard was in the position, so rare in public life, not only of being indispensable but of having his indispensability fully and publicly recognized.

On June 27th, during the debate upon the colonial estimates, Harcourt gave a long report on his stewardship as Colonial Secretary. He made his new policy for Nigeria a main item in his speech, and he spoke of Lugard in terms seldom used in the House of any public servant. The unification of Nigeria, he said, demanded both a method and a man.

" Happily the man is at hand with a tried and proved capacity to supply the method. Though I have been convinced ever since I came to the Colonial Office that this amalgamation was desirable, I frankly admit that I should not have thought the moment opportune unless I had happened to know and to command the services of the one man marked out for this great work, Sir Frederick Lugard. I have been able, greatly to the regret of Hong Kong, to induce him to leave that post and to take up what will shortly become the Governorship of the combined Nigerias. Northern Nigeria is in the truest sense the product of his foresight and genius. He reclaimed it from the unknown; he gave it a legal code, differing only in its civilization from the essential lines of native custom; he established a land system which, combining altruism with revenue, may well be a model and inspiration to other Protectorates . . . On my earnest solicitation he returns now to the field of his early and brilliant labours, to complete and consolidate what has proved, I think, to be the greatest tropical province of the Crown ".

He then went on to describe the special arrangements made for the tenure of the post.

"All the details cannot be settled now, but I shall hope that Sir Frederick Lugard will spend six months in the colony and six months at home, but the six months will not be treated and will not become leave, though they will act, I hope, for part of the time, in that capacity but he will be in close consultation and work at the Colonial Office."[1]

The "six months" was to apply only to the first year. Harcourt had made it appear as a continuing plan. When Flora pounced on this Harcourt explained that he could not be tied to it. " I am afraid that you will think me a hard taskmaster, but I suppose that is the fate of all Colonial Secretaries." (Harcourt to F. L., 1 July 1912).

Alfred Lyttelton, as the last Conservative Secretary of State, commended Mr. Harcourt for belatedly honouring the pledge he had himself given to Lugard and which had been repudiated by Lord Elgin. In his speech the influence of Flora could be detected. " One of the great drawbacks that our great Pro-Consuls are under in the tropical districts is the complete loss of family life because very seldom can their ladies accompany the Governors to these districts."[2] And he went on to take up the question of continuity of administration. There is some evidence that on this point Harcourt had allowed himself to be partly over-persuaded by his popular Conservative predecessor.

After the first year, according to Anderson's letter,[3] the normal division would be four months in England after eight in Nigeria, while the words in which both this arrangement and Lugard's status while in England were described were vague. The officials had been forced to retreat from the absolute negative which they had obtained under Elgin. But they had only fallen back upon their naturally strong position ready to advance again at the first favourable opportunity.

Lugard had now reached the summit of recognition and opportunity. The years of hard trekking and fighting, of almost desperate administrative improvisation, of uncongenial but successful service in Hong Kong, were over. He was now presented, in a chorus of eulogy, with the largest and most difficult task the colonies could then offer.

[1] *Parliamentary Debates*, 27 June 1913, V. 40. 512.   [2] *Ibid.* 542.   [3] See above p. 364.

He could approach it with more than his ordinary self-confidence. He knew his Northern Nigeria; the summer would suffice for him to master on paper all he did not know of the southern part. He had secured his Scheme in full for the first year, and in part for those succeeding, and he could thus indulge the two strong desires which had pulled him in opposite directions, the one to maintain uninterrupted control of his territory and the other to spend as much time as possible with his wife. To conclude this satisfying list, he was to have his brother to work with him in the specially created post of Political Secretary.

Flora had regained much of her strength during the long voyage home from Hong Kong and she set to work at once to plan the new life. Even before she left Hong Kong she had seen what she must do. She must have a house in London,

> " and a fairly roomy one, so that we may have a sense of home, and that when Fred is in England he may dispense hospitality of the easy kind he likes to his officers and to the many people whom he will need to see officially . . . It will be my business to see that, when he comes home each year, he shall find his relations with the London world in proper trim." (F. L. to E. J. L., 6 December 1911).

With her resilient mind, she saw how she could make the best of what had to be.

> " To me, I must say, London is a delightful prospect and if Fred likes the African work when he gets to it again the separation will be mitigated for both of us; for me, by the thought that he is doing a fine work and enjoying it—for him by the thought that I am living permanently in a climate which agrees with me, surrounded by conditions which I like." (F. L. to E. J. L., 14 January 1912).

She quickly found a suitable house at 51 Rutland Gate, bought the lease for £5,000 and proceeded to the happy task of redecorating and furnishing it. With the expenditure of another £2,400 she made what she felt was a fitting London headquarters. As her biographer admits, she now gave free rein—her husband's biographer would say, too free a rein—to her expansive promptings.[1] She had meant, as an economy, to let Little Parkhurst, but when the time came the attractions of a country house to supplement a London residence proved irresistible. After all, she could argue, there was a proper standard for a Governor-General and his salary *was* £6,000 a year.

[1] Bell, *Flora Shaw*, p. 273.

While accomplishing all this Flora had to face returning ill-health. In Flora Lugard had married anxiety. His unceasing devotion to her only made the burden heavier. For the rest of her life she was subject to intermittent illness, made bearable by short intervals of vigour and by her gay and resolute spirit. The wound made by the knife of the American surgeon in Japan refused to heal and further operations and various drastic treatments were attempted. The constant worry and the periodic crises added greatly to the strain of Lugard's life when they were apart and deepened his determination to fight for the fullest possible version of his Scheme.

He left England on September 18th, 1912. On the voyage he renewed his friendship with Eaglesome, his Director of Railways and Works. This friendship, which was to be lifelong, was not only precious personally but most useful officially, in view of the importance of the tasks now awaiting of railway development and public works. Another passenger was Ah You, Lugard's silent and perfect Chinese servant, who had chosen to accompany him to England and now to Africa.

As in Northern Nigeria, so through the years of his Governor-Generalship, Lugard's letters to Flora supply an intimate revelation of his actions and thoughts. Lugard—it was typical of him that he kept a careful record—wrote an average of four pages a day to Flora, making, for his periods in Nigeria, 3,375 closely written pages. Of these, 272 were lost during the war through the torpedoing of ships. The great bulk is of an intimate personal nature but, intermingled with this, there is a running commentary on his official activities. To Flora Lugard could release all the accumulated pressures and frustrations of the day. Some of his major grievances, such as those against the Colonial Office and his least congenial officers, run as continuous themes in these letters. When quotations from them are given, they need some mental subtraction, but not to an extent that cancels out the whole sum of his indictments. There is another continuous theme. As we have seen before, he was a phenomenal worker, or overworker, and he could only keep up a pace that would have broken most men by setting himself what seemed impossible tasks, and then astonishing himself at their achievement. But, if he were to break all these imaginary records, then Flora must support him in this self-congratulation.

After calling upon his fellow governors in Sierra Leone and the

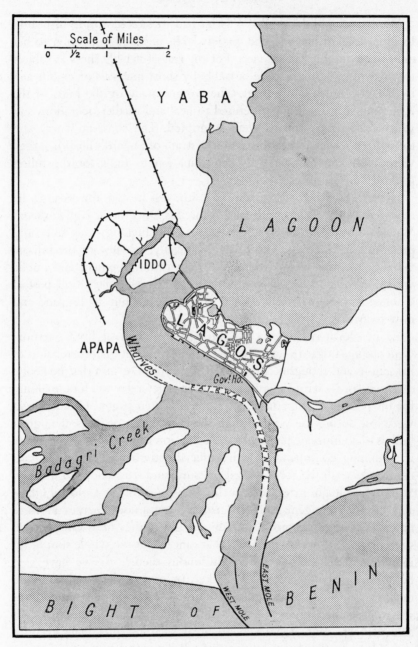

Lagos 1912

Gold Coast, Lugard reached Lagos on October 3rd, 1912. The port was not physically situated to give an easy welcome to its governor. The steamer had to lie two miles off the shallow bar, alongside which, at a cost of a million pounds, the great moles were then being constructed—a task of several years—to enable ocean-going ships to enter the harbour. Lugard's party arrived in pouring rain but this cleared before they got into the government "Lifeboat" and steamed past the eight British and German steamers lying in the roads and politely "dressed". Then across the bar, with a strong sea running and the boat tossing horribly on the broken water. The Acting Governor, Boyle,[1] had begged to be excused, as crossing the bar would incapacitate him for the day, and had sent the Acting Colonial Secretary, Donald Cameron,[2] a future governor of Nigeria, as his deputy. A drizzling spray broke over them and Lugard grabbed Ah You's mackintosh. Then another mile in the wide river-like channel which leads into the 50 square miles of branching lagoons behind Lagos, with all the further network of waterways leading out of it and running behind the coast. The bunting on the twenty ships in the harbour and on the customs wharf sagged in the rain as Lugard disembarked to go through the ritual of his arrival as the King's representative with its presentation of leading officials and unofficials. Landing on the western shore of the lagoon of Apapa, where the commercial wharves were already being constructed alongside the new railway, Lugard went on a long slow drive by motor-car circling round the Lagoon and over the two great bridges which span the creeks on each side of Iddo Island and so to the real heart of Lagos, which had been an African town before the British annexed it sixty years before. This is another island, crowded with shops and warehouses, churches and government buildings and a vast warren of African houses containing some 80,000 people. Finally, the procession of cars went along the shore road, the Marina, to the point just opposite that at which he had landed.

" The Marina, along which we drove at a snail's pace, was lined with

[1] Boyle (later Sir), Alexander George, K.C.M.G., 1872–1943; 1893–5 Colonial Service, Straits Settlements, 1895–1910 Colonial Service, Uganda; 1910 Colonial Secretary, Southern Nigeria; 1914–20 Lieutenant Governor.

[2] Cameron, (later Sir) Donald, G.C.M.G., K.B.E., 1872–1948; 1890 entered Colonial Service, British Guiana; 1904 Assistant Colonial Secretary, Mauritius; 1908 Assistant Secretary, Southern Nigeria; 1911 Principal Assistant Secretary; 1914 Central Secretary, Nigeria; 1921–3 Chief Secretary and Deputy Governor; 1924–31 Governor, Tanganyika; 1931–5 Governor of Nigeria.

crowds of natives shouting and seemingly very delighted, waving their hands and gesticulating and universally enthusiastic if they caught my eye ... I must say there seemed a dash of genuine intention about all this, and I believe the common people who all knew of me by repute ... seemed genuinely glad—the women flung up their arms and shouted things in Yoruba at me and one small boy in a boisterous excitement slowly ejaculated ' God save the King '." (L. to F. L., 3 October 1912).

There were many triumphal arches, bearing legends " Ekoile " [Lagos, your home]; " Governor Lugard "; " United Nigeria "; on the Lagos club was hung a vast " Floreat Rossalia ", doubtless the work of an old boy. More ambiguous, but referring, perhaps, either to the relationship between north and south or between the two races, was another placard, "Entente Cordiale". He thought it would all have pleased Flora, " even though you, like myself, might have judged it to be of little meaning and that they may be hooting me in the streets before long."

The motor at last turned in through the big gates and confronted the solid, square, white, two-storeyed house which was to be Lugard's headquarters for nearly six years. It was already some thirty years old and it has changed little in the succeeding years. A fair-sized garden held back the crowded city. The rooms led off galleries running round a central well, so that for all its size, the house had remarkably little accommodation. Lugard's office was in front, over the porch, looking out over the harbour. At the house were the Acting Governor and a large party, and the Chief Justice in his scarlet robes, ready for the ceremony of swearing in the new Governor. Then the heavens opened and a deluge came down and drenched the guard of honour and filled the grounds with water. After the ceremony Lugard turned to look at the great pile of telegrams of congratulations, cherishing one more than all the rest. "Welcome, doing well." " I confess I was worrying," he told her, " I was in a state of tension and nervous strain to know if it would come." And he sadly remarked that night that at times their love " seems to bring more anxiety and pain than joy." (L. to F. L., 3 October 1912).

Lugard had decided merely to pass through Lagos and Southern Nigeria on this occasion and to go on the next day to his other territory, Northern Nigeria. It was a very new experience for him, with thousands of miles of African " foot slogging " behind him, to embark on a train to take him to the northern capital, Zungeru, the site which he had to cut out of the bush ten years before. A special train awaited him at the station, with six long carriages, designed by his predecessor, Sir Walter Egerton,[1] with luxuriously fitted rooms, bathrooms and servants' quarters. Following him on his first tour of inspection round the country will enable us to see with his eyes the immense and varied region which he had been commissioned to unify.

From Lagos his train ran north for a hundred miles through the green vegetation of the southern Yoruba chieftainships. Here, the scene is dominated by the oil-palm. From the air it seems as though the whole region is decorated with little green stars made by these beautiful palm trees, the chief wealth of Nigeria, showering their easy uncultivated harvest upon the southern tribes. In the clearings made for cultivation around the rectangular Yoruba houses of brown mud could be seen cocoa, maize, yams and other crops. Lugard went on past the large African cities of Abeokuta and Ibadan, through slightly drier land, with the oil-palm thinning out, making for the frontier of Northern Nigeria and crossing it at Offa, some 140 miles from Lagos as the crow flies.

The train may have *looked* luxurious but both the speed and the motion on the 3 ft. 6 in. gauge left much to be desired. Early on October 5th it reached the Niger at Lugard's old station at Jebba. He looked at the familiar reach of the river upon which in 1899, he had sculled out in a dinghy in order to read Flora's letters in peace. " Sad letters they were, but wonderful letters, and they taught me to know you at a time when neither of us dreamed that we should ever be married to each other." (L. to F. L., 7 October 1912). There was, as yet, no bridge over the river, so the train was ferried across to run for another six hours to Zungeru. Here all the same ceremonies which had marked Lugard's arrival at Lagos were repeated.

He still felt ignorant and therefore troubled about the south, but he had looked forward eagerly to stepping upon the familiar soil of his own Protectorate. Yet it was at Zungeru that the first shadow fell upon his administrative prospect. After Lagos, the wooden Government House he had built there now looked a poor thing, with Flora's furni-

[1] Egerton, Sir Walter, K.C.M.G., 1858–1947; 1880–1903 served in Straits Settlements; 1903 High Commissioner, Southern Nigeria; 1904 Governor, Lagos; 1906–12 Governor, amalgamated Southern Nigeria; 1912–17 Governor, British Guiana; 1931 Member of Malta Royal Commission.

ture and hangings suffering Africa's rapid decay. (Ah You, with Hong Kong standards, and already bewildered by black Africa, was horrified at such accommodation for his master.) But this troubled Lugard much less than the disturbing reception which he was given by the Acting Governor of Northern Nigeria, C. L. Temple, the senior Northern Resident who would be Lugard's most important colleague. Boyle, the Acting Governor of the Southern Provinces at Lagos, had not only vacated Government House but had received his new chief with every possible honour. But Temple, tall, untidy, dreamy, meeting Lugard with his charming smile, had not only remained in Government House but, explaining that he had expected Lugard to stay on the train—two miles away, with the temperature of a baking tin when standing in the sun—gave him and his staff inadequate and makeshift quarters in a few minor rooms of the house. " I had," Lugard told Flora, " a small bed with a tiny camp mosquito net on four sticks tied to it and the *necessary arrangements* were abominable."(L. to F. L., 5 October 1912). Even more unpleasantly significant, Temple seemed to assume that he would retain his private secretary and aide-de-camp as if he were still acting the governor's part.

Temple was to play a large part in Lugard's life during the next five years in the north and was to leave his own very individual mark upon the region. He was a man who, at a time when social background was a stronger source of confidence than it is now, could claim to hold his own with Lugard. His father was Sir Richard Temple, first Baronet, a very eminent member of the Indian Civil Service, who added to high offices in India the parts of writer and member of parliament. A recent historian of India has raised some doubts as to whether this father was a wholly attractive character, and asserts that he was not greatly liked by his more junior colleagues.[1] The young Temple must have breathed in administrative ideas and ambitions and the atmosphere of public life from his infancy and it is surprising that he did not follow his father into a service which then offered so much both of adventure and prestige. Instead, he began by striking out upon lines very much his own. As a result, in 1901 Sir Richard Temple had approached Lugard through Goldie, explaining that though his son, then thirty years old, was a rising young officer in the consular service, he was ready to sacrifice his prospects for the chance of serving with Lugard in

[1] P. Woodruff, *The Men Who Ruled India: The Guardians* (1954), p. 57ff.

Northern Nigeria. His qualifications included some unusual items. He had already distinguished himself as a geologist and had won recognition for experiments in surveying by astronomical observations. As a boy he had ridden alone on a mule across South America in order to study the life of the Indians. Stranger still, he was an artist, both in spirit and in his ability to make quick sketches in virtue of which he was able later to illustrate his book with caricatures which hit off the dignities, humours and villainies of his African charges and at least tried to capture the beauties of the African scene.

Once in Northern Nigeria Temple's enquiring mind turned eagerly to the study of native customs: he became expert in the Hausa language and regarded the African through the eyes not only of an artist but also of an amateur psychologist, amused, affectionate but without illusion. He chose a wife who matched him, both socially and professionally. Olive Temple was the younger daughter of Sir Reginald MacLeod, the head of the MacLeod clan, and she, too, became an expert upon Hausa society, lecturing in Britain and writing a serious book upon the subject.[1] As a further and rather unexpected item of his character, Temple appears to have been abnormally sensitive about his status.

It is, perhaps, hardly necessary to describe Lugard's response to his reception at Zungeru. He felt that Temple " had not appreciated the position, and when we began to talk business in the evening I found it necessary to explain to him very clearly that he was now Secretary and I was the Governor." In spite of this Lugard could not help liking him. " He was most nice; not bumptious or disagreeable at all, but simply muddle-headed, and he had addressed me a long series of letters, speaking as Governor of N.N." (L. to F. L., 7 October 1912.)

Lugard was soon back in Lagos. It would have been asking too much of him after his experience with the Hausa and with the monarchical Baganda, not to be repelled by the social atmosphere of the capital of Southern Nigeria. And he had now to make his first contact with one facet at least of the stumbling block in the way of Nigerian unity— the deep differences between north and south. Writing three days after his return to Lagos he confessed to Flora " I am somewhat baffled as to how to get into touch with the educated native . . . To start with, I

[1] Mrs. C. L. Temple, *Notes on the Tribes, Provinces, Emirates and States of Northern Nigeria* (Lagos, 1922).

am not in sympathy with him. His loud and arrogant conceit are distasteful to me, the lack of natural dignity and courtesy antagonize me." (L. to F. L., 10 October 1912).

Part of the trouble was Lugard's sense of being in a new and strange country after the familiar North. Then, upon his return from Zungeru, he had a heavy attack of malaria, that most depressing of fevers. Fortunately, he had his brother to take charge of the situation, and Ah You to sleep at his door and wait upon him. In spite of his indisposition he used what time he had to inspect the large new harbour and other works started by his predecessor and to entertain the Lagos official and commercial community. Among his guests were the local African leaders—barristers, doctors and members of the Legislative Council. Some of these he liked, especially two men who, cultivated and successful, had almost become part of the British system. " Carr is more like a very intelligent European, and he appeared to hold much the same views on the subjects we discussed as I did myself." The next day he had a long talk with the other leading educated African, Kitoyi Ajasa, who had been educated in England, but whom he found rather less well-informed. " Still it is something to get a little in touch and hear their views." (L. to F. L., 24 October 1912). Both these Africans were later knighted.

Lugard spent only three weeks before setting out upon the next part of his preliminary tour. This was to the city of Ibadan. It was only eighteen years before that he had struggled through the northern part of the Yoruba region on foot as a pioneer explorer. But again he was more critical of the railway than grateful for it. African trains are seldom speedy and this one moved at 20 miles an hour along the 120 mile run from Lagos to Ibadan, and jolted so terribly that Lugard was unable to work with his pen or to write to Flora, a waste of that precious element, time, which exasperated him now and upon every journey.

In Ibadan he was seeing a great Yoruba centre, the largest negro city in Africa, with a population of some 170,000—it is now half a million—a genuine native city which existed before the European came into the interior.[1] Ibadan presents an almost unbroken sheet of tin roofs covering one-storied African huts or houses. These now give

[1] For a brief description of Ibadan in 1930 see Perham, *Native Administration*, pp. 178-200. For a full, more recent description see G. Parrinder, *Religion in an African City* (1953).

a reddish appearance from dusty and rusty tin, but in Lugard's day the houses were still largely thatched. Ibadan sprawls over seven hills and, like most indigenous cities in Nigeria, the majority of its people are only semi-urban in their way of life, as they live alternately in the city and on their farms with which it is surrounded. Ibadan was, and is, a place with an independent spirit. It was then ruled over by a complex gerontocratic council of civic chiefs.

Lugard drove for miles about the city in his motor-car in tornadoes of rain; interviewed the old chiefs; learned all he could of Yoruba religion and custom from the Resident, Captain W. A. Ross, and gave dinner parties to the local officials and traders. He found both classes " a bit casual " and made his first close acquaintance with an administrative situation distastefully different from the one he had imposed on the north. Already he could feel a nasty nip of opposition in the political air. He sent Flora some Lagos newspapers from Ibadan.

> " You will see the class I have to deal with. They say that the Lagos people will not be reduced to the ' futile condition ' of North Nigeria without a protest, and a big noise. They had emissaries all over Ibadan, Oyo and all the Yoruba towns stirring up the people to resist loss of their lands and taxation. They regard it with suspicion if I blow my nose, and think it means some deep-seated plot. I am beginning to think they are hopeless and that any attempt to make any reform with their co-operation is impossible."　　　　　　　　　　　　　(L. to F. L., 2 November 1912).

And he pointed out that the Government had to pay rent for land taken for the railway, which had enormously increased the wealth of Ibadan and so " Government pays to be allowed to confer benefits." These were only first impressions—depressions he called them—of questions which had to be squarely faced later.

From Ibadan Lugard re-visited Oyo, which he had reached from the north during the race for Nikki in 1894, and saw again that high dignatory, the Alafin of Oyo, with his vast entourage of courtiers. This time it was a different Alafin, and Oyo certainly saw a different Lugard from the ragged, imperilled traveller who had managed to struggle alive out of the wilderness of Borgu.

His next move was north again to spend nearly three weeks at Offa wrestling with the arrears of files and the jungle of Nigerian finances and to prepare his budgets for north and south with an eye to the coming amalgamation. Here Lugard really began to grapple with his task, though he was suffering agonies from a dental abscess. (It must be the minor ailments too slight to demand a complete intermission of work which are the greatest plague to public men). Those engaged in general administration find it hard to explain what they are doing in their long days in the office. But, writing from Offa to Flora, he gave a description which shows the number and variety of the problems presented in 1912 by an African region where large-scale modern developments were just beginning.

" Generally speaking I have taken over the actual Gov. of both these countries and all papers which should go before the Gov. come to me . . . The task of grappling with two new Administrations at once has been a colossal one. In this division of my work the subjects I have dealt with wholly defy recapitulation. There are literally hundreds (or thousands). In N. Nigeria the current papers include a large number of Mining questions . . . In S. Nigeria . . . large issues press for immediate decision as, for instance, whether the New Wharves and Railway to them shall be gone on with at a cost of $1\frac{1}{4}$ million (some of the plant costing £200,000 being already under order) . . . how to meet present congestion, without embarking on an ill-digested scheme which may prove money wasted, including also a coal wharf and Petroleum (dangerous goods) wharf. Then there are similar questions in regard to the Electric Supply, and the Tramway . . . shall Gov. do what is necessary or get a private Company, and if so on what terms? The same applies to a new dock costing I think it is £30,000 which has been wrecked on its way out—shall we replace it? I am for private enterprise instead of Gov., but the conditions involve much thought . . .

In Administration there seems to be a perfect chaos, and a great deal of crime and also of official incapacity, etc. Yesterday I had a case of 744 murders by ordeal, also accusations in a different district against a Gov. Officer of horrible things, including aggravated rape and possible murder. Today I have 6 murder cases to consider, a trial of two separate officers with a view to dismissal, a decision regarding the recent police mutiny in the ' Egba free state ' and so on . . . It is clear that this Administration wants regularly cleaning out like the Augean Stables. . . The problem of these ' Independent States ' baffles me at present. But my primary task has been the Estimates. These I have revised and recast both in N. and S. Nigeria, going through them from page to page and item by item over and over again, personally redrafting a good deal of the N.N. Estimates in my own hand. Then there are in addition the Combined Estimates which meant the reorganization of the Railway and an exhaustive examination into the whole Loan expenditure of S.N. . . . the Marine, Customs, etc., these Estimates alone have proved a colossal task, but it is now practically finished, and both are now drawn up in a form to facilitate Amalgamation. Of course in addition to this work there has been the inevitable interruption of interviews, entertaining and journeys, so I have been pretty well occupied." (L. to F. L., 13 November 1912).

From Offa he went back to Lagos for the big week of the year in this city, when the meeting of the Legislative Council coincided with a three-day race meeting on the course which makes such a pleasant green space close to Government House. The Governor must attend this event each day, and see the homebred northern ponies compete against imported stock, most of them owned by British and Syrian traders. The Legislative Council, which legislated for Lagos Colony and Southern Nigeria, met in the hall of Government House, with the rituals common throughout the colonies, though for the parchment-coloured locals Lugard had known in Hong Kong there were black Africans among the six unofficials who confronted the seven white-uniformed officials, as Lugard, in a frock-coat, read his message to the Council.

On top of all this work of governing the large and still separate colonies while starting to create a new one out of the two—a task which the Colonial Office were probably right in thinking that no one without Lugard's energy could have attempted—there was a round of social functions, dinners, a great ball, marquees on the lawn, a visitation of Frenchmen from Dahomey with their ladies, diversions which the central figure called " tomfoolery " and " very incongruous at a time of stress like this."

On December 2nd he sailed from his wharf just opposite Government House upon his next tour of investigation. Southern Nigeria was then divided into three provinces, Western, Central and Eastern, in addition to the Colony of Lagos, and he had now to visit the Central and Eastern Provinces. As on land, so on sea, the luxurious fittings of the Governor's new transport did not compensate for the horrible motion, caused by her necessarily shallow draught, and Lugard was seasick for the first time in his life as the *Ivy* left the Lagoon and took to the open sea on her way to Forcados, the westernmost branch of the vast island-studded delta of the Niger.

Here, as everywhere, he had two tasks. One was to get a grasp of the administrative situation by seeing the country and by meeting his officials, and the African chiefs and their councillors; the other was to study the whole range of material development, especially as concerned railways, wharves and other public works. For this reason he took Eaglesome with him throughout his tours. At every station all the European officials and unofficials of the district came in to be presented to him; he would go to dinner parties and return them, and inspect any important buildings and activities the place could show.

Forcados, as a terminus of the Niger, was the headquarters of the all-important marine department of Southern Nigeria. There Lugard saw the workshops for the fleet of government ships, the floating docks and slipways. The volume of trade which came here from up the river was clearly displayed by the agencies and warehouses of the many firms. Close to Forcados was Burutu, the former coastal enclave of Northern Nigeria and the headquarters of the Niger Company, now shorn of its administrative status but commercially busy under its Agent-General with his large house and princely salary. Eight thousand casks of palm-oil, each holding nearly a ton, were piled on the Company's wharf or being fed into large ocean-going steamers, which, in the Forcados river, were able to come alongside. The place had therefore become the main commercial outlet for the river-system of the interior, though it was to be rivalled by Lagos, with its railway, as soon as the moles and harbour works should allow the entry of large ships. Forty or fifty Europeans were here living on a piece of land reclaimed from the surrounding swamps. Forcados was no social health resort; as the tide went out a stench arose from the waste ground which was crawling with crabs and mud fish.

Lugard now sailed eastward, past the Niger mouths and along the coast. One of the main purposes of this tour was to explore the southeast coast for a site at which he could build a port. This would be the outlet for the projected eastern railway. In a canoe, drenched with sweat, Lugard and his staff probed the steamy hot creeks and mud flats, over which the canoe had at times to be hauled. A fringe of uncanny looking mangrove trees stood in the water, while behind rose the densely forested banks. Lugard and Eaglesome found the head of an inlet near Okrika which seemed suitable and which Lugard afterwards named Port Harcourt in honour of a Colonial Secretary towards whom, at that date, he still felt extremely friendly. That then virgin site is now Nigeria's second port with a population of 72,000.

Lugard was everywhere greeted by the coastal chiefs and people, energetic amphibious traders who had been in some touch with the western world for two centuries or more. They were now in protesting mood. The commercial importance of the coastal settlements had already been partly outflanked by the Niger Company's monopolistic penetration up the great river—hence the horrible Akassa raid[1]—and Lugard's railway plans must still further undermine their position. He was, moreover, already studying the long-established local system known as House Rule. British opinion, quick to smell a whiff of slavery, had been expressed by questions in parliament about House Rule and there were demands for the abolition of a system which had been legalized in 1901. Yet, in spite of present problems and future difficulties, the people of the creeks and estuaries at Forcados, Bonny, Opobo and Calabar, turned out to give the Governor their own kind of water-borne welcome, one very different from that of either the Yoruba cities or the Hausa states.

The main port of call was the relatively old town of Calabar, which had been the capital of the former Southern Nigeria before it was amalgamated with Lagos in 1906. It was now the headquarters of the Eastern Province. The *Ivy* turned into the wide estuary of the Cross river and steamed up to the pleasantly sited town, with its three hills and fine trees, a welcome relief after the dull flat maze of creeks and mangroves. Half the population seemed to be on the banks of the river and the rest on the water. Edward Lugard counted 40 large canoes, each holding 30 to 40 rowers, cutting round the *Ivy* at a great pace, with horns and trumpets blowing. Most of the crews of very strong-looking men were naked but for a loin cloth, others were got up in some kind of fancy uniform. One crew wore firemen's brass helmets. With streamers of coloured paper flying, Lugard went ashore in a shining " Governor's gig ", manned by smart Southern Nigerian marines. His motor-car had been brought on the *Ivy*—another striking contrast with his former conditions of travel—and in this he made a tour past the usual guard of honour and thousands of school children. Calabar, though very different from the old indigenous Yoruba cities, was even then a town with a long history, for it had

[1] See Vol. I, p. 530.

been an early centre for Western traders, while the missionaries had been there from the eighteen-forties, long before any European government had been established. The parade of chiefs was striking, though in a very different way from those in the west and north. The Eastern tribes had no culture or national dress of their own comparable with those of the north and west. They were borrowers, eager and not always discriminating. So the chiefs, when lined up, presented a strange spectacle, some in well-cut European suits from Britain but with tinsel crowns, others in top hats of all colours, one dressed as an admiral but with a gold crown. Lugard bowed to them gravely and later had long discussions with them. He was struck by the command of English shown by many of these coastal traders. He found there were so many mission institutions that he had to spend an extra day in order to make a really thorough inspection.

His first impression of south-eastern administration was poor. He quickly decided that nothing less was required than " the creation of an administration, for but little exists . . . native policy is non-existent. The two Provincial Commissioners were in practice Lieutenant Governors who did as they pleased. . . My policy is revolutionary and these fellows do not know where they are. But I find them a nice lot and I find I have a reputation here which makes it easy for me to do what would be practically impossible for any other man." This strong self-confidence was further nourished on this tour. At Opobo, for example, a usually very assured chief had shown himself highly nervous, and Lugard was told that his reputation, based upon what he had done in the north, was such that he was regarded with awe. " It always seems to me so odd," was his comment, " that anyone should be in awe of me, and I always fear that I am too familiar and easy-going." At Calabar a French missionary told Lugard that the people had come away from the event saying " This is the man for we." Lugard asked whether, after the way his northern land policy had been traduced in the south, they could think he was sympathetic towards them. " No," replied the Frenchman, " it is not that. They say you are a ' Leader' of men and they are proud to have as a Governor a man who is a ' Leader'." (L. to F. L., 12 December 1912).

Before he left Calabar, Lugard met another inhabitant of the place, who can justly be described as one of the greatest women of her generation. This was Mary Slessor, the Scottish mill-girl who had

worked with the Presbyterian mission in this region since 1876, and
had gone alone into the lands behind Calabar, armed only by her
faith, and a down-to-earth sort of courage that impelled her to box
the ears of huge murderous men, to struggle against slavery, twin
murders, poison ordeals, inter-clan fighting, and all the fierce and
terrible customs of the forest people. " Ma ", as the Africans called
her, was now sixty-four. So great was the influence she had built up
over the people that the Government had treated her as an unofficial
District Commissioner and made her president of the local native
court. But she was the last woman to present herself upon any public
occasion, and it seems that when Lugard came to Calabar she had to
be fetched from the bush. She honoured Lugard so far as to put on the
hat, the shoes and the stockings which she generally did without. The
worn, shabbily dressed little woman was brought up to Lugard, standing in all his plumed official dignity, and the two kinds of authority
confronted each other. Lugard took her hand and said he was proud
to do so. He was already plotting against her, being determined that,
even against her will, her work should be given public recognition.
In Lagos he and his brother had read her record and been deeply
affected by it. Edward Lugard wrote in his diary upon this day:

" Reading her life story—as I recently had occasion to do in drafting a
dispatch to the Secretary of State asking for H.M.'s bestowal of some
recognition of her great service (this is *confidential* and must not be repeated
until the award appears), a great lump rises in one's throat. The long
years of *not* quiet but fierce devotion—for they say she is a tornado—
unrecognized and without hope of, or desire for, recognition, in these
blatant days of self-advertisement. Her great work has been combating
witchcraft and the awful custom of murder of twins, and she has established twin villages and farms, and always has some little black urchin
about her. But she has not feared to go under fire to separate warring
tribes . . . "

It may be imagined how great was Edward's disappointment when
he found that Miss Slessor had slipped back into the bush as soon as
her presentation was over. But Lugard's proposal of an award was
accepted. She was made an Honorary Associate of the Order of St.
John of Jerusalem in England. It was no easy matter to get her down
to Calabar for the presentation by Mr. H. Bedwell, the Provincial
Commissioner. She took the honour as one conferred upon the

mission as a whole, while for herself: " May this be an incentive to work and to be better than ever I have been in the past." And in an address to the children she told them to be faithful to the government for, at bottom, it was Christian and, as her silver badge proved, friendly to the missions. When news of the award was known congratulations came to her from all over the world. Lugard sent his own " appreciation of this well-earned reward for her life of heroic self-sacrifice." " I shall never look the world in the face again until all this blarney and publicity is over," was her comment.[1] Three years later she died.

On December 12th Lugard was back at Lagos to spend a few days before going north. Among many other tasks he had to interview the Eleko, head of the so-called White Cap chiefs and of the former royal dynasty of Lagos. "He came attired in a hat trimmed with heavy silken lace and a silver crown in front of it, also a heavy brocade or Taborette cloth such as you have for heavy winter curtains. It was gorgeous, but I think, hot." (L. to F. L., 12 December 1912).

By December 25th, he was in his jolting special train again. He stopped on the way north to visit another large Yoruba chieftainship of Southern Nigeria, that of the Egba group, with its centre in the city of Abeokuta. Lugard was already turning a very critical eye upon the little Egba state with its high degree of internal self-government. But the reckoning was not quite yet; this was merely a quick, courtesy visit. The leading chief, the Alake, showed the usual southern indulgence in gorgeous array: " On his hands massive rings of gold like the links of an anchor chain and massive necklets of gold." His bodyguard, on horse-back, wore "an arrangement of different coloured plush cloaks, feathers, gold lace and tinsel." (L. to F. L., 24 December 1912).

On again, over the Niger, and back to Government House, Zungeru where, if the décor was depressing, the administration, in spite of his doubts about Temple, raised his spirits.

" Perhaps I should not say it since I am in principal part responsible for the creation of the N. Nigerian Administration, but the contrast between it and S.N. is extraordinary. N. Nigeria runs itself . . . In S.N., on the other hand, papers *pour* in and they have large questions of policy etc. which might have been decided 12 years ago."

(L. to F. L., 24 December 1912)

[1] W. P. Livingstone, *Mary Slessor of Calabar* (46th edition, 1935), pp. 304-7.

From Zungeru he went on to Kaduna, to which he was already thinking of transferring the northern capital, and on the last day of the year reached Kano, where a great Durbar had been arranged for New Year's day.

Lugard had already sent letters and the customary formal presents to all the northern rulers. In the Lugard Papers is a great sheaf of their replies in the Hausa language but inscribed in large Arabic lettering, and sometimes on fine parchment and with coloured illuminations. How much genuine feeling lay behind the emirs' courtly expressions? Certainly the manner and the speed of Lugard's occupation of their country could not fail to have impressed them with both his power and his generosity, and their loyalty, shown in the Satiru crisis was soon to endure successfully another searching test. There follow a few translated phrases taken from their letters, the expression of an isolated Muslim culture as utterly distinct from that of southern Nigeria as from that of Britain herself, the expression, indeed, of another age.

" *The Shehu of Bornu.* Letter from the Slave of God, Abu Baku. To our good helper, our prop, the solver of our difficulties . . . the one who carries our heavy burdens, Governor Lugard. With salutations more scented than the musk perfume and sweeter than honey." After that, " may God prolong your life, the helper of those who help others . . . "

The Emir of Bida sent " . . . salutation and good will shining bright as to the planets and constant as their light as the return of morn and eve. Oh! my Chief, my Leader, we ask God to prolong your life in prosperity and health. My present to you is a sword in a silver scabbard and two gowns . . . "

From the Emir of Yola, to the deputy of the King of England, the Governor who holds all our country in his hand and rules it all. A thousand salutations and fealty and homage repeated."

From the Emir of Jamaa, " I and my peoples, all of us, will not refrain from praying for you morning and evening . . . I told my people to rejoice . . . " (i.e. at Lugard's safe return) " We rode our horses and raced. I read your letter morning and evening and it makes me very happy."

From the Emir of Nupe, " Many beautiful salutations, a clean love, etc. . . my present to you is two turkeys, 1 package of plantains and 1 of limes."

399

There was one letter which Lugard sent which received no answer
It was to the pagan " king " of Kiama. " You, Kiama," wrote Lugard
" are my oldest friend in the country. Since I returned as Governor
have fulfilled the promises I made to you in 1894, when you made a
treaty with me, and I rejoice to think that you are now in peacefu
possession of your country. May you live long and prosper." Bu
Lugard's old friend, whose all but tragic story has been told, was no
more. " Poor old Kiama died the other day " wrote Lugard sadly.

The Durbar at Kano was a great occasion.[1] On the race-course, on
the level plain of Kano, some fifteen thousand horsemen, and an un
counted number of footmen, each grouped round their chief, deployed
in front of Lugard. There were 800 of the West African Frontie
Force, with some 300 Mounted Infantry, who, in their smart turban
and lances with pennons, led the proceedings with a gallop past. Thei
smartness and precision rejoiced the heart of Lugard, who had created
the Force only fourteen years before.

" Then each Emir came past with all his horsemen, and some of them ha
most interesting processions, led horses most wonderfully clad in ricl
clothes—court jesters mounted and unmounted. Heralds and trumpeter
and native bands. In one there was a company of women jesters to
entertain the Emir on his travels. In some there were camels, in som
there were men in chain armour. I cannot describe the variety of th
distinctive officers, all of them I presume date back for centuries. The
came the Pagans, almost naked, skipping and dancing and yelling an
brandishing clubs—some in most weird array . . .When, at last, the las
had gone past, they began the salute. Each Emir with a picked band c
horsemen . . . charged down at full gallop halting a yard or two off in
whirlwind of dust. The Emir dismounted and came and knelt on th
ground and made obeisance."   (L. to F. L., 1 January 1913)

It was a relief to Lugard after all this to be alone for a few moment
with his letter to Flora. " I have hardly heard your voice at all thi
last day or two," he told her, " what with the dust and the shoutin;
and braying of trumpets, and the noise. I have been treated here jus
as if I were a King, and I am wanting to get back into my own prope
sphere, and on to my office stool. . . . This is somewhat demoralizin
and fatiguing, though perhaps I should like it better if you were her
and I could lay it at your feet."

[1] See *The Times*, 5 and 27 February 1913. The latter prints Lugard's dispatch to Harcou
describing the Durbar. See also the *Illustrated London News*, 15 March 1913.

As follow-up of the Durbar, he saw all the leading chiefs individually and the lesser ones in groups. Temple acted as Lugard's interpreter. The next day there were sports.

" All the Emirs were seated together—a marvellous sight when one recalls the bitter jealousies which formerly possessed them . . . Even the Chinese have little or nothing to teach these Emirs in the way of courtesy and good manners . . . But the Pagan dances were simply wonderful. There were tumblers and contortionists from Ilorin, and wrestlers and also pugilists. These latter impressed me more than anything. Round their right hands they had matting bound with rough native string making a most formidable ' boxing glove ', much more severe than a naked fist. With this they dealt each other blows in the face or body with their whole strength, sparring with the left hand. The blows were so heavy that I wondered serious damage was not done, but the surprising thing was the absolute good humour with which they were taken, and the genial way in which when a man was knocked down and vanquished, he accepted defeat. And so also among all these vast crowds of horsemen and footmen during all these 3 days belonging to rival Emirs who had grievances against each other, and each trying to aggrandise their own lord—not a single quarrel or even altercation did I see or hear of! Everyone kept saying to each other that it was a really marvellous sight which they would not for the world have missed. And so it was!"

(L. to F. L., 5 January 1913).

Perhaps the most surprising thing about this great gathering was for these proud Muslim emirs to associate with naked pagans who, until the recent coming of the British, had been their natural prey.

Before leaving Kano, Lugard inspected the city. Outwardly it had changed little since its conquest by him nine years before. Yet there were some significant changes. The long red walls of the city were beginning to crumble. Even if the Pax Britannica had not made them superfluous there was no more slave labour to keep them in repair. Inside them the vast red hive of the city looked much the same. But Lugard was shown the new clean prison which had replaced the suffocating black hole of the past, the new Treasury, the re-organized market, all administered by the emir's government, and the first rather tentative schools. It was significant too, that Kano now contained a hundred Europeans.

The next stage in Lugard's tour of inspection was a visit to the plateau. Going from Zaria, with its new cotton mill, in a light railway which was being built to serve the tin mines but which had not yet quite reached them, Lugard found himself once more in camp in grass huts at the railhead. From here his car climbed up to the wide level plateau, going up some 2,000 ft. from the hot dust-laden plains to the cool uplands; and from the cities and farms of the long-robed Hausa to the pagan tribes who had found a vast place of refuge in the high level land scattered with granite outcrops. Here he found naked men riding naked ponies, controlling them without any bit but with only a leather rope tied round the animal's nose and a single rein. The only clothing worn by the men were greaves made of bark or grass or of iron soldered on for life. The women, too, were naked, except for the tribute to modesty of two small bunches of leaves, worn fore and aft. This nakedness, so striking by contrast with the surrounding Hausa and upon such chilly uplands, and also the style of horsemanship, were still the vogue when the writer visited the plateau nearly twenty years later.

Lugard's task here was to go to Naraguta to meet the tin miners who, with the metal at £230 a ton in a world which was short of it, were crowding into this primitive country and beginning to tear up its virgin surface with their machines, turning the shy pagans into "labour" and drawing the Hausa up to highlands hitherto inviolate from them. The whole of the mining law was, in Lugard's view, in a hopeless muddle. None of his officers seemed to have any understanding of this very complex subject, branching into questions of survey, demarcation, prospecting, land rights, water rights, timber rights, tailings, royalties, and the rest. And Lugard was confronted here with a hard-headed lot of men, some of them earning high salaries and with big money at stake, organized in a local Chamber of Mines, and in a state of indignation at various grievances. They were impatiently waiting for the railway to reach the mines, so as to allow them to get up their heavy machinery. In the meantime, much of the ore was being won by "calabashing", by men standing in the water and swilling the earth in iron pans until the heavier tin sank to the bottom. Lugard's experience upon his Kalahari expedition was now of much use to him. Taking the whole thing into his own hands he spent the best part of a week hammering out the substance of a new Minerals Ordinance and new Mining and Survey Rules, drafting them himself and, in the interests of the natives, forcing some unpalatable restrictions upon the mine managers.

The experience enlarged his economic education and showed why mining was a lure which could draw capital into the rawest spots in the heart of Africa, while it fought shy of those larger and more arduous enterprises so necessary for the balanced development of the continent. " The process is most simple," Lugard told Flora of the mining companies, " it costs them 2½d to 3½d a lb. including every kind of expense (depreciation of plant, buildings, wages, etc.); the cost is £28 a ton. Put transport at £20 and royalties at £2, total cost is £50 and the London price is £220! The profits must be immense, at least 400 per cent." Later he raised his estimate of working cost to £100 but the price was to rise to £400.[1] These figures made Lugard writhe, less from economic principle—there is, of course, a case to be put in defence of high mining profits—than from hunger for revenue for his territory. One fact was especially exasperating. "It is cruel that we have all the expenses to bear and the Niger Company gets half the royalties, fees, licences, etc." (L. to F. L., 20 January 1913).

From the tin miners Lugard went back to Zungeru for ten days with the boxes which, in the interval, had filled his room. He struggled to achieve that full understanding with Temple which was so essential to him in view of his imminent departure to England from which country he meant still to administer Nigeria. He felt that he had failed; for all Temple's charm and Lugard's efforts the barrier remained. From Zungeru he went down to Baro on the Niger, the post from which the Kano railway made contact with the considerable river transport of the Niger. He took his officials with him and worked every day on board, all the way down the river in steamy heat, and with every crack shut up to keep out the clouds of insects.

This was the last lap of his long survey. He went on south down the river to Lokoja and on to Onitsha, the riverside town of the vast Ibo group. Here he visited the Church Missionary Society centre under Bishop Tugwell, and laid the foundation stone of new buildings. The impression the visit made upon Lugard was mixed. He could tell himself that the missionaries based their work upon something that lay outside ordinary worldly considerations. But, to an overworked

[1] *Nigeria: Report, by Sir F. D. Lugard on the Amalgamation of Northern and Southern Nigeria, and Administration, 1912–1919*, (1919), Cmd. 468, p. 37.

Governor, to be unworldly was to be unbusinesslike, and he suffered also from their determination, very natural to isolated institutions in Africa, but very exhausting for the visitor, to show every single item of their work. He wrote of

" Their ignorance of the usages of the world, their efforts to please and their damned bad tea. Their unconscious assumption that nothing matters except themselves, their mixture of sound work and stupid dress for their adherents. It is difficult to describe and complicated to understand. Sir H. Johnston described it without sympathy after accepting their hospitality, and earned their bitter resentment. I would sooner speak with respect and sympathy but one feels one is in another world. The surroundings are often those of an N.C.O. in the married quarters of a barrack—the soul of the thing is often grand. We entered a small mud hut of 2 rooms in which various negro children in absurd mission dress ran about and a small and pretty white child born at, and named, ' Zaria ', full of life, presented me with a bouquet. I was then asked to sit down and offered drinks but before I could well do either I was begged to come and view with all my staff, a new born (6 weeks old) baby . . . I learnt with feigned interest its weight, and the number of pounds it had put on in a given time, and I left the tiny object sleeping as I found it. Again I was urged to sit down (which I did) and immediately requested to come and be introduced to a number of Mission people, male and female, whose work was described in glowing terms at each introduction. I made efforts to get on to a rational plane . . . but I had little time . . . Then I visited the male and female hospitals, etc. We came back and the Bishop arrived and caused another flutter. Then they all robed and marched in procession between large groups of fantastic natives who were either over clothed by the Missions or almost nude on their own account. Hymns were sung and speeches made and prayers, and I made my address."

(L. to F. L., 6 February 1913).

A quite different impression was made by this visit upon Lugard's brother, who thought it a great function, and deeply admired the medical work of the mission. But then Edward was wholly at one with the purpose which underlay the superficial gaucheries of the missionaries.

From Onitsha the party sailed on down the widening Niger, learning about the Udi coalfields with their promising outcrops. They then transferred to the seagoing *Ivy* and turned westwards round the delta to Sapele. From here Lugard drove inland to Benin, the historic town of the Beni people, an off-shoot of the Yoruba, who had been in touch with sea-borne civilization from at least the early Portuguese visits. The town became famous as "The City of Blood" from its reputedly wholesale practice of human sacrifice and the massacre of an unarmed party of British and Africans in 1896,[1] an event followed by annexation. The Benin chiefs presented themselves to Lugard stripped to the waist, a widespread sign of respect in Africa. The Benis, Lugard decided, were intelligent and law-abiding.

> "They had, like the Baganda, established a regular form of government and, like them, their kings had degenerated into monsters of cruelty. It must be a very ancient kingdom dating no doubt to the 13th or 14th century, and the home of the highest art discovered in Africa outside Egypt, I suppose . . . Of course we talked much of *the* Massacre . . . and of the subsequent army under Dawson which broke the power of Benin. It took a strong force of, I believe, upwards of 2,000 blue jackets with artillery etc., and they had heavy fighting. That was in 1897, just when I came from South Africa to raise the W.A.F.F."

Then, as if to typify the new age,

> "The chiefs only raised one question—the water rate—for Benin has a laid-on water supply."   (L. to F. L., 12 February 1913).

"Truly," is the remark on the same day in Edward's diary, "the British raj, whatever its shortcomings, let some light into dark places."

Lugard now returned to the comforts of Government House, Lagos, for a strenuous four weeks before leaving for Britain.

It was strenuous for the Lagos secretariat too. Lugard had not been there a week before it was reported that all the officials were at breaking point and longing for him to go and relieve the intolerable pressure. "They have it in small doses," was Lugard's comment, "first at Lagos, then at Zungeru, then at Kano, then at the Mines, then at Calabar, and so on, but Ned and I have it all the time. It makes us both very fit and well." (L. to F. L., 19 February 1913).

Wherever he went, Lugard showed his immediate assumption of mastery. When he met incompetence or insubordination, his treatment was severe. One example may be given. A senior Resident—we will call him Mr. X—in the Yoruba country had been so long in one district that he believed he had a permanent right to it. As soon

[1] For an account see A. Boisragon, *The Benin Massacre* (1897).

as Lugard learned that he was still working towards the goal, attributed
to Sir William MacGregor, of building up little independent states,
Lugard at once posted him to another station. Mr. X protested to the
Colonial Office, which telegraphed to ask Lugard if he had abolished
X's Residency or promoted him. Lugard's brief answer was "neither".
X then telegraphed to Lugard his own protest at being moved. Lugard
ignored this. Finally, on his tour, Lugard did meet X. " I told him
his telegram had been most improper and I absolutely declined to
admit that any single officer in the country had a presumptive right to
be quartered in any place . . . My policy, I said was the very opposite
of MacGregor's . . . It was time that he was made to understand his
position clearly for his head is swollen exceedingly. I fancy he has a
clearer idea now." Lugard was mistaken. Later in the day he had to
report that a note arrived from X in which he wrote that " I desire to
confirm my oral assent of this morning to Y.E's proposals regarding
the future of Yorubaland " and ending " Y.E. may take it that we are
agreed in principle." Even Lugard was at a loss. "A man who can
write with that self-assurance after what I said to him has a head of no
normal dimension!" (L. to F. L., 12 December 1912).

Lugard equally exacted what he regarded as proper behaviour from
Africans. When the head of the Lagos chiefs, the Eleko, arrived at
Government House very late for his interview—an unpunctuality
which, it seems, was his usual custom—he was told that the time for
the interview was over. Next time he came punctually and wrote a
letter of humble apology, thanking Lugard for not reporting him to
the king.

The two officers who meant most to Lugard were, of course, the
two senior men whom he had found Acting Governors in Lagos and
Zungeru, and who were to be his Lieutenant-Governors after amalgamation. Boyle, of the south, suited Lugard perfectly, too perfectly, a
critical observer might have said. But the rift with Temple widened.
Lugard's account of it throws light upon all three men. Speaking of
Temple, he wrote:

" I spoke very frankly to him (as I have done several times before) telling
him that the proposed scheme by which I shall work at home at the
Colonial Office cannot succeed unless I can count on absolute loyalty at
this end . . . later I hope to delegate more. He assured me of complete
loyalty and indeed I do believe he means it. He is a nice nature and a

gentleman ... Boyle is *full* of common sense and as loyal as a man can be. He works for his Chief. Temple works partly for himself, partly (and I think chiefly) for ideals and objects of his own creating, and not for the policy of his chief. He thinks and acts as though *he* were the Guardian of the real interests of Nigeria ... He desires to safeguard his ideas from the possible encroachments of Governors by invoking Colonial Office support in the lower ranks. Boyle is incapable of that ... I rarely read a Minute of Temple's but that I feel that it is either an attempt to obtain power or else falls short of the real policy by some shortsightedness. When I read Boyle's Minutes almost invariably I say to myself ' Well, that is just exactly what I think ' ... Boyle is liked and respected and never seeks to force respect. Temple is in a nervous condition of sensitiveness that everyone is trying to minimize his power and position and to laugh at him ... Says he can't maintain his position unless the Commandant and all officers salute him, and if I don't agree demands that I shall refer it to the Secretary of State." (L. to F. L., 4 February 1913).

It is not difficult to reconstruct from this a different Temple from the one Lugard saw. It is doubtful if Lugard ever understood the inner meaning of Temple's attitude towards him, one which will be better understood when we come to consider their differences over native administration.

Lugard's survey was now over. He had been wherever the old river and the new rail communications could have taken him in his first short period which gave no time for the long marches to reach the provinces of Sokoto, Bornu and Yola, and Lugard's old march-land of Borgu. He had now surveyed the future Nigeria. In his last letter before he sailed he reckoned up, for Flora's benefit, the sum of his work in this first period of his dual governorship.

" The amount I have learned about the Administration of S.N. and all its chief questions and also of the Adm. up to date of N.N. is much. It seems impossible that it is less than 5 months since I landed here. I think I can claim I have done a year's work in the time ... Yes, it has been an eventful year, and counting our lives as one, and our interests as one and indivisible—all our years as each goes by are eventful and even this is hardly more eventful than its predecessors for many years back. And I do thank God that He has ' set my feet in a large room ' with large work to do and with a wife to help me and sympathize with me and believe in me ... " (L. to F. L., 23 February 1913).

CHAPTER XX

THE CREATION OF NIGERIA

THE NINETEEN-FIFTIES saw the leaders of the many Nigerian peoples trying to find a workable constitution for their vast area. In 1954 they compromised upon a federation of which the disproportionate constituents were the Northern, Western and Eastern Regions and the Southern Cameroons.[1] They thus diminished the administrative unity achieved by Lugard in 1914. But these very words " Nigeria ", " unity " and " federation " may make us forget what this study should recall, that this territory was no more than a large and populous block of Africa around which a foreign power had drawn a line—we have seen the part Lugard played in the drawing—to mark off its sphere against those of rival powers. What Lugard unified in 1914 was the administrative system of the ruling power. It was a re-organization from above. This was a very different process from that which has been attempted these last few years, the creation from below of a national and democratic unity by the peoples themselves. To the student of history the difficulty the African leaders have found in constructing their own version of Nigeria can cause no surprise. Rather we may marvel that after so brief and enforced an association of such different peoples, " Nigeria " should have become sufficiently a reality for its peoples to attempt even a federal structure of national unity.

If the modern Nigeria is, as a state, wholly a British product, no single person played a greater part in deciding the form of its unity than Lugard. Amalgamation is a dry word but as planned and carried out by him it became an all-embracing design incised upon the region with the deep-cut mark of his personality, with its limitations as well as its merits. It is this design, rather than the intricate mechanism of the fusion, which we must consider.

[1] The present (mid-1959) populations of these regions are Northern: 19,158,000; Western: 6,861,000; Eastern: 8,074,000; Southern Cameroons: 841,000; Lagos (Federal Capital): 350,000; making a total of 35,284,000 people.

It required no great fertility of mind in anyone looking at the map of a large square-ish piece of Africa under the rule of one colonial power, to think it ought to have a unified government. But the Colonial Office had flinched from what it knew would be a very large task, and the decision taken in 1912 was due to the appearance at the same time of the most urgent practical reasons for amalgamation with that of the man who could carry through the task.

The practical reasons mainly concerned railways and revenues.

In Britain we take our more than century-old inheritance of railways for granted. Moreover, we had a system of communications before the steam-engine was invented. In most of the old Africa—the northern parts of Nigeria were an exception—men and goods had never moved more than a few local miles from home. Railways, with the auxiliary roads and tracks which developed round them, brought the first possibilities of effective large scale government, of large internal and external trade, and of the movements and mixtures of peoples which could lead hundreds of tribes towards national unity. The account given in the previous volume of Lugard's marches to and from the coast to Uganda and through Borgu will have shown, as the journals of Mungo Park, Livingstone and many others showed before him, what it meant to walk through pre-European Africa. But the long drawn-out difficulties which accompanied the building and financing of the Uganda railway had given British Cabinets a dread of running again into costly and embarrassing ventures in colonial communications.

In the Niger region political and physical facts combined to present a most complicated transport problem. Britain had naturally drifted into using the native city of Lagos, her first acquisition and the main port, as a capital, and its development only proved how naturally unsuited it was for both functions. The site was one of very low islands in a lagoon, flanked with odorous swamps. At the entrance a shallow and unstable bar necessitated the expense and hazard of transhipping all cargoes well out in an ocean that was often turbulent. Many millions had to be spent over the years—and the task is not yet finished—in order to deepen the bar, clear the channel, construct deep-water wharves, bridge the islands, drain the swamps and reclaim land from the sea. From this difficult port a railway, begun in 1901, was carried to Ibadan and then on to Ilorin, and by stages to the frontier with the north until, in 1909, at Jebba, it confronted the wide Niger which it crossed by ferry and so on to Zungeru. Meanwhile, Lugard's Royal Engineer successor in the north, Sir Percy Girouard,[1] insisted upon his own northern transport system based on the north's traditional river system. He therefore, on the credit of the revenue of the reluctant Governor of Southern Nigeria, built what was, in effect, a competing rail and river system by linking Kano with Baro, at the highest point on the Niger to which ocean-going vessels could reach in the season of full river. As the length of that season proved to have been over-estimated, and as the cost of dredging the Niger had proved very heavy, this northern plan was not a great success. The two lines met at Minna near Zungeru, and the northern section to Kano was opened in 1911. Bad planning and construction led to the southern section costing the then appalling sum of £13,000 a mile, as against £3,800 for the northern section. Yet, though the southern section cost £4¼ million, even so, such was the productivity of the country, the railway was showing a net surplus of more than £¼ million by 1913. By 1912 the development of the whole eastern half of Nigeria was crying out for a railway. How far would the two governments be able to agree this time on the co-ordination of the southern and northern sections? How were they to be paid for?[2]

Here railway policy merged in the wider problem of finance. From a Treasury point of view the position was absurd. Nothing, apparently, but a political line drawn by Britain herself separated a rich region with a handsome surplus and a mounting graph of trade[3] from a poor region with a deficit. In defiance of the current principle of colonial self-subsistence, the British taxpayer had had to make good this deficit for eleven years with an annual subsidy for the administration in addition to the cost of the West African Frontier Force. The answer was obvious.

It will be convenient to look at the manner of amalgamation before the matter. First something must be said about the time-table. Lugard was appointed in May 1912. He sent in his first proposals in 1913;

[1] Girouard, Major-General Sir Edouard Percy, K.C.M.G., 1867-1932; 1896 Director of Sudan railways; 1898-9 President, Egyptian Railway Board; 1899-1902 South African War; 1902 Commissioner of Railways, Transvaal and Orange River Colony; 1907 High Commissioner, Northern Nigeria; 1908 Governor, Northern Nigeria; 1909-12 Governor, East African Protectorate.

[2] Geary, *Nigeria under British Rule*, p. 141.

[3] See *Annual Reports for Southern Nigeria*, 1906-12, especially the diagram in the *Reports*, 1909, p. 35.

amalgamation as a constitutional act was officially achieved on January 1st, 1914. But he continued to work out its many implications until he left Nigeria late in 1918. His solid final report upon it was written when he was in England, pending retirement. It was presented to parliament in December 1919, and finally published in 1920.[1] But in this account, except in one or two central matters, there will seldom be need to distinguish the stages of amalgamation, especially as they were mostly developments rather than revisions of Lugard's original plan.

In travelling round his vast area and daily administering two widely different territories, he frequently complained that he had no time in which to think out the answer to the formidable problem of amalgamating them. Yet, after returning to England on April 6th, 1913, and taking up his room at the Colonial Office with only his brother and one typist to assist him, he was able, on May 9th, to send to the Secretary of State a dispatch which covers thirty-seven printed foolscap pages, and contains the complete plan for amalgamation. This plan stood the test of almost every criticism and of six years' progressive implementation, emerging at the end as a working system substantially unchanged from his original design. As before, in Uganda and in Northern Nigeria, he seemed to *know* from the very first moment what he would do. And it was not as though he saw his work as simply a piece of administrative joinery. He made of it a work of re-organization, indeed of reform, in almost every department of government.

The plan was, moreover, nearly all his own. The officials, Northern or Southern, nurtured within their own separate traditions contributed little. It owed hardly anything to the Colonial Office where his plan was accepted almost unchanged. There most of the attention was given to an attack upon the Scheme. During mid-summer, from his room in the Colonial Office, Lugard launched one long dispatch after another, supporting his proposals with historical and analytical studies, draft laws and staff and salary lists. By the beginning of September Harcourt, advised by officials who, in spite of their growing objection to Lugard's way of doing things, were impressed by the results, gave his general agreement to the plan of amalgamation.

Lugard returned to Nigeria, after five strenuous months in England, at the beginning of October 1913. Upon January 1st, 1914 he went through the necessary amalgamation ceremonies in a spirit of dogged

[1] *Amalgamation Report.*

routine. To Flora he reported the great event in the minimum of matter-of-fact words:

" The ceremony went off as the Commandant said ' like clockwork ', and I received congratulations on every side regarding it, as well as on my new appointment as Governor-General—we started sharp at 9 at the Court House, and I made my speech first, then the instruments of Government were read—then 21 gun salute, then I was sworn—17 more guns—then Boyle and Temple and I read the King's and Harcourt's telegrams. Then I addressed the populace from the balcony, and drove home. I came all alone—the streets being lined with soldiers, blue-jackets and police and I returned with Boyle and Temple and Ned—then I swore in James and the C.J. at Government House then the Legislative Council, and Executive Council and we finished I think about ½ past 12. It was suffocatingly hot in the Court House and I was wet right through."

Immediately after the ceremony Lugard went up to the north.

The Colonial Office had sent out Strachey to be present at this event, and to travel round Nigeria and see it at first hand, at this period rather an exceptional procedure. He was a distinguished member of a distinguished family, who had come over from the Foreign Office to the Colonial Office. Charming, humorous, musical, with a fine brain intent upon the larger issues, he was popular with everyone. Except Lugard, who had opposed his coming. He could hardly see the man behind the Colonial Office intruder and he found the sight of this enquiring visitor disturbing.

" I wonder if he (Strachey) realises that the function he saw like a gala day in Europe might, if it had been the wrong thing and done in the wrong way, have given cause for riots! But of course these are Colonial office men who know everything from the office point of view and cannot be aware of the kind of forces with which they are dealing. He is sufficiently absorbed I expect in assimilating the oddity of seeing naked children running about the streets and in the local colour and temperature!"

(L. to F. L., 2 January 1914).

In making his declaration of the unification of the country Lugard pronounced little by way of oratorical benediction upon his plan. In brief words he made an appeal and a promise.

" To succeed in such a task would be impossible unless I have the goodwill and co-operation of all classes, Official and Unofficial, irrespective of race or creed, and I take this opportunity of earnestly asking for that co-operation and loyal assistance, assuring you at the same time that, so far as in me lies, I shall not spare myself nor find any work too hard or arduous, if I can thereby advance the true interests of this country and of each individual person in it, whatever his race or creed or however humble his rank."[1]

In the first volume we saw Northern Nigeria as one of the squares on the African chess-board on which the European powers played their giant game. In this volume, with his appointment to occupy and govern it, a much closer look at this part of the country was taken. Now we must take a third view, as if looking over Lugard's shoulder, at the map of the whole country which, in 1913, hung in his new office in Lagos.[2]

Lugard's journeys of 1912–13 through the familiar north and the mainly unfamiliar south, had shown him the human and physical diversities with which he had to deal. Between Southern Nigeria and the old emirates lay the zone where the Fulani advance of the early nineteenth century had penetrated only partially, and where the emirates were lightly extended amongst pagan groups, some subject and some independent. Though in Southern Nigeria there were large sections, running into millions, such as the Yoruba and Ibo, which were fairly homogeneous in culture, this by no means meant political unity and the number of wholly independent groups within the borders of the new Nigeria ran into hundreds, indeed, probably into thousands if all the fiercely independent little societies of the Ibo and the hill pagans of the north are counted. The separate languages were between two and three hundred according to the classification of " separateness ". Lugard, pondering over the map of his territory, was not dismayed by its irregular mosaic. His task, it must be repeated, was to unify administrations, not peoples. Even administratively, however, and especially at the level of what was then called " native administration " and is now called " local government ", Nigeria, as the next chapter will show, held problems enough.

First Lugard had to design the general shape of his unified government. Here, since the size and inadequate communication of the country forbade close administration from a single centre, there were

[1] Speech by the Governor on the occasion of the declaration of the Constitution of the Colony and Protectorate of Nigeria. L.P.

[2] For accounts of Nigeria at this date, see Geary, *Nigeria under British Rule*, A. C. Burns, *History of Nigeria* (5th edition, 1955), A. N. Cook, *British Enterprise in Nigeria* (Philadelphia, 1943); C. R. Niven, *A Short History of Nigeria* (1937); and Perham, *Native Administration*.

two main options. He could accept the division between north and south which he had inherited, or he could break the country into several large provinces with boundaries drawn with some relation to tribal and religious affinities. Several such schemes were presented to him. E. D. Morel drew up one dividing the area into four great provinces, in one of which Borgu and Ilorin were put in with the Yoruba.[1] Temple drew up one which would have divided the country into seven large provinces. Accepting the three southern provinces and Lagos colony he proposed that the north should be split into three. First, the Hausa states of the north-west; secondly the Chad territories, covering Bornu, Bauchi and Yola; thirdly the Benue provinces, containing the remaining southern and western districts along the Niger. This was very altruistic advice upon Temple's part since it would have abolished his own potential post of Lieutenant-Governor of the Northern Provinces in favour of three Chief Commissioners.[2]

Lugard rejected this advice. He decided to retain the division between north and south, bolted together by the strong Governor-General he meant to be. He gave as his reason for retaining the identity of what were now to be called the Southern and Northern Provinces that this would cause the minimum of administrative disturbance. Legislatively, he pointed out, the two parts were under quite different sets of laws and it would take a long time to assimilate them. Until that were done it would be difficult to disturb the existing boundary. These were solid reasons. But we should also see here the first sign of the very special Lugard character stamped upon the design. The dominant theme of the pattern was authority, an authority to be wielded by the Governor-General, and by one who meant to spend part of the year administering Nigeria from England. A closer unification or a new regionalization upon Temple's lines, both untried innovations, would equally have thrown a great deal of day-to-day work upon the Governor, preventing him from travelling, and would have demanded a strong deputy in his absence. This would have undermined the Scheme. But, under his plan, the Lieutenant-Governors could carry on with their dual routine much as before, while he, whether in Nigeria or Britain, held the control of all major policy in his own hands and gradually remoulded the country upon his own

[1] E. D. Morel, *Nigeria, its Peoples and Problems* (2nd edition, 1912), pp. 201-10.
[2] Temple to Lugard, February 1913 (with map), L.P.

lines. In his first dispatch to the Colonial Office on amalgamation Lugard made no secret of this reason.[1]

The Governor-General's powers were therefore defined in the largest terms. Lugard even induced the Colonial Office to give statutory recognition of the Scheme in the Letters Patent, so as to allow of his being continuously in charge of the country and merely appointing a deputy during his leaves instead of handing over to an Acting Governor.[2] He was supplied with the wholly official Executive Council usual at that period. But the Legislative Council, which had been extended in 1906 to cover the whole of Southern Nigeria, was not, as might have been expected, extended now to cover the whole territory. On the contrary, it was demoted to its former status as the legislature for the small Lagos colony only and its numbers reduced to four (nominated) unofficials, two of them European and two African, and six officials. This, too, was a typically Lugardian measure. But this does not mean that he had not good reason for it. He argued that the size of the new territory, coupled with its lack of communications, would make the periodic calling of a really representative legislature highly inconvenient. The European unofficials were mere agents of firms whose principals were in England and could not, therefore, take an independent part in a legislature. And the powerful and intelligent emirs who, at that stage would best represent the north, were wholly unready for such an institution. This meant that

" The native unofficials necessarily represented only the small, though important, class of educated natives of the coast . . . Few, I believe of the intelligent native gentlemen who, for many years past, had represented Southern Nigeria on the Legislative Council had even visited the coast ports outside the Colony proper and none, I think, had any personal knowledge whatever of the interior tribes, other than the Yoruba-speaking communities to which they belonged."

In these circumstances, he decided, a legislature would be of little value. He then went on to define a principle which he was later quite consistent in applying to the reverse racial situation in Kenya, but which British governments were to depart from in central Africa.

[1] Report enclosed in Lugard to Harcourt, 9 May 1913, *Correspondence (May 1913 to January 1914) relating to the Amalgamation of Northern and Southern Nigeria.* Colonial Office Confidential Print, African (West) No. 1005 (1914), p. 6. L.P.

[2] *Colony of Nigeria; Letters Patent constituting the Office of Governor and Commander-in-Chief,* 29 November 1913, pp. 7-8.

" It is a cardinal principle of British Colonial policy that the interests of a large native population shall not be subject to the will either of a small European class or of a small minority of Europeanised natives who have nothing in common with them, and whose interests are often opposed to them."[1]

Certainly his first experience in 1912 of the Legislative Council, as it then was, did not alter his quick judgment of its value. The estimates came on last after a long morning. The unofficials " were getting desperate hungry for lunch. As a result they voted over a million sterling in under three minutes! It shows how little use the Legislative Council is." (L. to F. L., 23 November 1912). This conclusion was natural enough. Yet the incident might have been taken to show how much African leaders needed the education which service in the Council could give.

By Lugard's settlement, Lagos Colony, though it retained its Legislative Council, was no longer to have a separate senior administrator and secretariat. The Lieutenant-Governor of the Southern Provinces was to administer it, treating it, with due provision for its status as a British Colony, much as any other province.

In place of a Legislative Council, Lugard invented a wholly novel type of body to be called the Nigerian Council. It was to be composed of the major officials with six nominated Africans, three from the north and three from the south. Its main function at its one annual meeting was to hear a long statement upon the past year's events and the plans for the future. Lugard made its meetings an important social occasion outside the council chamber, and he claimed, in 1919, that " So far as I am aware the opinion is universal that the Council serves a very useful purpose." It had, however, its critics both in Nigeria and at the Colonial Office, as being no more than an audience for the Governor-General's speech. Lugard's successor, Sir Hugh Clifford, in order to bring Nigeria into line with other British territories and to provide " the politically-minded section of the public with a legitimate outlet for their energies and aspirations," restored the power of the Legislative Council to legislate for the Southern Provinces.[2] But this was in 1922, after eleven years' experience of a united Nigeria; years, moreover, in which much had happened both to stimulate the

[1] *Amalgamation Report*, p. 19.
[2] Address to Nigerian Council, 26 February 1923, pp. 7-14; also, The Nigeria (Legislative Council) Order in Council, 21 November 1922.

political consciousness of the Africans and to demonstrate their loyalty.

These measures left legislation in the hands of the Governor-General after review in the Executive Council. Lugard wished to legislate without waiting for the approval of the Secretary of State. It was only after a long struggle, during which Lugard was on the verge of resigning over the issue,[1] that a compromise was arranged by which there was a two months pause between enactment and publication. This allowed just time for the ordinances to reach England and for a reply to be sent back by the Colonial Office.

The retention of the old division between south and north, with Lugard's special reason for it, led him to keep as many departments as possible in duplicate. But the main economic reason for amalgamation demanded the early establishment of some common services. Among these were the treasury, railways, (with the colliery), survey, military, audit, posts and telegraphs, judicial and legal, though with a legal adviser for each Lieutenant-Governor. Directors of medical and forestry services and for public works were appointed as central advisers to the Governor even though the departments were divided. Marine and customs, at first centralized, were later, for obvious reasons, included among the Southern Provinces' departments. This list represents a compromise. Lugard had strongly disagreed with the Colonial Office about the number of centralized departments. He had opposed them over the treasury, posts and telegraphs, and survey. He told Flora that the Colonial Office policy

" means that I shall get a large centralized secretariat which, as I have told them, is wholly opposed to my policy until there are better communications . . . It will also mean a duplicate Governor-General and then goodbye to continuity and the esprit de corps which a one-man rule can create but which is lost in alternating Governors."

(L. to F. L., 24 October 1913).

Provided with the necessary departments, the Lieutenant-Governors were left in direct charge of their regions submitting to the Governor-General any question which affected Nigeria as a whole. They were to present their annual budgets for incorporation in the general budget. They had their own secretariats. Lugard himself had a central Secretary, with a very small secretariat, and his brother was his

[1] Lugard to Harcourt, 26 October 1913, L.P.

Political Secretary, a title by which Lugard attempted to define the indefinable status of an *alter ego*, albeit a very subordinate one. There was, of course, a private secretary and an aide-de-camp. But Lugard's staff was unprecedentedly small for such a large appointment. At first this may seem hardly consistent with his high estimates of his powers and position. In reality it was a further example of them. Lugard wanted his powers to be at once flexible and fully within his own hands. He seems to have feared that, as with the central departments, so with a large secretariat, he would be chained by it to the capital and unable either to dispense with an Acting-Governor or to take his powers with him to England when he went on his unique kind of " duty-leave ". The Colonial Office strongly disapproved of his refusal to have a proper secretariat. Sir Hugh Clifford created one in 1921 and at the head of it he placed Cameron who afterwards wrote in withering condemnation of Lugard's attempt to govern with " no co-ordinating link save the memory of one man ".[1]

We have seen that finance provided the main urgency for amalgamation. It might have been thought that here the Colonial Office, with the Treasury behind them, would have provided both the initiating mind and the controlling hand and that Lugard, the promoted pioneer, would have been prepared, in this sphere at least, to play the subordinate. But he had fully grasped the importance of the financial side of his task. He soon decided he had taken over no officers up to his standard in this department, and he therefore undertook himself the greater part of the drudgery of working through four sets of past accounts, those for Northern Nigeria, for its native treasuries, for Southern Nigeria and the Colony. He re-cast them, item by item, into four new budgets, for the Southern Provinces, the Northern Provinces, the central departments and a much revised native treasury budget. No part of his work pleased and impressed the Colonial Office more than the speed and competence of his first budget for Nigeria.

The marriage of wealthy Southern Nigeria, with a revenue in 1912 of two and a quarter million pounds and a surplus of a million, to its impoverished northern neighbour, with its bare half million of local revenue, including a customs allowance of £70,000 from Southern

[1] Sir Donald Cameron, *My Tanganyika Service and Some Nigeria* (1939), p. 142; see also pp. 16-17.

Nigeria, was bound in face of the total expenditure, to bring both into insolvency. This was the more certain as Lugard was eager to draw upon southern funds to build up the still undermanned northern administration, while there were many development projects by which a united Nigeria should be signalized and advanced. In this age in which not only poor colonies but poor independent nations are regarded as having a right to development at the expense of richer nations, it is difficult to recall the hard limits within which Lugard had to make his plans. Britain was still working to a rule laid down sixty years before by Earl Grey, referring, as it happened, to West Africa, that " the surest test for the soundness of measures for the improvement of an uncivilized people is that they should be self-supporting."[1] Though Chamberlain's conception of the undeveloped estate was really incompatible with this principle, it was to be many years before, with the addition of three letters to his adjective, the full meaning of the obligations contained within this idea would be recognized. Lugard was thus forced to follow a policy of rigid economy and even, if there were to be any development, of an ingenuity bordering on trickery—that legitimate trickery to which most devoted colonial officials, from the District Commissioner upwards, have resorted in the interest of their people. Lugard first showed his skill in this line during the process of financial amalgamation during 1912, and he laid bare the process to Flora.

" I think you would laugh if I explained the lines on which I have done this thing. I amalgamate the Railways—an absolute and immediate necessity—also the Marine, equally necessary for different reasons. The bulk of the Public Debt I transfer to Railways on which it has been incurred, and I therefore take over the Public Debt (Interest and Sinking Fund) into my Combined Nigeria Estimates. This involves a net expenditure of about ½ a million. So I take over the Customs also (of course in each case both the Revenue and Expenditure) and as this has a Rev. of about 1½ millions, I have nearly a million at my disposal to meet the deficits of both Budgets. The S.N. Revenue is reduced to £108,000 from £2,000,000 by this process! and in order to make the process palatable to S.N. I tell them that it is necessary to transfer the Customs to the Central (Combined) Estimates in order to save them paying the usual £70,000 to N.N.! ! They will never arrive at the fact that in reality they leave me with

[1] Earl Grey, *The Colonial Policy of the Administration of Lord John Russell* (1853), p. 281, quoted by Sir Alan Pim in M. Perham ed. *Mining, Commerce and Finance in Nigeria* (1948), p. 226.

a large sum which I can devote to either N. or S. Nigeria as I like. . .
The net result is that I have prepared the way for Amalgamation, which
from the financial point of view has already been to a large extent effected.
This has involved a re-cast of the whole Estimates. I actually came out
with a surplus of £200,000 instead of a deficit to the same amount which
the C.O. writing to the Treasury demonstrated was the best they could
possibly hope. This surplus I have not of course allowed to appear, but
have absorbed it in Railway Capital works, much of which is more
properly debitable to Loan Account. This I can do later on, if I want the
surplus to build the new capital! Whether the C.O. will appreciate this
bit of juggling I don't know. I think they will as I have made it fairly
clear in my covering dispatch."   (L. to F. L., 22 November 1912).

It is to be hoped that the reader will be ingenious enough to " appreciate this bit of juggling "!

When Lugard wrote this he did not know that a world war was
coming which would cut brutally across all his plans for finance and
development. These will therefore best be reviewed at the end of this
section when Lugard drew up the final accounts of his stewardship.
But we should take up now his reference to a new capital.

Lugard did not like Lagos. Certainly it is possible to admire the
spirited people of this city with their large measure of sophistication
and their pride in what, for all its modern accretions, they can claim
as historically a tribal city. Yet it is not easy, at least for a European,
to find much that is congenial in its setting. Its physical defects as
a port have been mentioned. To the lagoons and swamps must be
added the often leaden skies reflected in the grey waters, the hot and
heavy atmosphere during much of the year, and the vast maze of
long-established slums which, at a density of 30,000 to the square mile,
in the hands of determined owners with the rights of British subjects,
have been the despair of a long succession of town-planners and sanitary
officers. Night-soil had to be taken out on a tramway and deposited
in a neighbouring lagoon on the tide, but it ceased to be possible to
deal with it all on the ebb. Lugard wrote "the flood brings it back
into Lagos with disgusting effluvia." He seldom felt well in Lagos.
From his office over the porch of Government House he looked at the
steamers passing by with dismal hoots while, more distantly from
across the stretch of dull water from the wharves of Apapa, came the
grind of working winches, the scream of whistles and sirens and clouds

of smoke. Small wonder that, when he got clear of Lagos and of the shrouding monotony of the southern forests and stepped out of his train into the dry air of the north and the open, windy plains, and tasted again the atmosphere of graded authority, he felt a new man, or rather the former man, the untrammelled High Commissioner.

His mind naturally turned to the finding of a new capital for the new Nigeria. He admitted now that Zungeru could only be defended for its temporary use as an advanced base for the occupation of the north. Its heat, its mosquito-infested rocks, and now its rotting wooden houses, all suggested its abandonment. Lugard chose Kaduna, central, high and fertile, on the river of that name, already headquarters of the Frontier Force and a suitable point for the junction of the western line with the projected eastern railway. Here he could plan a capital on a virgin site with an eye to vistas, and express, on the grand scale, that soldier's love of orderly lay-out which he had shown long ago at Karonga, at Fort George and at Kavalli. He asked Flora to make an ideal town plan for Kaduna and his officers called upon her when on leave to discuss their proposals. His hope was to make Kaduna his main capital, while residing at Lagos as occasion needed. But not at Lagos proper. His other hope was to shift the government offices several miles further inland to a higher site at Yaba. " Government House," he wrote hopefully but untruthfully, " would make an excellent hotel." It was not to be: war and the need for economy forbade it and successive Governors have had to remain confined between lagoon and ocean and watch from their windows an ever-increasing number of ships pursue their smoky way up the lagoon, while Chief Commissioners or Lieutenant-Governors enjoyed the airy amenities of Kaduna and of the new and verdant regional capitals of Ibadan and Enugu.

CHAPTER XXI

FIRST MEASURES IN THE SOUTH

THE AMALGAMATION of Lagos and Southern Nigeria in 1906 had not led to much assimilation between the two administrations. Nor, previously, as British rule had spread northwards from the coast, had there been even assimilation of Lagos Colony with Lagos Protectorate. Thus the three parts out of which Southern Nigeria had been composed still bore the stamp of British rule which they had been given by different men at different periods of policy. Lugard was, therefore, faced with a much more complicated pattern than that presented by a major contrast between north and south.

We saw that in the amalgamation settlement he had left the old territorial boundary as a line between the two groups of provinces. But it was no longer to be a barrier. His policy was assimilation and for him only one kind of assimilation was imaginable. It is true that in his Amalgamation Report he dealt politely with the question. " I regard it," he wrote, " as a means whereby each part of Nigeria should be raised to the level of the highest plane attained by any particular part. Thus regarded, each of the two Administrations had much to learn from each other."[1] He might *say* this but there was never any doubt as to his real view. The one superiority he allowed to Southern Nigeria was the wealth created by its material development, most of which was, of course, due less to the government than to the happy accidents of its coastal position, its palm trees and the enterprise of its traders, both white and black.

In every other way the contrast in his eyes was to the overwhelming advantage of the north. Indeed, Lugard looked at the government of the south with something very close to disgust. " The whole system and policy on which this country has been run, not only in the old

[1] *Amalgamation Report*, p. 8.

days but right up to now, seems to me wrong," (L. to F. L., 18 October 1912). Colonial administrators who were successful enough to travel round the Empire on the wings of promotion often tended to idealize the environment within which they passed their creative prime and the people whom they believed they had done most to mould. Lugard, who did not hesitate to suggest in his report that Northern Nigeria was largely his own creation and one which he looked upon as very good, had some better reasons than this to support his partiality. In this system, as we have seen, under the wide powers of the governor, everyone, British official, emir, counsellor, alkali, district-head, village-head and commoner had his place and knew it. By contrast, the administration of the old Southern Nigeria seemed to sprawl without unity or purpose. It had been handed down from a period before " native administration " came to be regarded as a specialized branch of government with principles of its own, one which was, indeed, waiting for its full development at Lugard's hands.

Britain's dependencies in the later nineteenth century belonged to a country not deeply interested in annexing colonies and still less in their methods of government, a sphere in which governors were free to do very much what they liked. In Southern Nigeria Lugard now found himself applying what we may call a twentieth century policy to a situation which had been shaped in the nineteenth. Southern administrators, men like Baikie, Beechcroft, Casement, Burton and Macdonald had all been, in the main, gradualists. They had represented the cautious, economical approach, one which relied upon treaties and agreements, and had a respect, both moral and legalistic, for native rights, except where, as in Benin and later with the domination of the oracle known as "Long Juju of Aro Chuku ", there seemed no alternative to force.[1] The new attitude was more urgent, positive, and businesslike than the old. It revived something of the determination and, at times perhaps, a little of the ruthlessness, of the eighteenth century. Certainly Lugard, as an administrator, had no patience with half-measures or for what he regarded as weakness or pretence.

He fell first upon the provincial organization. The drawing of provincial and district boundaries and the establishment of their head-quarters are not merely technical dispositions. Nor can they be constant. They have to be adjusted from time to time to changes

[1] See *Reports S. Nigeria*, 1902; also Perham, *Native Administration*, pp. 28-9.

in such matters as communications, finance, and urban development. Yet the earliest administrative distribution of still plastic
native groups may influence the shape in which their new and widening loyalties are set. And they always present the problem of how best
to deploy a handful of European officials over the tens of thousands
or even millions of the population within the unit they administer.

Lugard soon decided that the three divisions of Southern Nigeria
outside the Colony of Lagos, the Western, Central and Eastern
Provinces, were quite out of proportion to his less populous northern
provincial divisions; their Provincial Commissioners had almost the
status of Lieutenant-Governors and were under little direction from
the Governor. They ordered their own stores and equipment directly
from Britain, and appeared to be in almost complete control even of
the departmental staff. He therefore cut up the three provinces into
nine smaller ones. These were very approximately comparable in
population, though not in size, with his twelve northern provinces
and the change left most of the provincial populations at a little more
or less than half a million. The exceptions were Kano, estimated to
reach nearly three and a half million, and three south-eastern provinces, each of which topped the million. The southern provinces,
we may note, covering 76,684 square miles, were then held to
contain seven and three-quarter million people and the northern,
within their 255,700 square miles, nine millions. Each southern
province, as in the north, was now put under a graded staff of Residents
and their assistants, averaging twelve to a province, and charged to
concern themselves mainly with Lugard's new forms of native administration. The departmental heads were put in charge of their own
subordinates under the general co-ordination of the Resident.

Next came judicial reforms. In the north Lugard's system of Indirect
Rule was closely bound up with the judicial structure he had introduced there. According to this, it will be remembered, the Supreme
Court had jurisdiction only over Europeans and in European-made
cantonments. Elsewhere judicial powers were in the hands of the
political officers in what was known as the Provincial Court system,
or, as regards the vast bulk of cases, in those of the graded Native
Courts, the highest of which could inflict capital punishment.[1]

Lugard's faith in his northern system was further strengthened

[1] See above pp. 158-61.

during his second period in Nigeria. This was due, in part, to his determination to be in ultimate control of all aspects of government; the British judges of the northern courts were, above all, *his* administrative agents, trained in his philosophy and practice, and not the subordinates of the Chief Justice who, with his direct commission from the Crown, reproduced in the Colonies the British independence of the judiciary towards the executive.

The system, both in the very large powers it sanctioned in the highest grade of the Native Courts and in the placing of judicial powers in the hands of administrative officers, could now be clearly seen, in contrast with the South, as the judicial complement of Lugard's conception of Indirect Rule. His system differed from that of his French neighbours who maintained the tradition of the later Roman Empire and had consciously used their own law and justice as assimilative and civilizing forces. The writer, while studying the French system in Equatorial Africa and the Cameroons, was often told by French officers that they regarded the native systems as barbarous and incapable of development, and could not understand the English recognition of them. To Lugard law was not something fixed and almost outside and above the workaday sphere of government: it was the continuously evolving expression of Britain's peculiar experience as a nation. The men of that nation, who brought the common law with them as part of their inheritance, could therefore be trusted with a wide discretionary power in adapting the rigidities of law and of judicial procedure to the customs and needs of another people. It could be assumed that they would approach African legal institutions with the same respect they accorded to the whole native political system, or at least to their own conception of that system.

With such ideas in his mind, Lugard reviewed the judicial problem of the south. He quickly decided to sweep away a system which his predecessors had been developing for some fifty years and to replace it by one he had created only a dozen years previously in the north. The Chief Justices, Sir Edwin Speed[1] of Northern Nigeria and A. Willoughby Osborne of Southern Nigeria, accepted the consequent reduction in the sphere of their Supreme Court jurisdiction. Since their status and dignity protected them from anything firmer than influence

[1] Speed, Sir Edwin Arney, 1869-1941; 1893 called to the Bar; 1899 District Commissioner, Gold Coast; 1900 Attorney-General, Lagos; 1906 Attorney-General, S. Nigeria; 1908 Chief Justice, N. Nigeria; 1914-18 Chief Justice, Nigeria.

by the Governor, the case against the Supreme Court must have been strong indeed to bring them in agreement with Lugard on this issue. With the help of memoranda by these two Chief Justices, (one of whom, Speed, had worked in Southern Nigeria before appointment and was to become Chief Justice of the new Nigeria), Lugard was able to build up his indictment against the system of courts in Southern Nigeria. The Supreme Court, instituted to extend throughout Southern Nigeria, operated fairly satisfactorily in the small Lagos Colony and Lugard could not challenge its long established position there. It extended patchily over the Yoruba country along the railway line, and in certain chieftainships, by usage or by local agreements such as those with Oyo, Ijebu and Ife. But much of the region was outside any British jurisdiction. Here there were native courts called Councils with wide powers in which British officers sat with minor courts under them. English legal procedure was being copied and appeals lay to the Supreme Court.

Nominally this Court also covered the south-east but the obstructive physical character of the country and the very incomplete pacification of the people, with the shortage of judges, meant that the court hardly functioned outside the few main centres. Supreme Court justice was thus inaccessible to the greater part of the population and many of those who did appear before it had to take long journeys, which on arrival were often followed by delays. Witnesses had to be detained almost like prisoners. As a result, crime often went unpunished. Administrative officers, with little training or supervision, held their District Courts as Commissioners of the Supreme Court upon which procedure was modelled. According to the Chief Justice of Southern Nigeria, the admission of legal practitioners to the Supreme Court meant that the less successful African lawyers from Lagos, and others from Sierra Leone and the Gold Coast, went to the south-east, where they were strangers to local custom, and battened upon the ignorant natives. This was especially true in land and tribal boundary cases which they were said even to foment for the sake of the fat fees, frequently upsetting arrangements made executively by the administration. In the opinion of the Chief Justice himself, the effects of this influx had been enough to undermine the efficacy of the Supreme Court, and led him to the conclusion that " the Supreme Court is not the most suitable form of tribunal for territories in the opening stages of civilization . . . "[1] As to the efficient administration of the Criminal Law, here, Speed said, " the greatest enemy to an efficient administration of the Criminal Law is delay, and delay is inherent in the Supreme Court system . . . The Supreme Court system has been tried in the Southern Provinces and has, in my opinion, proved a failure. If ' the bringing to the African of English justice is one of the most valuable assets to him,' then the system stands condemned, for that is exactly what it failed to do." [2]

Below the Supreme Court in this region were the native courts. These had many defects. Responsibility was lost by division, both between the very large number of so-called chiefs, who were really family elders and who, as many as sixty at a time, sat in rotation as judges, and again, between them and the District Officer who was president. Procedure was a mimicry of that of the Supreme Court to which went the ill-documented appeals. The real power in the court was generally the semi-educated native clerk who kept the records and managed its affairs. The Northern Chief Justice declared that " the main and, to my mind, insuperable objection to the Southern Nigeria native courts is that they are not native courts at all."[3]

Lugard thus advanced to his indictment of the Supreme Court with his two Chief Justices as his counsel and seems easily to have won his case with the Colonial Office. His reforms, in effect, re-defined his northern judicial system and extended it to the whole country. The Supreme Court outside the Colony was, as in the North, to be restricted to a few urban centres. The Provincial Court system was extended to the Southern Provinces. Its courts were to have concurrent jurisdiction with the Supreme Court over all non-natives' cases. Such cases could be transferred, as could all civil cases over £50, from the Provincial to the Supreme Court with the consent of the Chief Justice. The Provincial Court in each Province was to be staffed, as in the north, by the political officers, with full powers for the Resident and lesser powers for his subordinates. No legal practitioners could appear in the Provincial Courts. It was the duty of the judge to put the case both for and against the accused. Appeals no longer went to the Supreme Court; all sentences in excess of six months' imprisonment, 12 strokes, or £50 required confirmation by the Governor-

[1] *Amalgamation Report*, p. 75.   [2] *Ibid.* pp. 77-8.
[3] Minute by Speed, 3 February 1913, enclosed in Lugard to Harcourt, 21 May 1913, *Amalgamation Correspondence* (1914), Confidential Print, p. 75, L.P.

General. This power, which he had no longer time to exercise himself, he delegated to the Lieutenant-Governor in the Northern Provinces, advised in capital cases by the Chief Justice, and to the Chief Justice in the Southern Provinces. The reason Lugard kept the power of delegation in his own hands, instead of allowing appeals to go direct to those he commissioned is characteristic. It was because the government could not

" always count upon having as Chief Justice a man with the breadth of view, the wide experience of the country and the sympathy with the Provincial Executive which Sir Edwin Speed had acquired during his eighteen years' service there . . . By vesting the power of delegation in the hands of the Governor-General a wise discretion is, in my judgment allowed."[1]

The Native Courts, as we saw, ranged in the north from the Judicial Council of each leading emir and the court of his chief alkali down to the rudimentary tribunals of the Plateau and Benue pagans. Each court was carefully graded from A to D, according to its powers, and was under the supervision of the political officers who themselves worked under the careful instructions of Lugard's *Political Memoranda*. It was upon this pattern that Lugard now re-organized the southern native courts. In the south-east their tendency to model themselves upon the procedure of the Supreme Court was checked, their powers were reduced and they were confined to matters of native law and custom. The District Officer was now to supervise but not to preside; the membership was diminished and—a matter more easy to decree than to enforce—the clerk was to be the servant and not the master of the court.[2]

Lugard's judicial measures were an extension, large in area and confident in spirit, of what was sometimes called, though the terms are open to misconception, political or administrative justice, at the expense of professional justice. Lugard claimed the advantages of convenience for this system in that it brought a simple and speedy British court almost to the door of every African. He could claim also the merit of economy in that his political officers were dual-purpose men and saved the scanty revenues from the burden of the large staff of

[1] *Amalgamation Report*, p. 25.
[2] Lugard's Judicial Legislation was contained in four Ordinances of 1 October 1914: No 6, " The Supreme Court Ordinance ", No. 7, " The Provincial Courts Ordinance ", No. 8, " The Native Courts Ordinance ", and No. 9, " The Criminal Procedure Ordinance ".

judges and Crown counsel, by which alone the Supreme Court could
have been stretched to cover the country effectively. But he claimed
even more positive merits for his system. Among these was the value
of using as judges men who knew and understood the customs and
the language of their people, and the freedom of their courts from
elaboration of procedure and of legal technicalities bewildering to the
African peasant. By the extension of this system to the south junior
political officers had now more restricted powers than they had before
as Commissioners of the Supreme Court, but they exercised a more
summary procedure; they were subject to training and examination,
while the new Provincial Courts were more widely distributed.
Lugard could remind the southern Africans that a combination of
executive and judicial functions was almost universal in their own
societies. Writing in retrospect he did not hesitate to advance his case
further into a much more vulnerable position. " Moreover, in a
country recently brought under administration, and in times of
political difficulty, occasion may arise when the strictly legal aspect
must give way to expediency."[1]

As was to be expected his measures caused an immediate outcry in
Lagos. Petitions were sent in to the Colonial Office. The Anti-Slavery
Association took up the matter.[2] It was raised a number of times in
the House of Commons by questions and in debate.[3] The opposition
was founded partly upon exaggerated reports, such as that junior
administrative officers were to have capital powers, but partly upon
a very strong sentiment in favour of retaining for the Southern
Provinces what was held to be the best kind of British justice. There
was disapproval of a system by which southern Africans could now
be condemned to death without being defended by counsel. Lugard
was quite unmoved by the opposition, whether in Britain or Nigeria,
and he was steadily supported by Harcourt. But he did make one of
his rare appearances in the Legislative Council early in 1914 in order
to deliver a long speech fully explaining the reasons for the new
measures.[4] And he also published in *The Gazette* a defence of them by

---

[1] Lugard, *Dual Mandate*, p. 539. See also the whole of this chapter, and *Amalgamation Correspondence* (1914), Confidential Print, pp. 38–77, L.P., and *Amalgamation Report*, pp. 20–5.
[2] See below p. 590.
[3] See, for example, *Parliamentary Debates*, 31 July 1913, V. 56. 843, 849; 5 March 1914,
V. 59. 594; 9 March 1914, V. 59. 878; 1 July 1914, V. 64. 339, and 30 July 1914, V. 65. 1543–6.
[4] Speech to Legislative Council, 12 March 1914.

the Chief Justice, Sir Edwin Speed.[1] But Lugard had small sympathy with the lawyers for, although their main plaint was the injustice of depriving accused murderers of counsel, he was informed they had shown little inclination to take up those unremunerative cases and their concentration had been upon profitable land cases. Looking back on the struggle, he could declare to his wife that " if I did nothing else during my time in Nigeria but effect this great reform I should feel I had not worked without result." (L. to F. L., 17 March 1914).

Opinions will differ now, as they did then, as to whether this was indeed the great reform which he believed it to be. But if critics at the time were often blinded by interest or sentiment, the fault of later critics may suffer from an inability or a refusal to recreate the problem of the time, especially in its practical limitations of money and communications. And the Supreme Court was at that time, over much of the Southern Provinces, a misleading sham, and Lugard had no patience with shams. But his reforms were not the end of the story. The tendency of Indirect Rule was to exalt and perpetuate the powers of the administrative staff. If he had dwelt on the inherent virtue of his system, the two Chief Justices had emphasized more its immediate and, by implication, temporary necessity. When, in 1931, Sir Donald Cameron, Lugard's able assistant, succeeded his chief, he decided that the system should be corrected again in the direction of professional justice by the division of administrative and judicial duties, and he took the opportunity to condemn the view that the judgment of administrative officers had some permanent and inherent merit. He declared that

" if the decision of the Court may properly be swayed by political or other non-juridical consideration within the knowledge of the Administrative Officer . . . then, in my judgment, the Court has ceased to be a judicial tribunal and the officer has ceased to be a judicial officer."[2]

He therefore revised the system, establishing the new Protectorate Courts, to be staffed with qualified judges as these became available. In 1945 the Protectorate Court was merged into the Supreme Court.

Those who wish to pursue the controversy further can follow it to the other side of the continent when the administrative justice of East Africa was arraigned by a Commission under a legal chairman and

---

[1] Reprinted in *Amalgamation Report*, p. 77.
[2] Speech to Legislative Council, 6 March 1933.

defended by the governors[1], whose view was, for the time being, supported by the Colonial Secretary. And on that side of Africa they will learn that Cameron himself, before he returned to Nigeria, had introduced Lugard's system into Tanganyika.

The subsequent changes made in Lugard's system were less striking than the continuity of its main structure, that of a dual system of courts linked together by the supervision of the administrative officers who were also judges in the British courts. It was considered later by a judicial Commission that Cameron's reforms which modified this close link came to soon. But whatever may be said of the British courts, the Native Courts system which found its apotheosis in Nigeria, even in rapidly changing conditions, showed through the succeeding years at least four merits. These were the flexibility of their grades from A courts with capital powers down to the crowded benches of primitive elders; their suitability for land cases; their social necessity as the judicial aspect of each native administration unit; and their ability to deal cheaply with a vast mass of litigation. As an instance of the latter merit we may note that in 1930, whereas the Nigerian Supreme and Provincial Courts dealt with just over 15,000 cases, the Native Courts handled more than 300,000. Even as late as 1952, when a Commission of Inquiry investigated the Native Courts of all these Regions, only minor reforms were proposed. Indeed, like other parts of Lugard's system, it was so successful in its day and for long after that the British authorities hesitated to press those year-to-year adjustments which were needed in an Africa which was becoming part of a wider world.[2]

Provincial reorganization and judicial reform, which affected the whole of the Southern Provinces, could be quickly enacted. But when it came to the extension of native administration proper Lugard had to reckon with the very great difference between the south-west and the south-east which arose not only from the earlier difference in British policies, but from the deeper pre-existing differences in the African societies.

In the south-west, with its large chieftainships, Lugard found him-

[1] *Report of the Commission of Inquiry into the Administration of Justice in Kenya, Uganda and the Tanganyika Territory in Criminal Matters* (1934), Cmd. 4623.
[2] In Lord Hailey's *African Survey* (1957), there are passages too numerous to list on these judicial questions. See also the three Reports on the Northern, Western and Eastern Regions of the *Native Courts Commission of Enquiry* (Lagos, 1952).

self baulked at the very outset, even before he could study their structure, by the constitutional uncertainty, which did not present itself in the south-east, as to whether he had the necessary authority to enact reforms at all. We saw that Lagos itself, largely because it had been an outlet for the slave trade, had been annexed outright in 1861 as a small Colony, in the constitutional sense, and the equalitarian principle of the day had extended to it the rights of British subjects, with Supreme Court Jurisdiction and a Legislative Council.

Lagos port and its surroundings were to have been the total of annexation but, as in India and South Africa, Britain, like Rome, was to find it all but impossible to draw a settled frontier between strength and weakness, order and disorder. From Lagos British trade and influence flowed over the several Yoruba states which, partly because of the temptations of the lucrative slave-trade, indulged in the nineteenth century in frequent inter-state wars and imported firearms for the purpose. While, as we saw in the first volume, Lugard had been among the very first Europeans to make contact with some of the northern-most Yoruba towns,[1] the more southerly groups had long been in touch, directly or indirectly, with the commerce of the world. The influence of the Governor of Lagos, like that of his colleague in the Gold Coast, always going a little further than imperial policy sanctioned, gradually spread inland in the attempt to arbitrate between warring groups, suppress the slave trade, discourage human sacrifice, control the traffic in arms, protect trade and offer a permissive British justice to those who sought for it. More than fifty years of tentative and piecemeal extension by usage, consent and formal and informal agreements had left the government with an authority which was equally tentative and piecemeal. There were British Residents at the major towns but their authority was undefined and they tended to be rather more like consuls and advisers than administrative officers. They were confronted by spirited groups, very ready to question any further claims which did not suit their interests or their pride.

Such a constitutionally indefinable situation was unacceptable to Lugard. We have seen how resolute he had been in the north to claim full and immediate authority by right of conquest, and how, from the

[1] Vol. I, Chapters XXII–XXIV. The writer must confess to an error on page 490 of this volume where it is stated that no white man had, before Lugard, come alive out of Borgu. Richard and John Lander had passed through it in 1830 on the way from Lagos to the Niger at Bussa. See R. & J. Lander, *Journal of an Expedition to the Niger* (1832), vol. i, pp. 198 ff.

unquestioned eminence of that sovereignty, he had given back to the emirs by grace and delegation some of the large powers they had lost by right. Armed with this apparently successful experience, he now set to work to clear the south-west of the constitutional litter, as he saw it, left by the faltering administration of his predecessors. It was difficult for him to find out just what the legal situation was. The archives at Lagos were said to be in " a chaotic state " and his enquiries drew from a senior official the astonishing reply that " it was the custom under the old Lagos administration to destroy records after a few years' retention ".[1] He also learned, with disapproval, that it had been Sir William MacGregor's intention " to create a number of completely independent states, each, I believe, with its own fiscal frontiers."[2]

Lugard recognized the seriousness of this constitutional check. He asked his Attorney-General to make a legal analysis of such treaties as existed and set the Chief Justice to work writing a historical and judicial report on the whole situation.[3] The latter succeeded in producing a list of some eighty-three documents, dated from between 1861 and 1912, but mostly between 1887 and 1900. These included treaties, agreements and declarations dealing with extensions of judicial authority in cases concerning non-natives; with the abolition of human sacrifice; with land, especially for the railway; with trade and with other matters by which British power had been exercised and accepted by the rulers. Lugard's conclusion was that, except in the case of the resolute little Egba state of Abeokuta,[4] which had a clear treaty of internal independence dated 1893, and the rather less definite case of Oyo, the Crown could at least claim to have acquired jurisdiction over what had been the former Lagos Protectorate. The Lagos Colony itself was undeniably British territory but the difficulty here, one typical of the hazy state of the administration, was that its boundaries were quite uncertain.

Lugard wrote a long dispatch on the problem.[5] In this he did not

---

[1] Lugard to Harcourt, 30 June 1913, *Amalgamation Correspondence* (1914), Confidential Print, pp. 91 and 117-18, L.P. Mr. Colin Newbury, who has been working upon this period in Nigeria, informed the writer that this excuse for failing to find them was not wholly true.

[2] *Ibid.* p. 95.

[3] Enclosure 2 in Lugard to Harcourt, 30 June 1913, *loc. cit.* pp. 103-17.

[4] Abeokuta was the chief city in the state of the Egbas, sometimes called Egbaland or simply Egba, which, between 1898 and 1914, was under the Egba United Government. Except where the sense obviously dictates otherwise, the name Abeokuta will be used here to cover both the town and its dependent territory.

[5] Lugard to Harcourt, 30 June 1913, *loc. cit.* pp. 91-125.

hesitate to dig down to the roots of the nature of colonial sovereignty. The question he had to answer may be put thus: " What right has Britain to obliterate all the remaining autonomy of the Yoruba states and impose her own authority?"

Lugard began by putting to himself and to the Colonial Office a realistic question prior to the legal one. " What *need* has Britain to take this action?" In pursuit of the answer he sent F. S. James on a tour of inquiry round the Western Province to report upon the efficacy of the administration.[1] James gave him all that he wanted. His report is, indeed, a surprising document. This official had for long been a senior Provincial Commissioner and, as Acting Colonial Secretary, had signed three of the last four annual reports upon Southern Nigeria. Yet he now wrote sweeping condemnations of the administration of the Western Province almost in the tone of a critical outsider. From this report Lugard was able to make some telling extracts to send to the Colonial Office. " The more," James wrote, " I visit and enquire, the more chaotic does the condition of our administration in this Province appear . . . bribery and extortion is rampant . . . this Province has been allowed to run itself from the very early days." Referring to one district, he reported, " There is no sign of any administration at all."[2]

There was plenty that Lugard could add to this to impress the Colonial Office which was showing itself, in his view, too legally minded. He asked them to look to the future. Was it a wise policy to tolerate semi-independent states with fiscal frontiers astride a railway that was to be the main economic artery of Nigeria? Human or cattle epidemics might spread unchecked. Minerals might be found, followed by the influx of a European mining community. These states at present had British commissioners appointed by the Government but if they developed their autonomy further they might employ advisers of their own choosing. Abeokuta, with its undoubted rights by the treaty of 1893, was chiefly in his mind. This state, while it demanded the trappings and privileges of autonomy, was, Lugard

---

[1] James, (later Sir) Frederick Seton, K.C.M.G., 1870-1934; 1896 Assistant District Commissioner, Niger Coast Protectorate; 1906 Provincial Commissioner and member of the Executive and Legislative Councils of Southern Nigeria; 1914 Administrator of the Colony; 1924 Colonial Secretary, Straits Settlements; 1924-30 Governor and Commander-in-Chief, Windward Islands.

[2] James to Lugard, 11 and 14 March 1913, enclosed in Lugard to Harcourt, 30 June 1913, *loc. cit.* pp. 117-18.

insisted, unable to sustain itself without the support of the Government's troops. Britain had recognized as ruler the Alake, the most important of the four leading chiefs. In 1906 the Alake, threatened by his own chiefs, had been obliged to call upon the British government for armed support. The same thing had happened again a week after Lugard's arrival. Lugard had, moreover, grave doubts about the quality of the justice and of the education in Abeokuta. It was important to ascertain, he said, whether there were " elements of permanency in such creations."[1]

Moving from the issue of need to that of right, Lugard pressed the question back upon its international setting. He started from the right of conquest, or of acquiescence in annexation, both of which were recognized as valid by international law and which, in his view, certainly conferred upon Britian full rights in the Eastern and Central Provinces of the south as they had in Northern Nigeria. He went on to a consideration which, as we have seen before, was often in his mind. Britain had accepted international obligations with regard, for example, to the trade in arms and spirits, the preservation of game and the protection of the subjects of foreign nations. She must therefore assume the powers needed to fulfil those obligations. In the light of modern controversies it might be asked how decisions made between European states could confer rights binding upon the annexed peoples, but at least Lugard had justifiably shifted the ultimate responsibility by several removes away from himself. Finally, returning to expediency, he claimed that it would be impossible for him to carry out his main purpose of reforming the administration unless he were given unquestioned power to do so. Amalgamation offered a fitting opportunity for finally settling this issue. The new Letters Patent should " assert in unequivocal terms the right of the Crown to legislate for the whole of Nigeria, and to exercise executive powers while the courts should be vested with full jurisdiction."[2] Egbaland, he admitted, would have to remain an exception though here he proposed, as a " New Policy", a revised agreement to limit in several matters the inconveniences of its autonomy. Finally, he promised that, if he were given the powers for which he asked, he would avoid " drastic and sudden change " but would introduce his reforms gradually. Having made this case Lugard confidently asked for full authority.

[1] *Ibid.* pp. 96-7.   [2] *Ibid.* p. 98.

He received a very guarded reply. Harcourt agreed that the onus of proof, with regard to the Crown's jurisdiction, should in future rest in each case upon the native community and not upon the governor. But he refused to omit from the Letters Patent the saving clause that the authority of the Crown was subject to all existing treaties and agreements and he would not accept Lugard's "New Policy" for the curtailment of the rights of Abeokuta.

Fortune, or misfortune, according to the point of view, played into Lugard's hands and he was fully ready to catch the ball thrown to him. In July and August 1914, some disorders broke out in Abeokuta. The exact nature of these disturbances was not without an interest which will lead us to look at them again when we consider the affairs of Abeokuta in more detail. For the moment Lugard, who was in England when the news came, was concerned only with the issue of sovereignty and he at once advised the Colonial Office that the Alake should be told he must renounce his treaty. If the head of an independent state had to appeal for external help to support his authority then, Lugard argued, he was no longer capable of sustaining that independence. Nor was it right that the colonial government should send troops to suppress disorders when it could not know whether such suppression was justified. The existence of such a state in this ambiguous position was a source of danger, especially now that the British Empire was in a state of war. He succeeded in his aim of abrogating the treaty of 1893. "Did I tell you," he wrote to his wife, "that I had squashed the Egba treaty and made a new one. In the course of time I shall create a very different state of things in these Southern Provinces." (L. to F. L., 27 October 1914). He was thus able to state in his final report "I informed the Alake that I could no longer consent to suppress by force disturbances the causes of which were outside my control and which for all I knew may have originated from gross misrule . . . With the concurrence of the Secretary of State I invited him to reconsider, with his chiefs and advisers, the treaty of so-called independence . . . The Alake gladly adopted my suggestion." A new agreement abolished Abeokuta's fiscal frontier, brought the state within the general judicial system, and placed it "unreservedly" under the Protectorate government.[1] Harcourt and his officials, though they

[1] *Amalgamation Report*, pp. 13-4 and p. 75.

had shrunk from acting in anticipation, were very pleased with the accomplished fact.

It was constitutionally easier to carry out the same policy towards Oyo as its Alafin had no formal treaty. And Oyo was a far more sizeable gain since under the Alafin were a number of important towns and an estimated million of subjects. Having thus removed the two most difficult obstacles, Lugard was able to plane down the rest of the constitutional irregularities of the Yoruba units to a surface which appeared to be smooth enough to take the northern system of Indirect Rule.

CHAPTER XXII

INDIRECT RULE
AND WESTERN OBSCURITY

IN THE south-west, Lugard's policy demanded for its success—as success can be measured in colonial government—a full knowledge of Yoruba society. Such knowledge is only now, as this chapter is written, being systematically collected by anthropological research; in 1914 it would have been difficult, even if not quite impossible, for Lugard to acquire it. He did not know how much lay below the surface waiting to be revealed but, even if he had, it is doubtful whether he would, or perhaps could, have delayed action while he waited for the revelation. Looking back with our present knowledge there is a deep and at times an almost tragic interest in reconstructing the picture of Lugard, with his strong will but only partly comprehending mind, as he tried to re-mould these societies.[1]

It will have been clear already that the Yoruba were clamant in their demand for his attention. They surrounded him in his Lagos capital and stretched away north and west between him and the rest

[1] For this chapter I am greatly indebted to the writings and to the comments of Dr. P. C. Lloyd who has been working for ten years upon Yoruba sociology. He does not wholly agree with me that Lugard could not have discovered more about the nature of Yoruba societies and their diversities and refers to the evidence upon land tenure submitted to the committee appointed in 1912 by the Colonial Secretary to advise upon land policy in Southern Nigeria. It amassed a great volume of evidence, including that of Africans, but, owing to the outbreak of war in 1914, it never reported. Lugard states in *The Dual Mandate* that he made use of this evidence for his own instruction. Perhaps he did not find time to study the material fully until after his retirement. Or, perhaps, he did not appreciate, as anthropologists have done since, the closeness of the relationship between forms of land tenure and other parts of native society. His staff were thin upon the ground and became fewer with the war; they were also somewhat deranged by the wholesale changes in policy for the south and, perhaps, insufficiently vocal in face of their masterful chief. Dr. Lloyd's publications are, ' The Traditional Political System of the Yoruba', *South Western Journal of Anthropology*, vol. X, Winter 1954, ' The Yoruba Lineage ', *Africa*, vol. XXV, July 1955; ' The Development of Political Parties in Western Nigeria ', *American Political Science Review*, vol. XLIX, September 1955. See also Daryll Forde, *The Yoruba-Speaking Peoples of South-Western Nigeria*, Ethnographic Survey of Africa: Western Africa, Part IV (1951); and William Bascom, ' Urbanization Among the Yoruba ', *American Journal of Sociology*, vol. LX, March 1955.

of Nigeria. Numbering today in British territory—for they stretch over the border into French Dahomey—almost five millions, they are a linguistic group with much cultural but no political unity, being divided into some twenty-five kingdoms with populations varying from 25,000 to nearly half a million. There is no written evidence as to when and how the population came to be in their present home, where they fill the best part of a block of 160,000 square miles, but it has been conjectured that an invading people, bringing with them the concept of the "Divine King", were in process of dominating the region during the centuries 800 to 1200 A.D. Fortunately we need not speculate here about millennial migrations. We can start from the important fact that in the seventeenth or eighteenth century—dates cannot be exact before about 1800—the supremacy was with the Alafin of Oyo whose power, though not inclusive of all the Yoruba, stretched from the western borders of the present Ghana to the Niger. But this power was already in decline when the Fulani, who, as Lander's fascinating first account of the region shows, were in the eighteen-thirties already infiltrating right to the coast, drove down from the north, seized the Yoruba city of Ilorin and ravaged into the heart of Yorubaland. There began a time of troubles which extended over much of the nineteenth century. There were wars with the Fulani and frequent wars between the states into which the old Oyo empire had dissolved. The country was dotted with large walled cities. A high level of social life was attained by these semi-urbanized peoples, with their weavers, dyers, traders, and metal workers, their extensive inter-state trade and their strong cultural affinity. This did not restrain them from that constant warfare among themselves and that inability to unite against a common foe for which, had they known the history of the world, they would have found eminent precedents in Greece and Italy. But it should be remembered that it was the traders of some European nations who through much of the nineteenth century, brought to the coast the guns which made war so destructive and their demand for slaves which, at least up to the 'forties, still made it so profitable.

The annexing British were thus confronted by a number of independent states. Among them was the reduced but still large chieftainship of Oyo; and those of Ife, Ijebu-Ode, Abeokuta, Ondo and Lagos, with some less prominent groups. These seemed to Lugard closely comparable with some of the larger and smaller emirates and as he had declared that the indirect rule principle was applicable even to the smallest pagan groups, it was natural that he should regard the Yoruba states, and especially that of Oyo, as most promising material upon which to exercise his proved administrative system. But the appearance, we can now see, was deceptive. It may well be that before the Muslim penetration of many centuries earlier, the greater part of Nigeria, except where the forests and hills offered refuge for the more primitive groups, was covered by relatively large pagan societies not so very different in essentials from those Lugard was now contemplating near Lagos. It is possible to detect dimly in the emirates traces of the old order under the pattern of the new. But the long penetration of Islam produced its effects, assimilating, simplifying, and centralizing. Then came the sudden sweeping military conquest by the alien Fulani which further levelled down the Hausa states under a more autocratic set of Muslim rulers than before. Whatever intricacies and varieties might still lurk beneath the relatively autocratic power of the emirs, that power gave the British administration the obvious and effective fulcrum it needed for its own superior power.

By contrast the texture of the Yoruba states, as we now begin to understand them, almost defies description in ordinary English terms, certainly in the abbreviation which must be used here. They present successive layers of complication. They were built up, cell by cell, upon the principle of kinship and lineage, from the natural family into the groups of families living in their large compounds under the authority of the oldest males and of councils of elders, through the widening groups claiming common descent in larger and larger units until at last all the millions of the Yoruba could regard Ife as the sacred house of their first founder, Oduduwa, and a million or more could look to the Alafin as the lineal descendant of his son Oranyah.

The lineage system was linked with the real or mythical settlement of the group upon a given location producing in time a resultant series of cells contained within larger ones as in a Chinese box, and each looking to a—at least supposedly—lineal head. Unfortunately for the neatness of the simile the wider ties of clan linked the " boxes " with those in other settlements. The Hausa, too, had their extensive kinship groupings but these had ceased to perform what might be called a subpolitical function. But if, to change the metaphor, lineage provided the dominant strands, there was a number of less organic elements crossing or reinforcing the existing threads so as to produce an intricate and very irregular pattern. Most of these elements were due to later developments away from the original simplicity of begetting and migration. The Yoruba, at least for some centuries before British annexation,[1] had taken to living in towns, and were indeed the most urban-minded of all African peoples, though it must be remembered that the people thus concentrated were still mainly farmers. Unfortunately for British administration, the towns were not the simple agglomerations they appeared, since the new bonds of civic propinquity had not obliterated the lineage ties of the groups which had come together. These remained to form what the British called wards, or townships within a town, and were often linked with kindred rural groups or with subordinate towns.

Urbanization had, moreover, bred new forms of association. There were craft guilds for dyers, traders, weavers and the like, both for men and for women, and groups formed for thrift or recreation. War also had bred its own institutions and in Ibadan this took the form of a dual set of graded chiefs, civil and military. And while most towns were linked with superior towns by ties of blood, real or supposed, others had been forced into subjection during the nineteenth century wars and might be only unwillingly subservient. Little scope was thus left for centralized powers by the crowned heads or Obas. Even when at last through this maze of component authorities we reach in our survey the great mud palaces, with the three steep thatched gables which were the perquisite of royalty, such powers as were wielded by Obas were derived not only from divine descent but also from a large measure of public consent. Their exercise was further subject to elaborate checks at the centre. There might be a group of councillors, as at Oyo, who chose the ruler from the eligible males of the royal family, one of which group had the duty of politely sending his king a gift of parrots' eggs when he decided that it was the time for that ruler to make a final exit from the stage. The hint, it is said, would always be quickly taken though Dr. Lloyd believes such invitations were rare. There was also the group of palace women, eunuchs or trusted slaves who wielded their large and

[1] Bascom, *op. cit.* p. 448.

441

immediate influence. The all important point is that though the Oba must be a member of the royal lineage, tracing descent from Oduduwa, the choice from among the candidates rested with the generally large group of chiefs. There were also conventions which prevented other members of the dynasty obtaining any privileged position.[1] Finally there were the so-called secret societies, sometimes centred upon one of the four hundred lesser deities which surrounded the supreme Yoruba god. Among these were the important Ogboni societies which might wield very large powers, political and judicial, including those of life and death. Since the sociologists are still unable to define exactly these powers, which, indeed, varied from state to state, it is not surprising that some British administrators were tempted to regard such societies as pathological growths.

Two last Yoruba complexities must be listed. There was no uniformity in the political shape of the several states, yet the same terms were often used in different states with different content. Secondly, the original patterns had been distorted in varying degrees by more than seventy years of European influence.

Here, then, are some of the reasons why Lugard failed to discern the multiple parcelling of authority among the Yoruba, and, above all, the sharp distinction between the northern Emir and the south-western Oba. There was another distinction to which he gave inadequate weight. The striking practical success of his system in Northern Nigeria had been due not only to the presence there of chiefs with large regions and large powers, but also with large revenues. We saw that these were based upon a settled system of taxation which Lugard had been able to regularize. In this the northern Muslim states were almost unique in negro Africa. Many systems of local government in colonies, and not only in colonies, that have seemed excellent upon paper have declined into semi-paralysis without the quickening power of an ordered revenue. Colonial treasuries were seldom affluent enough to be willing to sacrifice large grants-in-aid to very experimental local governments. By 1912 it was clear how closely the success of the northern administration was founded upon taxation and treasuries. Here lay the obstacle. The negro of the coast had to pay occasional dues to his ruler but he was quite unfamiliar with regular taxation and, unlike his less sophisticated and less assertive fellow-Africans on the

[1] I owe some of these points to an unpublished article by Dr. P. Lloyd.

east coast, he was very ready to resist this attribute of civilization. The British had not attempted to impose direct taxation upon the Gold Coast where, fortunately, the prosperity of the cocoa trade allowed of a very adequate revenue from customs. In Sierra Leone the attempt to introduce a hut tax in 1898 had caused a very serious revolt, only put down with a heavy loss of life. The Commissioner who reported on the incident found excuse for the rebels and advised that the tax should not be imposed again.[1] E. D. Morel, one of the best informed unofficial experts of the period, in his book on West Africa published in 1912, had given a strong warning against any brusque introduction of tax in Southern Nigeria after fifty years of association without taxation.[2]

In Lugard's mind, however, taxation was a financial necessity. It was also much more than this. The case he made for his first scheme of taxation in Northern Nigeria has been given.[3] But now he carried his arguments further. The British income-tax payer would hardly be able to recognize the unpleasant necessity to which he submits as the same institution which Lugard exalted as the source of all civic health. The salutary influence which he had extolled in the north seemed to him even more needed in the south. Without any exact knowledge of the diffused mass of tributes and services in the Yoruba states he pictured them as a fetid swamp from which wealth was oozing and evaporating. His taxation would reclaim it by canalizing and controlling the stream of revenue until it flowed in a single clear river to the Native Administration headquarters, there to bifurcate into central and local revenue, the latter flowing back to irrigate each level of native administration. All illegal exactions and oppressions would be cut away; each peasant would have the clear, free status of the tax-payer; slavery, in all its forms, would become superfluous; chieftain-ship would be at once strengthened and controlled; every public official and judge would be paid for his services and the hosts of parasites would be starved out of existence. While he would never use taxation as a means of enforcing labour, it would have the indirect effect of stimulating production, for men would know they must pay tax but would be free to keep their surplus. From the government side tax was not only a recognition of sovereignty; it brought the

---

[1] *Report to Her Majesty's Commissioner and Correspondence on the Subject of the Insurrection in Sierra Leone Protectorate, 1898* (1890), C. 9388.

[2] Morel, *Nigeria, its Peoples and Problems*, p. xiv.   [3] See above pp. 164-6.

administrative officer into closer contact with the peasantry than any other of his functions, one, moreover, in which he would appear, not as a hard exploiter, but as an agent who would free the common man from the burden of heavy and capricious exactions. Much of this paean in praise of taxation he poured, with his usual lavishness of argument, into a long dispatch to the Colonial Office in support of taxation in the Yoruba states in 1915.[1]

Before writing this dispatch, Lugard, who was not unaware of the need for knowledge of his people even though he often had to act without it, had selected one of his most outstanding and most anthropologically-minded northern Residents, H. R. Palmer,[2] to tour round the south and to report upon the situation, especially with regard to the introduction of direct taxation. The mind Palmer brought to bear on the region had, of course, a northern slant. He confirmed that " In the past there has been no ' Native Policy ' "; that the former Native Courts, almost the only institution introduced by the government, had been used as executive as well as judicial organs; that the powers of chiefs were in decline but could be restored; and that in the southwest, at least, there were many forms of tribute which could be consolidated into a single tax. The introduction of the new Provincial Court system was already cutting away their takings from the many authorities who before had a hand in the large profits from fees and fines. He reported, however, that southern officials believed that the northern system of direct taxation was inapplicable to the south. This, much too easily, he put down to their " innate conservatism " and also to a quite untenable view that all Africans north of the boundary were quite different from all Africans to the south, even though the French on the west and the Germans on the east were successfully taxing their very similar " southern " peoples. He recommended the introduction of taxation at once into the three most favourable areas, Benin, Oyo and Abeokuta.[3]

This was exactly what Lugard wanted from his investigator. The plan which, early in 1915, he put up to the Colonial Office was a complete scheme for the three provinces. He urged the additional

[1] His views can also be found in *Memoranda*, 1918, pp. 163-215.
[2] The writer has been helped by information and documents supplied by the late Sir Richmond Palmer about this period of his work.
[3] " Reports of a Tour in the Southern Provinces in 1914 by H. R. Palmer." Typescript in L.P.

advantages that the chiefs' losses from the reform of the old native courts could be made good and the immoral duties from spirits could be gradually replaced. Above all, the further disintegration of the native authorities, which was, he believed, very largely the result of their being flouted by Christian converts and " educated " clerks, could be checked.[1]

The Colonial Office would have none of it. The Sierra Leone incident was well in mind and Secretaries of State dreaded serious unrest, with costly punitive expeditions which might cause financial embarrassment with the Treasury and political embarrassment with humanitarians inside and outside Parliament. It was held that in time of war, with Nigeria denuded of troops for the Cameroons campaign, the risk could not be taken. The refusal caused Lugard more than the usual personal exasperation. " This," he told Flora,

" is the psychological moment when I have repealed the old treaties (with their consent) and introduced the new courts and new provinces. It can be done, I am assured, not only with no difficulty but with hearty approval. The C.O. method means that I must wait till that moment has passed. Then they will take, I expect, a month to consider it and finally send me orders drawn up by some junior C.O. official which will render it a failure and the nett result will be disturbances with which they will credit me!" (L. to F. L., 29 January 1915).

He persisted, however, and early in 1916 he had the satisfaction of introducing his system of native administration with taxation into the large Oyo unit. After all that has been said of the nature of Yoruba society it can come as no surprise that this innovation led to troubles which showed the contrast between European and African conceptions of government.

The first trouble was in Oyo, the large northern area grouped around that town. It was natural that Lugard, seeking the source of political power, should find it in the palace of the Alafin, that impressive figure which, surrounded by courtiers and slaves, he had first seen in 1895. Even as late as 1918 he could write " In Yoruba-land " (an expression then often used to describe the region dependent upon Oyo) " the position is practically identical with what I have described as prevalent in Fulani States prior to British Administration, but owing to the character and ability of the Alafin, it has not perhaps degenerated

[1] Lugard's views can be further studied in *The Dual Mandate*, pp. 230-79.

quite so much as it did in them."[1] This sentence advertises at least two important mistakes.

The first concerned the kind of power this Yoruba potentate wielded. The ritual at Oyo seemed to exalt his power. Each Alafin when he first entered the Afin (the palace) did so through a new doorway cut into its wall and stepped over the blood of a sacrificed man and woman; he then retired into his inner sanctum to eat his predecessor's heart. Here, indeed, it seemed, was a high and semi-sacred being! But his was a kind of royal sanctity unknown in Britain even when the most extreme doctrine of the divine right of kings was being promulgated. The Alafin, unlike any Tudor, Stuart or even Bourbon, had to veil his face behind a fringe of beads; he could never leave the Afin save on three special occasions in the year. Small wonder that, to quote Lugard, " the loyal and enlightened ruler, the Alafin, is anxious to accept the same status as the paramount emirs of the North "![2] Small wonder, also, that at first this desire had to be kept secret or both the Alafin and his Resident would have been in danger of their lives.[3]

There was a second major difficulty in trying to make an emir out of the Alafin. Within his dominions, among many other by no means docile towns, lay the largest of all, the great sprawling city of Ibadan which, as we saw, Lugard had visited soon after taking up his post. The city had grown into importance during the wars as a place of refuge and an armed camp with considerable military strength. It had no Oba or crowned head, not even a minor one, but it did have a gerontocratic council, with graded civil and military elders under a town-head known as a Bale, and it possessed a very independent spirit. It claimed, Yoruba fashion, primacy over several populous subordinate towns. Here was a monstrosity unknown in the North. But Lugard did not, perhaps could not, know this. To him it appeared that all the northern Yoruba, numbering over a million, owed allegiance to the Alafin but that for many years there had been a tendency for the Ibadans " to flout his authority and to set up a separate rule under their own Bale ".[4] He believed that the northern system could be imposed upon this situation. " The course most in consonance with the history

---

[1] *Memoranda*, 1918, No. 5, p. 175.   [2] *Ibid.* p. 305.
[3] Lugard to Harcourt, 30 June 1913, *Amalgamation Correspondence* (1914), Confidential Print, p. 99, L.P.
[4] *Amalgamation Report*, p. 13.

and tradition of the country," he wrote in his *Political Memoranda*, " and the one most likely to result in a sound administrative organization would seem to be that the whole of the Ibadan and other divisions of Yorubaland should be divided into districts under headmen directly responsible to the Alafin, and hence independent of the Bale who himself would rank as a District Head."[1] Here Lugard was taking the Ibadan citizens' respectful acceptance of the fatherly primacy of the descendant of Oduduwa as a basis for novel and powerful forms of executive authority imported by the British. It is not surprising that his decision was the beginning of a long struggle between the growing city of Ibadan and the Alafin in his small, sleepy headquarters at Oyo, which lay outside the main currents of influence which were flowing into the towns along the railway. The writer happened to visit the region when the tension was at its height in 1931. Three years later Ibadan at last won its independence as a major unit of local government.[2]

Ibadan was not the only town nominally under the Alafin to exhibit restlessness under Lugard's reforming hand. While he was in England in October 1916 disorders broke out in the important town of Iseyin, some sixty miles west of Oyo, and at the head of the list of those murdered was one of the new District Heads and one of the judges of the new Native Court. Lugard, after his return, admitted that but for the prompt action of the Resident, Captain W. A. Ross, and the loyal and energetic support of the Alafin, the revolt might have spread much more widely through Yorubaland. Among the grievances of the people were antagonism towards the new Native Courts, especially on the part of those who had lost their former places or profits; the introduction of " new men " as District Heads and alarm at a so-called " voluntary " collection for the Red Cross.

Iseyin was held to be a town with a history of stubborn self-will and Lugard thought some punishment was needed. The eight men who had murdered the native officials appointed by the government were executed publicly before the people of the town and delegates from others nearby. Lugard believed that, if the government were to enforce its reforms throughout the Yoruba country, it must take the occasion of this revolt to show its mastery. He felt able to charge the

[1] *Memoranda*, 1918, No. 5, p. 177.
[2] For a fuller account see Perham, *Native Administration*, pp. 178–200.

Colonial Office with delaying consent to the taxation out of which
the new court members and other officials could have been properly
salaried in lieu of the old bribes and tributes. The Office, on its side,
was able to blame Lugard for not reporting until April 1917 upon a
serious outbreak occurring in November 1916. This was a result, the
officials were quick to point out, of Lugard trying to administer from
England. One good result, in Lugard's reckoning, was that he persuaded the Office to allow him to take advantage of his punishment
of the dissidents to introduce that taxation by which he believed he
could make his reforms at once complete and acceptable.

A further example of Lugard's dealings with the Yoruba is found
in Abeokuta, where there was a serious outbreak in 1918. The whole
Abeokuta story is rich in evidence about the difficulties of African
administration and shows how a governor's policy could err not only
from his own lack of understanding of native institutions, but from the
faultiness of the agents through whom he must administer that policy.
This city state of the Egba group of the Yoruba has already demanded
attention and we saw how Lugard had to deal with it as part of the
sovereignty issue in the south-west. Now we must look more closely
into its history and constitution, for there were special reasons why it
proved even more violently recalcitrant against his policy than Ibadan.
Lying only about thirty miles north of the boundary of Lagos colony,
in an excellent position to interfere with the main trade routes, Abeokuta
early received much the same influences from European missionaries
and traders as did the port. Its independent spirit was partly due to the
militant nature of the people who had colonized this forested region,
presumably during the Middle Ages, and played a vigorous part in the
nineteenth century wars. The city itself dates it foundation from 1830
when four separate groups of fighting men set up their joint camp or
refuge under the grey crag which dominates this place.[1] The early
missionaries, arriving some ten years later, had encouraged the
separatist tendencies of the Egba by working, in a way not uncommon
in this period, towards a state dependent upon their advice and as far
as possible immune from other interventions. Thirdly, there had been
early in the century migrations of freed slaves from Sierra Leone back
to Abeokuta, bringing with them a measure of sophistication and a

---

[1] S. O. Biobaku, *The Egba and Their Neighbours 1842-1872* (1957), chapters 1-3; see also his
'Historical Sketch of Egba Traditional Authorities', *Africa*, vol. XXII, January 1952.

knowledge of firearms. Abeokuta, often at war against Dahomey with its Amazon soldiers, and with its other neighbours, and also within itself, became increasingly warlike and independent in spirit.

It was in recognition of this spirit that the Governor of Lagos had made a treaty with the little state in 1893 promising that " its independence shall be fully recognized ". Abeokuta agreed to accept a British Commissioner, to maintain freedom of trade and of trade routes, and to cease the human sacrifices which stained its presiding rocks.[1]

The Abeokuta leaders were now secure, as they thought, in their miniature independence. They built up a state modelled on what they believed was the British colonial pattern, the only European form of government they knew. A very remarkable educated man, Edun, was, under the title of Secretary, the moving spirit. With advice from the British Commissioner and the missionaries he built up an elaborate system of administration known as the Egba United Government, printing an official gazette in English and Yoruba. He drew up estimates; issued large numbers of Orders in Council and regulations; set up a secretariat with heads of departments, and even recruited British as officials. E. D. Morel, who inspected the institutions of Abeokuta just before Lugard came back to Nigeria, was impressed " with the industry and businesslike air which reigned within them."[2] The roads were excellent; so was the water-supply, built out of a £30,000 loan from the British government. The British Commissioner, P. V. Young, was exhibiting the special talent of his countrymen in such situations, that of wielding unofficial influence without official power, and using it to build up the little state in increasing self-containment.

This policy was not one which could commend itself to Lugard. His first task was to show his staff the error of their ways and educate them in his own. He described this rather painful process to his wife.

" . . . I spent my morning with Boyle, James and Young (the Dist. Cmsr. of Egba) explaining my views on the policy to be followed in Egba land. Young is a keen officer and he has been Resident there for the past 7 years. His policy has been to model the Egba Govt. on the Lagos Gov. and himself to be the ' Uncrowned King '. Through his initiative the Egba Council have passed laws which render our position very difficult. I asked if before pressing these ' reform laws' on the Alake he had communicated

[1] Burns, *History of Nigeria*, pp. 332-3.
[2] Morel, *Nigeria, its Peoples and Problems*, pp. 78-9.

with the Lagos Government whose servant he is, or obtained the approval of the Governor. He admitted he had never done so. I pointed out that the latest which he takes pride in having ' forced through the Council ' by his personal influence, is contrary to the Treaty. I pointed out with unmerciful logic the ultimate drift of his policy. He would not gainsay me and only urged (as all others do) that he thought he was doing what Mr. W. Egerton wanted but had never been able to get any instructions or guidance. James, then temporarily Officer Administering the Government, had lauded this policy in a letter to the Alake and no doubt felt very uncomfortable when he found himself emphatically agreeing with my arguments. It was a useful conversation though I am very sorry for Young who suddenly finds that the ideals he has followed all these years are shattered—not by a despotic decree which he could resent, but by a sober dispassionate exposé with which he finds that he himself agrees. The policy of the future is immensely difficult and all I can do at present is to put a stop to progress on wrong lines, and try to find a way through the wood to the right path. That is never an easy task."

(L. to F. L., 23 February 1913).

Lugard was at least right to foresee that the modern, pseudo-colonial pattern of government super-imposed upon the old Yoruba constitution was not likely to be stable.

The riot which allowed Lugard in 1914 to abrogate the treaty of 1893, was a most unhappy event. One of the opponents of the Secretary, Edun, by name of Ponlade, was arrested and died in the native prison. It was largely because of the discontent caused by his death that the Alake and Young had appealed to the government for troops. When these arrived the malcontents came in to what they regarded as a parley but which the young officer in command of the troops regarded as a riot. The result was a lethal fusillade which became known as the Ijemo Massacre. The deaths were followed by angry accusations and counter-accusations about what had actually happened. The event had left behind it a deep sense of fear and of bitterness towards the government.

By 1918 Lugard felt secure enough in Abeokuta to persuade the Colonial Secretary to allow him to introduce taxation. This was done early in 1918. The innovation seemed to have been accepted calmly, and towards the end of May, 1918, Lugard was congratulating himself that any restlessness in Abeokuta was directed against the native government and was the result of the people

" learning for the first time under my scheme of taxation that they have been bled in the past, and all the abuses and iniquities of the old 'independent' government of Egba are coming to light. The people are anxious everywhere to adopt the tax scheme in spite of all the misrepresentation which the interested parties can make. It is my private conviction that since 1913 a revolution has been worked in the south."

(L. to F. L., 21 May 1918).

Even as Lugard wrote these words, a revolution of a somewhat different kind was on the way. On May 29th he could still maintain that all the hostility was directed against the still-surviving Edun. On June 13th the news came of a rising that did not quite fit Lugard's interpretation of the trouble. " The Egbas," he told Flora, " have broken out and torn up the railway, looted trains and railway stations." He had hurried police and troops to the scene.

" Well, never mind the details—it does not worry me *much* but in this country you have always to look out for the heather catching fire and though I have most positive and repeated assurances that it has nothing to do with this new tax started in Egba the C.O. will be only too delighted and too keen to say it has. This is not a matter to be depressed about, it is part of the normal burden of administration accentuated by the knowledge that the C.O. are only too eager to ' get a knife into me ' if they can. That they should have had no opportunity for 6 or 7 years past in a country so difficult as this is, I think, remarkable."

(L. to F. L., 13 June 1918).

The next day came news of losses to the troops and murders of Europeans. Much of it was proved later to be exaggerated, but it caused Lugard to exclaim that this was the worst disaster since Satiru and to criticize those who had given him misleading accounts of the situation. But the crisis differed from that of Satiru, differed, too, from what it would have been even the year before, in that he had ample forces just returned from fighting in East Africa. He needed them. The city of Abeokuta was calm, the movement being confined to one part of the Egba country. But here the rebels were tenacious, and highly destructive, especially of the railway stations and rolling stock. Not only the warlike tradition of the Egbas but the hand of the trained ex-soldier could be seen. The rioters killed one of the leading chiefs who refused to join them but it was soon proved that only one

451

European, a trader, was murdered, though there was much looting of stores.

We are reminded, as after the Satiru affair, that the severity of repression after a revolt is generally proportionate to the fear, however brief, which it has aroused. Lugard supported stern measures. The people continued to resist, but 1,000 well-armed African troops, even when hampered by torrents of rain, were a formidable punitive force and at least 500 of the rebels were killed.

But the suppression of the revolt left Lugard in no easy position. He believed the Colonial Office would debit the outbreak to his policy. He had little other British criticism to fear at this tense final stage of the world war but at least the new London weekly, *West Africa*, demanded a full enquiry. It pointed out uncomfortably that if an autocratic governor takes all power into his own hands then he must bear all the criticisms for a breakdown, and this one must be "something of a personal humiliation" for Lugard. Surely "the middle of a great war is an excellent time to go softly even though the manufacture of Ordinances and Regulations at Lagos should suffer a brief interruption."[1]

The death of the rebels and of those they murdered was not lightly taken by any of the authorities. Clearly, the cause for such violence must be discovered. Lugard already had his own opinions about the general cause of the outbreak.

"These people, within 20 miles of Lagos, have been so mismanaged by successive governors and by the Colonial Office that here in 1918 we have them tearing up the Railway, cutting the telegraph, looting many thousand pounds' worth of goods, murdering a white man and taking away his head for fetish rites. This is the outcome of Independent Native Rule started by Macgregor and Co. The cause of the outbreak is very obscure but it seems to be ancient misrule—recent reforms had exasperated chiefs who had lived for years by plundering the peasantry, and now, seeing their day is gone, they have spread lies and excited this rising."

(L. to F. L., 17 June 1918).

For such a serious occurrence something more was needed than the Governor-General's verdict. The practice of this century in the British Empire of appointing a commission of enquiry to report upon disorder and bloodshed was followed. And since disorder was often the only

[1] *West Africa*, 24 August 1918.

way in which illiterate tribal people could express their undefinable discontents, these commissions, especially when their reports were published, have frequently led to important changes of policy. Lugard was too certain of the rightness of his reforms to be very apprehensive about an enquiry. This Commission was chaired by Dr. James Maxwell,[1] one of his own Residents and another future governor, and included a Wesleyan missionary, a member of John Holt's trading firm, a police magistrate and the African barrister, Eric Moore. The Commission did its work with courage and detachment, collecting a vast mass of evidence. Finding Lugard's assessment was much too simple, it reported in terms which went far to condemn the local officials and to excuse popular discontent. The main fault, it was stated, lay with the administration, and especially the officers directly in charge. Not one but many mistakes had been made by them in their application of Lugard's policy and they had been too far out of touch with the people to observe their accumulating discontent.

Thus the Commission. But was Lugard, as the policy-maker, wholly free from blame? The issue could not be simplified to that of the new taxation. That, as we saw, was part of a whole structure based on the northern model. But, as with Oyo, it was clear that the simple pattern of a single dominant ruler with District Heads under him to conduct the administration and to collect the new tax simply did not fit the Abeokuta system which was at once looser and more complex. The Alake himself was not, by origin, comparable with an emir, but was the chief among the four heads of the four component groups of the city. The exact part played in government by the secret societies was still unknown.

The new District Heads were sent out into the countryside to the affiliated towns to form the connecting link between them and the city of Abeokuta and so by-pass the large ruling class at headquarters. That this sudden change was linked with the introduction of direct taxation was not likely to make either innovation popular. Taxation, by Harcourt's order, was to be voluntary but it requires little knowledge of African administration to realize how difficult it is to give this character to any measure emanating from the strong foreign power which controls appointments and salaries, police and military. How-

[1] Maxwell, (later Sir) James C., K.C.M.G., K.B.E., 1869–1932; 1897 District Medical Officer, Sierra Leone; 1914 First Class Resident, Nigeria; 1920 Colonial Secretary, Sierra Leone; 1922 Colonial Secretary, Gold Coast; 1927–32 Governor, Northern Rhodesia.

ever, it appears that the Alake and the other chiefs did accept the principle of taxation and that this was carefully explained to the people by the able but unpopular Edun. A first assessment for taxation can never be a very cheerful process. The people had been promised, in return, an end of all "free" labour on the roads and other public works. But when the time came in 1918 to pay the tax the forced labour was still exacted. Simultaneously the reorganized native courts were stimulated to hasten sanitary reform by the sanction of fines. It is difficult to decide, in the history of colonial administration, whether forestry measures which interfered with the freedom of hunting and with shifting cultivation, or sanitary measures which sent ill-trained native jacks-in-office poking into the private women's quarters, have caused more indignation. Here was inflammatory material in good quantity and widely scattered. The spark was supplied by a threat that if the indignant people did not behave themselves troops would be sent. The minds of the people at once went back to the Ijemo "massacre"; it was still the popular belief that on that occasion the soldiers had fired upon a peaceable delegation. And had not Ponlade died after protesting against forced labour? It was upon the old argument of the sheep and the lamb that a section of the people took to their arms. All this came out in the report which finally suggested, in courageous criticism of the Governor-General, that it had been a mistake to push through a major reorganization during the war and with great shortage of staff.[1]

The report followed Lugard home after he had left Nigeria and he answered it from Abinger. He naturally underlined the point that taxation in itself had not been the main cause of the trouble.[2] He took full responsibility for the constitutional reforms and stood by them. As in the north he could not accept that hundreds of chiefs should live in the city, in his view neglecting their districts. He had first, he said, seen this undesirable African tendency in Uganda; he had dealt with it in Northern Nigeria and he had carried through the same reform in Abeokuta only after gaining the understanding of the Alake and Edun.

[1] *Report of the Commission of Enquiry into the disturbances in Abeokuta Province.* (An undated copy of the report in the Lugard Papers).

[2] I am indebted to Mr. Newbury for pointing out that the revenues of the independent Abeokuta, derived from their control of trade, had risen from about £13,000 in 1904 to about £40,000 in 1911. The loss of these as a result of full incorporation within Nigeria, and in spite of new services and salaries, must have fallen heavily upon this small state and especially upon many of the traders.

He had postponed making any major changes too soon after the abrogation of the treaty. " But the government could not indefinitely postpone its responsibility for the good government of the country." Nor could he accept the view that it was unwise to press reforms with a depleted staff. There was a psychological moment for action which it would have been unwise to miss. " It is not possible to stand still and mark time indefinitely."[1]

Though the report was not published it was not consigned at once to a shelf. It seems to have been very fully considered at the Colonial Office where it was felt that, though Lugard was not likely to admit it, the trouble had been due, at least in part, to the new direct taxation. But the Office appears to have concluded that the Commission had gone too far in condemning the Nigerian officials and rejected its plea that the offending region be forgiven a special tax which was to be levied in order to make good the destruction that had been caused.

How different riots and rebellions seem after fear and anger have evaporated, the dead are buried, and the causes of discontent are laid bare! The anonymous and unfortunate rebels are generally proved to have had good reasons for their discontent. This plunge a little below the surface into the detail of native administration throws light upon Lugard's difficulties and also upon both his weakness and his strength as a ruler of Africa. His chief difficulty here was that he had to govern, and govern resolutely from day to day with quite inadequate knowledge of the societies he had to handle. He could not make sense of the condition of Abeokuta at this time, a relatively new state and one open to the influence of the nearby and even more restless influences of Lagos, a point which we must take up elsewhere.

There are limits to the responsibility of a colonial governor both for the total situation he takes over and for the purposes he has been ordered to fulfil. Admittedly Lugard's character and period gave him a larger personal responsibility than most of his class, and certainly of his successors. Yet he would have been entitled to ask a critic of his Yoruba policy whether he could have restrained all action while the variations and complexities of these swiftly changing societies were being investigated. Would these Africans have suffered more or less if he had hesitated to enforce reforms directed towards their more orderly and humane government? If he had lived into the second half

[1] Lugard to Milner, 5 April 1919, L.P.

of this century, might he not have asked whether the record of the newly emancipated dependencies did not bear out all the evidence of history that the uncivilized and tribal parts of the world could often be forced into larger and more viable shapes only by rough hammering? We may be endeavouring today to build up new nations by more rational and humane processes but in Lugard's time this possibility lay just outside his horizon. Yet, when all is said, it must be recorded that there remained a disquiet in Lugard's own mind. Some twenty-six years later, when it was known that the writer was to be his biographer, he said "You will blame me about Abeokuta!" This was a remark he made about no other incident in his life.

CHAPTER XXIII

INDIRECT RULE AND EASTERN INTRACTABILITY

EVEN THE critics of Lugard's dealings with the Yoruba people would admit that he had a policy for them and that he applied it with deep and lasting effect. This cannot be said of the south-east which presented him with an entirely different administrative situation which he was unable to master. Scattered references have been made to the peoples of this region but we must now, with better evidence than was available to Lugard, summarize the difficulty they presented.

The first problem which faced the government was on the coast and it proved the least troublesome. Here in creeks and estuaries had been built up the so-called Houses. This unique institution had arisen during the long years of commercial contact with the west in order to deal with the trade first in slaves and then in palm-oil. Their chiefs were vigorous and sophisticated traders who had collected round them hundreds, and in some places, thousands, of supporters and slaves who worked to produce food, manned the canoes and went inland to collect the trade goods, human or vegetable, for shipment at the coast. These chiefs had commercial and diplomatic contacts with British consuls and traders. According to Dr. Diké, an African historian, himself an Ibo, who has made the first, full scholarly study of the delta region in the mid-nineteenth century, the House was " at once a co-operative trading unit and a local government institution."[1] The scale upon which some of the Houses conducted business is shown by the story of the House Chief Nana. His stronghold was attacked by H.M.S. *Alecto*, whose return from her first repulse Lugard had witnessed.[2] When the ship returned to the attack again and, with the help of three naval consorts, stormed the chief's riverside fortress, it was

---

[1] K. O. Diké, *Trade and Politics in the Niger Delta 1830-1885* (1956), pp. 34-6.
[2] Vol. I, pp. 497-9.

found to contain a hundred and six cannon, three hundred cases of gin and five thousand slaves. This action, like the bloody attack of the men of Brass upon the Niger Company's station in Akassa, which Lugard only just escaped, was part of the resistance of the African traders of the coast to the British penetration inland which threatened their long-established position as middle-men.

Lugard's problem was whether to attempt to use the House as the basis for his Indirect Rule. In spite of its being founded upon slavery, Lugard's predecessors, in default of other sources of order, had passed laws to support the authority of the heads of these Houses over their members and given them power to recapture runaways. But Lugard had spent too much of his life in the struggle against slavery to sanction any compromise with the institution. Harcourt, for his part, knew that the old anti-slavery sentiment was still very much alive in parliament. By an ordinance of 1914, following due notice, all legal support was therefore taken away from the Houses and they were left to die the slow natural death of institutions left behind by the course of economic and political change.[1]

The real difficulties of administration were met only as the British pushed inland behind the relatively sophisticated coast into the main mass of the Ibo and Ibibio peoples. From the first the south-eastern region had depressed and daunted Europeans. To a contemporary writer this is a somewhat embarrassing fact. Today we British can smile as we read the depreciations of the rude habits of our forefathers by Julius Caesar or by later visitors to our island. " Who the first inhabitants of Britain were . . . remains obscure:" wrote Tacitus, " one must remember we are dealing with barbarians."[2] But in Africa events have moved so swiftly that the grandsons of wholly uncivilized tribesmen may now be our colleagues and friends in the common task of preparing Nigeria for full self-government, while in the remoter forest or bush there may still linger some of the old customs which may now be as repellent to them as to the Europeans. It is natural that the modern African should find the study of this immediate past un-congenial and, since science has largely discarded the old theories of inherent racial differences, he can claim that it is also irrelevant. But neither anthropology nor history can indulge in such dismissals. It is

[1] *The Native House Rule (Repeal) Ordinance, 1915,* 31 December 1914, No. 15.
[2] Tacitus, *Britain and Germany,* new translation by H. Mattingley (1948), p. 61.

certainly part of Nigerian history, and the reason for Lugard's first recoil from the prospect of work in this region,[1] that the way of life of these forest peoples made the task of their administration seem unattractive. Since the groups of the south-east have no history before the coming of the Europeans, it is not possible to estimate how far the effects of living in the hinterland of a coast which catered for the European slave-trade had been an additional handicap upon an already isolated population. Be that as it may, the psychological handicap certainly affected British officials. As early as 1894 an annual report struck this note. " It is very greatly to the credit of all concerned that an administration of any kind was maintained under the dispiriting influence of a deadly climate and a feeling fostered at home that the West Coast was the land of the lost and had better be severely left alone."[2]

It is, therefore, an important administrative factor that the first impression which the forest peoples made upon most Europeans was one of gloom and strangeness. Cannibalism, twin-murder, the poison ordeal, human sacrifice, the confinement of girls in " fatting houses " before marriage, were among the customs found in this region and they made a combination especially uncongenial to the European. Even today it is difficult to pass into a village within the intense shadow of the tall forest, which at once isolates and conceals, and see evidences of juju beliefs, with the skulls of cruelly sacrificed horses nailed to the poles of the huts, without a sense of encountering something dark and alien. Admittedly, the mind of the observers may be already stored with early accounts of the local customs, which lost nothing in their telling by reporters of " Darkest Africa ", or they may have received a later impression from the nightmares of Amos Tutuola.[3] Long before, a sixteenth century sea captain set the fashion by describing a coastal group in this region as a " people of beastly living, without a god, laws, religion or commonwealth."[4] But recollection of the return of some of the reputedly highly civilized and Christian nations of Western Europe to calculated cruelties upon a vast scale should act as a restraint upon this old, easy ascription of special depravity to any African tribe.

" Without commonwealth." This, at least, was only too accurate.

[1] Vol. I, p. 609.

[2] *Report of the Administration of the Niger Coast Protectorate, 1891–4* (1895), C. 7596, p. 2.

[3] e.g. A. Tutuola, *The Palm Wine Drinkard* (1952); *Simbi and the Satyr of the Dark Jungle* (1955).

[4] Burns, *History of Nigeria*, p. 58. See Perham, *Native Administration*, pp. 21–23, for a fuller description of this question.

The problem of the south-east was the problem of all the small, scattered, pagan groups of the north but it was seen here upon a vast and solid scale. The Ibibio now number about a million and the Ibo, covering the central block of the region, nearly five millions. They had no bond but a common language, in its several dialects, and similarities of culture. Crowded though they were, unlike the northern Muslims and the Yoruba they had no cities. Lugard could appreciate the formidable fact of their social fragmentation but, as with the Yoruba, it was many years after his regime that the anthropologists began to give exact definition to the obstacles which faced the administrators. Dr. C. K. Meek, Nigerian government anthropologist, and Dr. Margaret Green, who lived for two years amongst the Ibo, have revealed something of the minute cellular composition of the society.[1] The only really functioning social unit was the group of kindred families, containing up to a few hundred persons and called in official language, not very accurately, a village. Above this could be discerned a number of such kindreds, officially called a village-group, or, far less appropriately, a town. These groups varied widely in numbers which might run into some thousands. But this large group was of little service to British officials; its members might claim a common ancestor and might share a common market place and combine for defence, but that was usually—for variety added its difficulties to multiplicity—all they had of unity. Indeed, they were not seldom at war with each other and the only really certain mark of their community was that they would not eat each other.

The difficulties of administering this amorphous mass of humanity were preceded by those of occupying their country. Up to the 'eighties Britain's relations with this coast were mainly peaceful gropings up the waterways. The formal annexation of 1885 was, at the time, intended rather to warn off external competitors than to introduce internal administration. But, by degrees after this date, Britain began to go in behind the coast and the Houses and make contact with the interior peoples. The ensuing struggle was prolonged because, as a 1903 report complains, " to establish a foothold . . . it is necessary to deal with each and every ' town ' therein . . . There are thousands of these so-called ' towns '," and, with these, diplomacy, without a

[1] C. K. Meek, *Law and Authority in a Nigerian Tribe* (1937); M. M. Green, *Ibo Village Affairs* (1947). See also Daryll Forde and G. I. Jones, *The Ibo and Ibibio-speaking peoples of South-Eastern Nigeria*, Ethnographic Survey of Africa: Western Africa, Part III (1950).

Sir Ladipo Ademola, K.B.E., the Alake of Abeokuta

Pagan dancers from the plateau

The Yandaka Gate, Katsina

strong escort, was quite ineffective.[1] Penetration northwards through this roadless forest country was difficult and it was by no means fully pacified even when Lugard took office. Attention had to be given mainly to the task of extending and maintaining control, and the reports of the first years of this century are one long record of patrols and small expeditions. The chief agencies of government were the courts which the early consuls had established as courts of equity to deal with matters of slavery and trade. As the British hold on the country gradually increased, the tendency was for the courts to become not only judicial centres but to act, under their British official presidents, as councils to pass local laws and it was even expected they would " carry out work of administration and control which otherwise in all probability could not be coped with."[2]

These courts were still the main administrative instrument which Lugard took over. We have seen how, on the judicial side, he took them away from the Supreme Court, put them under the Provincial Court manned by political officers, and removed their British presidents. He also increased the number of courts and reduced the lists of those holding warrants as court members. But he was well aware that he was very far from having found the complete answer to the question of administration in the south-east. In his *Political Memoranda* we can see him groping for a solution of what was to prove almost beyond discovery. He had rejected the former pretentious pseudo-European type of court. Yet he did not believe in abrupt changes imposed from the centre. He would impress upon his southern staff " the maxim which I regard as vital in all African Administration, that only harm and distrust is [sic] wrought by sudden and radical changes and dislocation of procedure." The pattern must be adapted by each Resident to the special conditions of his Province. But all " towns " should be represented on a court, and he was even ready to accept the principle of election of " chiefs " and abandon that of descent. Some court members could be taken out of the court to become executives in official Native Authorities. If there were too many eligible members, even when the number of courts had been increased, members could sit in rotation. The boundaries of court areas must always be those accepted by the people.[3]

[1] *Reports, S. Nigeria*, 1903, p. 39.   [2] *Reports, S. Nigeria*, 1898–9, p. 10.
[3] *Memoranda* 1918, No. 8, pp. 272 ff.

Many detailed suggestions were added, including those for controlling court clerks and simplifying the rules of procedure; he added
injunctions that constant explanation and education were essential
Regarding taxation as essential to any advance in local government
he wished to extend to the south-east the simple form of capitation
tax applied to the northern pagans. But this the Colonial Office forbade.

The spirit of Lugard's instructions seems at once humane and
realistic. The great emir may have been the arch-type upon which
his system had been founded but, at least by the end of his time in
Nigeria, there was no vestige of even unconscious contempt or impatience in his treatment of the most primitive of his charges. His
basic principle could be extended to all levels. The spirit of his voluminous instructions is perhaps best shown in this paragraph:

" It may hardly seem worth while to set up a crude Tribunal consisting of naked Pagans, who can hardly be called Chiefs, and have
but a limited control over a few families, but from such small beginnings alone is it possible to create the rudiments of law and order, to
inculcate a sense of responsibility, and evolve among a primitive community some sense of discipline and respect for authority. A Resident
in such cases will doubtless feel that it would be much less trouble to
do the work himself, than to place even the smallest reliance upon so
ineffectual an instrument, but I desire earnestly to impress upon every
Administrative Officer that, even though the judicial work be not so
well done as it would be by himself, it is only by the patient training
of such a Court that better Tribunals can be evolved and real progress
achieved. The close supervision of such a Court will involve more
labour and personal effort than direct administration, but it is worth
the effort."[1]

Lugard had a strong, though not quite constant, awareness of his
own ignorance which was to make him a vigorous patron of African
sociology. He would, he said, have liked to have been able to equate
the village elders with the Indian *panchayat*, " but there is little accessible and reliable information regarding the social organization of the
tribe and the village among the primitive races of the Southern
Provinces." He proposed to inaugurate a system of records by experienced officers " with a view to co-ordinating and comparing the evi-

[1] *Memoranda*, 1918, No. 8, p. 273.

dence submitted and arriving at some really reliable data regarding each tribe of importance."[1] For the south-east, as elsewhere, he was anxious for his staff to learn the local languages, no easy task in Iboland where the language is tonal, like Yoruba, and varies in dialect from district to district.

Much of the *Memoranda*, like much of *The Dual Mandate*, often represents what Lugard tried to do rather than what he actually accomplished. This was especially true of the south-east. To deal with a difficult people with a language all but unattainable by a peregrinating political officer, he had a staff always inadequate in numbers and capacity for his large demands, and one that was still further reduced under both heads during the war which filled four out of his six years. It was a period which saw no little restlessness in parts of this region. We may note that he did not consider these Eastern disturbances to be serious. On one occasion he reported to Flora:

" My local news is not much. We have scotched the Kwale insurrection' only to find that the Udi business is very widespread and no progress is being made. Yesterday I arranged for *that*. This evening late I hear the Ogonis are up. Moorhouse came to tell me and read the telegram that they had eaten two persons. ' What sort of persons ' I asked, " were they Govt. employees?" He said oh no, they were no-one in particular. Then let them eat some more, I said. If Ogoni eats Ogoni my withers are unwrung! These things are trivial, the only trouble is that my last man is with Dobell in the Cameroons and I have absolutely no-one except some untrained scalawag police to send."

(L. to F. L., 15 November 1914).

Lugard was therefore forced to leave Nigeria in 1918 without having discovered how to administer the peoples of the palm-forest. His successors advanced little further. The Palmer report which he had ordered was followed by the Grier report in 1922 which was highly critical of the inefficiency and corruption of the courts. Then, in 1923, came the Tomlinson report which concluded that the courts, from which it had proved impossible to abstract their executive authority, were not so bad as Grier had reported.[2] Yet the old abuses of the so-called " warrant ", or government created, chiefs and the omnipotent

[1] *Ibid.* p. 306.
[2] *Report on the Eastern Provinces by the Secretary for Native Affairs* (S. N. Grier), Lagos, 1922; *Report on a Tour of the Eastern Provinces by the Assistant Secretary for Native Affairs* (G. Tomlinson), Lagos, 1923. See also Meek, *op. cit.* pp. 325-55 for a summary of administrative experiments after Lugard's time.

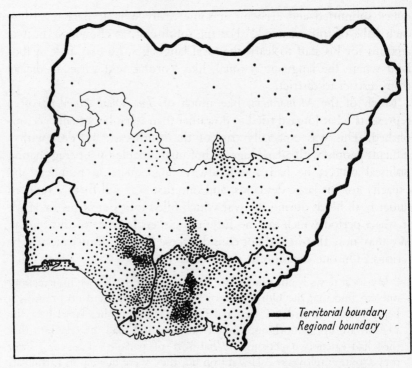

Map to illustrate the uneven distribution of Native Administrations, 1946-7. Each dot represents one Native Administration or Subordinate Administration. The thin line marks the administrative boundary which follows the approximate southern boundary of the old Hausa-Fulani states. Reproduced from K. M. Buchanan and J. C. Pugh, *Land and People in Nigeria* (1955)

court clerks were rampant. In 1927 came the belated decision to take up Lugard's rejected policy and to extend taxation to the region. In confirmation of Colonial Office fears this was followed at once by riots in Warri in 1927 and in 1929 by the extensive and serious women's outbreak, generally known as the Aba riots, when the "warrant chiefs" were attacked.[1] These troubles were followed by two or three hundred intensive investigations into the basic kinship groups, and a policy of decentralization down to these smallest units in the hope that these would rebuild themselves voluntarily into larger organs of

[1] For an account of these riots see Perham, *Native Administration*, pp. 206-20.

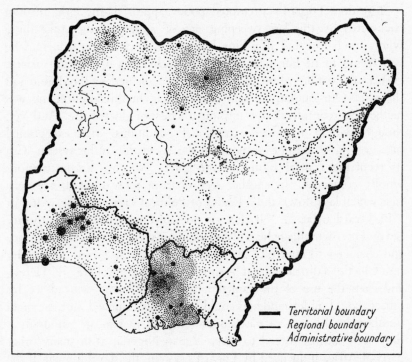

Map showing distribution of population in Nigeria, based on 1952 census. One dot represents 5,000 people; towns with population of more than 10,000 people are shown as spheres. The thin line marks the administrative boundary, which follows the approximate southern boundary of the old Hausa-Fulani states. Reproduced by permission of A. T. Grove

local government. These painstaking reforms, resulting in the creation of more than 500 native authorities of thirteen different types, can hardly be regarded as successful. The people themselves, deeply and swiftly changed by economic and educational influences, had no sooner begun to take over their own destinies as the new Eastern Region in the middle 'forties than the attempt to base Indirect Rule upon their complex indigenous pattern was thrown overboard. They chose instead a system of local government, largely taken from the British model, of County Councils, District Councils (Urban and Rural), and Local Councils, based mainly upon straight election.[1]

[1] Lord Hailey, *Native Administration in the British African Territories*, Part III: West Africa (1951), pp. 182 ff.

How does Lugard's attempted policy appear in the light thrown backwards by this last sweeping act of appropriation? Like those who came before and after him, but with a much clearer principle, he was trying to fit European rule to the actualities of African society, even to the baffling dispersal of authority presented by Ibo, Ibibio and the rest. Our quotations have shown that, in this attempt, he was neither overconfident, nor unsympathetic nor doctrinaire. And yet, though willing to meet exceptional conditions with exceptional measures, he could not escape from the association of his system with its recurring central figure of the chief. Nor are his instructions wholly consistent. In another section from those quoted, the very first which lays down the " Duties of Political Officers ", he writes of " Backward tribes ". " If there is no Chief who exercises authority beyond his own village he will encourage any village Chief of influence and character to control a group of villages, with a view to making him Chief of a district later if he shows ability for the charge."[1] Here— and even the use of the capital letter is significant—was advice his officers could understand and could take, which, indeed, in their small numbers in the face of vast undifferentiated masses of " kindreds ", they were almost forced to take. Yet in Nigeria, as in many other parts of Africa influenced by Lugard's system, the development of the instruction " Find the Chief!" into " Make the Chief!" was almost bound to lead to unsatisfactory results.

The truth is that in south-eastern Nigeria, as in many other parts of the territory and, indeed, of Africa, the real problem was that " administration " and " authority ", as understood and applied by the British, were concepts utterly unknown to the people. The problem was not only the obvious one of scale but also of character. Dr. Green, Dr. Meek, Mr. G. I. Jones, and other sociologists have shown us that Ibo society was not so invertebrate as appeared at first sight. The smallest unit, that of the extended family, could manage most of its affairs so effectively that even the kindred or village had few regular powers that could be listed. Duties and privileges were dispersed between heads of families, heads of kindreds, priests, oracles, rain-makers and diviners, age-grades, holders of titles in the many " societies " and even men of exceptional wealth or of oratorical or other gifts. Through the attachment of women from outside the exogamous unit, and through

[1] *Memoranda*, 1918, No. 1, p. 11.

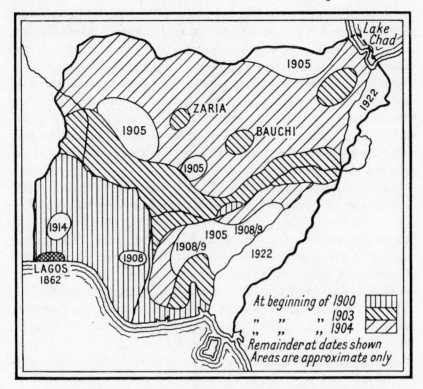

Nigeria, showing approximate areas and dates of British occupation. Reproduced from C. R. Niven, *A Short History of Nigeria* (1937)

the titled societies extending outside the village, there were subtle personal ties between what in most ways were small independent groups. It followed that for government to select, with the best intentions, a man who appeared to be an accepted leader and to invest him with their " warrant ", often to carry out novel and unpopular duties for them, was to make him automatically unacceptable and to drive him to irregular measures to support his new authority. It is small wonder that neither Lugard nor any other European administrator could devise a wholly effective means of administering the omnigenous millions of the south-east. They did not suffer this misunderstanding in silence. Tomlinson compared the vocal easterners to the northerners with their " capacity for silently enduring oppression."[1]

[1] *Report on Eastern Provinces*, p. 4.

Are we then to assume that the attempt to adapt the fundamental principle of Indirect Rule to these intractable human conditions was no more than a long misdirection of effort? Surely not. If the " warrant chiefs " system had been maintained with unyielding continuity as an agency of foreign rule this might have led either to much more extensive revolts or at least to a much deeper passive alienation of the people than actually occurred. But the very attempt, which the principles of Indirect Rule demanded, to find the true leaders, with its constant readiness to try and try again, mitigated the potential harshness of the policy.

It is not surprising that the apparently backward Ibo, spurred on by poverty and over-crowding, should have made an immense contribution to the material development of Nigeria, not only in their own Region, but elsewhere, and especially in the north. They form a large element of the new towns outside the Muslim cities, supplying the technical and clerical skills, and energetically building up their own social and educational life. Vigorous individualists, untrammelled by the bonds of chieftainship, socially mobile and assimilative, they were the first, under the exciting leadership of Dr. Azikiwe, to form an effective political party. They demanded not only freedom from colonial rule but undiluted democracy for which they could claim, with justice, that they were excellently prepared by their own equalitarian institutions. Their other very natural and very pregnant demand, as they thrust their way all over Nigeria, was for national unity.

CHAPTER XXIV

INDIRECT RULE
AND NORTHERN CONSERVATISM

THE SYSTEM devised by Lugard for Northern Nigeria in the first years of the century has been described and discussed in Chapters VII and VIII. When he returned as Governor-General it appeared that except for the important innovation of the Native Treasury, which will be described presently, he found the northern structure very much as he left it. It also appears that after his six years' tenure of office he handed it over to his successor, Sir Hugh Clifford, still almost unchanged. Our main interest in this chapter must be to ask how far this double appearance of continuity was real and, if it were, whether such continuity was in the interests of the northern peoples.

The close, almost verbal similarity of the doctrine and methods of Indirect Rule between their first formulation in the 1906 and in those of the 1918 *Political Memoranda* was pointed out in the latter many times by Lugard as a matter of pride. This similarity can best be judged by comparing the first model with the definition, concise and comprehensive, which he gave to his system in his 1919 report and which may be taken as his final definition of it as governor.

" The system of Native Administration in the separate Government of Northern Nigeria had been based on a recognition of the authority of the Native Chiefs. The policy of the Government was that these Chiefs should govern their people, not as independent but as dependent Rulers. The orders of Government are not conveyed to the people through them, but emanate from them in accordance, where necessary, with instructions received through the Resident. While they themselves are controlled by Government in matters of policy and of importance, their people are controlled in accordance with that policy by themselves. A Political Officer would consider it as irregular to issue direct orders to an individual native, or even to a village head, as a General commanding a division would to a private soldier, except through his commanding officers. The courts administer native law, and are presided over by Native Judges (417 in all). Their punishments do not conform to the Criminal Code, but, on the other hand, native law must not be in opposition to the Ordinances of Government, which are operative everywhere, and the courts . . . are under the close supervision of the District Staff. Their rules of evidence and their procedure are not based on British standards, but their sentences, if manifestly faulty, are subject to revision. Their prisoners are confined in their own native gaols, which are under the supervision of the British Staff. The taxes are raised in the name of the native ruler and by his agents, but he surrenders the fixed proportion to Government, and the expenditure of the portion assigned to the Native Administration, from which fixed salaries to all native officials are paid, is subject to the advice of the Resident, and the ultimate control of the Governor. The attitude of the Resident is that of a watchful adviser not of an interfering ruler, but he is ever jealous of the rights of the peasantry, and of any injustice to them."

He went on to extend his principle to the more primitive groups of the north, which were not to be put under Muslim rule.

" This system is clearly only adapted in its fullest application to communities under the centralized rule of a paramount Chief, with some administrative machinery at his disposal and finds its best exposition in the Moslem communities of the North. Nevertheless, its underlying principles are applied to the varying extent to which it is possible in each case to apply them, even to the most primitive communities in the North. The first step is to endeavour to find a man of influence as chief, and to group under him as many villages or districts as possible, to teach him to delegate powers, and to take an interest in his ' Native Treasury ', to support his authority, and to inculcate a sense of responsibility."[1]

The aim of this system, he explained, was not " to impose a form of British rule with the support of native Chiefs—which is a very different thing." The aim was rather that " the regeneration of Nigeria may be through its own governing class and its own indigenous institutions."[2]

Lugard wrote this during his final leave in England. In order to answer the questions that have been set in the opening paragraph, we must first go back to the time when he left Northern Nigeria and see

[1] *Amalgamation Report*, p. 14.   [2] *Political Memoranda*, 1918, No. 9, p. 317.

how the two governors who filled the six years of his absence from the country handled his system.

Colonial governors can usually expect only a few years in which to make their individual mark and they often show a very human tendency, if not to reverse some of their predecessors' work, at least to turn away from it while they strike out upon some new lines of their own. Both Sir Percy Girouard and Sir Hesketh Bell[1] appear, however, to have treated the work of their predecessor with almost reverent acceptance.

Sir Percy Girouard, as a Royal Engineer and an expert upon transport, concentrated his chief attention upon developing the railways. But he spoke warmly of Lugard who had handed on to him a government " which he had initiated, improved and perfected ". He considered the possibility of changing to a more direct rule and rejected it.[2] He praised and maintained Lugard's *Political Memoranda* as enjoining the proper balance between co-ordination and flexibility. He even censured one of his Residents for departing from Lugard's Memorandum enjoining support for Fulani rule, underlining in his letter the words " I adhere absolutely to the policy laid down in Memorandum 18 . . . "[3] The changes which he *did* make emphasized only his inability to live up to the standard of industry set by Lugard. Thus he abandoned Lugard's plan of dealing directly with all the political work himself and acting as the sole link between thirteen provinces. Instead, he set up a normal colonial secretariat. He also handed over to the Chief Justice the arduous task of going through all the cause lists of the Provincial Courts which, it was pointed out, took his predecessor a whole day a week.[4]

Sir Hesketh Bell in his turn remarked that " the policy of ruling through and with the native rulers . . . has been pursued with undeviating fidelity in the Northern Emirates."[5] It may be noted, however, that annual reports now shrank greatly in size, mainly at the cost of the full, rather personal and dramatic accounts of political work

[1] Bell, Sir Henry Hesketh Joudou, G.C.M.G., 1865-1952; 1882 Colonial Service, West Indies; 1890-3 Colonial Service, Gold Coast; 1894 Receiver-General, Bahamas; 1899 Administrator, Dominica; 1906 Commissioner, Uganda Protectorate; 1907 Governor, Uganda Protectorate; 1909 Governor, Northern Nigeria; 1912 Governor, Leeward Islands; 1916-25 Governor, Mauritius.
[2] *Reports, N. Nigeria*, 1907-8, pp. 5-6.
[3] Sir Richmond Palmer, ' Some Observations on Captain Rattray's Papers', *Journal of the African Society*, vol. XXXIII, January 1934, pp. 37 ff.
[4] *Reports, N. Nigeria*, 1907-8, p. 32.   [5] *Reports, N. Nigeria*, 1910-11, p. 32.

which had swelled Lugard's records. The two succeeding Governors seem to have regarded their work with far less sense both of personal commitment and of personal achievement.

The interval saw one most important new development in the sphere of native administration. This was the organization of the emirs' share of direct taxation, generally a half, into a regular native treasury, known as the Beit-el-Mal. This reform, which seemed so indispensable once it had been achieved, had spread from an innovation made by Palmer in Katsina. He had worked out the system with an intelligent new Emir who, not being of the traditional Fulani line, was exceptionally dependent upon British and native support and wished to demonstrate publicly what he did with his revenue.[1] The Emir's revenues were now paid into an official Treasury and a simple budget drawn up to cover all the salaries and to distinguish them from the various other expenses of the administration, such as public works, education and district and village administration.[2] Before Lugard returned this procedure had been gradually extended to other emirates.

Apart from this important addition and a good deal of attention to problems of land tenure, a problem too large and complex for inclusion here, everything seemed much the same to Lugard when he first went up to the north from what he regarded as the ill-ordered south. He could, we saw, upon first arrival, exclaim with relief that, by contrast, " the north runs itself." He was going to his administrative home, the one he had built himself, and where he had counted upon being wholly welcome and happy. Yet he soon felt in the air something like opposition.

The truth was that he had not made the imaginative effort to reckon up the effects of time and change since he left the country.[3] In the first six hectic years his administration had necessarily been almost a one-man show and his political staff, built up from zero and very largely from men with no appropriate experience, had been wholly dependent upon his direction. Their docility, we saw, was wearing a little thin in parts even before he left. After his departure this staff, now thoroughly indoctrinated, confronted two governors who were

[1] *Reports, N. Nigeria*, 1910-11, pp. 3-4, also Perham, *Native Administration*, pp. 70-2 for a description of these events based on Sir Richmond Palmer's verbal account to the writer.

[2] *Reports, N. Nigeria*, 1910-11, p. 33, and 1911-13, pp. 29-30.

[3] In what follows, the writer owes much to information from some of Lugard's Residents, mainly Sir Richmond Palmer, Sir William Gowers and Sir George Tomlinson, supplied in letters written between 1948 and 1955.

at once new to the country and far less dominating in character than Lugard. This was especially true of Sir Hesketh Bell whom Palmer called "kindly—but conservative and neutral". Girouard, though a much more positive character, was converted rather than dominated by his staff. Moreover, he gave them a very free hand. He came like "a breath of fresh air," Sir William Gowers told the writer. The officials might still be called Lugard's school but it was a school in which, while the master had been away, the pupils felt that they had more than learned his lesson, a situation which is often painful for an ambitious and self-confident teacher. They had built up a working partnership with his emirs; they had created the Native Treasury system which had given a new and solid strength to his Native Administrations. They felt that they had turned a rough improvisation into a settled system. In a dozen or so years of day-to-day and down-to-earth administration they believed they had carried Lugard's ideas to their logical conclusion.

But had Lugard ever understood the logic of his own ideas? It was doubt upon this point which led some of the senior officers to regard with apprehension the return of the master. Among these was the scholarly Burdon, now an expert in his field and an enthusiastic friend and supporter of the senior Emir of Sokoto. Above all there was Temple who had been Girouard's friend and chief of staff and had been given a very free hand with the northern administration as Bell's Deputy Governor. Sir Richmond told the writer that when he met Temple in St. James's Street, just after the announcement of Lugard's appointment as Governor-General, he found him quite dismayed. Temple was a close personal friend not only of Girouard but also of Charles Strachey at the Colonial Office and Sir Richmond believed that they had all three wanted the appointment of Girouard, and had confidently expected it. Their hope had been both to develop the northern system further and to extend it to the south. But now, Temple told Palmer, he felt very pessimistic about this extension and, indeed, about the future of Indirect Rule generally. He feared also for the continuance of that free hand which, they felt, had enabled them to accomplish so much.

The institutional and impersonal surface of any system of administration is very thin and we are reminded, especially at times of failure, or at least of strain, that its success depends almost wholly upon the relations between persons. Their individual ambitions, fears, prejudices and ideals make up very sensitive units. These, when clamped together by the demands of the machine, are often chafed raw if not severely wounded by the forced conjunction. Lugard and Temple, each a man of high character and ability, were human parts which simply could not be effectively articulated.

Temple's background and his first contacts with Lugard have been described.[1] The well-informed Morel had felt sympathy for his governor, Lugard's predecessor. Writing to John Holt, head of the important West African commercial firm, he said:

" Whatever Hesketh Bell may do, he is in future tied to a tiger which he will have very great difficulty in shaking off. Temple, the Senior Resident, whom I have got to know extremely well and who is a man of great power and personality, (although like you and me absolutely against the Governor's present unfettered control) has been appointed Deputy G. to take Hesketh Bell's place when the latter returns on furlough . . . I don't envy Hesketh Bell if he is going to run on wrong lines! I have conceived a very great admiration for Temple who is by no means popular, but he with Burdon . . . and Orr constituted the triumvirate which has been able to steer the ship of State in N.N. through many rapids unknown to the general public who do not realize anything beyond the Governor's name whoever the Governor may be . . ."[2]

There were three major ways in which Temple differed from Lugard. To begin with in their general politics Lugard was increasingly a Conservative while Temple was a rather speculative and individual kind of Socialist. Secondly, while Temple had a really intimate knowledge of the Hausa and their language, Lugard, though he realized with increasing certainty the importance of such studies for his staff, never built this intimate bridge between himself and the people he ruled. He respected native society on principle; his system was founded upon this respect. But Temple, working his way up in the administration, had seen it closely from the inside, and though he could observe and satirize its corruption and oppression, he yet believed almost fanatically that it should be kept inviolate from the disintegration of western influence. He developed his ideas in his very remarkable book, *Native Races and their Rulers*,[3] enlivened by his own

[1] See above, pp. 388–9
[2] Morel to John Holt, 21 September 1910, Holt Papers.
[3] Temple, *Native Races and their Rulers*, p. 71. The quotations which follow are all taken from chapter IV, pp. 49-79.

drawings. The importance of Temple's position in Northern Nigeria for so many years and the attitude of mind he must have diffused in the service would demand attention even if there had not been a subtle but important conflict between his ideas and those of his chief.

He believed that the path the natives must follow was " the natural evolution of their race ", which was quite different from that of the white man. Yet he did not believe " that one race can remain subject to another for an indefinite length of time." And certainly the rulers should not impose a heavy bureaucratic rule. If, he surmised, William the Conqueror had been an efficient direct ruler, the government he established might have saved us from the Wars of the Roses. But should we have been a contented people? Britain could only prolong her rule over the Hausa states if she gave " scope for the higher yearnings of human nature " and allowed native communities to manage their own affairs and permit to the native leader " the exertion of his talent ". He believed that " if the policy of Indirect Rule should be consistently and intelligently applied " the larger Fulani and Yoruba states might attain full internal self-government within one or two generations, presumably as a number of independent or federated states. The more backward units would take longer. (But, in comment, these were smaller, much more numerous, and widely scattered). In order to achieve this end Temple laid down a number of conditions. First of all " you must shut your eyes, up to a certain point," to a great many practices reprehensible in our present civilization. (Here followed some colourful quotations about Elizabethan bribery). Secondly, the Resident must " keep his authority in the background and concealed, if not from the Emir and his entourage, at all events from the people generally." Otherwise the emir's prestige would be impaired. This concealment was even more important with backward groups. (Though, surely, much more difficult?) These conditions led on inevitably to another. The Resident must be given an almost completely free hand. " In a vast number of matters, and important matters, the Resident only is in a position to give a right judgment." In addition, his status with emir and people depended upon his " moral prestige " among the natives and this was undermined by interference from, or even references to, the centre. In any case he could obtain little help from outside sources. " So subtle are often the bases on which he arrives at a decision that he may sometimes find considerable difficulty in making a good case on paper . . . In my humble opinion he should not be called upon for such justification." If these conditions were observed the Resident under Indirect Rule " can wield an enormous power for good " over the destinies of the people. He " takes the place of the influence of public opinion as a controlling force over the Emir's actions . . . "

Even when due allowance is made, as is only just, to the special circumstances, practical and ideological, of the time, the dangers of these ideas, which as we saw in earlier chapters on Indirect Rule were latent in the system, can readily be seen after some forty years more of Nigerian history. The surprising thing is that Temple, with his feeling for history, his speculative mind and his capacity for satire, should have led himself on into these extremes. Perhaps the key lies in Palmer's evidence in letters to the writer. They record how strenuously Temple rebuked Palmer for some deviation from the true gospel. " He devoted his life to Northern Nigeria and the policy of Indirect Rule was his ideal. His point of view was quite different from Lugard's." Palmer also said that Indirect Rule was Temple's religion and that at times he verged on the fanatical.

It will have become more evident why Temple and Lugard were so discordant. Temple, for all his streak of fanaticism, could be detached and speculative, his mind could range both widely and forward into the future. By contrast, Lugard was practical, concentrated, with hardly a moment when he could laugh at himself or his work; his mind reached a certain distance out into the future and stopped where such exploration seemed to be a mental indulgence. But Temple, casual, philosophic, artistic, lived in a different mental world. No wonder when the two met, Lugard noted his awkwardness and silence and gave him low marks for intelligence. And it is significant that when Temple wrote his book upon Indirect Rule, he hardly mentioned the name of his chief or made any reference to Lugard's writings or to the part he had played, during twelve out of Northern Nigeria's eighteen years of existence, in founding and building the system which the book described.[1]

It is regrettable that, as with Lugard's conflict with Macdonald, recounted in the first volume, the abundant criticism from Lugard

[1] The book has no index, but there seems to be only one very casual reference to Lugard in the chapter on Justice, p. 191.

cannot be balanced from much material providing the other side of the case. Fortunately, in contrast with the Macdonald affair, and perhaps because this time it was Lugard who gave the orders, he continued to like Temple and his wife personally. Explaining him to Flora, he wrote:

> " He has a great personal charm, and is wonderfully in touch with every single thing in the Protectorate, but very opinionated and obstinate. I think anyone but myself would find him very difficult to deal with but I can say (in more civil terms of course) ' whether you like it or not *this* is my policy and you jolly well do it,' and my position is too strong for him to resent it. Besides, I am convinced that he is thoroughly loyal to me and thoroughly in earnest and speaking from knowledge and conviction when he differs from me. Naturally, therefore, I attach great weight to all he says, and for the present I have let him have his own way in one or two matters on which we differed, pending my fuller and more up-to-date investigation."　　　　　　　　　　(L. to F. L., 20 November 1912).

A year later he exclaims

> " I had the same feeling of despair come over me that I so often have with Temple—a feeling that he is utterly unsuited for a responsible position. . . Fortunately I am entirely his master—poor Hesketh Bell was not !"
> 　　　　　　　　　　　　　　　　(L. to F. L., 10 November 1913).

Lugard assumed that, upon amalgamation, there would be no escape from having Temple as Lieutenant-Governor of Northern Nigeria. The only other possibility, since he seemed to be well esteemed at the Colonial Office, was that he might be promoted elsewhere as a governor. Lugard was therefore startled during 1913 by an unexpected episode. A pagan group had killed a tin prospector who insisted upon arranging his survey marks in a way which offended their customs. It appears that because Temple sent in an inadequate report upon the rather fierce repression of these offending pagans, he put Harcourt into difficulties over a parliamentary question—a very serious hurt to a politician. Temple received an unusually strong rebuke. He was told, in an open dispatch, that Harcourt had lost confidence in him and that he had removed his name from the list of those he was considering for promotion. Upon this matter Lugard felt for Temple. After telling Flora the story he concluded " I think he has been very hardly used." (L. to F. L., 28 February 1913). As a result, Temple was not promoted away from Nigeria and was among the few of Lugard's most senior officers not to become a governor.

In spite of this the Office, and especially his friend Strachey, supported him increasingly against Lugard for the rest of the Governor-Generalship, an external support which, to say the least, weakened Lugard's vaunted " mastery " of his Lieutenant-Governor. " There is nothing," Lugard decided gloomily, as he looked ahead on the eve of amalgamation, " I think, in the future under Amalgamation that gives me greater uneasiness than Temple . . . " (L. to F. L., 28 December 1913).

What were the actual issues which divided the two men? It would be difficult to find any that did not. They held different views even about the proper sartorial turn-out of a senior official so that Lugard, who thought him slovenly, was reduced to telling Mrs. Temple a story in the hope that she would realize its indirect relevance to her husband. They disagreed about land tenure, Temple being fascinated by the theories of economic rent and nationalization. They disagreed about the form amalgamation should take. Their most serious disagreement, lying at the very heart of their work about Indirect Rule was closely bound up with Temple's difference with his chief about the character of their official relationship. In his amalgamation proposals he put in a clearly heartfelt plea for decentralization, almost every word of which implied a criticism of Lugard. With increasing centralization, he wrote, the administration was becoming " more and more mechanical ". " A great deal of work is now being done by the Governor which could, I submit, be done quite as well by the senior political officers, and thereby a great deal of the former's time, which is at present spent on duties of an almost routine description, is wasted. That time might well be employed in considering questions of policy which have a wide embrace and a far-reaching importance." Under this defective system a senior official was so clearly devoid of real responsibility that he had influence neither with the emirs nor with his own junior staff. His scheme of amalgamation was therefore devised to reduce the Governor's powers of control. Lugard's scheme, as we have seen, was devised with the exactly opposite purpose.

Lugard soon recognized that many of the northern officials shared this attitude of mind with Temple. This naturally made him feel anxious when Strachey went up north to gather impressions. " It is curious," he reflected,

" that I have no misgiving as to whom he collected his impressions from in Southern Nigeria. It is in Northern Nigeria that I fear my policy may be distorted. In the old days, with my loyal staff in Northern Nigeria, I should have felt absolutely indifferent if a waggon-load of Stracheys had been turned loose. Since I left there has grown up under Bell and Temple a disloyalty and a swollen-headedness which has spoilt N.N. Every Resident, including the best, writes at large on the policy we must pursue . . . The Governor is left out." (L. to F. L., 28 December 1913).

He even felt at times, when he was on tour in the north, that some of the Residents, Gowers for instance, wanted to prevent him from coming into direct contact with their emirs—those emirs whom, for the most part, he had himself subjected, chosen and installed. He recognized one reason for this attitude, which, the writer observed, was still persisting in some Provinces seventeen years later when Sir Donald Cameron was trying to introduce reform into the northern provinces. " They naturally want to aggrandize the Province and their Emir." (L. to F. L., 11 January 1914). To do this was at once to enlarge their own power and to diminish control from the centre. The Residents were asking from their governor that wide sphere of initiative which he was asking for himself from the Colonial Office. The proper degree of delegation is one of the most difficult of all administrative measurements but the history of colonial policy seems to show that though central control, whether from colonial or imperial headquarters, often led to immediate errors, over a long term it was dangerous for colonial officers and their charges to settle down into a backwater almost outside the stir of the main stream of policy.

Some of the Residents, confident that immense progress had been made in building upon Lugard's foundation after he had left, felt that upon his return he looked with disapproval upon their edifice. " When Lugard returned," wrote one of them, " he certainly left the impression upon those of us who were whole-hearted ' indirect rulers ' that though he could hardly quarrel with the results achieved he was very doubtful about the methods employed and thought we had gone too far in encouraging the growth of live units of local governments, especially from the financial point of view."[1] " It is putting it mildly," wrote

[1] Sir William Gowers to M. Perham, 26 November 1949.

another, " to say that Lugard did not approve of the method and extent to which Indirect Rule had been pushed since he left in 1906."[1]

Native administration was a wide enough area over which to disagree, but perhaps the most definite point at issue was that of the control of the Native Treasuries, with which was bound up the whole character and future of the larger Native Administrations. It was a very good thing, declared one of his staff, that the system of Treasuries was firmly established before he returned. " When he came back we always felt that he looked at them a little sourly with his odd combination of penuriousness and distrust."[2] It may be that since the Treasuries had been developed after Lugard left Northern Nigeria, they were the component of the system which the Northern service could best defend from their Governor. And, of course, they opened out new possibilities, especially to the larger emirates, of increasing their powers and status. For the whole seven years of his period Lugard fought his Lieutenant-Governor, his staff and the Colonial Office over the question of the financial status and allocations of the Treasuries.

The struggle began immediately after his return. In the first general estimates which he prepared he included the details of the Native Treasuries and also showed their surplus as if it had been part of government revenue. The Office strongly disapproved, and Harcourt informed Lugard that the emirs ruled and that they were in control of their revenues, being advised by the government only as far as necessary. Therefore their accounts should not be included in the government estimates. This was out-Lugarding Lugard with a vengeance. To Lugard it appeared that it was not only that the Office, like the staff, had learned Lugard's old principle too well, but that Temple and his colleagues had carried it even further. They had encouraged a quasi-independent status for the emirs and buttressed it with the Treasuries, and nothing could shake their adherence to what had become a matter of faith rather than reason. When in Nigeria at the end of 1913, Strachey collected the strong views of Temple and his staff on this matter, he must have warned his colleagues in Downing Street to regard any attempt of Lugard to modify the system as an action on the level of treachery or even of political dishonesty. From

---

[1] Sir Richmond Palmer to M. Perham, 17 December 1949.
[2] Sir G. Tomlinson to M. Perham, 19 January 1950.

now on the Office seemed to be always on guard ready to pounce upon the Governor at the slightest sign of such turpitude.

Lugard's point of view is interesting. To most students of colonial administration it will come as a surprise that the originator of Indirect Rule struggled to modify his own original system in the direction of greater centralization at the expense of the native authorities. And yet the really surprising thing, when a close view is taken of his character, is that a man who was so dominant and industrious, a natural centralizer, should ever have fathered a system based upon such a large measure of delegation to African emirs and chiefs. It seems as if the explanation must be that Lugard, as early as his Uganda or even his Indian days, accepted the *theory* of such delegation and the circumstances of Northern Nigeria in 1900–6 enforced the *practice*. He brought the two together in his early reports and memoranda and yet all the time the practice in its full expression was really in some measure—for this point must not be exaggerated—against his own strongest natural tendencies.

Lugard had, however, an argument as well as an instinct. He was quite ready to admit that Temple and his colleagues had done a fine thing in developing his own plan for the emirs' revenues into a system of official Native Treasuries. But Lugard could still learn, and what he had seen of quasi-independence in Egbaland and Ibadan had influenced his views. He explained that the ideal at which he would aim in the present state of development was the maximum of European control that was consistent with the fostering of a keen interest in their own financial affairs by the Native Administrations. But, he thought, it would be a grave mistake to allow the Native Administrations to strike off on lines of increasing independence in their relations with the central British administration. The response of the Office was to favour this tendency by ordering that the native revenues were to be kept quite distinct from general revenues. When Lugard came home, the official who was, it seems, least unsympathetic towards him, Sir John Anderson, talked to him and delivered the blow in person. It seems as though Lugard was quite unable to understand how there could be any doubt of his good intentions. Sir John made it clear to Lugard that he was regarded in the Office as a man who thought he was a perpetual ruler of Nigeria whose wisdom and ability were equally beyond question.

481

Lugard certainly felt the blow. The Office had, he told his wife, humiliated him publicly by cancelling his action. He was also refused permission to have any proper audit of the Native Treasury accounts and he now found them full of the wildest errors and discrepancies. According to him, Temple was utterly incompetent at figures and hardly knew the difference between debit and credit, so that Lugard, in spite of working hard himself upon the muddled accounts of some fifty treasuries, felt the gravest misgivings as to how far their revenues, the total of which by 1918 had risen to £414,000,[1] were being properly audited, spent and accounted for.

Defeated over the issues of an all-inclusive budget, and of proper official audit, Lugard now attacked the position from another side. Believing that the revenues of the bigger native administrations were growing too large for their needs or their status, he hit upon the idea of getting " reimbursements-in-aid " from them to the Protectorate government for various services and for works ostensibly done for them. But the Office, alerted by Strachey, was ready to man the walls at this new point. Their view was that if the Treasury revenues were too large the basic proportion of their allocation should be re-considered but there should be no tampering with their current revenues. This time Lugard was treated to a really serious rebuke by Harcourt himself and a very difficult interview took place. After it Lugard wrote to Harcourt a strange apology that on the personal side reads rather more as a regret at being misunderstood than as a true apology, while on the official side it was by no means a recantation. He had thought, he said, that as governor he was entitled to make such changes without Colonial Office supervision. His aim was different from that of the Office. He was obliged to agree that the ultimate object was " the creation of dependent states, guided and con-trolled by British officers ". But he believed that the Native Admini-strations should remain in a tutelary stage for some years though he was fully prepared for further progress when their education and experience should have justified it.

The Colonial Office must have thought that with this solemn rebuke from the Secretary of State the struggle was over. But Lugard's head was still unbowed. The estimates of the Native Treasuries excited his

[1] Northern Provinces, *Native Administration Estimates 1918* (Lagos), p. 167.

passion for economy as well as for control. Writing to Flora, to whom he reported every move in the game, he said:

"I am in the greatest difficulty regarding them. I will not agree to squandering money on projects which are wholly unnecessary merely because the Native Treasuries have more cash than they know how to spend. Yet that is what Mr. Harcourt insists upon my doing at a time when the Revenue of Nigeria is reduced by about £1,000,000 in consequence of the war . . . So I have decided that surplus monies shall be passed to reserve so that I shall have an enormous sum to invest at a time when they are demanding increased expenditure on Education, Forestry, Veterinary, etc. It is extremely embarrassing and adds greatly to my difficulties." (L. to F. L., 19 December 1914).

He had just done more than this. When he sent in the Estimates for 1915, accompanying them with 44 explanatory pages, whereas Temple had sent in nothing to him, it was found that he had charged Native Treasuries with costs which might be regarded as being for central purposes. Once more the Office firmly instructed him to comply with the previous instructions and to send in the fullest details to prove that he had ceased to disobey.

Still Lugard would not accept defeat. He had now been beaten off in three attacks but, carefully reconnoitring the Office position, much as he had secretly surveyed the Arab stockade on Lake Nyasa nearly thirty years before, he saw two other weak places. One was provided by the war and we shall have to refer to it again. Briefly, it was to use contributions from the emirs towards the cost of the local campaign and thus release government revenue for other purposes. The Office must have been astounded when they saw the double purpose of this move, the legitimate and indeed laudable public purpose, which it was very hard for them to reject, and the old private purpose which Lugard had so long pursued. Lugard had gratefully accepted the grants from the emirs before the Office had time to act and he naturally pointed out that they would be gravely offended at the rejection of their gift. In spite of this, Harcourt insisted that the gifts should be returned. He followed up this repulse by an attack on Lugard's own position, laying down that the contributions should be made, insofar as they could be afforded, *after* the war and direct to Britain. This was more than a defeat for Lugard, it was an indignity.

" The Emirs will be wholly bewildered. They will probably think the King despises their gift, the Governor is humiliated, and the financial problem of refunding money already credited in accounts upsets all our figures. Were I free to do so I would, I think, really be inclined to resign my appointment. I cannot do so, for I *must* serve my time and far above this I would not send in my resignation during the war, even if they told me to publish throughout Nigeria that I was an incompetent ass."

(L. to F. L., 7 April 1917).

Lugard had detected another possibility of attack over the question of audit. His direct assault over this issue had been defeated, but he fell back upon mining and sapping operations. He appointed not auditors but " supervisors of Native Revenue " whom he sent round with instructions to reduce the accounts of the Treasuries to some orderly common system. The Office, however, through its contacts with Temple and other critics of their chief, soon heard of these agents, and that they were known as " H.E.'s spies ", and that they were sent out by him into provinces without any warning to the Lieutenant-Governor. It is, however, interesting to note that at this stage—the middle of 1915—Temple had shifted his position so far as to agree with Lugard that if these inspectors reported purely upon the *arithmetic* with no element of *inspection* they could be useful. He showed here a slight tendency, which Lugard frequently remarked after 1915, to be less wholeheartedly antagonistic to his Governor than he had been at first. Indeed, a point seems to have been reached when the Office remained more critical than the local dissidents. But Lugard was in a strong position in insisting that some £400,000 of what he regarded as public revenue should not be managed by emirs, native clerks, and the financial amateurs of the political service without proper control. When, in 1917, he put up a scheme for official " examiners of Native Accounts " the Office did not feel able to reject the proposal out-of-hand, but decided that it could wait until after the war, a somewhat barren concession for a shortly retiring Governor.

Lugard had still one more stratagem up his sleeve. Observing that almost all the plans *he* put up to the Office were turned down, while the advice of some of his officers was solicited, he hit upon the idea of presenting some of his proposals in their names. He told Flora that

" I have long recognized and accepted the fact that my own opinions count for nothing at the Colonial Office . . . It is astonishing how difficult it is to efface oneself to the proper degree . . . I rarely dare speak of any-thing in regard to the Native Administration in the North unless I can base myself upon Temple." (L. to F.L., 17 February 1916).

But in 1917 Temple left Nigeria. His health was not good, and it had been further worn by his continuing difference with his Governor not only over his concept of Indirect Rule but over the closely related issue of the denial to the Residents, as he saw it, of a proper measure of freedom. He retired first to South Africa where he wrote his book, which shows some reflection of local views of social segregation, and then to Granada. Here, after turning his remaining energies to a study of the local gypsies, he died, leaving his wife, his devoted partner in all his work, to an inconsolable widowhood. The resignation of Temple gave Lugard his chance. He had in Goldsmith,[1] a Senior Resident, just the co-operative man he wanted and he obtained his appointment in succession to Temple. This appointment was criticized, and he himself afterwards felt some misgivings as to whether Moor-house were not the better man.[2] But he was now able to put forward his northern plans not only with Goldsmith's hearty concurrence but over his name. Lugard believed that the Office had supported the stand of Temple and Gowers against his attempts to cut down the wide dis-cretionary power of the Residents over Treasury finances. They now found, in 1918, Goldsmith actually going back on Temple's proposals and suggesting that control over Residents should be tightened rather than loosened. This was shocking, but with Governor and Lieutenant-Governor in accord, the Office was at least out-manoeuvred.

The history of this long disagreement has been given because, from 1900 to the time of independence, the exact content of Indirect Rule has been the central question for the Northern Provinces, and, indeed, for Nigeria as a whole. And finance was its inner core. Was the ultimate purpose, in the interests both of unity and efficiency, to level down the large northern—and by imitation the large southern—native societies, until they reached the proportions of units of local government? Or were they to grow upwards with an increasing measure of autonomy until they, or at least the larger ones, became self-governing native

[1] Goldsmith, H. S., C.M.G., 1873–1945; 1899 entered Colonial Service, Nigeria; 1918–21 Lieut.-Governor, Northern Provinces.
[2] Moorhouse, Lieut.-Colonel (later Sir) Harry Claude, C.M.G., 1872–1934; 1900–8 Colonial Service, in West Africa; 1908 Chief Assistant to Colonial Secretary, S. Nigeria; 1914 Secretary, S. Provinces; 1921–5 Lieut.-Governor Southern Provinces; 1928 Special Commissioner to the Solomon Islands.

states? This was the question which was to continue for many years to haunt thought and practice in this, as in some other dependencies. It was one to which no final answer could be given in the decade under review. Yet human societies somewhat resemble trees in their tendency to grow according to the shape to which they are pruned in youth.

The determined stand which the Colonial Office made in favour of the native states principle was based upon genuine conviction, derived partly from experience elsewhere in the Empire but also, very largely, from Lugard's original teaching and its dilation by his senior Residents. The officials were convinced that they were representing continuity of policy and that Lugard, through an inability to delegate to anyone, black or white, was playing the unnatural part of a man murdering his own child. Theirs was, we must admit, a high-minded view since the continuation of Treasury aid to Nigeria was necessitated only by the paucity of revenue in the north, and the Office might well have been tempted to win the favour of that powerful department by laying hands upon the large surplus funds of the Native Treasuries.

Yet Lugard's opposing view rested upon something much more respectable than an appetite for power. Far from murdering his child he contested that, while they wanted to keep it permanently stunted, he wanted it to grow, but in a different way. " It is amazing," he exclaimed, " that these people should think I have gone back on a policy evolved through a series of years against the most strenuous opposition. I would suggest to them the conception as an alternative that possibly, having devised the original policy, I may be the best man to guide its development. They have grasped only its rudiments." He went on to accuse some of his own officers of going behind his back to gain the ear of the Colonial Office. This conduct, he said, was opposed " to all the loyal traditions of old N. Nigeria " and indeed one of Temple's colleagues told the writer that the Lieutenant-Governor's behaviour in this matter was, in his view, very open to criticism. Disloyalty, no easy word to use in the context of administration, was to be the cause of further conflict between Lugard and the Office. " Well," Lugard concluded wearily,

" I suppose that as I can't be here for ever, Strachey and the C.O. ' Continuity ' will win in the end, and a few years hence will prove their error too late. Still I will lay my own line of bricks so long as I am here. After I go, they can do what they like. The present point is that the C.O.

order me to allow the Emirs to prepare their own Estimates and control their own expenditure. I say they are not ripe for it. These very men were only a few years ago practising extortion and supporting it by torture too revolting to describe. Only today I have the case of the Emir's son and heir (of Zaria) caught for the second or third time in embezzlement and this is the most intelligent of them all . . . "

(L. to F. L., 6 April 1916).

Two days later he went on:

" You were speaking of my Native policy. The point at issue is that Strachey and Co. thinking that they know more than me, are busy trying to convert the Native rulers into much more independent chiefs than they are at present fitted to be." (L. to F. L., 8 April 1916).

The words " at present " raise a further question. Did Lugard differ from the Office only in the timing and not in the principle of much greater independence? If we turn to his book, *The Dual Mandate*, written only a few years later, we fail to find a definite answer to this important question, upon which Temple's views have already been given. But he shows there his belief that the ultimate development of the African territories into complete independence " is not yet visible on the horizon of time ". Hence there seemed no need for him to deal in final goals. But it may be judged from what has been recorded in this chapter, that if he had not been obstructed both by the Colonial Office and by some of his own senior staff, and by the distraction of the war, he would have developed a much closer control of the emirs, with its corollary, a much closer control of the Residents by the Governor. The subtraction of revenue from the Native Authorities would have been a subtraction of power. Some retired Residents with whom the writer, while working upon this volume, has discussed this issue, point out that the conservatism of the northern administration was an unavoidable response to the conservatism of the rulers and their people. To press British control and reforms beyond a certain point would have meant the loss of their essential co-operation. This belief, held by men of the time and on the spot, demands serious attention but, like its opposite, must remain a hypothesis. The issue will arise again in the context of education. In the writer's view Lugard's policy was at least well worth attempting since, if the new direction he tried to give to policy had been steadily followed by his successors, the Northern Region today might have been more uniform in its administration, more centralized, with more fully developed central services. Secondly, it would have presented today rather less of a political contrast with the Southern Regions. Thirdly, as the system which many British governments in Africa and elsewhere soon came to regard as the archtype of native administration, it would have been a little less remote both in spirit and form from the more modest realities of these other colonies.

CHAPTER XXV

LUGARD TURNS EDUCATIONIST

IN THE field of education the Colonial Office assumed that Lugard, the soldier-explorer, would recognize his own incompetence. They fervently hoped that he would. They were wrong. Lugard had to work through departments but there was nothing departmental about his mind. He saw the life of the people he was administering as a whole and his own policy as a total response to their needs. Far from regarding education as no more than one part, however important, of these needs he saw that it must govern their whole future development. Of the problems presented by amalgamation, he asserted, " there was none comparable in importance and in urgency with that of education."[1] He told his wife that he regarded the education question as " *the* most important both at Home and in our Colonies and I read anything of importance regarding it." (L. to F. L., 2 October 1912). His papers frequently show him referring to his studies of the subject in Britain, Asia and Africa.

Education, especially in its administrative aspect, still more when treated to abbreviation, can be a very dull subject: the central figure of the child becomes lost in a forest of statistics and curricula while the exploration of principles can move quickly outwards from that small human centre until it becomes lost in the universal.

Lugard was quite ready to follow it that far though he had to find his way there conscientiously through problems of educational finance and administration. The Colonial Office seemed to have forgotten that Lugard had played no small part in matters educational in Hong Kong, or perhaps, when reminded of the devotion he had given to his university, they felt able to dismiss this as a piece of very localized experience.

---

[1] *Amalgamation Report*, p. 59.

There will be no need, in order to show his contribution, to write a chapter in the history of Nigerian education; the briefest background will suffice. There must, as in native administration, be two backgrounds since, when he began to examine his two Nigerias as fields for educational policy, he found them so different that he was in large measure forced to deal with them separately.

Since 1914 an immense volume of material upon the problems of colonial education, pedagogic, administrative and sociological, has been built up. But in his day Lugard, for a governor, was rather a pioneer in his intense concentration upon the subject. He was quick to foresee that the then inseparable combination of Christianity and western education could destroy the discipline of Africans as members of families, of tribes and as subjects of a colonial government.

The education problem made its impact upon him almost immediately upon his landing in Southern Nigeria. Here the dichotomy between the educational and the political actions of Britain was the more complete in that two quite separate metropolitan agencies were at work, the missions and the government. The missions here, as in most parts of British tropical Africa, had long provided an education inseparable from evangelization. Their penetration into the interior, dating from the 'forties in Yoruba and Efik country, preceded government and by 1914 the two were still only tenuously linked by control or subvention. A few figures will sketch in the picture better than many words. By 1918 there were more than 600 European missionaries with some 5,000 African assistants.[1] There were between 37,000 and 47,000 children attending school, and of these only 4,600 were in government schools, including 50 at the one government secondary school, King's College, Lagos. The vast majority of the rest were in mission schools, but only 12,500 of these were in schools of a standard to qualify for a share of the few thousand pounds which represented the total government assistance. The rest were unaided schools and in 1912 government control over them was negligible. The typical bush-schools of this period were mostly enlarged huts in which a native evangelist-teacher, hardly literate himself, struggled with inconstant classes of all ages and capacities. The provision was inadequate by any standard whether of quality or of quantity. For the latter, Lugard reckoned that amongst the estimated eight millions

[1] James S. Coleman, *Nigeria: Background to Nationalism* (California, 1958), p. 94.

of Southern Nigeria only one child in 180 was in any kind of school.

Viewing this picture from Government House, he naturally first measured the educational situation he found in Southern Nigeria by a political yard stick. " The primary function of education should in my judgment be to fit the ordinary individual to fill a useful part in his environment with happiness to himself, and to ensure that the exceptional individual shall use his abilities for the advancement of the community and not to its detriment or to the subversion of constituted authority. The local press presumably writes what its readers demand and if it may therefore be taken as a criterion, we must admit that education has not brought happiness or contentment to the educated community of Nigeria. It should be the aim of our new system to train up a generation who shall exchange this bitter hostility for an attitude of friendly co-operation, and who shall be able to recognize and achieve ideals of their own, without a slavish imitation of the European and be proud of a nationality with its own clear aims and future."[1]

This definition bristles with assumptions which later experience has taught us to question. But Lugard could support his point of view from the public statements of two leading Europeanized Africans who were as puzzled and shocked as himself. Sapara Williams, the senior African member of the Colony Legislative Council, declared that, " Sometimes parents feel that it is far better children do not go to school at all than come out as they do at present filled with ignorance, pride and stupidity."[2] Henry Carr described the products of the schools as " ill-educated, unreliable and lacking self-control " and he admitted that the local press, as a product of western education, was doing " grievous harm."[3]

Some European administrators, when first confronted with this problem, have urged concentration upon agricultural and technical education instead of " book-learning ". But even if Lugard had not possessed a streak of genuine liberalism in the authoritarian marble of his character, the practical demands of the new Nigeria would have ruled out this difficult reversion. Modern government is based upon the clerk, a being who can read, write, count and use a typewriter, and if the few and costly expatriate white men were not to be used up in very elementary clerking, its local provision was a first necessity.

[1] *Education in the Colony and Southern Provinces of Nigeria* (Lagos, 1914), p. 4, L.P.
[2] *Ibid.* p. 10.
[3] *Amalgamation Report*, p. 60.

Lugard reckoned that there were already 4,500 African clerks employed by government and commerce in Nigeria, that the demand was rising rapidly and that there were only 272 boys receiving anything that could be called secondary education. The gap was partly filled by recruitment from the older and educationally more advanced British colonies along the coast, and also, most incompetently, by boys leaving school as soon as they could put their minimum of literacy upon the ready market. Thus the supply of higher competence, especially for the teaching profession, was leaking away at the source.

With his usual celerity Lugard devised a policy of reform. It had five main heads. (1) The strengthening of government control over all education. (2) More and better government education. (3) Co-operation with the missions and more grants-in-aid for their schools. (4) A stimulating form of government inspection. (5) Emphasis upon character training both by religious and secular moral education.

A few comments will show that these were more original than might appear today.

The first, the strengthening of government control, was only one more example of Lugard's determination to master the whole range of government action. He therefore increased the inspectorate, drew up a full new ordinance, and himself wrote an education code. He desired power not only to control the creation of new schools, but also to control the existing unassisted schools, even if it were a power held in reserve. With memories of Uganda, he also wanted to prevent conflict between denominations by assigning them to separate regions.

His second purpose was for government itself to play a much larger part in education. Before deciding what this part should be, he sorted out the several aims of education in Nigeria so as to make a simple classification of schools. He distinguished three main types of education. First came the more advanced literary training needed by clerks and teachers. The best schooling of this type would be given by King's College which would prepare the pick of the youth to a standard which would allow some of them to go to England for university courses. But he wanted to see a lower level secondary school set up by the government at each provincial centre, but well away from the town. These were to house boarders; they would always have British headmasters, the prefect system, and much emphasis would be placed upon English games. Through these Lugard hoped

Lord Harcourt, Secretary of State for the Colonies, 1910-15

Sir Hanns Vischer

Charles Temple, Lieutenant-Governor,
Northern Provinces of Nigeria, 1914–17

to be able to share the English values in which he had so much confidence and which he had himself been given through his training as a gentleman at home and at his public school. Secondly there would be rural day-schools, with elementary schooling and native arts and crafts. Thirdly there should be training for those who, after some education at a provincial school, aimed at technical work of the European kind, which he saw made quite different demands from those of native craftsmanship. This training would be carried on mainly by the government departments for their own employees, and also through an apprenticeship system. Alas! war with its distractions and its diversion of staff and money, prevented all but a very partial fulfilment of this large, clear and, for its period, not illiberal plan.

On the third head Lugard's desire for government control and extension was not aimed at supplanting the missions; the new vigour of government would be shown in a greater capacity to lead and assist them. He had never forgotten his admiration for those men whom he regarded as the very best of missionaries, Dr. Laws in Nyasaland and Bishop Tucker in Uganda. Yet he was a severe critic of some of the results of mission teaching, especially of its tendency to destroy respect for chiefs and beneficial tribal customs. But he saw clearly how much was owed to their long pioneer efforts and how impossible it was, above all financially, for government to take over the large activities which they provided almost gratis. And if the two agencies were to co-exist it must be in intimate and fruitful partnership. He therefore entered from the very first into full discussion with the leaders of the missions both in Nigeria and also in London. Here, as the records of the Church Missionary Society show, their headquarters' staff were frequent visitors at Rutland Gate. In the Southern Provinces he set up a Board of Education, with the Lieutenant-Governor in the chair, in which the Directors of Education and others of his staff could solve their problems " with the good will and assistance of those who have daily experience of the practical work of education."[1] He also set up in each Province school committees upon which local Africans could sit.

His fourth reform was a complete change in the method of inspecting assisted schools. This had been done mainly by means of examinations. To Lugard, here somewhat in advance of his age, this was a

[1] *Amalgamation Report*, p. 62.

soulless method. He wanted his inspectors to stimulate and help the schools and pay attention to other matters than mere examination marks since he rated the training of character above that of intellect. He therefore laid down that inspectors should in their reports allow the school only 40 per cent for examination results, allotting 10 per cent for buildings and equipment, 20 per cent for the quality of the staff, and 30 per cent for " tone, discipline, organization and moral instruction." He tried to meet the admitted difficulty of this last assessment both by his emphasis upon continuous co-operation with the missions and also by insisting upon a very high quality in the government staff. After discussion with the Readers in Education at Oxford and Cambridge, he arranged for this staff to take courses in educational theory at those universities.

By 1917 Lugard was able to boast to Flora that his southern measures had won " a consensus of approval ". The Education Department, the Protestant missions and the Roman Catholic bishop were all "enthusiastic". (L. to F. L., 17 February 1917). This report was largely true. The records of the Church Missionary Society, which worked closely with other non-Roman missions, show that their leaders were impressed by the Governor's eagerness to help them and also by his emphasis upon the moral side of education. The C.M.S. London Committee formally thanked him for the friendly tone in which he communicated his plans to them and his readiness to consider their new suggestions.[1] Yet, within their agreement about the moral aspect of education, there was room also for a most interesting disagreement, one which throws much light upon Lugard's mind.

Resentful of any boundaries to his power, he was unwilling to recognize one at the point where his control of secular education ended and the realm of morals began. Having lost his old faith he groped for some system by which to explain his own morality. His wife, in much the same spiritual situation, seems to have led the way in tailoring a new philosophy to meet their special needs. While they still found much moral sustenance in the Psalms, they rejected the God of David in favour of their own interpretation of theories of natural law and of Truth immanent in the Beautiful. " It may be," wrote Lugard one day, " that the triumph of Right over wrong and of Liberty over

---

[1] F. Jones to Manley, 9 February 1915 (Yoruba Mission), No. 8, Church Missionary Society Papers.

tyranny is as much a Natural and immutable Law as the combinations which produce explosives or the colouring and form and shape of a flower . . . The beautiful plant covered with blossom is also the *healthy* plant. It is Natural and that is Divine. So in the never ending conflict between Right and Wrong, the Right, which is also the beautiful, must succeed." (L. to F. L., 19 January 1915). To this conviction, which he still held in the second year of the first world war, he added the pride of the agnostic. " It is so easy," he wrote a year later, " to pray to God—still easier to pray to an Intercessor with God— possibly easier still to pray to a woman who shall intercede with the Intercessor—instead of trying to *will* the thing you wish by strong thoughts addressed to the Universal Law of Nature or to the vital principles and the vital essential forces of the person for whom you plead." (L. to F. L., 2 February 1916).

It followed naturally from such ideas that Lugard should think the influence of the missions useful in the making of good men and good citizens, but also that they were insufficient. Moreover he was up against a problem with a long history—that of the place of religion in government schools. In searching for that " something else " which he needed he must turn to Flora for help and together they found what they were looking for in the teaching of a body called The Moral Education League. Lugard had already faced the problem of teaching morality unsanctioned by religion in Hong Kong university. He now drew up an elaborate instruction for Nigerian schools to supplement the teachings of religion and he persuaded one of the School Inspectors to compile readers under his guidance. His official definition of what he was attempting, written early in 1915, ran as follows: " I conceive that if a short period daily be devoted to placing before children, in an attractive way, the social and other incentives to gentlemanly conduct, the success which rewards self-control and industry, with similar lessons by the aid of illustration and anecdotal biography, it would form a valuable adjunct to the inculcation of the same ideals of right living as enforced by religious precept and sanction."[1] He therefore wished his staff to add to their other training two weeks of Moral Instruction run by The Moral Education League. The missionaries, however, thought that " moral instruction without a systematic and definite religious basis is not of sufficient force to

[1] *Amalgamation Report*, p. 63.

overcome the natural proclivities of the African boy,"[1] and the Colonial Office also recoiled from this project.

The disagreement of the Colonial Office with this particular plan was only one item of an opposition which covered almost the whole of Lugard's education policy in the north. For the Southern Provinces their opposition was much less and was mainly shown in delaying tactics. Lugard wore himself out with repeated requests for the acceptance of his new ordinance and code. The ordinance was to apply to the whole of Nigeria; the code of regulations to the assisted schools only to the south. He had drafted these early in 1914 with great enthusiasm and, having circulated them to all school managers for their views, he sent them to London in November of that year. For a year, according to him, the Colonial Office completely ignored them and it was not until December 1916 that, after much pressure on his side and criticism upon theirs, the new law was enacted. The Office, among other things, disliked his assumption of wide powers, especially over unassisted schools, though he was later able to claim triumphantly that in this he had anticipated the Fisher Act of 1918 in Britain. They disliked his plans for training his British staff. They objected above all to his project for moral education. In this the officials detected the hand of Lady Lugard. Indeed, he was proud to proclaim her help.

In his plans for the Northern Provinces Lugard received from the Office not only delay but almost complete condemnation. Their opposition began with their determination to retain the boundary between south and north as a real division. Lugard, with whatever local adjustments, wanted to have the same general administrative structure for both parts. Surely, he argued in 1915, when the Office brusquely cut out from his proposed legislation all that concerned the north, the educational problem for both regions was basically the same and the whole purpose of amalgamation was to level up the standards to the highest point attained in any one part and to help each to learn from the other. But the Office insisted that the north was entirely different and must be treated as such.

Certainly the differences were large and obvious. In the Southern Provinces Lugard could control, assist, and extend. But education remained predominantly in the hands of the major missions, long

---

[1] Minutes of C.M.S. educational committee, received 13 July 1915 (Y), No. 59, C.M.S. Papers.

established and based upon their strong headquarters in Britain, these in turn resting upon the nationwide moral and financial support of their own churches. In the Northern Provinces the situation was wholly different. It was not only that the British government had arrived much later than in the south and had been much poorer in resources, or that the missions had hardly yet begun to operate. The main problem was, of course, the existence of strong Muslim states, based not upon a variegated and crumbling paganism but upon a world religion. And this religion was inseparable from that social and political structure upon which it was the purpose of Indirect Rule to build.

Lugard was facing here the profound social-religious aspect of the problem he appeared to have solved so swiftly and easily on the political plane. It was and is—for this issue is still, and even more consciously, with us today—bound up with European domination over peoples of different race, culture and religion. How much should or could Britain offer—or impose? How much would the people need or accept? And, if the receiving culture were indivisible, could the imposing culture be carved up for selective application?

Before we consider the form in which these questions were presented to Lugard as Governor-General and argued with the Colonial Office we must take a brief look backwards in order to see how far he had dealt with them as High Commissioner.

We have seen how he had made his settlement with the emirates at a time when he was deficient in military power, revenue, staff and communications. The emirs had been defeated and mastered but the true measure of their suspicion and conservatism had still to be taken. In the emirates were to be found some six million Muslims, who professed a common world religion, possessed their own system of some 25,000 Koranic bush schools and were, for all their isolation, proudly self-sufficient in their own culture.

Lugard had won the acceptance of British rule by chiefs and people very largely by his reiterated promise, which it would be useful to quote here, to respect their religion. " Government will in no way interfere with the Mohammedan religion. All men are free to worship God as they please. Mosques and prayer places will be treated with respect by us."[1] Policy as well as poverty therefore prompted Lugard

---

[1] Speech of Lugard at Kano, 21 March 1903, *Reports, N. Nigeria*, 1902, p. 106.

to postpone any educational measures. Yet he did not postpone interest in the matter. In his report for 1901, with the most important part of the territory still to be occupied, he gave " Education " as a heading. Under it he apologized that he had so far been able to accomplish little except some beginnings of apprenticeship by government departments and announced his intention to start what came to be called " domestic science " for the older girls in his home for freed slaves.[1]

It was just short of the truth to say that in Northern Nigeria government had arrived ahead of the missions. First, in 1894-5, there was a preliminary reconnaissance for the Church Missionary Society by the Reverend C. H. Robinson.[2] After this, five pioneers of this Society under Bishop Tugwell, after three of them had been to Tripoli to study Hausa, travelled up to the north in 1900 almost simultaneously with Lugard and found him at temporary headquarters in Jebba. One of the five was Dr. Walter Miller, who was to be a unique figure in the history of the Protectorate, not only because he worked there for the next fifty years as a doctor and also became a great Hausa scholar, but because he was the one continuous European resident in the region who could both act as an independent observer and critic and also put his views vigorously on to paper. This he did not only in the correspondence of the Society but in four books.[3]

It was early in 1900 that his party paused, in their hazardous journey, to call upon the new High Commissioner. It might have been thought, for more reasons than one, that Lugard would have been hardly in the mood at that moment to welcome five pioneering missionaries. But the impression he and the young doctor made upon each other was immediate and favourable.

" On the top of the hill," wrote Miller, " overlooking the two branches of the mighty Niger River, where it divided to form an island, was Government House and there I was first introduced to His Excellency. How rare it is to find men of great experience and achievement willing to listen to, and be interested in, the aspirations and hopes of younger men! Here was one great enough to do so.

---

[1] *Reports, N. Nigeria*, 1901, pp. 22-3.   [2] C. H. Robinson, *Hausaland* (1896).
[3] W. R. S. Miller, *Reflections of a Pioneer* (1936); *Yesterday, Today and Tomorrow in Northern Nigeria* (1938); *Have We Failed in Nigeria?* (1947); *Success in Nigeria? Assets and Possibilities* (1948). A very interesting and well-informed discussion of the mission case will be found in A. Victor Murray, *The School in the Bush* (1929).

As I talked with Sir Frederick of the language, the future of the country, education and other matters, notably what script was to be adopted for the schools and all literary purposes, Arabic or Roman, he was never impatient, but encouraged all that was sane and reasonable in one's ideas. At all times, then and since, I have received kindness, courtesy and real friendship from the Governor."[1] The impression was mutual. " The best type of missionary I have ever met," wrote Lugard, " . . . an ideal missionary—and one of the best of men, for whom I have a more wholehearted admiration than I have for—well—very few!" (L. to F. L., 30 January 1906).

The little party pressed on northwards to the still unconquered Kano where on Easter Day, 1900, for the first time within those walls they celebrated the Eucharist. Regarded, not surprisingly, at that date, as spies by the Emir of Kano, they were lucky to get back with their lives. They paid the usual and accepted price of early missionaries. One of them died on the journey, another broke down and had to be sent back to England. A village-head who showed them kindness was killed by the Emir of Zaria by the novel method of throwing him repeatedly up against the palace ceiling. As soon as they could struggle back, ill and exhausted, into contact with the British, Lugard courteously but firmly forbade them to renew the attempt.

In the year following this encounter Lugard came to two conclusions about missions. The first referred to the emirates. " I am myself of opinion that it is unwise and unjust to force missions upon the Mohammedan population, for it must be remembered that, without the moral support of government these missions would not be tolerated. In effect, therefore, the mission obtains its footing on the support of British bayonets and if they are established by order of government, the people have some cause to disbelieve the emphatic pledges I have given that their religion shall in no way be interfered with."[2] Yet he felt it possible in that first education report in 1901 to say that the heads of the C.M.S. and of the Toronto Industrial Mission " afford me every confidence that both missions will be of great value in the work of civilization and progress," and added that missions should be given small grants.[3] He wanted to encourage missions to go to pagan areas, even those under Muslim rulers.

[1] Miller, *Reflections of a Pioneer*, p. 37.   [2] *Reports*, N. *Nigeria*, 1902, p. 77.
[3] *Reports*, N. *Nigeria*, 1901, p. 23.

The following year he gave a flexible interpretation of his pledge. While he would not *force* emirs to accept missions he would *encourage* them to do so and he could therefore report in 1904 that the C.M.S. had started work in Nupe where the Emir of Nupe was actually sending his son to their school.[1] The next year Dr. Miller, who had already achieved his ambition of speaking Hausa so well that in the dark he could be mistaken for a native, was invited to Zaria by the Emir who established such close personal relations with him that they were able to have discussions upon religious and social questions. A number of the mallam[2] class were taught Roman characters, an all-important beginning in Lugard's view since it would enable them to write to officials who had not learned Arabic. Lugard reported with enthusiasm upon Miller's medical and educational work. " Not only has there been no hostility but the people have manifested a desire ' to read, to hear and to consider.' " This success was due to Miller. The mission, Lugard went on, was intending, with the Emir's consent, to open a station next year in Kano, while the Emir of Kontagora was " quite anxious to allow them to come."

Lugard naturally longed to make a start with government education and was already planning several types of school. In all his plans Dr. Miller was giving advice and offering co-operation. Lugard ended up sadly with a comparison of what mission education had achieved gratis in little Nyasaland compared with the small beginnings in Northern Nigeria.[3] Thus, when he left Northern Nigeria, the political weather seemed to be " set fair " for a modest beginning of education, including mission education, not only in pagan but in Muslim areas.

In the interval, 1907 to 1912, while Lugard was in Hong Kong, this promising start in co-operation between government and mission came to a halt. The tendency, already described, of Lugard's school of administrators, under Temple's inspiration, to deepen and harden his policy was as apparent in education as in administration. Gowers, as Resident in Kano, the most influential Hausa city, was a strong opponent of the mission. Girouard, presumably believing that he was developing Lugard's policy, bent to their bias. The emphasis of the annual reports changed. In that for 1907–8 Miller's mission at Zaria

---

[1] *Reports, N. Nigeria*, 1904, pp. 124-5.
[2] Literate man, teacher or scribe.
[3] *Reports, N. Nigeria*, 1905-6, pp. 118-121, 1906-7, p. 39.

was written off as a " failure " with the addition, quoting Cromer's policy in the Sudan, that " it appears advisable to educate Moham- medans along their own lines and compulsory attendance at a Christian school is inconceivable and might prove disastrous. It is, moreover, in opposition to the promises of my predecessor." This, we can see, was not a wholly valid interpretation of what had been attempted. Moreover, mission schools in pagan areas were treated to the sweeping judgment that they failed in " inculcating and increasing a respect for native customs and institutions where not at variance with higher standards of morality ". The premature teaching of English led to " utter disrespect for British and native ideals alike, and to a denational- ised and disorganized population."[1]

It followed from this attitude towards missions that the government itself must take a hand in education. The following year, 1908, a most unusual and interesting political officer was seconded to take charge of education. He was Hanns Vischer.[2] He was the son of a successful Swiss businessman who had abandoned commerce in order to devote himself to religious works. Admiring England, he sent his sons to Cambridge. The elder became an Anglican priest. Hanns was also deeply religious, choosing Saint Francis of Assisi as his hero-saint. He volunteered for the mission field and went out under the C.M.S. to Northern Nigeria in 1901. He had not been there long before he felt he could do more constructive work in the administration and applied to Lugard for appointment. Lugard, as he afterwards told the writer, was a little disconcerted at this request from a foreigner and apprehen- sive about the effect upon the Muslims of appointing a Christian missionary. So, like the king in the fairy tale, he set him a number of hard tasks which he never expected him to perform. Among these he was to become naturalized, to master the English and the Hausa languages, and the Maliki Muslim law, and to gain the diploma of the Royal Geographical Society for surveying. Two years later the aspirant faithfully presented himself declaring that he had passed all these tests. Lugard was obliged to appoint him. So began a career of brilliant service to Africa and to Britain and a forty-five year friendship with

[1] *Reports, N. Nigeria*, 1907-8, p. 70.
[2] Vischer, (later Sir) Hanns, 1876-1945; 1900-1 C.M.S. Hausa Mission; 1903-8 Political Service, N. Nigeria; 1906 crossed the Sahara; 1908-15 Director of Education, N. Nigeria; 1915-18 seconded to War Office; 1923-39 secretary of the Secretary of State's Education Advisory Committee, Colonial Office; 1926-45 Secretary-General (hon.) International Institute of African Languages and Culture.

Lugard which ended only one month before the latter's death and drew from the survivor his last published writings.[1]

Vischer was the real initiator of government education in Northern Nigeria, and, though he found his way to this congenial task in the interval between Lugard's two periods of service he wrote to his old chief in Hong Kong about his plans. His mastery of the local language became so perfect that he earned from the people the unique title of " dan Hausa " or " son of a Hausa ", a valuable recognition for a man who had to struggle with the deep distrust of these isolated Muslims towards western education. (Early in 1960 the writer found his picturesque mud-brick house in Kano carefully preserved and still in use.) After going on tour to study education in the Gold Coast, Egypt and the Sudan, he built up the educational side of what may be called the Temple school and was thus in opposition to his old missionary colleague, Miller, who was at least his equal in mastery of Hausa language and customs.

By the time Lugard returned to Nigeria Vischer, working in the closest alliance with the Residents and some of the emirs, but still in the face of intense Muslim suspicion, had started a five-sided experiment at Nassarawa, just outside Kano city. It included an elementary school—but the adjective would really cover the whole complex—a school for sons of chiefs, scribes and clerks; workshops for local crafts, and a survey class. The cost was largely borne by the emirs from their treasuries. Some 320 pupils, from ages 6 to 60 had been recruited, some of them from distant emirates where they had parted from weeping parents who feared they would never see their sons again. Vischer, with his genius for giving and evoking understanding, succeeded against all obstacles. He himself attributed the results attained in the first two years to his basic principle " the preservation of the native", on lines adapted to his mental and physical condition.[2]

Meanwhile, the C.M.S. were still represented in the emirates only in Bida and Zaria. In Zaria Miller was running up against serious difficulties. The missionaries had never accepted their exclusion from the other emirates. When they appealed to Girouard and cited Lugard's earlier offer to allow them in Kano he replied that since then there had

---

[1] *The Times*, 6 March 1945. See also Lugard's tribute in *Africa*, vol. XV, April 1945.
[2] *Reports, N. Nigeria*, 1911, pp. 11-13.

been the fanatical outbreak at Satiru. In Hesketh Bell the missionaries seem to have found a much more responsive governor and they drew from him a promise, in confirmation of Lugard's earlier intention, that they should start work at Kano. But the Colonial Office, already in strong support of Temple's ideas, had been still further moved by Vischer's infectious idealism, and was against this extension. Bell's exit from Nigeria seems to have been clouded by a rather humiliating defeat over this issue. Harcourt put the whole problem to Lugard when he was appointed Governor-General and asked him to think it over and then decide. Lugard hesitated. He might well do so. He was confronted with an absolute opposition of ideas which, containing on both sides the intractable element of faith, was unamenable to the usual British solution of compromise.

At the furthest extreme, upon one side, stood Temple. His view was frankly political, an attitude, he believed, shared by the emirs themselves. Their power was not so strongly established that they could afford the entry of strangers with revolutionary ideas if these had behind them the sanction of the European and his government. " Now, in a sense," argued Temple in his book, " the British government is today in the same position as were the Emirs formerly," and " we are threatened with grave danger of administrative difficulties . . . if we allow the authority of the native administration to become ineffective." He feared " a kind of national decay, a crumbling away of the character and individuality of the native." He would cease to be " though primitive, robust mentally and physically." Mistaken government policy, of course, could achieve this result equally with the " well-meaning but misapplied efforts on the part of the missionary." Thus he reached his conclusion " Any and every influence, I contend, which outrages the pride of race should be opposed by the Government in the interests of the governing as well as of the governed races." Strangely enough he thought that because " The primitive pagan is a robust fellow . . . there is little or no danger of his losing his characteristics readily or of his trying to ape the white man." Missions could therefore be allowed to reach him. But as soon as pagan society showed any signs of being undermined the government would have to restrict missionary activities. Once a native state had become fully efficient and had developed enough pride of race the missions might be allowed in again. He calculated with satisfaction the small proportion of natives which had so far been Europeanized. The number should be kept to the minimum; quite enough had been denationalized in order to provide the necessary clerks.[1]

Temple not only led the northern Residents in this matter but greatly influenced his friend Strachey who, in turn, influenced the Colonial Office. Newly coined ideas often have a very high currency value and here was further evidence that the preservative ideal, which Lugard had done so much to put into circulation a few years ago, was proving very attractive. It was inevitable that the northern Residents should want it to embrace education as well as administration.

What was the extreme opposite of the views? It was put strongly by the missionaries and especially by the C.M.S. It was, of course, based squarely upon the universal validity of the Christian faith. To the uncompromising Miller the official policy was a " deliberate abandonment of a part of Christ's kingdom to the devil."[2] If to Englishmen Christianity was the true faith was it not a form of superiority to deny it to the Hausa? Referring to the old formula " Islam is more suitable to them," Dr. Miller wrote " It is surely necessary to be convinced that Islam is more suitable for *everyone* before using a phrase suggestive of contempt in speaking of its value to subject peoples!"[3] The second argument was that by excluding missions, by " playing up " to Islam, and by the fact that the British staff's fidelity to their own faith was not very obvious to the Africans these were confirmed in their belief in the universal superiority of their own religion and the inferiority of Christianity. A later Christian critic of this policy remarked a hesitancy in the British temperament to undertake responsibilities with a moral aspect, allied with a perverse quixotism so that " The less the authorities themselves believe in Mohammedism the more likely they are to favour it!"[4] Certainly the missionaries living obscurely and almost continuously in Zaria or Bida close to the people, saw the life of the Muslim at closer range than the officials, and at a level far below the impressive ceremonial and trappings of its surface, and they were not inclined to admire it. They saw the corruption, oppression, cruelty and disease, the treatment of women and animals, and they longed to be given the chance to make

---

[1] Temple, *Native Races and Their Rulers*, pp. 211 ff.
[2] Enclosure in Jones to Manley, 18 February 1918 (Y), No. 14, C.M.S. Papers.
[3] Miller, *Have We Failed in Nigeria?* p. 82.
[4] Murray, *The School in the Bush*, p. 280.

a beginning, however small, in the introduction of new standards of probity and social justice and, not least—for Miller was a doctor—of hygiene and medical care.

The political and religious aspects of the controversy could not be separated. Archdeacon Jones, who was consecrated Bishop of Lagos in 1919, reported to the C.M.S. headquarters his belief that " The objection to Miller politically is that he knows and learns too much of the oppression which goes on under the aegis of the Emir to please the authorities."[1] He believed, after a discussion with Temple, that what the authorities feared was not a religious rising but " much more the supposed danger of the education and enlightenment of the native which will make him more difficult to govern."[2] The missionaries were not convinced about the way Lugard's original pledge had been interpreted after he left in 1906, and they were determined to hold on to his promise about Kano. Miller claimed that in his thirty-five years in Zaria there had never been a single incident in which a missionary had caused any trouble to the administration.[3] The pledge was, he argued, so employed that the officials' great influence over the emirs was used to encourage them to forbid entry to the missions. Far from protecting, the Governor, overcome by Temple and his clique of Residents, was according to Alvarez, Secretary of the Northern Nigerian Mission, rehabilitating a "corrupt and effete Mohammedism."[4]

On Lugard, in his exposed position between these two irreconcilable parties, rested the responsibility for decision. The struggle did not reach the deeper levels of his own conscience, but even as a political problem it was painful enough. In his dilemma he was driven into indirect courses quite foreign to his nature. He gave the impression to some of the missionaries both in London and Nigeria that he was more sympathetic than he dared to show. He admitted that he was " in a cleft stick ", and hinted that since it was difficult for him to override his own Lieutenant-Governor in such a matter he would like to see the missions move the Secretary of State to do so.[5] To the impatient missionaries, for all his sympathetic tone, he seemed unable

---

[1] Jones to Manley, 18 January 1918 (Y), No. 8, C.M.S. Papers.
[2] Jones to Manley, 19 July 1916 (Y), No. 82, C.M.S. Papers.
[3] Miller, *Reflections of a Pioneer*, p. 94.
[4] Alvarez to Manley, received 5 July 1912 (N.N.), No. 81. See also Macintyre to Manley, 24 August 1912 (N.N.), No. 110 and Lugard to Alvarez, 10 January 1913 (N.N.), No. 30, C.M.S. Papers.
[5] Interview with Strachey, 4 December 1916 (Y), No. 120, C.M.S. Papers.

to make them any concession in the north and they concluded that he did not want to have the same " rough handling " on the issue which his predecessor, Bell, had suffered from the Colonial Office. As early as 1912 one of the C.M.S. leaders in the north decided that Lugard " plays with Miller as a cat with a mouse." He was " always delight-ful to meet, and apparently a well-wisher—but it does not come out in action." When, advised by Lugard, the mission did go to the Colonial Office they met the same evasiveness. Strachey spoke of the difficulties caused by the war but, when pressed for some decision, " confessed to personal disinclination to take the initiative in such a matter."[1] He knew that a frontal clash with church interests in Britain must be avoided at all costs. The missions could only guess what was happening behind the scenes and they could not know how long and hard Lugard fought the Colonial Office. In struggling to give a liberal interpretation to his orginal pledge to the emirs, he was fighting on their behalf. And he would have given them more opportunities and support in the pagan areas than the Residents were willing to allow.

He might have beaten either the Residents or the Colonial Office but not both. Strachey was not only the friend and supporter of Temple; he and his colleagues were fascinated by Vischer whose educational policy seemed the perfect complement to Indirect Rule. Even when Vischer's brilliant cosmopolitan abilities were borrowed by the War Office in 1915 for intelligence work, there is evidence that he still continued, unknown to Lugard, to advise his Colonial Office friends, who were just across the road in Downing Street, about the Governor's educational proposals. As with his Native Administra-tion the officials marvelled that Lugard seemed unable to appreciate that he had taken over not only the right policy but the perfect adviser in Vischer, for here he was spoiling the one and ignoring the other.

We find, therefore, a long series of attempts by Lugard to liberalize northern education turned down by the Office. Among them were his proposal to treat education for Nigeria as a whole; his plan for a northern Board of Education by which he hoped to bring government and non-government education together in order that the missions should be offered co-operation and not suppression; and his proposal

[1] *Ibid.*

506

to assist the missions to conduct schools in pagan areas to save the expense of government schools, which needed a British headmaster and his replacement on leave.

A further issue concerned language and syllabus. In the south Lugard did win Office approval by cutting Latin, Chaucer and much English history out of the King's College syllabus. But his desire that, even in the north, instruction in English should play an important part, was opposed. His opponents insisted upon the prime importance given by the Muslims to Arabic. The people must be protected from the sudden unsettling influences of modern civilization. When Lugard strongly urged the need for a supply of properly qualified clerks, with which he could at least begin to replace the southern ones, he ran into a settled fear of over-production in this profession. The emirs were said to despise clerks as " white men's boys ". Above all, it was urged, a rift must not be created between the western educated minority and the rest. As a result Lugard could still report in 1918 that among its estimated nine millions, " the Northern Province does not at present supply a single clerk or artisan for the Government service from its intelligent population."[1]

This was not the last of Lugard's reverses. He wanted to use a benefaction to found a modern technical school to train well-qualified schoolboys in the handling of power-driven machinery. This clashed against the Vischer policy that northerners should be taught to improve their own arts and crafts. Indirect Rule in education, moreover, meant that buildings should be in native, not European style. And the pupils for these handicraft schools should be carefully chosen as morally sound and come only from government schools, and not from mission schools since the Christian teaching of equality was regarded as un-settling. Lugard had to give way. Government, commented Alvarez, was attracted to " cringing but insincere Muslims " rather than to the " more sturdy products of mission schools which turn out far manlier and more independent types."[2] Finally, there was Lugard's Moral Instruction. The Office, of course, objected to this even more in the north than in the south. It was argued, in this case with some reason, that in the numerous little Koranic schools to which the people were much attached, they already had a religious education and that the

[1] *Amalgamation Report*, p. 64.
[2] Alvarez to Manley, received 27 April 1914 (N.N.), No. 28, C.M.S. Papers.

European's secular Moral Instruction would be anathema to the devout believer.

It is not surprising, since Lugard had been forced to make some surrenders of his position on the main front of native administration, that he was less able to make a successful defence on the educational flank. War-time shortage of men and money came to reinforce the conservatives. In 1918, in the hope that the restrictions of the war period could be relaxed, the C.M.S. mission pressed for a statement of future policy. But Lugard was just leaving Nigeria. There was little he could do at the eleventh hour. He just managed to get his northern Board accepted. But he gave up his claims to control the Koranic schools. And he finally agreed to the principle that the missions should be allowed to enter pagan areas only.

It seems in retrospect that, except for his aberration about Moral Instruction, Lugard's middle position between Vischer and the missionaries was sound. The case for caution was strong. The tension of the early days of occupation needs to be recalled; many Muslims would shift out of the shadow of an " unbeliever " or spit after he had passed. Miller could argue that in the emirates Britain was not protecting vital authority but rehabilitating one that was effete and oppressive, and that the emirs were in no position to revolt. But the responsibility of acting on his advice would have been grave. There was also wisdom as well as knowledge in Vischer's understanding of Islam and respect for a religion and culture that appeared to foster unity, discipline, self-respect and contentment. It was natural for northern officials to point contemptuously, by contrast, to the headlong, clamorous assimilation of the south. They were right in their belief that the conservatism of the north was deep and persistent. As late as 1932 the writer heard the Native Authorities in Bornu protesting bitterly that the whole work of their chief government school was not centred upon the teaching of Arabic which was almost another name for Islam.

It must be remembered also that Harcourt, his officials, Temple, Vischer and the rest were not being merely locally opportunist in Nigeria. British governments had by 1914 a long-established tradition of curbing evangelists of their own nation and faith. Such control had been practised in India: it had been thought politic in the northern Sudan and in Somaliland. Lord Salisbury had defended the tradition since " you are dealing with a force which a sincere though mistaken theism gives to a vast population." Premature attempts at conversion might cause bloodshed and so prove a permanent obstacle to that conversion which they all hoped to see one day.[1] Chamberlain's mind was in agreement. In 1901 he had endorsed a minute by Ommaney, " I wish it were possible to keep the missionaries out of the Mohammedan districts for the moment."[2] This was a policy natural to a people who had themselves painfully acquired the practice of toleration, with the virtual secularization of the state, when they were confronted with a subject people amongst whom religion and society were still inseparable. Political liberalism and personal courtesy would help to support this attitude of mind. And it may have been reinforced then, as it certainly is today, by the sense that it was not in accordance with the spirit of Christ that He should be presented as an incident of imperial conquest.

Yet we may ask whether this policy, conceived less in the interests of the governed than of the government—the linked government of Britain and the Fulani emirs—was not carried too far. The deliberate attempt to preserve so completely the cultural immobility of a people suddenly brought from isolation into direct contact with the civilized world was to risk future adjustment in the interests of present stability. It seems possible to pay the highest tribute to Vischer's success in starting education at all in Northern Nigeria and yet to question whether, once the period of beginnings was over, it did not fall just short of that almost prophetic quality which could sense the movement of change even if it could not foresee the headlong course it would later follow.

These doubts should induce a further appreciation of what Lugard attempted—his plan to bring north and south nearer together under one education system; his encouragement of the missions in the pagan north; his readiness to permit them, where the emirs were willing, to enter the Muslim states; his advocacy of the teaching of English— " no greater benefit," he wrote, " can be conferred on the African . . . than the teaching of English as a universal medium "[3]—his plans to train northerners as government servants and as modern mechanics. All these items of policy went to prove one thing, that he did not believe that the success of Indirect Rule in the north depended upon keeping

[1] Speech at Exeter Hall, 19 June, 1900, quoted in Lugard, *The Dual Mandate*, p. 591.
[2] Minutes on Lugard to Chamberlain, 17 February 1901, C.O. 446/14.
[3] Lugard, *The Dual Mandate*, p. 454.

that region inviolate from the influences of the modern world. His un-inhibited mind can best be seen in the two chapters he gave to educa-tion in *The Dual Mandate*. Here he insisted that "not only as trustees for their advancement are we pledged to afford to the races of the tropics the best education we can give to fit them for an increasing share in governmental and municipal duties but that the irresistible material progress of the country demands an ever-increasing supply of Africans with both a literary and a technical education."[1] Lugard never said or wrote what he did not mean. This was written in 1921. If between 1912 and 1918 he had been able to infuse northern education with his own careful measure of liberalism there might not be today, between the northern and southern élites, quite such an uneven level of modern education and therefore of attitudes to the world. The northerners, at present bitter at their dependence upon southern skills, would not be able to level at Britain their not wholly just accusation that our neglect is responsible for the disparity. We might not see the Muslim North, once so proudly superior towards the southern pagans, re-garded by the impatient southerners as the backward region which, for lack of that knowledge and experience upon which modern states depend almost for their existence, has acted as a brake upon the evolu-tion of a united and independent Nigeria.

Dr. Miller, in spite of all his own reverses, knew where Lugard's heart lay. He knew him at close quarters for half a century, and he also knew and revealed the dark "underside" of Indirect Rule. Yet he never wavered in his respect for Lugard. He judged that his friend's own version of Indirect Rule was honest and beneficent and it was to others that he ascribed its misdirection, or rather its crystal-lization. It was evidence of this belief that he dedicated his most considerable book, with all its perhaps too sweeping criticisms," To Lord Lugard, Africa's Friend."

One final caution is needed. Whether with reference to government or education, the balance of our judgment—and more important, that of the Nigerians—inclines for or against Lugard's views, two things must be remembered. One is that the differences between him and the conservatives was in the degree and not the kind of policy. The other is that an imaginative reckoning must be made of the condi-tions of the times, both those of Lugard and subsequently. The first

[1] Lugard, *op. cit.* p. 459.

will emphasize the dangers and difficulties of the early administrators, the other will remind us that in the first decades of the century no one could have foreseen how little time remained within which Britain would have to prepare the contrasting societies of Nigeria for unity and independence.

Those who defend the line taken by Vischer, the Office and the Residents can point out that if some progress in the north was lost, at least as far as the evidence of 1960 can be trusted, a most valuable condition of future association was retained in the goodwill of rulers and people towards Britain.

CHAPTER XXVI

DOWN TO EARTH

THE ACTIVITIES and struggles of Lugard which have been described were mostly ones of pen and pencil directed from his office desk in Lagos. But, though he was perhaps too much at this period a man of the desk, there were times other than the earlier occasions which have been described, when he set out on tours with his brother and a small staff, and made contact with provincial and district realities, meeting chiefs and peasants, Muslims, pagans and Christians and moving about, in heat and discomfort, amongst forests, savannahs, plateau, mud cities or thatched villages, across the immense surface of Nigeria. Early in 1915, for example, he went on tour in the South East, driving the first train along the 16 miles of rail between Port Harcourt and Imo river. From there he went north into the heart of the densely populated Ibo country visiting the coal-field and calling at the headquarters of districts. He was greeted everywhere by the forest people, the women giving him the almost universal greeting of female Africa of shrill " lululuing ". (Many of the women of all ages were absolutely nude and Ah You, quite shocked, turned his back on them.) Coal and railway-cutting focused his attention more upon geology than humanity. But he had an eye for the natural beauties of Enugu, the future Eastern capital, which was then almost virgin bush.

He went to Benin to discuss with the Oba and chiefs, his new scheme of taxation to which " they very cordially agreed ". He visited Nana, the chief whose dangerous stronghold and slave depot had been blasted out by the navy in 1894. The contrast between then and now was dramatic. He found a " new model village and saw his house, a really wonderful piece of native design and construction. His four or five sons educated at Accra had built it and the design would not have disgraced the Public Works Department . . . The town was laid out with good roads and wonderfully clean." Finally, he summarized his tour, "We have done in the last 12 days about 1,000 miles of which 550 miles have been by sea and river, and 450 miles by motor, and 40 by rail." (L. to F. L., 26 February 1915). And in 1916 he toured the region again.

There were also, of course, visits to the much more accessible Yoruba towns at which it was always easy to break his journeys to and from the North. In February 1917, after the serious Iseyin rising, he went up to Oyo, Ibadan and Abeokuta to bring home to these cities the stern lesson of the punishment of Iseyin and to congratulate the Alafin and other chiefs upon their loyalty.

But his longest tours were in the Northern Provinces. These covered such a vast area that travel here was a more serious affair. Here, with the rulers of large and settled states, it was possible to talk of administration upon equal terms. It was these tours that he described most vividly to Flora. In order to visualize him at work on the move it is therefore best to draw upon his letters describing these journeys.

The catalogue of vast concourses of people, of parading and charging horsemen in their array of coloured cloaks, gay equestrian furnishings, chain mail and the rest need not be repeated for the reader as often as it was, in heat and dust, for Lugard. There are, however, a few such incidents that are worth recording because they present the Nigerian scene, and some of its inhabitants, from potentate to peasant. Here are some extracts from an account of Lugard's visit in 1916 to the Emir of Katsina, the man, it will be remembered, with whom Palmer had first worked out the Native Treasury system. The party went by car along a road the Emir had made for the purpose.

"The country on this side is wonderfully fertile, and well timbered. Huge tamarinds—most graceful of trees—and enormous lucust bean trees, Shea, dunia, figs and very many others, whose names you would not know, dotted all over the country. Palmer tells me that, where now we see a succession of prosperous villages, a thick population and acres and acres of cotton, and other crops, only 10 years before was uninhabited jungle. At each village of any importance there is an imposing Rest House built, of course, of mud, but coloured a deep brick red, often with a crenellated front and a series of arches inside. They are delightfully cool, and the moderate light inside is a relief from the outside glare. The villages are very proud of them and keep them beautifully clean. We stayed to breakfast in such a one, the villagers bringing leeks and tomatoes and rice, wood and water in profusion. As we travelled North, when within some 30 miles of Katsina, I saw the first Dum palm (branching palm), the Herald of the Desert, and the country began to change. The noble trees were scarcer, and the Baobab, Dum, Euphorbia and Acacia take their place. The surface, dust-blown sand, becomes deeper, but the road for the whole 150 miles had been swept and the streams ramped, and the ruts repaired with clay. The labour must have been prodigious— long lengths were prepared like a mud tennis court—in honour of my visit. About 3 miles from the City, Katsina and the two minor Emirs awaited me with an immense crowd and some thousands of horsemen. Katsina has a motor car which is driven admirably by a Katsina man, who, I am told, can make all ordinary repairs &c., after having been taught for 3 months only at Ibadan . . . What a change from the day when in 1903 I entered Katsina on my way back from Sokoto, and they spent the night in discussing whether they would fight me the next morning or not."

Another example of this Emir's quite unusual modernity was his purchase of an American buckboard in which he drove a pair of horses. With this and his motor he had an interest in good roads. Lugard thought him by far the best Emir in Nigeria. He went on to give a piece of past history, which deserves recording.

" When we had that crisis at Sokoto just before I left Nigeria . . . the then Emir of Katsina became very disaffected. Palmer, who was then in charge, was told to build a fort. He asked the Emir how many men he could provide. He said 23. The next two chiefs said that it was the season of the crops and they could get no men. The present Emir was the third Chief. Palmer asked him how many he could provide. He replied at once 5,000, and he brought over 6,000 and built the Fort. He is absolutely loyal."

There were other Emirs present besides Katsina.

" Daura, an enormously bulky youth, is, Palmer tells me, hardly less loyal than Katsina himself. He is Habe (not Fulani) with a pleasant and ex- tremely black face, jovial and fat. Palmer tells me he is the direct repre- sentative of a dynasty which goes back fully 1,000 years. He is a very good ruler. Kazaure (the third Emir) was also good. His family dates back to about 1600—comparatively modern! Then we got into our cars and I paid the Emir [of Katsina] a return visit, and he showed me again over his house, and over the splendid school he has built. There are 99 pupils, and I have limited the number to 100 at present . . . The boys were called out of the Mosque to see me. A very intelligent-looking lot of youngsters, among whom were several of the Emir's sons. Thence we drove to the new Mosque in building, which is a wonderful structure. They have been building for two years and when completed it will be the finest in Nigeria. Nothing in Kano or Sokoto can touch it."

There was one sight which was deeply gratifying to Lugard. Many of the villages they passed had been built by ex-slaves. Some had become headmen or held high positions. They showed a greater sense of discipline than the Fulani who were apt to let things slide. There was evidence of the economy of Indirect Rule.

" The whole staff here paid for by Govt. is one District Officer and one clerk. The revenue has risen from £25,000 to £52,000 of which half goes to the Native Administration." (L. to F. L., 15 January 1916).

From Katsina Lugard returned southwards to Kano, where Palmer, increasingly an expert on Muslim Nigeria, was now in charge. Kano, as usual, put out the most impressive numbers of horse and foot to greet him.

" Abbas, though a man I like, and a loyal Emir, is a curious character, a prey to suspicion, jealousy, and fear. Palmer tells me that in anticipation of each of my visits he has been in a state of much misgiving and spent large sums by way of presents to Mallams to pray that I have not come to depose him." (L. to F. L., 16 January 1916).

In 1917, Lugard travelled up to Bornu in the north-eastern corner of the Protectorate. It had only been visited once before by a Governor, and that had been thirteen years before when he had made the first visit after the annexation. The visit meant then, as it still means— though a railway is projected—a long journey by motor-car over the treacherous black cotton soil which is a morass in rains, while in the dry season it bakes into deep cracks over which the car has to be invited at times to make dangerous jumps.

" . . . Yesterday I saw the Emirs of Jemaari and Katagum . . . and the especially loyal and gallant Emir of Little Missau. The trouble is that they all bring huge presents out of all proportion to their means to the ' Great Governor ' . . . I feel very sorry only to spend five minutes or so with these men, who with their horsemen have come long distances to see me—or to fly past a village with a wave of the hand without stopping

515

when they have waited for me since daybreak, but what can one do? If I stopped at every village I should never reach Bornu. We did 134 miles today. . . . We nearly ran into a herd of giraffes; there are very great numbers in this long stretch of jungle." (L. to F. L., 22 May 1917).

At last they reached Maiduguri, the new capital of Bornu.

"At 8 a.m. we started in the motor-car for the 'Shehuri'; the place is built on the model of the old town of Kuka [Kukawa], where last I saw the Shehu, a broad open space, perhaps 200 yards by one hundred, quite flat, ends in the mud archway which leads into the Shehu's labyrinth of dwellings—the native town is on either side . . . I mounted a handsome horse (having on my new white cord breeches) and pranced up to the saluting base. The mounted infantry then marched past and galloped past, and saluted in line (this being Empire Day) and then left the ground . . . The Shehu then " processed " to his house amid the shrieking of hundreds of women, the braying of scores of trumpets, the beating of drums and the shouts of the populace. He received me in a courtyard under the spread awning of a tent, he at the end of a small dais and a mass of velvet cushions, myself on a chair of gorgeous hue with embroidered velvet carpet. . . . Then he proceeded to have a confidential talk, a great storm broke, and the rain came down in torrents, so we went into the house. He laid all his requests and complaints before me . . . Then he brought his present, I cannot pretend to remember it all. Two beautiful horses, seven great rams; and then samples of the work of Bornu, fans and cushions, and fly switches and spears and boomerangs and swords and knives, and I don't know what besides. Then two mountains of native food, and then a score or so of leopard skins and so on. This done, he wanted to show me his house and we wandered through room after room, all bare and with sandy floors, till he came to his great triumph, a European brick built two-storey bungalow with more rickety doors and windows made of old packing cases or adzed wood and painted green. It was built for him doubtless for a large sum of money by a European trader. Finally we mounted up mud stairs to the room over the entrance arch, looking down the long vista of the parade ground with masses of people on either side, and the galloping salute began. The noise was deafening and you could not hear yourself speak. Men in armour, men in all kinds of weird costumes, brandishing swords or spear, came up at a wild gallop, succeeded by others, group after group. The Shehu himself galloped twice, and Dikwa [the neighbouring Shehu of Dikwa] several times; the excitement was obviously great, men swaying to the music and almost trying to dance in their saddles. This went on a long time—the shouting and noise seeming to intoxicate the people. Horses dashed into each other at a gallop, and how neither man nor horse got speared was a mystery and a mere accident. No-one looked where he went or what he did with his spear. In the firing off of guns yesterday in honour of the Shehu when I met him, I hear that one man discharged his piece thro' the brains of another—but it wasn't even mentioned."

Lugard staggered off, dazed with heat, noise and the dust of the journey, and fell asleep, to be woken by two immense storms and hurricanes of rain in quick succession. After the native potentates came the officials.

" At 4 p.m. I had the three political officers (Tomlinson[1] is one) up, and talked of the principles of taxation and particular difficulties and Native Courts and so on, and answered their points. It was quite interesting. At 5.30 I went off to see the Fort and the prison, but it came on to rain."
(L. to F. L., 24 May 1917).

The return journey was difficult. It was almost an impossible task to get the cars across 300 and more miles of black mud, and over recently empty river-beds, suddenly swirling with sandy water. It is a good corrective to over-critical judgments of the past, whether in administration or economic developments, to remember what most of Africa was like until very recent years, what, indeed, much of it is still away from the air routes, railways and main roads, which the visiting observer generally follows. But it is in these moments of difficult trekking that Africans show themselves as the best of companions. We must picture Lugard, with his cars stuck deep in mud, leaving them and walking for miles in pouring rain, in search of a village and finally, at darkness, lying down under a tree. Then " during the night we heard the arrival of the big lot of men from the far village with shouts and drums. But what was our amazement to hear when we got up, that in the pitch inky darkness of the night, they had extricated the car, entirely by themselves, without ropes or help. It is as great a mystery how they did it as how the Egyptians built their pyramids! But it was a fact." (L. to F. L., 27 May 1917).

But that was not the worst. A little further on they found their road

---

[1] Tomlinson, (later Sir) George J. F., K.C.M.G., 1876- ; 1903-4 Transvaal Education Department; 1907 Assistant Resident, N. Nigeria; 1910-11 Director of Education, Gold Coast; 1911-21 Political Officer, N. Provinces, Nigeria; 1925-7 Acting Secretary Native Affairs, Nigeria; 1929-30 Member of Committee on Colonial Appointments; 1930-9 Assistant Under-Secretary of State, Colonial Office.

blocked by a turbulent river almost as broad as the lower Thames, covered with great masses of foam, and even as they watched the last islands of sand in the middle were covered.

" The local Emir (Jemaari), who has been Emir here for 34 years and is very old was sitting by the Bank on his mat with scores of his men around him all stripped while others swam and shouted in the water. It was already in places several feet deep. I said we must, of course, abandon the cars and ride in (100 miles) on native saddles. Old Jemaari said we could still cross if we did not delay, and as I do not pretend to know anything of a motor, I agreed to let them experiment with the Ford. It was not merely the depth of water but the shifting sand at the bottom into which the cars would sink axle deep. Whether they would be serviceable even if they ever got through I had no means of knowing. Well, the Ford started in surrounded by a black mass of yelling humanity which took a tortuous course and gradually got further and further from our bank and nearer to the other, pushing, lifting and pulling with ropes, and eventually the car was across having been completely submerged. They now urged me to let the big car go. I considered it sheer madness, but the men were all absolutely confident. The river by this time had risen so far that in places it was unfordable and over a man's head. They took it after we had dismantled it of everything detachable. It very slowly moved across. At the worst place there was a long check and I thought it had gone for good, but they pulled it through with long ropes by sheer force. . . . It is *amazing* how they did it. The loads were taken across on rafts of calabashes and I followed on a raft pulled by 13 or 14 men who, in one place, were swimming for a long distance and had only their heads above water! There was great yelling and shouting, and when I reached the shore they hoisted the entire raft with me on it on their heads and carried me over the loose sand for some distance and deposited me in safety. The old Seriki [the Emir] had got on a raft as soon as my car took the water and remained there refusing to leave the raft until every single car and every bit of luggage was across."

The operation took some eight hours.

" Then came the examination of the cars and the attempt to get them started. All the machinery was, of course, full of water and sand. After some hours of work the Ford was able to go, and by 5 p.m. or so my car was able to start. . . . I had, after crossing the river, got on the horse of some high native official with a saddle cloth of gold and silver embroidery and rode to the rest camp a mile off."

The *finale* is typical.

" Then I sat in a hut and read my *Times* till at last the car towed in by the
Ford arrived."   (L. to F. L., 28 May 1917)

Just as the cars were at last capable of movement another great
storm fell, covering the ground with water and immobilizing the
party again. The next day Lugard and his staff were carried on rafts
over a mile of swamps by " a vast concourse of yelling men."

" Many of them preceded us shouting perpetually ' Hankali!' (carefully·
carefully) and gesticulating to the men who bore us at a snail's pace.
Eventually we reached the main stream of the river and got into a canoe
escorted by about 100 men each lying on a hollow gourd of about 18
inches to 2 ft. in diameter and paddling himself with legs and arms. You
cannot imagine a more bizarre sight—' Human tortoises' Carter called
them—but I wished I could have had a cinema photo as we approached
the bank. It baffles description, some in bravado made the calabashes
spin round and round, their 4 arms and legs waving in the air, and the
shouts were deafening . . . "   (L. to F. L., 31 May 1917).

In 1918 he visited the province of Sokoto, even today lying away
on the periphery of the Northern Provinces but all-important as the
starting point of the Fulani conquest. The next words can be echoed
with feeling by the writer, who has at successive times travelled over
these northern steppes on horseback, and then by car, and lately
visited the Sultan of Sokoto by aeroplane, from which this country
can be seen, in all its harsh emptiness, not indeed of man but of the
visible works of man.

" This is a *dreadful* country! A howling N.E. wind blows like a blast from
a furnace over the bare loose sand and black laterite rocks. Loose sand of
unfathomable depth everywhere . . . a plain of black laterite, heated to
oven-heat by the blazing sun, and over it the wind came in a hot blast.
Not a tree to break the burning heat. I said that I thought it would be an
arid spot to live in, and they would suffer from the heat of the laterite.
Arnett [the Resident] said he loved it. That this scorching wind was
almost damp and cool compared to the Sirocco which blows in March,
April and May."   (L. to F. L., 26 February 1918).

There was the usual ceremonial parade.

" Sokoto was followed by 45 different retinues, each separate District

Head coming past with his horsemen. Then Gando followed, and then all *his* district heads; then Argungu and *his* district heads. It seemed that the procession would *never* finish. Arnett said there were over 6,000 horsemen, besides masses of footmen. Many were in gorgeous silks of every hue and the ceremony was most picturesque. I suppose that the procession lasted well over an hour!"

There was a new Emir to instal; Lugard's first ritual being faithfully followed.

"I enclose the Oath which I drew up long ago and which each Emir repeats word for word (in Hausa) after the Resident or myself. First by Moslem custom he washes his hands and face and feet (attendants bring the water in enamelled (!) kettles for the purpose), for he may not lay his hands on the Koran and swear by Allah until he has done so. Then, seated on his state carpet, both hands laid flat on the open Koran held by the Alkali (Native Judge) who scrupulously sees that the Emir does not miss a word, or fail to keep his hands glued to the book—he repeats the Oath. I say a few words—wish him a long and prosperous rule, regret the death of his predecessor, express my confidence in him, and so on, and the ceremony is complete. The Emirs and Sultan go off to the big Court House where we are to talk, out of the sun and dust, and I slip into my house and change out of uniform, and get a drink to take the dust out of my throat."

Lugard now had a private talk with the Sultan, the titular head of all the emirs.

"Had he any matter of any kind to talk over with me?—not necessarily by way of complaint or protest, but just for a friendly talk? No, he had nothing. He had absolutely nothing. He had only thanks to God for his prosperity and peace, and for my visit which had filled him with pleasure and completed his happiness. Was his country doing well? Had there been any cattle disease, were the crops promising well? Yes, all was well. There had been less disease than usual, the rains had been good. He thanked God for all his blessings—I said this was the first time I had met him as Sultan, and I deplored the death of Atahiru—whom I had installed in 1903, then *he* was himself one of the Councillors who elected him on the morrow of the defeat of the Sokoto Army by us. I congratulated him on the progress since made, especially on the solution of the troublesome slave question and the signal loyalty and justice with which the Alkali of the Native Courts had since that day dealt with this matter and liberated many *thousands* of slaves by redemption and otherwise."

No achievement gave Lugard more joy than this. What followed is a good reminder of the solid practical content of British Rule.

" I spoke of road-making, of the progressive dessication, and our proposed Artesian boring—of Vaccination and isolation camps, talking in their own mode of thought (i.e. revaccination about which they are now keen), I observed that, as circumcision was imposed by their religious law, so vaccination was imposed by our secular law, with the result that in England we had practically stamped out smallpox. I told him of our recent successful treatment of leprosy, and added that we British considered it to be our Mission, and the reason of our presence in the country, that we should bring to it the gains of civilization, whether in producing water in the desert by Artesian boring, or by the restraint of disease among men or among cattle by scientific methods. He said they were most grateful (as indeed they are) for all we had done. I replied that we were advisers and helpers, the real progress of the country and the happiness of its people lay in the hands of its own rulers. *He* thanked *me*, but I in turn thanked him, for the progress was due to his loyalty and that of his Chiefs and District Heads. I talked of Forestry and the projected reserves which had a double object—first to conserve the water-supply at the sources of the rivers, and secondly, to produce an annual increment of forest produce for use. Of education I had *much* to say, but you will be tiring of this talk—no, I am quite sure you are *not* tiring, but if I were to go and tell you of all I said on each of these matters, I should not complete tonight. Not that it took long to say, but it takes so long to write. He left, I think, very well satisfied and pleased, and was followed in turn by Gando, and Argungu and Illo, to each of whom I said more or less the same, though not at quite such length . . . "

The other half of Lugard's duty on these tours was to instruct and encourage the officials who spent their hard but interesting lives in these lonely stations.

" I should like to have told you of my conversation with Arnett, the burden of which was that it was necessary to look, not only at the apparent needs and expediency of the moment, but also to the *direction* in which any policy was leading us, and this was especially my function. So that, however slowly we progressed (and I did not want to press the pace), we should be going towards a definite goal and not on a line which, though attractive at the moment, meant retracing some of our steps later on. More especially in the question of the relations between the Technical Depts. and the Political (or Administrative) officers of a province.

Nigeria, 1912-1918

It is a perennial and an *inevitable* difficulty. Arnett as usual was full of sense and quick to see my point of view and the larger issues."

(L. to F. L., 27 February 1918).

At such moments, exhilerated by a sense of constructive work and of partnership with emir and official, Lugard could forget the Colonial Office.

From Sokoto town back through all the weary miles to " the land of electric light and iced drinks " at his new Northern capital of Kaduna. Then a week or two later to Lagos " a place of greenery and flowers and with the comforts of a spacious Government House " but also to the military and economic anxieties of the war and the pinpricks of the local press.

But, though this was the year 1918, there was one more tour to be done, so back north he went to Jebba. Here he saw for the last time the rock that had been such a feature of his adventures in Nigeria. Again he remembered sitting in his Thames dinghy and reading long letters from Miss Flora Shaw. That was eighteen years before. " They have been busy and eventful years but the outstanding gain and the greatest change and happiness is that I am married to you. For the rest there is no great difference in my life and work. I am doing almost exactly for the South what I did in those years for the North, but with a larger experience and on a larger scale." (L. to F. L., 11 August 1918).

When he went on tour along the Middle Niger and the Benue he was moving amongst primitive pagan tribes who, though they did not know it, owed much to his protecting hand. The tour was mainly by boat and he took with him, for the sake of his education, a newly arrived officer, Alan Burns,[1] who like so many of his school was to become a governor. He was also to be a historian of Nigeria. Some extracts from Lugard's letters of August 1918 will reflect the nature and conditions of his officers' work in pagan lands along the rivers as he stopped at one station after another. Here, in one, was an older D.C. who had lost his son in the war " one of the most difficult cases I have to deal with . . . the keen, earnest hard-working official to whom God has given no brains at all." Then, scratching and cursing amongst

[1] Burns, (later Sir) Alan C., G.C.M.G., 1887– ; 1905–12 Colonial Service, Leeward Islands; 1912–24 Nigeria; 1924 Colonial Secretary, Bahama Islands; 1929 Deputy Chief Secretary to Government of Nigeria; 1934 Governor, British Honduras; 1940 Assistant Under-Secretary of State for the Colonies; 1941 Governor of the Gold Coast; 1947–56 Permanent U.K. Representative on the Trusteeship Council of the United Nations; published *History of Nigeria* (5th edition, 1955).

522

the Benue sandflies " I do feel very strongly for these men doing the Empire's work here. There is sleeping sickness and yellow fever, endemic (we lost two and nearly a third from the latter last year). They have more than their share of blackwater and malaria. They are cut off from all intercourse and get their mails a month or two after they reach Lagos. Their work is among primitive pagans (one was killed and eaten last year)." At Numan he found a young man, a noted University runner, administering all alone, and " I asked him how he managed to get any exercise, for the country all round is flooded. He said he had put up hurdles and jumped them for exercise—when the natives weren't looking—they would think him clean mad."

On up the Benue to Yola, where the Emir and the ruling class were pure Fulani " and look on Hausa as a slave's tongue ". Here the Resident, G. W. Webster, " of a very good old Scotch family " and " one of the best " spoke fluent Hausa and Fulani, and the Emir was " after Katsina ", the most remarkable ruler in Nigeria. " His breadth of view and foresight and capacity rival any European." This Emir had actually had the good sense and humanity, when pagan tribes had been put under him in 1913, to point out the resentment of the tribes and the danger that his own Muslim District Heads, once they had got over their fear of the pagans, would oppress and enslave them.[1]

Back down the Benue again, to be greeted by tribes formerly truculent, some cannibals and head-hunters; in one place there were some 15,000 of them dancing naked on the river bank, to the accompaniment of drums and every conceivable kind of flute and whistle and jingling bells, while a refrain went up from their lusty throats. We must wonder what ideas of Lugard these dancers had as they rejoiced in his presence. One dance was given by a large number of absolutely naked girls with pieces of wood through their nostrils. They danced to him with intense excitement and happiness before their contemptuous Fulani Emir. Then downstream to Ibi, where Lugard found the Resident, Jack Fremantle, a famous character, in bed with blackwater fever, but so full of high spirits and talk that Lugard could hardly get in a word. Next to the point on the Benue where the great railway bridge was to be built. Here representatives of the large pagan Munshi or Tiv people came to meet him. Here he could see at once the spirit of the old Africa, which is nowhere so un-

---

[1] *Memoranda*, 1918, pp. 302-3.

restrainedly expressed as in the dance, and also the new forces already playing with effect upon this lush growth of isolated humanity.

" . . . Here a vast concourse of Munshis, 5,000 or 6,000, from all the clans near and far, had come to salute me. They drummed and danced in their naked masses, carrying all kinds of weird effigies—one at least not too decent. A small boy clad completely in a leopard's skin fitted close to his body simulated the beast on all fours. Others with masks of oxen faces were carried aloft, and they danced incessantly, old grey and white headed men joining in with intense seriousness—unable to resist the fascination. Round and round my dais they danced streaming and glistening in the sun with perspiration, each absorbed in the step or the contortions of the dance. All intensely happy and good natured—shouting salutations. A free and jovial throng looking on the British as their friends—effusive in their desire to please. And these are the *dreaded* Munshis, who in the days of the Niger Company fired arrows at each passing steamer, who drove out the white man from his silver mines at Orofu and pitched his machinery into the pit he had dug. In those days an expedition against the Munshis was looked on with something akin to dread for their poison was reputed so deadly that a mere scratch was death. Now the Munshi school cannot accommodate the pupils who desire to enter it. A detachment of School boys paraded for my inspection. Half of them were stark naked, and looked droll as they stood at attention, unconscious as Adam of the fact. The rest wore the small but really pretty and well made Munshi cloth, of which I am buying you some samples. I had a long talk with Rev. Bargery, ex-missionary, and now a superintendent of Education in the Service of Nigeria—a very excellent man who has acquired the Munshi language and is absolutely *devoted* to his work. He lives alone at the school, but ' never had a moment to miss the society of white men '. The day was not long enough to cope with the work, and the interest of it was absorbing. That is the spirit here. That is the spirit which has transformed this dreaded tribe into one of the most docile, easily managed of all the pagan tribes, and without exception all the officers who deal with them are devoted to them. Their sturdy independence and fearlessness wins esteem. Their tax this year has been practically doubled, and collected with no difficulty at all in the early months of the year. It is a wonderful example of the genius of our race for controlling subject races."

The day ended for Lugard with a very encouraging compliment. He asked whether his Memoranda were useful. Fremantle replied that one of his officers had said to him that: " Reading them was like read-

ing the Bible, the more you read it, the more you found there was in
it!"

He had spanned the circle of the Northern Provinces, through its
problems and its diversities, from the northern Muslim city states, each
with its own character, to the little naked dancing clans of the Benue,
still pagan and independent. They were all taking in their different
ways the influence of Britain through the medium of Lugard and his
staff, and were beginning to adapt their lives to something they can
never have known through all their history—peace.

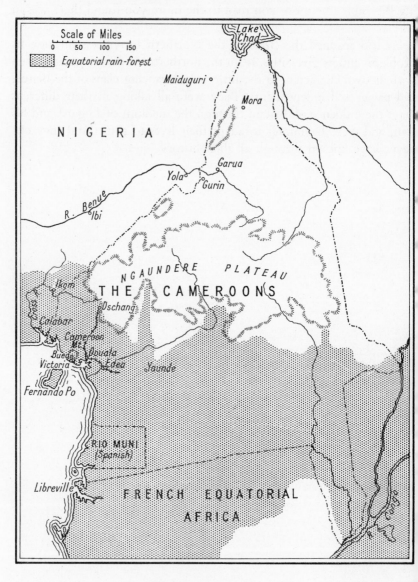

The Cameroons 1914-16

CHAPTER XXVII

WAR 1914-1918 [1]

ON AUGUST 4th, 1914, Lugard was on leave in England. We have therefore no record of how he and his wife met the moment when the stroke of war fell upon the nation. On the official side the event seems to have been taken very calmly, both by him and by the Colonial Office, and after dealing with a number of military and routine matters he left for Nigeria, where he arrived early in September.

A Governor with less natural confidence than Lugard might have seen plenty of cause for anxiety. The war had struck Nigeria only eight months after the enactment of amalgamation which, in many departments of government, was still far from having settled down into a smooth-running system. The conquest or occupation of the strong Muslim states of the north had been completed only eleven years before, and in the south there were many symptoms of unrest, both of the sophisticated and of the primitive kinds, the first among the Yoruba groups and the second in the still not fully administered regions of the south-east.

As Lugard voyaged out along the west coast, through seas in which the whereabouts of the German gunboats *Panther* and *Eber* were still unknown, the map of the neighbouring territory of the German Cameroons must have been his chief study. It was a strange-looking map. The territory covered 300,000 square miles; it ran in a vast wedge, some 530 miles wide at its equatorial base, and tapered to a point nearly 1,000 miles north at Lake Chad. From this lake, down

---

[1] For this chapter use has been made of Sir Julian Corbett, *History of the Great War*, vol. i, Naval Operations (1920), p. 267; Sir Charles Lucas, *The Empire at War* (1924), vol. iv, Africa (chapters on the Cameroons Campaign, Nigeria, 1914-16 and the Nigerian Brigade in East Africa); Brig.-Gen. E. H. Gorges, *The Great War in West Africa* n.d.; History of the Great War based on official documents, *Military Operations, Togoland and the Cameroons*, 1914-18 (1931), compiled by F. J. Moberly.

the eastern side of the triangle and along its base to the sea, ran French Equatorial Africa. As a result of the settlement following the Agadir crisis, the French had lost to Germany some 100,000 square miles of their Congo territory, an addition which rounded out the German colony on the south-east. This subtraction had occurred only three years before the war, and the French were therefore certain to be eagerly bent upon regaining it. Nigeria's border ran with the west of the Cameroons for over 1,000 miles. Three important places which have already come into these chapters lay close to the frontier—negro Calabar in the green south, Fulani and pagan Yola on the Benue river, rather more than half-way up, and Kanuri Maiduguri, capital of Bornu, and a possible base of operations, in the extreme north. But the place in the Cameroons of most immediate interest to the directing brains of a naval and commercial power such as Britain was the deep water port of Douala, the only good harbour between Sierra Leone and Cape Town, and the seat of the German government. It had two short railway lines striking out from it eastwards and northwards. The political map reveals another important feature of the Colony, a biggish square of Spanish territory, Rio Muni, cut out of the coast to the south and destined to play an important part in the campaign for the Germans.

The narrow German strip of Togoland, further west along the coast between the Gold Coast and Dahomey, fell almost at once to French and British forces. It was expected by many concerned with the military plans that, for all its greater breadth, the Cameroons would not take very much longer to overrun. It lay remote from Germany, and was surrounded on nearly all sides by hostile land or naval forces, while it was reported that the Germans had only about 170 white men and 2,000 Africans under arms, an estimate which proved pretty accurate.[1] A description of the military operations would take us too far from our subject. But, having been able to travel round this territory, it is possible for the writer to picture some of the physical reasons why the campaign there was prolonged far beyond Lugard's hopes and greatly to the embarrassment of his administration.

The northern part is dry, open country, like the corresponding zone of Nigeria. But it was then almost wholly lacking in communications and, as Lugard's experiences on trek will have shown, even its scarce

[1] Moberly, *op. cit.* p. 53.

rains can make movement very difficult. A spine of rocky hills runs south from Lake Chad, and there are outlying peaks, notably Mounts Mora and Banyo, which the Germans were able to make into almost impregnable fortresses. The Benue breaks the chain of hills, and Yola, on its banks, looked towards the strongly fortified German town of Garua, 50 miles up-river. Southwards along the frontier, the hills become less rocky, their gaunt grassy shoulders stand bare until near Dschang, some 200 miles north of the sea, the forest begins. It deepens and finally sweeps round the base of the magnificent Cameroons mountain. This, standing almost in the sea, rises to a 13,000 foot summit. High on the mountain was the German hill station of Buea, green with mist and rain. It looks across twenty miles of blue water to its twin mountain on the Spanish island of Fernando Po, and at the rare moments when the two giants strip themselves clear of rain and clouds there is to be seen one of the most majestic sights in a continent rich in scenic grandeur, whose effect on the European, or at least the English mind, is more often one of amazement rather than charm and inspiration. A few miles eastward from Buea and its port of Victoria, but then almost inaccessible by land, lies Douala, set deep inside a tangle of islands and lagoons. Behind Douala, and especially south of it, can be seen the real reasons for the difficulty of the campaign, the rivers and swamps and all the obstructive vegetable products of heavy rain in an equatorial latitude, chief among them the truly terrible forest. Where road or rail cuts a way through it this forest can be seen like a solid cliff, formed not only by immensely tall trees growing close together but by the creepers and ferns which weave in the interstices a mat so thick that even the gaudy flowers which embroider it fail to relieve the sense of green menace.

In 1914 the plan of attack, quickly made, was to muster all available troops from the West Coast dependencies and to send them, with naval forces and with French co-operation, to seize Douala and to invade the Cameroons, starting up the railways. Meanwhile sections of the Nigerian forces were to be posted at the three obvious bases on the long frontier, ready for attack or defence.

Lugard's position was not an easy one. He was, as Governor, titular Commander-in-Chief; he was a soldier, skilled in African warfare and the chief creator of the West African Frontier Force. It rested with him, moreover, to put his territory and all the resources it contained at the disposal of the army and navy. Temperament as well as experience impelled him to play a rather more active part in the campaign than that of a helpful civil administrator. But he was, of course, in no sense presiding over the military operations, and the Colonial Office, which was the department responsible for the local forces was, so he told Flora, very quick to remind him of this fact. This was done in so many words at the outset of the fighting and was emphasized, according to him, by a studied policy of ignoring even the legitimate and, indeed, vital part he had to play as Governor of Nigeria in furthering the campaign.

This negative treatment did not restrain him from trespassing upon forbidden ground. The first task he took upon himself was highly unpleasant. He had no faith in the commander of the Nigerian forces, nor, as he well knew, had the officers. Could he, at the eleventh hour, act upon this opinion at the risk of upsetting the operations? "The situation," he wrote to his wife, "was very grave. Perhaps you can hardly realize how very serious it is to interfere with the Commander of a Force a few days before it takes the field." He telegraphed to the Colonial Office. Fortunately they consulted the War Office " and *their* reply was a foregone conclusion." In *that* quarter, he wrote, "Men like myself are credited with some reliability and their views are promptly acted upon." There was left to him the hateful duty of breaking the news to the man who was to be removed, and who might, Lugard feared, be driven even to suicide. Fortunately the worst did not happen. "In my private heart I believe that I have saved many lives and perhaps a disaster." (L. to F. L., 6 September 1914). One result, however, until General Dobell[1] should arrive to take over command of all the land forces, was that "I am more or less doing Commandant as well as Governor." Colonel Cunliffe,[2] for whom Lugard felt an admiration and friendship which were fully returned, was put in command of the Nigerian forces, but he had gone up to Yola and he remained throughout the campaign operating across the frontier from the north-west.

Lugard, like most of his contemporaries, regarded the war with a

---

[1] Dobell, Brig.-General (later Sir) Charles McPherson, K.C.B., C.M.G.; 1890 entered army; 1905-6 served in W.A.F.F.; 1907-11 General Staff; 1910-15 A.D.C. to the King; 1913 Inspector-General W.A.F.F.

[2] Cunliffe, Brig.-General Frederick H. G., C.B., C.M.G.; 1889 entered army; 1904 joined W.A.F.F.; 1914 commanded Nigeria Regiment; 1955 died.

mixture of incredulity that such a monstrous thing could happen in 1914, and a lofty sense of dedication to the cause it represented. What he wrote at this time will recall to those who experienced it the atmosphere of that period which now seems so very distant across the intervening years of two periods of war and two of troubled peace.

As news poured in of the response of Britain to the fact of war he could exclaim that "we belong to the very finest nation God ever made. Let us never be pessimistic again!" His response to wider news as he read the King's proclamation to the Empire and the details of the Indian rajahs' response in men and money, invites perhaps a more questioning retrospection today. "I was reading it out and I found such a lump in my throat that I could hardly go on in an unconcerned voice. Truly, our rule has been wonderful. Peace brings sedition and bombs and agitation, but when the Empire has to fight for life these are all swept aside. Here, in Nigeria, heads of tribes in German territory are coming over to declare their desire to be under our Rule. It is times like these that makes us proud of the name of Englishman." (L. to F. L., 10 September 1914). Upon one point his satisfaction was premature. The natives of the Cameroons did not, as the British rather expected, turn against their rulers *en masse*. It is interesting, in view of the Nigerian peoples' attitudes, to recall that while there was disaffection in the southern towns, the Muslim group, further north, remained especially loyal to the Germans.[1]

The mood of exaltation was not constant. It often happened that Lugard and his staff broke off in the early hours exhausted by the strain of dealing with the work of the war on top of the ordinary routine of Nigeria's administration, with cipher telegrams coming in for decoding at any time of the day and night. He would then see another side: "What a lot of human energy a war involves and just for the object of destroying the creations of human industry! Europe will be set back 50 years, I suppose, by the results of this war." As he watched his staff take up the burdens of war he could see the humorous as well as the noble sides of his nation. "Our ideas of 'secrecy' must make the Gods laugh . . . X, for instance, who is in charge of the most confidential documents will lock them up in a ponderous safe with an air of mystery and then discuss them over a meal in a stentorian voice in front of English-speaking servants. They are all the same.

[1] Moberly, *op. cit.* p. 53.

They will write a most secret document and tear it in half and throw it in the waste-paper basket. It is hopeless to teach an Englishman to keep a secret. He simply *can't*. I am much the same myself." (L. to F. L., 17 September 1914). Then he would come back again to the deeper thoughts evoked by the war.

> " I have taken the psalm book out of my box, and I am going to read your psalms . . . I have read them—both morning and evening and perhaps at this moment you may be reading them too and we shall meet in thought—in spite of interrupting telegrams on which I have to give decisions. They are wonderful psalms and I know just the verses which will arrest your thoughts, the words you have so often quoted to me ' The Lord sitteth between the cherubim be the Earth never so unquiet'. ' There is sprung up a light for the righteous and for such as are true-hearted '. ' The King's power loveth judgment ' and so on. Really I would have to quote the *whole* were I to try and recall those you loved. Taken as a whole it leaves a grand impression of impassionate justice presiding over the destiny of all, of faith in the triumph of Right and with it all the Paean of gladness and thanks and gratitude for the Triumph of good and Justice and Truth".
>
> (L. to F. L., 19 September 1914).

Lugard was deeply anxious about Flora and now with much more reason even than before. Though her health was still very poor she had, in the mood of indignant compassion caused by the invasion of Belgium, forestalled official response by going at once into action. By August 17th, she had begun improvising an organization to deal with the first refugees from that country. She wrote an appeal to the press for help of every kind, which produced 1,000 letters the same evening and 2,000 the next morning, all giving or offering help of every kind. After a few days of heroic over-work, taking possession of empty factories and other quarters, it became clear that the flood of refugees must become a national rather than a private responsibility. But Flora retained a large part of the work, concentrating especially upon the allocation and care of the professional and propertied refugees, which she regarded as a " task of consolation " as much as one of practical help.[1] The immense burden of committee work and administration which, in defiance of her poor health, Flora undertook with brilliant success, filled Lugard with pride. But pride fought with a gnawing anxiety which his letters written to her during the first

[1] Bell, *Flora Shaw*, p. 278 ff.

October of the war reveal. Here was one written at one o'clock in the morning:

" I take up your letter and find no rest in it. You are too dead tired, worn out with heavy work, and with the terrible strain and depression of that time [the end of August and first days in September] when, as you say, every day brought news of fresh slaughter, and desperate fighting, and every day a fresh retirement ' for strategic reasons ' . . . Then again I read of your heroic efforts far beyond your strength, and while my heart swells with pride of you it cries with anxiety lest you overdo it . . . taking years off your life, and I can't spare an *hour*. You will say ' Do *you* wish me to do less when all we have and are is being exerted for the sake of our country '. It is hard to answer . . . that if you did something less there would be others equally capable who would make up for it. I can't say that because I do not believe it. There is no-one else in England—and certainly not out of England—who could replace you because you combine such a wonderful diversity of qualities. You have the brain and organising capacity which no other woman has, you have the tact which no-one else has, you have the charm, the feminine compelling charm which makes them all love to help you and serve you, you have the sympathy and womanly feeling, the *heart* which is so essential to the work . . . "

" You may be justly proud," he wrote a few days later as news came from her,

" and *I* am—of the achievement. In 3 weeks over 3,000 Belgians actually housed. The House of C. carrying by acclamation a resolution to offer the Hospitality of the Nation—an organization—albeit with a most troublesome Committee—in full swing. It is a *great* record . . . Only my darling I fear for you. You are ageing yourself by anxiety and sympathy. There is really no cause for it. You have already achieved your great object . . . Remember I too have some vested rights in my wife. She made some promises to me when she put her hand in mine in the church . . . Let them fight if they want to! Let them resign 50 at a time— who cares! I am inclined to guess that it would not be an unmitigated disaster if they did. But *you* go quietly, dear, and now that you have brought it to the stage it has reached through you, there is no fear. And so I beg you to take more ease—merely for my sake."

(L. to F. L., 15 October 1914).

It was for her great services for the refugees that Flora was created a Dame of the British Empire in 1916.

The beginnings of war in his own sphere continued to keep Lugard very busy. A nation which can hardly foresee the possibility of war until it breaks in upon their unreadiness must endure initial reverses. West Africa now supplied a local example. Nigerian forces were thrown across the frontier from their three widely separated bases. From Maiduguri a column attacked the German mountain post at Mora and was beaten off. Another, from Yola, tried to take the German town of Garua and was repulsed with loss. A third column from Ikom in the south was surprised and soundly defeated by the Germans. The casualties were heavy, especially in the loss of trained officers who would be hard to replace.

But Britain was not unready at sea and the attack upon Douala soon corrected the balance. This was a large operation. First arrived Captain Fuller,[1] who was in charge of the naval side, with a couple of gunboats to reconnoitre the neighbouring bays of Victoria and Douala. The Nigerian marine service, which was turned overnight into a war department, went to work with a will, hammering armour plate upon their large flotilla of little ships, which were mainly meant for river transport. Then came General Dobell in the Elder Dempster *Appam* converted for war service. He picked up contingents from the British colonies along the coast as he came, with the French following on from Dakar with their warlike Senegalese. To this combined force, numbering 4,300 coming from outside, Nigeria contributed 1,260 African troops with 65 British officers and N.C.O's, and 79 British civilian volunteers. Along the Cameroons frontier, under Cunliffe, were another 2,040 rank and file, and 92 British officers and N.C.O's.

At Lagos, inside and outside the harbour bar, there were now warships, and a Government House full of officers and talk of the expedition. Inevitably the senior men came to depend much upon Lugard, not only as Governor but also as soldier. Cunliffe, in command of the frontier, deferred often to him, and Dobell also consulted him. Yet Lugard had just received a dispatch—"not," he said, "a model of courteousness"—which said bluntly: "You will understand that General Dobell is in entire and sole command." "Yes," was Lugard's comment, "I understand . . . nor have I ever in any remote degree

[1] Fuller, (later Admiral Sir) Cyril Thomas Moulden, K.C.B., 1874–1942; 1914–16 with Togoland and Cameroons Expeditionary Force as Senior Naval Officer; 1919-20 Head of the British Naval Section, Paris Peace Conference; 1920-22 Chief of Staff, Atlantic Fleet; 1923-5 3rd Sea Lord and Controller of Navy; 1930-2 2nd Sea Lord.

been accused of interfering with the Military Commanders." He went on:

" I think there should be small chance of a Governor getting swollen head! What between the scurrilous invective of the local press... and the constant little snubs from the C.O., a man would have to be armour-plated to suffer from vanity. The difficulty is to assure oneself that, in spite of the constant evidence to the contrary, one is not really a scoundrel or an idiot." (L. to F.L., 17 September 1914).

The little expeditionary force sailed from Lagos on September 20th, 1914. Lugard judged favourably of Dobell and was enthusiastic about Fuller. " They have a tough proposition but I now believe they will succeed all right." It was important for him that they should succeed, as already there was news of unrest here and there in the Southern Provinces, and this made him uneasy to see the country denuded of troops. Lagos itself might be in danger, since the German cruisers *Dresden* and *Stuttgart* were believed to be at large in the area, and Lugard had to stimulate those who should have been responsible to make some plan of defence for the capital. Soon he was exclaiming in surprise that Dobell and Cunliffe seemed to be planning for a twenty years' war. " I am so young and impetuous. I feel that these old fogies have not enough dash." (L to F. L., 7 October 1914).

He became anxious about the main expedition. Douala lay far back from the sea flanked with swamps and masked with defensible points. News came that the Germans had blocked the fairway with sunken ships. Fuller himself thought the task a very ugly one. To quote Lugard, who rarely praised unreservedly:

" He was, however, a splendid fellow who commanded the confidence of all whom he met. He went at it in the dogged true British way, and the extraordinary efficiency of our Marine workshops assisted him greatly. He swept up the Mines, he got round the sunken ships. He took heavy risks and scored. He sent the *Dwarf* to scour the creeks—he himself searched all round Fernando Po. He was splendidly efficient. The net result was that Douala surrendered to a naval bombardment before Dobell had landed a single soldier. And I am obsessed by the efficiency of our navy. Fuller did it admirably."

This, however, as Lugard foresaw, was by no means the end.

" But at home they seem to have supposed that the fall of Douala meant the end of the business. That is not so, but it has relieved *me* immensely. I had feared either a reverse or at best a terrific list of casualties, for it was a place you could not get at, and the Germans had had *months* to render it impregnable. I can't understand their abandoning it. It would have cost us a terrible death roll to have stormed it. Still we only occupy the area of the town and a very small space besides. . . . The pressure of war is almost lifted off me locally—at least all cause for anxiety re local matters is gone. We have still a good deal of fighting I daresay, but all these fellows are longing for that and will be keenly disappointed if they don't get it— so let it be!" (L. to F. L., 30 September 1914).

Lugard's next problem was to cope with a stream of German prisoners being sent back from the Cameroons. He had neither quarters nor guards for them. Among them were women, some of them pregnant, and children. He was quite astonished at the way his officials reacted to the arrival of the prisoners. It seemed they could not do enough for them, especially for the women and children.

" Really we are an extraordinary nation! I thought I was a fairly humane man but I find I am the Brute who has to be propitiated."
(L. to F. L., 1 October 1914).

When Lugard planned for the men to be put in a camp and the women to be billeted out amongst missionaries and others, he was accused of harshness in separating wives and husbands and had to rearrange his plans. " Then Boyle, Hood and others went down to see after the comfort of these women and each in turn came to me to plead for indulgences." Edward Lugard joined them. As the women brought no luggage with them, and as he found the Lagos stores had no " combinations " of the type they liked, he was reduced to offering his pyjamas, which were refused. Then it was argued that Lagos was not healthy enough for them. The next thing was that they objected to the company of an American woman who had been brought away with them because, they said, she had a tarnished reputation. Dobell had promised that all the missionaries should go free, but when one of them, who had twice been caught trying to blow up the little gunboat *Dwarf*, was questioned by Lugard he replied he was a soldier first and a missionary afterwards. The German spokesmen for the prisoners were full of complaints about their treatment, especially by the French, and since truth is always one of the first casualties of war, the German

Governor of the Cameroons sent him a long letter about the " barbaric treatment of the women and children". Lugard sent a long civil reply explaining that they had been treated more as guests than as prisoners, " but when," he commented to Flora, " one thinks of German barbarities in Belgium, it is like the Devil quoting scripture to hear a German quoting the terms of the Hague Convention. However, I forbore to say a word in this sense. We will not lower ourselves to their standard or take reprisals on women, even to the extent of comparing our method with theirs. Our reprisals will be of a sterner and more manly kind." (L. to F. L., 8 January 1915).

This was not quite the end of the story. The prisoners were all convinced that the Allies were already defeated in Europe and that London was in flames, and only smiled when the real news was given them. Then Lugard found one of the prisoners' chosen leaders writing to his wife, evacuated to Norway, to say that they had been welf treated but that he had set himself to give Lugard the maximum ol trouble by frivolous complaints etc. He told his wife to send him German papers in British wrappers for " the English are very stupid". He reported also to her that he had been sent north where he lived with the Secretary, " The next man to the Governor," and had been asked to lunch by the Governor. " Temple!" exclaimed Lugard, " I am in despair with my countrymen!" He could laugh, however. " He begins his letter ' Dear Treasure ' . . . I felt inclined to kick him for that much more than for bragging that he had wasted my time . . . at *that* I laughed, but he has no right to address his wife as ' Dear Treasure ' . . . " (L. to F. L., 22 October 1914).

By the end of October, 1914, Lugard managed to ship all the unwelcome guests to Britain. But from there they sent back a number of claims, one from a man stating that he had left behind in the Cameroons 6 hens, 6 ducks and $1\frac{1}{2}$ lbs. of flour. He wanted these items traced and the hens and ducks fed and valued.

Though Lugard might chide his officers for lacking any sense of proportion in their dealings with the prisoners, his wife had plenty of evidence of his real feelings. He told her of his joy that " we are setting to the world a new standard of fighting ethics. Our men, and our women, too, at home, and our press and our public men are creating a new ideal of warfare to set against the German philosophy of Bernhardi and N. and T. (I can't spell their beastly names). Since wars must be it is a magnificent thing that we should . . . in the face of Europe and America . . . be showing to the world how war can be waged with chivalry." (L. to F. L., 23 October 1914). To balance the picture it should be added that Lugard reported more than once that the German officers in the Cameroons had behaved well.

At the end of November 1914, he sailed to the Cameroons on the mail boat *Karina*, to inspect the conquered port and the forty miles radius around it which had now been occupied. He sailed into Douala in his own steam yacht, the *Ivy*, which had served in the expedition, through a lane of captured vessels and of British ships of all sizes, with all their crews standing to salute and cheer.

" Then as I approached the wharf the guns rang out from cruisers and from shore a tremendous salute. Everything was done with the most perfect precision and seamanship, we were alongside the pier and the gangway down in a jiffy and along its whole length was a double guard of honour. French along one side, British on the other. I think you would have felt a little thrill if you had been with me. . . . We drove to Govt. House where a room and an office had been prepared for me. The wall between the two had been carried away entirely by one of the *Cumberland*'s shells (she only fired 27 all told!), but it had all been mended up splendidly. We started almost at once on a tour and inspected the hospital. . . . Then we went thro' one store after another full of most valuable material captured from the Germans. The whole thing is simply amazing. This place was absolutely impregnable. Even our 6-in. gun shell fire could not have done them any very great harm if they had stuck it out, for we could not have afforded an unlimited number of shells. They surrendered at once without a struggle, abandoning shipping worth £½ million or £1 million, and houses, stores, even a battery of guns without even trying to blow up their magazine and wireless station, and damaged the machinery of a few ships, but that was all. The houses stand as the Germans lived in them. I lunched opposite a picture of Moltke riding on a lone horse."

There were deputations of native groups to interview. Then the German prison " where a white bearded old scoundrel who has served some years for theft knelt and asked me in passable English for pity. I let him out! That is not good business! Poor devil! They had men chained together, two and two, which I did not like." Then to the new native towns, "excellently planned" and the waterworks, "on a wonderful new principle " all leading to the conclusion " We have much to learn from these Germans." (L. to F. L., 24 November 1914).

Then followed a trip up both the railway lines and over broken bridges, all heroically patched up for the next round of fighting. " It still remains a mystery," Lugard remarked, "why the Germans abandoned such defensive positions with hardly a fight, and yet only yesterday they made a futile attack on Edea and suffered great losses . . . I cannot understand *fighting to lose*." (L. to F. L., 25 November 1914). He saw the sites of a " gallant little battle " that had been fought a few days before and the dense forest and swamp. For hours at night he sat listening while Fuller read to him the dispatches he had drafted for the Admiralty, with Lugard tactfully cross-examining him and suggesting amendments. " There is no doubt that they have done splendidly and there is also no doubt that they have had the most amazing good luck." Everyone praised Fuller as the real author of victory and everyone seemed to love him.

The next day he sailed the short distance back westward to Victoria, where the battered little *Dwarf* lay at anchor. He went up the great Cameroons mountain, through miles of well kept cocoa and rubber plantations intersected with light railways, to the Germans' twin-capital of Buea. He passed through miles of road hedged with roses, and up to the Governor's high *schloss*, with its avalanche of flowers falling over the stone balustrades from terrace to terrace, a sight which made the writer reflect sadly that, whatever their faults as colonists, the Germans showed in their buildings an imaginative taste that seemed to have been denied to our Colonial Service, or at least to our Public Works Departments. " We went," wrote Lugard, " to Government House, which was just as the Governor left it. The house, silver and linen all in place, the latest books and periodicals. Here, as at Douala, I hear that almost every house was full of the most obscene pictures and literature . . . They have shown quite amazing stupidity. They could have defended Douala, Victoria, Buea, and we simply could *never* have taken the former—naval guns notwithstanding. (L. to F. L., 27 November 1914). He could only think that they were so sure of the victory in Europe that they did not want to destroy, either by fighting or by dynamite, all that they expected so soon to repossess.

The first question in his mind as he surveyed what had been con-quered was naturally " Who is to own and govern all this?" His mind passed through phases. As he steamed along the Nigerian coast towards the Cameroons he showed a moderation at which he could later have been astonished. " I am not anxious that England should take over all the German colonies. Germany has a great population and her colonies are her outlet. We have not waged this war for greed of Germany and I should like it to be marked with restraint in our claims. Still, we ought fully to adjust our frontier. . . . We should also keep the sea port and naval base of Douala." (L. to F. L., 22 November 1914). As he surveyed the excellent plantations at the base of the Cameroons mountain, he remembered that, as private property, they could not be confiscated by conquest. Yet he could provide no men either to cultivate or to guard them. He seemed to forget that by the same international law there had to be this inconvenient suspense before the final war settlement should be made. Instead he grumbled, " I wish I could get the Home Government to realise how essential it is to come to a decision as to whose flag is to fly in this country." He reflected gloomily that he would be the last person the Colonial Office would consult about the allocation of the Cameroons or its administration. The long report he now sent in upon his visit of inspection to the conquered area, giving his views upon its management, was not even acknowledged. By the end of the year those views, however, were changing, and Germany was to be a total loser. He was prepared, he told Flora, to give the French what they had lost over the Agadir incident, confine Britain's share to rectification of the frontier, and give the rest, with Douala, to Belgium as compensation for her injuries, at the same time neutralizing it. " It would prove to the world that we have not embarked on this war in any land-grabbing spirit, and *that* is the great point of my proposal. . . . Do you think you could lay it before Austen Chamberlain or Bonar Law, and perhaps Milner?" (L. to F. L., 22 and 25 December 1914).

Lugard left the Cameroons just as the fighting there was beginning its second and unexpectedly long and intricate period. Upon his return to Nigeria the most pressing of his many problems was that of staff. The expanding Nigerian forces needed a flow of officers, and clearly the men most ready to train and lead Africans were the junior and middle ranks of the political staff. Most of those were naturally eager to volunteer for this duty. Other non-combatant posts created by the demands of the war drew heavily upon all departments. Tropical war is an extravagant employer. The list of casualties from enemy weapons continued to mount, but there was a longer list from sickness as men marched and fought and camped in heavy rains and in malarial swamps and forests. Yet Lugard had to keep a watchful eye upon Nigeria and to hold the balance as even as possible since staff shortage meant loss of contact with the people, and that meant loss of control and confidence which, in turn, could soon lead to disorders and a call for troops inside the frontiers.

It was not an easy balance to keep. He had intervened sufficiently in the conduct of the war to bring about a division of commands between Dobell, operating with the large and very mixed force in the south, and the all-Nigerian forces along the eastern frontier; and since the latter, with the local French troops, were under Cunliffe and Major Wallace Wright, V.C., both close friends and admirers of Lugard, there was small chance of misunderstandings. But the several columns had to be fed with men, guns and supplies over very long lines of communications. The Colonial Office was intercepting Nigerian staff in Britain and telegraphing to him to keep both Nigerian forces fully supplied, and suggesting that he was not doing his full share. Yet " The Cameroons campaign has simply existed on us from a shirt button to the supply of all the essential men and ships and everything." (L. to F. L., 7 May 1915). The strain upon Lugard was very heavy as he struggled to carry his war duties and both maintain and reform the administration of his huge dependency. He worked eleven hours a day. He had no leisure and seldom any exercise. Once or twice his brother managed to drag him out for a quick walk and bring him back exhausted and streaming with sweat. But he could rarely be persuaded to take this unattractive diversion of walking " in a muggy atmosphere and great heat between two evil-smelling swamps along a causeway." There were moments when the strain was such that he almost envied his Chinese servant, Ah You, as, with a face of utter calm, he laid out his master's clothes in the regular unhurried routine of a life wholly dependent upon a higher will.

Lugard was, however, spared the worst anxiety. The outbreak of war failed to shake even for a moment the loyalty of the Muslim emirs to their new overlords. This was the more surprising as there was much fighting along their eastern frontier with Bornu and Yola in the fighting line, and Germans even raiding into their territories. And there was a very anxious moment when Turkey came into the war in November, 1914. Lugard called the large Muslim community in

Lagos together and made a long reasoned speech upon Britain's record of friendship towards Turkey and her respect for Islam throughout the world.[1] But there could be no disguising the scantiness of the British forces or the initial failures and defeats. The word " loyalty " has been used but it is difficult, without deeper insight into the minds of these rulers, to know what is the proper word to explain their unanimous refusal to make use of their apparently Allah-given opportunity to regain an independence so lately lost. On the contrary they were quick to encourage recruiting, to make gifts to war charities and to vote sums in aid of the cost of the campaign; they sent impressive letters to Lugard to assure him of their allegiance, and even offered prayers for Britain's victory. No analysis of their motives can deprive Lugard of the credit for this solid practical result of his policy. It allowed him to continue with his development of native administration in the emirates almost irrespective of the war.

But if the Muslims were steady and remained steady almost without exception throughout the war, the Southern Provinces had a more mixed record. This was true of the Yoruba groups, including Lagos, of which more must be said later. Lugard believed that in the less sophisticated parts these troubles were caused by rumours, spread by German agents, that the British were leaving the country, and the withdrawal of troops and of political officers would support such belief. Some troubles were due to recruitment for carriers or to the fear of it, others to a recurrence of old inter-tribal hostilities. Some outbreaks led to the murder of British and African officials and of Hausa traders. But there is no need to list all these expressions of unrest. Lugard was never alarmed by them but only worried by the demands they made for troops or police who could be ill-spared. On the large surface of Nigeria, the areas of discontent were small and isolated. But the tendency during the war was to treat rebellion or disorder sternly, making up with severity for the lack of numbers in the security forces.

As 1915 went on, Lugard became increasingly impatient at the continuation of the local war. Large and increasing forces under British command, with Nigerian, Gold Coast and Sierra Leone contingents, and also French and Belgian colonial troops, were trying to surround the Germans in the Southern Cameroons, but making

[1] Undated typescript in Lugard Papers.

little progress in spite of the growing Allied superiority in numbers and supplies. Dobell wrote to Lugard admitting that honours lay with the Germans. In the north, Cunliffe was running short of men. He had at first found chaos on the British front, and said it was rather a matter of the Germans besieging Yola than of his besieging Garua. Presently news came of a successful German attack on a Nigerian post at Gurin, and next that Garua could not be attacked until a big gun was got up there and that had to wait the rising of level of the Benue. The gun arrived at last, and after a regular siege Garua fell on June 10th, 1915. Cunliffe was now free to march south in command of French as well as of Nigerian forces, and provide the northern arc of the columns converging upon the German positions some 300 miles to the south. The capture of the key-point of Garua also allowed Lugard to go to England where he spent some five months administering Nigeria from his room in the Colonial Office, returning to West Africa towards the end of 1915. During this time, on the invitation of his old friend General Willcocks, he spent a week on the western front, having as close as possible a view of the costly fighting of that summer.

By the time Lugard got back to Nigeria at the end of December the Cameroons fighting was at last coming to an end, the final action being the capitulation of the northern mountain stronghold of Mora on February 18th, 1916. By the end of the campaign the Allies had about as many thousands of troops as the Germans had hundreds, yet the Germans, who had fought well after their initial abandonment of Douala, escaped encirclement and got away safely into the neutral Spanish quadrilateral of Rio Muni in the south. It must be remembered, in explanation, that the campaign had thrown a heavy strain upon communications in areas where human carriers alone could be used for transport. It had also been an intricate and delicate task of organization. A number of columns coming from different directions had to converge at a given point upon specified dates, while co-operation at all levels had to be attained within a combined force which was under three European governments, recruited from different colonies and from different races, including in the end some Indians. The Germans had the advantage of unified force, of knowing the country and of fighting from a central position. Lugard called the final phase of the war, with the escape of the Germans, a fiasco. Though he believed that Cunliffe and Wright had done brilliantly in the north, he had been critical of the conduct of the southern part of the campaign from the moment the main naval operation was finished. Allowance must be made for the feelings of a soldier who had to stand and watch from the side-lines.

A further blow was to fall. We have seen that Lugard had at first been inclined to disapprove of Britain annexing German colonies. But " earth-hunger ", as his old opponent Sir William Harcourt had called it, is very catching. And his restraint had not meant that he was ready to see the major part of the conquered region go to France. He was therefore dismayed to receive a telegram from the Colonial Office early in March, 1916, announcing that much the greater part of the Cameroons was to be handed over at once to French administration.

" . . . I have been able to locate the boundary of the Cameroons on the map. We are giving the whole to the French with the reservation of such an insignificant little strip, that it was hardly worth reserving at all . . . The port of Douala is a very important matter. It is the finest on the coast.

. . . For the rest, as you know, I am not sorry except for the disappointment to the natives who have so loyally helped us—especially the Emir of Yola, who has no doubt been led to expect that he would get some at least of his old territory back." (L. to F. L., 14 March 1916).

The next day the situation looked no better:

" I am to take over the Adm. of this narrow little strip varying from 40 to 80 miles broad which we have taken as our 'sphere' south of the Benue. I am 'of course to consult Dobell' and so on and so on. Why in the world people can't just leave a man to do it, without all these platitudes at 2/2 a word." (L. to F. L., 15 March 1916).

Lugard was not the only man to be upset by the partition.

" . . . Poor Fuller is desperately disappointed. He has worked for a year and a half improving the harbour of Douala, perfecting the workshops &c. (and I am told he is a desperate hard worker). It was his child. He alone captured it now he has to hand it over to the French. Dobell is no less sick and most anxious to get out of the country. I do think that it would have been a far better business to have handed the *whole* Cameroons provisionally over to the French till the end of the war instead of sticking to this wretched little strip—smaller than most of the provinces of Nigeria. By creating two 'spheres' we appear to have made a sort of

544

bargain, and no-one in England stops to look at the size of each . . . It is a wonderful country, and from the French point of view almost worth a war to obtain it . . . The little bit I have got to take over will give me as much work as a much larger area, and it is full of difficult problems as it contains these vast plantations and private estates belonging to German companies—hitherto worked by more or less forced labour."

Lugard never knew that upon this occasion at least his chief at the Colonial Office was in agreement with him and had as bitter a grievance against his own chiefs as ever Lugard had cherished against himself and other superiors. Harcourt had put the strongest case in the Cabinet for retaining Douala and had made the most of Lugard's arguments. In February 1916 he told the Prime Minister that he was " aghast " to find that, without even consulting the Cabinet, Douala had been handed over by the War Cabinet to the French.[1] It had not even been used as a price with which to bargain over certain outstanding questions with the French in the New Hebrides and Jibuti. He demanded that " my utter dissent " should be recorded from a decision " which has been arrived at without any consultation or concurrence on my part." To this protest Asquith and Grey made the lame reply that it was a provisional settlement![2] Harcourt regarded this action " a great imperial disaster."[3] He was not, he said, speaking in a spirit of greed for acquiring colonies at Germany's expense. He would have demanded an equal division with France and would then have handed the British half to Belgium as a neutral state to save future trouble with France, an interesting commentary upon Anglo-French relations in the middle of the war. Lord Islington and Harcourt agreed angrily that M. Cambon could always bluff the Foreign Office.[4]

In April, Lugard went to inaugurate the administration of his strip of the Cameroons. His visit to the German botanical gardens deepened the admiration he felt both for the efficiency of the Germans and for the beauty of the country. It is well to record his impression for it was as scientists that the Germans, in their mixed record in Africa, made their best contribution.

" A broad mountain stream rushes babbling over stones through the middle. In one place it is dammed up and forms a waterfall, and above

---

[1] Harcourt to Asquith, 25 February 1916, Harcourt Papers.   [2] 28 February 1916, *loc. cit.*
[3] 1 March 1916, *loc. cit.*   [4] Islington to Harcourt, 7 March 1916, *loc. cit.*

is a pool covered with lilies of many kinds, large flowering Cannas, all
kinds of exotic flowering rushes etc. There are banks of every kind of
fern and the Germans had introduced every kind of tropical tree and
palm, each neatly labelled with an enamel plate with its name &c. Acres of
all kinds of young trees, special varieties of cocoa, rubber, &c. of fruit
trees of many kinds in bearing, of gay croton shrubs &c. The soil as rich
as you can imagine—the whole plan like the inside of a most magnificent
Kew hot-house. Around on every side towers the Cameroon mountain
capped with clouds, 14,000 ft. high—avenues of almond trees lead to an
herbarium with dried specimens and bottles and masses of literature now
lying about and all in a mess. Another still larger and palatial house is the
Agricultural laboratory with the Curator's living house on the upper
storey, then there is the school where natives were taught scientific agriculture, the ice house where ice is made by power from the mountain
stream." (L. to F. L., 10 May 1916).

He went up the Cameroons mountain again to Buea and there, dining
in the German Government House with the newly installed British
officials, he found himself facing three portraits hanging on the wall.
He was fascinated by the contrasts they presented.

" The old Emperor William, a fine head with a most kindly face, whiskers
and moustache in the old military style like the photo of my Uncle in my
bedroom at Abinger, and you felt here was a kindhearted soldierly old
man . . . Then the Emperor Frederick. A fine intellectual face, very handsome and aristocratic. And, between them, a *photo* of the Kaiser, doubtless one he liked and therefore presented to Govt. House of one of the
three of his greatest colonies. It is a singularly evil, brutal and ruthless face.
The great development of the jaw *laterally*, makes the facial oval with the
broad end downwards! and the narrow end at the top of the head. His
moustaches turned up at a right angle, and a cold, cruel and fierce eye.
There was the old king who made modern Germany, and beside him the
King who has destroyed it, and dragged its honour and reputation in the
mud and slime. I wished there had been a 4th picture of the Crown
Prince with his sensual face and ' village idiot' look, and I think the
group would have been a singular study in degeneration."
(L. to F. L., 12 May 1916).

The direct effects of the war upon Nigeria by no means ceased with
the end of the Cameroons campaign. True, the Nigerian troops were
returning, with Lagos giving them a gaudy and vociferous welcome.
" And the stolid Hausas in rags, with scowling honest faces, quite

imperturbable. One company lost 34 killed." (L. to F. L., 2 April
1916). These were the first to return: others were on their way. All
had been promised the leave to their widely scattered homes, and the
period of rest with their families that they needed after the arduous
and unhealthy campaign in which 1,000 men out of the 7,000 had been
casualties. But now arrived an urgent telegram from the Colonial
Office demanding more than 2,000 men of the W.A.F.F. to be sent
immediately to serve under General Smuts in East Africa. Lugard was
much disturbed. Half of them were sick or lame. Their trusted
officers had been taken for other service. Cunliffe agreed with Lugard,
who remembered the Sudanese mutiny in Uganda, that to break their
word to these weary men, who had not volunteered to serve overseas,
might well mean mutiny. Lugard wired to this effect to Bonar
Law, now Colonial Secretary. The result was that it was not until
Lugard returned from England in November that he waved farewell
to the ships gliding past Government House and carrying some 3,000
Nigerians setting out for service in East Africa under their own
General Cunliffe. They carried with them another batch of officers,
many of whom Lugard had sacrificed from his depleted civil staff.

Hardly had the contingent embarked, leaving Nigeria almost
denuded of troops, when a storm cloud suddenly blew up beyond the
Sahara border in the north. The Tuareg tribe revolted and with arms
brought down from Tripoli besieged the important French post of
Agades. This outbreak might have had wide ramifications in Muslim
North Africa. The French asked for help and Lugard gave it with a
speed which allowed scant reference to the Colonial Office, rapidly
pushing up through Nigeria French troops sent from Dakar, and
dispatching a small supporting force to guard the frontier. After he had
already acted, Lugard received a wire from the Colonial Office giving
various belated instructions. "If," was Lugard's comment "the French
asked assistance, it would be a matter of extreme urgency and seeing
that both Zinder and Maradi are close to our frontier it would be a
matter of self-preservation. And they tell me that ' of course ' I would
do nothing without consulting them first! That might mean waiting
for two or three days for an answer. . . . It makes one blaspheme."
(L. to F. L., 5 January 1917).

He authorized the Nigerian troops to cross the frontier and help the
French if the officer in command thought it necessary. A few days

later, he told Flora "Mr [Walter] Long[1] telegraphs that he leaves the question of assisting the French to my discretion! He is utterly unable to do anything else and might have done it at first instead of endeavouring to delay things . . . If we could calculate the number of gallant lives which have been wasted because the men in power (and in comfort) at home would not *realize* or take the necessary action until too late, they would form a terrible army of accusants!" (L. to F. L., 8 and 10 January 1917).

After prolonged fighting all went well, except for the Tuaregs. Lugard hated the whole business because he believed the French, when they regained control, would use terribly severe repressive measures against these black-veiled nomads. He went up to the frontier and could again congratulate his emirs and himself upon the steady loyalty of the Muslim states. Some of the rulers even offered to raise levies to help the regular forces.

From this date, the spring of 1917, there was to be no more fighting upon any of Nigeria's borders. Lugard's anxieties were bound up with the main course of the great struggle which at certain moments at this period seemed likely to end in defeat for Britain, as a result of the submarine war, before the United States could deploy her newly committed strength. This phase of the war was not, of course, without some direct local effects upon Nigeria. The intensification of submarine war threatened to cut communications between Britain and West Africa. It took a heavy toll of Lugard's most scarce and most valuable commodity, his trained European officials. By June 1918, Lugard reported that out of Elder Dempster's fleet of twelve passenger ships, seven had been sunk. Ninety-eight military and civil officers from Nigeria were lost on these ships and in addition to these there was a tragic loss of the lives of women and unofficials. It had been difficult enough to spare officials to go away on leave: now it was dangerous. The effect of anxiety and of loss upon such a small community of British was a grave addition to the general strain of the war. There were even moments, after a submarine had shelled a mail boat not far from Lagos, when the possibility of one surfacing in Lagos harbour and shelling Government House had to be seriously considered.

[1] Long, (later Viscount) Walter Hume, P.C., F.R.S., 1854-1924; 1880 entered Parliament; 1886-92 Parliamentary Secretary to Local Government Board; 1895-1900 President, Board of Agriculture; 1900-5 President, Local Government Board; 1905-6 Chief Secretary for Ireland; 1916-18 Secretary of State for the Colonies; 1919-21 First Lord of the Admiralty.

Nigeria's main military task in the later years of the struggle was the recruitment and training of troops for the East African campaign. We have seen that in November 1916 General Cunliffe embarked with the first contingent of some 3,000 Africans. These forces went out to some very severe fighting in the river-veined Rufiji area in the south-east of German East Africa.[1] A year later when a reinforcement of five hundred troops left Lagos it was Lugard's part to give them a send-off. " I addressed the sea of black faces with their little woollen green fatigue caps, wishing them good luck etc. which an excellent inter-preter rendered in Hausa and Yoruba. I ended up by asking them if they were ready to go and conquer just to give them the chance for the yell of applause which they love. The interpreter rendered ' Governor wants to know if you are ready to kill all the bastards' and the yell of applause was great and then they gave the usual three cheers for me with splendid enthusiasm. They are a fine lot—as good as any we have sent and fully trained." (L. to F. L., 9 December 1917).

In the spring of the year following Lugard had to meet these troops as the transports came back. The contrast between the going and the coming back of fighting men is nearly always tragic, behind the cheering, even if they have been victorious. And victory, against the brilliant endurance of General von Lettow-Vorbeck in East Africa had been a costly prize. In Nigeria there was a special element in the sad-ness in that the troops, volunteers mainly from the more martial peoples of the north, could have only a limited understanding of the cause for which they had fought. " What," Flora asked her husband, " did the Nigerian soldier think of the issues for which he fought so splendidly?" Lugard maintained that " he fights, above all, for an ideal which he values immensely as his white officers do . . . Yes, he knows himself now to be a British soldier." And then the historic fear of those who employ mercenaries creeps in, " He also knows how to kill white men, around whom he had been taught to weave a web of sanctity of life. He also knows how to handle bombs and Lewis guns and Maxims—and he has seen white men budge when he stood fast. And altogether he has acquired much knowledge which he might put to an uncomfortable use some day." (L. to F. L., 19 June 1918). That

[1] *Record of the Overseas Contingent, Nigeria Regiment, West African Frontier Force, Dec.,1916— June 1917*, privately printed, Lagos; see also Lucas, *Empire at War*, pp. 135-148.

day, if we except the actions of some Yoruba ex-soldiers, a few weeks after this in the Abeokuta rising, has never come.

There were great preparations in Lagos for the soldiers' return early in 1918. The bunting was up; the usual " indefatigable ladies " were there dispensing food and drink, cigarettes and the more traditional stimulant of the kola-nut was ready. The weather was unkind. The big troopships could not enter the harbour and the soldiers, many of them diseased and wounded, had to be transhipped in rough seas outside the bar. Deluges of rain, crashing thunder and a tornado which shook even Government House, greeted the home-comers. But as Lugard went down day after day to greet the batches of men as they were brought in he saw that nothing could damp their joy. He observed " the great excitement of the men, who are almost too excited to eat— their wild and resonant cheers as they steam up the harbour and hear the bugles sound, and see the red coats of their comrades which they have not worn for so long, the cheery fellows limping on behind with bandaged feet or legs, the bronzed officers and British N.C.O's in tattered uniform, and the all-pervading cheeriness." (L. to F. L., 19 and 20 March 1918). One centre of interest was a sergeant who, with his mouth shot away, smoked his cigarette through his nose.

It was sad, indeed, to hear that men were dying of pneumonia on the troopships before they could be disembarked. Tragic, indeed, thought Lugard, "to have been through so strenuous a campaign and to get back to Lagos harbour and die without landing." He heard more to depress him at night when he entertained General Cunliffe—"the same dear old hearty fellow as ever "—and his officers. His judgment, as an armchair critic, on the conduct of the East Africa campaign was severe. He believed there had been excessive losses, especially of carriers, muddled and expensive administration. But at least he could be proud, if not quite impartial, about the fighting men he had sent to the other side of Africa. " There is no doubt that it was the Nigerians who won the campaign. They alone could stick the starvation and the malaria, and showed indomitable pluck in action."

The last months of the war were complicated for Lugard not only by the crisis of the Abeokuta rebellion but also by symptoms of unrest within the ranks of his tired and isolated British service, while the railway staff was on the verge of a strike for more pay. There were other economic and financial difficulties in plenty. And there was his increasing shortage of staff. Yet early in 1918 he had a most urgent demand for still more men capable of serving as officers, especially in the Near East. The Cabinet demanded that everything must give way in order to meet the crisis facing the empire. Unessential departments, Lugard decided, must remain in abeyance: even in the administrative sphere normal development must be arrested. He was obliged to admit to himself that he must come down to bedrock in numbers and scrap efficiency. We can imagine the unhappiness with which he told his staff " I shall not expect the same results as under more normal circumstances." There was, as there had to be, a slipping back in Lugard's urgent plans for advance. Those, and especially Africans, who try to assess the colonial record of Britain in the last half century, should make allowance, in the short colonial record, not only for the first years of incomplete control and for the great slump but also for the effects upon administration and development of two periods of world war.

At the very end of the war, Nigeria, like most of the rest of the world, was visited by the influenza epidemic which struck Lagos hard during October 1918, and pushed his staffing problem to desperation. It reached into Government House and claimed the secretary, Mr. Browne, so that Lugard himself became a " contact ". Soon there were ninety Lagos Europeans laid low—the Africans were down by thousands, and there was hardly a messenger or a clerk left in any of the offices. The military officers, too, were nearly all in hospital, and as a result there was discontent, desertion and near-mutiny among the men. Lugard handled in person a dangerous situation among the troops at Zaria with understanding and commonsense. He himself refused to take any special precautions from the epidemic and maintained his usual working day. The sand-flies kept him awake all night, " but it never makes me tired to miss a night's sleep." The connection between Lugard's success as a tropical Governor and his steely constitution had never been more clearly shown than in these last war-years in Nigeria.

At last came the great news of November 11th, with Lugard sharing the immediate reaction of many of his countrymen about the Kaiser. " I would hang him as high as Haman—they should deliver over to us ' to be dealt with according to law ' all the persons principally responsible for atrocities. Responsibility for the war is a different matter, and I do not feel so strong on that." It was not, however, only aggressive and revengeful emotions which the war had bred in Lugard and which he had shared day by day with his wife. Their correspondence had never shown a fuller intimacy of thought upon public as well as private matters as during the period of the conflict.

"I have said to you often and I cannot say it too strongly that I regard this war as our salvation. I think that the horizon was very dark when the storm broke. There was Ulster and civil war in sight, but that was a minor question. The cleavage between the classes and the masses was a far more serious matter. Lloyd George and his Land policy, the domination of the Trades Unions, the bitterness of the Labour Party—the coming war between the Haves and Have-nots. Apart from this was the growing increase of the idle rich living in extreme luxury—I see that even still men's handkerchiefs are on sale and *being sold* in Bond St. at 20 guineas a dozen. This canker could only be excised with a knife. The war has been the surgical operation needed, and it will, I have no doubt myself, postpone our decadence as a nation for half a century or more."

(L. to F. L., 20 March 1916).

One effect of the war upon Lugard was a burning desire to work harder than ever now this further great cause had been added to his other purposes. Flora had urged that he should do all his work both for the sake of duty and of his love for her. "Don't" she said, "scamp even a ridiculous petition from some illiterate who appeals to you." But now a deepened patriotism drove him still harder. When, on the same day he heard of the German bombardment of Scarborough and of the decision of his brother, whose only son was already in the army, to rejoin his regiment, he "felt rather a mean cuss and a coward that I am doing nothing." He felt the same as he saw the work that Flora was doing. "At times there comes over one a sense of the insignificance and pettiness of the routine in which one is engaged when such momentous issues are being fought out in Europe and men's lives are being lost by thousands, when you are engaged in succouring a whole nation . . ." (L. to F. L., 19 December 1914). He continued to enter with the most intense interest into every detail of her work. He was, however, still tormented with anxiety about her health. Though she had rallied to the challenge of the task she still suffered from the unhealed wound from her operation in Japan. One sultry night, as he lay awake persecuted by flies and with a storm brewing up

" Fear began to creep in ". He called into his mind verses from Deuteronomy bidding him trust in the Lord. " I still write, but I say to myself: ' If she were still alive on this planet would she not have sent a telegram in reply to mine praying for news?' I telegraphed again today—urgent—begging for news. Still no reply. My God! I have suffered today as badly as I did in Hong Kong. Will you ever see these lines . . .? As I lay on my bed this morning suffering a perfect hell of thought Ah You came in with a telegram. I set my teeth as I opened it, not knowing what news it might contain." It said: "I have cabled regularly" and then their code word: " Reassured ". " Somehow, in an irrelevant way, it occurred to me and I almost said aloud, ' the change from deep pathos to bathos is like dancing a hornpipe in a cathedral.' "

Lugard's power to love and to suffer had not weakened, it is clear, since those far-off days when, after the breaking of his first great love, he had drifted almost insane down the east coast of Africa. With his life now fused with that of his wife he was divided between admiration of the great public work she was doing and a kind of jealousy that she was using up upon others the small and precious remnants of her strength which belonged to him, or rather to both of them together.

When it became impossible for him to leave Nigeria and he stayed out for two years, he found some consolation for the wretchedness of the separation in a reflection which is a comment upon the record of this chapter: "At last I am personally doing something and suffering something in this great crisis."

CHAPTER XXVIII

COLONIAL HOUSEKEEPING

LUGARD'S NAME has been so much associated with colonial administration that it would be easy to forget that, as a governor, he had also
to deal with finance and economics. The union of the two Nigerias had,
of course, problems in these spheres. Further, these are days of strongly
aroused interest in " under-developed " countries and also of attacks
by the peoples of these same countries upon the exploitation of
colonialism. These current ideas lend an extra interest to the economic
activities of an undoubted colonialist and to the policies followed in
his generation.

In justice to Lugard we must recall the background of economic
thought of his day. It might be said that, apart from trade which was,
of course, the nation's first interest, government before the First
World War was still conceived of mainly in political terms. The
conception Lugard would carry from Britain to Africa of the functions
of the state in the economic sphere would, by contrast to those of 1960,
be very modest. He certainly thought of himself as primarily a political
man. He had been given the mainly classical education of the public
school system; thereafter his apprenticeship had been military.
Economics was still a pioneer subject of which, it is probable, he had
hardly heard. The political officer—and the adjective is significant—
represented the political authority of the Governor and was the
dominant figure in province and district where the few so-called
" technical " officers, who attended to the material aspects of government, were in a definitely subordinate status. Indeed, the growing
need for the revision of this traditional relationship continued to
embarrass African administrations for many years to come.[1] Although
the political officers were in general charge of their regions it is notice-
able that in Lugard's very full instructions to them, as revised in 1918,

[1] See Perham, *Native Administration*, p. 299 ff.

there are no sections which deal with economic matters other than those on land, which treat mainly of the laws governing title; forestry; and an unexpected heading " goods and vessels in transit " necessitated by the problems of Niger transport. Yet, within the confines of the thought of his day, Lugard's attitude to economic affairs showed neither indifference nor ignorance. His need to popularize his policy of colonial annexation had long ago impelled him to advertise to British opinion the latent riches Africa might yield to British trade. Nor was he the man to be content with throwing out a vague allure: his lectures and writings were full of businesslike observation of Africa's products, actual or potential. To his thrifty, practical mind there was an appeal in the economy and finance of a territory. This went far beyond the simple imperative which forced every colonial governor to pay close attention to the production of that trade out of which he must raise most of his revenue; all the more since, like the medieval kings, he was always being told that " he must live of his own ".

Since Lugard's day there has been an immense development of Nigeria's economy, or rather its economies, for these can be distinguished to some extent as foreign and indigenous, commercial and subsistence, and also by regions, though the political unity of the country has fostered the development of economic unity. Since his day, also, and especially during the last twelve years or so, authoritative economists have revealed the structure of Nigeria's economy while sociologists have probed into the native societies to show the deeper effects of bringing a piece of Africa within the exchange system of the world.[1] But in the years 1912 to 1918 some of the most striking current features of Nigeria's economy either had not appeared at all or had not developed far enough for identification. Certainly the economic points in the future nationalists' case against their rulers had hardly been framed. Lugard had to work within narrow limits created by the situation he took over and the ideas of his time. These concerned mainly the freedom of trade and enterprise, the sphere of state action and the economic role of a colony within the empire. He

---

[1] It is possible to mention here only a few of the many works upon this subject. A. McPhee, *The Economic Revolution in West Africa* (1926); W. K. Hancock, *Survey of British Commonwealth Affairs*, Volume II, Problems of Economic Policy 1918-1939, Part I (1940), Part II (1942); M. Perham, ed. *The Native Economies of Nigeria* (1946); M. Perham ed. *Mining, Commerce, and Finance in Nigeria* (1948); P. T. Bauer, *West African Trade* (1954); K. M. Buchanan and J. C. Pugh, *Land and People in Nigeria* (1955); an excellent summarizing chapter in Coleman, *Nigeria: Background to Nationalism*, pp. 63-90; International Bank for Reconstruction and Development, *The Economic Development of Nigeria* (Baltimore, 1955).

must take his measures with little knowledge of those revolutionary effects upon the people which only time could show. Yet since he was working under his own principle that the interests of rulers and ruled must be and could be harmonized it is proper to judge his policy by the degree to which he maintained this balance which he afterwards defined as " the dual mandate ".

To begin with finance, its sources and its deployment. We have seen that amalgamation resembled the enforced marriage of an aristocratic bankrupt with a wealthy parvenu, one whose riches were not all derived from respectable sources. When Lugard, as Governor in 1912-13 of a still single Southern Nigeria, reviewed the revenue, he found the main facts and figures impressive enough. There was a total trade in 1912—the last year of complete separation—of £11¾ millions. Of the £5¾ millions of exports, £4¼ millions represented palm-oil and kernels. A revenue of £2¼ millions allowed of some £400,000 to be spent on capital works, roads, bridges, Lagos harbour and a railway, this last item already showing a profit unusual for young African railways.[1] These figures had to be contrasted with his poor Northern Nigeria's revenue of less than half a million, with a deficit made up by the Imperial Exchequer.[2] But Lugard brought morality into the scales. Northern Nigeria was not only aristocratic; nearly all its own scanty income came from what he regarded as the virtuous source of direct taxation. By contrast, of the £1½ millions of Southern Nigeria's revenue raised from customs, more than £1 million came from what Lugard regarded as the disgraceful source of the duty upon spirits.

In spite of these difficulties Lugard could set to work upon his first estimates for amalgamated Nigeria with reasonable hopes. It was agreed that the Exchequer grant, reduced from an average of about £300,000 odd to £100,000 a year, should cease after five years. (The last grant was actually paid in March 1918). The plans to build a unified railway system, beginning with the eastern Port Harcourt terminus and running up through rich palm country to the new coalfield at Udi, and the general atmosphere of confidence evoked by the unification of such a large and promising block of Africa, aroused expectations of rapid economic advance. Lugard could state, though admittedly in the almost compulsory optimism of an after-dinner speech, his belief that " we were on the threshold of the conquering innovation of rail-

[1] *Reports, S. Nigeria*, 1912, p. 5 ff.   [2] *Reports, N. Nigeria*, 1912, p. 4 ff.

way extension and the opening up of the world's markets for the products of the tropics."[1] Eight months after amalgamation came the outbreak of war. It was at first difficult to foresee what its effect upon West Africa would be. But Lugard was never discouraged. He was determined to carry on to the utmost that was possible with his plans for the development of Nigeria, and where the Colonial Office was for caution, especially in the matter of continuing with the construction of the eastern railway, he was in favour of going forward.

The first economic effect of the war was to advertise the startling fact that Germany was as large an importer from Nigeria as was Britain herself, that she took the great bulk of the palm-kernels, and that German firms played a large part in the economic life of the territory. Shipping was disorganized; exports piled up and deteriorated at Lagos, there was scattered unrest in the provinces, and there was a local war with Germany on the border, of which Nigerian revenues had to carry part of the cost. It was natural that there should have been some pessimism about the finances. Yet Lugard was able to claim triumphantly that instead of the deficit of £200,000 which, even on the assumption of peace, the Treasury had estimated for the first year of amalgamation, he had closed his first budget with a surplus of £80,000. His next triumph was to build the eastern railway from Port Harcourt to the Udi coalfields out of revenues and reserves and without calling upon the loan which the Treasury was prepared to pay.

Economically there were three periods during the war. The first was one of shock and dislocation. Then a new economic pattern began to take shape. Hungry Britain found she needed Nigeria's oil-products and must therefore allocate shipping for them, while America came in as a customer to take up some of Germany's share of import and export trade. But the last part of the war, with the effective submarine attack, produced a new crisis with the shortage of shipping and the high costs of freight and insurance, and a service dispirited by overwork, lack of leave, and the high cost of living.

Fortunately, the last critical period ended with the peace before the serious loss of shipping became fatal for trade, and Lugard was able, in 1918, to hand over very impressive accounts of his financial stewardship. In spite of war and of the loss of the £1 million of the dues from

[1] Report of speech to an African Society dinner, *Morning Post*, 17 May 1912.

spirits, the revenue had been raised from £3 million to £4 million. A large programme of public works had been carried through out of revenue. Among the major ones, in addition to the eastern railway, had been the new Port Harcourt; the new capital at Kaduna; the large harbour works at Lagos; and the big bridge across the Niger at Jebba. Nigeria had contributed some £1,400,000 in extra expenditure for the war including the whole cost of the northern sector of the campaign in the Cameroons. In addition to this Lugard had, as we have seen, almost forced the Colonial Office to accept from Nigeria an engagement to pay the interest and sinking fund upon £6,000,000 of Britain's war debt, though payment was not to begin until after the war. The charges upon the territory's total debt of about £8½ millions, mainly incurred for railways, would easily be paid, Lugard asserted, from their working profit, though the further extensions after Lugard left were to show very much less favourable railway accounts. The growth of revenue had been due, in part, to the increased royalties on tin, the profit of railways and harbours, and Lugard's extension of direct taxation.[1]

A few figures will show the commercial assets upon which Lugard had to build his finances. In 1913 he found that the total trade of both Nigerias amounted to £12,798,000. The exports at £7,097,000 were largely supplied from Southern Nigeria, palm products accounting for no less than some £5 million of the total. From Northern Nigeria, except for half a million pounds' worth of tin, the exports were negligible. By 1917, in spite of war, there had been a great increase and a movement away from something like monoculture. The total trade was now £14,411,078 and of this Northern Nigeria's ground nuts and hides now supplied £1,597,294, while the value of its tin had trebled. Access to the northern products was made possible by the linking of the southern railway system to Kano in 1912, though the Jebba bridge was not built until 1913.

Since the support of the West African Frontier Force might properly be regarded as an imperial charge, the total grants-in-aid made by the Treasury on account of the civil revenues of Northern Nigeria amounted by 1918 to £4,261,000. To this could be added the £865,000 grudgingly sanctioned by parliament in 1899 for the expropriation of the Niger Company. Lugard claimed that if the total profits made by the

[1] *Amalgamation Report*, p. 46.

Treasury over its handling of the Nigerian coinage were allowed for, the total cost of the occupation had been £4,700,000. If, he went on, Britain now accepted the war aid which he had offered, it could be calculated that Northern Nigeria had been acquired at no cost whatever to the British taxpayer.[1] The cost, he might have added, had been in the heavy percentage of life and health upon the military and civil officers and also of the African troops who had been engaged in the occupation and the defence of the country, both in Nigeria and abroad.

Lugard was, of course, the head of a large service whose good work under his direction, and in all the difficulties and shortages of war, made possible the success which lay behind these statistics. Yet some of his most senior officers came and went, while he remained in control for two years of peace and four of war. And it is worth repeating here that the Colonial Office, which differed from Lugard upon so many questions which have been or will be described in this book, including some political aspects of taxation, more than once showed approval and confidence over the all-important matter of the annual budget.

From this survey of the figures of revenue, we must go on to look at some of the economic policies and facts of which they were the result.

First we must look more closely at what lay behind the loss of the largest item of revenue, the duties on spirits. We saw in the first volume with what enthusiasm he had taken up this issue and how first Goldie and then Lugard had completely prohibited the trade in Northern Nigeria.[2] As with the slavery question, he seemed to stand somewhat apart from those who took up these causes in a state of humanitarian fervour. By some process in which morality and reason combined, he would make his decision that a certain matter was wrong and would then set to work to try to bring it to an end by action rather than words. On the liquor question, after he had fought such a brilliant opponent as Mary Kingsley, he still had to meet much solid opposition. The financial aspect, in Nigeria's poor and still hazardous condition, might have been thought convincing. Here was a solid £1 million of revenue easily collected from the palm-oil producers upon an undeniable luxury. Such taxation, upon the British precedent, seemed justifiable, even orthodox. Yet, the slavery issue being settled,

---

[1] *Amalgamation Report* pp. 47-8.
[2] See also F. Lugard, 'The Liquor Traffic in Africa', *The Nineteenth Century*, vol. XL., November 1897.

the humanitarians in Britain, with the temperance societies as their spearhead, fastened upon this one evil to the exclusion, as Morel observed, of all the many other questionable effects of European influence upon native societies.[1] Observers, partial and impartial, pointed out that, strange though it might seem, the small sophisticated minority of the southerners, who were the main customers, could absorb more than $3\frac{1}{2}$ million gallons of gin a year without apparent demoralization. A Commission which was sent out in 1909 to make a thorough enquiry in Nigeria came to the same conclusion, adding that the " trade spirit " imported for African use was not of deleterious quality.[2] The terrible ravages made by drink upon the peoples of the Pacific, the Coloured group in South Africa, and earlier upon the Red Indians, may have led the Brussels Conference in 1892 to prohibit the spirit trade in Africa where it was not already established. Sir Nevill Geary reckoned the percentage of convictions for drunkenness in London to be nearly eight times more than that in Lagos, though of course the effectiveness of policing in the two cities was hardly comparable.[3] Further arguments against prohibition were the dangers of smuggling; of increased use of local spirits made from grain or palm trees, to the injury of food and oil supplies; and the potential use of home-made stills which it would be impossible to repress in crowded forest country. Geary also questioned the morality of the non-abstaining British imposing upon Africans what amounted to a discriminatory prohibition.[4] The bottle of gin, " old square face ", had from early days been a major article of trade, an essential at African ceremonies and a form of currency. Spirits had been a continuous merchandise from the days of the slave trade. Early in the nineteenth century an African chief had summarized his system of commerce with striking brevity: "We want three things, powder, ball and brandy, and we have three things to sell, men, women and children."[5]

Lugard, however, never wavered in his determination to destroy the trade now that he had the power to do so. He raised the duty upon trade spirits from 5/6 a gallon in 1913 to 10/- in 1918, while at the same time reducing the spirit content of the gin. In 1916, on the same day

[1] Morel, *Nigeria, its People and Problems*, p. 246 ff.
[2] *Report of the Committee of Inquiry into the Liquor Trade in Southern Nigeria* (1909), Cd. 4906.
[3] Geary, *Nigeria under British Rule*, p. 258.   [4] *Ibid.* p. 260.
[5] T. F. Buxton, *The Slave Trade and its Remedy* (1840), p. 280, quoted by Burns, *History of Nigeria*, p. 230, n. 7.

that he felt bound to tell the Colonial Office his fear that Nigeria was in a state of " financial collapse ", he also declared his intention of abolishing the traffic in spirits altogether, though the Office was horrified at the cost of the sacrifice in revenue. He introduced in 1917 a comprehensive Liquor Ordinance to strengthen the enforcement of absolute prohibition in the Northern and parts of the Southern Provinces, to impose licensing and prevent local distillation. As a result of this measure, and also of the difficulty and cost of shipping spirits from Rotterdam during the war, the importation of trade spirits was reduced from 4,500,000 million gallons in 1913 to 269,000 in 1917, and the proportion of revenue derived from it from 34 per cent in 1913 to 1.23 per cent in 1918.[1] In 1919, by a Convention signed at St. Germain-en-Laye, the importation into Africa and the sale of trade spirits was prohibited by international agreement among the Allies.

Lugard's attitude throughout is interesting. His desire for economy struggled with his principle and lost. But what exactly was his principle? In his final report and in *The Dual Mandate* he gives the arguments upon the other side so fairly that it is difficult to regard his own reasons as superior. He states that the question of demoralization is still an open one and that he thinks many of the evils attributed to drink are really due to venereal disease. But he went on, " however this may be, no one can deny that it is a sterile import, upon which the native wasted one and a half million sterling annually without securing any improvement in his standard of comfort or increasing productive output, that it is a disgrace to an Administration that the bulk of its Customs, and nearly half its revenue, should be derived from such a source; and that it is a foreign product, and *pro tanto* decreases British imports of a more useful character."[2] (There was no hypocritical deceit here: Lugard strenuously opposed the substitution of British for German spirits.) To the argument that the Africans would increase their making of native liquor he merely retorted: " I do not regard it as a moral and legitimate argument, that if they must have liquor we should supply and make a profit out of it." (L. to F. L., 22 October 1917). Finally, he pointed to Britain's policy, at considerable sacrifice, with regard to the prohibition of opium. Here he might have remembered that his own attitude in this matter as Governor of

[1] *Amalgamation Report*, pp. 55-6.　　[2] *Ibid*, p. 55.

Hong Kong had been more tolerant and gradualist. It seems likely that the intensity of his antagonism to the trade sprang from his puritan upbringing, with its resultant hatred of waste and self-indulgence. He was himself abstemious though not an abstainer. But he felt his government to be a "trustee for the welfare of the native population" and he was convinced that he knew what was right for them.[1]

For the rest of his life, especially in his work on the League of Nations, he maintained his active interest in the liquor question. Though the support his policy had in certain quarters in parliament was recognized, there appears to have been no enthusiasm for it at the Colonial Office. There is a letter from Strachey in Lugard's papers putting the case strongly and effectively on the other side (13 September 1913). Lugard, therefore, had the double satisfaction of carrying through a plan very dear to his heart and proving the Colonial Office to have been wrong. He wrote of the duty on spirits, "I have balanced without it, and though the C.O. never calculated its extinction, they assumed I must borrow £1¾ million from the Treasury to carry on and complete the Udi line. We have not borrowed a cent! We are now solvent, and the Liquor Revenue has gone!" (L. to F. L., 22 October 1917).

Another matter affecting his accounts which vexed not only Lugard's sense of economy but also his great desire for himself and for his staff to join in the sacrifices of war, was the difficulty he had in stopping the supplies of food sent from Britain to Nigeria, which was by 1917 importing from America. This was, of course, food for Europeans or for Africans on a European diet; except for the accidents of famine the African population could feed itself. When Cameron reported to him that Nigeria needed so many tons of butter a month, "I brushed it aside as being mere nonsense, and appointed a Committee under Boyle to whom I had very freely expressed my own views." Lugard, clearly no great believer in the impartiality of committees, thus got his own way. "They practically asked for nothing except tea, provided the monthly service from the U.S.A. was maintained. I passed this in Ex. Co., but if tomorrow I were told that the service was stopped, I should tell the S. of S. we could do without even if the whole Ex. Co. disagreed." (L. to F. L., 6 March 1917). Soon, to personal economy and desire for war sacrifice, he added a third motive for indignation,

[1] *Amalgamation Report*, p. 55.

the recurrent theme of Colonial Office ineptitude. Immense quantities of scarce foodstuffs were still pouring into Nigeria in spite of Lugard's protests. To Flora he wrote: " It is a scandal . . . Really I wish you would show this up! I have telegraphed to the S. of S. and have also written a strong dispatch. Fancy *you* and all those at home being on short rations while *we* are importing these foodstuffs. We have 3 or 4 million cattle and I forget how many millions of sheep and goats and swine, and we are importing meat! ! . . . But it ' raises my gall ' to think of you going short and this atrocious waste continuing." (L. to F. L., 19 March 1917). It is possible that some of his overworked staff did not altogether share Lugard's taste for austerity, which included beef coming down on the hoof from the north and the reduction or disappearance of tea. It was their misfortune, at such a time, to have a chief who had not only iron principles but an iron constitution.

All aspects of the economy were, of course, ultimately dependent upon the productivity of the country and especially upon that percentage of production, by no means large, which could leave the country by way of exports. For Nigeria was very largely self-supporting with the Yoruba and northern Muslim sections of the population living at a high standard of life for Africa, and therefore with a considerable internal trade. It was over the export trade that there flared up, during the last three years of the war, a controversy of imperial as well as Nigerian significance, and Lugard was severely tested by it.

Professor Hancock has given a brilliant account of the affair. He has shown how British and Dominion politicians and capitalists lost their heads for a time as they were gripped by the needs and fears of a war which, for Britain, resembled a siege. In this mood of fear, of hate, and of hectic counting of resources, they took stock of the empire and resolved to carry over into peace the controlled economic unity which had been forced upon them by the war. Professor Hancock writes that in the stress of war, " the problem of supply dominates . . . An emotional torrent, whirling through narrow channels of heroism and hate and fear, drowns criticism and even memory . . . The besieged citizens cannot or will not remember those customary activities of busy commerce in an unsundered world which have been the foundation of their peace-time comfort and a preparation of their war-time strength."[1]

[1] Hancock, *Survey*, Vol. II, Part I, p. 94 ff.

When the issue was survival Britain laid desperate hands upon such colonial products as she needed. The question now was whether, as the nations planned for the transition from war to peace, and for the years that should follow that transition, it was good economics or good politics to prolong the grip of imperial control.

We are on the edge of a subject long in history and deep in complexity. Critics of British colonial policy have assumed that, whatever our political professions, the bread and butter of the subject peoples were always subordinated to the furnishing of the rich imperial table. The economic incidents which follow provide one test of the criticism and also an incident in the economic struggle between state control and laissez-faire which, it seems, continues until it is finally smothered under the blanket of totalitarianism. Lugard was called upon to play a part in this large controversy on five main occasions when he was caught up into its fringes.

The first occasion was over the issue of the palm-kernel trade. Here Germany had certainly stolen a march upon Britain—a legitimate peace-time march. To understand the problem we must look a little more closely at the oil-palm itself. It covers the coastal strip of West Africa with its shapely but rather gloomy dark green plumes. Its fruit is contained within a fleshy peri-carp, from which the oil was easily but not always efficiently expressed by the Africans. The hard kernels of the fruit were sold for export to Europe, where they needed special machinery to break them and release an edible oil. The Germans had been quick to make full use of them. In 1913 they were importing 181,000 tons from British West Africa as against Britain's 36,000. They had internal waterways for conveying the bulky product to the river or dock-side factories; specially adapted crushing mills; a sale of much of the oil to Holland for making margarine; while they used the residual matter to make cattle-cake for their own herds. Conservative British manufacturers had as yet no proper crushing mills. Conservative British farmers had not yet seen the value of the cake. The sudden loss of the German market for kernels was thus a blow to Nigeria and an opportunity for Britain.

A Committee was set up in June, 1915, with Arthur Steel-Maitland, Under-Secretary of State for the Colonies,[1] in the chair, to consider

[1] Steel-Maitland, (later Sir) Arthur, P.C., 1876-1935; 1915-17 Under-Secretary of State for the Colonies; 1917 Joint Under-Secretary for the Foreign Office, and Secretary to the Board of Trade; 1924-9 Minister of Labour.

the question. Lugard and his Gold Coast colleague, Sir Hugh Clifford, sat on it when they were in England. Its other members were politicians, traders, experts and civil servants. It reported that British manufacturers would not take the risk of setting up the special crushing machinery unless they could be sure of their supplies and could be protected from what would otherwise be the certainty that Germany would recapture the trade after the war. An export duty of £2 a ton should therefore be put upon palm-kernels and remitted to British buyers.

This discriminatory duty at once became a focus of conflict. The new wave of monopolistic feeling dashed against the old but shaken rock of economic liberalism. There was a strenuous debate in the Commons in which Liberal and Labour members reproached the Government for abandoning the true principle of British trade and injuring the interests of their African wards. The Committee had admitted that there was a risk that the limitation of the market *might* lower the price paid to the native producer, but had continued, in words which betray the spirit behind their recommendation, to affirm their belief that " whatever risk there is in the matter is worth taking for the proposed term of years in view of the objects to be obtained."[1] The " risk ", it should be remembered, was the Africans'; the "objects" were those of the merchants, or, more charitably, what were believed to be those of Britain.

Ramsay MacDonald was able to make good play with this, and the other liberal and humanitarian attacks make excellent reading.[2] The other side made much of the fact that the two Governors had belonged to the Committee and had assented to its findings. In fact neither had been in Britain in the later stages of its sittings and had not signed the report. The Liberal M.P., Mr. Wiles, who himself signed a minority report, said that the Governor of the Gold Coast never once spoke.[3] But it was stated in the report that Lugard had agreed that the risk of a combine to depress the price was not serious. Bonar Law, the Colonial Secretary, made useful play with Lugard's name. " I have seen him and I have discussed the matter with him. He believes that this will help the natives." Then, as if realizing this was going rather too far, " At all events, he seems pretty sure that, though there is a

[1] *Report of a Committee on Edible and Oil-Producing Nuts and Seeds* (1916), Cd. 8247, p. 23.
[2] *Parliamentary Debates*, 3 August 1916, V. 85. 529-66.
[3] *Ibid.* 605.

risk of its injuring them, that will not be the effect." " With regard to the effect on the natives," said Steel-Maitland, " really and truly, the wish of the Governor-General of Nigeria to do justice to the natives is quite beyond question."[1] He instanced the gifts and offers of support which had poured in upon Lugard from the chiefs, and asked " is it possible that the man under whose rule you get all these spontaneous gifts is a man who is likely to have a lack of care for the natives?"[2]

Looking back today it would be generally agreed that the export duty was not only monopolistic even against our allies; but was economically unsound since palm-oil production, which could easily be extended outside Nigeria and was also threatened by several substitutes, was a most unsuitable item for monopoly. Where, then, did Lugard, whose name was doubly employed to justify this policy, stand in the matter? The answer is that he *had* agreed to the duty. He had to find a quick market for the product and he recognized Britain's need in the war for the oil as a food and as a constituent for explosives. But, in the report and more certainly in the debate, the strict conditions within which he had set his agreement do not gain their proper importance. The Committee first recommended that the duty should be used not only to gain the kernel-crushing industry for Britain but to *retain* it, and that the duty should be levied for five years after the war, when the advisability of continuing it could be considered.[3] Lugard insisted that the duty could be accepted only as a " temporary war measure ". If the firms combined and there was a decrease in the local price " the duty can at any moment be abolished by the light of such experience. And were it thus misused I should myself be the first to press for its withdrawal."[4] He later justified it upon the principle upon which Adam Smith had more than justified the Navigation Acts that " defence is of far greater importance than opulence. " He believed that the defence was a common interest between Nigeria and Britain, for which it was fair that as a wartime measure Nigeria should bear some sacrifice, and he saw, of course, that the " opulence " that was threatened was that of the Africans, and this he was determined to watch over. In the event the duty was not imposed until 1919 and, after continuing controversy and a changing position with regard to supplies, it was dropped after less than four years.

---

[1] *Parliamentary Debates*, 3 August 1916, V. 85. 634.   [2] *Ibid.* 632.   [3] Cd. 8247, p. 24.
[4] Proceedings of the Nigerian Council, 29 December 1916, p. 20, and Lugard, *Dual Mandate*, p. 267 ff.

Lugard's very conditional agreement was an exception to his general principles. The opportunity to express these came at the end of 1916. He was presented with a request from the Colonial Office to consider the economic policy of Nigeria in the wide context of the war and post-war situations. The request arose from the conference in Paris in June of that year, at which the Allies tried to extend their military solidarity into the economic field. Their recommendations had been passed on to a British committee under Lord Balfour of Burleigh, in which the interests of " the nation " bulked more largely than those of " the Allies ". Lugard was hardly in a position to resist pressures from such august sources at such a moment, but he made it clear, both when he presented the questions to his Nigerian Council and again in his subsequent reply to the Colonial Office, that he was not prepared to go to extremes or to sacrifice the interests of Nigeria, as he saw them, to any new short-sighted and acquisitive policy.

Having declared, though with strong reservations, the acceptance of the export duty on kernels, he warmly commended the British Empire Cotton Growing Association as an instrument for progress. His admiration here was barbed with criticism for those who could not measure up to its standards. He emphasized that the Association depended upon stimulus and not monopoly or control, and believed that the interests of the cultivator must come first.[1] On shipping he protested against the monopoly of the Elder Dempster line and urged healthy competition, even if this demanded the help of a subsidy. Similarly, although the representatives of the firms urged that they could supply all the capital required to develop the country, he urged the need for wider participation by non-enemy capital and by the people of the country. This led him on to a statement that was still more liberal when the date and the ideas prevailing at the time are remembered. To the official question " How can the sources of supply be prevented from falling under foreign control?" he stated—and we must remember that Keynes' famous book, *The Economic Consequences of the Peace*, had still to be written—his disbelief that " the industrious and intelligent population of Germany and Austria, numbering some 121,000,000 of people, should or could be excluded from the trade and commerce of the world. Were it possible to do so—which it is not— we should suffer almost as much as they." The most to which he would

[1] Lugard, *op. cit.*, pp. 271-2.

agree was that Germans should not be able to acquire land for a period of years. Lugard took this stand in the middle of a total and still un-decided war, in which hatred of the enemy was far less diluted with the more fatalistic philosophy of the second conflict. Lugard took the opportunity also to declare his own guiding principle, " I hold that the very foundations of the British Empire rest on its tolerance and the ' Open Door ' which it has always afforded to all the world. This alone has disarmed the opposition of other nations to the growth of the Empire and secured their goodwill."¹

Nor was this all. He pressed another point which cannot have been wholly palatable to the Chambers of Commerce whose influence upon policy was now so strong. He had used the war as an opportunity to push on the development of local products. Among these were coal, meat, lime, tiles, timber, furniture, oil-casks, gunny-bags, solder, and other items. By saving on unnecessary imports he hoped to release more money for railways and other public works. Thus he hoped to afford employment to " our own people " in a twofold direction— "First, in that they themselves produce those articles, and secondly, by the labour employed in the construction of the Capital Works which we undertake with the aid of the revenue saved."² It is to be noted that to him " our own people " meant the Nigerians. This was in itself an involuntary rebuke to the monopolistic spirit and in the tradition of a service whose members have often protected their native charges even against their own country.

The debate that followed in the Nigerian Council revealed some views far less liberal than those of its President. This was one of the occasions when the African Ajasa exhibited the intense loyalty of his class, his character and his period. Of course, he said, Africans would accept any necessary restrictions. " The loyalty of the native is not measured by the pounds, shillings and pence he can now make ... but by the duty he owes to his country and the Empire he is proud to belong to." He was wholly in opposition to his Governor's tolerance. " I am one of those whose cry is ' The Empire for the Empire!' that is, for those who owe allegiance to her ... I am sorry I have to differ with your speech in one particular. I do it Sir, with the greatest diffidence—I refer to the policy of the ' Open Door '. It will be driving a great part of the trade of Nigeria into German hands." He would never

¹ Proceedings of the Nigerian Council, 29 December 1916, p. 22.
² *Ibid.* p. 24.

allow the Germans back—" No, Sir, no more forging a sword for others to cut our throats."[1] The representatives of the British firms who followed showed a much more grudging attitude than Lugard's not only towards the ultimate restoration of economic relations with Germany, but towards neutrals and even allies.

The third issue which provoked Lugard into a defence of his economic principles was the sale of the German properties in Nigeria. There were interests in Britain which wanted to form a combine to buy up all the properties, or at least to confine purchase to British buyers. Lugard strongly resisted this. Although, as we saw, he was willing to see Germans prevented for a period from gaining control over land in Nigeria, he would agree to no further restriction. It appears that the government acted upon his advice. In a debate in the House of Commons Steel-Maitland declared himself opposed to the accumulation of enemy property in the hands of any combine of British West African merchants, and he went out of his way to criticize the Liverpool merchants for profiteering during the war at the expense of the African producers. Sir Edward Carson attacked the government bitterly over this and accused them of having accepted Lugard's views. Mr. R. McNeill, also speaking in support of the motion, said that while Lugard was a very zealous and capable public servant, after the strenuous years in Nigeria he " has not got the larger perspective of the consequences of the European war which," he went on to say with only too much truth, " have undoubtedly modified the opinions which many men in this country hold on questions of imperial policy. I sympathize with him if that is so." It was misguided loyalty which prevented the Colonial Secretary from throwing over the man on the spot. No personal susceptibilities should stand in the way of a great principle of policy.[2] Sir Edward Carson also employed his forensic ability to discredit Lugard's position. " I have nothing to say against Sir Frederick Lugard. I should be sorry to do so. His vision is Nigeria. I think our vision ought to be somewhat greater." He urged that no loyalty towards Sir Frederick Lugard should prevent at least a postponement of the decision to have an open sale. But the government stood firmly behind their Governor-General.

Lugard, reading the debate, rejoiced in the support given to his

[1] *Ibid.* pp. 25-6.   [2] *Parliamentary Debates*, 8 November 1916, V. 87. 265-6.

policy. But remembering, perhaps, what he had mistakenly sacrificed only two years before under Carson's spell, an incident still to be described,[1] he made a wry face. The " Nigerian vision " riled him. " Parliamentary lawyers . . . can of course be depended on to realize imperial necessities and 'to think imperially'." He thought, however, that Steel-Maitland's attack upon the Liverpool merchants was a little intemperate and as " I am universally regarded by the merchants as the prompter of that speech and that the statistics he evolved were supplied by me", the results were likely to be uncomfortable for him. (L. to F. L., 6 December 1916, and 20 January 1917).

His fourth round in his defence of the Open Door and of the interests of " our own people " is a more obscure episode. The Colonial Office informed Lugard in the late summer of 1917, of a plan of the Ministry of Food to form a joint Anglo-French Oil Seeds Executive, buying oil and oil nuts at a fixed price from the merchants f.o.b. in Nigeria and itself shipping the produce to Europe. The merchants would, in fact, be acting as Commission Agents for the British government. Lugard was therefore asked to find out the produce price paid at up-country buying stations. Lugard attacked the scheme with little scruple in his choice of words. It was not only its utter impracticability in the absence of an immense staff to carry out the necessary investigations at scores of up-country buying stations. It would be equally unacceptable to the Africans and to the established merchants. It would destroy competitive pricing. Asked whether the colonial government would care to have a share in any profits, he showed his contempt for the scheme. The only recipient of any profits should be the colonial government, " which is the direct trustee for the merchants and natives alike and applies every cent of the money to the benefit of the country . . . I answer with the unanimous approval of my Executive Council that this Government does not desire to take any profits thus collected." He preferred to see African wealth increasing and, if revenue were needed, to raise the rates of taxation. " These are normal processes for which this Government has no desire to substitute a state monopoly in which it would be a partner." Why, he asked, was the British Government, while refusing to accept the open voluntary gifts from the Native Treasuries, resorting to a scheme which " by deflecting the profits of trade which belong to the people

[1] See below pp. 623-7.

of Nigeria would in our view be contrary to the traditions of the Empire." (Lugard to Walter Long, 21 October 1917.)

The dispatch, covering eight pages of print, is a model of clarity and of informed reasoning aimed like a missile at its target. The reader who remembers the burden and strain of the war, of overwork and of the climate, which Lugard had carried for two years without leave, or even a day's holiday, must commend the man who wrote it, and also his refusal to be pushed by his masters away from his principles of economic right and wrong. It was a dispatch written *con amore*. He sent it to Flora for her approval and also for some of the desired but improper action it was his custom to ask from her, in this case to show it confidentially to Lord Scarbrough. But he added "I feel that the Gov. Scheme is so monstrous that I can smash it myself." He confessed to his difficulty in writing with any restraint. "I am so glad you think with me on this subject, but I knew for certain you would. Like you, I regard it as an attempt to strike a vital blow at our theories of Colonial Empire." (L. to F. L., 15 January 1918).

Lugard's fifth round in the economic sphere was with the Empire Resources Development Committee, a self-appointed group of M.P.s and businessmen who tried to turn the new sense of imperial solidarity, and the vague hope that Britain could recoup her losses by a centralized exploitation of imperial resources, into a definite system.[1] Since the Dominions were not amenable to such ordering from Britain, attention was concentrated upon the Crown Colonies and India, since these were " assets of the Empire " and " Imperial estates ", places unlikely " ever to receive any large measure of self-government, and there will be less difficulty in regarding them mainly from the standpoint of estates of the Crown."[2] The language of the counting house was lightheartedly applied. The German colonies were " a new estate of great dimension and promise. This estate is clearly an asset which should be set off against the costs of the war ", and used to liquidate the war debt.[3] A central board should consider the assumption by the state of promising enterprises, or its participation in them. But this should apply only to those which, according to expert opinion, were certain to yield a return of at least 10 per cent.[4] There was even wilder stuff than this. "Colonial industries," said Mr. Bigland, one of the chief

[1] *The Times*, 29 January and 22 March 1917. [2] Hancock, *Survey*, Vol. II, Part I, p. 107.
[3] H. Wilson Fox, M.P. in articles in *The Times*, 28, 29 September 1916.
[4] *The Times*, 22 March 1917.

exponents of the new mercantilism, " should disburse the entire cost of the war . . . not only would we be helping and giving of the wealth we are blessed with to our Allies, but we would combine in one great force and become dictators of the earth, and no one would dare oppose our power."[1]

From this modest programme it was soon found that India had to be dropped. Attention was therefore concentrated upon West Africa. Its native population was one of our " undeveloped assets ". The natives would benefit since their labour would be harnessed to the chariot of progress and productiveness. Here, in truth, was colonialism as its critics love to portray it. But unfortunately for them the sample is not at their disposal, nor is there any need for future West African historians of colonialism to waste much powder and shot upon these aberrations: there was more than sufficient contemporary fire-power, in parliament and outside, to shoot them down. Professor Hancock, some of whose liveliest pages deal with these " ju-ju economics ", finds a measure of excuse for them in the narrow margin by which, owing to shortages of supply, the nation had escaped defeat, in the new emotional but unrealistic awareness of the empire, and in the gross ignorance of the propagandists about their subject.[2] It could be added that for all their blind selfishness, the errant committee was struggling, though from the wrong end, with a very real problem. In the years since the First World War it has not proved easy to find a way of squaring the need of the Colonies for development with the hesitation of much needed private capital to enter the field under the restrictions demanded by a genuine trusteeship.

The interest of these abortive attempts is that they provoked Lugard to clarify still further his own colonial economics against their contrasting background. His views can be read in *The Dual Mandate*[3] and they recur in his letters to Flora. She discussed the dispatch mentioned above with Lord Scarbrough, and reported his strong agreement. Lugard was no unqualified admirer of the West African merchant firms, but at least they knew their coast and had no desire to see the abrupt intervention of amateur control boards or state

[1] From an address given by Alfred Bigland to the United Ward's Club, reported in *West Africa*, 24 March 1917.
[2] Hancock, *op. cit.* pp. 107-9.
[3] p. 273. See also ' The Crown Colonies and the BritishWar Debt', *The Nineteenth Century*, vol. LXXXVIII, 1920.

monopolies into their established trade. Lord Scarbrough, however, was not unduly worried. He asserted that no one enjoying great public confidence had joined the Empire Resources Committee in their projected raid upon the colonies. Lugard agreed that " these schemes of interference imposed by a bureaucracy unhinged by its exercises of power are too opposed to the genius of the English people to last." (L. to F. L., 4 March 1918). The prophecy was correct; all the more as the scheme proved to be economically unsound.

As regards Lugard's part in this affair it appears that Lord Scarbrough, as quoted by Flora, advised that he would have to remain muzzled until retirement should give him freedom of speech. " I do not share this view," was his comment, " I am not the servant of either Mr. Long or Sir G. Fiddes and I shall take pleasure in opposing all their schemes which in my judgment are contrary to the interests of the Empire or the particular country whose interests I represent." (L. to F. L., 4 March 1918). It was an unusual definition of the constitutional status of a governor. It was not one which made for harmonious conduct of affairs behind the scenes. But in the long run of our constitutional history as much has been achieved by breaking as by keeping the rules, and this independence of spirit in defence of the native people, which Lugard shared with some other outstanding governors, may have saved Britain from some of the errors committed by other colonial powers.

Professor Hancock concludes that the monopolist policies bred by the desperate experiences of war were defeated by the alliance of experienced and " decent " merchants, of the missionary-humanitarian group and " the humane administrator ", as represented by Lord Lugard.[1] It is probable that if Professor Hancock had had the time and opportunity to follow up Lugard's activities as we have done here, he would have underlined even more this authoritative commendation. True, in the unavoidable ignorance of the British public about the subject, the debate upon colonial policy in West Africa was largely carried on by these three elements. But these parties were not always in agreement. This was probably just as well in the period before the people most concerned, the Nigerians, were ready to join the discussion. The more experienced Gold Coast unofficials unanimously rejected the export duty on kernels in the Legislative Council. We

[1] Hancock, *op. cit.*, pp. 109-10.

shall see in the following chapter that Lugard, the administrator, was less in accord with organized humanitarian and liberal opinion, than Lugard the economic director. We must now see another sharp angle of this complex pattern of disagreement between the parties by considering his critical attitude towards the main agency in the western development of Nigeria, the merchant community.

His first objection was really political. It sprang from his high estimate of his own duties as a governor. He believed that the firms ought to have stationed some of their principal men in Nigeria, instead of sending out subordinate staff while the principals remained in Britain. He could give the obvious reason that commercial policy should be made in Nigeria by the men closest to Nigerian realities. But his deeper reason was that under this arrangement he, as governor, was reduced to dealing with men who had no powers of superior decision. This mattered less so long as he could maintain his scheme of continuous administration since this allowed him to deal with the heads of the firms, during his periods in Britain, more continuously than in the hurried round of meetings and dinners which were the routine between organized commerce and governors on leave. This possibility had been one of his main arguments in favour of the Scheme. But with the war and his longer spells of duty in Africa, it irked him greatly to know that economic policy was being settled in Britain between the firms and the Colonial Office. The status of the local managers prevented them even from giving authoritative advice to the Governor, and also subtracted from the prestige and the efficacy of his Nigerian Council, upon which some of them sat. In spite of the delicacy of the question, in the intimacy of the small circle of the British in Nigeria Lugard made no secret of his view. But the firms were not prepared to change their policy: they remained extra-territorial companies in the fullest sense of the adjective.[1]

In the last year of his governorship one of the leading figures in West African trade, and Chairman of the West African section of the Liverpool Chamber of Commerce, Mr. G. A. Moore, rejected Lugard's criticism, not without a touch of arrogance. " We send out the best men for the work they have to do, but we hold that the duty of advising the Government is not part of their work, but that the

---

[1] For a discussion of the position and organization of the Nigerian firms see the section upon this subject by J. Mars in *Mining. Commerce and Finance in Nigeria*, ed. M. Perham.

Government should come to us who have the permanent interests of
the country at stake." He had, he said, succeeded in getting Sir George
Fiddes to recognize this at the Colonial Office. Lugard was un-
convinced. "The merchants who gain wealth from Nigeria," he
wrote in his final report, "have a duty to the country which transcends
the task of safeguarding their purely personal interests."[1] And he
returned to the question again in *The Dual Mandate*.[2]

He had other criticisms of the merchants which went deeper. We
have seen that upon closer contact with the work of the Niger Company he had lowered the high estimate he had first formed of it. There
are a number of references in his letters to Flora about the methods
employed by the Company, especially in the Benue region, in handling
the African producers. In case Lord Scarbrough, as head of the
Company, should be ignorant of these, he asked Flora to enlighten
him. She was to tell him that the system of barter by which Company
agents sometimes refused to pay cash for produce but unloaded unsale-
able goods upon the Africans was undermining the Company's reputation. Fortunately, the Africans had already found a way of escape:
some of them had taken to ordering goods direct from Britain, sending
postal orders and receiving parcels. He had a further complaint that
there was a tendency for the African trader, and especially the up-
country Hausa, to be put out of business by the firms, since they could
not get goods at wholesale rates. When, furthermore, he considered the
poverty of his revenues it was with a sense of bitterness that he fulfilled
the ninety-nine year obligation to pay the Company half of all the
royalties won in the area which contained the tin-mines. It was, he
said, shortsighted for the suzerain power "to barter these assets". An
outright money payment should have been made, even if it had
remained a charge on the revenues. As it was, Lugard found himself
in 1917 paying out £70,000 for that year and the sum was rising.[3]

It is clear that the merchants, though they showered compliments
upon Lugard at his appointment, were apprehensive about his attitude
towards them. When Lugard was appointed Morel wrote to
Jonathan Holt, of the old-established West African firm of that name,
to warn him to go and see Lugard as soon as possible. "Lugard is not
a small man," he said, "but a very big man—a big minded man, and

---

[1] *Amalgamation Report*, p. 35.   [2] p. 116.
[3] *Ibid*. pp. 349-50. The Company was acquired by Lever Brothers in 1920.

if you get on the right side of him it will be of immense importance to you. He is essentially an autocrat by temperament: on the other hand he is a diplomatist with a natural inclination to justice and common sense and, as I say, not *petty* at all."[1]

The firms had reason to be wary of the new Governor. He was, from the first, on the alert against any tendency amongst them to combine. He very early warned Mr. Cowan of Miller Bros., who seems to have been one of the few senior men amongst the firms who spent much time in Nigeria, and whom Lugard greatly respected, that he was opposed to monopoly and meant to watch the firms very carefully in the interests of the Africans. Cowan reported to Lord Scarbrough upon his interview and begged him to take Lugard fully into his confidence as, apparently in spite of their personal friendship, Lord Scarbrough was not much inclined to do. Cowan's letter gives us another picture of Lugard, this time from the merchant's viewpoint. "Sir Frederick is much too fair a man," Cowan urged, "to wilfully misunderstand a position so put before him . . . he would gladly welcome such co-operation as business interests can offer to the Government of a country only partially developed. At the same time I am just as satisfied Sir Frederick would be about the first man to view with grave suspicion the consolidation of big interests where there was even a hint that the policy might be reactionary rather than one of progress and framed only for the accumulation of profits without any regard whatever to the ultimate good of the country . . . "[2]

Lugard's fears were well-founded. At the Edible Nuts Committee in 1916, he had stated his view that a combination of merchants was unlikely. Later, in 1917, he appears to have discovered that a combine was even then in existence and so informed the Colonial Office in his dispatch, already cited, of October 21st, 1917. The secrecy with which the arrangement was shrouded gave rise to criticism of the merchants' actions, much of it, he believed, unfounded or exaggerated. They had planned for a loss and found that exports actually increased during the war, while imports from Europe decreased with an immense resultant rise in prices. Just how far the firms had the will or the power to control the unforeseen effects of the war is not easy to say. Lugard recognized that they had to face difficult conditions, with the risk to

[1] Morel to Holt, 10 September 1912, Holt Papers.
[2] Cowan to Scarbrough, 12 February 1913, L.P.

shipping, the high freight and insurance and the congestion and deterioration of merchandise on the Lagos wharves. He believed that they had intended not only to steady produce prices but to reduce them to the lowest possible limit, while being prepared to pay that price even at a loss to themselves. He believed, also, that the merchants made what he felt to be very high profits, though he did not command the figures which would have allowed him to prove his point.[1] He trusted, however, that so long as the state, in this case represented by his government, refused to assist the monopoly, it would be difficult to maintain it intact. His attitude towards combination was taken over by the Africans as soon as they were aware of its effects, and the day came when they were able to answer it with their own kind of combination. It was the long sustained boycott of the firms' "pool" by the Gold Coast farmers in 1938 which was the dress rehearsal for a nationalist movement aiming at something much larger than economic freedom. It was a movement not without its influence upon Nigeria. It will be seen from the account that has been given that the later widespread belief amongst the political leaders that the government and the big mercantile firms were in alliance against their interests was quite unfounded as far as Lugard's period was concerned.

This account does not contain the whole range of Lugard's economic policy: an active governor in a large territory covers a lot of ground in six years. Much of the work was, of course, in the hands of the directors of departments and their staffs. Lugard was, for obvious reasons, far less critical of these than he was of some of his political officers. Though he judged that the general standard of the Nigerian service was inferior to that of Hong Kong, there were times, especially in the later years, when he broke into enthusiastic praise of members— " I've got some officers here whom I simply *love*—they are so capable and efficient and do their work so well." (L. to F. L., 9 December 1916). There had been Captain Child, R.N., Director of the Marine Department, who brilliantly improvised a fleet out of the Niger transport, and who was unfortunately drowned upon active service. Eaglesome, in the immense field of public works was both friend and partner. None was more valuable to him than Cameron who, with his clear, dry mind and his confident grasp of economic and financial realities, was the perfect complement for Lugard's more subjective

[1] *Amalgamation Report*, pp. 30-31. See also Lugard, *The Dual Mandate*, pp. 472 ff.

and temperamental approach. The writer, who knew Cameron well in his years as a governor, witnessed a slight cooling of their later relationship, and some unwillingness on Cameron's part to acknowledge the full measure of his debt to Lugard's system in the extension of Indirect Rule to Tanganyika. But at this time the two men made a very effective partnership. Yet if other men entered efficiently into Lugard's labours there was no sphere where he recognized any frontier against his own understanding and active control. In these long days and nights, when he sat within a wall of files which he steadily and happily demolished, he dealt among other things with the encouragement of old and new products; with research and experiment; with communications and freight charges; with transport, the new colliery, the processing of local products, the control of adulteration, currency and many other economic matters.

Among these was labour. He was now able to continue what he had so well begun in Northern Nigeria, and preside over the steady, rational supersession of the system of slavery. His expert interest in this question led him to an understanding of its natural sequel in labour problems, where, at least among " men on the spot ", his ideas and practice were in advance of his time.

The end of slavery has often seen the beginning of forced labour. The difficulty at that period of obtaining adequate and regular labour for large public works led to grave abuses in other territories, especially in some foreign African colonies. The writer will not forget the sight in the French Cameroons of trainloads of enforced northern tribesmen being transported to work on the railway construction in what was to them the unhealthy southern forest region, notorious for the loss of life among the labourers. Lugard, however, insisted that his government " was radically opposed to coercion in any form, even for works of such urgency and importance to the country as railways and roads." He warned employers that they must attract labour from their often lucrative work as independent farmers by good wages regularly paid, kind and fair treatment and decent housing. The men must be allowed time to purchase their food, to return at proper intervals to sow or reap their fields, and there must be " an entire absence of blows and rough usage." He also believed in promoting Africans to skilled and responsible work at the earliest possible moment and he commended the colliery managers for this policy. He was amongst the earliest of those who saw the mistake of assuming that African labour was un-limited and he pressed employers to start at once installing power-plants and labour-saving machinery.[1]

Does this review of Lugard's policy for the development of Nigeria suggest that he worked to any guiding principles? We can certainly detect an opposition to monopoly, whether of his own nation as against foreigners, or by combines of firms against producers. He was also determined to keep out concessionaires, whether the rights were to be over land or produce, and he looked with disapproval at some French, Belgian and Portuguese methods. He was, however, pre-pared to see a few ranches or plantations developed by Europeans as models and experimental enterprises.[2] His views upon this subject lay behind his support of the sweeping Land and Native Rights Ordinance, of which he had laid the foundation in 1902. This legislation armed the government equally against European land speculators and the short-sighted African who might have fallen to his lure. Lugard scouted the idea that there were large areas of land in Nigeria which, with ready labour, would allow of European enterprise, whether by companies or settlers. He can, of course, be given only a share in the credit for the policy that has kept Nigeria free from European settlement or conces-sions. He took over in Southern Nigeria a well populated country where the people had a rich export crop and could supply a fully adequate revenue from indirect taxation, while in the North he had strong rulers who might have been alienated by European economic intrusion. But he and his successor, Sir Hugh Clifford, steadily sup-ported Nigeria as a country of African peasant farming. Even though its main products had to run the risk of competition from the modern methods of European enterprise elsewhere, they kept out planters or concessionaires. Though the British firms had built a vested interest in a trade based upon native peasant production, Messrs. Lever, at least, wanted the plantation method. But the shadow left by the Congo atrocities was long in fading: it hung over discussions of even the most moderate schemes for improved handling of palm-oil put forward by Messrs. Lever.[3] It stimulated the vigilance of the Liberals and humani-tarians in parliament as well as the attitude of Lugard and his successor, who were determined to protect Africans from the mere possibility of

[1] *Amalgamation Report*, p. 43-4 and 53.   [2] *Ibid.* pp. 36, 39.
[3] See Mr. Maidman's advocacy of British Settlement in the Nigerian Council, 29 December 1916, p. 33. See also *Parliamentary Debates*, 31 July and 12 August, 1913, V.56. 787 ff.

exploitation. It is not surprising that he later showed little sympathy with white settlement in Kenya and he could rest satisfied that Nigeria faced a future from which this complication at least was absent.

In spite of the satisfaction he found in wielding the power of the state, Lugard had no temptation to be a state socialist. " I have never varied in my belief that it is no part of Govt. to supersede private initiative and enterprise," he explained to his wife, and he referred to " the strong line I have always taken in support of individual responsibility and against Gov. interference." (L. to F. L., January 1918). But the narrow range of European enterprise and investment left a wide sphere open for government initiative. Lugard was quite ready to take it. He and Harcourt seemed to be in full agreement that the government should " nationalize " the Udi coalmine since it had to build the railway which gave access to it—a method not without its critics.[1]

Everything comes back to Lugard's dominant idea that in economics as in politics, by wise management and adjustment of the balance according to day-to-day realities, he could harmonize the interests of metropolis and colony. It may be that by the standards of haste forced upon governments today his plans were too leisurely. Had he been able to forecast the storm of change which the second world war would release upon the world he might have injected into his economic activities an urgency that at the time seemed not only superfluous but harmful. He was not, at least in later life, given to extremes in action or in language. At the end of his book he wrote a conclusion which, while it gives the keynote to the whole of his work, refers especially to economic policy, and which asks for the same reasoned judgment which it expresses.

" Let it be admitted at the outset that European brains, capital and energy have not been, and never will be, expended in developing the resources of Africa from motives of pure philanthropy; that Europe is in Africa for the mutual benefit of her own industrial classes and of the native races in their progress to a higher plane: that the benefit can be made reciprocal, and that it is the aim and desire of civilized administration to fulfil this dual mandate."[2]

[1] See correspondence in *The Times*, 2, 5 and 6 January 1914.
[2] Lugard, *op. cit.* p. 617.

CHAPTER XXIX

THE LAGOS OPPOSITION

THE AUTOCRACY of the Governor-General was not unquestioned. From time to time he encountered some African criticism and even opposition. The view he held of his critics is unlikely to be the same as ours since, during the nineteen-fifties, we have seen the rapid and astonishing political growth these small seeds of discontent have made. A first glance at this subsequent history seems to suggest that the critics have been proved to be in the right. We cannot set aside this retrospective knowledge but unless we are careful to reconstruct the contemporary situation, it may make us too severe with Lugard as the authoritarian and too complimentary to his opponents as the pioneers of nationalism.[1]

Lugard's mind was fixed upon the whole of his vast Protectorate, 342,000 square miles of it, inhabited by some 20,000,000 people. He visualized them all as being in need of everything he was working hard to bring to them, whether they were Hausa groups requiring guidance and reform, or primitive tribes in need of everything a civilized government could supply. According to his plan the whole population was divided into its tribal units now set within the framework of the over-all state supplied from Britain. Each unit, large or small, was to be administered by a direct partnership between its native rulers and the political officers whose large discretionary powers emanated from the supreme discretion of the Governor-General. The plan was flexible in shape and management but not in principle. Its fulfilment depended, in Lugard's view, upon its covering the whole country and upon all the levers of ultimate control being in his hands.

It was difficult in this plan to make allowance for Lagos. The Colony,

[1] Just before this book was finished the writer was fortunate enough to see Professor James Coleman's book *Nigeria: Background to Nationalism* (California, 1958). This is a most valuable contribution to the subject with the early stages of which this chapter deals. Fortunately it has been possible to insert some references to it.

and much more the town, spoilt the whole pattern. As he saw it, he was dealing with the real Africa but his headquarters happened to be placed in the unreal Africa of the capital. Its constitution was the expression of the much earlier British attitude, which has been discussed under the name of the policy of identity, by which British institutions were as far as possible extended to the first coastal annexations. As a Colony, created in 1861, Lagos therefore had its Legislative Council and its British judicature and its inhabitants were British subjects.

It was, however, the social character of Lagos which enabled its residents to exploit their special status. An old Yoruba city, it had been in touch with Western influences long before its annexation and it had naturally drawn to itself a large number of European traders, missionaries and officials and these in turn had attracted Africans from outside Nigeria and from the hinterland. By Lugard's time the town contained an upper class which had adopted, more or less superficially, the European way of life. Many of them had visited England, a few of them had been educated there, especially in law;[1] they lived in European-style houses and sent one or two of their children to England for their schooling. There were at least five newspapers which reported social events, describing in appropriate journalese the dresses worn at English-style weddings. They also, for the most part, kept up a ceaseless criticism of the government. The most sophisticated residents were those who had come to Lagos from other parts of the West Coast, from the Gambia, Sierra Leone and the Gold Coast, drawing upon a still older phase of western influence. These threw themselves fully into the social and political life around them. Among them and among the Yoruba the freed slaves were an important element. The tap-root of their culture having been cut or, at the least, weakened, they had naturally drawn fully upon the alien civilization through which they had been both transported and liberated and from which they often borrowed their names. One group which had been repatriated from Brazil contributed some important families.

A picture of the life of Lagos may be gained from the account of her childhood given by Miss Kofoworola Moore, as she then was, the daughter of a leading lawyer and the first African woman to enter

---

[1] Coleman, *op. cit.* p. 141, estimates that by the early nineteen-twenties there were 30 Nigerian university graduates and 200 who had completed post-primary education. The bulk of these would be in Lagos.

Oxford University. She is now Lady Ademola, M.B.E., having married the son of the Alake of Abeokuta, who became Chief Justice of the Western Region in 1955 and is now Chief Justice for the Federation of Nigeria.

" I was born in Lagos, 21st May, 1913, being the second daughter of my parents . . . I was brought up against the background of essentially Western ideas, and from my earliest childhood my mind was formed in relation to Western culture and not to the background of untouched tribal life. My grandparents on both my mother's and father's sides were well educated. My great-grandfather was an ordained minister of the Church of England and my grandfather was at an English public school before he was likewise ordained for the ministry. The paternal branch of my mother's line originated from America. We are still in touch with these relations. Two of our cousins have visited Nigeria and my mother and elder sister have been in America in recent years. My father was educated at Monkton Combe School near Bath. Afterwards, he studied at the Middle Temple, London, and returned to Nigeria qualified as a barrister and solicitor. I can recall scenes in my childhood when my sisters and I used to listen with rapt attention to the accounts of his adventures in his student days in England. We were amused by his experiences in trying to drive a coach-and-four and fascinated by his riding in the Row. On his return to Nigeria my father set up a practice at Lagos. He was nominated by the Crown to the Legislative Council in 1915 [the date was actually February 1917] and from that date he has continued his services to the Assembly. In 1934 he was elected First Member of the Lagos Division of the Legislative Council. My mother was educated at the C.M.S. Girls' School, then called ' the Seminary '. Later she proceeded to England for the general ' finishing ' course available to ' young ladies ' in those days. A friend who knew her told me she was a most accomplished young lady. My parents did not set themselves to be blatantly Westernized, but naturally, due to their own education, they brought us up on Western lines. My sisters and I were made familiar early with everyday things of English life. We learnt, moreover, to converse in English with our parents: their method was to make us speak English the whole day every Sunday . . .

Changes were not as rapid in Lagos ten years ago as they are today; I have still vivid memories of settings with a strong tribal flavour. The average European in Lagos does not, I think, realize to what extent we preserve vestiges of our old traditions, especially in such ceremonies as marriages, christenings and burials.

I started going to the Church Missionary Society Girls' School in 1916 and continued there until I came to England in 1924 at the age of eleven."[1]

Some of the Lagos leaders of Lugard's day were still to be met when the writer first went there in 1931-2. Among them were Sir Kitoyi Ajasa and Mr. Eric Moore, who have appeared already in these pages, and Mr. Sam Pearce, who lived in his capacious Elephant House and would show visitors his American electric organ. There was also Mr. Herbert Macaulay, who demands some description.

Herbert Macaulay, looked back to as The Grand Old Man by later nationalists, was for most of his life (1864–1946) the leading critic of the government. Like so many Africans who first entered the western setting of administration and commerce, he had failed to keep its unfamiliar laws of financial probity and had gone to prison for embezzlement. His consequent exclusion from public office may have given an extra edge to his opposition. He took up all the main causes against the government but he concentrated especially upon the defence of the rights of the dynasty of the chiefs of Lagos, the House of Docemo. The degree to which, at least in Lugard's day, he conceived of his opposition as resting upon a Lagos, a Yoruba, or a Nigerian basis is hard to estimate, a difficulty which illustrates the still fluid state of political thinking in these early years. In discussion with him in 1932 the writer, to whom he presented his book *Justitia Fiat*,[2] was chiefly impressed by his moderation and old-fashioned liberalism.

The leaders did not stand alone. They had a growing following. The town at this time had a population of some 76,000 and from amongst the mass an increasing number were pushing up into a middle stratum of clerks, mechanics, small traders and servants in European houses. This class was naturally open to the political and social example of their leaders. And behind them, if material for demonstrations or riots were needed, were the adherents of the Eleko or the White Cap Chiefs, and especially the market women, organized in their guild, whose robust, humorous almost Billingsgate character still impresses the visitor.

These were the people, with some outlying individuals in other Yoruba towns, and in the old Efik mission station and port of Calabar

[1] Margery Perham ed., *Ten Africans* (1935), pp. 323-5.
[2] Herbert Macaulay, *Justitia Fiat: the Moral Obligation of the British Government to the House of King Docemo of Lagos* (1921).

584

far to the east, with whom Lugard had to reckon. Those at the top, detached more or less from their own African societies, felt justified as British subjects not only in claiming for themselves the right to be treated as such but also to judge by British standards Lugard's policy for the rest of the country. With much effort, and often with much educational expense, they had, they believed, entered into the heritage of Britain's culture. They had learned at school about the liberties which Englishmen had begun to wrest nearly three hundred years before from Charles I, if not indeed, from John at Runnymede. They now wished to appropriate these ready-made rights and use them against the present King's representative in order at once to defend and to justify their own first political assertions. The gradual and tentative advance of British power had left Lagos and other Yoruba peoples with a sense of self-confidence so that they did not regard themselves as a conquered people, but rather as torch-bearers of progress who had kindled their flame at Britain's hearth and were eager to go into partnership with the government in its task of civilizing their more backward brethren.

When a new governor arrives in a West African colony there is usually a brief honeymoon period while the press is still taken up with denunciation of his predecessor. With Lugard the period was short: his reputation was too positive and had been gained too near at hand to leave much room for hope. The Northern Provinces, as seen by the urban élite, were a place of despotism and it was easy, or at least politically useful, to portray Lugard as coming down from the north clanking the chains with which he meant to shackle the south. By early 1913 the *Lagos Weekly Record* had decided " Lugard is a disappointment to Nigeria." He was " A man whose walking stick is a pistol and whose thoughts by day and dreams by night are punitive expeditions and military patrols. Stirring tales were told of his negrophobia, his anti-black proclivities, his distant attitude to all men in general."[1] What one of the African lawyers said in a letter to the Anti-Slavery Society about Lugard's judicial reforms can be quoted to illustrate the attitude they asserted towards all those British institutions which could be regarded as bulwarks of freedom.

" If that system stands condemned in Africa, why is it so much admired in every part of the habitable globe! Is the African not human, and is he

[1] *Lagos Weekly Record*, 8 March 1913.

so dense as not to be able to discern between what is evil and what is good? How many a time since, fifty years ago, Lagos was given the advantage of English justice, has a discordant tune been raised against the system; not once. Our cry is not against English justice, as we are bred to it, and love and admire it, but against the endeavour now being made to deprive us of that justice and relegate us back to the first ages of barbarism . . . for if English justice stands condemned in Africa it must necessarily be so in England herself, since, what is good for the goose is also good for the gander."[1]

We saw Lugard's almost immediate sense of incompatibility with Lagos. He formed his first impression of the new phenomenon of the educated negro a few days after his arrival. " I am somewhat baffled how to get in touch with the Educated Native. To start with I am not in sympathy with him. His loud and arrogant conceit are distasteful to me, his lack of natural dignity and of courtesy antagonize me." It is, perhaps, only fair to add what followed: " Nor do I find it any easier to get on with the European agents of Liverpool merchants." (L. to F. L., 18 October 1912). At his garden parties he compared the dignified courtesy of his Muslim guests, in their long robes, with the southerners dressed in the latest and smartest European fashion, but some of them, inevitably, with insufficient knowledge of the European manners that should have gone with this attire.

There were times, also, when, like many others before and since his time, he was stung into anger by the dishonesty or apparent unteachability of his personal servants. Some of them broke or stole his razors, were absent without leave, told lies to explain their truancy, grovelled on the floor when reprimanded, and seemed incapable of understanding reiterated orders. The resultant exasperation sometimes drove him into comprehensive denunciation of their race. " It made me moralize," he wrote to Flora after a particularly unhappy episode, " on the African in contrast with the Chinaman or White man, ' Unstable as water thou shalt not excel '. It is the character of the race and it is their curse." (L. to F. L., 5 December 1916). Here he spoke before the sociologists had become so insistent that races do not possess inherent mental characteristics, and without that understanding of a people who had been hustled into a moral no-man's-land between the lost sanctions of their old society and those, still unattained, of the new. Yet Lugard's

[1] Osho Davies to Travers Buxton, 20 October 1914, The Anti-Slavery and Aborigines Protection Society Papers, G. 236.

reaction here is worth recording because servants may be those members of the people with whom a European has his most intimate contact and where the necessary understanding is most difficult to acquire upon either side.

Many officials who served in the north of Nigeria made depreciation of the educated southerner the obverse side of their pride in the northerner. Even Morel, who greatly admired Lugard's Northern Nigerian system and whose " torrents of praise " had, in Lugard's view, helped to turn the heads of his northern officials, was highly critical of the educated southerners.[1] He could write in 1910,

> " I fear and distrust for the welfare of Africa a large section of the educated natives of Southern Nigeria more than I do all the Stock Exchange financiers put together. Some of them are all right but some of them are pursuing their own ends and those ends are not for the good of their fellow people. In fact, our educationary methods and our missionary propaganda between them appear to turn a large section of the educated natives against their own race."[2]

It is well also to remember, before too much responsibility is ascribed to Lugard for his strained relations with the Lagosians, that even before he took over, Morel had prophesied trouble. He believed that the element in Southern Nigeria most closely identified with European influence provided the " persistently hostile critics of the Administration, begetting unrest and disloyalty to Government."[3] These views are worth remarking in a man to whom some left-wing writers dedicated a recent book as " The Great Champion of African Liberties."[4]

With these causes of difference between the city and the governor it is not surprising that his tenure was marked by a series of clashes. These concerned the status of the city, the judicial reforms, the position of the Lagos dynasty, the imposition of a water rate, the intervention of the Lagosians in the affairs of the other Yoruba states, and the activities of the press.

The first rift appeared quickly. Some of the provisions of the amalgamation were felt by the intelligentsia to be blows aimed straight

[1] Morel, *Nigeria, its Peoples and its Problems*, pp. 220-1.
[2] Morel to John Holt, 21 September 1910, Holt Papers.   [3] Morel, *op. cit.*, pp. 81 ff, 221.
[4] F. le Gros Clark, and others, *The New West Africa* (1953), ed. B. Davidson and A. Ademola. Upon European attitudes to the educated Africans see a very interesting discussion in Coleman, *Nigeria*, pp. 145-52. He admits that in Lugard's day there was some reason for regarding the educated Africans as being unrepresentative of the masses.

at them and their Colony. We have seen that it was part of Lugard's plan to reduce the constitutional status of Lagos by abolishing its separate secretariat and putting it under the Lieutenant-Governor of the Southern Provinces. He also showed his opinion of the city clearly by his two plans, which were to remain unfulfilled, to make Kaduna the central capital in its place and to move the capital of the Southern Provinces from Lagos to Yaba. The Lagos press was quick to see that Lugard wanted to get away from the " storm-centre " and Morel came in for some bitter denunciation for agreeing, in his *African Mail*, with Lugard's plan.[1]

Another part of the amalgamation was the reduction in the status of the Legislative Council. He confined its powers, which formerly covered all Southern Nigeria, to the Colony and made its unofficial membership almost the same as that of the municipal council. Meanwhile he established his wider advisory Nigerian Council. Thus the opposition was hurt not only in its pride but in its political ambitions. For was not the Legislative Council a parliament in embryo? Now, they complained, it was reduced to a mere municipal board. And Lugard added insult to injury by a deliberate neglect to attend the Council except upon rare occasions. "The present Legislative Council," complained one of the leading newspapers, " is an effete body . . . The Governor-General does not attend at, or preside over its sittings . . . as in the good old days of the Ancient Colony . . . " The writer concluded that it would be more honest (that is in accord with the new spirit ruling Nigeria) to abolish it.[2] Further, Lugard's scheme for his continuous administration of Nigeria was felt to cut the people off from such appeal as was possible over his head to the Secretary of State. In any appeal in the future, went on the writer, using a not wholly appropriate simile, " It will be a case of going from Philip drunk to Philip sober."[3]

These clashes were no more than preludes to the real battle. This was fought over Lugard's Provincial Courts Ordinance. In an earlier chapter the opposition to this reform was recorded,[4] but it was not discussed as the deepest reason for the alienation from Lugard of the educated class even though it did not apply to Lagos. There were three reasons why this measure was so much hated.

[1] *Times of Nigeria*, 17 February 1914.   [2] *Times of Nigeria*, 2 February 1915.
[3] *Ibid.* 10 March 1914.   [4] See above pp. 429-30.

The first was that at this time, though it is impossible to give exact figures, the majority of the leading Lagos citizens and politicians who had been educated in Britain were lawyers and, as we saw, their exclusion from the new Native Courts in the Southern Provinces hit their pride and their pockets very severely, and it was surely from no excessive share of original sin that they resented this loss. The second reason was that, as lawyers, they cherished, and had communicated widely to their supporters, a knowledge of British constitutional law. It seems that, over and above their self-interest, British law and judicial procedure had a real fascination for them. Litigation played a large and leisurely part in their own societies and their minds were very ready to grasp even the subtleties of English law and to study the constitutional history in which it was embedded. Moreover, since most of the British staff who wielded judicial powers were not legally qualified in this sphere, the African lawyer could challenge them from the height of superior attainment.

The third reason has to be sought deeper in the consciousness of the educated African. To belong to the primitive mass was to be raw material for " native administration," in other words to be under the discretionary power of a political officer, himself in partnership with uneducated and possibly despotic chiefs. But British law recognized " natives " as persons; it had been sterilized long ago in Britain from the arbitrary will of kings and lords and—in theory at least—of bureaucrats. And now it could be used to emancipate Africans from dependence upon the will of foreign men of authority; it could endow them, of right, not of grace, with the status of persons, of citizens, equal with each other and with the white rulers themselves, equal in the eyes of the sovereign. This potentate, new and distant though he might be, was revered as a very real being by the educated Africans, especially by the Yoruba with their ancient royal houses. The survival of this deep respect was brought home to Britain by the enthusiastic reception given to the Queen upon her visit in 1956.

Is it surprising then, that the Lagos élite fought with all their strength against a measure which, as they saw it, seemed like a dark cloud spreading down from the " servile " and " barbarous " north to overwhelm the dawn of British justice in their city? Perhaps, it was suggested, the new Ordinance was the beginning of an attempt to exploit West Africa on the lines of East Africa, since

" it is easier to enslave the Native on his own soil than to transport him to far-off lands at great expense to the trader and purchaser alike . . . Or is it that the Anglo-Saxon fears the rapid intellectual and industrial strides the darker races have made . . . There are 60,000,000 white persons holding down 400,000,000 coloured persons in subjection . . . It was the proud boast of these darker races that they were under the British Crown and were British citizens. There was the celebrated case of the Jew of Malta which enabled Lord Palmerston to deliver one of the most telling orations on the rights of the British citizen. Is there any Liberal Minister today who dares to stand up for the rights of any dark citizen of the British dominions?" [1]

No, concluded the writer, Britain was becoming decadent. According to another paper, Lugard's object in devising the new judicial system was to create " a nation of convicts ".

The opposition to the judicial changes did not stop at the laments and warnings of leader writers. A public meeting of protest was called in Lagos; delegations were sent to interview Lugard. There were protests and petitions not only from Lagos but also from the few coastal towns in the south-east, with Calabar in the lead. The opposition had an even more powerful weapon. An appeal was made to British public opinion. A letter from Osho Davies to Travers Buxton, the Secretary of the Anti-Slavery Society, announced the determination of the Africans to continue to fight the new measure even after it has been passed into law since " in British justice the African builds all his hopes, and therein he rests all his all—it is the indestructible palladium of his liberty, his shelter and safeguard against the insolence of Officialdom and his impregnable bulwark against Patrician domination." [2]

It was in the tradition of the Society to act upon such appeals. Buxton took up the question by writing letters to Lugard himself, and to Harcourt at the Colonial Office. Sir William Byles, M.P., a member of the Executive Committee of the Society, after vainly approaching Harcourt, raised the matter in parliament. The Africans persuaded Buxton to engage a retired judge from Southern Nigeria, William Stoker, K.C.—a precedent for many such assignments—to advise them on the formation of the Nigerian Reform Association. This was a body to organize public opinion against the Ordinance. A British

[1] *Times of Nigeria*, 14 July 1914.
[2] Davies to Buxton, 20 October 1914, A.S.A.P.S., G.236.

lawyer, Sir Nevill Geary, wrote articles and pamphlets against the measure. The lawyers' indignation against the author of the Provincial Courts Ordinance was, however, too deep to be assuaged by reasonable expositions and wild and bitter attacks were made.

Lugard, if unyielding, was not as indifferent to this treatment as he wished to appear. He recognized the opposition, as we saw, by giving full explanations for the change of system; he published a defence of it by Sir Edwin Speed in *The Gazette*; he allowed delegations to question him, and he went to the Legislative Council early in 1914 to expound his policy. But he never retracted an iota of his reform in deference to the opposition. To Flora he wrote,

" I am having some trouble over my new judicial system. There was a public meeting of protest in the Glover Hall here a day or two ago, which was led by the most influential natives here and resulted in a petition. I also have a petition from the local bar at Calabar and the local press is fulminating in its most virulent way . . . I am shattering the reputation I had gained, by these bills. They are as a matter of fact the charter of the country when properly administered. Reform in this country however, is not easy, and one must expect plentiful abuse."

(L. to F. L., 9 February 1914).

He had to confess later of the Ordinance that

" It has cost me the whole of my popularity with the natives here and I regret that because up to a certain point popularity is valuable. Whatever I do now, they are apt to say ' Here is another monstrous act, another Provincial Courts Ordinance ' and that, to some extent, makes it harder to do things. But I stolidly go on and by the time I have finished these Southern Provinces will be very different."

(L. to F. L., 22 April 1915).

He was right about the habit of opposition. His next serious disagreement with Lagos was over his decision to impose a water rate upon the city. A proposal to do so had caused an angry outcry in 1908. In 1915 works had just been finished to supply piped water and a small rate was proposed to pay about a quarter of the annual cost. The result was a riot. The Lagosians declared that they had always had plenty of water and did not want the government's new supply. They declared firstly that " Taxation is against our national tradition"; secondly that they had not been consulted; and thirdly that it was all for the benefit of the Europeans.[1] Lugard treated the outbreak temperately and the next year was able to report that the rate had been collected without difficulty. But the incident left a further deposit of bitterness behind it.

Next came the affair of the Eleko. It might have been expected that at least the most advanced of the new Yoruba intelligentsia would have been opposed to the institutions of kingship and chieftainship which dominated most of the Yoruba country. But though the position of the rulers' families might be complicated and weakened by the new influences, it was too strong as yet to be seriously threatened. Some of the intelligentsia therefore tried to make use of the old loyalties centred upon these institutions and mixed themselves up with great vigour in the struggles for power. In Lagos itself the head of the ruling dynasty, descended from the viceroys appointed from conquering Benin in the late eighteenth century, had been pensioned off in 1861 by the British government. But the local Yoruba remained loyal to the titular " prince " and to the fourteen or so " White Cap " district chiefs who surrounded him. The restoration of the status of the dynasty became the main activity of some of the educated leaders. While Herbert Macaulay was its chief supporter, even Lagos residents from other parts joined in this recognition. Though a small pension was still paid to the chief, this was on condition that he renounced his kingship and it had long been government policy to ignore him politically. Lugard might have taken this vigorous survival, which continued to be a major problem for government for many years after his time, as a confirmation of his belief in the vitality of African chieftainship, even when it had been overlaid year by year for half a century by the increasing weight of a great modern seaport and capital. [2] It appears that soon after his arrival he did consider the possibility of putting the White Cap chiefs in charge of quarters of the city, but he was persuaded by the very Europeanized Henry Carr that " it would be impossible to give quite uneducated men authority in a city containing so many who were educated." (L. to F. L., 24 October 1912). Lugard soon came to regard the Eleko Eshugbayi, the titular

[1] R. L. Buell, *The Native Problem in Africa* (New York, 1928), vol. i, pp. 661-2; and *Reports, Nigeria*, 1916, p. 37.

[2] See Perham, *Native Administration*, pp. 264-71; Buell, *op. cit.* vol. i, pp. 662-7; Coleman, *Nigeria*, pp. 195-7. In February 1960 the writer found the holder of this chieftainship still recognized as the titular head of Lagos and engaged in building a new modern " palace " beside the one founded, he claimed, in the eighteenth century.

chief of his day, and the factions of his court as little more than a nuisance.

The opposition within Lagos would not have disturbed Lugard so much if it had been contained within the port and the Colony. But he had to reckon with the penetration of what he regarded as seditious influences from Lagos into the Yoruba States where he was engaged upon the difficult task of extending Indirect Rule. This extension has been described but it belongs to this chapter to discuss Lugard's view that much of the trouble he met in the Yoruba region was due to the new influences of which Lagos was the centre. For Lagos was, after all, one of the Yoruba city states. Many of its residents came from further north and remained passionately interested in the affairs of their homes. The Lagos newspapers professed to be the mouthpieces of " the Yoruba nation".[1]

Lugard decided upon his first visit to the Yoruba country that the Lagos opposition and their newspapers were stirring up the states of the south-west against his policy. It was natural that he should be tempted to ascribe Yoruba discontent more to external influence than to any internal flaws in his system of native administration. " It appears," he wrote in his Annual Report for 1916, speaking of the serious outbreak against the Alafin at Iseyin in October of that year, " to have been due, in part, to reports spread by a few seditious persons that the Government was no longer able to maintain order, and that the British were being defeated by the Germans who would presently return and be the rulers of Nigeria." " In part," he said, the trouble " was due to the spirit of lawlessness and defiance of all author-ity which had been growing for many years in the guise of a claim to independence of the Central Government the tolerance of which had become incompatible with peace and good order."[2] To his wife he confessed that the Iseyin revolt had reached the proportions of a " wide-spread rising " which, in the shortage of staff and troops, had caused him serious embarrassment and to her he indulged his accumulated anger with Lagos.

" There is the chronic and abiding trouble of the secret sedition and dis-loyalty of Lagos. It is practically certain that they are at the bottom of this Yoruba trouble and the people have been misled by specious lies with the result that 50 have been killed in the fighting while their Lagos instigators

[1] Morel, *Nigeria, its People and its Problems*, p. 77.   [2] *Reports, Nigeria, 1916*, p. 37.

sit safe here and laugh over it. It is really pathetic and troubles one badly. These people here are seditious and rotten to the core. They are masters of secret intrigue and they have been plotting against the Government ceaselessly. They produced a riot among the ignorant the other day in Lagos . . . I have no time to go into details but I could show you that Lagos has for 20 years past opposed every Governor and has fomented strife and bloodshed in the Hinterland . . . I have spent the best part of my life in Africa, my aim has been the betterment of the Natives for whom I have been ready to give my life. But after some 29 years, and after nearly 12 years as Governor here, I am free to say that the people of Lagos are the lowest, the most seditious and disloyal, the most prompted by purely self-seeking money motives of any people I have met."

(L. to F. L., 9 December 1916).

It would be difficult now to verify just how far Lugard was right in ascribing the Iseyin trouble to influences from Lagos. But Abeokuta provided in 1915 a good illustration of the way in which Lagos influence could reach out to the north and ultimately to the British public and parliament.

The Colony and Abeokuta lay together and shared early contacts with the outside world. Once old commercial rivalries were forgotten, close ties could develop between the educated and trading classes. One Lagos newspaper, the *Nigerian Chronicle*, devoted itself almost wholly to Egba affairs especially when these were disturbed. It seems that two Africans, Alder and Green, had been dismissed by the Egba government and were therefore anxious to revenge themselves upon the Secretary, Edun. They were arrested early in 1915 on the charge of fomenting trouble after the unfortunate Ijemo shooting.[1] Lugard decided that the question of whether the usual enquiry into such an incident should be held should await the upshot of their trial. The Lagos lawyer, Eric Moore, contested this view.[2] When a commission of enquiry was appointed he made another protest against its being entirely official and also deplored the lack of notice and publicity.[3] The *Lagos Weekly Record* declared that without a native representative the commission of enquiry was "more or less a farce ".[4]

[1] *Nigerian Chronicle*, 4 April, 27 June 1913, 17 July 1914 and weekly until publication ceased in March 1915.
[2] Moore to Lugard, 15 March 1915, A.S.A.P.S. G.237. For the Ijemo affair see above p. 450.
[3] Moore to the Secretary, Southern Provinces, 19 April 1915, *loc. cit.*
[4] *Lagos Weekly Record*, 17 April 1915.

The Lagos critics now succeeded in gaining the support of the Church Missionary Society. Missionaries are always in a difficult position in colonies when their flocks have a strong political grievance against the government. Bishop Tugwell of the C.M.S. decided to take up this one with the Governor-General and told him that recent events had been due to " the exasperation of an oppressed people ";[1] the oppression, presumably, being that of the Alake. If, he said, there were no enquiry, loyal subjects of the Crown would for long chafe under a sense of injustice. Lugard, though it was the government opinion that the ignorant Ijemo had been stirred into disorder by the so-called " Christian faction " and that these were themselves linked with the " seditious " elements in Lagos, was obliged to take a Bishop's intervention seriously and to reply at length.[2]

The agitation did not end here. An auxiliary branch of the Anti-Slavery Society had been founded in Lagos in 1910 with help from the active British humanitarian, Mr. J. H. Harris. This branch wrote to the parent British section and set the Secretary, Travers Buxton, working upon their behalf. He moved Sir William Byles to press the Government, both in private and in parliament, to publish the report of the enquiry,[3] though it seemed that the Society did develop some doubts about the truth of the accounts they were getting from their African informants.[4] Harcourt stalled off these attacks but, of course, demanded full explanations from Lugard. The matter dragged on into 1916 with the Africans prodding the London Anti-Slavery Society. In the end Bonar Law decided against publication and the Colonial Office took a high negative line with the humanitarians at home. The customarily low priority of Colonial affairs fell to the bottom with the crisis over Ulster and then the world war. At such a time parliament could hardly be expected to concentrate upon what the Lagos newspapers called " the tragedy of Ijemo ".

Lugard was naturally inclined to ascribe to Lagos influence the far more serious Abeokuta revolt of 1918 though, as we saw, the Commission of Inquiry considered that the outbreak was due mainly to internal causes. Yet the existence of a free platform and a free press ceaselessly criticizing the Governor from a Yoruba city within the

---

[1] Tugwell to Lugard, 9 September 1914, L.P.
[2] Lugard to Tugwell, 10 September 1914, L.P.
[3] *Parliamentary Debates*, 25 November 1914, V. 68. 1147.
[4] Travers Buxton to Bishop Johnson, 23 February 1915, A.S.A.P.S., G237.

privileged position of a Crown Colony, must have made it difficult to maintain the absolute authority which the government at that period felt obliged to wield over fellow-Yorubas just across the Lagos border.

Certainly the Lagos opposition had by the end of Lugard's period built up a large armoury of weapons. This included speeches at political meetings, mass demonstrations, petitions, appeals to the Anti-Slavery Society in England, petitions to the Secretary of State, delegations to England and the employment there of British lawyers, with the threat of riots as a last resort. There were provocative rejoicings when Herbert Macaulay was released from prison. (Lugard might call him a jail-bird but he should have weighed carefully the fact that in the eyes of the Lagosians his punishment added rather than detracted from his prestige). The assumption behind these appeals to Caesar over the head of the colonial government was that the local officials were not expressing those British principles of " justice and fair-play " which were so frequently invoked in the press and on the platform. But the most important weapon, new and crude, but to be perfected in the future, lay in the Press.

A study of the nascent colonial press of many countries reveals how infant nationalism, in its stage of non-responsibility and subordination, is fed upon a ceaseless and undiluted diet of political indignation, spiced with ridicule and personal abuse. The critics poured their indignation into the exciting new vehicle of print, their native eloquence, of which some examples have just been given, clothing itself always sonorously and sometimes impressively in their newly adopted language. Their use of it at times recalls at least the rhythm of Burke or of some of the classical lawyers they had studied; at times there is an echo of Shakespeare or Gibbon. Here is a typical example.

> " The absolute security of life and property under the old regime was a source of constant delight to the community and a firm belief in its more beneficent working under the union was the article of faith of individuals concerned."[1]

They enjoyed the inevitable comparison of Britain with Rome.

> " When Rome gave herself up to luxury and the getting of wealth, forsaking the old traditions in a saturnalia of universal greed, she began to

[1] *Times of Nigeria*, 29 December 1914.

oppress her subject peoples. Rebellion became rife throughout the Empire and Rome fell amidst the execrations of the civilized world."[1]

The journalists showed an early skill in finding joints in the armour of their rulers in which to insert their needles. There was no hesitation in singling out the Governor with the reiterated refrain " Thou art the man!" According to one of the papers he was the " Napoleon of Nigeria ", the man who had brought " one-man rule " and " unadulterated autocracy ". And the whole colonial hierarchy was no better. A new Litany was devised:

" From a prancing pro-consul who must have his own way and does not care one iota for the safety of the innocent people under his charge;

From a born and bred-in-the-law Chief Justice who mercilessly drafts out oppressive Ordinances in order to maintain the prestige of autocratic officials to the detriment of 16 million of souls;

From a set of ' influential' Englishmen who live only to suggest and support drastic measures to deprive the poor native of his right;

From a Colonial Secretary who, having been influenced by ' the man on the spot ', deliberately deafens his ears and shuts his eyes to the moans and groans of an oppressed people and

From negrophobism, colour-prejudice, oppression and deceit,
Good Lord Deliver Us."[2]

A rumour that Sir Hugh Clifford was being sent to Nigeria to replace Lugard was greeted as being " too good to be true ".

The " prancing pro-consul " and the preference for Clifford certainly went home. " One goes on with this ceaseless grind and the thanks one gets is the execrations of the Lagos Press." It was natural that Lugard should refer to the " scurrilous local yellow press" and should, like so many other British governors then and since in many colonies, look round for some way of curbing its " monstrous freedom ". However, he was powerless to deal with it, " for the Colonial Office and the Faddists would never tolerate any infringement of the right of the Press to be as libellous and seditious as it pleases." (L. to F. L., 16 October 1913). In the Criminal Code, however, which Lugard had drawn up for the united Nigeria, there was, as one of the journalists was quick to point out, " a clause 8, section 61 under which it is possible for the Editor of this Journal to be sent to prison as a felon

[1] *Ibid.* 14 July 1914.   [2] *Ibid.* 24 March 1914.

for three years . . . for some criticism of his [the Governor's] policy which is calculated to interfere with the free exercise by him of the duties or authority of his office."[1]

The war seemed to give Lugard the opportunity to obtain a stronger control of the press. Harcourt, however, a good Liberal, stood fast upon his disapproval of any such restriction, and the Office saw through Lugard's attempt to fuse the quite different issues of peace-time and war-time control. When Lugard made the same attempt again in 1917 he met with the same refusal. Even with regard to what might be called legitimate control in the emergency of war Lugard had his difficulties. When, in 1916, he showed the Chief Justice a news-paper statement that the Africans preferred German to British rule and hoped that Britain would be defeated in the war, the judge, Lugard reported " argued that it was justifiable journalese comment. I wholly disagree and I am glad to say that the editor was tried and is ' doing time ' in gaol." (L. to F. L., 9 December 1916). In 1917 he managed to get agreement to a measure under which editors had to enter into a bond.

Lugard considered at one time a more positive way of dealing with the problem of the press. In 1915 he made a proposition to his com-mercial friend, Mr. A. A. Cowan. He pointed out that the local papers " pour out columns of venomous abuse often bordering on sedition or libel and there is no means of explaining in sober language the real objects and motives of reforms and the reasons for any especial piece of legislation." (L. to Cowan, 13 October 1915). The public, including the schoolboys of the south, were being brought up on race-hatred and contempt for government. It was impossible to counter with the truth all the misleading journalism they read. Morel's English weekly for West Africa had, he said, turned pacifist and pro-German since the outbreak of war. He wanted to see a really high-class and rational, but interesting, weekly published in England, with affiliated papers in each British West African territory. It should have a good English editor with a sense of humour. He realized that a newspaper subsidized by the government could " give colour to a charge of partisanship " but papers such as he suggested, started with the support and the advertise-ment of the firms interested in West Africa, would meet the urgent need for public enlightenment which he had described. Cowan

[1] *Times of Nigeria*, 14 December 1915.

598

answered sympathetically but for the time being nothing came of it.

The unhappy aspects of Lugard's relations with his critics have been given in some detail because, unfortunately, they largely predominate and were highly significant for the future. But even towards Lagos Lugard was not wholly illiberal while, upon their side, negro Africans, then and since, have shown a capacity to interrupt their political antagonism from time to time with gestures of response and with laughter. There were, therefore, a few rifts in the clouds of mutual antagonism.

For example Lugard, though he did not cede a single point to his opponents over the Courts Ordinance, was yet glad to feel that his sincere attempts to meet criticism with the fullest explanation had some mollifying effect upon them. To Flora he wrote that

> " the local papers, even the most bitter and scurrilous of them, referred with approbation to my having published the C.J.'s memo. in *The Gazette* and said it seemed to be a fulfilment of my promise to take the people into my confidence. Now that is just what I found in Hong Kong . . . The Officials acted as if they were little tin gods whose wisdom could not be questioned. I started a new regime. I had informal discussions with the unofficials . . . I have not here the same intelligent public opinion but it fancies itself quite as much and, being secretly aware of its deficiency, it is all the more sensitive. The agitation has been fomented by the large group of black lawyers; they are the brains of the native community, and they have supplied all the arguments."   (L. to F. L., 12 March 1914).

Again, soon after his arrival he agreed to meet the Lagos auxiliary of the Anti-Slavery Society. He admitted to Flora his doubts as to whether he was right to do so since he believed the Society " comprises the leading spirits of the disloyal factions ". He asked for an advance summary of what they had to say, partly lest they should tread on forbidden ground and partly because one member said he wished to speak for an hour!

> " I find the subjects are on the borderline, and though expressed in courteous terms, I feel some doubts as to whether I ought to let them speak on such matters, but if I refused, with a semi-educated and cunning people like this, they would say I was afraid to meet their arguments . . . On the whole it is perhaps best to hear them and I must do my best to answer judiciously."   (L. to F. L., 27 February 1913).

We have an account of the interview from the other side, from no other than Herbert Macaulay. He led the deputation and they put forward their grievances about the Eleko, land, colour discrimination and other matters. Macaulay said that in spite of their grievances about land " We [in Lagos] have carefully studied the colonial policy of the French, the Germans, Spaniards and Portuguese . . . and we are all satisfied that there is no other but the British nation whose colonial policy is so perfect, just and philanthropic." Lugard, upon his side, said he was glad to meet them because it was very much preferable that they should bring matters which were agitating them to the Governor and ask for information, " instead of holding meetings and writing in the press before you are sure of your facts." The meeting ended in laughter because, when the Africans demanded dispensaries, as in Hong Kong, Lugard, striking at the Lagos attitude to taxation, remarked of his former Chinese subjects, " They proposed to the Government to erect dispensaries and offered to supply the funds. I commend their action for your imitation."[1]

On another occasion he reports an amicable and workmanlike talk on the water-rate problem. He admitted that " The questions raised are by no means easy." (L. to F. L., 28 April 1915). This last remark suggests that Lugard's mind was not closed to the impressions the Lagosians tried to make upon it. This is borne out by an incident a year later.

" I have spent three solid hours in talking! and I am quite tired of it. The Editor of one of the Lagos rags—but by far the best of them—asked for an interview and proposed to discuss an enormous list of difficult subjects. So ' I took him on ' and went very fully into all his arguments and grievances. I found him very intelligent (I had never seen him before) and I was anxious to show that I am always accessible to any reasonable enquiries. I hope my interview may have done good . . . If I were here long enough I would have all these Lagos people in my pocket!"

(L. to F. L., 19 April 1916).

It was, perhaps, not that he was not there long enough but that the routine he had set himself reduced such personal contacts to an unfortunate minimum.

But perhaps his most successful interview was in 1917 when he saw

[1] 28 February 1913, A.S.A.P.S., G.230.

a number of African merchants and shippers who were complaining about the distribution between local shippers and producers of the shrinking ocean tonnage space. The leading spirit was Sam Duncan.

" You may remember that one ' Sam Duncan ' got the entrée to *The Times* and was largely quoted in the Nigerian Sales debate . . . In the midst of his torrent of language I interrupted to ask how it was that he had represented the Gov. allocation of tonnage Committee to be concerned in the Lagos (Lagoon) trade, when he was well aware it was confined to rail-borne trade . . . that, if he was so ignorant of the A.B.C. of the whole matter, he was a very improper delegate. His Black friends roared with laughter at his discomfiture. Again, when he and others talked of the 73 Native firms who had no justice or fair play, I asked how many were dummies—they were moved to hilarity. One of them very frankly said that the list included Stewards and Caretakers and any dummies. I could have wished that Bigland, and the Editor of *The Times* and some others who swallowed whole all they were told had been present! . . . I had not set out with the idea of exposing or snubbing young Duncan of whom I have a considerable opinion, (and I have asked him to an official dinner on Saturday), but this was the *result* when confronted with straight questions . . . The interview was most useful, and as a net result they had practically nothing to ask Govt. to do or to complain of."

(L. to F. L., 15 February 1917).

Africans' capacity to laugh at themselves has certainly been a saving grace in political struggles which have held so much material, real and fancied, for bitterness and misunderstanding. Lugard's critics were not wholly insensible to his co-operative gestures. After a meeting in the spring of 1916 the *Lagos Weekly Record* commented that " on that occasion he revealed himself as the very incarnation of patient and sympathetic hearing and displayed a versatility and knowledge which was equally surprising and impressive."[1] The writer felt that, with regard to the water rate, Lugard had been unjustly saddled with the sins of his predecessors. The active lawyer-politician, Osho Davies, writing to Travers Buxton, made a reasoned analysis of Lugard's character as a governor which may be quoted not only to throw light upon Lugard but to illustrate the calibre of some of his critics.

" Sir Frederick Lugard has not realized the great expectations I had anticipated of him. Of course, his task of governing with such a scanty

[1] *Lagos Weekly Record*, 4 May 1916.

check almost amounting to no control of a country almost half the size of India with a population well nigh 20,000,000, is an arduous one, and faults and some mistakes there must be, because he is but human—but his policy of attempting to arrest progress, stopping the diffusion and dissemination of knowledge, refusing to allow the high standard of civilization in S. Nigeria from streaming to the Northern, and to seek to enforce this by legislation staggers me, and my reasons fail me in attempting to reconcile it with his public utterances—The G.G. may perhaps think all this to be expedient but it is an admitted principle that if the rule of expediency were followed there would be neither right nor law at all . . . I, however, give him credit for good intentions . . . H. E. too is a military officer of a high reputation and it is not an easy task, for one who has been used to the hard and fast rules of the military code, to adapt himself to the easy and protracted rules of the civil code; this also is an excuse which ought to be put much in the G.G.'s favour."[1]

Lugard had not only apologists but also some friends and admirers among the educated leaders of Lagos. Chief among these were the two outstanding men who have already appeared in the narrative, Henry Carr and Kitoyi Ajasa. Both men gave Lugard steady and public support for his policies, Ajasa using for this purpose a newspaper he owned. They courageously faced the opposition and in their loyalty to him and their scorn for the character and opinions of some of their fellow Africans they may sometimes have misled Lugard. Their position rested not upon African support but official nomination. They were, indeed, among the first of those Africans to enter so completely into the social and political heritage of Britain that they had almost moved out of their own society and could turn round and view it with European eyes, all the more as they had not only views but characters which commended them to their British associates. British rule and influence seemed so strong and permanent that they did not have to pay for this mental and social transit so dearly as their many successors, Africans and others, who have been caught, like unanchored ships, in the stormy period when British power was giving way before the strong forces of racial-national movements. Yet they did have to endure some criticism from their fellows as being some " of the few natives on whom the Governor relies for information as regards native opinion . . . because they occupy high positions they have no influence . . . they do not intermingle freely among their people; they treat the

[1] Davies to Buxton, 28 July 1914, A.S.A.P.S., G. 232,

majority with barely a patronising glance and nod and the great bulk with mingled contempt and scorn . . . " Their information was therefore, their critics claimed, without weight and their advice misleading.[1]

Speaking of the Lagosians, " They are beginning," Lugard told his wife, " I think, to realize, as was said of Dr. Benson, that he was a beast—but he was a *just* beast." This may have been true. But the Lagosians were unable to estimate fully his sense of justice, because the evidence in his favour remained largely hidden or was exercised within the complexities of economic policy.

In one matter, for example, deeply affecting the southerners but which remained buried in the files, Lugard showed himself more liberal than some of his northern officials. There was sometimes a tendency among British administrators to identify themselves so closely with the group in their charge that they even imbibed their prejudice against what could be regarded as rival groups. This attitude led some northern officials into what Lugard called gross injustice towards the southern clerks and other southern employees who held those posts for which the Hausa were unqualified, and who filled those alien settlements, the Sabon Garis, on the fringe of northern cities. These emigrants knew well how to make their grievances public. Their case was taken up by the Lagos press and in 1913, through the Anti-Slavery Society, it was raised by Sir William Byles in the Commons when he horrified the House by an account of southern clerks being stripped naked and publicly flogged for playing football in the market place and for refusing to prostrate themselves, according to northern custom, before the magistrate.[2] The story had, of course, lost nothing in the telling. Harcourt got the true account from Lugard. It was that two clerks had persistently disobeyed orders not to kick footballs about in the middle of the market, creating disturbance and damage, and had been given ten strokes in the same market place as an example.

But for once Lugard was largely in sympathy with the Anti-Slavery Society. Indeed, he had already dealt with the matter, censuring the officer concerned, and refusing to assist him over an action he started

---

[1] *Times of Nigeria*, 5 June 1917.
[2] *Parliamentary Debates*, 31 July 1913, V. 56. 845-6.

in the Lagos courts for defamation. Lugard felt very strongly about the whole matter.

> " I fear that the treatment of the Coast clerks in N.N. has been very bad. They are often most disagreeable persons, insolent, unbelievably conceited, drunken etc. but that is no reason for treating them unjustly. The example has come from the top, Temple and Co., and is one of the most serious developments in N.N. My attitude is, I fancy, bitterly resented, but it can't be helped. The whole attitude of the European on the Coast to the trousered Black is wrong—one slips into it oneself in an unguarded moment."　　　　　　　　(L. to F. L., 29 December 1913).

He was especially worried about the question because these abuses inflamed the antagonism of the southerners against the northern judicial system.

> " The difficult point is that they truly say that this is the Northern Nigeria system and point to some monstrous things which have been done in N.N. There were four separate instances of Native clerks being publicly flogged in the market place. One occurred since I returned to Nigeria. It was wholly illegal—as well as outrageous. It was done by H. . . . Yet I censured him and ordered £10 compensation to be paid to the man . . . A native parson was badly treated by a Resident. I had a Court of Enquiry on it and the papers are with the Colonial Office—probably the Resident will be degraded as I have recommended. I apologized to the Parson. But they do not know or they ignore these things and only quote the incidents. These were the outcome of Temple and Co's trying to carry the native administration system to extremes."
>
> 　　　　　　　　　　　　　　(L. to F. L. 9 February 1914).

The last sentence is very significant.

Lugard went on to show that he was still sufficiently master of his own system to correct its excesses by standing out against the subjection to the northern Native Courts of natives from other parts of West Africa and those from the Colony who had the status of British subjects. Lugard wanted the law changed and twice took up the matter with the Colonial Office. As he argued later in *The Dual Mandate*, he did not think these people should be justiciable to the Native Courts unless they had become permanent residents or by their own consent.[1]

Lugard had some sympathy with the educated element upon

---

[1] Lugard, *The Dual Mandate*, p. 550, and *Memoranda*, 1918, No. 8, p. 277.

another issue. One of the main grievances of the dissidents concerned African entry to the government services. Here again, though the standards were too high for many Africans at that time, he did what he could. He urged the Colonial Office that African doctors should be encouraged to join the Nigerian medical service. He wanted to encourage a larger number of African doctors to work as private practitioners and to throw open to them the dispensaries and hospitals in the larger cities. He expressed the view that to centralize all institutions in the hands of the government was to retard the natural development of the people and to withhold the opportunities for private initiative which alone would bring them to the sense of responsibility and independence which it had always been his aim to foster.

This readiness to recognize and promote ability and loyalty was shown by his decision, early in 1918, to make Henry Carr the Resident of the Colony, a high post in the political service. He carried through this appointment in spite of doubts at the Colonial Office about a step which, as they pointed out, meant that British District Commissioners would serve under an African. As long ago with Chief Khama, once an African had earned his respect, he treated him as an equal.

These were no more than exceptions and alleviations to the general state of opposition between Lugard and his educated neighbours in Lagos. Its underlying cause is clear. His opponents had a view of their position as political and potential national leaders which he did not share. The Lagos intelligentsia, in Lugard's view, had no direct part in the great task of administering the Protectorate; they should use their education as independent professional men, as officials in the service of the government, or by graduating into increasing responsibility within their own municipality.[1] By the accident of history Lagos was fully committed to British institutions. But he regarded these as irrelevant for Nigeria as a whole. When he worked out the question more fully in *The Dual Mandate* he wrote of the coastal intelligentsia that " it would be unjust to place under their control the interior tribes, who themselves have a right to a measure of self-rule." In this lies the key to his attitude; he recognized Indirect Rule as the true, soundly based self-government, even if it were still in a preliminary stage.

Even in his day there were some who could see further than this.

[1] Lugard, *op. cit.*, p. 225.

The editor of *West Africa*, in a review of an article by Temple, remarked that his view of Indirect Rule was now impossible, at least for the non-Muslim regions. "Every school, every book, newspaper, bicycle, motor-car, railway, every article of commerce exposed for sale, every sight of a steamer, every exercise in the use of the English language is a sapping of its foundations. They are new wine. The old bottles will not serve for them."[1]

To use a different simile, the British democratic tradition was like the tiny egg of a parasite, laid in the organism of a colonial government. Both lived and grew together but the intruding influence gradually consumed its host from within until in the end it emerged through the dead husk of imperial power as a would-be independent nation which owed its very existence as a nation to that upon which it had been nourished. Britain herself, the parent organism, not being subject, fortunately, to the laws of the insect world, lived on, and could adopt the new nations as foster children of whom she could be proud, and even claim that this was the result she had intended from the first. She has thus been able at last to reconcile, hastily and incompletely perhaps, the conflict between the principles of empire and freedom which had troubled her from the time of the American Revolution. Those who took the chief strain of this metamorphosis were those agents Britain sent out still holding the old commission to uphold imperial power. They found themselves carrying their heavy responsibility before the final results of that shift of principles could be realized as inevitable, still less desirable. This was Lugard's position. He carried out his work of creating, as far as colonial administration could create, a single Nigeria out of the immense area under his rule. It might be argued that, with that prophetic sense which he sometimes showed, he might have treated the handful of 'prentice nationalists of Lagos with greater understanding. He might have fostered their political education. But it can hardly be argued that at the early stage of Nigeria's development he could have shared with them his responsibility for the government of the whole country.

[1] *West Africa*, 2 November 1918.

CHAPTER XXX

CONFLICT WITH
THE COLONIAL OFFICE

WE SAW that in 1906 Lugard had extracted from Alfred Lyttelton a promise that he should remain in continuous charge of Northern Nigeria, spending about half his time in Africa and half in the Colonial Office, and that when the Liberal government replaced the Conservatives in 1906, Lord Elgin reversed the decision. Calling this action a breach of faith Lugard resigned his post. When, in 1911, another Liberal Secretary of State, Harcourt, wrote to Lugard offering him the task of amalgamating the Nigerias and making no secret of his indispensability—" in fact, if I cannot secure your help, I think I shall let the project drop for the present . . . "—Lugard grasped this opportunity to try to dictate his own terms. He was able to extract less indeed than the full Scheme, but he did obtain an agreement to have four months in England after eight in Nigeria.[1] His two passions, for his work and for his wife, pulled him in opposite directions: the Scheme alone would allow him to indulge them both.

We must recall the several ways by which Lugard sought to ensure the Scheme by building it into the structure of Nigeria's amalgamated constitution. To emphasize his exceptional authority he obtained the title of Governor-General. He appointed his brother to the specially manufactured post of Political Secretary. In his draft of the Letters Patent he attributed to his office the power to legislate without prior reference to the Colonial Office. He retained the existing division of Nigeria in two parts so that the two Lieutenant-Governors, whom he hoped would be loyal and docile agents of his policies, could carry on in his absence in much the same routine as the two former governors. He fought against a large central secretariat or the creation

[1] See above pp. 364-5.

of more than the minimum number of central departments because, in his absence, these would have demanded for their control an Acting-Governor with full powers, responsible directly to the Secretary of State. Instead he was to have the power himself to appoint his own deputies who would be responsible to himself. He therefore had written into the Letters Patent the unprecedented clause that, whenever the Governor was absent from the territory, except while upon passage, "he may continue to exercise . . . all and every the powers vested in him by these Our Letters Patent . . . , and may . . . appoint any person or persons to be his Deputy or Deputies . . . Every such Deputy shall conform to and observe all such instructions as the Governor shall from time to time address to him for his guidance." And the appointment of such Deputies should in no way abridge the Governor's power and authority.[1] To facilitate further the execution of his policies he tried to gain complete control over appointments and promotions.

The Colonial Office opposed every item in this list of powers. Harcourt, by no means a figurehead, tried, especially in the first years, to support Lugard as the man of his choice but, like most politicians in this office, he was forced to bow before the officials' knowledge of the numerous and exotic territories. His Permanent Under-Secretary, Sir John Anderson, a reserved, bearded and respected senior, at first followed his chief in defending Lugard from the more extreme attacks in the Office. Not so Fiddes, his Assistant Under-Secretary, a hard, strong person, who wore and wagged menacingly an even longer beard. He was especially repugnant to Lugard and Flora who were well aware of his settled hostility to their Scheme. Then there was Temple's friend, Strachey, whom we have already met. As head of the Nigerian Department he was most intimately concerned with Lugard's work. His Assistant Principal was A. J. Harding, a Yorkshireman, whose mathematical mind was outraged by what he regarded as Lugard's muddled methods.

These three men, Fiddes, Strachey and Harding, showed from the first a settled opposition both to the Scheme and to the special status Lugard built up for himself in his amalgamation proposals. On the question of legislative powers even Sir John Anderson felt that one

[1] *Letters Patent Constituting the Office of Governor and Commander in Chief of the Colony of Nigeria*, 29 November 1913, pp. 7-8.

man could not be given the uncontrolled power over millions of people with no check but an Executive Council composed of his own officials.

It was only by assuring his staff that the Scheme was personal to Lugard and only experimental that Harcourt obtained their agreement. They remained certain that it *would* fail and even more certainly resolved that it *should*.

Lugard returned to England on April 6th, 1913, after his brief preliminary visit to Nigeria. He was given a room in the basement of the Colonial Office. In this were two desks, one large and one small. Every morning the two brothers arrived, generally by nine o'clock but never later than ten. Lugard took the larger desk and Edward the smaller. They were allotted one female typist. The whole of the incoming mail from Nigeria, dispatches, telegrams and the rest, were brought, first and unopened, to this office, by a messenger, and placed in Edward's " In " tray. From his " Out " tray they were taken away by the messenger, presumably for some form of registration, and then brought back for the elder brother's " In " tray. Lugard would work through this material, would amend or rewrite the dispatches and send them on to the Nigerian Department with his own signature. Officials from Nigeria would come to his office for interviews.

His inability to keep his hands off details was illustrated to the writer by Lord Davidson, who at this date was private secretary to Harcourt. Upon visiting Lugard's office he found him busy writing a memorandum. Looking up Lugard remarked " You know this is rather an interesting question." It concerned a request from second-class administrative officers that they should be issued with a certain domestic piece of china-ware which was supplied only to first-class officers. Lugard, it appears, was engaged in composing a refusal to this request on the grounds that a bush at the bottom of his compound had been good enough for him in his young day.

The first leave passed without too serious a breach. The Office was, as we saw, deeply impressed by the work Lugard had put into his task of administering two large territories at once and at the same time planning their amalgamation. Harcourt was friendly and admiring. He was sensitive enough to take a clear impress of Lugard's character. At the summer dinner of the Colonial Service Corona Club, on June 17th 1913, Harcourt, who clearly took a great deal of trouble over his language in this annual speech, paid an elaborate compliment to Lugard. "Last year," he said,

" at this dinner I spoke of Sir Frederick Lugard as a figure of hope, promise and, to some of you, anxiety. Today he has become the token of execution and achievement. With relentless activity he has covered in his preliminary tour nearly all the essential centres of his future work. . . . From the Splendid Durbar of the Emirs he returns on so-called leave—which comprises no holiday—to a humble room in the Colonial Office. And that room is today the crucible of amalgamation. . . . Sir Frederick Lugard is a happy man to have returned to the field of his great and early labours. I am a happy man to have induced him to do so. (Applause). Sir Frederick Lugard is no prancing pro-consul—he is a man of irresistible, relentless—I had almost said stealthy—approach, the result of a highly finished but human genius for complete achievement."

These almost honeymoon relations were threatened soon after Lugard returned to Nigeria in the autumn by his discovery that the Office had, in his view, gone back upon their promises to give him powers to legislate without waiting for assent from London. He saw any restriction upon his powers as a threat to the Scheme and he wrote a very stiff dispatch. At the end he drafted a sentence offering his resignation as, he said, it seemed that he no longer had Harcourt's confidence.[1] But Edward persuaded him to cut it out and Flora, to whom a copy of the draft was sent, congratulated him upon his second thoughts. The same day she wrote this Flora received a telegram from her husband referring to the compromise fixing a two months' delay between the passing and promulgation of legislation, "Letters Patent settled amicably." And then she went on to draw a useful lesson from her own experiences:

" As for the C.O., I know there is no use in taking it heroically. It is not heroic. The kind of things that look most serious to outsiders are often done by a kind of haphazard: somebody was in or not in, saw or did not see a given dispatch, heard or did not hear a bit of gossip or a biting comment. Above all some question asked of somebody of no importance is looming over the Secretary of State in the House of Commons and the mere thought of the light of publicity being turned on to his most harmless actions unbalances his nerve. Even Chamberlain was not altogether above that. And it is not only the C.O. The same may be said of most

[1] Lugard to Harcourt, 26 October 1913, copy in L.P.

offices. I had an opportunity during the Jameson crisis of comparing from the inside the panic of the C.O. and the panic of *The Times* and it was six of one and half a dozen of the other."

(F. L. to L., 8 November 1913).

This psychological and intellectual treatment was effective. Lugard was able to admit that Harcourt's conditions were really very favourable, "and I have been treated with the greatest kindness and consideration and I am keenly alive to it." (L. to F. L., 17 December 1913).

He had at this time another and rather surprising cause for satisfaction. Herr Solf, the German Colonial Secretary, visited Nigeria. Upon leaving, he wrote to Lugard in English from his ship in terms surprising for the minister of a jealous, indeed rival, colonial power. " It is with a feeling of great admiration that I see the work which is being carried out in Nigeria and more especially so with regard to the Northern Protectorate . . . my admiration for this system is so sincere that I consider with the Governor of the Cameroons, who is a fellow passenger, whether we should adopt the same principles and introduce them into the northern provinces of the Cameroons." He accepted Lugard's views about the preservation of African law and custom but, " I am afraid that those representatives of the European capital who offer the boons of our civilization to the natives cash down in the shape of roof-iron and cheap prints will give much more trouble if they find the 13 gateways of Kano shut! Also the missionaries of different denominations!" (13 October 1913.) He begged Lugard to allow him to have for his own use the confidential *Political Memoranda*. Lugard, of course, replied warmly and helpfully, welcoming the chance " to promote cordiality between our respective nations." (L. to Solf, 10 November 1913.) Up to the end of July 1914, Solf was still writing to Lugard. He told him that he had already adopted several of the ideas he had learned from Nigeria.

At the time his pleasure at this most unsolicited testimonial from Germany was the greater because it was public. Solf told him that he had on various occasions in the Reichstag pointed out the wonderful achievements of Nigeria and Harcourt later quoted Solf's praise in one of his speeches, with a pleasantry that reads sadly in retrospect. We seem to be looking at the people living on the slopes of a volcano, unaware that it is on the point of eruption. " I believe," said Harcourt, " that he was sent up country on a train whose engine was covered with the German imperial emblems and flags, which induced me to tell Herr Solf that at last the long awaited German invasion had taken place.''[1] As a mark of gratitude for this reception the German Emperor presented a polo cup to the Nigerian Service.

Germany's unsolicited testimonial was needed. The year 1914 proved a difficult one for Lugard. This was due not only to the strain of war but also to the worsening of his relationships with the Colonial Office. The year opened badly with the visit to Nigeria, already recorded, of Strachey, and this in a period when such excursions from the Colonial Office were very rare. For most people Strachey's unusual personality was of a kind to interest and attract. But to Lugard he was not only Temple's friend but also, in a sense, his official master. He anticipated that after wandering about " doing the role of the ' Innocent Abroad ' . . . by the time he gets back to Downing Street he will know much more of Nigeria than I do and his two months will weigh in the balance against my twenty odd years and the years will be found wanting." (L. to F. L., 17 February 1914).

The next issue arose from this operation in reverse. Nigerian officials were pouring criticism of the Scheme and of much else into some of the ready ears at the Office. The contacts between officials on leave and the Colonial Office staff can, obviously, be encouraging to the first and enlightening to the second but they open up embarrassing possibilities whenever, on either side, discretion is relaxed. And Lugard had reason at that time to have doubts about the discretion. But his reaction was drastic. At the end of 1913 he issued a circular laying down that members of the Nigerian Service while on leave in England should, except on routine matters, communicate with the Colonial Office only through him. There was great indignation in the department. It was too much even for Harcourt, who was still trying to reserve as large as possible a sphere of action for Lugard. Flora defended her husband to Harcourt. If junior officers, she said, were encouraged to go behind his back it would be destructive of all discipline and good administration. Harcourt dissented. A stiff dispatch, he told her, had therefore been sent to Lugard. One reason given was that such interviews enabled Colonial Office officials to " obtain information which it would be otherwise difficult to obtain." Lugard called it outrageous that the Office should frankly own that they meant

[1] Speech at the Corona Club, 18 June 1914, L.P.

to elicit information from juniors behind the Governor's back and he would very much like to know if Harcourt personally saw this dispatch or not. (L. to F. L., 9 February 1914). Flora had been able to enlighten him. Harcourt had, he told her, toned down Anderson's first draft but confessed, speaking of his staff, that he had had some difficulty " in softening them down for their feathers were very much ruffled." (F. L. to L., 24 January 1914). Lugard was obliged to withdraw the offending circular.

The year was still young when other causes of offence began to pile up. The grave disagreement over the Native Administration revenues, already discussed, was, of course, perennial. But early in 1914 the Office, ignoring the large questions of policy which lay behind his estimates, asked him why £70 had been spent upon a cook-house and demanded a full list of all roads under construction, their length, breadth and whether or not they were metalled. Then, writing about the Port Harcourt railway which had already been well begun at both ends, they said that the line to be taken had not yet been sanctioned. Lugard, fulminating to Flora, said that even he himself would not think of interfering with the able engineer in charge but the Office in England felt fully qualified to do so. " I shall laconically tell them the facts and they can censure me if they like. My action will have saved thousands—tens of thousands—of pounds . . . " (L. to F. L., 23 February 1914).

This was followed by a somewhat interesting grievance. The doctors were almost on strike for more pay. The Medical Advisory Committee in England was active in the matter. Another active body which advised the Office was the Survey Committee. These committees, which have so multiplied since his day, seemed to Lugard just one more device by which governors could be over-ruled from a distance by persons deficient both in responsibility and knowledge. It perhaps did not occur to him that by conceiving broods of new ideas which the civil servants had to bring to executive birth, they were not always popular with the Office.

The accumulated friction in early 1914 drove Lugard to the view that the Colonial Office was endeavouring to administer directly. He reflected that while for Hong Kong, small but complex and internationally important, he had only been obliged to send some 300 dispatches a year, in Nigeria he was forced to send some 3,500! Calling history and natural history to aid his arguments he declared that because the Colonial Office, " being a species of blind insect with no horizon, do not genuinely know where they are and what are their functions," they had in the colonies, as formerly in the white Dominions, made the same mistake of excessive interference. That was why Dominion self-rule had not been foreseen or conceded but extracted by forces too powerful to control. Dimly, for the first time, the idea of continuing the fight with pen in his hand and his wife at his side came into his mind. " But the Crown Colonies have grown too, but have not yet found a voice. Shall we find them that voice—you and I?" (L. to F. L., 27 February 1914). If the Office was blind, did not Lugard suffer here from shortsightedness? The Colonies would certainly one day find a voice, but it would not be that of an ex-governor but one of the same popular kind as that in which the Dominions had demanded their freedom.

These irritations led Lugard to a diminished estimate of his present master. Chamberlain had known well how to keep his department in order, but Harcourt, he decided, was lath and plaster, painted to look like iron. (L. to F. L., 13 March 1914). However, as he had written a few weeks earlier " it has been said that ' a reasonable amount of fleas is good for a dog' and it is profoundly true. The Colonial Office supply the fleas." Unfortunately, these sometimes bit very hard.

The date of Lugard's leave was always a contentious question. Lugard read the original agreement as allowing four months a year in England: the Office interpreted it as four months *after* eight months in Nigeria. So, whereas he asked to return in April, the Office instructed him not to return until July. This ruled out the careful programme of work of a kind he could do only in England, re-casting laws and instructions so as to allow of the extension of his system to the South. There were also officials and others he must meet before the summer holiday which, in that golden age of leisure and prosperity, scattered all the important people to distant retreats where they remained for long *incommunicado*.

Lugard sat down to write one of his broadside dispatches. Judges came back for the same period of four months of continuous leisure. *He* was not asking for a rest. " It is no doubt a personal idiosyncrasy but I do not need and do not remember ever to have required a holiday . . . I shall not spare myself, Sir, if you will allow me to carry out this work for the present in the one way in which it appears to me possible to do it."[1] The officials were unmoved. Their not unreasonable view seems to have been that Nigeria should not be left so long to subordinates, that his overworking was the reverse of meritorious, and that it would be better if he did half the amount of work in Nigeria and none in England. Harcourt agreed that he should return in April for four months. But there was a sting in the tail of his telegram deeper than the customary flea-bite. It concluded " that any attempt to control details of administration whilst in this country is a physical impossibility and not conducive to promptitude and efficient conduct of affairs. Harcourt."[2] This was the first overt attack on the Scheme.

These exchanges should have been confined to Downing Street and Lagos. But three parties were involved. Harcourt had to mediate not only between his officials and Lugard: he had to placate Lady Lugard.

Thousands of miles apart, the Lugards yet shared their lives far more fully than many of those who live together in one house. One night on the train running north he wrote " I lay on my bed thinking of you for an hour. I lay awake thinking of many things but chiefly talking to you and this more nearly expresses it than thinking of you. I am literally talking to you in my mind . . ." And again, when most exasperated with the Office, he said " It does not make me unhappy. Nothing but bad news from you can make me unhappy . . . I serve, thank God, a higher master than the C.O. I serve my wife and my conscience and so long as they do not tell me to do anything which militates against those high allegiances (which are one in effect) I will do it."

Flora, upon her side, surmounted the brutal fact of their long separations, since " the wonderful thing is that I am more and more *with* you every day. Space separates us less and less. This winter I hardly seem in spirit to have been divided from you." Though she encouraged him by her faith she also, tactfully, almost insensibly, urged him towards self-restraint and acceptance of inescapable conditions. She, too, found night the best period for mental communication. "I lay thinking a lot about it both last night and this morning. The opportunity which you

[1] L. to Harcourt, 4 February 1914, copy in L.P.
[2] Harcourt to L., 28 February 1914, copy in L.P.

have been given in this vast territory of Africa is so great that it must not be thrown away for any aggravation or pin-pricks or annoyance which the misconceptions of the C.O., whether under Mr. Harcourt or another S. of S., may lead them to inflict." She referred to his annexation of Sokoto in 1902-3. "You took the responsibility. You did that which has resulted in the peaceful organization and opening up of that vast country to civilization, that which has freed slaves, has practically abolished slavery, has established schools, has placed civil life on an orderly basis, has brought, in a word, peace, prosperity and progress to countless millions of people." Now, at least, the Colonial Office had given him the chance of carrying that work much further. That choice, at least, was large-hearted and comprehending. "Let us be content to rejoice in that and in the great field which lies before you ... That is the final word that came out of my thinking. Do it, go in and do it!"

She set herself to carry out her side of the task by dealing with the Colonial Office officials and, above all, with Harcourt. There took place a series of meetings at her house which must represent a unique relationship between a Colonial Secretary and the wife of a leading governor, one, moreover, with whom he and his staff were at odds. The picture Flora gives of her visitor is full-length, one of a gentleman of the old school, a late Victorian rather than an Edwardian, a Whig rather than a Liberal, highly cultured, dressed in the height of fashion, yet with a suggestion of the old-world in his four-inch collar and rather Mephistophelian moustaches, "a beautiful creature" as one of his former secretaries described him to the writer. He would sit down to luncheon or to tea *à deux* with his beautiful hostess, and then settle his considerable length comfortably into a chair by the fire, gain permission to light his cigarette, and sit there for some two hours or more while they talked or while Flora read, with skilfully disguised omissions, from her husband's letters. "On the whole I managed to pull myself up fairly well when I was galloping along and found myself suddenly landing in things not intended for Secretaries of State! He would have opened his eyes if he could have seen how the story read to him so demurely was embroidered with love-making all round its edges."

Harcourt seemed fascinated: he was quite equal to guessing much that was omitted. When she stopped he would say "Go on! Go on!

It is most interesting and I am thrilled with it." " I was careful, of course," she wrote another time, " to expurgate any phrase which I thought might offend and read him what I thought, if I were Secretary of State, it would be good for me to hear as the private opinion of a man of your experience. As the passages recurred again I said ' You are sure you don't mind this frankness,' and he again reassured me. ' No. No, I like it. I esteem it a privilege.' And at the end he said ' You are lucky to have a husband who can write to you like that. You share the whole of his life though he is away from you.' " Maps and photographs were brought out as Lugard's tours were followed. " He was like a nice child (as all the best sort of men are) learning it all and listening with the greatest interest." Sometimes he would suddenly remember he should be in the House and would rush away promising to come back the next day, or the day after, for more.

In this warm atmosphere official discretion seems at times to have melted away. At an early meeting Harcourt discussed with her the inadequacies of Temple. She hesitated at first and then, by quoting Montaigne, neatly put the responsibility upon him. "*Un parler ouvert ouvre un autre parler et le tire hors comme fait le vin et l'amour.*"[1] And before long they were discussing whether the offending Temple ought not to be moved from Nigeria and where he should be sent. Instructed by the copies of his dispatches which, quite improperly, she was getting from Lugard, she argued out with Harcourt every point of disagreement.

From her conversations with the relaxed Secretary of State she was able to give Lugard an intimate picture of what went on both in his mind and in the Colonial Office. One day they discussed Lugard's dispatch over his legislative powers as defined in the Letters Patent in which he said he must have lost Harcourt's confidence. " I was absolutely amazed," declared Harcourt, " I couldn't believe it. I said to Anderson ' He must be ill! The strain is too great and it is telling upon him.' I have done everything a man could do to show the confidence I feel in him. I have overborne the Office on my own initiative to please him and to give him his way about working the Scheme half in England and half out there. I have done everything to secure him in the first instance and to let him have his own way when

---

[1] The quotation will be found in the first essay, ' Books ', *Essais*, Pierre Villey ed. (1923), p. 12. It is not easy to translate. "Frank speech evokes frank speech, drawing it out as does wine and love."

I had got him. And then because of a little thing that I won't trouble you with he thinks I have lost confidence in him."

" But it was not a little thing," she replied and plunged into the problem of Lugard's legislative powers in the Letters Patent. They argued it out in detail, agreed that Lugard was, perhaps, ultra-sensitive, and Harcourt finally left urging her that she *must* explain. " You mustn't let him be so sensitive . . . You must tell him that he has my absolute confidence. I am awfully sorry . . . " No wonder that Lugard and his brother found such passages in Flora's letters enthralling.

Upon her side the main theme of all Flora's talks with Harcourt was the Scheme. All her own art and her selections from the letters were directed to prove what she so wholly believed herself, that an exceptional man with an exceptional task needed exceptional conditions. Was not he, upon his side, ready to sacrifice everything to the task he had undertaken, his leisure, his health, even what he most valued, her happiness and well-being! Harcourt once confessed to Flora that when he had in prospect a disagreeable interview hauling a man over the coals it made him physically sick for days before. He had, therefore, prevaricated about the all-important date of Lugard's return for leave, putting off the moment when he must encounter her indignation. So, when the blow had fallen, and he did call on March 7th, his first remark, as he stood hesitant in the doorway, was " Am I in disgrace?" to which Flora replied " Yes, indeed you are!"

He came in and set himself to use all his very great charm to such effect that Flora actually told her husband that she could hardly convey to him " the sympathetic nature of the conversation, how very well he seemed to understand your point of view." He assured her that " I have told the C.O. over and over again that he must have his head, that he must do it in his own way." He did not flinch even when Flora read him some of the strongest condemnations of the Office which Lugard had thrown on to paper. " I said to him at the end ' I have been very frank!' " He said " Yes, I am very grateful to you for trusting me." Then he added " I think it is good for him, too, to know that I hear what he really thinks and to know what I think, which is so rare." Flora soon came back to the Shceme. " I asked him point blank whether the Office was so set against it that it was really pre-doomed to failure." It seems that Harcourt could not look into her eyes and utter the full truth. " No! No ! No !" he said. " Get that out of your mind. It is not so at all. They don't like it. It is contrary to their traditions." " But you yourself," she pressed him, " are in favour of it !" " Yes," he said, " I am in favour of it."

For all her involvement in the issue, Flora could consider the general question that lay behind the experiment. Where did the watershed run between ultimate metropolitan control and immediate gubernatorial authority? Lugard had said in one of his letters that even Anderson, perhaps because he was an ex-Governor, had admitted that the Office had been intervening too much in detailed matters. Flora now quoted Sir Hugh Clifford, whom Harcourt had freely—too freely—discussed with her, to the same effect. He had told Lugard that he had nearly dropped off his chair when a certain Ellis, a relatively junior man at the Colonial Office, had told him that " for twenty years the Gold Coast has been administered from this room."

Harcourt had once confided to Flora that he liked the Colonial Office because he loved administering. So she pressed him to a definition of the terms governing and administering. " It is my duty," she argued, " to provide a good cook and see that my husband and his friends are decently fed. That belongs to my province of government. But if I were to go into the kitchen and wish to cook the dinner, nothing but confusion would ensue." If Harcourt chose Lugard, because of his experience, to enact amalgamation, that was an act of government. Surely he should be left to use that experience to carry out the task. Harcourt agreed. " Your husband has an unrivalled experience in Africa. He is the greatest living authority on African affairs. And I do assure you that when they come to me at the Office and want to disagree with something that he has laid down I shrug my shoulders and say ' I don't know but I trust Lugard to know better than any of us and he must have his way '."

He had something to teach even Flora about the difficulties of his responsibility to parliament. He told her that " generally speaking, if anything is done that the House of Commons don't like, I have to stand up to be shot at. It is right. I think that they should, but I must have the power to defend myself by deciding what should be done." But he also explained that he might have to take the responsibility of evading parliamentary control. He referred to an incident considered in the last chapter, that of Sir Hesketh Bell and the permission he gave to missionaries to settle within the walls of Kano. " Now," he said, " What am I to do in a case like that? It is altogether wrong that they should go there: but nevertheless he would have had popular opinion in the House of Commons on his side if the matter had come up for debate. On the whole I must take the responsibility, and I think it is right that I should take the responsibility . . . "

She saw, of course, that Harcourt himself, not unnaturally, wanted to be well in the picture. The self-confidence of the aristocrat had not expunged the public vanity of the politician. He was clearly delighted that Lugard had called the new port, cut out of virgin creek and bush, after him. When Flora said she did not suppose he cared, he cried " Don't *care*! But I care immensely. I can't tell you how glad I am to have it called after me. But I wouldn't have asked for it for the world and I would like everyone to know I didn't ask."

Talk flowed on to home politics and where he stood in the contemporary party alignment. " You don't realize," he chided, " what an advanced Radical I am." Flora shook her head slowly and said " No, you are not! You may think you are but you are not . . . Dorothy Grey used to say the same to me sometimes about Edward . . . He is a philosophic doctrinaire . . . He has no child. He has nothing but ideas and altruistic theories. But you are not like that . . . you have your son to follow after you. You are fond of the flesh-pots. You can't be detached . . . Could you see your estate broken up, your pictures, your collections, dispensed to museums for the general good and your son forbidden to own more than £500 a year?" " I didn't think that such a thing could ever happen," was his reply.

There were days when Harcourt revealed his scientific and aesthetic interests, his delight in being a trustee for the Wallace Collection and the British Museum. He told Flora of the drudgery of public life, when he could hardly ever see his wife, with sittings at the Commons up to six o'clock on Saturday. " It's a dog's life." Flora's unsympathetic comment was " Yes, a dog's life, but you like it as all well-bred dogs do " and he laughed and agreed. When Mrs. Harcourt came to call and complained that people who said " So delightful to be Colonial Secretary!" did not realize how near it went to wasting all their private lives, Flora was well qualified to agree. " Of course," she said to herself, " she has the feeling of having brought him heaps of money," and later she remarked the sad contrast that was all too true, " I am not like Mrs. Harcourt—I bring you only expense, not money."

It must be remembered that Flora and Harcourt were having their talks in the feverish political atmosphere of early 1914, a time when Lugard was writing that he could not think why Lloyd George had not been assassinated. It was strange that a politically minded woman like Flora, Irish Protestant for all her French mother's Papistry, should be able to stay in the room at this date with a member of the Liberal Cabinet. When they strayed into the region of the Irish problems the air became stormy, and a coming event in the Lugards' story cast a shadow over the hospitable comfort of the room. She declared that Harcourt and his colleagues in the Cabinet had given no sign of understanding the first elements of the situation in Ulster. They went on to disagree totally about the Parliament Act and the position of the King in the crisis. Was Harcourt not reported to have said that the Crown was " rolling in the mud "? She threatened him with rebellion by her friends over the water and with civil war in England. Yet, so strong was the solidarity of the society to which they both belonged, that it still seemed impossible that the grave words they were using could really mean the things they represented. Flora felt " It is all deplorable . . . The Radical Party has wantonly mis-used their power and they have broken what I fear will never be mended. The distinctive features of England are dying under their hands. However, Englishmen made England, Englishmen may save it yet."

At last this cycle of letters comes to an end. " I am counting the days now to April 25th . . . Life seems almost too good to be true. And then I remind myself happily ' But it is the good which is true '!"

Lugard and his brother returned to England on April 25th, 1914, bringing with them an elegant crested crane, 2 white oryx, a secretary-bird and a ground horn-bill, huge and jet black, which, Edward said, " talked continuously like a creaking wheel and has got great eye-lashes like a human or more so." He presented the first creature on this list to Mr. Harcourt. He might have considered the last two appropriate for the Colonial Office, but these he gave with the oryx to the zoo. The brothers then setttled down at once in the grudging hospitality of their room in the Colonial Office and set to work to administer Nigeria from there. The attitude of the officials had hardened further : their comments became more caustic; they were quick to seize upon the not infrequent confusions caused by the mislaying of papers.

Harcourt's efforts to placate Lugard privately by means of his wife, while officially he acted at least in part upon the advice of his officials, had not been very successful. A joking remark, innocent enough for a man of the *beau monde*, and made to Flora herself, that his constant visits might lead to the suspicion that he was conducting an intrigue with her—it is, perhaps, necessary to explain in this context, that he meant an amorous intrigue—was coldly received by Lugard. He was never a man to enjoy that kind of joke even if Flora and everything connected with her had not been so sacred to him. In a note written in 1940, presumably for his biographer, he said—and the quotation is given more to illustrate the deep-cut impression upon his mind than as a balanced judgment upon Harcourt—" He boasted to her that he personally administered the Colonies . . . His wife said to Flora that Lulu was a born administrator . . . he constantly reversed my action as Governor . . . The Service under him was intolerable." This note was found attached to a bundle of pencilled papers which appear to have been written in preparation for a talk with Harcourt in May, 1914. It is impossible to read, unmoved, these almost desperate jottings. The handwriting is confused almost to the point of being unintelligible. In them he thrashes from side to side between expressions of loyalty and self-assertion, between thanks for personal kindness and anger at professional treatment. The total result is that he now does not know what to do.

" I was sent out to perform a task but its performance has not merely been taken out of my hands but in almost every particular of importance (esp. re N.N. in which when I was left alone I was able to create an administration which has been successful) my recommendations have been reversed. My object is to loyally carry out the task but continual reversal has made me afraid to suggest anything for fear of reversal which is read by every black clerk. I built up administration of N.N. on G.S.O.'s and Pol. Memos, am now afraid to write either for smallest details have to be sent to Colonial Office, G.M. of Railway has more power than I have.'

The notes become more elliptical and are heavily decorated with red underlinings.

" *Takes the heart out of* one the way *they worry. Can't sleep.* Gets on my nerves. $14\frac{1}{2}$ years as Governor 26-5 years in Africa. *All* in command.

He cannot be aware. Direct adm. by C.O. *Never in E. Af.* Not unsuccessful when left alone. Now impossible. Will he come R. Gate?"

Strange, indeed, with such an accessible master, and one so laudatory in his opinion of Lugard, so closely in touch with his wife, and with that wife now present to console and restrain, that this should have been the state of Lugard's mind at this date. There is no evidence as to what happened at the interview which must have followed this desperate preparation.

This is not surprising. Midsummer in England that year was darkened by a storm which broke the unity of the nation and shook what had seemed the most deeply founded constitution in the world. Lugard was drawn into the Ulster vortex. This was, of course, due to Flora. Deserting his desk in the Colonial Office for a few days he went with her to Belfast in the second week of July. They were the guests—this was surely the first unwisdom—of Lord Castlereagh, and they mixed with the other leaders of the Ulster Unionists. What happened can most briefly be recalled by quoting from the central news page of the *Irish Times* for July 11th. It carried the following as its headlines over its main double column:

SIR EDWARD CARSON IN BELFAST
MEETING OF THE PROVISIONAL GOVERNMENT
EMPHATIC DECLARATION AGAINST HOME RULE
ARRANGEMENTS FOR INDEPENDENT GOVERNMENT
MINISTERS CHARGED WITH STIRRING UP STRIFE
MACHINE GUNS FOR THE VOLUNTEERS
SIR FREDERICK LUGARD'S HIGH ENCOMIUM

Among the lesser news items on the page there was reported the death of Joseph Chamberlain. There was also news of the arrival at several ports of guns and ammunition. A leading column called attention to the speeches of Lord Castlereagh as he reviewed the regiment of the Belfast Volunteers who, in khaki and with rifles, were drilling in preparation for their rebellion. After Lord Castlereagh had addressed them, speaking of the leader's reliance upon them to carry the conflict to the very end, the report continued as follows:

SIR FREDERICK LUGARD
Sir Frederick Lugard, who also addressed the men, said he came to

Belfast that morning with the object of seeing for himself what he had heard so much about, and he had seen what he should remember as long as he lived. He was not an Ulsterman nor an Irishman, but he had served his country almost entirely overseas. He wanted to tell them that the example they were showing in Ulster of the grit and determination in the people of the United Kingdom would never be forgotten. They were putting heart into men like himself. They who had the interest of the Empire at heart sometimes felt that things were going to the bad in the old country, and they were doubtful if a crisis came and there was a call to arms whether there would be any response. Ulster had given that response. He could assure them that the attitude they had taken up had rung through the Empire from one end to the other. He wished them God speed, and hoped the time would never come when they would be called upon to fulfil the terms of their Covenant. Should that time come he knew there would be men who would do all they should. He warmly congratulated them, and in the name of the Overseas Dominions which, perhaps, he might claim to represent, he thanked them heartily, for the encouragement they had given.

Cheers were then given for the King, Lord Castlereagh, and others.

The party subsequently motored to various drill centres, where other sections of the regiment were seen at work.

At the hall in Dock Street Sir Frederick Lugard again addressed the men on parade.

This press report hardly needs comment. The outbreak of the world war soon overlaid, at least in England, the feelings which had been aroused over Ulster and a generation which did not live through those weeks can hardly recreate, even with the help of recent books on the subject, the depth of the feelings aroused against the Government. It was signalized by the Curragh " mutiny ", when the class which most prided itself upon its service to the state believed—a belief fostered by some of the Conservative Party leaders—that loyalty could best be shown in rebellion. That Lugard should at least sympathize with such feelings was natural, and his wife's allegiance to the cause of her country and family and the electrically martial air of Belfast in those July days did the rest and swept him on to the platform. Almost the moment it was over there came some realization of what he had done and he wrote to his brother in London:

" The fact is I got carried away at an inspection of the special service troops last night, and being asked by Lord Castlereagh to address them I did so and it is in all the papers this morning. My host, Sir Robert Kennedy, an ex-diplomat, assures me that I need have no fear but that the Nationalist Members will ask a Question in the House as to what right I have to engage in these polemics and it is probable that Harcourt will agree with him! Unfortunately I thanked them in the name of the Overseas Dominions. This show is enough to carry any man off his legs. Monday is *the* great day, Orange Day and the Lord knows what it may produce. Flora, of course, is spoiling for the fray. We are announced as part of Carson's party. Carson is *worshipped* here. It is extraordinary." (L. to E. J. L., 11 July 1914).

Lugard was back in London on the 15th, and on the next day the blow fell. At 5 o'clock a messenger arrived with a note in Harcourt's own hand. Rather than a note it was a statement without beginning or end except for his name at the top and Harcourt's at the bottom. It enclosed a cutting of the report in the *Irish Times* and ran as follows:

15.7.14 Colonial Office,
Downing Street, S.W.

" The enclosed report of a supposed speech by you in the neighbourhood of Belfast has only just reached me. I shall be obliged if you will at the earliest moment send me any explanation you wish to offer and at the same time return the cutting."

The choice open to him in writing his reply was not wide. Short of a grovelling apology, there was no comment he could usefully make upon the affair. But he attempted one.

15.7.14 51 Rutland Gate.

" Sir,

The circumstances in which I addressed a regiment of volunteers in Belfast were as follows: I went to Ulster for the weekend. Lord Castlereagh was going to inspect some volunteers in the evening and invited me to accompany him as a spectator, and I did so. I had no intention of taking any part of any kind, but after he had addressed the men on parade, he asked me if I would say a few words to them. On the spur of the moment I did so. The gathering was characterized by extreme loyalty, the Union Flag was exhibited and the King was cheered with great enthusiasm. I said nothing regarding His Majesty's Government and though I cannot vouch for the accuracy of the report enclosed in your letter, I presume it is substantially correct. I had no notion that there were reporters on the ground and I regret that it appeared in the papers.

Your obedient servant,

F. D. Lugard."

He wrote this answer within the hour and sent it round to Harcourt's house by hand. He then sat down to write a more private letter to send by post. Again, it would appear, that short of the abject retraction that was impossible for the man he was, every additional word at that date to a member of Asquith's Cabinet could only give further offence.

15.7.14   51 Rutland Gate.

" Dear Mr. Harcourt,

May I supplement my formal reply to your letter by expressing to you my apologies for the irregularity of my action which, as I have told you, was quite unpremeditated. I almost think that, had you been there, and seen the extraordinary self-sacrifice, the devotion, the earnestness, and the intense loyalty of these men, you would yourself have been carried away by admiration, whether you agreed with their ideas of liberty or not.

Sincerely yours,

F. D. Lugard."

Lugard passed the night and the next morning not knowing whether or not his career was to end in a summary dismissal. About noon another messenger arrived at 51 Rutland Gate with a further statement in Harcourt's handwriting.

16.7.14   Colonial Office,
Downing Street S.W.

" Sir Frederick Lugard. After anxious consideration—and consultation with the Prime Minister—I have decided to accept the apology in your letter of last night for your very grave breach of the best traditions of the Colonial Service. If your speech becomes a matter of public comment and criticism I shall have to state that I have received and accepted this apology. I am sorry to be obliged to add that this incident must in the future gravely affect my estimate of the value of your judgment and discretion.

L. Harcourt."

Harcourt told his secretary to show the whole correspondence to his staff at the Colonial Office—" and say that I hope they approve of my merciful decision and unmerciful language."[1] To Harcourt's letter Lugard returned two lines of formal acknowledgment. His interpretation of the correspondence was shown in a letter, written the next day, enclosing it in confidence to Captain Craig, M.P. (later Lord Craigavon). " I was careful " ran his annotation " not to retract a word I had said but in my second (private) note I apologized for the breach of Colonial Regulations." Captain Craig, explaining, understandably, that he was " up to the neck in work," promised to keep the correspondence confidential " except so far as Sir Edward Carson is concerned, as he, above all others, would enjoy hearing about the correspondence. May I put my conclusions in a short sentence—you are a brick."

It was all very well to be in with the " Outs " but Lugard was now out with the " Ins " and they were in control of the department he served. It is doubtful whether Asquith would have seriously considered dismissing outright so well-known and respected a governor as Lugard. He was certainly not the only public servant whose " loyalty " was not, for the occasion, towards the government, and the Cabinet's uncertain handling of the officers of the Curragh " mutiny " may have reassured Lugard and Flora as they waited through that night for the decision. But to have given the Colonial Secretary and his department a legitimate cause to condemn and distrust him, in addition to the long score they already held against him, was serious enough. Was Flora penitent about this result of her influence? Did Lugard ever reproach her? There is no evidence upon either point but we can be sure the answer to both questions is " No ".

The outbreak of war twenty days after Harcourt wrote his reply substituted external for internal conflict for the nation. This, at least for the moment, strengthened Lugard's position. There could be no question now of transferring or demoting the man who knew Nigeria so well and was so well known there: he alone was likely to have at once the political authority and the military sense to hold this large territory in order with war certain to break out along its frontier. And Lugard, looking back upon the incident more than four years later, declared that he took no exception to Harcourt's letter of reprimand. " I think he was fully justified."

Though Lugard remained in his post, the armistice between the

---

[1] 16 May 1914, Harcourt Papers.

warring parties in Britain did not extend to his own conflict with the government. Harcourt seems to have largely withdrawn the protecting shield he had from time to time interposed between Lugard and the stabs of the official pens and the criticism of the Office grew sharper.

Meanwhile, war or no war, Nigeria had to be administered. Lugard returned in September to a West Africa already at war. We have seen something of the long series of disagreements between him and the Office that marked the years which followed—the problems connected with the war; the conflicts over the Native Administration and its finance; the new capital at Kaduna; land questions; the Egba rebellion and the threatened railway strike; disagreements raised by the conduct of the local war, the handling of the Cameroons, the emirs' gifts and the Senussi revolt. Even this list is not exhaustive. He was convinced that " since that Ulster episode Mr. Harcourt has let it be known in the Colonial Office that I am a man to be kicked whenever opportunity offers. The tone has changed." (L. to F. L., 13 March 1915). He was naturally delighted to hear on May 27th, 1915 that Harcourt had gone back to the Office of Works and had been replaced by Bonar Law, who " will make a 100 per cent better Colonial Secretary than Chamberlain [Austen]." Unfortunately for him Bonar Law was far too much involved with the war to give much more than the minimum of routine attention to colonial affairs. His biographer, Mr. Robert Blake, makes only the briefest mention of this side of his work.

The war, of course, completely changed the setting, already unfavourable enough, for the Scheme. Lugard believed that while the war lasted Nigeria was his front-line. But in the early summer of 1915 it appeared as though even the iron Lugard was on the edge of a breakdown. In May Temple, and perhaps other officials, must have been to the Colonial Office to complain about him, especially about his tendency to over-centralization and to report that he was in frail health and that his memory was becoming defective. The Colonial Office took this news as just what they had expected. Fiddes regarded the whole situation as deplorable and likely to bring discredit upon his own department.

Certainly Lugard, for the first time in his life, confessed that he was feeling the strain. Even the loyal Edward, going ahead of him on leave, was forced to admit this much. To be precise, Lugard's own admission was not that he was tired but that he was *becoming* tired.

" A man who is himself over-strained or tired is worse than useless
here while all nerves are sensitive . . . One only wishes that a Harcourt
or a Bonar Law could come and shoulder this burden himself in this
climate, with these surroundings, and served with this staff and see
what it means." (L. to F. L., 17 June 1915). He asked Bonar Law for
leave to come home for the summer though declaring himself quite
ready to stay on if required. This was an opening for which the officials
had been waiting. He was told he could come but was warned that
the Scheme of continuous administration should now come to an end,
and that he was therefore to bring no papers home.

Soon after his return in July he had several talks with Bonar Law.
In these he put his side of the case about the Scheme, complained how
he had been overruled again and again and pleaded for a larger latitude
in which to work. His new master, showing both strength and a
sense of honour, told him that though he was himself opposed to the
Scheme on principle, as a pledge had been given, he did not feel able
to revoke it.

This reprieve meant that the old conflict with the Office continued.
During the summer months almost every Nigerian question became
one of controversy. For one thing, Lugard, in the Office view, was
demanding decentralization on paper while in practice he centralized
everything into his own hands. Upon his side Lugard was especially
incensed about Colonial Office delay over education. On the return
voyage, working on his papers, he found that the Office had ignored
his education dispatch of just a year ago, itself the product of a year's
hard thinking and working. " Things are no better," he concluded,
" under Maitland and Bonar Law than under Harcourt." Then, as
so often, he had a sudden fear that *he* might be at least partly in the
wrong.

" This comes of being so damnably opinionated and cocksure. A more
merciful judgment would, perhaps, say it comes of being so much in
earnest . . . The difficulty is to *visualize indifference*, to realize that the man
you are writing to on a matter which moves you to tears doesn't care a
twopenny damn and looks on it merely as an office paper. His first idea is
to make a clever criticism, and when it is shown to be absolutely untenable
(owing to things he did not understand) to ' keep his end up ' and ' not
to give away the office '—My dear, you'll soon be as sick of Education as
I am at this minute! But if I suffer from myopia remember I am in a

10 ft. cabin stuffed full of 'Education' with no other diversion in the world except a weevil-eaten cigar plastered round with a cigarette paper, a cascara pill and a temperature which makes one realize that we are in the tropics once more. At the back of one's mind there is a hungry gnawing for news of an overworking wife and of a terrible war which is at a crisis." (L. to F. L., 12 November 1915).

Had Lugard, as his ship went its dangerous way through the Gulf of Guinea, known what had happened at the Colonial Office, he would have been somewhat comforted, with almost the first comfort of its kind since his appointment as Governor-General. It was true the officials had fallen upon some of his education proposals but when their criticism went up higher something very novel happened to them. Sir John Anderson regretted " the total inability of the Niger Department to consider any proposal emanating from Sir F. Lugard without animus, and of persistently asking his subordinates to criticize his policy behind his back . . . " At the next stage, Steel-Maitland defended himself by saying that he was " as anxious as anyone not to disagree unnecessarily with Sir F. Lugard's proposals." What had caused this revolution? The paper reached the top and the reason became clear. For Bonar Law the education issue had been swallowed in the wider matter. His decision ran as follows:

" I have read with grave misgiving Sir John Anderson's criticism of this department. During the time I have been here I have seemed to detect on a good many occasions an inclination in this Office to disagree without adequate cause with the views of the Gov. I hope that in every department the C.O. will start with the assumption that the man on the spot is likely to be right and will not interfere with him unless there is a real necessity for doing so. I wish this Minute to be circulated to every dept."

It is clear from this what influence had led Anderson at last to write his firm criticism of his staff. It is doubtful if Lugard ever knew what he owed in that dark autumn of 1915 to the overworked Conservative leader who thus validated, at least for his biographer, Lugard's long case against the Office. Yet, in so far as Bonar Law imposed an armistice upon the conflict with the Office, it was only partial and temporary. Even so it gave Lugard some relief. He was able to get his way about building Kaduna and getting on with the eastern railway; he was at least allowed to *enquire* into the possibility of taxation in the south-west; he prevented the calling up of his weary Nigerian soldiers for East Africa; his financial measures were generally approved. On the level of personal contact, too, relations seemed easier. " Fiddes and Strachey receive me with great apparent cordiality," he told Flora later. (L. to F. L., 6 April 1916).

But there had been no fundamental change in the attitudes of either side. Flora was, for obvious reasons, unable to reach Bonar Law. But she did the next best thing, and in place of the imposing figure of Harcourt at her table for tête-à-tête meal and fireside chat she now entertained his Under-Secretary, the young Arthur Steel-Maitland.

He came at eight and did not leave until near midnight. He began, like Harcourt, with a panegyric of Lugard and an assertion of " the high admiration and sympathy with which Bonar Law and he regard you." Then came regret that you should have " got across the Colonial Office " and an endeavour most kindly and frank to find the cause of it. They got on to the major issue of Lugard's native policy and his belief that " you are inclined to abandon your own old policy of development through the natives and to impose a modern commercial development." On the recurring problem of delegation Flora asked, " Why send a Governor-General of experience to Nigeria if Mr. Strachey is to govern Nigeria from Downing St.?" His reply was " How is continuity to be preserved if Downing St. does not maintain continuous traditions and watch over their observance?" The only practical conclusion from this argument was that Lugard should keep the personal touch with the two political heads of the Office by writing them private notes. When the rejection of the Nigerian offer to undertake part of Britain's war debt was mentioned, he exclaimed " Now, there is a case! A few personal lines—half a sheet of notepaper might have been enough—to either Bonar or me would have given us the note of what it really meant." (F. L. to L., 8 March 1916).

Flora, thinking over this long talk, and remembering her disappointments over Harcourt, felt depressed " to find still under new men the old system in full force of administration from Downing St. . . . They talk of delegation but they don't seem to know what delegation means." Obedient mediocrity was all they wanted. She reminded Steel-Maitland of Milner and " his services finally rewarded by a vote of censure and his abilities unused by the State." Lying in bed, sleepless, longing to find the encouragement for her husband which the interview had failed to supply, she reviewed in her mind all Lugard's long career.

" And with it came a consoling thought. . . . I like to think of you as a servant of England, not of the Colonial Office. The Colonial Office is also a servant of England, and both of you no doubt in your own way doing your best, and England is worth working for. The views of any given Colonial Minister take their proper proportion when one thinks of England as your mistress. I love to think that you have worked for your country and that you have served it well. You talk of being proud of me. I wish you just knew with what pride of you I fall asleep."

(F.L. to L., 9 March 1916).

Lugard's response to Steel-Maitland's proposals could be anticipated.

" The result arrived at is that I am to write private letters to Bonar Law or Maitland to support any official dispatch which I consider of importance . . . The confounded day is only 24 hours long. . . . ' Half a sheet of notepaper ' about the six millions of National Debt! ! Was I to imagine that a dispatch dealing with an offer of 6 millions (13 millions in all before it was paid off) was so unimportant that unless it was accompanied by half a sheet of notepaper to Maitland it would escape attention? . . . What then was the half sheet to contain? ' It would have given us the note of what it really meant '. I read those words with simple amazement and I may add that not a word has ever come in acknowledgment except the very snubbing telegram . . . I detest all these back-door notes of which there is no record on the files and which hopelessly mislead a successor. It is not the way that the Empire should be run."

It is, perhaps, less easy to agree with him upon the next question he raised, that of continuity. " It is for continuity that I work all my leave in England. I have been the prophet of Continuity. They did not know the word or its meaning until I raised it . . . " (L. to F. L., 5 April 1916). True, that by a combination of both unusual qualities and unusual circumstances he was stamping Nigeria with a pattern which was to endure for long. But it was part of his intense preoccupation with his own contribution, at once a strength and a weakness, that he would not see that the ultimate source of continuity must be in the Whitehall department and not in the sequence of governors working under it.

Lugard came home for the summer of 1916. Nothing spectacular occurred during this period. In December, Walter Long succeeded Bonar Law as Colonial Secretary. Lugard heard the news with regret. He had hoped for Milner. He remarked that this was the seventh Secretary of State under whom he had served as a governor.[1] There would be only one more, Milner. And Sir George Fiddes, whom Lugard regarded as the most rude and unsympathetic of the officials, replaced the more congenial Sir John Anderson as Permanent Under-Secretary.

The heavy cost of separation from his wife was brought home to Lugard early in 1917 by the news that he had nearly lost her. She had taken, for that date, the rather daring step of putting herself into the hands of an osteopath and, while he was actually manipulating her, she collapsed. She very nearly died, and two famous medical men who were treating her, Sir Thomas Parkinson and Sir Arbuthnot Lane, were incensed both against the osteopath and against her for resorting to him. It was a great tribute to Flora's rationality that, even in the midst of the crisis, she remained in command, and when " Parky ", who was most attentive and kind, clenched his fists and said that if she had died he would have been delighted to sue the offending " quack " for manslaughter, "it left me profoundly unmoved." "After all," she added, " Heart failure on the operation table is by no means an unknown occurrence." Sir Arbuthnot Lane said " You dear nice clever women, it is always you who make the greatest fools of yourselves." He seemed to think osteopathy was mixed up with hypnotism but Flora said that she had experienced the brawny muscles of a strong man rather than any other form of suggestion. She would make no promise not to resort again to osteopathy. (F. L. to L., undated. ? late December 1917).

With the appointment of Long the officials now realised that they might succeed in abolishing the long-hated Scheme. They were right. On April 16th, 1917, the minister signed a dispatch which reached Lugard on May 17th to say that he had decided to end the system. The letter covered five pages of typed foolscap and it referred to the circumstances in which the plan had been started, emphasizing its originally tentative nature and the later questioning of it by Harcourt and Bonar Law. In the second part Long spoke of the many delays and inconveniences, especially the difficulty of having papers in the right place, which were caused by the system. He referred also to the long delay,

[1] Chamberlain, Lyttelton, Elgin, Crewe, Harcourt, Bonar Law, Walter Long.

while Lugard was in England, in reporting a serious outbreak in the Southern Provinces. He could find, he said, no compensating advantages. He had therefore decided to amend the Letters Patent and Order in Council and to insert the customary provisions about the position of the Governor on leave.[1]

The whole tone of the dispatch was coldly legalistic and accusing. There was not one word of appreciation of Lugard and his work, nor any admission that even under the condemned scheme an immense administrative task had been carried through. The dispatch was a great shock to Lugard though we might think, after all that had passed, that the decision should not have been a very great surprise. Before any reply could have been received, so he told his brother, " with indecent haste (lest my reply to Mr. Long should enlighten him as to the un-truths of what they have told him and also to the pledge made to me)" the Office telegraphed to say that the Letters Patent had already been altered with effect from June 1st. They knew, he said, he had resigned before upon the issue in Lord Elgin's time and he supposed they counted upon his resigning now. But " Perhaps I have got somewhat insensitive owing to my being kicked so often and so hard by the C.O." (L. to E. J. L., 2 June 1917). Almost simultaneously the Office sent a cable to him from Flora begging him not to come on leave because of the submarine danger. So the embarrassing question of when he was to take leave under the new plan did not arise.

Lugard therefore stayed on grimly without answering either the letter or the telegram. He was, of course, tempted to resign. But he wanted to round off the task of amalgamation by a revision of his Political Memoranda and Standing Orders and a consolidation of the laws of the two former territories, an immense labour when taken into Lugard's thorough hands. The Colonial Office were opposed to the first project as being unnecessary and did not appear to have been at all interested in the second. Many another man in Lugard's position might now have somewhat relaxed the intensity of his efforts. He was fifty-nine years old: he had overworked mostly in hot and gloomy Lagos for five years, some of them years of war. He had never taken off more than a few week-ends even when in England. Yet now he continued, with seemingly unabated energy, to work for two more years without leave.

[1] Long to Lugard, 18 April 1917, L.P.

As the final months of Lugard's tenure ran out, the fortunes of his little war with the Office varied. He managed to win a few battles but failed in his struggle for additional staff; in his request for more control over the local press; in his plea to be excused full reporting upon punitive expeditions. He was criticized, among other matters, foi his handling of the railway " strike ", while the Egba rebellion which so tragically marked his final period was taken, in justification of the Office view, as a result of his much-criticized taxation policy. In the last days, exhausted by overwork, with his staff down with the influenza epidemic, racked with anxiety about news of Flora being ill, he yet had to drink the last strong drains of his bitterness against the Office.

> " But to all men the moment comes when they have to lay down the trowel . . . I have done over the usual time for which a Governor holds office. . . . I believe in my own secret heart that I am regarded with so much dislike (and perhaps jealousy) by the C.O. officials that they would be delighted to see the last of me. I hope by the grace of God to temper that pleasure by making them devoutly sorry they released me from the galling control of the C.O.'s red tape—but that is another story."
>
> (L. to F. L., 2 September 1918)

That story, of course, referred to his plan of continuing the conflict as a free man with his pen.

As soon as he returned Lugard wrote Walter Long the letter he would have written in Nigeria if he had not felt that " No Governor was justified in raising a serious personal issue during the war." The contents of the letter can easily be imagined—a reiteration of the pledge he had been given, a defence of the Scheme and a protest against the " misleading information " about it which must have been supplied to the Secretary of State by the officials. Walter Long replied with an indignant defence of his staff and an even stronger attack upon the Scheme. Lugard answered expressing agreement in general with what the minister had said about the high traditions of the Civil Service and announced that his task in Nigeria was now completed. The minister promptly took this as a resignation from the Colonial Service, offered him official thanks for his work, referring to his amalgamation of Nigeria, the development of its material resources and the maintenance of the loyalty of its peoples, and finishing by offering to recommend him for the G.B.E. Lugard's reply was that he had not intended to resign from the Service and now offered himself for further work. But he refused the honour and said he had nothing whatever to ask by way of recognition. The reply made it clear that he was unlikely to be offered any other appointment.[1] And it must be admitted that it would not have been easy, even if relations had been idyllic, to find a post suitable for Lugard's age, character and attainments. There was a most unhappy exchange with Fiddes who wrote asking Lugard for an apology for having brought against himself and some of his colleagues "one of the gravest charges that can be made against servants of the Crown" that of "misleading" their minister. Lugard's reply, distinguishing a complaint against unjustifiable public conduct from one against personal honour, can have given small satisfaction.

It is not enough to conclude this chapter with the exclamation "The pity of it!" still less to assume that Lugard's sense of suffering persecution from the Colonial Office might have been some three parts imagination to one of reality. Certainly some of this evidence carries the taint of exaggeration. There were both periods of co-operation and large areas of agreement between the two sides. There were moments when Lugard admitted that Harcourt had been generous in experimenting with the Scheme at all; that his personal relations when he was actually meeting the officials were quite good, and also that he himself was a difficult, "three-cornered" man to deal with. Even so, there is sufficient external evidence to show that there was a settled bias in the Office against Lugard, a readiness to criticize almost everything he did.[2]

Yet Lugard can hardly be acquitted of an almost wilful blindness in insisting, in the face of all precedent and criticism, upon the continuance of an expedient devised to suit his own peculiar temperament and convenience. It was bound to embarrass the officials, both those acting for Lugard in the territory and those in Whitehall, and to throw an impossible strain upon any governor who lacked Lugard's extraordinary strength of body and of will and his devotion to his task. His presence in the Office jeopardized a most important principle of the Civil Service, its anonymity under the signature of the Secretary of

[1] Correspondence between Lugard and Long, 30 November 1918—2 January 1919, L.P.

[2] See for example the reference of Sir Donald Cameron to seeing "a dispatch to a very senior governor to whom the state owed much conclude in discourteous terms which I do not think any Secretary of State that I have known would have endorsed." *My Tanganyika Service and some Nigeria*, p. 259.

State. The officials, therefore, had a good case. Where they erred, surely, was in their incapacity to recognize the quality of the man with whom they were dealing, the difficulties within which he was working, and the size both of his task and of his achievements. Such recognition, once the pledge had been given, would have demanded that the best should be made of what could only be a temporary deviation from official propriety.

There is a wider aspect. If Lugard, upon his side, suffered in excess from the not uncommon incapacity of men of his powers to run obediently in departmental bit and bridle, the men of the Office erred, as Flora had divined, in overstepping the boundary between the sphere of Whitehall and that of the Colonial government. This functional boundary may have been hard to demarcate at that time. Lugard later called to his support the articles written by Hemming, censuring the interference of the "junior clerks" of the Colonial Office.[1] But Sir Donald Cameron, though by no means a docile character, after long but later experience as a governor, discounted this view and declared himself "quite satisfied with the manner in which the Colonial Office treated me during those years of my Governorships."[2] In an interesting discussion of the issues that have been raised in this book he concluded that by his day the Office had changed. It had "mellowed". Nor, among many other comments, does another governor, who once served under Lugard, make the criticism of over-interference.[3] With time and experience the line of division between the tasks of the department and colonial governments became so much clearer that Colonial Secretaries could reiterate in parliament their renunciation of any desire to administer. Later governors, indeed, have not seldom complained to the writer of receiving too little rather than too much guidance upon large matters of policy.

For Lugard himself in 1918 his unhappy relations with the Colonial Office had a future as well as a past. He believed that there was a settled policy to make no use of his experience, but to leave him isolated and neglected as far as any official contact was concerned. The writer remembers that when, in the late nineteen-thirties, Arthur (later Sir Arthur) Dawe, a senior Colonial Office official, came to Abinger to consult him, Lugard remarked that this was the first event of its kind

[1] Lugard, *The Dual Mandate*, p. 160.
[2] Cameron, *op. cit.*, pp. 252-63.
[3] Sir Alan Burns, *Colonial Civil Service* (1949).

since his resignation. The record of the earlier volume is an illustration of the fact that in certain conditions able men can force their way into positions of power. These later chapters provoke the comment that, within the complex structure of a modern government, great ability is needed to recognize and use great ability. By this test the story is not all unfortunate. Harcourt and his staff had, as Flora pointed out, sufficient capacity to choose and appoint Lugard, even if they had not enough to make the fullest use of him. It is perhaps one of Lugard's claims to greatness that in spite of this and other adverse conditions, not excluding some features of his own temperament, he carried through his work in Nigeria, if not to perfection, at least with an undeviating purpose which has made his name one of the greatest among colonial administrators.

PART FOUR

The Last Years 1918-1945

Frederick Lugard

Flora Lugard

CHAPTER XXXI

WORKING TOGETHER

THE OFFICIAL retirement of Lugard in 1918 places his biographer in a difficulty. The sixty years of his life, forty of them packed with adventure and achievement, have been recorded upon a scale which the richness of the material allowed and seemed to justify, and two substantial volumes have been filled. The years of retirement lie before us. In most biographies, with the exception of those of Prime Ministers who in our day sometimes reach their apogee in the late winter of life, the final years can be covered in one, or at the most two, brief chapters. But Lugard never retired. The last twenty-six years of his life saw him enter upon a new series of activities, most of them fruitful and some of them creative, in which he worked the same long hours as before and which did not end until a few days before his death. To explain these activities and also define his own contribution to each of them would go a fair way towards writing the history of colonial policy between the two world wars and during the course of the second one. This task would be worth attempting and it may yet be done. But it will demand its own volume, one in which the work of Lugard becomes less independent and more contributory, as he gave to a number of contemporary movements and organizations what each needed from his experience, his knowledge, or his powers of leadership.[1]

The moment of retirement in November, 1918, was bitter-sweet. The bitterness was towards the Colonial Office which had, in his view, all but dismissed him and seemed determined not to use his services again. The sweetness lay in the thought that at last the long separations

---

[1] Hitherto, in dealing with Lugard's history it has been proper to use the impersonal form for the few personal statements that have been made. But in this final part, and especially from 1929, I was much involved in the affairs described, either as a student of current colonial matters or, to some minor extent, as a participator in them, but most of all, as a close friend of Lugard and an associate in many of his tasks. I shall, therefore, use the direct form. M.P.

from Flora were ended and they would live together at their home on Leith Hill.

Little Parkhurst now became the base for Lugard's activities for the rest of his life. The little Surrey sandstone cottage which Flora had enlarged into a building fit to house a governor and his guests stood in a very isolated position just off the road leading up Leith Hill. Its lawns were almost surrounded by a wall of beech and pine. This rather formidable background was enlivened by flowers and most of all, in early summer, by the gorgeous array of azaleas and rhododendrons flourishing in the local greensand. The house was planned for modest entertaining with its large hall, the gay rose-chintz and green Edwardian drawing-room, and guest-rooms. It was also planned for work. Lugard had a study, with a large desk facing north and a small connecting room to hold his ever-increasing mass of carefully docketed papers. Leith Hill is 965 feet high—Lugard used to claim that it was the highest point on a line drawn between the Alleghanies and the Urals— and it was cold in winter. But then every room blazed with fires of logs supplied from the surrounding woods.

Lugard's first task upon returning to England was to round off his work for Nigeria by thoroughly revising his *Political Memoranda* and seeing to the official publication of his comprehensive report upon the amalgamation. His second task was to get on to paper all his long accumulated ideas about colonial government.

The first work was soon finished. The second was swiftly completed by December 1921 and it was published early the next year by William Blackwood as *The Dual Mandate in British Tropical Africa*.[1] It was, of course, dedicated to Flora and, being written by Lugard in his study with his wife next door in the drawing-room, he could discuss every point of style or principle with her. But the book is wholly his own both in content and character, the work above all of a practical administrator. The first and lesser part, " Europe and Tropical Africa ", contains some sound history and a survey of the peoples and their government. Part II which, under the title " Special Problems ", is some five-sixths of the whole, gives two chapters to most of these following subjects: methods of ruling native races, taxation, land tenure, minerals,

---

[1] Four editions of *The Dual Mandate* were published: 1922, 1923, 1926 and 1929. Apart from the addition of a section on East Africa in the last edition, the differences between editions are not substantial.

slavery, labour, education, transport, trade, economic development, and law and justice, with two chapters on " other problems " and one in conclusion. This list shows that the book is indeed comprehensive. But the first word that must come into the mind of a reviewer is " solid ". And time has found little chaff to winnow from the grain. Each idea seems to be derived either directly from experience, or from a carefully chosen comparative fact, obtained less from books than from his daily reading and cutting of *The Times*. Into this book Lugard, quite unconsciously, put the whole man, character, experience and ideas.

From the mass of material in the book two main ideas seem to stand out. Firstly—and this was not then so obvious to the public— that empire was no monolithic layer of mastery, whether beneficent or oppressive, but had to be broken down into a dozen or so branches of administration. These, the products of European experience and concepts, had to be intricately adjusted to their points of contact with the hundreds of the separate tribes of Africa. Lugard explained, of course, the part which he believed his indirect principle could play in at once softening and activating the contact. The second main theme, which gave its title to the book, was the mutuality of the colonial relationship, expressed in an unemotional calculation of the economic advantages for both sides and in the apprenticeship to civilization given to Africans. In his almost eighteenth century distrust of " enthusiasm ", or at least of its expression, he sometimes tended to play down the courage and idealism of the pioneers, missionaries and others in a tropical Africa that was only then emerging from the pioneer phase, just as he had little to say of the opposite extreme of European brutality and greed.

The second theme seems to have most impressed the contemporary reviewers. A Labour Party pamphlet, priced at twopence, on the government of Africa, which appeared shortly before Lugard's book, had advocated the placing of all colonies under international control. Reviewers felt that *The Dual Mandate* was an overwhelming negation of the Labour views. But Mr. Leonard Woolf, who seems to have been largely responsible for the pamphlet, and whose book of un-mitigated condemnation of the European occupation of Africa had recently appeared,[1] claimed that Lugard having, like Balaam, come to

[1] Leonard Woolf, *Empire and Commerce in Africa* (1920).

curse the Labour Party for its ideas, was forced in many cases to bless it by adopting them.[1]

The word " classic " was at once widely applied to the book and it received large and laudatory attention in all the major newspapers. Sir Harry Johnston wrote an article in *The Times* which was a fine tribute to the writer's career as well as to his book. Lugard, he said, was not egotistic and the reviewer, though he had been in Africa several years before Lugard, found himself " almost everywhere in agreement with its author." Considering how Lugard's star had waxed while his had inexplicably waned, this was generous indeed.[2]

Two reviewers hit off the main character of the book, one by asserting that nothing quite like it had existed before and that its supreme merit was " that it had not only been written. It has been lived,"[3] and the other by concluding that the book was in itself " almost a deed."[4]

The book was so full that, as one reviewer almost complained, it led the reader in " endless directions ". One of these led towards a reform of the Colonial Office. It included an advocacy of the famous Scheme, which Lugard was at last free to urge publicly and which he called " the continuous administration scheme."[5] His presentation of it was firm and full but in criticizing the Office he mixed much less venom with his ink than might have been expected from the earlier threats with which he had relieved his feelings.

Lugard's method of writing does not facilitate the selection of striking quotations or even of generalizations which provide the keynote of the whole book. But those who wish to obtain or renew a contact with it may well, after assessing the weight of the chapter headings and their analyses of contents, turn to the final chapter, remembering that it was written by a man who had found his way into parts of an Africa on the eve of European annexation, and had left them after he and others had given them twenty-five years of British government. Reviewing this changed Africa and his own country, he assessed the effects of the contact between them. He saw the largely " waste and ungarnered products of Africa " developed in the interests both of the producers and of " the hungry people of Europe," the trade of Nigeria alone

[1] *Leicester Pioneer*, 31 March 1922 and *New Statesman*, 1 April 1922.
[2] *The Times*, 6 March 1922.
[3] ' Sir Frederick Lugard on Principles of Empire', *The National Review*, November 1922.
[4] *Birmingham Post*, 7 March 1922.
[5] Lugard, *The Dual Mandate*, pp. 102-13.

having increased from some £2,000,000 to £42,000,000 a year. He saw the wider order and the new humanity which now reigned. " When I recall the state of Uganda at the time I made the treaty of 1890 which brought it under British control, or the state of Nigeria ten years later and contrast them with the conditions of today I feel that British effort—apart from benefits to British trade—has not been in vain."[1] On the political side " if there is unrest and desire for independence " among Africans, then " their very discontent is a measure of their progress."[2] The words nearest to a general conclusion are those already quoted " that the benefit can be made reciprocal and that it is the aim and desire of civilized administration to fulfil this dual mandate."[3]

It is possible that the part of this book which will seem to be most dated, especially to Africans, is that which deals with their own character, then in the first phase of European education, and which contains doubts of their competence, at least in the foreseeable future, to embark upon the British form of parliamentary government. It may well be that those who a few years ago ridiculed this last fear, which Lugard entertained for Asia as well as Africa, may be a little less sure today that he was so utterly misguided.

The book's price of two guineas was certainly high for the period. Sales were slower than the emphatic approval of reviewers seemed to promise. By 1937 Lugard noted that, after four editions had been printed, 2,242 copies had been sold and he showed the proceeds to have been divided as follows—publishers £2,428; booksellers £1,214; author £1,066. This makes an interesting comparison with similar allocations today.

The book finished, he was able to take part in some of the many enterprises which were demanding his services.

Among the first and most important of these was the Permanent Mandates Commission. He was, we know, at once a nationalist and an internationalist. These attitudes were not contradictory; the second grew out of the first. His deep understanding of the colonial problems of his own country was not closed in by his patriotism but opened out into an understanding of the problems of other nations. His travels, and indeed, conflicts, in a continent parcelled out amongst half a dozen powers convinced him, once the parcelling was finished, of the need

---

[1] Lugard, *op. cit.* p. 617.   [2] *Ibid.* p. 618.   [3] *Ibid.* p. 617.

for co-operation between them. He had from the first tried to respect in act as well as word those international agreements which had been signed at Berlin and Brussels. In 1922 he was asked by the Duke of Devonshire, as Colonial Secretary, to replace Mr. Ormsby-Gore (later Lord Harlech), as the British member upon the Permanent Mandates Commission. The appointment was made by the League Council: the governments could only nominate and the member must not hold any appointment under his own government. Lugard's scruples about his inadequate knowledge of French, and his fear that acceptance might bar him from being transferred to some government post even nearer his heart, were overborne.

Thus began a thirteen years' servitude. If he had known the weight of the burden he was undertaking, above all the separations from Flora which it demanded, he might well have refused. As she pointed out in a letter to Mr. Amery, he had to spend up to thirteen weeks abroad at the Geneva sessions, while an exacting task of correspondence, interviews and the study of documents overflowed into the intervals. And all this, for a man who had only his pension, with no more return than expenses. At this rate, she exclaimed, with a rare descent into the colloquial, the Commission would soon have only " duds " in its membership.

That his appointment was fortunate for the system is clear when its main features are recalled. It was an elaborate compromise hammered out in Versailles between national acquisitiveness and international idealism, with some admixture of international jealousy. It was founded upon the three quite different concepts of the Roman mandate, of tutelage and of trusteeship. It placed the fourteen territories which had changed hands during the First World War, containing some twenty million people, into a category new to international law. Under the famous Article 22 of the Covenant of the League, their government was defined as " a sacred trust of civilization ". They were to be administered by those individual Allied powers which had been most concerned with their conquest. Each territory had its own mandate, a document containing conditions designed mainly for the welfare of the inhabitants. The territories were divided into A mandates, covering the advanced states of the Middle East taken from Turkey; B mandates, covering most of the African Territories, Tanganyika, Ruanda-Urundi, the two Cameroons and the two Togolands; and the C mandates, South-West Africa, Samoa, New Guinea, Nauru and the ex-German islands in the North Pacific taken by Japan. The system was new not only in the conception of the mandate but in the setting up of a body which should supervise the execution of an international agreement by reporting to the Council of the League. The system was in action from 1921 until 1939. It piled up a vast documentation of reports by the mandatory powers and the Commission and it evoked an immense literature of comment.[1] The cynics expected—or hoped—too little of it: the idealists expected too much. In the event the results came somewhere between the extremes, but most serious observers seem to have inclined the balance of judgment somewhat in favour of the idealists.

If they are right Lugard did much to weigh the scales. His tenure of the office was long. Perhaps the Permanent Mandates Commission's greatest advantage was the high degree of continuity in its membership, higher than any other organ of the League. It had (after a German was added in 1926) ten members. A majority had to be from non-mandatory powers. One of these was from Italy, which provided, in the Marquis Theodoli,[2] its chairman for the first sixteen years. Holland sent M. van Rees[3] who sat from 1921 until his death thirteen years later. The Swiss Professor Rappard[4] sat from 1924 for the remaining fifteen years of the Commission. Scandinavia sent, in succession, the only women members; one of these, the Norwegian Mlle. Dannevig, sat from 1928 until 1939. Portugal's second appointment ran for ten years. Among the representatives of the mandatory powers, the Belgian, M. Orts,[5] sat for the whole eighteen years. Five French

[1] Among the most useful general studies are Freda White, *Mandates* (1926) (with foreword by Lugard); D. F. W. van Rees, *Les Mandats Internationaux* (Paris 1927); H. Duncan Hall, *Mandates, Dependencies and Trusteeship* (1948). I am much indebted to Dr. Margaret Bates for allowing me to see some of her notes analysing the voluminous proceedings of the Commission.

[2] Theodoli, Alberto, Marchese di Sambuci, 1873-1955; Civil Engineer; served as Under-Secretary of State for Colonies, and as Minister of Foreign Affairs; 1919 delegate to the Peace Conference; Senator of the Kingdom of Italy.

[3] van Rees, Daniel François Willem, 1863-1934; 1882-1914 Netherlands East Indies Civil Service; 1905-8 Secretary-General of the Netherlands East Indies Government; 1908-14 Vice-President of the Council of the Netherlands East Indies; Secretary-General of the Colonial Institute.

[4] Rappard, William, 1883-1958; Professor of Economic History and Public Finance, and Director of the Institute of International Studies, University of Geneva; served on diplomatic missions to Paris, London and Washington; 1920-5 Director of League of Nations Mandates Section; 1928-39 member of Swiss delegation to League of Nations; 1945-55 Swiss delegate to International Labour Conferences.

[5] Orts, Pierre, 1872-1958; 1898-1920 member of the Belgian Diplomatic Service; 1917 Secretary-General to the Ministry of Foreign Affairs; 1919 delegate to the Peace Conference; member of the International Colonial Institute of Brussels.

members sat in succession and three Japanese. Lugard's own membership was for thirteen years, from 1923 to 1936.[1]

But continuity alone would not have given the Commission prestige and authority if amongst the long-term members there had not been some who combined a reputation for high character with great experience in colonial administration. Here the three important men were Lugard, Orts and van Rees. And both as man and expert the two others would have accorded primacy to Lugard with his record of deep and wide colonial experience, and the power to rationalize it so lately shown in *The Dual Mandate*. These three men, and especially Orts and Lugard, besides bringing their individual authority and judicial capacity to the Commission, acted together in a responsible accord. " My meetings with you," wrote Orts to Lugard upon the latter's resignation, " were one of the charms of my visits to Geneva. The death of van Rees leaves me very much isolated morally. From the beginning we found that we had a common way of thinking on all important questions. How many times have we three not formed a ' bloc ' which had to be reckoned with !" (Orts to L., 19 August 1936). When, in 1936, Monsieur Rappard begged Lugard to reconsider his resignation it was because of the loss to the Commission of prestige as well as wisdom and he added that " I have certainly learnt more about colonial administration from you than from any of my other colleagues." (Rappard to L., 7 August 1936).

To Lugard's prestige and knowledge should be added his impartiality. Britain held six[2] out of the fifteen mandates, and these contained nearly half of their total population. And three members of the British Commonwealth, Australia, South Africa and New Zealand, which were not represented upon the Commission, were mandatory powers. Yet on all sides tributes were paid to the equal treatment Lugard meted out to all territories, problems and persons. He was often in the position of cross-examining representatives from British or Dominion mandates and these knew that though, like other representatives, they would be treated by the British member with understanding and courtesy, they would be given no favour and must endure from him the most experienced probing they would get from round that table. Sir Edward Grigg (later Lord Altrincham), who

[1] See the table in Duncan Hall, *op. cit.* pp. 181-2.
[2] Iraq, Palestine, British Togoland, British Cameroons, Tanganyika. The mandate over Nauru island was shared with Australia and New Zealand.

wanted closer union between the East African territories and chafed against the barrier of Tanganyika's mandatory status, found Lugard " not at all helpful " and " inclined to exalt his independent position."[1] Dr. Weizmann, who had only too good reason for close contact with the Commission, said that the " rather dry functionaries " from the Colonial Office sometimes complained about having to account to a lot of foreigners, ignorant of British traditions, about their administration of Palestine. " They usually forgot that amongst the members of the Mandates Commission there was Lord Lugard, an Englishman, and a magnificent administrator who understood their methods only too thoroughly and did not by any means always approve of them." To the Jewish leader Lugard seemed " a personality of great power, commanding respect and affection . . ." His most remarkable feature " was his complete impartiality in dealing with a matter closely affecting the interests of Great Britain . . . In conversation he always made on me the impression of a great judge called upon to try a complicated case."[2]

This impartiality towards British interests was one side of a coin of which the other was lack of prejudice against any foreign causes and persons coming before the Commission. This quality in a man of Lugard's nationality, background, and patriotism, shown in a sphere hot with controversy and jealousies, had much influence both within and beyond the Commission. Admittedly one or two rare occasions can be found when he reacted with momentary sharpness to what he felt to be unfair criticisms of British conduct. But there seem to have been only two really important exceptions which go to prove this fine rule of conduct.

The first is, perhaps, defensible. He was strongly critical of South Africa's performance of her mandate in South West Africa. This much oppressed ex-German territory was one of the most difficult about which to obtain information but Lugard discovered enough to press the South African representatives very hard about the treatment of the Africans by the administration, both for what he regarded as its harshness and its neglect of education and other services. He also showed up the Union government's evasion and delay in face of criticism.[3]

---

[1] Grigg to Colonel C. W. G. Walker, 10 May 1934, Altrincham Papers.
[2] Chaim Weizmann, *Trial and Error* (1949), p. 465.
[3] See, for example, *Minutes of the Eleventh Session of the Permanent Mandates Commission*, June-July 1927, pp. 87 ff. and *Fifteenth Session*, July 1929, pp. 61. ff.

His dealings with this mandate sometimes revealed strong feeling and spilled over into something like a general criticism of South African native policy, which he always severely condemned.

The second of his lapses from impartiality was more serious and raises a difficult question. France's unhappy conduct of her mandate in Syria had led in the summer of 1925 to a rebellion which the French High Commissioner, General Sarrail, repressed with great severity. In the course of the long-drawn-out resistance the French twice bombarded the city of Damascus.[1] This was, perhaps, the most serious test for the Mandates Commission which had now to deal with a state which was at once a great power and a leading member of the Council of the League of Nations to which the Commission was subordinate.

An extraordinary session was held in Rome early in 1926 at which the incident was investigated. In addition to M. de Caix, the accredited mandatory French representative, M. de Jouvenel, and the new High Commissioner, was called to the table to account for the government's actions and especially for the methods used in suppressing the revolt. The Commission's lobbies were thronged with protesting Syrians, five hundred petitions having been sent in by this ubiquitous people. There were allegations of ruthless methods and of torture. It was a tense moment in international relations and all eyes were directed upon the Mandates Commission. Much was expected of Lugard, with his authoritative position in that body. To the astonishment of all he was silent. The Italian Chairman drew barbed attention to this strange behaviour at a big dinner. " Everyone is asking me whether Sir Frederick is ill. They say there must be something the matter with you because you don't speak. You can't be acting under orders and yet you do not join in the discussion as is your custom." (L. to F. L., 20 February 1926). We now have the key to the mystery. Rappard, in a letter written to myself in 1947, drew attention to this one instance of Lugard behaving out of character. He also discovered the reason. " At the session . . . Lugard long remained silent in spite of his obvious interest in the matter." Much surprised, Rappard questioned him, as they walked back together one night from a dinner. Lugard replied " '. . . I find myself greatly embarrassed. Before leaving London I was asked to see our Foreign Secretary (Austen Chamberlain). He told me

[1] For a full account of these incidents see A. J. Toynbee, ed. *Survey of International Affairs 1925, vol. i, The Islamic World* (1927), pp. 416 ff.

that, well aware of the independent status of the members of the Commission, he had neither the right nor the wish to give any instructions. He added, however, that I should realize that whatever views I expressed in Rome would, in Paris, be attributed to him and to the British Government. Now, where is my duty?'" There followed Rappard's comment, "A truly moving and extremely enlightening ethical conflict!"[1]

It is easy to endorse Rappard's description but not so easy to judge the ethics. Lugard's and Flora's letters give us more evidence for judgment. Not only Sir Austen Chamberlain but also the Colonial Secretary, Mr. Amery, had summoned Lugard before he left for Rome in order to lay this equivocal burden upon him. It was the more difficult since Flora sided with the ministers. She told Amery, when sending him extracts from Lugard's letters, that " he realizes that the higher issues must take precedence over the lower and he determined, with your warnings in his mind, to go and do his best." (F. L. to Amery, 22 February 1926). For Lugard this distinction between lower and higher was not as easy as it was to Flora, much of whose career had been in the anterooms of statecraft. He suffered anguish during the session as he struggled to find a compromise position in which publicly he was almost silent while privately he saw Syrian petitioners, coached his special friends on the Commission and helped to draw up reports that were by no means composed wholly of whitewash. " Does Amery appreciate such a position? . . ." he asked. " This is a horrid position to be put in. I am not a diplomat and never pretended to be." (L. to F. L., 17 February 1926). His political, though not his moral, dilemma was slightly eased in that he did not think the Syrians were quite ready for self-government and that, on the assumption that France would now reform her administration and cease her methods of repression, he did not believe that Syria would gain at this stage from a change. In any case it did not lie in the Commission's power to withdraw a mandate though they could make its further maintenance almost impracticable.

But the moral dilemma remained. It was made no easier as a result of his confiding it to his friend, Orts. For the Belgian, faced before leaving home with the same issue, had consulted his government and had been assured by them that he was *absolutely* free. Could he even

[1] Rappard to M.P., 1 September 1947.

draft the report, knowing that the drafter's identity always leaked? "Certainly, you can do as you like," was the answer. It was a humiliating moment for Lugard. "I felt very guilty for my government. For the first time I, too, had consulted my government and got a reply exactly the opposite. And the result is deplorable. The whole Commission believes that I am under orders not to speak and therefore [the result is] to identify England with France's action." (L. to F. L., 21 February 1926).

Amery sent the extracts from Lugard's letters on to Austen Chamberlain. "Please thank Mr. Amery," wrote Chamberlain's secretary, after getting the first batch of letters, "and tell him how grateful Sir Austen is for his most potent and useful intervention *auprès de* Sir F. Lugard."[1] The archives of diplomacy sometimes give off such a strong smell of realism that the layman recoils. Does Lugard emerge tainted from this episode? Defiance would have been nobler than obedience but it was a difficult gesture for an ex-soldier and ex-governor to give. The main regret must be that Britain's ministers were in this matter less honourable than those of Belgium.[2]

To balance this, when we look at Lugard's contribution to the structure of the Commission, we find him by no means reflecting the views of Chamberlain. The eliciting of full and significant information being the Commission's main task, Lugard urged that it should, in certain conditions, hear petitioners in person. The Commission also drew up a long questionnaire of some 118 heads. When these proposals went to the Council in September 1926, Chamberlain exploded with wrath. The questionnaire was "inquisitorial", it would undermine the mandatories' authority: the proposal about petitions was "imprudent, even dangerous." Briand, Ishii and Vandervelde concurred and Mr. Smit, the representative of South Africa, not surprisingly added that the Council's reaction would give pleasure both in his country and in South West Africa.[3]

---

[1] L. Selbey to A. Edgcumbe, 1 March 1926, L.P.

[2] It is impossible to resist giving M. Rappard's wider comment in his letter upon this incident. Referring to the authors of the provisions of the U.N. Charter by which members of the Trusteeship Council are to be national officials appointed by governments, he says, "It is, perhaps, unfortunate that they should not have had the opportunity to ponder over the far-reaching implications of the story of how Lord Lugard was once silenced and thereby paralysed, even in his capacity as a private individual, by his renown as a long trusted and faithful servant of the British Crown."

[3] Fortieth Session of the Council of the League of Nations, *Official Journal*, pp. 1231 ff. Also van Rees, *Les Mandates Internationaux*, p. 102 ff. and Duncan Hall, *Mandates, Dependencies and Trusteeship*, p. 206.

Although the rejection of the proposed reforms set certain bounds to the further development of the Commission's powers, Lugard continued staunchly to support what he regarded as its proper rights with regard to questioning, and in other procedural matters he showed no tendency to go into full retreat before ministerial disapproval. The minutes of the Commission show how much he contributed year by year to the competence of the institution, not only by his firm but temperate handling of representatives, but by his advice on constitutional matters which recognized at once the potentialities of the system and its unavoidable limitations.

While, of course, he was at his most effective in discussions upon the important African B mandates, he became an expert on Samoa, Iraq and Palestine. For his knowledge of Samoa I can vouch personally as I visited the islands in 1929 and came back to find not only a most eager but also a very informed listener to my report. Each member of the Commission specialized upon certain subjects. His assignments were finance (especially native treasuries), land and liquor. But he was naturally expert in the whole field of native administration and led the Commission towards a useful service in cross-fertilizing the ideas of the mandatory powers' official representatives with experience from the entire field of the mandates and beyond. And, of course, the minutes and reports of the Commission were carefully studied in all colonial circles.

He resigned from the Commission in 1936, finding the burden of its work too great, especially since his increasing deafness made it difficult for him to follow the rapid French. The testimonies which followed his resignation defined his contribution. One thing that struck his contemporaries was his humanity. Never emotional or exacting, the minutes show his constant care, in details as well as principles, for the interests of the governed, a care he well knew how to express in very practical interrogation. As the observant Weizmann remarked, " He was humane in his outlook, sympathizing with the submerged and the dispossessed . . . He felt the Jewish plight deeply . . ."[1]

The years of industry had a cumulative value but at a high cost to himself. Freda White, then a close and lively student of the Mandates system, wrote: " Thirteen years of that service is a long spell. Thirteen

---

[1] Weizmann, *op. cit.* p. 464.

years of bumpety P.L.M. trains, of hotel meals, of stuffy secretariat rooms, of Italian, French and Norwegian English. Fourteen[1] mandatory reports a year, documents whose omissions are as prolonged as their contents: fourteen wary mandatory representatives to question on their omissions . . . How often, reading the minutes, one laughs with satisfaction at one of his questions, dead on the point." Very exact is her next estimate of " a mind working so true that it reaches its conclusions with no apparent effort." Watching only this late harvest of his work, she could conclude " Greatness is not an analyzable thing . . . " and statesmanship is seen only once or twice in a generation. " It is statesmanship which Lord Lugard has given at Geneva to the service of subject peoples."[2]

These were views from the outside. From inside comes the picture drawn by his colleague Rappard. This Swiss professor was regarded by Weizmann, as one of the really effective triumvirate, in place of van Rees. With no colonial background his energy and brilliance yet made him a dominant figure at the Commission table. Part of the long letter he wrote to me has been given but much of the rest demands quotation. He begins by recalling the rather apprehensive anticipation of the Commission as to what a mature man of action would make of " the collective, wordy and indecisive deliberation of an international body" whose main task was to talk and to draft reports.

" Well, whatever Lugard may sometimes have felt, he appeared to his colleagues, from the first day to the last, as the most patient, courteous, actively interested and indeed discriminatingly inquisitive member of the Commission. No meeting ever seemed too long or too tedious, no investigation too minute and too searching to exhaust the resources either of his erudition or of his curiosity or even of his temper. It was only on rare occasions, when he had thoroughly convinced himself of the ignorance of a witness, or of a wilful desire to disguise or to mislead on the part of the representative of a government whose report was under review, that Lugard's attention relented. Even then, however, he never allowed any harsh words to fall from his lips. Sometimes, towards the end of a prolonged interrogation, in the latter stages of making up his mind about an official's incompetence or insincerity, a storm seemed to be brewing on his brow. His eyes began to flash and his questions became briefer and almost angry. Then of a sudden he was through. He had had enough. His discouragement or his disgust had at long last outrun his patience.

[1] Iraq became self-governing in 1932.   [2] *Headway*, September 1936.

But invariably the storm broke into a fit of merriment, most often discreet so that only his nearest neighbours could hear him murmur under his smiling moustache: ' That man's a fraud,' or, more kindly: ' Poor fellow, he'll know better next time.' Sometimes it happened that Lugard's competent and logical questions led to revelations of ignorance or bad faith so disarming that the mirth was open and general. Sometimes the victim's sense of humour allowed even him to overcome his obvious dismay and to join in the laugh.

As a rule, however, witnesses being well-informed and having nothing to withhold, were accordingly able and eager to reply to Lugard's questions. Then it often happened that the meetings developed into dialogues between himself who questioned, always jotting down the answers in writing, and the official, who was flattered to arouse the interest of the great Lugard and sometimes only too happy to display his knowledge. What may have become of the hundreds, nay of the thousands of pages of notes in which a beautifully regular, but not all too legible, hand summarized the conversations between the British member of the Mandates Commission and the accredited representatives of the various mandatory Powers?

In his relations with his foreign colleagues, Lord Lugard was always extremely courteous but perhaps somewhat reserved. His slight deafness and his imperfect understanding of French—the *lingua franca* of the Commission—seemed to limit his intimacy with most of them. Those whom he favoured with his friendship will ever most gratefully and most affectionately remember his remarkable qualities of mind, of character and of heart. The extraordinary modesty of one who had so much to be proud of and the singular simplicity, purity and kindness of soul of one whose varied career in all parts of the world and amidst all kinds and all manner of men might well have inclined to cynical hardness, were a delight to experience and will ever remain a lesson."

(Rappard to M.P., 1 September 1947).

Lugard, of course, did all in his power to help his successor, Lord Hailey, to take over and his letters show his delight at hearing from his friends on the Commission how worthily the ex-Indian was replacing the ex-African governor.

Upon the international stage Lugard appeared in another manifestation. This was as an expert upon slavery, continuing the longest unbroken thread in the texture of his work. It is a highly coloured and variable thread. It can be said to start with his schoolboy essay and to run quickly from juvenile theory to the young man dropping back half dead from the attack on the Mlozi stockade in 1887, then through action in East Africa, and on to the vast measures of redemption from slavery in Nigeria both by conquest and by legislation. In Hong Kong he had to deal with the Mui Tsai, a Chinese institution which often came very close to slavery. It was not surprising that in 1924, when the League set up its first Temporary Committee on Slavery, he was the British member, and the first Slavery Convention accepted by the League Assembly in 1926 was largely based on his work. The link which bound his work to Livingstone through Sir John Kirk, the friend and partner they both shared, was finally endorsed when the latter wrote, looking back to Lugard's article ' Slavery under the British Flag ' in *The Nineteenth Century*, [1896] that it was " still referred to as the leading authority on the subject. I believe it has been more read than anything you ever wrote and has made a deep impression."[1]

Following upon this the Assembly set up a Committee of Experts on slavery to which he was appointed in 1932. In 1920 he had interrupted his work on *The Dual Mandate* to make a quick visit to Ethiopia in order to make enquiries about its concession for a British Company, the Abyssinia Corporation. The actual mission proved less important than its by-products, one of which was the acquisition of a great deal of information about serfdom, slavery and the slave-trade in this ancient Amharic empire which for many years continued to be the centre of interest in all anti-slavery movements. Until his death Lugard remained at once the chief practitioner and the chief living authority in this field, and his ceaseless activities are beyond even listing in this chapter. Among them were articles, speeches, confidential memoranda to the League and to ministers, close co-operation with the Anti-Slavery Society, and constant advice to the Emperor of Ethiopia. In 1928 he wrote the article on this subject in the *Encyclopaedia Britannica*. After working on the 1932 Slavery Committee, in 1933 he was suddenly and inexplicably dropped from the Permanent Slavery Commission which grew out of this, being replaced by Sir George Maxwell without even being warned by the government or consulted about a successor. There is a letter from Professor Coupland, himself an expert upon the history of slavery, which puts the question " Is it conceivable that you are regarded in British quarters as too

[1] Undated note by Kirk.

good a servant of the League . . . and an insufficiently selfish champion of British interests?" (Coupland to L., 17 October 1933). It was typical of Lugard that, though painfully wounded, he continued to do all he could to help the Belgian chairman, M. Gohr, who frequently drew from him long memoranda and advice about procedure. He arranged for a debate on the subject in the House of Lords in 1935 and though he was at work abroad when it took place he supplied material for other speakers. In 1938 he brought his *Encyclopaedia* article up to date. The end of the long thread must have been in 1941 when he recorded four broadcast talks on the subject.

It has been shown before in this book that Lugard realized that the conditions which favoured slavery in backward countries could easily lead to its replacement by forced labour. It was therefore a natural addition to his anti-slavery efforts that from 1925 until 1941 he should have been a member of the International Labour Organization's Committee of Experts on Native Labour.

Lugard's incursion as a governor into the field of education has had its own chapter. Freed from the control of officials who were sceptical of his capacity in this field, he was able to develop this interest freely. His most important service was given through the medium of the official Advisory Committee upon Education in Tropical Africa which was set up in 1923.[1] We can recall that he had once exclaimed against advisory committees as weakening and crossing the vital line of communication between Governor and Secretary of State. But the fifth wheel of a coach seems much less otiose to a critic when he is asked to supply some of its supplementary motivation himself.

The Committee took shape at a very important moment in the affairs it covered. The inactivity maintained by most of the British African governments had, up to the First World War, left some 95 per cent of education in the hands of those Christian missions which had begun to supply it before governments appeared. It was now realized that this could continue no longer. But if governments were to play a larger part they must have direction from Britain and if Britain were to have a policy she must find some principle upon which to base it. Hence the Committee. Upon the blank sheet before it a number of questions were quickly written. How and how far were governments

---

[1] In addition to the evidence of the voluminous Lugard and Oldham Papers on educational matters I am indebted to Mr. R. S. Harvey of the Colonial Office for some very useful notes he made on the history of this Committee.

to invade the field of education? What should be their relations with the occupying forces of the Christian missions? And also to the religion in which lay the origin and purpose of mission enterprise? And also, alas! to the missionaries' sectional divisions? What should be the content of education? What the language of instruction! And—in unavoidable sequence—what were Africans to be educated *for*? For continuing subordination or for self-government? As individuals or as members of communities? And what sort of communities? And how deal with the non-Christian religions—Islam and animism?

There was a spirit abroad in the early nineteen-twenties to give urgent and generous answers to these questions. As if in compensation for its cruelty war seems to create or to release a counter altruism. The Mandates system expressed international interest in educational needs. Lugard's own concept of the Dual Mandate emphasized them. But it was clear in Britain that authoritative answers to these immense questions and the continuous advice as to how to act upon the answers could be given only by a committee, and one heavily weighted both with intellect and experience. That such a committee was created in 1923 and that it went a long way towards succeeding in its almost impossible assignment was largely due to Lugard and Dr. J. H. Oldham and to the close friendship between them which began at this time.

It was one of the joys of Lugard's release from both the restraints of office and service overseas that he was now free to express his great capacity for friendship. His intimates were few but very close and, as with his marriage, personal devotion was almost inseparable from partnership in public service. And his partnership with Dr. Oldham was perhaps the most complete and effective of these later years.

Dr. Oldham is—for happily he is still with us—a man whose great gifts have had diverse expressions—ecclesiastical statesman, writer, administrator, teacher, and, as we shall see in another enterprise with Lugard, diplomat and politician.[1] He was destined to leave a deep if, in part, a secret mark upon Africa. It was through his interest in missions that he was drawn into educational problems. He had made an impres-

[1] Oldham, Joseph Houldsworth, C.B.E., D.D., 1874-   ; 1896-7 Secretary of Student Christian Movement; 1908-10 Secretary of the World Missionary Conference; 1921-38 Secretary of the International Missionary Council; 1931-8 Administrative Director of the International Institute of African Languages and Cultures; 1925-36 Member of the Advisory Committee on Education in the Colonies; 1927-8 Member of East African Commission on Closer Union; 1939-45 Editor of *Christian Newsletter*.

sive contribution to the important Edinburgh Conference on missions in 1910 and had been made Secretary of the International Missionary Council and Editor of its Journal. These duties led him on naturally to the sudden challenge of African education and this, in turn, brought him into contact with Lugard.[1] Sincere, selfless, thoughtful, a small man and very gentle, but with steel behind the gentleness, he and Lugard fitted perfectly in character and aims. In their immense correspondence they can be seen during the spring and summer of 1923 planning every detail of the projected Committee and even canvassing its membership, and all the time moving swiftly from acquaintanceship to trust and affection. They worked, of course, with others and, as Dr. Oldham has lately emphasized in a letter to me, the Committee could never have been created if it had not been for the deep and tireless interest of the Colonial Under-Secretary, Mr. Ormsby-Gore, who became its first chairman. The Secretary of the Committee was Lugard's old protégé, Hanns Vischer, with whom Lugard now greatly deepened his old friendship. Missionary leaders of the chief denominations were there, of course: they alone had the accumulated working experience of the subject. There were British education experts, practical and theoretical, and, for politicians, some working members of parliament who had shown some interest in the Committee's problems. There were the practical men from overseas—Lugard himself, one of the few governors who had at least worked out an education policy, and Sir James Currie who in this field had been both original and effective in the Sudan. Before this body came a procession of governors, and then of directors of education who suddenly found they had become significant. Even America, just awakening to awareness of Africa, appeared in the person of Dr. Jesse Jones of the Phelps Stokes Fund, leader of a commission making a study of education in Africa,[2] working in close contact with the new Education Committee and bringing experience of social work among the negroes of the Southern States to the service of Africa.

These and others brought their rich diversity of ideas to the Com-

---

[1] For Dr. Oldham's views upon African education at this period see J. H. Oldham and B. D. Gibson, *The Remaking of Man in Africa* (1931). The appendix B, pp. 151-82, containing an analysis of education throughout tropical and S. Africa, shows the high degree of dependence upon missionary services. For some light upon Oldham's political influence see R. Oliver, *The Missionary Factor in East Africa* (1952), pp. 250-72. Many of the educational problems discussed in the Committee appear in A. Victor Murray, *The School in the Bush* (1929).

[2] T. Jesse Jones, *Education in Africa* (New York 1922).

mittee and there bred new ones in common. Above all there was a new partnership between educationalists in Africa and those in Britain replacing the large degree of mutual ignorance which had hitherto marked their relationship. I was myself for some years a member of this Committee and I found it, with the Inter-University Council for Higher Education in the Colonies which grew out of it, one of the most, if not *the* most, constructive official body which I had ever attended. That was at a later stage. Perhaps the Committee was never so creative as in the first five years when it dealt solely with Africa and was obliged to face and to settle some of the major issues which were waiting for it. It could claim to be the most effective of the Colonial Office advisory committees, and its achievement in devising a coherent policy was at that time matched in no other non-technical branch of colonial government.

The first meeting, called to plan the venture, was on Derby Day, 1923, which the late Bishop Bell noted as a remarkable tribute to the devotion of public men to the new demands of Africa.[1]

Lugard was a productive member of the new Committee. He attended all the monthly meetings and served, generally in the chair, on a number of sub-committees. Among the subjects of his memoranda were " Education by Local Authorities ", " Professor Huxley's Proposals for Biological Education in E. Africa ", " Educational Grants-in-Aid ", " European Education in N. Rhodesia ", " Religious Teaching in Government Schools ". He was at least the chief author of a memorandum " On British Education Staff". These titles may sound prosaic, especially to the uninitiated, but they provided part at least of the foundation upon which African education was built up in the fifteen years following the war and education, as Lugard had come to believe, for good or ill would re-create Africa.

It is possible that the most important document put out by the Committee was its White Paper, *Educational Policy in British Tropical Africa*, published in 1925.[2] It contained the initial definition of principles which were to prove the basis of policy for many years to come. The drafting of this foundation document was largely Lugard's work, though Oldham and Sir Richard Sadler discussed and amended it. But to Lugard it did " not matter a row of pins whose it is so long as it is done. I have felt greatly elated at our success in getting it done and

---

[1] G. K. A. Bell, *Randall Davidson* (1952), p. 1234.　　[2] Cmd. 2374.

so has my wife who, I believe, dreamt of it last night."[1] " We should never have had it at all," Oldham replied, " unless you had started us on the track and your original framework has remained unchanged."[2]

The document, in effect, proclaimed the need for partnership between government and missions in education. It was an ungrudging endorsement of the part played by the societies and a promise to encourage and to aid them fully in the future. They were to come under general government supervision and work alongside schools which were to be conducted by governments. Advisory boards with mission representation should be set up. Religious and moral instruction was to be given the highest importance. The " indirect " approach was endowed with official sanction in the educational sphere. " Education should be adapted to the mentality, aptitudes, occupations and traditions of the various peoples, conserving as far as possible all sound and healthy elements in the fabric of their social life." This paper was sent out to all African governors, bringing with it a policy, which in many cases was entering a vacuum, and it was twice reprinted in the 'thirties for more general use. An article which Lugard wrote in 1925 for the *Edinburgh Review* upon this report was published by the Colonial Office in 1930 and re-issued in 1938. " A future generation," so ran his conclusion, " may look back with amazement at the comparative apathy of the British people today in a matter so momentous, and may regard the little noticed White Paper . . . as one of the principal landmarks of imperial policy in the twentieth century . . . "[3]

In 1929, so great had been the practical success of the Committee, that it was reconstituted with full scope over all the dependencies and renamed the Advisory Committee on Education in the Colonies.[4] Lugard continued to work hard upon it until 1937, a service of fourteen years. The Secretary of State himself, Mr. Ormsby-Gore, recognized his work as having been something even wider than a service to colonial education. " The system of securing expert technical advice in London through voluntary committees is now an essential feature of Colonial organization, and I feel that the successful establishment

---

[1] L. to Oldham, 11 March 1925, O.P.   [2] 12 March 1925, O.P.
[3] Sir F. D. Lugard, *Education in Tropical Africa* (1930), African No. 1135.
[4] Arthur Mayhew, C.M.G., C.I.E., was appointed as a second secretary to the Committee and he later surveyed its problems in *Education in the Colonial Empire* (1938).

of this system has been due in no small measure to your support of it on the educational side." (5 January 1937).

The Advisory Committee, with its long and heavy demands, was not Lugard's only activity in the sphere of education. He was nominated by the Nigerian government as its member upon the Governing Body of the Imperial College of Tropical Agriculture. He never ceased to watch over the affairs of his own offspring, the University of Hong Kong, remaining a member of its Court, and of its London consulting committee, where his main purpose was to urge the use of the bulk of the Boxer Indemnity funds for the benefit of Chinese education. This led on to his joining the Universities China Committee, while his representing Hong Kong on the Universities Bureau of the British Empire, where he sat on the executive committee, resulted in his being made representative there also of Malta and of Cape Town University and, in 1944, of South Africa generally. Almost inevitably he went on to the governing body of the School of Oriental Studies. Here he acted as a link with the China committees and worked hard for the establishment of a Chair in Chinese. He was a link also with the International African Institute[1] and he was successful in getting " and African" added to the name of the School. He showed his alertness to new ideas by entering enthusiastically into a plan to use the cinema as a medium for African education and in 1935 he became Chairman of the Advisory Council for the Production of Films for the Bantu People.

He was not content with co-ordinating and stimulating from above but played a direct educational role by giving numerous lectures on colonial administration, especially to colonial service courses at Oxford and Cambridge. I was able to persuade him to give the inaugural address at the two first Summer Schools on Colonial Administration which, with Professor Coupland, I organized at Oxford in 1937 and 1938. As a speaker he sometimes disappointed audiences drawn by the lure of his reputation as a great man of action by being too unemphatic and impersonal. He refused to believe that his hearers were mainly interested in *him*, his experiences and achievements. His presence, accessible and unpretentious, was deeply appreciated by the men of the Colonial Administrative Service who came from all over the empire to the two Schools. He was utterly humble about his

[1] See below p. 699.

performances. He came doggedly to these affairs largely to please me. He wrote to tell me that he had put together a string of platitudes and asked me derisively what was planned to happen next after the storm of applause had died down.

It is difficult to find any chronological dividing line in dealing with Lugard's so-called retirement because so many of his activities ran right through the period. One of his tasks, which seems to belong to the education group, was his work for the International African Institute. But as he continued as active Chairman up to the week of his death it may be left to the next chapter. Another quite different group of activities, that of his directorships of companies, was not unconnected with the needs of his uneconomical wife. Although they ran on after her death they certainly belong in origin to the period of her life.

We know that, in all that concerned himself, he was the most economical of men. But Flora made her house a centre of hospitality. Flora Shaw's cottage had been somewhat inaccessible, but by the time it became the Lugards' Little Parkhurst, some thirty miles southwest of London, it was easily reached by motor-car. A stream of visitors came to lunch, dine or stay the night or the weekend. This establishment could not be sustained upon the meagre pension of an official who had entered the Colonial Service relatively late in life, even with the small contribution made by the War Office. There seemed to be no way by which a British government could, or would, make any supplement to reward outstanding services. Lugard's mass of voluntary work exacted expense as well as effort. When, as was inevitable with a man of such distinction, the chairmen of companies began to feel after his services, the temptation seemed beyond resisting. Yet Lugard refused to become a director in any company where he did not believe his service could be of value to Africa as well as to himself. The companies which sought him must have known that his name on the balance sheet would be no nominal advertisement of honourable intentions towards native peoples and that he would be no dummy director.

In this spirit, after consulting the Colonial Office, he went on to the boards of four concerns. Perhaps the most important, certainly the most arduous, was that of Barclay's Bank. In 1922 he went on to the Court of the Colonial Bank (which in 1925 was incorporated as the Dominions, Colonial and Overseas section of Barclays), and on to its

East African sub-committee, and in 1928 he joined Barclays Central Board. He attended meetings every Tuesday and every other Thursday, never missing until a fortnight before his death, unless he was ill—a very rare occurrence—or abroad upon other public work. As he had no motor-car of his own, and could not bring himself to spend money upon his own comfort and convenience, when returning from these and other of his numerous journeys to London, he would take the Guildford 'bus from Dorking, get off at the nearest stop, and walk three and a half miles, mostly up a long steep hill. He felt, he said, like a beetle crawling up a wall. Even when the 'bus came nearer he still had a mile uphill of unlighted and forested road to climb. Towards the end he at last gave in to the Bank's insistence that he should accept the cost of using the ramshackle local taxi.

There was plenty of work which Lugard could do as a director. The governor of a bank feeling its way into new lands had to be very sensitive to conditions at all levels. Within a given colonial territory there were really no limits to the conditions which could usefully be studied. There were contacts to be made with colonial governments and governors, British and foreign; a large staff, white, brown and black to be recruited and administered. Lugard was always pressing for policies that would be of even more direct help to the local people than the undoubted benefit of an efficient and stable banking service. He wanted to see the banking staff encouraged to study the local conditions; to enter into close relations with the leaders of native society; to be given a regular service of books and reports. He urged a study of the conditions under which the Bank might capitalize native agriculture. He wanted it to give scholarships for the further education of the natives. He considered it discreditable, in view of the generous American financing of educational and other projects in British Colonies, that British financiers did not play a larger part. He greatly enjoyed the weekly lunches at which the Bank entertained leading figures of all types and nationalities. In the course of his work he made a close friendship with the leading figures in the Bank, Sir John Caulcutt and Sir William Goodenough, both men of great charm and wide public interests.

As a governor Lugard had always found the Empire Cotton Growing Corporation a most helpful agency for stimulating the production of cotton in the colonies. Soon after his leaving Nigeria he became a

Vice-President and Chairman of the West African Sub-committee. The Corporation nominated him to represent it upon the Kassala Cotton Company which appointed him a director. This Company was a southern extension, upon seasonally flooded land, of the great Gezira irrigated enterprise on the Blue Nile managed by the Sudan Plantations Syndicate. The Hadendowa, the semi-nomad Fuzzy-Wuzzies of Kipling's verse, were in danger of being exploited during their first bewildering contact with modern capitalist methods of production. It was the impossibility of finding a compromise between the clashing interests of Big Business and the small peasant which led to the Company's concession being transferred to the Gezira. Lugard was a friend of Douglas Newbold who fought hard and successfully for the rights of the Hadendowa.[1] He made at least one interesting contribution to the general policy of both companies over the question of the repayment of a loan by the Sudan government to finance operations. He framed the two questions: " Why should the living pay for the benefits received by the dead?" and " Why should the living pay for posterity?"[2]

The fourth company which Lugard joined was the *Huileries du Congo Belge*. This was an off-shoot of Lever Brothers. Lord Leverhulme had failed to gain from Sir Hugh Clifford concessions for palm plantations in Nigeria, but, indefatigable and somewhat romantic about Africa, he switched his project to the Belgian Congo where he saw the prospect of " very big things indeed." He was drawn, he said, not only by money but by the lure of business " because business is life."[3] The Company which resulted was dissociated from Lever's in order to avoid British taxation and became a purely Belgian company. When I first learned about this, being then somewhat critical of certain aspects of the Lever subsidiary, the United Africa Company, or haunted, perhaps, by memories of the old Congo scandals, I must have registered some slight surprise at Lugard's association with the enterprise. My fear was unworthy. Quick to perceive it he shortly after wrote to me about it and sent also a bundle of documents. These together told the whole story. The Belgian government had taken over the Congo as a colony in 1908 and King Albert was anxious to show the world that Belgium's new Colonial Charter of native rights

---

[1] See K. D. D. Henderson, *The Making of the Modern Sudan* (1943), pp. 37.
[2] A. Gaitskell, *Gezira* (1959), p. 167.
[3] Charles Wilson, *The History of Unilever* (1954), vol. I, p. 187.

was being honoured. But he was hampered by the large concessions made to Belgian companies. The H.C.B. as a new British company, gave him the opportunity to demand that it should be a model concern. Onerous obligations with regard to amenities were imposed upon the new Company. It became Lugard's work during his twenty-two years as director and chairman, not only to make them more onerous still, or at least more intelligent, but also to do all that he could to ensure that the rules were actually enforced. He was in a very strong position to do so. King Albert greatly valued his joining the Company; so did Lord Leverhulme and with the help of Orts, his Belgian friend on the Mandates Commission—" a man of fearless integrity " as he told me—and of the influential Count de Merode, he was able to experiment in new measures for the well-being of the labour force with regard to recruitment, family settlements at the plantations, medical services, diet and rights to land. The papers Lugard sent me showed that when criticisms were later made both in Belgium and America about the treatment of native labour in the Congo, the H.C.B. was excepted and was, indeed, warmly praised.

It was typical of Lugard not only that he did not resent my doubt but that he answered it by going over the mass of company papers that had accumulated in twenty-two years. I was distressed to discover that a chance word, almost an inflexion, of mine had imposed such a labour upon him at the age of eighty-six, a few months, indeed, before his death. He did not see it that way. " I had had some misgivings," he told me, " as to my continuance on the Board, but I feel considerably relieved by this examination and I think I am justified (to myself) both as regards my work for the Company in defence of its policy and because I may be of use to the ' humanitarian ' aspect by remaining as a Director." (L. to M. P., 27 December 1944).

Should ex-governors become directors of companies, especially those connected with the colonies where they have served? It will soon become a question of merely historical interest. But the question can fairly be asked of Lugard's period and for some time after. That ex-governors must live is not the proper answer: a grateful British government should assure them of an adequate pension. It is certainly valuable for the companies to have the knowledge and perhaps the restraining influence that such a director should supply. But rules are made for the avoidance of abuse and the prospect of such accommodation might influence a far-seeing and self-interested governor to deal too indulgently with the large firms operating in his territory.

Lugard was innocent of this weakness. He never for a moment ingratiated himself with the business concerns at work in his area. If anything he went too far in the other direction with the result that as a governor he was far from popular in commercial circles. The record of his papers show that in all the companies he directed his special concern was the defence and promotion of the interests of the native peoples. Finally, his acceptance of these posts was absolutely consistent with the theory of the mutual benefits of the Dual Mandate, and he meant to do all in his power to prove his thesis.

The fees derived from these directorships, every penny of which he earned by serious work, enabled Lugard to give the remainder of his numerous working hours to unpaid public service. He was also able to satisfy his own and Flora's desire to turn their house into a kind of high-level conference centre for the discussion of colonial, and mainly African problems. And, thirdly, he was able to give his wife, during the few years in which he was able at last to live with her, a fitting home.

But she provided the most impelling motive. Her tendency to extravagance seems to have grown with the years. It was not only that she gave help and hospitality to her relatives, or even that she conducted her house with what she felt was a proper standard of dignified hospitality. She had also begun, even before Lugard left Nigeria, an adventure in agriculture.

To begin farming late in life is nearly always hazardous, but to begin as a woman, a woman of fashion and an intellectual, with small stock both of knowledge and of capital, was to make quite certain of failure. Tempted by a conjecture of Sir Daniel Hall that the sands which overlie the greensand of this part of Surrey could, with proper treatment, be made fertile, she rented a small acreage from the Wooton Estate nearby, a property of the family of Sir John Evelyn, the diarist. Beginning in 1913, and stimulated the next year by the patriotic demand for war-time food-growing, she gradually extended operations until they finally covered 37 intensively cultivated acres rescued from the prevailing heather, gorse and pine-trees.[1] She advanced from vegetables to fruit and went on to poultry, rabbits and Berkshire pigs.

[1] For a fuller account see Bell, *Flora Shaw*, pp. 289-92.

A water-supply was brought; a communicating road, sheds and cottages for the staff were built, and lorries took the produce direct to Covent Garden. Here " Abinger Lettuces " were placarded, becoming famous for their quality, and a quarter of a million were sent in a single year. The pigs won prizes at shows. Pictures of the farm show vast gleaming rows of cloches and bell-glasses. There remains a lovely brochure illustrating hampers, cornucopias bursting with fruit and vegetables, which could be sent direct to buyers for 10/-, carriage paid, by passenger train. There is the characteristic addition " Each order receives individual attention. Customers are invited to express their wishes with regard to the contents . . . " the choice being from some forty odd items. And even, " Flowers and boughs can be included by request without extra charge." No wonder all Flora's friends and many others sent orders for these wonderful hampers! And no wonder, also, that year by year the deficit on these operations piled up! No wonder, as Edward Lugard, who looked after the farm during Flora's absences, remarked to me, that the lettuces looked splendid—they were manured with five pound notes. All Lugard's savings melted away in the farm while Flora studied all the latest books on soil science, always hoping that next year the tide of loss would turn and profit begin to flow in. It never did. Flora had even to consider reducing the household staff but as these all at once offered to stay for much lower wages, what was meant to be a business interview ended, she complained, in emotion. They planned to move into a cottage and let the house profitably. But this, too, came to nothing.

There could have been no fiercer practical test of Lugard's love for Flora than that he, with economy bred into his being from childhood, should have stood back and, for the sake of her health and happiness, allowed the drain to go on. When, one year, the auditor, aghast at his discoveries, ventured to voice his opinion of the whole operation, Lugard sternly reminded him that he had been employed to deal with figures and nothing else.

From January 1st, 1928, Flora might have claimed that a dignified way of living was proper to the Baron of Abinger, for the New Year Honours saw her husband raised to the peerage. She described his reception of the news when, according to custom, he opened his post at her bedside. Reading the official communication he broke off, " I can't understand this. What does it mean?"

"It means that the Government is offering you a Peerage."

"Me! A Peerage! What for?" She supplied a few reasons. He decided he ought to refuse.

"I am terrified at the idea of the House of Lords and I shall never dare to open my lips."

"It will only be the biggest of your many Committees," was her comment.

"I suppose you wouldn't like me to refuse?" She assented.

"Two hours later he came back to me, bathed, shaved and breakfasted and sat down to confide. 'Do you know, I believe the Lordship is coming out on me. I find that I am liking it very much. . . . This is going to make a great difference to Africa; the African Service has been a neglected service. . . . This has raised the African Service to the level of the other services.'"

He humoured Flora by ordering a box of linen handkerchiefs for her from Ireland, suitably embroidered. She fingered the coronet appreciatively saying, "This is the kind of present I like, one which has taken a lifetime to win."

The two certainly did win happiness in these ten years of his retirement. In their uninterrupted enjoyment of each other they were the happiest of their lives. But Flora's strength, strained by over-exertion and injured by incompetent operations, could not match her husband's. As the 'twenties drew to an end it became clear that she was failing. She could no longer read or see the colours of the flowers in the much-loved garden. She remained almost completely happy and peaceful. To a friend she wrote that her husband's public life brought into her own "a continuous stream of interest which carries on for me all the interests of my own public life without the labour and fatigue." And again "I am so happy that nothing seems to matter. A peace which passeth understanding seems to have come to me."[1]

This peace was disturbed by two anxieties. She and her husband had a high but reasoned estimate of the distinction of the other's career. Flora naturally wanted to take advance measures to ensure that his biography should be worthily written. Studying the appropriate writers and scholars of her day she very rightly decided upon Professor (later Sir) Reginald Coupland. His life of Wilberforce especially pleased her, while his work upon Sir John Kirk seemed to

[1] Bell, *op. cit.*, pp. 299-301.

lead naturally on to her husband as Kirk's friend and successor in the struggle against slavery. But a long and interesting correspondence led to a negative end. Coupland felt that by the time he had finished his East African trilogy,[1] in which Kirk figured largely, "I shall exhaust the emotion I feel about it. To do it justice, the *theme* must be repeated with freshness and vigour. Sir Frederick's career would, of course, be in fact, a new subject and a much wider subject than Kirk's. But justice will only be done to it by a writer who comes to it with a fresh enthusiasm for the inspiring cause . . . behind it all." Flora, who had poured out to Coupland all *she* felt the biography should cover, in other words an essay upon her husband's character and achievements, was deeply disappointed.

The second anxiety which shadowed her was much greater. It was the thought of leaving her husband alone. In these last years it was natural that their minds should turn much to questions of faith and morals. Flora, with a more voyaging mind than his, continued to seek for the ultimate reality. From her Bible, from Thomas à Kempis and other Christian writers, she turned to the philosophers: she studied and met Bergson, she peered into biology, astronomy and physics. Towards the end she even began to doubt her own disbelief in immortality. "I have no theories, only a great and growing trust in the goodness of God. The war has, I think, greatly strengthened the feeling that Death is not what it generally seems to be, but something sweeter, simpler and in the order of expanding life."[2] In a message to Lugard written just before she died, she wrote "As we feel near the edge, everything has a golden vision . . . It seems impossible that I shall know nothing of you when I have passed. Absolute truth must exist somewhere."

She died on January 25th, 1929, at the age of seventy-six. It is a frequent custom in literature as well as in life to pass quickly over the fact of death, yet it ranks at least equally with the other major events of life. Demographic statistics show that widows, generally the younger partners, greatly outnumber widowers. Human statistics, if such could be collected, would certainly show this to be the better way round. Lugard was not, of course, the man to drift rudderless after his wife's death. His life had been set upon a clear course before

[1] R. Coupland, *Wilberforce* (1923); *Kirk on the Zambesi* (1928); *East Africa and her Invaders* 1938); *The Exploitation of East Africa 1856–90* (1939).
[2] Bell, *op. cit.* p. 302.

he married her and after her death he continued to follow it. But life without her was only half a life, his suffering was of the same measure as his power to love. She had known and dreaded this for him. She left behind her " a word of farewell and love and gratitude for all these last happy years that we have enjoyed together. I want you never to remember anything but the joy and the peace of it. . . . " But he could not be comforted. It was at no unripe age that she had died. But he had married her late in life and he had now to live for sixteen years without her. To his brother he wrote, towards the end of the year of her death, " you, who know me better than any other living soul, must know that the blow which fell on me is one which can *never* be healed. I do not do things by halves and my love for her was part of my very being . . . I am *always* thinking of her and if I sleep I dream of her, as I did last night, and the vividness of a dream is more painful than thought . . . to the outside world I am no doubt just what I was a year ago. Life is still interesting even though all the sunshine and pleasure have gone out of it. Leave it at that." (L. to E. J. L., 11 November 1929).

Flora's death was rightly regarded as an event in the history of the empire and Amery was a Colonial Secretary well able to understand this. Among the many tributes to her was the one he gave at the Corona Club dinner on May 6th of the year of her death:

" There is one loss, not indeed in the ranks which gather round this table, but in the truest sense in the Colonial Service, that we must all deplore. Lady Lugard had already played a notable part in awakening the consciousness of this country to the opportunities and responsibilities of our Imperial heritage before she entered upon that wonderful partnership of kindred spirits inspired by a single lofty aim which was to be hers for so many years with Lord Lugard in West Africa, in the Far East, and in that ever active focus of interest on all the affairs of the Empire, their beloved home down in Surrey."

I did not know Lugard until some months after her death. But it needed no deep perception to recognize her spirit living on in his life. The house was as she had furnished it; the servants, especially her confidential maid, Florence Robinson, had been trained by her and had loved her; her portrait gazed down from above the drawing-room mantelpiece. Her favourite nephew, Reginald Brackenbury, a widower, and his sons came, as it was her wish, to live at Little Parkhurst. Her own room was kept unused and exactly as she had left it. "You would have found no change in the house and in our way of life as she left it," Lugard wrote in 1940, "for her spirit and the harmony she created, has lived after her." He was writing here in answer to one of Flora's most intimate friends. But ordinarily he could not speak of her. I remember once—I think in the late 'thirties— when some old acquaintance called and made a sudden passing reference to Flora. I had always taken the expression about a face "darkening" as novelists' license. But on this occasion something that seemed in truth to be a dark shadow passed over Lugard's face, and he at once turned the conversation. Work could provide a distraction from the pain of loss but the much-vaunted healer, time, found in Lugard a case quite beyond his powers.

Dr. J. H. Oldham

Margery Perham

Cartoon of the Joint Committee on Closer Union that appeared on 23rd July, 1931, in the weekly newspaper *East Africa & Rhodesia*

Lugard, with the Sultan of Sokoto and Sir Donald Cameron on his right, on his left the Emir of Kano and Sir William Gowers

CHAPTER XXXII

WORKING ALONE

FLORA'S DEATH meant that sixteen of the twenty-six years of Lugard's retirement had to be lived alone. The heavier volume of his work lay on the later side of the black line which, at the year 1929, cut the period in two.

A lifetime of merciless self-control and acceptance of public duty made it possible for him to continue his work with very little interruption after January 25th, 1929. The cost of this effort in continuity was revealed by Oldham. In a letter to me in 1945 he wrote of a visit he made to Lugard a few days after Flora's death:

" I had reason to think that the Government was about to take action in regard to Kenya which would be contrary to what Lord Lugard and I believed to be right. I could see no means of preventing it except an intervention by Lord Lugard . . . I travelled to Little Parkhurst . . . When we settled down in the study for a talk after dinner I explained to Lord Lugard the situation as I saw it, and said that I saw no way of arresting action which we both believed to be mistaken, except a letter by him to *The Times*. He visibly shrank from this suggestion, and said that it was contrary to his deepest feelings to come before the public in any way at such a time. I at once accepted this, and we talked for an hour about other matters. He then rose from his chair and went over to his desk, and began writing. I sat in silence while he did so. He came back and handed me a sheet of paper with the words: ' You can send that to *The Times* tomorrow.' It appeared in *The Times* the next day, and had, I believe, the effect we desired. I do not think that I have ever had a stronger sense than during that half hour of what is sometimes called the ' numinous ' or witnessed a greater manifestation of supernatural heroism and devotion to duty. It is impossible to convey the impression in a letter. One has to know what Lord and Lady Lugard were to one another, and the way in which his life was torn in two by her death, to understand the courage and iron resolve which enabled him to do what he did."

members of the Joint Select Committee on Closer Union depicted in the caricature on the opposite page are, reading the top left-hand corner: Mr. J. H. Hudson, M.P., Mr. J. Allen Parkinson, M.P., Mr. W. Wellock, M.P., Dr. ᵐmond Sheils, M.C., M.P., Lord Phillimore, Lord Lamington, G.C.M.G., G.C.I.E., Lord Cranworth, M.C., Rt. Hon. L. C. S. Amery, P.C., M.P., Lord Passfield, P.C., Lord Stanley of Alderley, G.C.M.G. (Chairman). Mersey, C.M.G., C.B.E., The Earl of Onslow, P.C., Lord Ponsonby, Lord Dickinson, P.C., K.B.E., Lord ᵃʳd, P.C., G.C.M.G., C.B., Sir Robert Hamilton, M.P., Major the Rt. Hon. W. G. A. Ormsby-Gore, P.C., M.P., ᵒhn Sandeman Allen, M.P., Lord Stanley, M.C., M.P., Mr. C. Roderick Buxton, M.P.

It is not surprising that the incident was connected with East Africa. This was the largest and most persistent public question which occupied Lugard throughout these years. The East African problem, with Kenya at its centre, has at least forty years of acute controversy behind it and branches into a dozen or more major complexities. A succession of British governments has tried and failed to settle it, and the stage the Kenya problem is reaching today gives Lugard's contribution an added interest. Behind all the luxuriant growth of controversy the root issue is quite simple. It arose from the sustained effort of a small but able and determined group of white colonists, who began to settle on the Kenya highlands some dozen years after Lugard made his 1890 trek across them, to win what they claimed to be normal colonial self-government. For precedents they could point to the earlier grants of " self-government " over native races in New Zealand, Natal and Southern Rhodesia. But in Kenya there were some special difficulties. The number of the colonists was very small in relation to the native population; they were isolated in a vast area of thoroughly black tropical Africa; there was a larger number of Indian immigrants; and finally, there was growing in Britain a new concept of trusteeship, which set up a moral barrier, though one of precarious and inconstant strength, across the path of the colonists.

Lugard was from the first determined to strengthen this barrier against the settlers' demands. It was not that he had any illusions about the readiness of the Africans at that time for self-government. And had he not, when crossing the highlands, only the second Englishman to reach Uganda by that route, been astonished at their emptiness and called in his book for Indian colonists to fill the void?[1] On the other hand he had been deeply alienated by what he had seen and heard of white colonists in South Africa and Rhodesia during his Kalahari expedition in the mid 'nineties. He had very strong ideas about native rights in matters of land and labour and he believed the settlers to have transgressed both. He had faith in what the paternal British government could do and none in a shifting division of power between its agents and the settlers. He thus became one of the leading opponents of the settler demands in the most critical years of their drive for self-government during which, at one or two moments, they seemed to be on the very edge of success.

[1] Lugard, *The Rise of Our East African Empire*, vol. i, pp. 487-91.

Working Alone

In the years between 1923 and 1936 there were issued in Kenya and East Africa no less than ten major imperial public documents, the most authoritative of all being the report of a Joint Select Committee of both Houses with its two volumes of evidence.[1] Behind the public struggle which these documents signalized there was carried on an intense conflict in which some fifteen to twenty characters played the leading parts. Prominent among these were Lugard and Oldham.

They went into the affair together. Their partnership in this joint enterprise began simultaneously with that on the Education Committee. They were not, like most of the others, officially involved in the affair. They were volunteers drawn in by their belief that this was a major issue of public morality. But in East African affairs they were neither of them new recruits. Oldham had entered, had indeed helped to initiate, the conflict in 1919–20.[2] For his part Lugard had had something to say about the Kenya problem in *The Dual Mandate* and in the 1923 edition he inserted his own solution, of which more presently, which he called " administrative separation."[3]

They first acted together in 1923 over the proposal to introduce a common electoral franchise for Europeans and Indians. The violence of the settlers' attitude at this time alienated Lugard still further from their cause. From January to July of 1923 the two friends were intensely busy behind the scenes and the technique of their long partnership, with its division of functions, began to take shape. Lugard provided the dignity of his name and age; he was the practical administrator with immense knowledge of Africa and Africans. As a member of the Mandates Commission he could now add international status and a new range of knowledge and contacts. Oldham was above all the diplomat. More than any man I have known he illustrated the meaning of that rather startling injunction of Christ, " Be ye wise as serpents and harmless as doves." A Christian of an oecu-

[1] *Memorandum on Indians in Kenya* (1923), Cmd. 1922. *Report of the East Africa Commission* (1925), Cmd. 2387. *Future Policy in Regard to Eastern Africa* (1927), Cmd. 2904. *Report of the Commission on Closer Union of the Dependencies in Eastern and Central Africa* (1929), Cmd. 3234. *Report of Sir Samuel Wilson on his Visit to East Africa, 1929* (1929), Cmd. 3378. *Statement of the Conclusions of His Majesty's Government in the United Kingdom as regards Closer Union in East Africa* (1930), Cmd. 3574. *Memorandum on Native Policy in East Africa* (1930), Cmd. 3573. *Joint Committee on Closer Union in East Africa* (1931), Vol. I Report with Proceedings of the Committee; Vol. II Minutes of Evidence and Index; Vol. III Appendices, Sess. No. 156. vii. 1. *Report by the Financial Commissioner on Certain Questions in Kenya* (1932), Cmd. 4093. *Report of the Kenya Land Commission* (1934), Cmd. 4556.

[2] Dr. R. Oliver gives an account of this and the Indian episode which followed in *The Missionary Factor*, pp. 245–62.

[3] Lugard, *The Dual Mandate*, pp. 317–24.

menical cast of mind, his political principles were based upon religious belief. He gave practical effect to these by working upon the people, *all* the people, who were in any way important in a given situation. His complete personal disinterestedness was a source of great strength. His method, of which I have myself been a willing object, was to meet them singly, study them with sensitive perception, emphasize all the points of agreement and draw them gently into at least some measure of constructive association with himself and others. Thus even his opponents looked upon him as a helpful adviser. He and Lugard— and Oldham in his unobtrusive way was captain of the team—would continue the treatment with further talk in clubs—especially, of course, the Athenaeum—or at week-ends at Little Parkhurst. Colonial Secretaries and Parliamentary Under-Secretaries of State at the Colonial Office came at the top of their list, but Prime Ministers and others in the Cabinet also occur. And the high-minded conspirators were quick to deal with possible successors to office. Thus, in 1924, Lugard even approached Sidney Webb " though it goes against the grain". Archbishop Davidson was a constant and powerful ally.[1] Not a single governor or other senior official, writer, or academic authority; no "weight-carriers" or "ice-cutters", or any who could be persuaded to enter the ranks of these political trades, were neglected. Lugard learned much from Oldham but he too, now he was no longer under the Colonial Office, was growing in moderation and wisdom. He had, also, a winning old-world courtesy and sense of honour in dealing with opponents as well as with allies. Both chose to work quietly in the background; both recoiled from extremists or clamant public egotists. For the decade following 1923, but especially from 1929 to 1931, there were many periods when they were often corresponding or seeing each other in London or Abinger several times a week and were even in daily contact during a crisis.[2]

They were increasingly taken up with Oldham's idea that the whole East African issue needed to be lifted on to the broadest constitutional plane and made the subject of thorough and comprehensive discussion in a Royal Commission. Oldham also pursued a plan for research which would reveal those basic facts about East Africa and its peoples

[1] See Bell, *Randall Davidson*, pp. 1229-35.
[2] The evidence is in the Lugard and Oldham papers and, especially for 1929-32, in the Altrincham Papers. For the critical years which followed I can supplement these sources from my own recollections and papers.

without which, he believed, the policy-makers were blind. More and more the central issue revealed itself. Oldham used a very exact metaphor in one of his scores of letters to Ormsby-Gore. Writing to him as Under-Secretary at the Colonial Office on May 5th, 1927, he said, speaking of the backwardness of the Africans in the body politic, " This means that the black man cannot pull his oar effectively and that consequently there must be a considerable strain on the rudder if the boat is to steer a straight course." The metaphor will stand extension. The rudder was largely in the hands of the local governors, either unable or unwilling to control the thrust of the settler oar. In the long interval before the Africans could pull their full political weight for themselves Oldham and Lugard wanted the imperial government itself to take a firm grasp of the rudder. But even Colonial Secretaries could not, in their view, always be trusted. They therefore wanted the nation, or that part of it which, in the troubled years of the later 'twenties, could be persuaded to consider East Africa, to lay down for many years to come the exact course the boat was to follow. But the clarity of the Kenya issue was confused by the larger question of Closer Union of the East African territories. For the form in which this was achieved must affect the internal situation of each territory and, above all, the position of the European settlers in Kenya.

To show Lugard's contribution to East African affairs we need do no more than pick out the main events. In July 1924 an all-party Parliamentary Commission, with Ormsby-Gore as chairman, was sent to East Africa. Its report, published the next year, emphasised, almost in Lugard's own words, the concept of the Dual Mandate. It advised against federation but was in favour of regular governors' conferences.[1] But in a matter almost of months the settlers, led by Lords Delamere and Francis Scott, were trying to get Closer Union in East Africa accompanied by an unofficial majority in the Kenya Legislative Council. Their hopes lay in the Conservative Colonial Secretary, Mr. Amery, and their new governor, Sir Edward Grigg.[2] He drew his inspiration from Rhodes and Smuts. He knew that

[1] *Report of the East Africa Commission* (1925), Cmd. 2387.
[2] Grigg, Sir Edward William Mcleay, 1st Baron Altrincham, P.C., K.C.M.G., K.C.V.O., D.S.O., 1887–1955; 1903 and 1908–13 Editorial Staff, *The Times*; 1919 Military Secretary to the Prince of Wales; 1921–2 Private Secretary to Lloyd George; 1922–5 M.P.; 1923–5 Secretary Rhodes Trustees; 1925–31 Governor of Kenya; 1933–45 M.P.; 1939–40 Parliamentary Secretary, Ministry of Information; 1940–2 Joint Parliamentary Under-Secretary of State for War; 1944–5 Minister Resident in Middle East.

Amery meant him to bring about Closer Union and could expect to be himself the first Governor-General.[1] The views of these two men and those who supported them must be set fairly against those of their opponents. They, too, had their ideal. They had come to put their faith in British colonists as the best agency for building up strong and prosperous dominions and of extending civilization. They believed, like many disinterested people who later supported the federation of Central Africa, that this policy was in the best interests of the Commonwealth, of Britain, of the colonists and, ultimately, of the Africans. Those of us who opposed them believed that a sound whole could not be built of unsound parts, that is, of unready or unwilling African populations. Insofar as unreadiness meant backwardness we could not agree that the white settler minority, with its interest in retaining power, was a better civilizing agency than the imperial government. I was myself chided by Lionel Curtis, Lord Lothian and Grigg about this time, for doubting their view that by being trusted with power over native populations white colonists would justify the trust. A quotation from Grigg will illustrate this view and show how far his assessment of the East African situation differed from Lugard's. " There is a real danger," he told Amery, " at present of claiming so much for the native that the reaction will set in and leave him in the end the worse for our ill-judged attempts to tie down future generations. His only real security must be in the goodwill of the higher race in Africa " (i.e. the settlers) " and the atmosphere in which that race approaches the era of political independence. I am as sure of that as I am that the sun will rise tomorrow."[2]

The summer of 1927 saw the beginning of what the dominating and liberal Governor of Tanganyika, Sir Donald Cameron, called " those tumultuous years " which ended in 1931. The East African governors were called to Britain.[3] Sir Edward Grigg wanted to go a long way towards the Kenya settlers' demands for Closer Union upon their own terms. The Lugard-Oldham axis and many other liberal elements which sensed the danger redoubled their counter-efforts.

Lugard was not merely negative. He had his own solution. From 1923, when he published his scheme in *The Dual Mandate*, until 1931, he did not cease to urge his plan of " administrative separation ". The

---

[1] Lord Altrincham, *Kenya's Opportunity* (1955), pp. 43 ff.; also L. S. Amery, *My Political Life* (1953), vol. ii, pp. 360-1.

[2] Grigg to Amery, 2 May 1927, A.P.   [3] Cameron, *My Tanganyika Service*, p. 220.

Colonial Office took his scheme seriously enough to print it for distribution in August 1927.[1] In this paper he pointed out that Grigg was pressing for an unofficial (if not yet wholly elected) majority in Kenya because "The settlers will accept nothing less and are in a position to *take* whatever they now consent to *ask* for, relying on the support of South Africa and Rhodesia." Even if this were granted there would be no finality, they would press for full self-government. " But self-government is one thing and the government of two and a half million of natives is quite another thing." Yet—a point he elaborated in many other papers—the alternative policy of working towards an African majority was also impracticable, since it "imposes on the majority a system of government not understood by them and contrary to their traditions, and would also make the legislative council the focus of a long conflict." He therefore proposed that Kenya should be partitioned. The settlers should be given responsible government within their "White Highlands", while in the African areas there should be a system of increasing self-government by way of councils, with a central advisory council at the top. The governor would hold a separate commission as the High Commissioner for the native areas, for which he should legislate. There could be, when necessary, joint sittings of the two councils. The services common to the whole country could be dealt with by joint boards. The scheme owed something to his experience of amalgamating selected services in Nigeria and of legislating on his own authority for the Northern Provinces.

The plan had attractions, if only as a way of escape from an intolerable dilemma, and in this and in other forms, though Oldham was somewhat dubious, it was from time to time considered by responsible persons and bodies. Even Amery and Grigg examined it seriously for a time. Upon my first public entry into the controversy soon after this I joined in its advocacy. But so long as the settlers thought the going was good for their own domination they were not likely to consider it.[2] " I hope," said Delamere to his constituents in January, 1927, " that Sir Frederick Lugard, one of the first pioneers here, will modify his opinion about that really quite impracticable scheme . . . We could never agree to be separated from our Coastbelt, our Port or from our Lake. If we were we should be completely devitalized as

[1] *The Constitution of Kenya and the Federation of the East African Dependencies* (1927), African (East) No. 1112, Confidential Print, L.P.
[2] Altrincham, *op. cit.* pp. 211–12.

a Colony."[1] The Africans, if they had had the knowledge and a common will at this time, might have accepted the plan. Today they reject it and, with the tables turned against them, it is some of the Europeans not only in Kenya but in Central and even in South Africa, who are inclined to the idea of some form of territorial and administrative separation between black and white.

At the time in Kenya there were other objections to the scheme. It made no provision for the largely urbanized Indians. Again, the railway from Mombasa to the Lake was the backbone to which the whole structure of Kenya was ribbed, with roads, freight rates and customs as common concerns. Thus, though the main black and white areas could, though not without some overlap, be demarcated, the colony was a bad subject for partition. Yet a very large degree of separation, with the vigorous development of the African as a citizen and a producer freed, if only in part, from the pressures and resentments of racial subordination in a unitary state, might have been a useful state of affairs, if only for a period. But a firm and constant imperial hand would have been needed to maintain and adjust the difficult mechanism of separation.

There was little chance of such constancy. Even as Lugard sent in his memorandum the Cabinet, to the despair of Amery and Grigg, was in dissension, suffering the opposing pressures from the settlers on the one side, and the growing forces against them in Britain on the other. And also from Cameron. Lugard admired his former assistant's administration in Tanganyika as an extension of Nigerian indirect rule to East Africa. He and Oldham realized that it would in time—and it needed time—be a challenging alternative to the Kenya system. Cameron was outspoken—Sir Samuel Wilson had to rebuke him for making speeches aimed at Grigg[2]—and he was well entrenched behind his international mandate. Oldham warned Grigg that Cameron held a key position with Labour and Liberals.[3] There was danger, especially in view of Germany's campaign for retrocession of her colonies, in seeming to pit Tanganyika against Kenya. At the height of the crisis Lugard, on his way to Brussels for his *Huileries* meeting, saw Cameron and got his account of what was happening at the Colonial Office and of how he had opposed Amery and Grigg.

"Amery, Ormsby-Gore and Wilson were greatly perturbed. There was

[1] *Ibid.* pp. 261-2. [2] Wilson to Grigg, 1928, A.P. [3] Oldham to Grigg, 9 March 1927, A.P.

a complete dead-lock. Cameron refused to budge an inch. . . . Then Amery said he wanted to speak to Cameron. He asked him bluntly whether or not any compromise was possible . . . Cameron said *No*. Amery said all right I will drop the proposals and send out a Commission to investigate the whole matter. Grigg (says Cameron) prayed on his knees against a Commission and wanted Amery to let him go back and make a statement to the settlers. Amery said ' No,' he would send a Commission. . . . Cameron is a splendid fellow. The way he told the Joint East African Board today his policy of Indirect Rule and that the native must come first was simply splendid. I should have admired it even had I thought otherwise. And he more or less carried the Board with him."

Well might Lugard, looking back, feel the changed climate in which Cameron worked.

" How times have changed! If Cameron had taken such a line with the S. of S. in the old days he would have been turned out and no-one would have been any the wiser as to the reason. Now they *simply daren't*. . . . The advent of the Labour Party has its uses."   (L. to F. L., 15 June 1927)

Cameron may have dramatised the incident a little but there is nothing in the Kenya governor's book to cast doubt on the story. In this way the idea of the Hilton Young Commission took shape. The government, suffering from opposing pressures, found in it at least a temporary escape from the strain of decision.

Oldham and Lugard welcomed it. Inaction was just what they wanted in order to build up, with others, a body of informed opinion against surrender to settler claims. How right Grigg had been to dread a Commission! And this one seemed to him " expressly designed to produce an anti-settler report."[1] He approved the chairman, Sir Hilton Young.[2] But Oldham was to be one of the four members of the new Commission and his now considerable knowledge of the issue combined with his subtlety and persistence of mind promised to make him a dominant element.[3] Of the other two, Sir George Schuster had behind him experience of the Sudan and Sir Reginald Mant of India.

[1] Altrincham, *op. cit.* pp. 214-15.
[2] Hilton Young (later Lord Kennet of the Dene), Edward, P.C., G.B.E., 1879-   ; 1915-23 and 1924-35 Liberal Member of Parliament; 1926 Chairman Royal Commission on Indian Currency and Finance; 1928 Chairman, Royal Commission on Closer Union in East Africa; 1931-5 Minister of Health; 1935 raised to Peerage.
[3] Upon reading this chapter in draft Dr. Oldham characteristically denies his was the dominant hand and ascribes the primacy to Schuster. Yet the document, especially when it deals with the racial issues, seems to bear the clear imprint of his mind.

Lugard was one of the very few in Britain to give formal evidence to the Commission upon its return and he also advised Oldham and one of the other four members, Sir George Schuster, upon draft chapters of the Report, which they sent him.

The Report, issued on January 17th 1929,[1] was a long, informative document, with a large place given to the interests of the Africans. It advocated the maintenance of imperial trusteeship and the refusal to the Kenya settlers of an unofficial majority. Sir Hilton Young wrote in some minority opinions. The Commission did not accept Lugard's " administrative separation ". They recommended a moderate and flexible form of Closer Union in which an authoritative governor-general would make imperial control, especially of native policy, a local and intimate reality.

The Report was hardly printed before it was condemned from the pro-settler side. To Grigg, who was in England, it was a " disastrous document ".[2] Lord Delamere, the settler leader, cabled a comprehensive denunciation of a Report which, in his eyes, banged the door on " responsible government " for Kenya and asked the settlers to stand still and wait for races twenty centuries behind them.[3] Oldham, with his keen political scent, must have been aware of the opposition even before the Report was published. The high-minded conspirators got busily to work. Oldham dealt with the press, not forgetting Scotland. He made contact with the Labour party—the political situation stimulated this activity—through De Lisle Burns and with the Prime Minister through the indispensable Tom Jones. He spoke at Chatham House with Lord Meston in the chair. Lugard put down a motion for debate in the Lords and there was much stage-managing of this coming event. Cameron arrived in England ready to back the Report and went down at once to stay the night at Little Parkhurst for a council of war. Grigg fought hard and feelings became strong.

Oldham felt that all he had fought for for so long was in jeopardy in spite of the Report. What more could he do? As a member of the Commission his freedom to act was limited. He told Lionel Curtis that of all his associates Lugard and the Archbishop were the most effective. But he said this on the day before Flora died. It was in this situation that he felt himself driven to break in upon

[1] *Report of the Commission on Closer Union of the Dependencies in Eastern and Central Africa*, (1929) Cmd. 3234.
[2] Altrincham, *op. cit.* p. 217. [3] *Ibid.* pp. 269-73.

Lugard's private anguish. The story has been told, but only up to the point at which Lugard wrote his letter. Oldham took it along to the Archbishop who thought, Oldham wrote to Lugard, " it is exactly what is wanted," so he sent it to *The Times.* " I cannot tell you," Oldham said at the end of his letter, " what last night meant to me." The letter appeared on February 7th. Lugard made no attempt in it to hide his personal loss; it was too well known, especially in *The Times,* for that. He confessed himself unable to play his part in discussing the Report; " The subject is one in which I have for long taken a deep interest and in which my wife's interest has been as deep as my own. Indeed, in writing this letter, I am giving effect to her last wishes." The rest of the letter was a plea for delay. An attempt was being made, he said, to break away from the traditional lines of Crown Colony government and the issue far transcended the importance even of the territories concerned. A general election was imminent and he believed that the new House of Commons should discuss the Report fully. A few days later, on the analogy of recent Indian affairs, Lugard and Oldham decided that the best way of ensuring full national con-sideration of the whole issue was to ask for a joint select committee of both houses. On February 25th, after a few busy days, a letter making this demand appeared in *The Times* over the signature of seven peers with Lugard's name at the top.[1]

Yet Oldham was still afraid he had not done enough to check some hasty action by Amery. The Colonial Secretary was, as we now know, hoping to circumvent the Report and was angry to find his Cabinet colleagues so hesitant that they appointed another Committee, this time a Cabinet one![2] Cameron again found himself " playing a lone hand " at the Colonial Office. " The machine was running away on another set of lines in quite a different direction and I was forced to intimate that if the new dispensations then being discussed were to come into effect I should return to Tanganyika merely to pack up my belongings and come home again." Grigg admired the courage of this threat to resign on the part of his arch-opponent even though " He had indeed made mincemeat of work which had taken me four years."[3] Cameron, whose self-assertiveness even his admirers, of whom I was one, must admit, boasted to his Secretary for Native Affairs,

[1] *The Times,* 25 February 1929. The other peers were Archbishop Davidson, Buxton, Cecil, Olivier, Reading and Southborough.
[2] Amery, *op. cit.* p. 362.   [3] Altrincham, *op. cit.* pp. 214 and 219.

that he had "fixed Amery, mobilized Ramsay MacDonald, Baldwin, J. H. Thomas, the late Archbishop and the Lord knows who," and killed Closer Union.[1] But in his own book he admits with more modesty and truth, that he had found upon his arrival in Britain " that an influential movement was already organizing opinion " against the Colonial Secretary.[2]

The debate which Lugard, as a leading member of this movement, had asked for took place on March 13th, 1929. He was to make his maiden speech. Flora had longed for this occasion; she had come to the House, only a few weeks before, when he had made his request for the debate. There was a moment when, diffident about public speaking in any circumstances, he felt he could not go through with it without her support. But, of course, he did appear. Cleverly concealing the papers upon which the speech he had composed in consultation with Oldham was written, he gave a good imitation of the impromptu. It was a long speech and much of its substance can be assumed. He sketched in general outline his idea of administrative separation. As the ex-governor of Nigeria he spoke of the building " on native lines " of African societies from the village upwards; as the pioneer of 1890 he spoke of his early treaties of friendship with the Kikuyu; as a member of the Mandates Commission he defined the special position of Tanganyika in any federation; as an enthusiast for education he urged greater understanding of the effects upon African minds of the educational and economic forces Britain had set in motion; from the wider statesmanship he was learning in these later years he pleaded for the local issue to be seen as one of " imperial magnitude", demanding no less than a break with past traditions of colonial government as creative as that made by Lord Durham exactly a century before. He pleaded with the settlers not to be " carried away by the arguments of those who assert that the country is theirs and they will not be dictated to by Downing Street—forgetful that the British taxpayer paid for the railway and the early grants-in-aid."[3] His main purpose was to ask for a Joint Select Committee of both Houses, following the recent precedent in Indian affairs, to deal with a question second only in importance to India. It should be remarked, remembering the date, and his admission that most of the East African tribes were still very

[1] P. E. Mitchell, *African Afterthoughts* (1954), p. 117.
[2] Cameron, *My Tanganyika Service*, p. 229.
[3] *Parliamentary Debates (Lords)*, 13 March 1929, V. 73. 469.

primitive, that he underlined the value of such a committee as " an unrivalled means of hearing the views of the African communities."

Lugard need not have dreaded the House of Lords. His debut was impressive. The tall, burly, bearded Lord Olivier, ex-governor of Jamaica and the uncompromising supporter of the under-dog, rose to give a glowing account of Lugard's career and something warmer than the ritual congratulations upon his maiden speech. Then he added that Lugard " speaks under the stress of great personal sorrow which has deprived him of one who, as is well known by all English people, has been an immensely vigorous assistant to him in his own imperial work." Lord Buckmaster, having been recently in Nigeria, assured Lugard of his great name among the people there. The Archbishop of Canterbury spoke of the permanent importance of Lugard's speech, one that would repay study by future generations. Only Lord Cranworth, soldier and writer, who spoke for the settlers, while complimenting the man " who first planted the Union Jack in Uganda " quarrelled with his proposal. Lord Plymouth, Under-Secretary for Dominion Affairs, though in the uncertain position of his government he was in no position to promise the Joint Committee, assured the House that anything said by Lugard, with his great knowledge and authority, would receive the careful consideration of the government. Altogether Lugard's première in the Lords was as solid a success as debate in that partially emasculated chamber allowed. Reporting to Cameron the following day, Oldham, who was always sparing of superlatives, wrote " Lugard was splendid. The outstanding feature of the Debate was the extraordinary expression of confidence in him from every quarter of the House. It is literally true to say that, in the opinion of the House, *he* was the Debate. The impression he made gives him a position of commanding influence which will be of great value in the future."[1]

The Colonial Secretary was in a difficult position. He could not bring himself to act upon the majority report, yet he could hardly, in the face of the well-organized and mounting opposition, act against it. The General Strike of 1926 had given a harder edge to party conflict and Labour might well take over in a matter of weeks. Once more recourse was had to the old form of relief—another Commission. (Lugard remarked that Britain's series of Commissions and pronounce-

---

[1] Oldham to Cameron, 14 March 1929, O.P.

ments was making her ridiculous on the continent.) Yet he and his friends preferred this delay to what they regarded as the wrong action. So, in April, three weeks after the debate, Amery sent " my right hand man," the permanent head of the Colonial Office, Sir Samuel Wilson,[1] whom the Altrincham papers show to have been in close sympathy with the ideas of Amery and Grigg, to East Africa to secure " by personal negotiation " some workable modification of the Report and try to find the unfindable element, a " basis of general agreement."[2] " Even now," Amery told Grigg, " I haven't abandoned hope of our getting through all, or a good deal, of what we are aiming at."[3]

Sir Samuel Wilson was back by July with proposals more favourable to the settlers than those of the Hilton Young Report. But his report embodied in an appendix its rejection by Cameron who, faithful to the line agreed with his friends, still demanded—the improper word is not too strong— " an authoritative Commission or Committee " and an end of " generalization " and " drift ". Wilson's report, which reduced the status of the High Commissioner to a co-ordinator of services, proposed for the Kenya Legislative Council an unofficial though not an elected majority, would have pleased Amery. But the Commissioner found upon his return that he had to present it to the bearded Fabian, Lord Passfield. Labour had in the interval, though lacking an over-all majority, come into office. For Lugard, Oldham and their circle of supporters this was a great opportunity and they turned towards the new ministers like flowers to the sun. But what they still wanted, especially as the new ministry was in no very secure position, was an *all*-party decision through a Select Committee. To ensure the appointment of this body they continued to bend all their efforts. Lugard saw much of Passfield and found him intent on " the prevention of oppressive policy on the part of the White Settlers ".[4] After dinner at Lord Passfield's house early in September 1929, the two went on talking until midnight, the minister taking notes and finishing by saying "He was most grateful for my advice. He was really entirely in agreement with me, but could only do what was practicable. The Colonial Office naturally wanted the line of least

---

[1] Wilson, Brig. Gen. Sir Samuel Herbert, G.C.M.G., K.C.B., 1873-1950; 1921-4 Governor, Trinidad and Tobago; 1924-5 Governor, Jamaica; 1925-33 Permanent Under-Secretary, Colonial Office.

[2] *Report of Sir Samuel Wilson on his Visit to East Africa, 1929*, Cmd. 3378, p. 5, and Amery, *op. cit.* p. 362.

[3] Amery to Grigg, 14 March 1929, A.P.   [4] Beatrice Webb, *Diaries 1924-32* (1956), p. 204.

resistance. He could not bind himself to do *nothing* without previously consulting me but he would do his best to do so."[1] Oldham reported to a friend that Lugard was especially useful in this quarter as Lord Passfield would deal only with peers! The new Prime Minister, Mr. Ramsay MacDonald, was reached by way of his son, Malcolm. Oldham and Lugard saw him before he left for the United States and extracted a promise that there *would* be a Select Committee. Relations were established with the new Under-Secretary, Dr. (afterwards Sir) Drummond Shiels, a wise and humorous Scot. There were meetings with Philip Kerr (later Lord Lothian) and with Geoffrey Dawson whose *Times* leaders were, on the whole, not unhelpful. The Archbishop was constant with influence and advice. Oldham was in touch with the university world and in Oxford mobilized Lindsay, the Master of Balliol, Professor Coupland, Gilbert Murray and others. Commercial interests were in touch through Lugard's close friend and ally, Sir Humphrey Leggett, chairman of the Joint East African Board.

In June 1930 Passfield declared his policy. He issued two White Papers, one on Native Policy[2] and one on Closer Union.[3] The first was a whole-hearted insistence upon African rights underlining the doctrine of the " paramountcy " of native interests first defined in 1923. The second restored the Hilton Young plan of a strong High Commissioner with power to co-ordinate native policy as well as joint services: the Kenya constitution was to remain unchanged except for an additional member to represent Africans while the idea of the dreaded electoral common roll was revived.

The White Papers, which gave the allies almost more than they wanted, provoked an outcry which rang from Kenya to the Cape. Passfield, moreover, accepted the Oldham-Lugard plan for a Joint Select Committee. This would consider the constitutional proposals. At the debate Passfield said the East African policy needed a sanction higher than that of any party government.[4] Lugard was in the position, not uncommon for non-party men on the edge of politics, of fearing to say too much lest he should lose in public that reputaion as at

[1] Note by Lugard, L.P. Since writing this chapter I have had the advantage of discussing it with Mr. George Bennett who is contributing a chapter upon this period of Kenya's history to the forthcoming three volume History of East Africa. He does not believe that at this stage of affairs Passfield's views were as liberal as Lugard was led to believe.

[2] *Memorandum on Native Policy in East Africa*, Cmd. 3573.

[3] *Statement of the Conclusions of His Majesty's Government as regards Closer Union in East Africa*, Cmd. 3574.

[4] Parliamentary Debates (Lords), 3 July 1930, V. 78. 288-9.

neutral expert which whould qualify him for membership of the proposed Committee. It was certainly a tribute to his character, and perhaps also to the discretion with which he had been exerting his private pressures, that Lord Cranworth, in attacking the plan for a Committee, could say that he could " only think of one man who seems an ideal member of that Committee " and that was Lugard.[1] But Lugard need not have feared: his inclusion was inevitable.

In a debate on November 12th 1930, he again pleaded for " a national verdict which no government could lightly set aside."[2]

The Joint Select Committee of both Houses duly met on December 4th, 1930. The list of its members contained the *ex-officio* names of the present and past Secretaries and Under-Secretaries, Passfield, Shiels, Amery and Ormsby-Gore. The other places were carefully distributed between the two Houses and the various interests and points of view.[3] Grigg commented that membership was " so composed that agreement upon it seems out of the question " and he added that agreement was undesirable. He thought it would "go on drivelling".[4] Neville Chamberlain had hoped to be a member but, as Chairman of the party, he had no time; but someone, he said, must be found to keep up the settler end. He urged Grigg to advise the Kenya settlers " to keep a stout heart " and not to think that the case had been lost " because the old nanny-goat has issued these two white papers." Perhaps " this inane government would be kicked out."[5]

Lugard, for his part, had no intention that this Committee should be either drivelling or indecisive. Membership meant arduous work. In the ten months before it reported it sat fifty-three times, with Lugard missing only six sessions while he was at the Mandates Commission in Geneva, and it examined fifty-one oral witnesses. All the chief protagonists of the East African controversy, including the three Governors, presented themselves before it, and Lugard saw his wish fulfilled in the arrival of African witnesses from all three territories. I was present at most of the sessions as I was commissioned to write articles for *The Times*.[6] As I watched the deep impression made upon

---

[1] *Ibid.* 293.   [2] Parliamentary Debates (Lords), 12 November 1930, V. 79. 77.
[3] The full list was as follows—Lords: Lord Stanley of Alderley (Chairman), Earl of Onslow, Viscount Mersey, Lord Lamington, Lord Cranworth, Lord Phillimore, Lord Lugard, Lord Passfield, Lord Dickinson and Lord Ponsonby of Shulbrede. Commons: Sir John Sandeman Allen, Mr. Amery, Mr. Buxton, Sir Robert Hamilton, Mr. J. Hudson, Mr. Ormsby-Gore, Mr. Parkinson, Dr. Shiels, Lord Stanley, Mr. Wellock.
[4] Grigg to Lord Francis Scott, 19 December 1930, A.P.
[5] N. Chamberlain to Grigg, 7 August 1930, A.P.   [6] *The Times*, 13, 14, 15 August 1931.

the Committee by the Africans, and especially by Mr. Kulubya of Buganda, who showed himself fully the equal of his interlocutors in bearing and intelligence, I felt that the majority race could never again be regarded as a passive, undifferentiated mass wholly dependent upon this or that decision of settlers or officials.

Lugard was active both in questioning witnesses and even more in all the inter-session discussions and memo-writing which accompany such a committee. He discussed every move with Oldham and others, and at week-ends Little Parkhurst reached its climax as a place of conference. Nearly all the more influential members of the Select Committee came. There were also serving officials, including the governors, Gowers, Cameron (and his Secretary for Native Affairs, Philip Mitchell) and Sir Joseph Byrne, Grigg's successor in Kenya. Lord Cranworth, Lord Francis Scott and Schwartze were there for the settlers. Julian Huxley and Professors Malinowski and Coupland represented intellectuals. Sir Samuel Wilson, Sir Humphrey Leggett, Sir Robert Hamilton and Lord Lothian brought their very various views. Oldham was, of course, a constant visitor, consulting at every stage, and I was often there myself.

The report, upon the drafting of which Lugard did much work, was written during the late summer and autumn of 1931. These were difficult days—dark shadows on the continent; in Britain the crisis of the pound and grave unemployment; the formation of the National Government at the end of August; the bitter General Election with its " National " victory in October. East Africa was a very secondary issue for Britain in those confused and somewhat inglorious days yet, in our group, we all pursued it as our major interest and refused to be either diverted or daunted by the larger issues.

The enormous amount of gestation which had preceded it may have made the report of the Committee, when at last it appeared on October 6th, 1931, seem somewhat mouse-like, but it certainly was not ridiculous.[1] Its tone was deflationary; its recommendations were clarifying compromises which, in sum, were rather negative. They were not the less important for this. Closer Union was rejected. The settlers no longer wanted it if they could not have it on their own terms with that added power in the Kenya Council which would have made them the chief influence in the Union. This Council, it was now stated,

---

[1] *Joint Committee on Closer Union in East Africa, vol. 1 Report, Sess. No. 156.*

should remain advisory, the only change being a larger representation for African interests. The controversial theory of African " paramountcy " was re-defined in more open wording that was less alarming to the settlers. Lugard's administrative separation which he had expounded at length to the Committee and in general support of which I had given written evidence,[1] was not accepted. But it made some mark in the Report. It was carefully described,[2] and the way was left open for a development in that direction by the emphasis upon the building up of native councils, reform in native administration based upon African social structure and a stronger position for the Chief Native Commissioner. And there were two important fields by which the work of the Committee was to be carried further and native grievances thoroughly investigated; the question of native lands and the division of revenue between Europeans and Africans. These were to be the subject of special Commissions.

Oldham and Lugard had reason to be satisfied. The Report rejected " responsible government " for the settlers, and it continued, with the great authority of its all-party membership and its thorough public investigations, the process of building up the African side of the Kenya structure. The settlers were not to be deflected from their very natural and unremitting search for security through political control. But though in practice it still remained hard for any British government or governor to hold the rudder against the strong pull from their side of the boat, in constitutional terms they never came so near success as during the Amery-Grigg combination. It would have been impossible for me, as an open if minor combatant in the conflict of policies that has been described, to pretend to any impartiality in narrating it. Subsequent events have strengthened my belief that Lugard and Oldham were right and Amery and Grigg were wrong in their views. But the two last-named were able and disinterested men and Africa is too young a continent in history for any observer to claim to have made an infallible judgment.

It remains to assess the reasons why the Amery-Grigg policy, which had so much Conservative support, failed. It was due to a combination of political events and personal efforts. Chief amongst the events were the advent of Labour to power with the appointment of Passfield as Colonial Secretary. His tenure was brief and he had his shortcomings.

[1] *Ibid.* vol. iii, Appendix 39.   [2] *Ibid.* vol. i, pp. 36-7.

Working Alone

But, as he told Grigg in rather rebuking letters, he approached the question not as a mere Labour doctrinaire, but as a trained administrator who had to see both sides of any issue, in this case the native as well as the settler side.[1] But perhaps no individual played a larger part from 1923 onwards than Oldham and we have seen that in the crucial years 1929-1931 Lugard and he acted as one. Sir Samuel Wilson could watch the building up of opposition more closely than Grigg and he not only wrote to the latter explaining that his advice carried little weight with his new Labour masters, with their wholly different approach from that of their predecessors, but that Oldham and the rest had done their work so well that he was now " regarded by these damned doctrinaires as the permanent official sent out by Amery and chloroformed by the settlers."[2] They had reduced the ministers to a state of utter indecision. But he had to admit that "There is a very live and very critical body of opinion in the country, both in and out of Parliament, which is intensely interested in the native policy of Kenya administration and which seems to become more so every day."[3] A little earlier he had given at least one important reason for the development of this new interest. " Oldham and Lugard . . . continue an intensive campaign in the Press trying to mislead the British public."[4] And Amery, returning to England from mountaineering in Canada after his loss of office, reported to Grigg, " Unfortunately I hear that Oldham and Lugard have been doing a lot of mischievous lobbying."[5]

The efforts of Oldham and Lugard did not cease with the Select Committee's Report. On February 16th, 1932, Lugard initiated a debate in the Lords. (This House, with the Commons too busy to give much time to East Africa, was the chief forum for the discussions about this region during these years.) To follow up the work of the Joint Select Committee, Lord Moyne[6] was to go out and report upon the allocation of Kenya's revenues and services between the races.[7] As a colonial administrator, Lugard dissected the elements in this

[1] Passfield to Grigg, 9 and 29 July 1930, A.P.
[2] Wilson to Grigg, 10 April 1930, A.P.   [3] Wilson to Grigg, 18 February 1930, A.P.
[4] Wilson to Grigg, 7 November 1929, A.P.   [5] Amery to Grigg, 22 October 1929, A.P.
[6] Moyne, 1st Baron (cr. 1932), Walter Edward Guinness, P.C., D.S.O., 1880-1944; 1907-31 M.P. for Bury St. Edmunds; member of Conservative governments in nineteen-twenties; 1932 Financial Mission to Kenya; 1938-9 Chairman, West Indies Royal Commission; 1941-2 Secretary of State for the Colonies, and Leader of the House of Lords; 1942-4 Deputy Minister of State, Cairo.
[7] *Report by the Financial Commissioner (Lord Moyne) on Certain Questions in Kenya* (1932). Cmd. 4093.

difficult task down to railway freights, import duties, the allocation of public services and local government finance, and demanded the widest and most thorough interpretation of his terms of reference. He warned the House that as a result of the series of reports upon East Africa " there exists in this country considerable misgiving as to whether native interests in Kenya have always received the consideration due to them."[1] Lord Moyne, whose tragic assassination in 1944 destroyed a man of great ability and liberalism, said that Lugard's speech had been of inestimable help to him.[2]

Lugard was equally active in the other matter arising out of the Select Committee's report. On March 23rd, 1932, he made a very long technical speech, of a kind which was so much more possible in the setting of the Lords than in the Commons, upon the whole land situation of Kenya, referring to the legal cases which had affected, and indeed, injured, native interests, and the many technical difficulties in giving general and individual title to tribal lands held communally. He spoke of the distress and bitterness caused by African fears for their land and concluded that " the land question is of transcendent importance to the African, bound up with his religious conceptions and his social life." He warned the House against the dangers that would one day ensue if they neglected the question now.[3] It naturally followed that as soon as Sir Morris Carter was appointed chairman of the Committee to investigate into the native lands he and Lugard made close contact. He greatly regretted, in view of the need for a wholly impartial approach, that a local European colonist was appointed to work with Sir Morris. When the report at last appeared[4] he strongly attacked the decision, after the allocation was made to the Africans, to cut them off from appeals to the courts in land matters, and to evict Africans from land admittedly theirs of right for the benefit of a racial minority. He also deplored the rejection of the Commission's recommendation that the Trust Board should be independent of any local interest.[5]

Even before the Commission reported, however, the discovery of gold in the Kavirondo reserve at Kakamega aroused a controversy in which Lugard, in letters to *The Times* and in the House of Lords, took

[1] Parliamentary Debates (Lords), 16 February 1932, V. 83. 592.   [2] *Ibid.* 607-8.
[3] Parliamentary Debates (Lords), 23 March 1932, V. 83. 1025.
[4] *Report of the Kenya Land Commission* (1934), Cmd. 4556.
[5] *The Times*, 29 May 1936.

a very strong line against the government in defence of African rights under the Native Lands Trust Ordinance. Working with him in this affair I could see how deeply he felt the shock to African faith in British promises.[1]

His abiding anxiety about the justice of British policy in Kenya kept that colony at the top of the list for his interest and studies and in our talks and correspondence. I visited Kenya several times before he died and he always wanted the fullest reports from me. One of his later writings upon the subject was the reasoned foreword he wrote for the book in which my controversy with Mrs. Huxley was published.[2]

Lugard's determination to defend African rights and interests from the ceaseless erosion of white colonists was not, of course, confined to East Africa. Where he had some personal connection his heart as well as head was engaged. He did not forget his friendship with Khama and he was sensitive to the needs of the people of Bechuanaland and therefore of the two other High Commission Territories in South Africa. As with Kenya this was a subject upon which we could work closely together and he warmly and publicly supported me in my conflict with Lionel Curtis, waged by means of articles in *The Times*. As the pressure of the South African Government for the transfer of the territories increased in the middle 'thirties he worked hard with his usual thoroughness to defeat this demand. He spoke in the Lords, in 1933, (December 17th), went on deputation to the Secretary of State for the Dominions in 1934, and wrote articles for the *Manchester Guardian* in 1935 (May 27th and 28th). He had two main points to press, that the administration should be better staffed and that it should be reformed on the indirect lines he always advocated. He was thus highly satisfied to see his Nigerian proclamation being used as a model in the heart of South Africa and especially in Bechuanaland. Secondly, while he opposed transfer until the territories were solvent and in good order, he believed that if it had to come some day it must be by means of a tripartite treaty in which the Africans were one of the signatories, a proposal worth remembering.

Nyasaland had for Lugard another tie of old association: he had left much of his blood and some of his bone on the shores of its lake. But

---

[1] *The Times*, 4 January and 13 March 1933, and *Parliamentary Debates* (Lords), 8 February 1933, V. 86. 548-59.
[2] E. Huxley and M. Perham, *Race and Politics in Kenya* (1944).

for several reasons the problems of the region, although basically similar to those of Kenya, never attracted such constant attention in Britain. They did, however, intrude themselves with the publication of the report of the Royal Commission in 1939.[1] Lugard's shyness, to which was added a growing burden of deafness, always made him dread appearances in the House of Lords but he forced himself to make his final appearance there in order to oppose any amalgamation which would extend the Southern Rhodesian colour-bar to the Northern Protectorates. Godfrey Huggins, the Prime Minister, later Lord Malvern, whose name is in the Little Parkhurst visitors' book, had earlier gratified him by ostensibly adopting the principle both of Indirect Rule and of administrative separation and had read aloud from *The Dual Mandate* in the legislature. But Lugard was neither so vain nor so old that he could not observe that Indirect Rule was not likely to flourish where the natives were scattered into some eighty separate reserves and half the country was set aside for Europeans. Moreover, his system of administrative separation demanded that the imperial government, and not a legislature of local Europeans, should be at the head of the two sections. All the co-operation needed in Central Africa could be provided by closer economic ties without political union.[2]

Africa, East, Central and South, were not, of course, allowed to crowd Africa West and, above all, Nigeria, out of Lugard's attention. From the moment he left there was a continuous procession to his house of the men who still called him " Chief ", while, with the exception of his immediate successor, Sir Hugh Clifford, each new governor, both before he went out and after he returned, would come to talk for long hours in his study. Much of the talk and also the correspondence, especially with Sir Bernard Bourdillon, governor from 1935 to 1943, turned upon the status of the emirates and Lugard always counselled against their evolution towards native states. In Nigeria he found his main theme for the scores of his speeches and articles and it was the Nigeria of the ever-changing present as well as of the past. My own studies of Nigeria and my travels round it in his footsteps enriched our friendship with the shared knowledge and discussions they allowed. There was no trouble he spared in encouraging me, in

---

[1] *Rhodesia-Nyasaland Royal Commission Report* (1939), Cmd. 5959.
[2] Parliamentary Debates (Lords), 31 July 1939, V. 114. 692-8.

reading the proofs of my book on the country and finally in reviewing it with affectionate bias at great length in the form of a general article. This, from his pen and upon this subject, had an importance beyond its immediate purpose.[1]

These contacts with the territory he had done so much to create were not confined to the British. Nigerians came to pay court to their old master, emirs from the north, obas from the south, journalists and others. He would discuss the old days, even the days when they had fought against each other. He would take them to the Zoo or—this for the equestrian emirs—to visit the Arab stud of his near neighbours on Leith Hill, the Vaughan Williams'. There they would see the small, splendid stallions pawing the earth of the Leith Hill woods instead of the dry open plains from which the emirs and the horses' own ancestors had come. The northern emirs and their suites would go out at sunset and prostrate themselves in the garden. The best known character among the southern rulers, the Alake of Abeokuta, added the brilliant colours of his robes and his state umbrella to the display of the azaleas as he strolled about the garden in constructive discussion with the man who had suppressed the independence of his state. With the younger men, and especially with Northern Nigeria's first journalist, Lugard was ready to discuss the future in new and liberal terms. I many times watched this cheerful epilogue to the long drama of conquest and " colonialism ".

Still other parts of Africa claimed his services. With Ethiopia his contacts were at once diverse and dramatic. It will be remembered that when, in his moment of despair in 1887, he flung himself out of England, he first tried to fight with Italy against Ethiopia believing, in so far as he then had a mind to think, that he would at least die in the anti-slavery cause. When he revisited the country thirty-three years later in 1920 he was at the same time attracted by Hailé Selassie and appalled at the prevalence of slavery and the slave trade. Upon his return he wrote to Lord Milner, then Colonial Secretary, to suggest that Britain might cede Zeila in British Somaliland to Ethiopia with a strip of access to this port in return for a promise, its fulfilment supervised by British officers, that slave-raiding and trading should cease. With the hope of settling the Ethiopian-Italian dispute he revived this plan, quoting the authority of my brother-in-law Major Rayne, who

[1] F. D. Lugard, ' British Policy in Nigeria', *Africa*, vol. X, October, 1937.

had administered Zeila for years, to show that the strip was practically uninhabited.[1]

In the anti-slavery campaign Ethiopia continued to be one of the main areas under discussion.[2] But over-indulgence in righteous indignation, which is generally the mark of those who isolate an evil from its deeper causes, was never Lugard's habit. Therefore, surprisingly in a ruler so sensitive and so delicately placed, Hailé Selassie never lost the respect and friendship towards Lugard which began with their first meeting. In 1931 he even asked him to come out to Ethiopia and advise him about the abolition of slavery. Through Colonel Sandford,[3] as a mutual friend, the Emperor remained in close touch with him. Upon British advice, the Emperor appointed Mr. Frank de Halpert, of the Egyptian Service, as his adviser to the Minister of the Interior with special reference to the suppression of slavery and in 1932 he asked this officer to consult Lugard upon this and upon methods of inducing his nomad Gallas to take to a settled life. It was in long conversation in Lugard's study that we made close friends with de Halpert and learned much of contemporary Ethiopia. With his sympathetic understanding of the country it may be imagined with what a deep shock of horror Lugard took the Italian aggression of 1935. I had never seen the businesslike calm with which he handled his many projects broken as it was then by the anxiety and shame which we shared. He wrote a letter to *The Times* on July 30th 1935, in which he marshalled every argument against the aggression and in favour of a strong lead for international action by the government but his feelings broke through his reasoning in the sentence " England has her opportunity at Geneva—God grant that she may not lose it through craven fear of being great." His outburst would have been stronger if he could have known the cynicism with which the British Prime Minister was handling the affair.[4]

When all efforts to prevent the impending tragedy failed there was still one melancholy but highly important work in which he could help. Acting, as he had throughout, with Lord Noel-Buxton, he became chairman of a committee formed to organize a Red Cross

---

[1] *The Times*, 10 July 1935. [2] See, for example, Lugard's letter to *The Times*, 3 August 1934.
[3] Sandford, Brig. Daniel Arthur, C.B.E., D.S.O., 1882–   ; 1910–13 Sudan administration; 1914 H.M. Consul at Addis Ababa; 1920–36 resident in Abyssinia, farming; 1936–40 in England; 1940–1 in Ethiopia with patriot forces; 1941–6 in service of Ethiopian government; 1946 farming in Ethiopia.
[4] Amery, *My Political Life*, vol. iii, pp. 174-5.

Ambulance Service for the war. Dr. John Melly, who had already visited Ethiopia, agreed to go out in charge. As the Foreign Office banned any public appeal before the war started and as the Red Cross hesitated to help, the British Ambulance Service in Ethiopia had to be launched with private subscriptions solicited through the post. Lugard worked with all his strength on this enterprise, and continued to do so after the war started. After this the Red Cross took over and help could be evoked upon a national scale. But the immediate task did not divert him from continuing to study and to write memoranda about the future of the country. Of the Hoare-Laval pact he wrote to me, " I knew you would feel as I do, thoroughly disgusted and humiliated. It has been a perfect nightmare as though of some personal disaster . . . Hoare must have been a sick man to have wrecked his career by such action. The Public will never trust him again." Our friends Dr. Melly and de Halpert, who had joined him, were in the middle of it and we would read the grim news coming back from them. The Italians bombed their Red Cross camp. In the chaos which followed the Emperor's flight from the capital, before the Italians marched in, both men went out among the mobs of armed and drunken looters in the attempt to save life and restore order. Melly was killed and de Halpert narrowly escaped. It was in character, however, that, when the Italian victory was complete, Lugard was quick to accept the inevitable and to turn all his energies to help the refugees, and to try, with incomplete success, to insure proper treatment for the exiled Emperor and honours for those who had distinguished themselves in the Red Cross work. For, I think, the only time in our friendship he chided me for not being equally realistic and continuing a vain pursuit of the question of "sanctions". He maintained his contact with the Emperor largely through their mutual friend, the courageous and devoted Sandford, until Hailé Selassie's triumphant if costly return to his throne. After Lugard's death, the Emperor cabled to Major Lugard his sympathy " on the death of your brother, a great Englishman and valued friend of ours."

Another great public wrong which deeply affected Lugard and drew him into a long campaign to put it right was the massacre of the Assyrians in Iraq in 1933. He felt especially responsible for these brave people because he was a member of the Mandates Commission which had brought the Iraq Mandate to an end in 1932 after the fullest assurances from the High Commissioner that this Christian people, who had provided fine troops to support the mandatory power, should be fully protected. He showed the persistence of the Good Samaritan in that he never rested until he had worked upon this difficult task to the very end. He himself collected some hundreds of pounds in order to rush out supplies to the survivors. He went on to the executive of the Archbishop's Committee and supported the protracted attempts to find some new home for this people. Brazil, British Guiana, Nyasaland were all considered in vain. Finally the remnant of the Assyrians were settled in Syria.

The last group of Lugard's activities which must be selected from the many that cannot be covered in these two chapters were concerned with research. In his headlong journeys into an unmapped Africa and in the crowded years of governing which followed, he had had no time to study the societies which he had to administer. But at least he knew his own ignorance. It was as though he made a kind of pact with himself that when the opportunity came he would do all in his power to promote the most thorough possible study of African languages and cultures and to spread this knowledge, especially amongst colonial administrators.

There were three main bodies in this sphere with which he was connected. Two of these can be mentioned in brief. One was the International Colonial Institute, based upon Brussels, which brought the colonial experts of Western Europe together for conference and published large collections of official and other documents. This was hardly research but it was a serious Institute and it met Lugard's view that the colonial powers should meet and co-operate upon the highest level for the communication of their studies and their experience. He was therefore willing to help to build it up on the British side and to preside over an important session held in London in 1936. The next meeting was in Rome but Lugard refused to go there to preside because of his strong feelings about Italy's aggression in Ethiopia.

The second enterprise in this category was the African Research Survey. Lord Lothian, and Lionel Curtis and—one might say, of course—Dr. Oldham, were the prime movers in this enterprise which partly fulfilled the hopes Oldham had formed in the late 'twenties. Lugard became a member of the General Committee and attended all but one of its six meetings. I was drawn in on the fringe and remember

one week-end in the grand setting of Lord Lothian's place, Blickling
Hall, where we discussed the problems of Africa which seemed very
far away as we ate out of gold plate while the lights around us were
directed upon world-famous Holbeins and Van Dycks. The affair
showed another side of Lugard's character. It would have needed
very little original sin in a man of his position as *the* great ex-admini-
strator and authority upon Africa if he had shown some slight sense of
disinheritance at the irruption into his field of an administrator from
India—for the choice of researcher fell at last upon Lord Hailey—to
whom Africa was a virgin field. But Lugard quickly appreciated
Lord Hailey's almost superhuman powers of absorption and synthesis.
He at once put all his own knowledge completely at his service, sending for his use the draft chapters of his own immensely revised *Dual
Mandate.* He also drew up for the other's use lists of experts who could
help him and, at an early stage, Lord Hailey spent an arduous week-end
with him, along with myself and my friend, the late Hilda Matheson,
the able and beautiful secretary to the Survey.

Lugard was well qualified to help in what was to be a great work
because he had for six years been in charge of an Institute of African
research.

This was the International African Institute, called in its earlier years
the International Institute of African Languages and Cultures. It was
born from the concern of Dr. Oldham and some of his missionary
friends that scientific research should be directed towards what they
recognized as one of the major problems of their age, the penetration
of African society by European influence. They put linguistic studies,
with all the massive detailed work of recording and orthography, first
among their purposes and they linked this with research into African
social structure in a phase of dangerously rapid change. The Institute
was to be international in the fullest sense, a centre for world-wide
contact between scholars and for the promotion of research and
publication. Conceived in 1924 it came quickly into existence with
Lugard as its first chairman, Dr. Oldham as its Administrative Director
and, to complete the trio of friends and fellow-workers, Hanns Vischer
as its Secretary-General. All these posts were, of course, honorary.

It is almost impossible to sum up the achievements of an Institute of
this kind. It can be said, however, that it has actually carried out the
high hopes of its first conception. This is due to the unselfish labours of

many people in western Europe as well as Britain, but most of all, at this stage, to the three friends at the main base in London. They built their devotion to Africa and their thorough standards into the structure of the Institute.

It was a joy to see them at any of the larger functions of the Institute —Lugard, a little shy, a little aloof, combining courtesy with dignity and quite unconscious of the great reputation that gave him the primacy: Oldham, far-sighted, sharing, perhaps, with some eminent continental in a quiet corner his understanding of the depth of Africa's problems: Vischer, handsome, witty, cosmopolitan, circulating confidently in three languages amongst the mixed company and making everyone feel happier and more intelligent as they sparkled in the glow of his humanity.

Lugard remained chairman for nearly twenty years, resigning—as we shall see—only a few days before his death. He was, of course, a real working chairman throughout. As a member of the executive of the Institute, I was able to see his work at close quarters. This work was never confined to the office in London. All connected with the Institute would sooner or later find themselves at Little Parkhurst. The anthropologists would come to get his blessing both before and after they disappeared into the long seclusion of the African bush. He would read their typescripts and often write the foreword to their publications. Distinguished women were especially to the fore, among them Dr. Lucy Mair and Dr. Audrey Richards with the three Margarets (Drs. Wrong, Green and Read) and all would testify to his kindness and genuine interest.[1] The second world war cut across the work of the Institute but Lugard, Vischer and Oldham, with Edwin Smith as Editor of the Journal, kept the Institute alive in London in the face of all difficulties so that it was ready to make a quick return to full life at the coming of peace. But then Lugard was dead.

If the final years could be claimed as ones of steady co-operative achievement they held, in his view at least, one failure. This was the revision of *The Dual Mandate*. It will be best to give the account in his own words. The letter is undated, and it must have been written about 1942 or 1943.

---

[1] For an account of the Institute up to 1934 see Edwin Smith, ' The Story of the Institute', *Africa*, vol. VII, January 1934. For accounts of Lugard's work by Lord Hailey, Dr. Oldham and M. Perham see *Africa*, vol. XV, July 1945.

Working Alone

My dear Margery,

I feel that the time has come for ' realistic ' action with regard to my new *Dual Mandate* and, since you have shown such—may I say?— affectionate interest in it, here are my conclusions.

Soon after the publication of *The Dual Mandate* in 1922 I began to make notes for a new edition. This soon took shape as a practically new book. I worked hard and rapidly but I soon found that the earlier chapters was already out of date and required revision. This process was repeated several times. After my wife's death . . . I realized too late with intense remorse how I had allowed my absorption in this work to monopolise the time and thought I should have devoted to her. I need not dwell on the agony of mind in such thoughts. I found relief in concentration on the problems which *The Dual Mandate* presented. I began all over again and worked incessantly, though with many interruptions which com- pelled me to lay it aside for weeks (even months) at a time. It became the old process over again! Instead of shortening the volume it increased in size with the rapid changes in colonial affairs of the last 10 or 12 years. . . . The volume extends to some 1,000 pages. I realize that a book of this size is now an anachronism, especially after Hailey's survey . . . The time has come to realize that the task to which I have devoted myself for nearly 20 years has been a failure such as I have never before had to admit to myself. It remains to be seen whether any salvage can be got from the scrap-heap . . .

Yours affectionately
Fred.

He then went on in this letter to put the material entirely into my hands to use as I thought best.

What he wrote was true. I had watched him devoting every hour left to him by his many activities to this immense work. I had seen it become a growing task in ever-increasing circles as each time he revised to the end he had to go back to the beginning to put in new developments and new ideas. After Flora's death he had a secretary, Miss Violet Townshend, who lived in the house and worked devotedly until the end of his life. All serious students of contemporary Africa, with its rapid developments and new revelations of its problems, endure this strain of chasing hopelessly after the swift wheels of change. Lord Hailey, with his amazing capacity for work, has followed hard upon their revolutions by producing new volumes and editions. His work alone, as Lugard saw, was more than enough to make any similar publication within the same period impossible. But Lugard's material differs in character from Lord Hailey's and as it lies on my shelves losing current relevance it gains in historical value and the time may come when, in whole or in part, his thorough work will find fulfilment in meeting the needs of students, and not least those of the new African nations. For most of these their brief recorded history, as distinct from tribal tradition, begins with the colonial period and the ideas and the work of those who handled them at this formative period must, when they have recovered from their first aversion from this phase of subjection, provide some of its earliest and most important chapters.

As the 'thirties wore on and voices from Germany became more menacing Lugard was drawn into one of his last controversies. There were some public men in Britain who felt that a colonial sop to the Cerberus in Berlin might prevent its bark from becoming a bite. There were others, Labour and Liberal men, who thought that some extension of international control might assuage the jealousy of the non-colonial powers. It was partly as an answer to these attitudes that the Colonial Empire Union was formed in 1937 with Lugard as its chairman.[1] He met the half-confessed sense of fear and guilt with the quiet voice of knowledge, and with three of the main ideas which had governed his public life. The first was his faith that, with all its faults, British administration was the best for the colonial peoples and that it would be a breach of faith to hand them over like chattels to another and less experienced nation. Secondly, pointing out the small proportion of world trade with Africa, the continent to be used in appeasement, he argued that what was needed was equal access. He had always advocated the "open door" which had recently been abandoned by Britain, and he believed that it would be within the powers of the Mandates Commission, which he did not wish to see stretched beyond its competence, to supervise. Thirdly, according to another almost life-long principle, he argued that Africa should not be regarded as an area of settlement. The Africans were densely crowded in the favourable parts and would need room for expansion.[2]

[1] *The Crown Colonist*, July 1937.
[2] See, among many other of his writings and speeches at this time, Parliamentary Debates (Lords), 25 March 1936, V. 100. 113-6, and 17 February 1937, V. 104. 184-9; 'The Basis of the Claim to Colonies', *International Affairs*, Vol. XV, No. 1, 1936; 'Some Colonial Problems of Today', *United Empire*, December 1936.

CHAPTER XXXIII

THE END OF THE LIFE

THE CHIEF activities and ideas of Lugard in the years of his so-called retirement have been described. It remains only to see him more closely, as I was able to see him myself in the years from 1931 when I was in constant touch with him.

The contact was possible because after my return, in 1930, from two years of travel, mainly in Africa, I went to live near him. My brother-in-law, Major H. Rayne, and my sister, both of whom had spent their working lives in Africa, bought a farm at Shere. I joined them there as far as research appointments in Oxford permitted. From our farm to Little Parkhurst was only some seven miles by road and it was even less to ride there along the fine Surrey escarpment and through the Abinger woods. I would put my horse in Lugard's garage and settle down in his study to discuss colonial affairs, the several organizations to which we both belonged, his current writing or mine and, perhaps, draw up some project for action. He would bring out all his latest papers, press cuttings, letters and so on, all carefully classified and docketed. Flora's photograph dominated his desk. A rare antelope skin lay before the fire. His largest ivory trophy was on one wall. On another was Chamberlain's portrait, affectionately signed. In the afternoons tea would be brought in at the elegant hour of five by a perfectly uniformed housemaid and placed on the table, the heavily embroidered Chinese cloth, the egg-shell tea cups and the perfect tea recalling his period in Hong Kong. In a grave and competent ritual, Lugard would himself make the tea from the boiling silver kettle, heating each cup with the water before pouring out the tea. Often I spent the day there or came for the night, especially when governors, officials or politicians came to discuss colonial matters. He would meet you at the door and hurry up the stairs with your suitcase. Dinner was formal—I need hardly say that he dressed every night—but not a moment was wasted in small-talk. Indeed, he had none of that useful currency. The guests were all there on serious business, and after dinner we would sit far into the night in his study talking hard and always with some definite action in view. And when at last we went to bed, he would go back to his big desk and work on into the small hours.

It was hard to identify the Lugard of the nineteen-thirties with the Lugard of the eighteen-nineties or indeed of the first two decades of this century. The fierce combativeness, the thrust of ambition, the furious chafing against control, local or distant, the bitter sense of frustration, the faults due to impatience and wrongheadedness which this record has not hidden—all these were gone. From being a fighting governor he stepped down to be a co-operative citizen, the friend and partner of all who came his way, except such few open egotists or careerists as he happened to encounter. The old lion, whose younger eyes look so hungry for action in the frontispiece of the first volume, had seemingly become as gentle and beneficent as one of the four couchant beasts which square the Nelson monument. I saw a hint of the old flash, with swift action to follow, only upon two occasions when he showed the door to men who had transgressed his code of manners, which was a code of character. All who came near him warmed themselves in this Indian summer of his kindness, from his many friends to the London refugees, who crowded his house at the outbreak of war and the servants who, in spite of the isolation of his house, stayed with him until their death or his. "His Lordship", wrote Miss Florence Robinson, who had been Flora's personal maid, "was the kindest gentleman and I am very proud that he counted me as one of his friends. I never knew him to be angry, he was always anxious for our comfort and to give us pleasure; he often sent us to places of amusement. He allowed all of us to have friends to stay. His Lordship seldom rang a bell to give an order; he would do any-thing to save us trouble although it was such a pleasure to us to do the smallest thing for him." Flora had bidden Robinson serve her widowed husband and after his death she worked with his elder sister and his brother Edward until he too died. One British N.C.O., who had served under him at the time of the Borgu operations of 1898 against the French, told me that in the forty-seven years which followed he had received nearly 200 letters from Lugard in answer to his own, and some of these brought him help for the education of his son.

Lugard's relations with me were, of course, inseparable from our mutual interests and work, and I was therefore deeply touched by the purely personal friendship he formed with my sister. Her daughter and three sons were all involved in the war and, though at this stage of his life he had no surplus of time or energy, he entered deeply into her anxieties and troubles with selfless understanding.

He never seemed to grow old. There was never anything of the pathos of age about him. His soldier's figure remained taut and square-shouldered. Remembering the man he had been, his modesty was as surprising as his gentleness. It is not always easy, and it certainly was not in his day, for a colonial governor, who is in truth a little king in his territory, to adjust himself to almost anonymous absorption in the ordinary life of his country and to exchange the dignities and comforts of Government House for a small private household. But Lugard had no pretensions. His dignity had not been put on with his uniform and it was not lost when this was put away.

To his family, of course, he turned the gentle side of his nature in full as he had from his earliest youth. That unity which bound together the little group under their mother in the cheap house in York was preserved unbroken to the very end. His sisters and his brother in their old age came to live as near to him as they could. Edward built a small house, Furzen Wood, a mile or two away at Abinger Common. No stranger who came to Little Parkhurst could have guessed the relationship between the brothers. Lugard would ignore Edward or give him gruff orders. But, as this book will have shown, this manner hid the devotion of eighty years. Edward had given almost his whole life to serve his brother. If he had not been a devout Christian it might have been said that he had made him his God, an attitude he once admitted to me that Lugard himself came very near to showing towards Flora. Each year, upon Edward's birthday, the elder brother, himself not rich, would send a cheque to the much less rich younger brother, and with it a letter in which he was able to put on paper some of the affection which he could never speak. Edward would acknowledge the gift with a similar unspoken revelation. After Lugard's death Edward continued his service by his work of sifting and re-ordering the vast mass of his brother's papers, with something not far from the reverence of a priest handling a sacrament.

It is usual, and surely forgivable, for the eminent aged to value the prestige they have won from capacities they no longer possess. This was not true of Lugard partly, perhaps, because he never ceased to work all and every day. His chief service now was the influence he wielded with and through others behind the scenes. On the public side he was always in request—to speak, to write, above all, to preside. While he did all and, indeed, too much that was asked of him, in his own words he " took small stock " of all this. By contrast his appreciation of others was sometimes absurdly generous and, applied to oneself, made one feel almost ridiculous. When, for example, I naturally wanted to dedicate my book on Nigeria to him, a book in which he himself made a large figure, he wrote:

> " I would like you to know how deeply I appreciate your thought of dedicating your book to me. I am very lame of speech and it is only the *wrong* thing that I ever express well but that you should have thought me worthy of the dedication is a memory I shall value. If I have seemed indifferent and even urged you to suppress references to me it is not that I undervalued *your* opinion, but because I felt that my part has been much over-recognized, and the Public are sick of hearing my name put forward as a " great Administrator " and the rest of it as though you and Cameron and others had not carried it to much further fruition than I ever did and taught me most of what I now preach. Well, enough of this! You are very imperious." (L. to M.P., 16 January 1936).

There is no embarrassment in quoting a compliment so absurd that all the credit goes to the writer.

The outbreak of war added to the stress of an old age passed in ceaseless work. The thick woods around his house were stacked with ammunition cases and there were some severe explosions of these. A plane fell in flames not far way. Towards the end of the war a " doodle-bug " exploded close to the house, flying bombs fell near and one destroyed the church at Abinger. These things, of course, had no effect upon the old soldier. Much more serious, the constant journeys to London were increasingly slow and uncomfortable as roads or railways were bombed; London itself became a more difficult place; food, service, light and heat diminished. Lugard seemed, though now in his 'eighties, not to notice these new burdens. His routine went on as before. He worked at his desk in a rug and wearing mittens, refusing an electric fire, and sent his elder sister into the garden to collect gum from the plum-trees so that he could make use of old envelopes. Nor was his work now mere routine. As late as January 10th, 1945, looking forward to the position of colonies after the war, a signed article by him appeared in *The Times* upon "A World Colonial Charter: the Welfare and Development of Dependent Peoples". In this he set the new and much more positive determination to help the Colonies against the historical background.

The end was in character with all the rest. Though some of his tasks diminished, many were carried right through the war, the most arduous being the Bank and the African Institute. He repeatedly tried to resign from the latter but no suitable man could be found who would take it over. Lord Harlech, Lord Hailey, Professor Coupland, Dr. Oldham, all declined. And so long as he was chairman he would not relax the efforts needed not only to maintain the Institute but to re-organize it as the end of the war seemed to be in sight. On February 3rd, 1945, his younger sister died and he brought his elder sister to live in his house. On February 19th Sir Hanns Vischer died. It was a deep personal shock as well as the loss of his mainstay at the Institute. Worn and distressed he struggled up to Newport Pagnell for the funeral. It was bitterly cold. Lady Vischer told me in a recent letter how in a kind of daze he sat " disconsolately upon the stairs, a true picture of grief. Twice I had to plead with him to come and sit with us in the library." During the next weeks he was in London for the Bank, for the memorial service to Vischer, but, above all, for the long business of re-organizing the Institute with new staff and going through its finances.

At last Lord Hailey, though himself a very busy man, agreed to succeed him. On March 28th, therefore, after having lunch together in London, Lugard and I went on together to a meeting of the Institute Bureau at which he was to preside for the last time before handing over. It was a very long meeting, lasting from three in the afternoon until twenty to six. It was also, most unhappily, a contentious one. He was worried about the large changes needed and made proposals which some of us, including myself, felt obliged to oppose. I could see that he was tired, though I did not realize *how* tired, and it was painful to increase the strain by opposition. After the meeting we went out into the familiar Lower Regent Street, where Florence Nightingale stood on her plinth close to the Institute offices. This was still black war-time London and for long there was no taxi to be had. It was an effort for him to catch his train and to make the cold, slow, dark journey back to Leith Hill.

He was not only tired but feeling deeply the loss of the Institute. On the two days following the meeting, he wrote a sheaf of letters—many in his own hand. He must have written all day long. The letters, or those of them that I can trace, went out to Nigeria, to a Hausa editor; to Belgium about the International Colonial Institute, and to my sister, to whom he was so much attached. He wrote to the new Director of the Institute, Professor Daryll Forde, and to the Secretary, Mrs. Wyatt, to thank them for all their arrangements; to Lord Hailey, to thank him for taking on the chairmanship, and to Professor Coupland. " I need not say," he wrote to him, " that it is a great wrench to give up what has been one of the chief interests of my life for the past 20 years." He must have answered Dr. Edwin Smith, the editor of the Journal, who wrote to him on March 29th, about an article he was to contribute, in a letter which ended, " I am sure you realized the heaviness of our hearts yesterday. To some of us the Institute can never be quite the same again without you to lead us." Dr. Oldham had also written to him the night after the meeting that " my feelings were so deep that I felt that any expression of them would be inadequate. What you have done for the African Institute cannot be measured and the association with you in its work for a period of years is among the happiest memories of my life." Lugard replied on March 30th that he was deeply moved by the letter and added three detailed pages about the work of the Institute for the future and finished up " This is my 'swan song' to my old colleagues and the reins are now in other—and very capable—hands, with new and illimitable opportunity if rightly used."

On April 1st he wrote to me in a hand in which there was no change from the old firm neat lines. I had come away from the meeting very unhappy with the sense that I had felt obliged to hurt him by my opposition at a sad and critical moment and I dreaded to open the envelope. I should have had more faith. The letter was full of affection and trust, of apologies for having been dull and distracted at our lunch together and of detailed enquiries about members of my family,

which was then somewhat stricken by the war, about my sister who
was ill, and about my own health. We were both to come in a few
days to stay with him, and he was promising to look after us well.
Most of the letter, which is probably the last he wrote, is too personal
for quotation. But some sentences can be given. He was finding
excuses for me for my not having written to him very often of late:

> " Oxford seems as far off as the West Indies [where I had recently been]
> and letter writing is tedious and takes up time which can't be spared from
> important work. I, too, have been pressed with work but without any
> useful result and I am increasingly conscious of the ineffectiveness which
> age brings with it and one must learn the meaning of ' acceptance ' as
> my dear wife used to say. You say I have too rigid standards and have
> adopted Lord Strafford's motto. What was it?[1] My dear mother taught
> me as a child that the verse in the Bible—'Whatever thy hand findest to do,
> do it with all thy might " should be the right motto and I have tried to
> adopt it. I must not write more now.
>
> Very affectionately yours,
Fred."

With this letter the story ends, as it began, with his mother and the
Christian training with which she had formed his character.

The next day, April 2nd, he was taken ill and remained unconscious
until he died on April 11th. He was in his eighty-seventh year.

This record of his life has been full and all those qualities which
sound so trite when listed—courage, endurance, industry, the capacity
to love—have been shown in action. But the whole was held together
within a quality for which it is not easy to find a word. " Order ",
" constancy " come to mind. All his actions seem to be within a
framework. Nothing was wasted, no efforts were spilled, no openings
given for irrelevant intrusions from outside. The two exceptions are
the great emotional catastrophe of his youth, though even that was
only a brief breakaway from the order of his life, and itself led him
quickly back to even more famous work. The other was the long and
surely ill-judged pursuit of his Scheme for continuous administration
into which his devotion to Flora led him. I have known no one else
who walked so closely along the line of a sustained purpose. He was
all of a piece, sincere in the real meaning of the word, solid marble
with no faking mixture of wax. Up to the end many people could

---

[1] ' Thorough '.

have echoed the exclamation made by Edward's wife when her brother-in-law was suddenly called away to leave them in the heart of Ngamiland, that when he was there " there was a feeling of someone so strong behind."

Because of this standing foursquare in his own strength, in every meeting with others he seemed always to be the giver and not the taker. Perhaps it was because of this, though he was not an orthodox believer, that Mrs. Oldham, who knew him so long and intimately and who, with her husband, must have met more devoted Christians than most people, wrote to Edward Lugard some months after his brother's death that she and her husband " have often thought and said to each other that in Lord Lugard, as in few others, we were conscious of the presence of Christ . . . To us his life was an inspiration."

His life all the years I knew him was just work and friendship, the two interlocked. The work was for Africa, or rather for Africans, and such others as needed his services. He would fear that Africans—at least some Africans—were being deprived of land, overtaxed, forced to labour, enslaved, given faulty education, maladministered through ignorance. These things must not be done anywhere but, above all, not by Britain. But they must be stopped not by emotional or doctrinaire protests, which sometimes relieve the feelings or promote the political interests of the protestor more than they assist the unfortunate. His remedial action was by quiet tireless work, by persuasion and instruction, in newspapers, in conversation, in memoranda, in committees, in the House of Lords, bringing every issue back to the principles of British justice, and with every argument based upon all the facts of the case.

The work of his twenty-six years of retirement seem to have been at least as effective in their different way as those of his fifty years of fighting, annexing, and governing. But such reckonings are, of course, too facile. There can be no precise assessment of the impact of his character, as a, perhaps *the*, chief figure in the sphere of British colonial affairs, upon the immense number of people, British and others, who, personally or indirectly, came into touch with him. And this during the several decades when the colonial empire rose to the height of its power and extent and began, if not to decline, to change its nature from domination to service. The peoples who are in the stage of a passionate recoil from subjection and who need a spring-board against which to find the impulse for their leap into independence have built up the concepts of imperialism. It has been constructed both of fact and of fancy. Perhaps there is no better method of discerning the proportions of these two constituents than by studying the actions and the character of this great imperialist.

List of Sources

I. UNPUBLISHED MATERIAL

A. OFFICIAL PAPERS

Colonial Office Records; at the Public Record Office.
Foreign Office Records; at the Public Record Office.

B. PRIVATE PAPERS

Anti-Slavery and Aborigines Protection Society; at Rhodes House Library, Oxford.
Chamberlain Papers, by kind permission of Mr. Julian Amery.
Church Missionary Society Papers; at C.M.S. Headquarters, 6 Salisbury Square, London, by kind permission of the Secretary.
Harcourt Papers; at Stanton Harcourt, by kind permission of Viscount Harcourt.
Holt Papers; at John Holt & Co., Liverpool, by kind permission of Mr. Cecil Holt.
Lugard Papers; at Rhodes House Library, Oxford.
Nicholson Papers; in the possession of Miss Perham.
Oldham Papers, by kind permission of Dr. J. H. Oldham.

II. PUBLISHED MATERIAL

A. OFFICIAL

Parliamentary Debates (Hansard).
Parliamentary Papers:

> C.7596 *Report of the Administration of the Niger Coast Protectorate 1891–4* (1895), C.7596. lxxi. 1.
>
> C.7977 *Report by Sir John Kirk on Disturbances at Brass.* Africa No. 3 (1896), C.7977. lix. 361.
>
> C.9372 *Papers relating to the Revocation of the Royal Niger Company's Charter and to the Government of the Niger Districts* (1899), C.9372. lxiii. 417.

List of Sources

C.9388 *Report on the Subject of the Insurrection in Sierra Leone Protectorate, 1898* (1899), C.9388. lx. 1.

Cd.1433 *Northern Nigeria; Correspondence relating to Kano* (1903), Cd.1433. xlv. 787.

Cd.2099 *Correspondence Relating to the Resignation of Sir Charles Eliot and to the Concession to the East African Syndicate* (1904), Cd.2099. lxii. 523.

Cd.3620 *Northern Nigeria; Correspondence relating to Sokoto, Hadeija and the Munshi Country* (1907), Cd.3620. lvii. 73.

Cd.4906 *Report of the Committee of Inquiry into the Liquor Trade of Southern Nigeria* (1909), Cd.4906. lx. 497.

Cd.6448 *Report of the British Delegates to the International Opium Conference held at The Hague, December 1911–January 1912* (1912), Cd.6448. lxviii. 743.

Cd.8247 *Report of a Committee on Edible and Oil Producing Nuts and Seeds* (1916), Cd.8247. iv. 15.

Cmd.468 *Report by Sir F. D. Lugard on the Amalgamation of Northern and Southern Nigeria and Administration, 1912–1919* (1919), Cmd. 468. xxxvi. 609.

Cmd.1922 *Memorandum on Indians in Kenya* (1923), Cmd.1922. xviii. 141.

Cmd.2374 *Educational Policy in British Tropical Africa* (1925), Cmd.2374. xxi. 27.

Cmd.2387 *Report of the East Africa Commission* (1925), Cmd.2387. ix. 855.

Cmd.2904 *Future Policy in Regard to Eastern Africa* (1927), Cmd.2904. xviii. 37.

Cmd.3234 *Report of the Commission on Closer Union of the Dependencies in Eastern and Central Africa* (1929), Cmd.3234. v. 353.

Cmd.3378 *Report of Sir Samuel Wilson on his Visit to East Africa, 1929* (1929), Cmd.3378. viii. 551.

Cmd.3573 *Memorandum on Native Policy in East Africa* (1930), Cmd.3573. xxiii. 105.

Cmd.3574 *Statement of the Conclusions of His Majesty's Government in the United Kingdom as regards Closer Union in East Africa* (1930), Cmd.3574. xxiii. 85.

Joint Committee on Closer Union in East Africa (1931), Vol. I. Report with Proceedings of the Committee. Vol. II. Minutes of Evidence and Index. Vol. III. Appendices, Sess. No. 156. vii. 1.

Cmd.4093 *Report by the Financial Commissioner on Certain Questions in Kenya* (1932), Cmd.4093. vi. 545.

List of Sources

Cmd.4556 *Report of the Kenya Land Commission* (1934), Cmd.4556. x. 229.

Cmd.4623 *Report of the Commission of Inquiry into the Administration of Justice in Kenya, Uganda and the Tanganyika Territory in Criminal Matters* (1934) Cmd.4623. ix. 653.

Cmd.5949 *Rhodesia - Nyasaland Royal Commission Report* (1939), Cmd.5949. xv. 211.

Other official material:

Correspondence (1899–1901) Relating to the Administration of Lagos and Nigeria (1902), African West No. 580, Confidential Print, L.P.

Correspondence (May 1913 to January 1914) relating to the Amalgamation of Northern and Southern Nigeria (1914), African (West) No. 1005, Confidential Print, L.P.

Northern Provinces [Nigeria], *Native Administration Estimates* 1918 (Lagos).

Report on the Eastern Provinces by the Secretary for Native Affairs (S. N. Grier), Lagos, 1922.

Report on a Tour of the Eastern Provinces by the Assistant Secretary for Native Affairs (G. Tomlinson), Lagos, 1923.

The Constitution of Kenya and the Federation of the East African Dependencies (1927), African (East) No. 1112, Confidential Print, L.P.

Native Courts Commission of Enquiry, Reports on the Northern, Western and Eastern Regions (Lagos, 1952).

ANNUAL REPORTS

Northern Nigeria

1900–01:	Cd.788–16 (1902) lxv. 473.
1901:	Cd.1388–1 (1903) xliii. 345.
1902:	Cd.1768–14 (1904) lviii. 153.
1903:	Cd.2238–14 (1905) lii. 253.
1904:	Cd.2684–22 (1906) lxxiv. 723.
1905–6:	Cd.3285–3 (1907) liv. 91.
1906–7:	Cd.3729–15 (1908) lxix. 243.
1907–8:	Cd.4448–3 (1909) lviii. 115.
1908–9:	Cd.4964–7 (1910) lxiv. 771.
1909:	Cd.5467–10 (1911) li. 601.
1910–11:	Cd.6007–4 (1912–13) lviii. 197.
1911:	Cd.6007–38 (1912–13) lviii. 245.
1912:	Cd.7050–26 (1914) lviii. 245.

List of Sources

Southern Nigeria

1899–1900:	Cd.431–7 (1901) xlv. 727.
1900:	Cd.788–23 (1902) lxv. 513.
1901:	Cd.1388–5 (1903) xliii. 381.
1902:	Cd.1768–10 (1904) lvii. 271.
1903:	Cd.2238–10 (1905) lii. 297.
1904:	Cd.2684–5 (1906) lxxv. 1.
1905:	Cd.2684–58 (1906) lxxv. 131.
1906:	Cd.3729–18 (1908) lxix. 347.
1907:	Cd.3729–47 (1908) lxix. 499.
1908:	Cd.4964–4 (1910) lxiv. 803.
1909:	Cd.5467–1 (1911) li. 631.
1910:	Cd.5467–31 (1911) li. 671.
1911:	Cd.6007–38 (1912–13) lviii. 287.
1912:	Cd.7050–23 (1914) lviii. 285.
1913:	Cd. 7622–16 (1914–16) xliv. 259.

Nigeria

1915: Cd.8434–7 (1917–18) xxii. 503.
1916: Cd.8434–33 (1917–18) xxii. 537.
1917: Cmd.1–31 (1919) xxxv. 545.

Hong Kong

1906: Cd.3285–8 (1907) liii. 649.
1907: Cd.3729–34 (1908) lxviii. 937.
1908: Cd.4448–26 (1909) lvii. 501.
1909: Cd.4964–33 (1910) lxiv. 549.
1910: Cd.5467–27 (1911) li. 421.
1911: Cd.6007–23 (1912–13) lvii. 725.
1912: Cd.7050–3 (1914) lviii. 23.

Proceedings of Lagos Legislative Council
Proceedings of Hong Kong Legislative Council
Proceedings of the Nigerian Council

B. Books Mentioned in the Text

Lord Altrincham, *Kenya's Opportunity* (1955).
L. S. Amery, *My Political Life, vol. iii* (1955).
E. J. Arnett, ed., *The Rise of the Sokoto Fulani* (Lagos 1922).
S. H. Bailey, The Anti-Drug Campaign, *An Experiment in International Control* (1936).

List of Sources

H. BARTH, *Travels and Discoveries in North and Central Africa* (1857).

P. T. BAUER, *West African Trade* (1954).

G. K. A. BELL, *Randall Davidson* (1952).

E. MOBERLY BELL, *Flora Shaw, (Lady Lugard, D.B.E.)* (1947).

J. H. BELLOC, *The Modern Traveller* (1898).

S. O. BIOBAKU, *The Egba and their Neighbours 1842–1872* (1957).

A. BOISRAGON, *The Benin Massacre* (1897).

E. W. BOVILL, *Caravans of the Old Sahara* (1933).

K. M. BUCHANAN and J. C. PUGH, *Land and People in Nigeria* (1955).

R. L. BUELL, *The Native Problem in Africa* (New York, 1928).

CHARLES BULLER, *Mr. Mother-Country of the Colonial Office* (1840).

A. C. BURNS, *History of Nigeria* (5th edition, 1955).

SIR ALAN BURNS, *Colonial Civil Service* (1949).

SIR DONALD CAMERON, *My Tanganyika Service and Some Nigeria* (1939).

VALENTINE CHIROL, *Indian Unrest* (1910).

W. S. CHURCHILL, *The River War* (eds. 1899, 1902, 1933).

F. LE GROS CLARK (and others), *The New West Africa* (1953) ed. B. Davidson
and A. Ademola.

JAMES S. COLEMAN, *Nigeria: Background to Nationalism* (California, 1958).

A. N. COOK, *British Enterprise in Nigeria* (Philadelphia, 1943).

SIR JULIAN CORBETT, *History of the Great War*, vol. i, Naval Operations (1920).

SIR R. COUPLAND, *Wilberforce* (1923).

    Kirk on the Zambesi (1928).

    East Africa and her Invaders (1938).

    The Exploitation of East Africa, 1856–90 (1939)

    Zulu Battlepiece, Isandhlwana (1948).

W. R. CROCKER, *Nigeria: A Critique of British Colonial Administration* (1936).

L. CURTIS and M. PERHAM, *The Protectorates of South Africa* (1935).

D. DENHAM, H. CLAPPERTON and W. OUDNEY, *Travels and Discoveries in
North and Central Africa in 1822, 1823 and 1824* (1831).

K. O. DIKE, *Trade and Politics in the Niger Delta, 1830–1885* (1956).

G. B. ENDACOTT, *A History of Hong Kong* (1958).

SIR GEORGE FIDDES, *The Dominions and Colonial Offices* (1926).

JOHN E. FLINT, *Sir George Goldie and the Making of Nigeria* (1960).

DARYLL FORDE and G. I. JONES, *The Ibo and Ibibio-Speaking Peoples of South-
Eastern Nigeria*, Ethnographic Survey of Africa: Western Africa, Part
III (1950).

DARYLL FORDE, *The Yoruba-Speaking Peoples of South-Western Nigeria*,
Ethnographic Survey of Africa: Western Africa, Part IV (1951).

SIR JAMES FRAZER, *The Golden Bough* (1890).

ARTHUR GAITSKELL, *Gezira* (1959).

List of Sources

J. L. GARVIN, *The Life of Joseph Chamberlain*, vol. iii (1934).

SIR NEVILL GEARY, *Nigeria under British Rule* (1927).

G. P. GOOCH and H. TEMPERLEY ed., *British Documents on the Origin of the War*, vol. i (1927).

E. H. GORGES, *The Great War in West Africa*, n.d.

M. M. GREEN, *Ibo Village Affairs* (1947).

VISCOUNT GREY OF FALLODON, *Twenty Five Years, 1892–1916* (1925).

EARL GREY, *The Colonial Policy of the Administration of Lord John Russell* (1853).

W. K. HANCOCK, *Survey of British Commonwealth Affairs*, Volume II, Part I (1940), Part II (1942).

LORD HAILEY, *African Survey, Revised 1956* (1957).
Native Administration in the British African Territories (1951).

H. DUNCAN HALL, *Mandates, Dependencies and Trusteeship* (1948).

K. D. D. HENDERSON, *The Making of the Modern Sudan* (1943).

E. HUXLEY and M. PERHAM, *Race and Politics in Kenya* (eds. 1944 and 1957).

H. INGRAMS, *Hong Kong* (1952).

International Bank for Reconstruction and Development, *The Economic Development of Nigeria* (Baltimore, 1955).

D. JARDINE, *The Mad Mullah of Somaliland* (1923).

W. I. JENNINGS and D. W. LOGAN, *A Report on the University of Hong Kong 1953* (1953).

T. JESSE JONES, *Education in Africa* (New York, 1922).

A. L. KENNEDY, *Salisbury* (1953).

MARY KINGSLEY, *West African Studies* (1899).

R. & J. LANDER, *Journal of an Expedition to the Niger* (1832).

W. E. LANGER, *The Diplomacy of Imperialism* (2nd edition, New York, 1951).

NORMAN LEYS, *Kenya* (1924).

LI CHIEN-NUNG, *The Political History of China 1840–1928* (New York, 1956).

W. P. LIVINGSTONE, *Mary Slessor of Calabar*, (46th edition, 1935).

SIR CHARLES LUCAS, *The Empire at War* (1924), vol. iv, Africa.

HERBERT MACAULAY, *Justitia Fiat; The Moral Obligation of British Government to the House of Docemo of Lagos* (Lagos, 1921).

A. McPHEE, *The Economic Revolution in West Africa* (1926).

ARTHUR MAYHEW, *Education in Tropical Africa* (1938).

C. K. MEEK, *A Sudanese Kingdom* (1931).
Law and Authority in a Nigerian Tribe (1937).

W. R. MILLER, *Reflections of a Pioneer* (1936).
Yesterday, Today and Tomorrow in Northern Nigeria (1938).
Have we failed in Nigeria? (1947).
Success in Nigeria? Assets and Possibilities (1948).

List of Sources

P. E. MITCHELL, *African Afterthoughts* (1954).

History of the Great War based on official documents, *Military Operations, Togoland and the Cameroons, 1914–18* (1931), compiled by F. J. Moberly.

E. D. MOREL, *Nigeria, its Peoples and Problems* (1912).

A. VICTOR MURRAY, *The School in the Bush* (1929).

C. R. NIVEN, *A Short History of Nigeria* (1937).

J. H. OLDHAM and B. D. GIBSON, *The Remaking of Man in Africa* (1937).

R. OLIVER, *The Missionary Factor in East Africa* (1952).

C. W. ORR, *The Making of Northern Nigeria* (1911).

H. R. PALMER, *The Bornu Sahara and Sudan* (1936).

G. PARRINDER, *Religion in an African City* (1953).

MARGERY PERHAM, ed. *Ten Africans* (1935).

Native Administration in Nigeria (1937).

ed. Daryll Forde and Richenda Scott, *The Native Economies of Nigeria* (1946).

ed. P. A. Bower, A. J. Brown, C. Leubuscher, J. Mars and Sir Alan Pim, *Mining, Commerce and Finance in Nigeria* (1948).

Lugard, the Years of Adventure (1956).

C. H. ROBINSON, *Hausaland* (1896).

W. McGREGOR ROSS, *Kenya from Within* (1927).

J. ROWNTREE, *The Imperial Drug Trade* (1905).

C. G. SELIGMAN, *Egypt and Negro Africa: A Study in Divine Kingship* (1934).

M. F. SMITH, *Baba of Karo* (1954).

ROBERT STANDISH, *The Three Bamboos* (1942).

D. S. STENNING, *Savannah Nomads* (1959).

C. L. TEMPLE, *Native Races and their Rulers* (Cape Town, 1918).

MRS. C. L. TEMPLE, *Notes on the Tribes, Provinces, Emirates and States of Northern Nigeria* (Lagos, 1922).

The Letters of Queen Victoria, Third Series 1886–1901, ed. G. E. Buckle, vol. iii (1930–2).

A. J. TOYNBEE, ed. *Survey of International Affairs 1925*, vol. i, *The Islamic World* (1927).

A. TUTUOLA, *The Palm Wine Drinkard* (1952).

Simbi and the Satyr of the Dark Jungle (1955).

S. VANDELEUR, *Campaigning on the Upper Nile and Niger* (1898).

D. F. W. VAN REES, *Les Mandats Internationaux* (Paris, 1927).

BEATRICE WEBB, *Diaries 1924–32* (1956).

CHAIM WEIZMANN, *Trial and Error* (1949).

DOROTHY WELLESLEY, *Sir George Goldie, Founder of Nigeria* (1934).

FREDA WHITE, *Mandates* (1926).

SIR J. WILLCOCKS, *From Kabul to Kumassi* (1904).

List of Sources

E. T. WILLIAMS, *A Short History of China* (New York, 1928).
CHARLES WILSON, *The History of Unilever* (1954).
P. WOODRUFF, *The Men who ruled India: The Guardians* (1954).
LEONARD WOOLF, *Empire and Commerce in Africa* (1920).
Record of the Overseas Contingent, Nigeria Regiment, West African Frontier Force, December 1916–June 1917, privately printed, Lagos, n.d.

C. ARTICLES MENTIONED IN THE TEXT

WILLIAM BASCOM, 'Urbanization among the Yoruba', *American Journal of Sociology*, vol. LX, March 1955.
S. O. BIOBAKU, 'Historical Sketch of Egba Traditional Authorities', *Africa*, vol. XXII, January 1952.
LORD HAILEY, DR. OLDHAM, and M. PERHAM, Tributes, *Africa*, vol. XV, July 1945.
P. C. LLOYD, 'The Traditional Political System of the Yoruba', *South Western Journal of Anthropology*, vol. X, Winter 1954.
'The Yoruba Lineage', *Africa*, vol. XXV, July 1955.
'The Development of Political Parties in Western Nigeria', *American Political Science Review*, vol. XLIX, September 1955.
F. LUGARD, 'The Liquor Traffic in Africa', *The Nineteenth Century*, vol. XLII, November 1897.
'The New African Crisis with France and Germany', *Blackwoods Magazine*, vol. CLVI, July 1894.
'Northern Nigeria', *Geographical Journal*, vol. XXIII, January 1904.
'British Policy in Nigeria', *Africa*, vol. X, October 1937.
LADY LUGARD, 'Nigeria', *Journal of the Royal Society of Arts*, vol. LII, 18 March 1904.
'West African Negroland', *Journal of the Royal Colonial Institute*, vol. XXV, June 1904.
SIR RICHMOND PALMER, 'Some Observations on Captain Rattray's Papers', *Journal of the African Society*, vol. XXXIII, January 1934.
FLORA SHAW, 'The Story of Zebehr Pasha', *The Contemporary Review*, vol. LII, September–November 1887.
EDWIN SMITH, 'The Story of the Institute', *Africa*, vol. VII, January 1934.

LORD LUGARD'S WORKS

Books
The Rise of Our East African Empire, 2 vols. (1893).
The Story of the Uganda Protectorate (1901).

List of Sources

Political Memoranda, Revision of instructions to political officers on subjects chiefly political and administrative, 1913–18 (1919).
The Dual Mandate in British Tropical Africa (eds. 1922, 1923, 1926, 1929).
Representative Forms of Government and 'Indirect Rule' in British Africa (1928).

Articles

(Lord Lugard's writings and speeches were so numerous and were reproduced in so many different forms that it is impossible, in spite of every effort, to claim that this list is complete. Many lectures and broadcasts did not appear in print.)

1889

'Coercive Measures for Suppression of the Slave Trade' (London, 1889).
'Lake Nyassa and Central Africa', *Manchester Geographical Society Journal*, vol. V, 1889.
'Nyassa-land and its Commercial Possibilities', *Proceedings of The British Association*, 42nd meeting, section E. 1889.
'The Fight Against Slave-Traders', *The Contemporary Review*, vol. LVI, 1889.

1890

'A Glimpse of Lake Nyassa', *Blackwoods Magazine*, vol. CXLVII, 1890.

1892

'British Officials and French Accusations', *Fortnightly Review*, vol. LVIII, 1892.
'Travels from the East Coast to Uganda', *Proceedings of the Royal Geographical Society*, vol. XIV, N.S. 1892.
'Characteristics of African Travel', *The Scottish Geographical Magazine*, vol. VIII, 1892.
'Captain Lugard on Uganda', letters to *The Times*, 8 and 17 October 1892 and 6 February 1893.
'Uganda, its Value to British Trade', *Manchester Geographical Journal*, vol. VIII, 1892.

1893

'Methods of dealing with East Africa and Uganda', *The Times*, 28 and 29 December 1893.

1894

'The War against Kabarega of Unyoro', letter to *The Times*, 26 March 1894.
'East and West Africa in Parliament', *Blackwoods Magazine*, vol. CLV, 1894.
(the following five articles appeared anonymously)

List of Sources

'The Uganda Protectorate', *Chamber of Commerce Journal*, vol. XIII, 1894.

'Imperial Interests in East Africa', *Blackwoods Magazine*, vol. CLV, 1894.

'The New African Crisis with France and Germany', *Blackwoods Magazine*, vol. CLVI, 1894.

'British Interests in East Africa', *Pall Mall Gazette*, vol. LVIII, 1894.

'The East African Question', *Pall Mall Gazette*, vol. LVIII, 1894.

1895

'An Expedition to Borgu on the Niger', *The Geographical Journal*, vol. VI, 1895.

'British West African Possessions', *Blackwoods Magazine*, vol. CLVII, 1895.

'England and France on the Niger, the Race for Borgu', *The Nineteenth Century*, vol. XXXVII, 1895.

'England and France in the Nile Valley', *National Review*, vol. XXV, 1895.

'New British Markets, Tropical Africa', *The Nineteenth Century*, vol. XXXVIII, 1895.

'Routes in Africa', *National Review*, vol. XXV, 1895.

'A Journey in West Africa and some points of contrast with East Africa', *Scottish Geographical Magazine*, vol. XI, 1895.

'The Extension of British Influence (and Trade) in Africa', *Journal of the Royal Colonial Institute*, vol. XXVII, 1895.

'British East Africa and Zanzibar', letter to *The Times*, 12 June 1895.

'The Borgu Treaties', letter to *The Times*, 22 August 1895.

1896

'Slavery under the British Flag', *The Nineteenth Century*, vol. XXXIX, 1896.

'Slatin Pasha and the Sudan', *National Review*, vol. XXVII, 1896.

1897

'Liquor Traffic in Africa', *The Nineteenth Century*, vol. XLII, 1897.

1904

'Northern Nigeria', *The Geographical Journal*, vol. XXIII, 1904.

1905

'West African Possessions and Administration', ed. C. S. Goldman, *The Empire and the Century* (1905).

1910

Memo regarding the restriction of opium in Hong Kong and China (Hong Kong, 1908)

'The Hong Kong University', *The Nineteenth Century*, vol. LXVIII, 1910.

Hong Kong University, objects, history, present position, prospects (Hong Kong, 1910).

List of Sources

1912

Hong Kong University, present position, constitution, objects and prospects (Hong Kong, 1912).

'The Problem of Universities in the East in regard to their influence on Character and Moral Ideals', *Congress of the Universities of the Empire, 1912.*

1919

Speech at dinner in his honour, *West Africa*, 29 March 1919.

'A new Partition of Africa', *The Times*, 29 March 1919.

'Tropical Africa', *Edinburgh Review*, vol. CCXXIX, April 1919.

'Liquor Trade in West Africa', *The Times*, 8 April 1919.

'Unrest in Egypt', letter to *The Times*, 16 September 1919.

'Our Mission in Africa', *African World*, 25 October 1919.

Speech at Nigerian Dinner Club, *West Africa*, 20 December 1919.

1920

'Palm Kernels', letter to *The Times*, 17 January 1920.

'The Crown Colonies and the British War Debt', *The Nineteenth Century*, vol. LXXXVIII, August 1920.

1921

'The Colour Problem', *Edinburgh Review*, vol. CCXXXIII, April 1921.

'Policy in Africa', speech reported in *West Africa*, 26 October 1921.

'Sir John Kirk, a personal tribute', *The Times*, 23 January 1921.

1922

'Peace in India', letters to *The Times*, 31 January and 22 February 1922.

'Carl. E. Akeley, *In Brightest Africa*', review in *Manchester Guardian*, 7 February 1922.

'J. C. B. Statham, *Through Angola*', review in *Manchester Guardian*, 21 March 1922.

'The Growth of Empire', *United Empire*, vol. XIII, 1922.

1923

'Chinese Education', letter to *The Times*, 4 January 1923.

'The Mandate System', *Edinburgh Review*, vol. CCXXXVIII, 1923.

'Our tropical Possessions', *Yearbook of the Bristol Royal Colonial Institute*, 1923.

'The Passing of Slavery in Africa', ed. Leo Weinthal, *Story of the Cape to Cairo, railway and river route from 1887 to 1922*, vol. i (1923).

1924

'Steps in Civilisation', *Outward Bound*, January 1924.

'Problems of Tropical Africa', *West Africa*, 16 February 1924.

'Indian Aspirations', letter to *The Times*, 21 March 1924.

'Les Progrès en Afrique', Société Belge d'Etudes et d'Expansion, *Bulletin*, No. 46, May 1924.

List of Sources

'Tropical Africa at Wembley', *West Africa*, 24 May 1924.
'The Mandate System and the British Mandates', *Journal of the Royal Society of Arts*, vol. LXXII, June 1924.
'British in Nigeria', letter to *The Times*, 24 December 1924.
'Quelques problèmes d'administration coloniale', ed. Franck, *Etudes de colonisation comparée*, vol. I, 1924.

1925
'The Prince's West African Tour', *West Africa*, 21 March 1925.
'Through Nigeria', *The Field*, 26 March 1925.
Presentation of the Gold Medal of the African Society, *Journal of the African Society*, vol. XXIV, July 1925.
'Education in Tropical Africa', *Edinburgh Review*, vol. CCXLII, July 1925. A revised edition of this article was printed in 1930 by the Colonial Office as African No. 1135, and reprinted in 1938.
'The Mandate System', *West Africa*, 8 August 1925.
'The Principle of Trusteeship for Backward Races', *Report of the Church Congress, 1925*, Royal Commonwealth Society Library, London.
'New Wine and Old Waterskins', *The Humanist*, December 1925.

1926
'The Under-Secretary in West Africa', *West Africa*, 16 January 1926.
With M. Ginsberg and H. A. Wyndham, *The Problem of Colour in Relation to the idea of Equality* (1926).
'Transport in Tropics', letter to *The Times*, 18 April 1926.
'Progress in Africa', ed. Smith, *The Christian Mission in Africa* (1926).
'Colonies, Protectorates and Mandated Territories', *Outlook*, 5 June 1926.
'Problems of Empire', *Daily Telegraph*, 5 October 1926.
'The British Dominions and Britain's Foreign Policy', *Overseas*, vol. XI, No. 129, 1926.
'The Food Supplies of the British Empire', *Overseas*, vol. XI, No. 121, 1926.
'Slavery, Forced Labour and the League', *The Nineteenth Century*, vol. XCIX, 1926.
'The White Man's Task in Tropical Africa', *Foreign Affairs*, vol. V, 1926.

1927
'C.M.S. Uganda Mission, Jubilee Year', report of speech in *The Record*, 27 January 1927.
'Problems of Equatorial Africa', *Journal of the Royal Institute of International Affairs*, vol. VI, 1927.
'Problems of Tropical Africa', *African World*, Supplement, 24 September 1927.

List of Sources

Report of speech at a dinner given by the Niger Company to President King of Liberia, *African World*, 23 July 1927.

'Training of Scientific Men', letter to *The Times*, 17 December 1927.

'British Tropical Africa, Training of Native Officials', letter to *The Times*, 30 December 1927.

'The Responsibilities of Rule in Africa', *United Empire*, vol. XVIII, 1927.

1928

'The International Institute of African Languages and Cultures', *Africa*, vol. 1, January 1928.

'Empire Trade Development', *The Financial Times*, 24 February 1928.

'Progress on the Gold Coast', *Manchester Guardian*, 3 April 1928.

'The Dependencies of the Empire and the Responsibilities they involve', Foundation Address to Birkbeck College, 1928.

'The Human Side of African Development', *United Empire*, vol. XIX, 1928.

'The Making of British West Africa', *The Times*, 30 October 1928.

1929

'The Future of East Africa', letter to *The Times*, 25 February 1929.

'Britain in East Africa', *The Glasgow Herald*, 14 March 1929.

'Nigeria Today', letter to *The Times*, 3 September 1929.

1930

Present-day Problems in British Tropical Africa', *Scottish Geographical Magazine*, May 1930.

'Aspects of Africa', letter to *The Times*, 9 January 1930.

'A Policy for East Africa', letter to *Spectator*, 3 May 1930.

'Native Policy in East Africa', *Foreign Affairs*, vol. IX, October 1930.

'The First Expedition from Uganda to Mount Ruwenzori', *Geographical Journal*, vol. LXXVI, 1930.

'Anglo-Belgian Co-operation and African Problems', *West Africa*, 12 August 1930.

'Evolution of British Rule in Tropical Africa', *West Africa*, 8 August 1930.

'The Ten Years Working of the Mandatory System', published by the Anti-Slavery and Aborigines Protection Society, 29 May 1930.

Speech on 'Anthropology in Administration', *Man*, vol. XXX, December 1930.

'The Forced Labour Convention of 1930', *International Review of Missions*, vol. XIX, 1930.

1931

Address to the Colonial Probationers at Cambridge, *Cambridge University Colonial Services Club Magazine*, vol. I, No. 4, 1931.

'Child Welfare in Africa', *Spectator*, 18 April 1931.

'The Administrative Aspect of the Colour Bar', *Spectator*, 13 June 1931.

'Africa in Transition', *Nature*, 24 October 1931.

1932

'A West African Centenary', letter to *The Times*, 27 January, 1932.

'Witchcraft in Africa', letter to *The Times*, 20 April 1932.

'The Five Year Research Plan in Africa', *Discovery*, July 1932.

'The Abolition of Slavery', letter to *The Times*, 3 August 1932.

'Does Lord Raglan Misunderstand the Systems he Condemns?', the *West African Review*, October 1932.

'Administration of Samoa', letter to *The Times*, 13 December 1932.

1933

'Education and Race Relations', *Journal of the African Society*, vol. XXXII, January 1933.

'Slavery in all its forms', *Africa*, vol. VI, January 1933.

'Gold in Kenya', letter to *The Times*, 4 January 1933.

'Gordon and Slavery', *Listener*, 17 January 1933.

'The Future of Kenya', letter to *The Times*, 13 March 1933.

'Slavery and the League', *Spectator*, 21 July 1933.

'Colonial Administration', *Economica*, vol. XIII, August 1933.

'Assyrians in Iraq', letters to *The Times*, 14 August 1933 and 18 August 1933.

1934

'Uganda Today', review of L. P. Mair, *'An African People in the Twentieth Century'*, *The Observer*, 4 March 1934.

'Studying our Primitive Races', *Daily Telegraph*, 30 July 1934.

'Slavery To-day', letter to *The Times*, 3 August 1934.

'The League and Native Races', *Listener*, 5 September 1934.

'Nigeria, Retrospect and Prospect', *Elders Review*, December 1934.

1935

'Kenya Natives', letter to *The Times*, 15 February 1935.

'Progress and Problems in Nigeria', *The Field*, 18 May 1935.

'South Africa and the Protectorates', *Manchester Guardian*, 27, 28 May 1935.

The Somali Strip', letter to *The Times*, 10 July 1935.

'Italo-Abyssinian Dispute', letter to *The Times*, 30 July 1935.

'Africa and the Powers', *The Times*, 19 and 20 September 1935.

'An Italian Brochure', letter to *The Times*, 7 December 1935.

'Lord Lugard and Abyssinia', *Manchester Guardian*, 7 December 1935.

1936

'The Claims to Colonies', *The Times*, 13 and 14 January 1936.

'Lord Lugard and Abyssinia', *Manchester Guardian*, 21 January 1936.

List of Sources

'Wounded in Ethiopia', letter to *The Times*, 18 February 1936.

'Basis of the Claim for Colonies', *International Affairs*, vol. XV, January to February 1936.

'The Problems of Kenya', letter to *The Times*, 27 May 1936.

'The Abyssinian Government', letter to *The Times*, 23 June 1936.

'The Value of Colonies', reviews on: Grover Clarke, *A Place in the Sun* and *The Balance Sheets of Imperialism*, in *The Times*, 7 August 1936 and *The Times Literary Supplement*, 15 August 1936.

'Arab and Jew', letter to *The Times*, 2 September 1936.

'The Right to Possess Colonies', *The Christian Science Monitor*, 14 October 1936.

'Some Colonial Problems of To-day', *United Empire*, vol. XXVII, December 1936.

1937

'Mandated Territories', letter to *The Times*, 22 February 1937.

'Hong Kong University', letter to *United Empire*, vol. XXVIII, May 1937.

'Lord Lugard on Colonial Problems', report of speech in *The Crown Colonist*, July 1937.

'Some main problems of Africa', report of Presidential Address to Colonial Summer School in Oxford, *East Africa and Rhodesia*, 15 July 1937.

'W. Bryant Mumford, *Africans learn to be French*', review in *Oversea Education*, July 1937.

'British Policy in Nigeria', *Africa*, vol. X, October 1937.

1938

'South African Natives', letter to *The Times*, 22 February 1938.

'Abyssinia and the League', letter to *The Times*, 28 April 1938.

'The Future of European Control', *News Chronicle*, 16 September 1938.

'Church Missions in Africa', *The Yearbook of the Church of England*, 1938.

1939

'Colonies and the Reich', *The Christian Science Monitor*, 18 February 1939.

'Germany's former Colonies', *Manchester Guardian*, 11 May 1939.

'Palestine Policy', *The Times*, 23 May 1939.

'Europe and Africa, new light on the scramble', review of R. Coupland, *The Exploitation of East Africa, 1856 to 1890*, in *The Times*, 1 June 1939; also reviewed in *Spectator*, 11 August 1939.

'Our Colonial Responsibility', letter to *Daily Telegraph*, 23 June 1939.

'Obligations of Empire', *Spectator*, 30 June 1939.

'The Case for Imperialism', *Spectator*, 13 October 1939.

1940

'The Future of the Colonies', letter to *Spectator*, 9 March 1940.

1941

'Federation and the Colonies', *Federal Tracts*, No. 7, Macmillan, 1941.

'The Democratic Principle in British Colonies', *The Crown Colonist*, May 1941.

'Der Treuhandgedanke in der britischen Kolonialpolitik', *Die Zeitung*, 17 June 1941.

'Future of the Colonies', letter to *The Times*, 24 July 1941.

'British Colonial Policy', *Britain Today*, No. 67, November 1941.

1942

'U.S. and British Colonies', letter to *The Times*, 26 November 1942.

1943

'The Colonial Empire', letter to *The Times*, 20 March 1943.

1944

'Some aspects of British Colonial Policy', *The Imperial Review*, March 1944.

1945

'A World Colonial Charter', *The Times*, 10 January 1945.

Forewords

Major Mintoft, *The Story of the W.A.F.F.* (1923).

Evelyn Sharp, *The African Child* (1931).

C. F. Strickland, *Co-operation for Africa* (1933).

Major G. St. J. Orde Browne, *The African Labourer* (1933).

Dr. D. H. Westermann, *The African Today* (1934).

H. B. Thomas and Robert Scott, *Uganda* (1935).

Nazi Activities in South West Africa, Friends of Europe publications (1936).

Dr. C. K. Meek, *Law and Authority in a Nigerian Tribe* (1937).

Mrs. Sonia Howe, *The Drama of Madagascar* (1938).

Mrs. Sylvia Leith-Ross, *African Women* (1939).

Royal African Society's Review of Lord Hailey, *An African Survey* (1939).

Index

Colonial Office, The: Chapter XXX; L.'s battle with, over finance and staff, 35, 37, 50, 89, 189–91, 192–3; concern over Kano operation, 95, 96–8, 105–6, 251; concedes his success, 135–6; constant disapproval of his methods as High Commissioner, 187–96; opposes his taxation policy, 191–3, 462, 559, 635; and flogging controversy, 199–200, 358; offers L. governorship of W. Australia, 224; opposes Continuous Administration Scheme, 225–6, 237, 241–2, 279–80, 411, 607–9, 610, 612, 615, 616–19, 628, 633–5; criticizes Munshi expedition, 247–50, 266–7; supports L. over Satiru, 258–9; criticizes his Hong Kong railway building methods, 309, 310; and opium trade, 322–3, 324, 326, 332, 335; opposes grant for Hong Kong University, 344–6; offers L. governorship of Nigeria, 363, 364, 365; constant friction over his work in Hong Kong, 367–8; accepts his plan for Nigerian amalgamation, 411; disagreement over secretariat, 417, 418; disapproves his taxation scheme for Yoruba states, 444–5, 448; disagreement over Native Treasuries, 480–7, 613; opposes L.'s education policy, 496, 504, 506–11, 629–30; approves his annual budgets, 559; doubts about Africans in government services, 605; L. accuses of excessive interference, 614, 619; censures his speech at Belfast, 625–7; and Closer Union in East Africa, 679, 680–1, 683, 685–6. *Mentioned:* 4, 11, 23, 47–8, 88–9, 110, 160, 163, 168, 169, 184, 262, 302, 409, 415, 429, 434–6, 452, 455, 477, 478, 503, 530, 541, 544, 547, 558, 562, 567, 570, 604
Conservative Party: 102, 266, 624

Continuous Administration Scheme ("The Scheme"): Chapter XI; rejection of, 244–5, 277, 279, 299; compromise on, 378, 380–1, 414–15; attacks on, 612, 615, 629–30, 635; abolished, 633–4; advocated in *Dual Mandate*, 644. *Mentioned:* 268, 411, 574, 608–9, 610, 618–19
Corona (steam yacht): 215
Coupland, Sir Reginald: 656–7, 662, 669–70, 687, 689, 708
Cowan, A. A.: 576, 598
Craig, Captain (Lord Craigavon): 627
Cranworth, Lord: 685, 688, 689
Crewe, Lord: 322–3, 331–2, 333, 335, 345–6
Cromer, Lord: 57, 240
Crown Agents for the Colonies: 4, 38, 310
Cunliffe, Brig.-General Frederick H. G.: 530, 534, 541, 543, 547, 549, 550
Curragh "mutiny": 624, 627
Currie, Sir James: 659
Curtis, Lionel: 682, 693, 698
Curzon, Lord: 74

Dahomey: 7, 439, 449, 528
Daura: 29, 514
Davidson, Archbishop Randall: 676, 682, 683, 687
Davies, Osho: 590, 601–2
Dawe, Sir Arthur: 637
Dawson, Geoffrey: 687
Delamere, Lord: 677, 679, 682
Denham, D.: 33
Departmental System: 310
Diké, Dr. K. O.: 457
Dikwa: 49
Dilke, Sir Charles: 99, 101, 102, 103–4
Dillon, Sir Martin: 13, 14–15, 16
District Courts: 426–7
District Heads: 447, 453
District Officers: 426, 427, 428
District Watch Force: 313
Dobell, Sir Charles: 530, 534–5, 543, 544

Lyttelton, Alfred: 193, 229–31, 234, 235–6, 244, 324, 326, 331, 381, 607

Macaulay, Herbert: 584, 592, 596, 600
McCallum, Sir H.: 10, 268
Macdonald, Colonel J. R. L.: 6
MacDonald, Malcolm: 687
MacDonald, Ramsay: 565, 687
McDowell, D. K.: 177
MacGregor, Sir William: 21, 201, 406, 433
Mackinnon, Sir William: 19
McNeill, R.: 569
Madeira, L.'s honeymoon in: 67, 69–75
Mahdism: 253, 254–5, 256, 262
Maiduguri: 516, 527, 534
Mair, Dr. Lucy: 700
Makafo, Dan: 253, 260
Malinowski, Professor: 689
Malvern, Lord (Sir Godfrey Huggins): 694
Manchester Guardian: 57, 59, 693
Mandates Commission, Permanent: 645–55, 688, 697, 702
Manson, Sir Patrick: 339
Mant, Sir Reginald: 681
Marchand, Captain: 5–6, 9
Marlborough, 9th Duke of: 233, 276, 278, 279
Matheson, Hilda: 699
Maxwell, Sir James: 453
Maxwell, Sir George: 656
May, Sir Francis Henry: 284–6, 287–9, 321, 356–7, 371
Medical Advisory Committee: 613
Melly, Dr. John: 697
Merchant community: 572–3, 574–7
Meredith, George: 58
Merode, Count de: 666
Middle Niger: 38
Miller, Dr. Walter: 264, 498–9, 500, 502, 504–6, 508, 510
Milner, Lord: supports Scheme, 240;

censured over Chinese labour, 243, 269, 270, 273–4, 631. *Mentioned:* 244, 271, 275, 633, 695
Mining: coal, 404, 556, 580; tin, 402–3, 558, 575
Missions and missionaries: in Hong Kong, 314, 338, 340, 341–2; and Nigerian education, 490, 493, 495–6, 506–7, 508, 657–8; L.'s co-operation with, 493, 494, 500, 506; L. encourages emirs to accept, 499–500, 509; criticisms of, 500–1; controversy over restriction of, 502–10; need for partnership with government, 661. *Mentioned:* 397–8, 403–4, 448, 620, 659. *See also* Church Missionary Society
Mitchell, Sir Philip: 689
Mody, Sir Hormusjee: 339, 341, 344, 347, 349, 350, 351, 370
Moloney, Captain: 92, 94, 97, 100
Moor, Sir Ralph: 10, 97, 245
Moore, Eric: 453, 584, 594
Moore, G. A.: 574–5
Moore, Miss Kofoworola (Lady Ademola): 582–4
Moorhouse, Sir Henry Claude: 485
Mora: 534, 543
Moradu: 126
Moral Education League: 495
Morel, E. D.: 414, 443, 449, 474, 560, 575, 587, 588
Morland, General Sir Thomas: expedition to Bornu, 51–2; and Kano, 105, 106, 107, 108–10, 113; in Sokoto, 127, 128. *Mentioned:* 24, 48, 95, 100, 178, 182, 258
Morley, John: 320
Morning Post: 231
Moyne, Lord: 691–2
Muller, Mrs. (later Lady) Max: 299
Munro, Sir Thomas: 142
Munshi people (Tiv): 39, 247–8, 250, 252, 256–65, 266–8, 523–4
Muri: 38, 87, 185, 209
Murray, Gilbert: 687

Muslim states: claims to rule pagan tribes, 156; and Mahdism, 254–5; missions in, 497, 499–502, 504, 508–10; loyalty during 1914–18 war, 541–2, 548. *Mentioned:* 10, 27, 152, 154, 261, 263, 440, 470

Nana, House Chief: 457, 512–13
Naraguta: 402–3
Nassarawa: 87, 91–2, 209, 502
Natal: 268, 269, 270–1, 278
Nathan, Sir Matthew: 290n.
Native Administration: *see* Indirect Rule
Native Chiefs: position under Indirect Rule, 155–6, 465–6, 469–72; effect of taxation on, 443, 444, 453; in Abeokuta, 453, 454; principle of election of in south-east, 461. *See also* Emirs
Native Courts: L.'s idea of, in Indirect Rule, 40, 140, 149, 158–61, 424–5, 431; political officers' supervision of, 140, 159, 161, 461; emirs and, 156; freeing of slaves, 172; reorganized in southern provinces, 428; merits of, 431; reform of south-eastern, 461–2, 463. *Mentioned:* 444, 447, 454, 604
Native Labour, Committee of Experts on: 657
Native Lands Trust Ordinance: 692–3
Native Races and their Rulers (Temple): 474–6, 503–4
Native Treasuries: 469, 470, 472, 480–7, 570
Nauru: 647
New Guinea: 647
New Territories of Hong Kong: 284, 287, 292, 296, 310, 312
Newbold, Douglas: 665
Nicholson, R. N.: 93–4, 136n., 182, 185, 215
Niger Coast Protectorate (Southern Nigeria): 11, 95, 142
Niger Committee (1898): 10

Niger Convention (1899): 9, 11
Niger River: explorations of, 27, 44; L.'s voyages along, 75–7, 393–5, 403, 404; railway to, 169, 410. *Mentioned:* 10, 38, 44, 47, 50
"Nigeria": origin of name, 11
Nigerian Council: 416, 567, 568, 574, 588
Nigerian Reform Association: 590
Nile River: 6–7, 9
Nineteenth Century, The: 656
Northern Nigerian Regiment: *see* West African Frontier Force
Numan: 523
Nupe: 39, 43, 207, 258, 500
Nyasaland: 693–4

Oduduwa, founder of Yoruba: 440, 442, 447
Offa: 391–3
Ogboni societies: 442
Oldham, Dr. J. H.: and Advisory Committee on Education in Colonies, 658–61; and Closer Union, 675–7, 679, 680, 681–3, 685, 687, 689, 690–1; and African Research Survey, 698; and International African Institute, 699–700, 708. *Mentioned:* 673, 710
Oldham, Mrs. J. H.: 710
Olivier, Lord: 685
Omdurman, battle of: 6, 250
Ommaney, Sir Montague: 98, 187, 194, 509
Onitsha: 403–4
Onslow, Lord: 96–8, 99, 102–4
"Open Door" policy: 564–72, 702
Opium trade: Chapter XVI; 292, 308, 309
Opobo: 395, 396
Ormsby-Gore, W. G. A. (4th Lord Harlech): 646, 659, 661, 677, 680, 688
Orr, Sir Charles: relations with L., 179–80, 182; policy advocated by, 185–6, 264; in Sokoto crisis, 255, 256–7. *Mentioned:* 157

743

744

746